Lecture Notes in Computer Scienc

T0238047

Commenced Publication in 1973
Founding and Former Series Editors:
Gerhard Goos, Juris Hartmanis, and Jan van Leeuwen

Klaus Schneider   Jens Brandt (Eds.)

Theorem Proving in Higher Order Logics

20th International Conference, TPHOLs 2007
Kaiserslautern, Germany, September 10-13, 2007
Proceedings

 Springer

Volume Editors

Klaus Schneider
Jens Brandt
University of Kaiserslautern
Department of Computer Science
Reactive Systems Group
P.O.Box 3049, 67653 Kaiserslautern, Germany
E-mail: {klaus.schneider,brandt}@informatik.uni-kl.de

Library of Congress Control Number: Applied for

CR Subject Classification (1998): F.4.1, I.2.3, F.3.1, D.2.4, B.6.3

LNCS Sublibrary: SL 1 – Theoretical Computer Science and General Issues

ISSN	0302-9743
ISBN-10	3-540-74590-4 Springer Berlin Heidelberg New York
ISBN-13	978-3-540-74590-7 Springer Berlin Heidelberg New York

Springer is a part of Springer Science+Business Media

springer.com

© Springer-Verlag Berlin Heidelberg 2007
Printed in Germany

Typesetting: Camera-ready by author, data conversion by Scientific Publishing Services, Chennai, India
Printed on acid-free paper   SPIN: 12115440   06/3180   5 4 3 2 1 0

Preface

This volume constitutes the proceedings of the 20th International Conference on Theorem Proving in Higher-Order Logics (TPHOLs 2007) held September 10–13, 2007 in Kaiserslautern, Germany. TPHOLs covers all aspects of theorem proving in higher-order logics as well as related topics in theorem proving and verification.

There were 52 submissions, and each submission was refereed by at least 4 reviewers, who had been selected by the program committee. Of these submissions, 26 were accepted for presentation at the conference and publication in this volume. In keeping with tradition, TPHOLs 2007 also offered a venue for the presentation of work in progress, where researchers invite discussion by means of a brief preliminary talk and then discuss their work at a poster session. A supplementary proceedings containing associated papers for work in progress was published by the University of Kaiserslautern. The organizers are grateful to Constance Heitmeyer (Naval Research Laboratory), Xavier Leroy (INRIA Rocquencourt) and Peter Liggesmeyer (Fraunhofer IESE) for agreeing to give invited talks at TPHOLs 2007.

The TPHOLs conference traditionally changes continent each year in order to maximize the chances of researchers from around the world being able to attend. Starting in 1993, the proceedings of TPHOLs and its predecessor workshops have been published in the Lecture Notes in Computer Science series of Springer-Verlag:

1993 Vancouver	LNCS 780	2000 Portland	LNCS 1869
1994 Valletta	LNCS 859	2001 Edinburgh	LNCS 2152
1995 Aspen Grove	LNCS 971	2002 Hampton	LNCS 2410
1996 Turku	LNCS 1125	2003 Rome	LNCS 2758
1997 Murray Hill	LNCS 1275	2004 Park City	LNCS 3223
1998 Canberra	LNCS 1479	2005 Oxford	LNCS 3603
1999 Nice	LNCS 1690	2006 Seattle	LNCS 4130

We would like to thank our sponsors: Fraunhofer IESE (Institute of Experimental Software Engineering), DASMOD (Dependable Adaptive Systems and Mathematical Modeling) Cluster, and DFKI (German Research Center for Artificial Intelligence).

July 2007

Klaus Schneider
Jens Brandt

Conference Organization

Program Chairs

Klaus Schneider
Jens Brandt

Program Committee

Mark Aagaard
Yves Bertot
Ching-Tsun Chou
Thierry Coquand
Amy Felty
Jean-Christophe Filliatre
Ganesh Gopalakrishnan
Mike Gordon
Jim Grundy
Elsa Gunter
John Harrison
Jason Hickey
Peter Homeier
Joe Hurd

Paul Jackson
Thomas Kropf
John Matthews
Tom Melham
Cesar Munoz
Tobias Nipkow
Sam Owre
Christine Paulin-Mohring
Lawrence Paulson
Klaus Schneider
Konrad Slind
Sofiene Tahar
Burkhart Wolff

External Reviewers

Behzad Akbarpour
Ulrich Berger
Stefan Berghofer
Pierre Castéran
Pierre Corbineau
Amjad Gawanmeh
Florian Haftmann
Osman Hasan
Nathan Linger
Claude Marche
Jia Meng
Paul Miner

John O'Leary
Sam Owre
Tom Ridge
Norbert Schirmer
Natarajan Shankar
Alan Smaill
Mark-Oliver Stehr
Christian Urban
Makarius Wenzel
Yu Yang
Mohamed Zaki

Table of Contents

On the Utility of Formal Methods in the Development and Certification of Software

Constance L. Heitmeyer

Naval Research Laboratory
Washington, DC 20375
http://chacs.nrl.navy.mil/personnel/heitmeyer.html

During the past three decades, many formal methods have been proposed whose goal is to improve the quality of computer systems. I use the term *formal method* to refer to any mathematically-based technique or tool useful in either hardware or software development. Recently, formal methods have played a significantly increased role in hardware design. More and more companies that sell microprocessors and hardware chips, including Intel, IBM, and Motorola, are using formally-based tools, such as model checkers, theorem provers, and equivalence checkers, to check hardware designs for flaws. While applied less frequently in practical software development, formal methods have, in a few recent cases, also been effective in detecting software defects. A prominent example is the set of tools developed in Microsoft's SLAM project which were designed to detect flaws in device drivers [1], a primary source of software defects in Microsoft programs. In 2006, Microsoft released the Static Driver Verifier (SDV) as part of Windows Vista, the latest Microsoft operating system. SDV uses the SLAM model checker to detect cases in which device drivers linked to Vista violate one of a set of interface rules.

This talk reviews several formally-based techniques of value in developing software systems, focusing on techniques for specifying, validating, and verifying software requirements [2], a primary cause of software defects. Next, the talk describes our recent experience applying formal techniques in the certification of a security-critical module of an embedded software device [3]. TAME [4], one formal technique applied in this effort, is a front-end to the higher-order logic theorem prover PVS. The benefits of using a higher-order logic are described.

References

1. Ball, T., Bounimova, E., Cook, B., Levin, V., Lichtenberg, J., McGarvey, C., Ondrusek, B., Rajamani, S., Ustuner, A.: Thorough static analysis of device drivers. In: European Systems Conference (2006)
2. Heitmeyer, C., Archer, M., Bharadwaj, R., Jeffords, R.: Tools for constructing requirements specifications: The SCR toolset at the age of ten. Computer Systems Science and Engineering 20(1), 19–35 (2005)

K. Schneider and J. Brandt (Eds.): TPHOLs 2007, LNCS 4732, pp. 1–2, 2007.
© Springer-Verlag Berlin Heidelberg 2007

3. Heitmeyer, C.L., Archer, M., Leonard, E.I., McLean, J.: Formal specification and verification of data separation in a separation kernel for an embedded system. In: Proc. 13th ACM Conference on Computer and Communications Security, ACM Press, New York (2006)
4. Archer, M.: TAME: Using PVS strategies for special-purpose theorem proving. Annals of Mathematics and Artificial Intelligence 29(1-4), 131–189 (2001)

Formal Techniques in Software Engineering: Correct Software and Safe Systems

Peter Liggesmeyer

Department of Computer Science
University of Kaiserslautern, Germany
Peter.Liggesmeyer@informatik.uni-kl.de
Fraunhofer Institute Experimental Software Engineering
Kaiserslautern, Germany
Peter.Liggesmeyer@iese.fraunhofer.de

In embedded systems, safety and reliability are usually important quality characteristics. It is required to determine these properties including hardware and software. Many techniques have been proposed to analyze, model and predict software and hardware quality characteristics on a quantified basis, e.g. fault trees, Markov analysis, and statistical reliability models.

Formal techniques are increasingly used to prove properties of critical systems. They support safety and reliability modelling by generating models based on formal analysis. Approaches for the automated generation of fault trees augment the traditional manual procedures.

We developed fault tree generation techniques that are based on finite state descriptions, and specifications of safety properties using temporal logic. Model checking is used to determine how specific failures can cause unsafe behaviour. This information is converted into a fault tree that propagates the failure probabilities of components, e.g. sensors, on residual risks on the system level. This is a combination of formal techniques, safety modelling and statistical analysis. Finite state machines are used to represent a system comprising a controller and a technical process under control. The controller is represented by a deterministic state machine. The process under control is, in general, non-deterministic, and so is the model. In the beginning, the verification by symbolic model checking assumes that the process may produce any arbitrary input for the controller. This will in most cases yield unreasonable inputs to the controller. By means of a process specification that is used by a model checker, transitions of the process are restricted to those transitions that are physically reasonable. Model checking is then used to determine whether unsafe states are reachable if certain failures occur.

Statistical reliability growth models are another approach that may be used to measure and predict reliability and safety. Since different software reliability models can produce very different answers when used to predict future reliability, users need to know which, if any, of the competing models are trustworty in a specific context. We developed a reliability assessment tool that helps in reaching such decisions and supports the reliability analysis of software-based systems. It incorporates reliability models and supports model selection based on observed failure data using statistically sound criteria. The tool was used to

K. Schneider and J. Brandt (Eds.): TPHOLs 2007, LNCS 4732, pp. 3–4, 2007.
© Springer-Verlag Berlin Heidelberg 2007

apply statistical reliability modelling to various projects within Siemens. These include, e.g., telecommunication software, railway systems, and medical applications. Although it only supports software reliability models, we also applied the tool to SW-/HW-Systems to get experience whether and how software reliability models can be applied to such systems. Model preselection, the selection criteria, aspects of the failure data used for model selection and calibration, scales (e.g., execution time vs. calendar time), the application of software reliability models to software-/hardware-systems, and the precision and usefulness of the results are discussed.

Safety and reliability analysis of complex systems will probably not be performed in a pure formal way. But formal and statistical techniques may contribute to enhance precision and reliability of the models. The traditional manual analyses are increasingly inappropriate. They are usually based on informal documents that describe the system. Considerable knowledge, system insight, and overview is necessary to consider many failure modes and dependencies between system components and their functionality at a time. Often, the behavior is too complicated to fully comprehend all possible failure consequences. Manual analysis is error-prone, costly and not necessarily complete. Formal and statistical techniques may be used to improve the reliability of the results.

Separation Logic for Small-Step Cminor

Andrew W. Appel[1,*] and Sandrine Blazy[2,*]

[1] Princeton University
[2] ENSIIE

Abstract. Cminor is a mid-level imperative programming language; there are proved-correct optimizing compilers from C to Cminor and from Cminor to machine language. We have redesigned Cminor so that it is suitable for Hoare Logic reasoning and we have designed a Separation Logic for Cminor. In this paper, we give a small-step semantics (instead of the big-step of the proved-correct compiler) that is motivated by the need to support future concurrent extensions. We detail a machine-checked proof of soundness of our Separation Logic. This is the first large-scale machine-checked proof of a Separation Logic w.r.t. a small-step semantics. The work presented in this paper has been carried out in the Coq proof assistant. It is a first step towards an environment in which concurrent Cminor programs can be verified using Separation Logic and also compiled by a proved-correct compiler with formal end-to-end correctness guarantees.

1 Introduction

The future of program verification is to connect machine-verified source programs to machine-verified compilers, and run the object code on machine-verified hardware. To connect the verifications end to end, the source language should be specified as a structural operational semantics (SOS) represented in a logical framework; the target architecture can also be specified that way. Proofs of source code can be done in the logical framework, or by other tools whose soundness is proved w.r.t. the SOS specification; these may be in safety proofs via type-checking, correctness proofs via Hoare Logic, or (in source languages designed for the purpose) correctness proofs by a more expressive proof theory. The compiler—if it is an optimizing compiler—will be a stack of phases, each with a well specified SOS of its own. There will be proofs of (partial) correctness of each compiler phase, or witness-driven recognizers for correct compilations, w.r.t. the SOS's that are inputs and outputs to the phases.

Machine-verified hardware/compiler/application stacks have been built before. Moore described a verified compiler for a "high-level assembly language" [13]. Leinenbach *et al.* [11] have built and proved a compiler for *C0*, a small C-like language, as part of a project to build machine-checked correctness proofs

---

* Appel supported in part by NSF Grants CCF-0540914 and CNS-0627650. This work was done, in part, while both authors were on sabbatical at INRIA.

of source programs, Hoare Logic, compiler, micro-kernel, and RISC processor. These are both simple one- or two-pass nonoptimizing compilers.

Leroy [12] has built and proved correct in Coq [1] a compiler called *CompCert* from a high-level intermediate language *Cminor* to assembly language for the Power PC architecture. This compiler has 4 intermediate languages, allowing optimizations at several natural levels of abstraction. Blazy *et al.* have built and proved correct a translator from a subset of C to Cminor [5]. Another compiler phase on top (not yet implemented) will then yield a proved-correct compiler from C to machine language. We should therefore reevaluate the conventional wisdom that an entire practical optimizing compiler cannot be proved correct.

A software system can have components written in different languages, and we would like end-to-end correctness proofs of the whole system. For this, we propose a new variant of Cminor as a machine-independent intermediate language to serve as a common denominator between high-level languages. Our new Cminor has a usable Hoare Logic, so that correctness proofs for some components can be done directly at the level of Cminor.

Cminor has a "calculus-like" view of local variables and procedures (*i.e.* local variables are bound in an environment), while Leinenbach's C0 has a "storage-allocation" view (*i.e.* local variables are stored in the stack frame). The calculus-like view will lead to easier reasoning about program transformations and easier use of Cminor as a target language, and fits naturally with a multi-pass optimizing compiler such as CompCert; the storage-allocation view suits the one-pass nonoptimizing C0 compiler and can accommodate in-line assembly code.

Cminor is a promising candidate as a common intermediate language for end-to-end correctness proofs. But we have many demands on our new variant of Cminor, only the first three of which are satisfied by Leroy's Cminor.

- Cminor has an operational semantics represented in a logical framework.
- There is a proved-correct compiler from Cminor to machine language.
- Cminor is usable as the high-level target language of a C compiler.
- Our semantics is a *small-step* semantics, to support reasoning about input/output, concurrency, and nontermination.
- Cminor is machine-independent over machines in the "standard model" (*i.e.* 32- or 64-bit single-address-space byte-addressable multiprocessors).
- Cminor can be used as a mid-level target language of an ML compiler [8], or of an OO-language compiler, so that we can integrate correctness proofs of ML or OO programs with the proofs of their run-time systems and libraries.
- As we show in this paper, Cminor supports an axiomatic Hoare Logic (in fact, Separation Logic), proved sound with respect to the small-step semantics, for reasoning about low-level (C-like) programs.
- In future work, we plan to extend Cminor to be concurrent in the "standard model" of thread-based preemptive lock-synchronized weakly consistent shared-memory programming. The sequential soundness proofs we present here should be reusable in a concurrent setting, as we will explain.

Leroy's original Cminor had several Power-PC dependencies, is slightly clumsy to use as the target of an ML compiler, and is a bit clumsy to use in Hoare-style reasoning. But most important, Leroy's semantics is a big-step semantics that can be used only to reason about terminating sequential programs. We have redesigned Cminor's syntax and semantics to achieve all of these goals. That part of the redesign to achieve target-machine portability was done by Leroy himself. Our redesign to ease its use as an ML back end and for Hoare Logic reasoning was fairly simple. Henceforth in this paper, Cminor will refer to the new version of the Cminor language.

The main contributions of this paper are a small-step semantics suitable for compilation and for Hoare Logic; and the first machine-checked proof of soundness of a sequential Hoare Logic (Separation Logic) w.r.t. a small-step semantics. Schirmer [17] has a machine-checked *big-step* Hoare-Logic soundness proof for a control flow much like ours, extended by Klein *et al.* [10] to a C-like memory model. Ni and Shao [14] have a machine-checked proof of soundness of a Hoare-like logic w.r.t. a small-step semantics, but for an assembly language and for much simpler assertions than ours.

2   Big-Step Expression Semantics

The C standard [2] describes a memory model that is byte- and word-addressable (yet portable to big-endian and little-endian machines) with a nontrivial semantics for uninitialized variables. Blazy and Leroy formalized this model [6] for the semantics of Cminor. In C, pointer arithmetic within any malloc'ed block is defined, but pointer arithmetic between different blocks is undefined; Cminor therefore has non-null pointer values comprising an abstract block-number and an int offset. A NULL pointer is represented by the integer value 0. Pointer arithmetic between blocks, and reading uninitialized variables, are undefined but not illegal: expressions in Cminor can evaluate to *undefined* (Vundef) without getting stuck.

Each memory load or store is to a non-null pointer value with a "chunk" descriptor ch specifying number of bytes, signed or unsigned, int or float. Storing as 32-bit-int then loading as 8-bit-signed-byte leads to an undefined value. Load and store operations on memory, $m \vdash v_1 \overset{ch}{\mapsto} v_2$ and $m' = m[v_1 \overset{ch}{:=} v_2]$, are partial functions that yield results only if reading (resp., writing) a chunk of type ch at address v_1 is legal. We write $m \vdash v_1 \overset{ch}{\mapsto} v$ to mean that the result of loading from memory m at address v_1 a chunk-type ch is the value v.

The *values* of Cminor are *undefined* (Vundef), integers, pointers, and floats. The int type is an abstract data-type of 32-bit modular arithmetic. The expressions of Cminor are literals, variables, primitive operators applied to arguments, and memory loads.

There are 33 primitive operation symbols op; two of these are for accessing global names and local stack-blocks, and the rest is for integer and floating-point arithmetic and comparisons. Among these operation symbols are casts. Cminor casts correspond to all portable C casts. Cminor has an infinite supply ident of variable and function identifiers id. As in C, there are two namespaces—each id

can be interpreted in a local scope (using Evar (id)) or in a global scope (using Eop with the operation symbol for accessing global names).

$$i \; : \mathsf{int} \; ::= \; [0, 2^{32})$$
$$v \; : \mathsf{val} \; ::= \; \mathsf{Vundef} \mid \mathsf{Vint} \; (i) \mid \mathsf{Vptr} \; (b, i) \mid \mathsf{Vfloat} \; (f)$$
$$e : \mathsf{expr} \; \; ::= \; \mathsf{Eval} \; (v) \mid \mathsf{Evar} \; (id) \mid \mathsf{Eop} \; (op, el) \mid \mathsf{Eload} \; (ch, e)$$
$$el : \mathsf{exprlist} \; ::= \; \mathsf{Enil} \mid \mathsf{Econs} \; (e, el)$$

Expression Evaluation. In original Cminor, expression evaluation is expressed by an inductive big-step relation. Big-step statement execution is problematic for concurrency, but big-step *expression* evaluation is fine even for concurrent programs, since we will use the separation logic to prove noninterference.

Evaluation is deterministic. Leroy chose to represent evaluation as a relation because Coq had better support for proof induction over relations than over function definitions. We have chosen to represent evaluation as a partial function; this makes some proofs easier in some ways: $f(x) = f(x)$ is simpler than $f \, x \, y \Rightarrow f \, x \, z \Rightarrow y = z$. Before Coq's new functional induction tactic was available, we developed special-purpose tactics to enable these proofs. Although we specify expression evaluation as a function in Coq, we present evaluation as a judgment relation in Fig. 1. Our evaluation function is (proved) equivalent to the inductively defined judgment $\Psi; (sp; \rho; \phi; m) \vdash e \Downarrow v$ where:

Ψ is the "program," consisting of a global environment (ident $\rightarrow$ option block) mapping identifiers to function-pointers and other global constants, and a global mapping (block $\rightarrow$ option function) that maps certain ("text-segment") addresses to function definitions.

sp : block. The "stack pointer" giving the address and size of the memory block for stack-allocated local data in the current activation record.

ρ : env. The local environment, a finite mapping from identifiers to values.

ϕ : footprint. It represents the memory used by the evaluation of an expression (or a statement). It is a mapping from memory addresses to permissions. Leroy's Cminor has no footprints.

m : mem. The memory, a finite mapping from blocks to block contents [6]. Each block represents the result of a C `malloc`, or a stack frame, a global static variable, or a function code-pointer. A block content consists of the dimensions of the block (low and high bounds) plus a mapping from byte offsets to byte-sized memory cells.

e : expr. The expression being evaluated.

v : val. The value of the expression.

Loads outside the footprint will cause expression evaluation to get stuck. Since the footprint may have different permissions for loads than for stores to some addresses, we write $\phi \vdash \mathsf{load}_{ch} \, v$ (or $\phi \vdash \mathsf{store}_{ch} \, v$) to mean that all the addresses from v to $v + |ch| - 1$ are readable (or writable).

To model the possibility of exclusive read/write access or shared read-only access, we write $\phi_0 \oplus \phi_1 = \phi$ for the "disjoint" sum of two footprints, where $\oplus$

$$\Psi; (sp; \rho; \phi; m) \vdash \mathsf{Eval}\,(v) \Downarrow v \qquad \frac{x \in \mathrm{dom}\,\rho}{\Psi; (sp; \rho; \phi; m) \vdash \mathsf{Evar}\,(x) \Downarrow \rho(x)}$$

$$\frac{\Psi; (sp; \rho; \phi; m) \vdash el \Downarrow vl \qquad \Psi; sp \vdash op(vl) \Downarrow_{\mathsf{eval\_operation}} v}{\Psi; (sp; \rho; \phi; m) \vdash \mathsf{Eop}\,(op, el) \Downarrow v}$$

$$\frac{\Psi; (sp; \rho; \phi; m) \vdash e_1 \Downarrow v_1 \qquad \phi \vdash \mathsf{load}_{ch}\,v_1 \qquad m \vdash v_1 \overset{ch}{\mapsto} v}{\Psi; (sp; \rho; \phi; m) \vdash \mathsf{Eload}\,(ch, e_1) \Downarrow v}$$

Fig. 1. Expression evaluation rules

is an associative and commutative operator with several properties such as $\phi_0 \vdash \mathsf{store}_{ch}\,v \Rightarrow \phi_1 \not\vdash \mathsf{load}_{ch}\,v$, $\phi_0 \vdash \mathsf{load}_{ch}\,v \Rightarrow \phi \vdash \mathsf{load}_{ch}\,v$ and $\phi_0 \vdash \mathsf{store}_{ch}\,v \Rightarrow \phi \vdash \mathsf{store}_{ch}\,v$. One can think of ϕ as a set of fractional permissions [7], with 0 meaning no permission, $0 < x < 1$ permitting read, and 1 giving read/write permission. A store permission can be split into two or more load permissions, which can be reconstituted to obtain a store permission. Instead of fractions, we use a more general and powerful model of sharable permissions similar to one described by Parkinson [16, Ch. 5].

Most previous models of Separation Logic (*e.g.*, Ishtiaq and O'Hearn [9]) represent heaps as partial functions that can be combined with an operator like $\oplus$. Of course, a partial function can be represented as a pair of a domain set and a total function. Similarly, we represent heaps as a footprint plus a Cminor memory; this does not add any particular difficulty to the soundness proofs for our Separation Logic.

To perform arithmetic and other operations, in the third rule of Fig. 1, the judgment $\Psi; sp \vdash op(vl) \Downarrow_{\mathsf{eval\_operation}} v$ takes an operator op applied to a list of values vl and (if vl contains appropriate values) produces some value v. Operators that access global names and local stack-blocks make use of Ψ and sp respectively to return the address of a global name or a local stack-block address.

States. We shall bundle together $(sp; \rho; \phi; m)$ and call it the *state*, written as σ. We write $\Psi; \sigma \vdash e \Downarrow v$ to mean $\Psi; (sp_\sigma; \rho_\sigma; \phi_\sigma; m_\sigma) \vdash e \Downarrow v$.

Notation. We write $\sigma[:= \rho']$ to mean the state σ with its environment component ρ replaced by ρ', and so on (*e.g.* see rules 2 and 3 of Fig. 2 in Section 4).

Fact. $\Psi; sp \vdash op(vl) \Downarrow_{\mathsf{eval\_operation}} v$ and $m \vdash v_1 \overset{ch}{\mapsto} v$ are both deterministic relations, *i.e.* functions.

Lemma 1. $\Psi; \sigma \vdash e \Downarrow v$ *is a deterministic relation. (Trivial by inspection.)*

Lemma 2. *For any value v, there is an expression e such that $\forall \sigma. (\Psi; \sigma \vdash e \Downarrow v)$.*

Proof. Obvious; e is simply $\mathsf{Eval}\,v$. But it is important nonetheless: reasoning about programs by rewriting and by Hoare Logic often requires this property, and it was absent from Leroy's Cminor for Vundef and Vptr values. ∎

An expression may fetch from several different memory locations, or from the same location several times. Because $\Downarrow$ is deterministic, we cannot model a situation where the memory is updated by another thread after the first fetch and before the second. But we want a semantics that describes real executions on real machines. The solution is to evaluate expressions in a setting where we can guarantee *noninterference*. We will do this (in our extension to Concurrent Cminor) by guaranteeing that the footprints ϕ of different threads are disjoint.

Erased Expression Evaluation. The Cminor compiler (CompCert) is proved correct w.r.t. an operational semantics that does not use footprints. Any program that successfully evaluates with footprints will also evaluate ignoring footprints. Thus, for sequential programs where we do not need noninterference, it is sound to prove properties in a footprint semantics and compile in an erased semantics. We formalize and prove this in the full technical report [4].

3   Small-Step Statement Semantics

The statements of sequential Cminor are:

$$s : \mathsf{stmt} \quad ::= x := e \mid [e_1]_{ch} := e_2 \mid \mathsf{loop}\ s \mid \mathsf{block}\ s \mid \mathsf{exit}\ n$$
$$\mid \mathsf{call}\ xl\ e\ el \mid \mathsf{return}\ el \mid s_1; s_2 \mid \mathsf{if}\ e\ \mathsf{then}\ s_1\ \mathsf{else}\ s_2 \mid \mathsf{skip}.$$

The assignment $x := e$ puts the value of e into the local variable x. The store $[e_1]_{ch} := e_2$ puts (the value of) e_2 into the memory-chunk ch at address given by (the value of) e_1. (Local variables are not addressable; global variables and heap locations are memory addresses.) To model exits from nested loops, block s runs s, which should not terminate normally but which should exit n from the $(n+1)^{th}$ enclosing block, and loop s repeats s infinitely or until it returns or exits. call $xl\ e\ el$ calls function e with parameters (by value) el and results returned back into the variables xl. return el evaluates and returns a sequence of results, $(s_1; s_2)$ executes s_1 followed by s_2 (unless s_1 returns or exits), and the statements if and skip are as the reader might expect.

Combined with infinite loops and if statements, blocks and exits suffice to express efficiently all reducible control-flow graphs, notably those arising from C loops. The C statements break and continue are translated as appropriate exit statements. Blazy *et al.* [5] detail the translation of these C statements into Cminor.

Function Definitions. A program Ψ comprises two mappings: a mapping from function names to memory blocks (*i.e.*, abstract addresses), and a mapping from memory blocks to function definitions. Each function definition may be written as $f = (xl, yl, n, s)$, where $\mathsf{params}(f) = xl$ is a list of formal parameters, $\mathsf{locals}(f) = yl$ is a list of local variables, $\mathsf{stackspace}(f) = n$ is the size of the local stack-block to which sp points, and the statement $\mathsf{body}(f) = s$ is the function body.

Operational Semantics. Our small-step semantics for statements is based on continuations, mainly to allow a uniform representation of statement execution that facilitates the design of lemmas. Such a semantics also avoids all search

$$\Psi \vdash (\sigma, (s_1; s_2) \cdot \kappa) \longmapsto (\sigma, s_1 \cdot s_2 \cdot \kappa)$$

$$\frac{\Psi; \sigma \vdash e \Downarrow v \quad \rho' = \rho_\sigma[x := v]}{\Psi \vdash (\sigma, (x := e) \cdot \kappa) \longmapsto (\sigma[:= \rho'], \kappa)}$$

$$\frac{\Psi; \sigma \vdash e_1 \Downarrow v_1 \quad \Psi; \sigma \vdash e_2 \Downarrow v_2 \quad \phi_\sigma \vdash \mathsf{store}_{ch}\, v_1 \quad m' = m_\sigma[v_1 \overset{ch}{:=} v_2]}{\Psi \vdash (\sigma, ([e_1]_{ch} := e_2) \cdot \kappa) \longmapsto (\sigma[:= m'], \kappa)}$$

$$\frac{\Psi; \sigma \vdash e \Downarrow v \qquad \mathsf{is\_true}\, v}{\Psi \vdash (\sigma, (\mathsf{if}\ e\ \mathsf{then}\ s_1\ \mathsf{else}\ s_2) \cdot \kappa) \longmapsto (\sigma, s_1 \cdot \kappa)}$$

$$\frac{\Psi; \sigma \vdash e \Downarrow v \qquad \mathsf{is\_false}\, v}{\Psi \vdash (\sigma, (\mathsf{if}\ e\ \mathsf{then}\ s_1\ \mathsf{else}\ s_2) \cdot \kappa) \longmapsto (\sigma, s_2 \cdot \kappa)} \qquad \Psi \vdash (\sigma, \mathsf{skip} \cdot \kappa) \longmapsto (\sigma, \kappa)$$

$$\Psi \vdash (\sigma, (\mathsf{loop}\ s) \cdot \kappa) \longmapsto (\sigma, s \cdot \mathsf{loop}\ s \cdot \kappa) \qquad \Psi \vdash (\sigma, (\mathsf{block}\ s) \cdot \kappa) \longmapsto (\sigma, s \cdot \mathsf{Kblock}\ \kappa)$$

$$\frac{j \geq 1}{\Psi \vdash (\sigma, \mathsf{exit}\, 0 \cdot s_1 \cdots s_j \cdot \mathsf{Kblock}\ \kappa) \longmapsto (\sigma, \kappa)}$$

$$\frac{j \geq 1}{\Psi \vdash (\sigma, \mathsf{exit}\, (n+1) \cdot s_1 \cdots s_j \cdot \mathsf{Kblock}\ \kappa) \longmapsto (\sigma, \mathsf{exit}\, n \cdot \kappa)}$$

Fig. 2. Sequential small-step relation. We omit here call and return, which are in the full technical report [4].

rules (congruence rules), which avoids induction over search rules in both the Hoare-Logic soundness proof and the compiler correctness proof.[1]

Definition 1. *A continuation k has a state σ and a control stack κ. There are sequential control operators to handle local control flow (Kseq, written as $\cdot$), intraprocedural control flow (Kblock), and function-return (Kcall); this last carries not only a control aspect but an activation record of its own. The control operator Kstop represents the safe termination of the computation.*

$$\kappa : \mathsf{control} \ ::= \ \mathsf{Kstop} \ | \ s \cdot \kappa \ | \ \mathsf{Kblock}\ \kappa \ | \ \mathsf{Kcall}\ xl\ f\ sp\ \rho\ \kappa$$
$$k : \mathsf{continuation} ::= (\sigma, \kappa)$$

The sequential small-step function takes the form $\Psi \vdash k \longmapsto k'$ (see Fig. 2), and we define as usual its reflexive transitive closure $\longmapsto^*$. As in C, there is no boolean type in Cminor. In Fig. 2, the predicate $\mathsf{is\_true}\, v$ holds if v is a pointer or a nonzero integer; $\mathsf{is\_false}$ holds only on 0. A store statement $[e_1]_{ch} := e_2$ requires the corresponding store permission $\phi_\sigma \vdash \mathsf{store}_{ch}\, v_1$.

Given a control stack block $s \cdot \kappa$, the small-step execution of the block statement block s enters that block: s becomes the next statement to execute and the control stack becomes $s \cdot \mathsf{Kblock}\ \kappa$.

---

[1] We have proved in Coq the equivalence of this small-step semantics with the big-step semantics of CompCert (for programs that terminate).

Exit statements are only allowed from blocks that have been previously entered. For that reason, in the two rules for exit statements, the control stack ends with (Kblock κ) control. A statement (exit n) terminates the $(n+1)^{th}$ enclosing block statements. In such a block, the stack of control sequences $s_1 \cdots s_j$ following the exit statement is not executed. Let us note that this stack may be empty if the exit statement is the last statement of the most enclosing block. The small-step execution of a statement (exit n) exits from only one block (the most enclosing one). Thus, the execution of an (exit 0) statement updates the control stack (exit $0 \cdot s_1 \cdots s_j \cdot$ Kblock κ) into κ. The execution of an (exit $n+1$) statement updates the control stack (exit $(n+1) \cdot s_1 \cdots s_j \cdot$ Kblock κ) into exit $n \cdot \kappa$.

Lemma 3. *If $\Psi; \sigma \vdash e \Downarrow v$ then $\Psi \vdash (\sigma, (x := e) \cdot \kappa) \longmapsto k'$ iff $\Psi \vdash (\sigma, (x :=$ Eval $v) \cdot \kappa)) \longmapsto k'$ (and similarly for other statements containing expressions). Proof. Trivial: expressions have no side effects. A convenient property nonetheless, and not true of Leroy's original Cminor.* ∎

Definition 2. *A continuation $k = (\sigma, \kappa)$ is stuck if $\kappa \neq$ Kstop and there does not exist k' such that $\Psi \vdash k \longmapsto k'$.*

Definition 3. *A continuation k is safe (written as $\Psi \vdash$ safe(k)) if it cannot reach a stuck continuation in the sequential small-step relation $\longmapsto^*$.*

4   Separation Logic

Hoare Logic uses triples $\{P\} s \{Q\}$ where P is a precondition, s is a statement of the programming language, and Q is a postcondition. The assertions P and Q are predicates on the program state. The reasoning on memory is inherently global. Separation Logic is an extension of Hoare Logic for programs that manipulate pointers. In Separation Logic, reasoning is local [15]; assertions such as P and Q describe properties of part of the memory, and $\{P\} s \{Q\}$ describes changes to part of the memory. We prove the soundness of the Separation Logic via a shallow embedding, that is, we give each assertion a semantic meaning in Coq. We have $P, Q :$ assert   where   assert = prog $\rightarrow$ state $\rightarrow$ Prop. So $P\Psi\sigma$ is a proposition of logic and we say that σ satisfies P.

Assertion Operators. In Fig. 3, we define the usual operators of Separation Logic: the empty assertion **emp**, separating conjunction $*$, disjunction $\vee$, conjunction $\wedge$, implication $\Rightarrow$, negation $\neg$, and quantifier $\exists$. A state σ satisfies $P * Q$ if its footprint ϕ_σ can be split into ϕ_1 and ϕ_2 such that $\sigma[:= \phi_1]$ satisfies P and $\sigma[:= \phi_2]$ satisfies Q. We also define some novel operators such as expression evaluation $e \Downarrow v$ and base-logic propositions $\lceil A \rceil$.

O'Hearn and Reynolds specify Separation Logic for a little language in which expressions evaluate independently of the heap [15]. That is, their expressions access only the program variables and do not even have *read* side effects on the memory. Memory reads are done by a command of the language, not within expressions. In Cminor we relax this restriction; expressions can read the heap.

$$\mathbf{emp} =_{\text{def}} \lambda \Psi \sigma. \ \phi_\sigma = \emptyset$$

$$P * Q =_{\text{def}} \lambda \Psi \sigma. \ \exists \phi_1. \exists \phi_2. \ \phi_\sigma = \phi_1 \oplus \phi_2 \ \wedge \ P(\sigma[:= \phi_1]) \ \wedge \ Q(\sigma[:= \phi_2])$$

$$P \vee Q =_{\text{def}} \lambda \Psi \sigma. \ P\sigma \vee Q\sigma$$

$$P \wedge Q =_{\text{def}} \lambda \Psi \sigma. \ P\sigma \wedge Q\sigma$$

$$P \Rightarrow Q =_{\text{def}} \lambda \Psi \sigma. \ P\sigma \Rightarrow Q\sigma$$

$$\neg P =_{\text{def}} \lambda \Psi \sigma. \ \neg(P\sigma)$$

$$\exists z. P =_{\text{def}} \lambda \Psi \sigma. \ \exists z. \ P\sigma$$

$$\lceil A \rceil =_{\text{def}} \lambda \Psi \sigma. \ A \qquad \text{where } \sigma \text{ does not appear free in } A$$

$$\mathbf{true} =_{\text{def}} \lambda \Psi \sigma. \mathbf{True} \qquad\qquad \mathbf{false} =_{\text{def}} \lceil \mathbf{False} \rceil$$

$$e \Downarrow v =_{\text{def}} \mathbf{emp} \wedge \lceil \mathsf{pure}(e) \rceil \wedge \lambda \Psi \sigma. \ (\Psi; \sigma \vdash e \Downarrow v)$$

$$\lceil e \rceil_{\mathsf{expr}} =_{\text{def}} \exists v. e \Downarrow v \wedge \lceil \mathsf{is\_true}\, v \rceil$$

$$\mathsf{defined}(e) =_{\text{def}} \lceil e \stackrel{\text{int}}{==} e \rceil_{\mathsf{expr}} \vee \lceil e \stackrel{\text{float}}{==} e \rceil_{\mathsf{expr}}$$

$$e_1 \stackrel{ch}{\mapsto} e_2 =_{\text{def}} \exists v_1. \exists v_2. (e_1 \Downarrow v_1) \wedge (e_2 \Downarrow v_2) \wedge (\lambda \sigma, m_\sigma \vdash v_1 \stackrel{ch}{\mapsto} v_2 \wedge \phi_\sigma \vdash \mathsf{store}_{ch}\, v_1) \wedge \mathsf{defined}(v_2)$$

Fig. 3. Main operators of Separation Logic

But we say that an expression is *pure* if it contains no Eload operators—so that it cannot read the heap.

In Hoare Logic one can use expressions of the programming language as assertions—there is an implicit coercion. We write the assertion $e \Downarrow v$ to mean that expression e is pure and evaluates to value v in the operational semantics. This is an expression of Separation Logic, in contrast to $\Psi; \sigma \vdash e \Downarrow v$ which is a judgment in the underlying logic. In a previous experiment, our Separation Logic permitted impure expressions in $e \Downarrow v$. But, this complicated the proofs unnecessarily. Having $\mathbf{emp} \wedge \lceil \mathsf{pure}(e) \rceil$ in the definition of $e \Downarrow v$ leads to an easier-to-use Separation Logic.

Hoare Logic traditionally allows expressions e of the programming language to be used as expressions of the program logic. We will define explicitly $\lceil e \rceil_{\mathsf{expr}}$ to mean that e evaluates to a true value (*i.e.* a nonzero integer or non-null pointer). Following Hoare's example, we will usually omit the $\lceil \ \rceil_{\mathsf{expr}}$ braces in our Separation Logic notation.

Cminor's integer equality operator, which we will write as $e_1 \stackrel{\text{int}}{==} e_2$, applies to integers or pointers, but in several cases it is "stuck" (expression evaluation gives no result): when comparing a nonzero integer to a pointer; when comparing Vundef or Vfloat(x) to anything. Thus we can write the assertion $\lceil e \stackrel{\text{int}}{==} e \rceil_{\mathsf{expr}}$ (or just write $e \stackrel{\text{int}}{==} e$) to test that e is a defined integer or pointer in the current state, and there is a similar operator $e_1 \stackrel{\text{float}}{==} e_2$.

Finally, we have the usual Separation Logic singleton "maps-to", but annotated with a chunk-type ch. That is, $e_1 \stackrel{ch}{\mapsto} e_2$ means that e_1 evaluates to v_1, e_2 evaluates to v_2, and at address v_1 in memory there is a defined value v_2 of the given chunk-type. Let us note that in this definition, $\mathsf{defined}(v_1)$ is implied by the third conjunct. $\mathsf{defined}(v_2)$ is a design decision. We could leave it out and have a slightly different Separation Logic.

$$\frac{P \Rightarrow P' \quad \Gamma; R; B \vdash \{P'\}s\{Q'\} \quad Q' \Rightarrow Q}{\Gamma; R; B \vdash \{P\}s\{Q\}} \qquad \Gamma; R; B \vdash \{P\}\mathsf{skip}\{P\}$$

$$\frac{\Gamma; R; B \vdash \{P\}s_1\{P'\} \quad \Gamma; R; B \vdash \{P'\}s_2\{Q\}}{\Gamma; R; B \vdash \{P\}s_1; s_2\{Q\}}$$

$$\frac{\rho' = \rho_\sigma[x := v] \quad P = (\exists v.\, e \Downarrow v \,\wedge\, \lambda\sigma.\, Q\,\sigma[:= \rho'])}{\Gamma; R; B \vdash \{P\}x := e\{Q\}}$$

$$\frac{\mathsf{pure}\,(e) \quad \mathsf{pure}\,(e_2) \quad P = (e \overset{ch}{\mapsto} e_2 \,\wedge\, \mathsf{defined}(e_1))}{\Gamma; R; B \vdash \{P\}[e]_{ch}:=e_1\{e \overset{ch}{\mapsto} e_1\}}$$

$$\frac{\mathsf{pure}\,(e) \quad \Gamma; R; B \vdash \{P \wedge e\}s_1\{Q\} \quad \Gamma; R; B \vdash \{P \wedge \neg e\}s_2\{Q\}}{\Gamma; R; B \vdash \{P\}\mathsf{if}\ e\ \mathsf{then}\ s_1\ \mathsf{else}\ s_2\{Q\}}$$

$$\frac{\Gamma; R; B \vdash \{I\}s\{I\}}{\Gamma; R; B \vdash \{I\}\mathsf{loop}\ s\{\mathbf{false}\}} \qquad \frac{\Gamma; R; Q \cdot B \vdash \{P\}s\{\mathbf{false}\}}{\Gamma; R; B \vdash \{P\}\mathsf{block}\ s\{Q\}}$$

$$\Gamma; R; B \vdash \{B(n)\}\mathsf{exit}\ n\{\mathbf{false}\}$$

$$\frac{\Gamma; R; B \vdash \{P\}s\{Q\} \quad \mathsf{modified\ vars}(s) \cap \mathsf{free\ vars}(A) = \emptyset}{\Gamma; (\lambda vl.A * R(vl)); (\lambda n.A * B(n)) \vdash \{A * P\}s\{A * Q\}}$$

Fig. 4. Axiomatic Semantics of Separation Logic (without call and return)

The Hoare Sextuple. Cminor has commands to call functions, to exit (from a block), and to return (from a function). Thus, we extend the Hoare triple $\{P\}\,s\,\{Q\}$ with three extra contexts to become $\Gamma; R; B \vdash \{P\}s\{Q\}$ where:

Γ : assert describes context-insensitive properties of the global environment;

R : list val → assert is the *return environment*, giving the current function's post-condition as a predicate on the list of returned values; and

B : nat → assert is the *block environment* giving the exit conditions of each block statement in which the statement s is nested.

Most of the rules of sequential Separation Logic are given in Fig. 4. In this paper, we omit the rules for return and call, which are detailed in the full technical report. Let us note that the Γ context is used to update global function names, none of which is illustrated in this paper.

The rule for $[e]_{ch}:=e_1$ requires the same store permission than the small-step rule, but in Fig. 4, the permission is hidden in the definition of $e \overset{ch}{\mapsto} e_2$. The rules for $[e]_{ch}:=e_1$ and if e then s_1 else s_2 require that e be a pure expression. To reason about an such statements where e is impure, one reasons by program transformation using the following rules. It is not necessary to rewrite the actual source program, it is only the local reasoning that is by program transformation.

$$\frac{x, y \text{ not free in } e, e_1, Q \qquad \Gamma; R; B \vdash \{P\}\, x := e;\; y := e_1;\; [x]_{ch} := y\, \{Q\}}{\Gamma; R; B \vdash \{P\}[e]_{ch} := e_1\{Q\}}$$

$$\frac{x \text{ not free in } s_1, s_2, Q \qquad \Gamma; R; B \vdash \{P\}\, x := e;\, \text{if } x \text{ then } s_1 \text{ else } s_2\, \{Q\}}{\Gamma; R; B \vdash \{P\}\, \text{if } e \text{ then } s_1 \text{ else } s_2\, \{Q\}}$$

The statement $\mathsf{exit}\, i$ exits from the $(i+1)^{th}$ enclosing block. A block environment B is a sequence of assertions $B_0, B_1, \ldots, B_{k-1}$ such that $(\mathsf{exit}\, i)$ is safe as long as the precondition B_i is satisfied. We write $\mathsf{nil_B}$ for the empty block environment and $B' = Q \cdot B$ for the environment such that $B'_0 = Q$ and $B'_{i+1} = B_i$.

Given a block environment B, a precondition P and a postcondition Q, the axiomatic semantics of a $(\mathsf{block}\, s)$ statement consists in executing some statements of s given the same precondition P and the block environment $Q \cdot B$ (*i.e.* each existing block nesting is incremented). The last statement of s to be executed is an exit statement that yields the **false** postcondition. An $(\mathsf{exit}\, n)$ statement is only allowed from a corresponding enclosing block, *i.e.* the precondition $B(n)$ must exist in the block environment B and it is the precondition of the $(\mathsf{exit}\, n)$ statement.

Frame Rules. The most important feature of Separation Logic is the frame rule, usually written

$$\frac{\{P\}\, s\, \{Q\}}{\{A * P\}\, s\, \{A * Q\}}$$

The appropriate generalization of this rule to our language with control flow is the last rule of Fig. 4. We can derive from it a *special frame rule* for simple statements s that do not exit or return:

$$\frac{\forall R, B.(\Gamma; R; B \vdash \{P\}\, s\, \{Q\}) \qquad \text{modified vars}(s) \cap \text{free vars}(A) = \emptyset}{\Gamma; R; B \vdash \{A * P\}\, s\, \{A * Q\}}$$

Free Variables. We use a semantic notion of free variables: x is not free in assertion A if, in any two states where only the binding of x differs, A gives the same result. However, we found it necessary to use a syntactic (inductive) definition of the variables modified by a command. One would think that command c "modifies" x if there is some state such that by the time c terminates or exits, x has a different value. However, this definition means that the modified variables of if false then B else C are *not* a superset of the modified variables of C; this lack of an inversion principle led to difficulty in proofs.

Auxiliary Variables. It is typical in Hoare Logic to use auxiliary variables to relate the pre- and postconditions, e.g., the variable a in $\{x = a\}\, x := x+1\, \{x = a+1\}$. In our shallow embedding of Hoare Logic in Coq, the variable a is a Coq variable, not a Cminor variable; formally, the user would prove in Coq the proposition, $\forall a, (\Gamma; R; B \vdash \{P\}s\{Q\})$ where a may appear free in any of Γ, R, B, P, s, Q. The existential assertion $\exists z.Q$ is useful in conjunction with this technique.

Assertions about functions require special handling of these quantified auxiliary variables. The assertion that some value f is a function with precondition P and postcondition Q is written $f : \underline{\forall} x_1 \underline{\forall} x_2 \ldots \underline{\forall} x_n, \{P\}\{Q\}$ where P and Q

are functions from value-list to assertion, each $\underline{\vee}$ is an operator of our separation logic that binds a Coq variable x_i using higher-order abstract syntax.

Application. In the full technical report [4], we show how the Separation Logic (*i.e.* the rules of Fig. 4) can be used to prove partial correctness properties of programs, with the classical in-place list-reversal example. Such proofs rely on a set of tactics, that we have written in the tactic definition language of Coq, to serve as a proof assistant for Cminor Separation Logic proofs [3].

5   Soundness of Separation Logic

Soundness means not only that there is a model for the logic, but that the model is *the* operational semantics for which the compiler guarantees correctness! In principle we could prove soundness by syntactic induction over the Hoare Logic rules, but instead we will give a semantic definition of the Hoare sextuple $\Gamma; R; B \vdash \{P\}\, s\, \{Q\}$, and then prove each of the Hoare rules as a derived lemma from this definition.

A simple example of semantic specification is that the Hoare Logic $P \Rightarrow Q$ is defined, using the underlying logical implication, as $\forall \Psi \sigma.\ P\Psi\sigma \Rightarrow Q\Psi\sigma$. From this, one could prove soundness of the Hoare Logic rule on the left (where the $\Rightarrow$ is a symbol of Hoare Logic) by expanding the definitions into the lemma on the right (where the $\Rightarrow$ is in the underlying logic), which is clearly provable in higher-order logic:

$$\frac{P \Rightarrow Q \qquad Q \Rightarrow R}{P \Rightarrow R} \qquad \frac{\forall \Psi \sigma.(P\Psi\sigma \Rightarrow Q\Psi\sigma) \quad \forall \Psi \sigma.(Q\Psi\sigma \Rightarrow R\Psi\sigma)}{\forall \Psi \sigma.(P\Psi\sigma \Rightarrow R\Psi\sigma)}$$

Definition 4. *(a) Two states σ and σ' are* equivalent *(written as $\sigma \cong \sigma'$) if they have the same stack pointer, extensionally equivalent environments, identical footprints, and if the footprint-visible portions of their memories are the same. (b) An* assertion *is a predicate on states that is extensional over equivalent environments (in Coq it is a dependent product of a predicate and a proof of extensionality).*

Definition 5. *For any control κ, we define the assertion* **safe** κ *to mean that the combination of κ with the current state is safe:*

$$\textbf{safe}\ \kappa \ =_{\text{def}}\ \lambda \Psi \sigma. \forall \sigma'.\ (\sigma \cong \sigma' \Rightarrow \Psi \vdash \textsf{safe}\,(\sigma', \kappa))$$

Definition 6. *Let A be a* frame, *that is, a closed assertion (i.e. one with no free Cminor variables). An assertion P* guards *a control κ in the frame A (written as $P\,\square_A\,\kappa$) means that whenever $A * P$ holds, it is safe to execute κ. That is,*

$$P\,\square_A\,\kappa \ =_{\text{def}}\ A * P \Rightarrow \textbf{safe}\ \kappa.$$

We extend this notion to say that a return-assertion R (a function from value-list to assertion) guards a return, and a block-exit assertion B (a function from block-nesting level to assertions) guards an exit:

$$R\,\boxed{\text{R}}_A\,\kappa \ =_{\text{def}}\ \forall vl.R(vl)\,\square_A\,\textsf{return}\ vl\cdot\kappa \qquad\qquad B\,\boxed{\text{B}}_A\,\kappa \ =_{\text{def}}\ \forall n.B(n)\,\square_A\,\textsf{exit}\ n\cdot\kappa$$

Lemma 4. *If* $P \,\square_A\, s_1 \cdot s_2 \cdot \kappa$ *then* $P \,\square_A\, (s_1; s_2) \cdot \kappa$.

Lemma 5. *If* $R \,\boxed{\text{R}}_A\, \kappa$ *then* $\forall s, R \,\boxed{\text{R}}_A\, s \cdot \kappa$.   *If* $B \,\boxed{\text{B}}_A\, \kappa$ *then* $\forall s, B \,\boxed{\text{B}}_A\, s \cdot \kappa$.

Definition 7 (Frame). *A* frame *is constructed from the global environment* Γ, *an arbitrary frame assertion* A, *and a statement* s, *by the conjunction of* Γ *with the assertion* A *closed over any variable modified by* s:

$$\mathsf{frame}(\Gamma, A, s) \ =_{\mathrm{def}} \ \Gamma * \mathsf{closemod}(s, A)$$

Definition 8 (Hoare sextuples). *The Hoare sextuples are defined in "continuation style," in terms of implications between continuations, as follows:*

$$
\begin{array}{l}
\Gamma; R; B \vdash \{P\}\, s\, \{Q\} \ =_{\mathrm{def}} \ \forall A, \kappa. \\
R \,\boxed{\text{R}}_{\mathsf{frame}(\Gamma,A,s)}\, \kappa \ \wedge\ B \,\boxed{\text{B}}_{\mathsf{frame}(\Gamma,A,s)}\, \kappa \ \wedge\ Q \,\square_{\mathsf{frame}(\Gamma,A,s)}\, \kappa \ \Rightarrow\ P \,\square_{\mathsf{frame}(\Gamma,A,s)}\, s \cdot \kappa
\end{array}
$$

From this definition we prove the rules of Fig. 4 as derived lemmas.

It should be clear from the definition—after one gets over the backward nature of the continuation transform—that the Hoare judgment specifies partial correctness, not total correctness. For example, if the statement s infinitely loops, then the continuation $(\sigma, s \cdot \kappa)$ is automatically safe, and therefore $P \,\square_A\, s \cdot \kappa$ always holds. Therefore the Hoare tuple $\Gamma; R; B \vdash \{P\}s\{Q\}$ will hold for that s, regardless of Γ, R, B, P, Q.

Sequence. The soundness of the sequence statement is the proof that if the hypotheses $\mathsf{H}_1 : \Gamma; R; B \vdash \{P\}\, s_1\, \{P'\}$ and $\mathsf{H}_2 : \Gamma; R; B \vdash \{P'\}\, s_2\, \{Q\}$ hold, then we have to prove $\mathsf{Goal} : \Gamma; R; B \vdash \{P\}\, s_1; s_2\, \{Q\}$ (see Fig. 4). If we unfold the definition of the Hoare sextuples, H_1, H_2 and Goal become:

$$
(\forall A, \kappa) \, \dfrac{R \,\boxed{\text{R}}_{\mathsf{frame}(\Gamma,A,(s_1;s_2))}\, \kappa \qquad B \,\boxed{\text{B}}_{\mathsf{frame}(\Gamma,A,(s_1;s_2))}\, \kappa \qquad Q \,\square_{\mathsf{frame}(\Gamma,A,(s_1;s_2))}\, \kappa}{P \,\square_{\mathsf{frame}(\Gamma,A,(s_1;s_2))}\, (s_1; s_2) \cdot \kappa} \ \mathsf{Goal}
$$

We prove $P \,\square_{\mathsf{frame}(\Gamma,A,(s_1;s_2))}\, (s_1; s_2) \cdot k$ using Lemma 4:[2]

$$
\dfrac{\dfrac{R \,\boxed{\text{R}}\, k}{R \,\boxed{\text{R}}\, s_2 \cdot k}\,\text{Lm. 5} \qquad \dfrac{B \,\boxed{\text{B}}\, k}{B \,\boxed{\text{B}}\, s_2 \cdot k}\,\text{Lm. 5} \qquad \dfrac{\dfrac{R \,\boxed{\text{R}}\, k \quad B \,\boxed{\text{B}}\, k \quad Q \,\square\, k}{P' \,\square\, s_2 \cdot k}\,\mathsf{H}_2}{}}{\dfrac{\dfrac{P \,\square\, s_1 \cdot s_2 \cdot k}{P \,\square\, (s_1; s_2) \cdot k}\,\text{Lm. 4}}{}}\,\mathsf{H}_1
$$

Loop Rule. The loop rule turns out to be one of the most difficult ones to prove. A loop continues executing until the loop-body performs an exit or return. If loop s executes n steps, then there will be 0 or more complete iterations of $n_1, n_2, \ldots$ steps, followed by j steps into the last iteration. Then either there is an exit (or return) from the loop, or the loop will keep going. But if the exit is from an inner-nested block, then it does not terminate the loop (or even this iteration). Thus we need a formal notion of when a statement exits.

---

[2] We will elide the frames from proof sketches by writing $\square$ without a subscript; this particular proof relies on a lemma that $\mathsf{closemod}(s_1, \mathsf{closemod}((s_1; s_2), A)) = \mathsf{closemod}((s_1; s_2), A)$.

Consider the statement $s = $ if b then exit 2 else (skip; $x := y$), executing in state σ. Let us execute n steps into s, that is, $\Psi \vdash (\sigma, s \cdot \kappa) \longmapsto^n (\sigma', \kappa')$. If n is small, then the behavior should not depend on κ; only when we "emerge" from s is κ important. In this example, if $\rho_\sigma b$ is a true value, then as long as $n \le 1$ the statement s can *absorb* n steps independent of κ; if $\rho_\sigma b$ is a false value, then s can absorb up to 3 steps. To reason about absorption, we define the concatenation $\kappa_1 \circ \kappa_2$ of a control prefix κ_1 and a control κ_2 as follows:

$$\mathsf{Kstop} \circ \kappa =_{\mathrm{def}} \kappa \qquad\qquad (\mathsf{Kblock}\,\kappa') \circ \kappa =_{\mathrm{def}} \mathsf{Kblock}\,(\kappa' \circ \kappa)$$
$$(s \cdot \kappa') \circ \kappa =_{\mathrm{def}} s \cdot (\kappa' \circ \kappa) \qquad (\mathsf{Kcall}\,xl\,f\,sp\,\rho\,\kappa') \circ \kappa =_{\mathrm{def}} \mathsf{Kcall}\,xl\,f\,sp\,\rho\,(\kappa' \circ \kappa)$$

Kstop is the empty prefix; $\mathsf{Kstop} \circ \kappa$ does not mean "stop," it means κ.

Definition 9 (absorption). *A statement s in state σ absorbs n steps (written as* $\mathsf{absorb}(n, s, \sigma)$*) iff* $\forall j \le n. \exists \kappa_{\mathrm{prefix}}.\exists \sigma'. \forall \kappa.\ \Psi \vdash (\sigma, s \cdot \kappa) \longmapsto^j (\sigma', \kappa_{\mathrm{prefix}} \circ \kappa)$.

Example 1. An exit statement by itself absorbs no steps (it immediately uses its control-tail), but $\mathsf{block}\,(\mathsf{exit}\,0)$ can absorb the 2 following steps:
$$\Psi \vdash (\sigma, \mathsf{block}\,(\mathsf{exit}\,0) \cdot \kappa) \longmapsto (\sigma, \mathsf{exit}\,0 \cdot \mathsf{Kblock}\,\kappa) \longmapsto (\sigma, \kappa)$$

Lemma 6. *1.* $\mathsf{absorb}(0, s, \sigma)$.
2. $\mathsf{absorb}(n + 1, s, \sigma) \Rightarrow \mathsf{absorb}(n, s, \sigma)$.
3. If $\neg\mathsf{absorb}(n, s, \sigma)$*, then* $\exists i < n.\mathsf{absorb}(i, s, \sigma) \wedge \neg\mathsf{absorb}(i + 1, s, \sigma)$*. We say that s absorbs at most i steps in state σ.*

Definition 10. *We write* $(s;)^n s'$ *to mean* $\underbrace{s; s; \ldots; s;}_{n} s'$.

Lemma 7. $$\frac{\Gamma; R; B \vdash \{I\}s\{I\}}{\Gamma; R; B \vdash \{I\}(s;)^n\mathsf{loop\,skip}\{\mathbf{false}\}}$$

Proof. For $n = 0$, the infinite-loop ($\mathsf{loop\,skip}$) satisfies any precondition for partial correctness. For $n + 1$, assume κ, $R \,\boxed{\mathsf{R}}\, \kappa$, $B \,\boxed{\mathsf{B}}\, \kappa$; by the induction hypothesis (with $R\boxed{\mathsf{R}}\kappa$ and $B\boxed{\mathsf{B}}\kappa$) we know $I\square\,(s;)^n\mathsf{loop\,skip}\cdot\kappa$. We have $R\boxed{\mathsf{R}}(s;)^n\mathsf{loop\,skip}\cdot\kappa$ and $B \,\boxed{\mathsf{B}}\, (s;)^n\mathsf{loop\,skip}\cdot\kappa$ by Lemma 5. We use the hypothesis $\Gamma; R; B \vdash \{I\}s\{I\}$ to augment the result to $I\,\square\,(s;(s;)^n\mathsf{loop\,skip})\cdot\kappa$. ∎

Theorem 1. $$\frac{\Gamma; R; B \vdash \{I\}s\{I\}}{\Gamma; R; B \vdash \{I\}\mathsf{loop}\,s\{\mathbf{false}\}}$$

Proof. Assume κ, $R \,\boxed{\mathsf{R}}\, \kappa$, $B \,\boxed{\mathsf{B}}\, \kappa$. To prove $I\,\square\,\mathsf{loop}\,s\cdot\kappa$, assume σ and $I\sigma$ and prove $\mathsf{safe}\,(\sigma, \mathsf{loop}\,s\cdot\kappa)$. We must prove that for any n, after n steps we are not stuck. We unfold the loop n times, that is, we use Lemma 7 to show $\mathsf{safe}\,(\sigma, (s;)^n\mathsf{loop\,skip}\cdot\kappa)$. We can show that if this is safe for n steps, so is $\mathsf{loop}\,s\cdot\kappa$ by the principle of absorption. Either s absorbs n steps, in which case we are done; or s absorbs at most $j < n$ steps, leading to a state σ' and a control (respectively) $\kappa_{\mathit{prefix}} \circ (s;)^{n-1}\mathsf{loop\,skip}\cdot\kappa$ or $\kappa_{\mathit{prefix}} \circ \mathsf{loop}\,s\cdot\kappa$. Now, because s cannot absorb $j + 1$ steps, we know that either κ_{prefix} is empty (because s has terminated normally) or κ_{prefix} starts with a return or exit, in which case we *escape (resp. past the* loop skip *or the* loop *s) into* κ. *If* κ_{prefix} *is empty then we apply strong induction on the case* $n - j$ *steps; if we escape, then* (σ', κ) *is safe iff* $(\sigma, \text{loop } s \cdot \kappa)$ *is safe. (For example, if* $j = 0$, *then it must be that* $s = $ return *or* $s = $ exit, *so in one step we reach* $\kappa_{prefix} \circ (\text{loop } s \cdot \kappa)$ *with* $\kappa_{prefix} = $ return *or* $\kappa_{prefix} = $ exit.) $\blacksquare$

6 Sequential Reasoning About Sequential Features

Concurrent Cminor, like most concurrent programming languages used in practice, is a sequential programming language with a few concurrent features (locks and threads) added on. We would like to be able to reason about the sequential features using purely sequential reasoning. If we have to reason about all the many sequential features without being able to assume such things as determinacy and sequential control, then the proofs become much more difficult.

One would expect this approach to run into trouble because critical assumptions underlying the sequential operational semantics would not hold in the concurrent setting. For example, on a shared-memory multiprocessor we cannot assume that (x:=x+1; x:=x+1) has the same effect as (x:=x+2); and on any real multiprocessor we cannot even assume *sequential consistency*—that the semantics of n threads is some interleaving of the steps of the individual threads.

We will solve this problem in several stages. Stage 1 of this plan is the current paper. Stages 2, 3, and 4 are work in progress; the remainder is future work.

1. We have made the language, the Separation Logic, and our proof extensible: the set of control-flow statements is fixed (inductive) but the set of straight-line statements is extensible by means of a parameterized module in Coq. We have added to each state σ an *oracle* which predicts the meaning of the extended instruction (but which does nothing on the core language). All the proofs we have described in this paper are on this extensible language.
2. We define spawn, lock, and unlock as extended straight-line statements. We define a concurrent small-step semantics that assumes noninterference (and gets "stuck" on interference).
3. From this semantics, we calculate a single-thread small-step semantics equipped with the oracle that predicts the effects of synchronizations.
4. We define a Concurrent Separation Logic for Cminor as an extension of the Sequential Separation Logic. Its soundness proof uses the sequential soundness proof as a lemma.
5. We will use Concurrent Separation Logic to guarantee noninterference of source programs. Then (x:=x+1; x:=x+1) *will* have the same effect as (x:=x+2).
6. We will prove that the Cminor compiler (CompCert) compiles each footprint-safe source thread into an equivalent footprint-safe machine-language thread. Thus, noninterfering source programs will produce noninterfering machine-language programs.

7. We will demonstrate, with respect to a formal model of weak-memory-consistency microprocessor, that noninterfering machine-language programs give the same results as they would on a sequentially consistent machine.

7   The Machine-Checked Proof

We have proved in Coq the soundness of Separation Logic for Cminor. Each rule is proved as a lemma; in addition there is a main theorem that if you prove all your function bodies satisfy their pre/postconditions, then the program "call main()" is safe. We have informally tested the adequacy of our result by doing tactical proofs of small programs [3].

Lines	Component
41	Axioms: dependent unique choice, relational choice, extensionality
8792	Memory model, floats, 32-bit integers, values, operators, maps (exactly as in CompCert [12])
4408	Sharable permissions, Cminor language, operational semantics
462	Separation Logic operators and rules
9874	Soundness proof of Separation Logic

These line counts include some repetition of specifications (between Modules and Module Types) in Coq's module system.

8   Conclusion

In this paper, we have defined a formal semantics for the language Cminor. It consists of a big-step semantics for expressions and a small-step semantics for statements. The small-step semantics is based on continuations mainly to allow a uniform representation of statement execution. The small-step semantics deals with nonlocal control constructs (return, exit) and is designed to extend to the concurrent setting.

Then, we have defined a Separation Logic for Cminor. It consists of an assertion language and an axiomatic semantics. We have extended classical Hoare triples to sextuples in order to take into account nonlocal control constructs. From this definition of sextuples, we have proved the rules of axiomatic semantics, thus proving the soundness of our Separation Logic.

We have also proved the semantic equivalence between our small-step semantics and the big-step semantics of the CompCert certified compiler, so the Cminor programs that we prove in Separation Logic can be compiled by the CompCert certified compiler. We plan to connect a Cminor certified compiler directly to the small-step semantics, instead of going through the big-step semantics.

Small-step reasoning is useful for sequential programming languages that will be extended with concurrent features; but small-step reasoning about nonlocal control constructs mixed with structured programming (loop) is not trivial. We have relied on the determinacy of the small-step relation so that we can define concepts such as $\mathsf{absorb}(n, s, \sigma)$.

References

1. The Coq proof assistant, `http://coq.inria.fr`
2. American National Standard for Information Systems – Programming Language – C: American National Standards Institute (1990)
3. Appel, A.W.: Tactics for separation logic (January 2006), `http://www.cs.princeton.edu/~appel/papers/septacs.pdf`
4. Appel, A.W., Blazy, S.: Separation logic for small-step Cminor (extended version). Technical Report RR 6138, INRIA (March 2007), `https://hal.inria.fr/inria-00134699`
5. Blazy, S., Dargaye, Z., Leroy, X.: Formal verification of a C compiler front-end. In: Misra, J., Nipkow, T., Sekerinski, E. (eds.) FM 2006. LNCS, vol. 4085, pp. 460–475. Springer, Heidelberg (2006)
6. Blazy, S., Leroy, X.: Formal verification of a memory model for C-like imperative languages. In: Lau, K.-K., Banach, R. (eds.) ICFEM 2005. LNCS, vol. 3785, pp. 280–299. Springer, Heidelberg (2005)
7. Bornat, R., Calcagno, C., O'Hearn, P., Parkinson, M.: Permission accounting in separation logic. In: POPL'05, pp. 259–270. ACM Press, New York (2005)
8. Dargaye, Z.: Décurryfication certifiée. JFLA (Journées Françaises des Langages Applicatifs), 119–133 (2007)
9. Ishtiaq, S., O'Hearn, P.: BI as an assertion language for mutable data structures. In: POPL'01, January 2001, pp. 14–26. ACM Press, New York (2001)
10. Klein, G., Tuch, H., Norrish, M.: Types, bytes, and separation logic. In: POPL'07, January 2007, pp. 97–108. ACM Press, New York (2007)
11. Leinenbach, D., Paul, W., Petrova, E.: Towards the formal verification of a C0 compiler: Code generation and implementation correctness. In: SEFM'05. IEEE Conference on Software Engineering and Formal Methods, IEEE Computer Society Press, Los Alamitos (2005)
12. Leroy, X.: Formal certification of a compiler back-end, or: programming a compiler with a proof assistant. In: POPL'06, pp. 42–54. ACM Press, New York (2006)
13. Moore, J.S.: A mechanically verified language implementation. Journal of Automated Reasoning 5(4), 461–492 (1989)
14. Ni, Z., Shao, Z.: Certified assembly programming with embedded code pointers. In: POPL'06, January 2006, pp. 320–333. ACM Press, New York (2006)
15. O'Hearn, P., Reynolds, J., Yang, H.: Local reasoning about programs that alter data structures. In: Fribourg, L. (ed.) CSL 2001 and EACSL 2001. LNCS, vol. 2142, pp. 1–19. Springer, Heidelberg (2001)
16. Parkinson, M.J.: Local Reasoning for Java. PhD thesis, University of Cambridge (2005)
17. Schirmer, N.: Verification of Sequential Imperative Programs in Isabelle/HOL. PhD thesis, Technische Universität München (2006)

Formalising Java's Data Race Free Guarantee

David Aspinall and Jaroslav Ševčík

LFCS, School of Informatics, University of Edinburgh

Abstract. We formalise the *data race free* (DRF) guarantee provided by Java, as captured by the semi-formal Java Memory Model (JMM) [1] and published in the Java Language Specification [2]. The DRF guarantee says that all programs which are correctly synchronised (i.e., free of data races) can only have sequentially consistent behaviours. Such programs can be understood intuitively by programmers. Formalisation has achieved three aims. First, we made definitions and proofs precise, leading to a better understanding; our analysis found several hidden inconsistencies and missing details. Second, the formalisation lets us explore variations and investigate their impact in the proof with the aim of simplifying the model; we found that not all of the anticipated conditions in the JMM definition were actually necessary for the DRF guarantee. This allows us to suggest a quick fix to a recently discovered serious bug [3] without invalidating the DRF guarantee. Finally, the formal definition provides a basis to test concrete examples, and opens the way for future work on JMM-aware logics for concurrent programs.

1 Introduction

Today, most techniques for reasoning about shared-memory concurrent programs assume an interleaved semantics, although modern hardware architectures and compilers do not guarantee one [4]. So there is a gap between languages with shared-memory concurrency and reasoning principles for them. Java aims to bridge the gap via a complex contract, called the *Java Memory Model* (JMM) [1,2], which holds between the virtual machine and programmers. For programmers, the JMM claims that correctly synchronised (data race free) programs only have *sequentially consistent* behaviours, which means that reasoning based on interleaved semantics is valid in this case. This is the *data race free* DRF guarantee. For compiler writers implementing the virtual machine, the JMM constrains permissible code optimisations; most prominently, instruction reordering.

To see why the memory model contract is needed, consider the simple program below, with two threads sharing memory locations x and y:

initially: x = y = 0	
1: r1 := x	3: r2 := y
2: y := 1	4: x := 1

The contents of the thread-local registers r1 and r2 at the end of the program depends on the order of serialisation of memory accesses. For example, the result

K. Schneider and J. Brandt (Eds.): TPHOLs 2007, LNCS 4732, pp. 22–37, 2007.

r1 = 0 and r2 = 0 holds if the order of the statements is 1, 3, 2, 4. On the other hand, the result r1 = r2 = 1 is not possible in any serialisation of the program, and most programmers would not expect such an outcome. But if a compiler or the low-level hardware reorders the independent instructions 1, 2 and 3, 4 in each thread, then the result r1 = r2 = 1 *is* possible, e.g., by executing the statements in the sequence 2, 4, 3, 1. This kind of reordering results from simple optimisations, such as write buffering to main memory or common subexpression elimination. To allow these optimisations, we need a *relaxed memory model* that provides weaker guarantees than global sequential consistency, but allows the programmer some kind of control to prevent unintended behaviours.

The Java Memory Model has already been revised after the initial version had serious flaws [5]. The current version is designed to provide:

1. *a promise for programmers*: sequential consistency must be sacrificed to allow optimisations, but it will still hold for data race free programs;
2. *a promise for security*: even for programs with data races, values should not appear "out of thin air", which prevents unintended information leakage;
3. *a promise for compilers*: common hardware and software optimisations should be allowed as far as possible without violating the first two requirements.

The first requirement gives us hope for intuitive understanding, and simple program logics, for data race free programs. Most programs should be correctly synchronised, as recommended by [6]. The second requirement makes a security promise for the "racy" programs: even though values may be undetermined, they should have an origin within the computation, and not, e.g., appear from other memory contents which may be sensitive. Considering these goals, Manson et al [1] published proofs of two theorems. The first theorem, stating the promise for compilers, was recently falsified — Cenciarelli et al [3] found a counterexample. The second theorem, which is the DRF guarantee, is the topic of this paper.

Contribution. We describe a formalisation of definitions of the JMM and a proof of the DRF guarantee it provides. We believe that this is the first theorem prover formalisation of Java's memory model. The exercise has provided significant clarifications of the official definition and proof, turning up notable flaws. Our formalisation reveals a design space for changes that preserve the DRF guarantee, enabling us to suggest fixes for the recently discovered bug while preserving the key guarantee for programmers. When testing our fixes on the JMM test cases [7] we discovered another flaw in the memory model and we offer a solution for it, as well. While we have intentionally stayed close to the informal definitions, we have made some simplifications. The most important is that we require executions to be finite, because infinite executions cause some tricky problems without, we believe, illuminating the DRF proof (see Sect. 4 for further details).

Overview. The rest of this paper is organised as follows. In Sect. 2, we introduce the basic definitions of the JMM, as we have formalised them in Isabelle, together with some commentary to assist the reader. In Sect. 3 we give our proof of the DRF guarantee. This considerably expands the informal proof of [8]. Sect. 4 summarises our results, collecting together changes to the JMM to repair the bugs, discussions of the differences between our formalisation and the official informal work, and the improvements we claim to have made. Sect. 5 concludes, mentioning related work on other formal methods applied to memory models, as well as our plans for future work building on the results here.

2 Formal Definitions for the JMM

The following definitions are from [2,1], with minor differences described at the end of the section. We use abstract types $\mathcal{T}$ for thread identifiers, ranged over by t; $\mathcal{M}$ for synchronisation monitor identifiers, ranged over by m; $\mathcal{L}$ for variables (i.e., memory locations), ranged over by v (in examples, x, y, etc.); and $\mathcal{V}$ for values. The starting point is the notion of *action*.

Definition 1 (Action). *An action is a memory-related operation; it is modelled by an abstract type $\mathcal{A}$ with the following properties: (1) Each action belongs to one thread, denoted $T(a)$. (2) An action has one of the following* action kinds:

- volatile read *of $v \in \mathcal{L}$,*
- volatile write *to $v \in \mathcal{L}$,*
- lock *on monitor $m \in \mathcal{M}$,*
- unlock *on monitor $m \in \mathcal{M}$,*
- normal read *from $v \in \mathcal{L}$,*
- normal write *to $v \in \mathcal{L}$.*

An action kind includes the associated variable or monitor. The volatile read, write, lock and unlock actions are called synchronisation actions.

In contrast to an interleaved semantics, in relaxed memory models there is no total ordering of all actions by time. Instead, the JMM imposes a total order, called *synchronisation order*, on all synchronisation actions, while allowing non-volatile reads and writes to be reordered to a certain degree. To capture the intra-thread ordering of actions, there is a total order, called *program order*, on all actions of each thread, which does not relate actions of different threads. These orders are gathered together in the definition of an *execution*. An execution allows non-deterministic behaviours because the order and visibility of memory operations may not be fully constrained.

Definition 2 (Execution). *An execution $E = \langle A, P, \leq_{po}, \leq_{so}, W, V \rangle$, where:*

- *$A \subseteq \mathcal{A}$ is a set of actions,*
- *P is a program, which is represented as a function that for each thread decides validity of a given sequence of action kinds with associated values if the action kind is a read or a write,*
- *the partial order $\leq_{po} \subseteq A \times A$ is the program order,*
- *the partial order $\leq_{so} \subseteq A \times A$ is the synchronisation order,*
- *$W \in \mathcal{A} \Rightarrow \mathcal{A}$ is a write-seen function. It assigns a write to each read action from A, the $W(r)$ denotes the write seen by r, i.e. the value read by r is $V(W(r))$. The value of $W(a)$ for non-read actions a is unspecified,*
- *$V \in \mathcal{A} \Rightarrow \mathcal{V}$ is a value-written function that assigns a value to each write from A, $V(a)$ is unspecified for non-write actions a.*

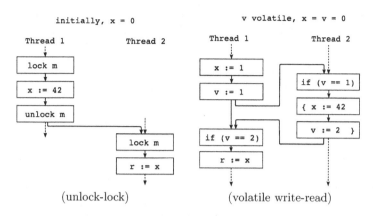

Fig. 1. Happens before by release-acquire pairs

Following Lamport [9], an approximation of global time is now defined by the *happens-before* relation of an execution. An action a *happens-before* b, written $a \leq_{hb} b$, if either: (1) a and b are a *release-acquire* pair, such as an unlock of a monitor m and a lock of the same m, where a is ordered before b by the synchronisation order, or (2) a is before b in the program order, or (3) there is c such that $a \leq_{hb} c$ and $c \leq_{hb} b$. A precise definition follows in Def. 4.

Fig. 1 shows two simple cases of the happens-before relation. In the first execution, the write x := 42 happens-before the read of x because the accesses to x are protected by the monitor m; the lock of m is ordered after the unlock of m by the synchronisation order in the given execution. Similarly, a volatile write and a volatile read from the same variable are a release-acquire pair. In the second execution, the happens-before includes two such pairs for the variable v. This means that the three instructions in thread 2 must happen in between the first two and last two instructions in thread 1.

The precise definition of the happens-before relation is provided via an auxiliary *synchronises-with* ordering. Each is derived from a given execution.

Definition 3 (Synchronizes-with). *In an execution with synchronisation order $\leq_{so}$, an action a synchronises-with an action b (written $a <_{sw} b$) if $a \leq_{so} b$ and a and b satisfy one of the following conditions:*

- *a is an unlock on monitor m and b is a lock on monitor m,*
- *a is a volatile write to v and b is a volatile read from v.*

Definition 4 (Happens-before). *The happens-before order of an execution is the transitive closure of the composition of its synchronises-with order and its program order, i.e. $\leq_{hb} = (<_{sw} \cup \leq_{po})^{+}$.*

To relate a (sequential) program to a sequence of actions performed by one thread we must define a notion of *sequential validity*. The next definition is new to our formalisation and was left implicit in [1], as was the notion of program itself. To be as abstract as possible, we consider programs as characteristic functions on traces, i.e., thread-indexed predicates on sequences of pairs of an action kind and a value. An action kind and value pair determines the effect of a memory operation (e.g. a read from a variable, or a write to a variable with a given value).

Definition 5 (Sequential validity). *We say that a sequence s of action kind-value pairs is* sequentially valid *with respect to a thread t and a program P if $P(t, s)$ holds.*

The next definition places some sensible restriction on executions.

Definition 6 (Well-formed execution). *We say that an* execution $\langle A, P, \leq_{po}, \leq_{so}, W, V \rangle$ *is* well-formed *if*

1. *A is finite.*
2. *$\leq_{po}$ restricted on actions of one thread is a total order, $\leq_{po}$ does not relate actions of different threads.*
3. *$\leq_{so}$ is total on synchronisation actions of A.*
4. *$\leq_{so}$ is consistent with $\leq_{po}$, i.e. $a \leq_{so} b \wedge b \leq_{po} a \implies a = b$.*
5. *W is properly typed: for every non-volatile read $r \in A$, $W(r)$ is a non-volatile write; for every volatile read $r \in A$, $W(r)$ is a volatile write.*
6. *Locking is proper: for all lock actions $l \in A$ on monitors m and all threads t different from the thread of l, the number of locks in t before l in $\leq_{so}$ is the same as the number of unlocks in t before l in $\leq_{so}$.*
7. *Program order is intra-thread consistent: for each thread t, the sequence of action kinds and values[1] of actions performed by t in the program order $\leq_{po}$ is sequentially valid with respect to P and t.*
8. *$\leq_{so}$ is consistent with W: for every volatile read r of a variable v we have $W(r) \leq_{so} r$ and for any volatile write w to v, either $w \leq_{so} W(r)$ or $r \leq_{so} w$.*
9. *$\leq_{hb}$ is consistent with W: for all reads r of v it holds that $r \not\leq_{hb} W(r)$ and there is no intervening write w to v, i.e. if $W(r) \leq_{hb} w \leq_{hb} r$ and w writes to v then[2] $W(r) = w$.*

2.1 Legal Executions

The definition of *legal execution* constitutes the core of the Java Memory Model, but it appears convoluted at first sight.

Definition 7 (Legality). *A well-formed execution $\langle A, P, \leq_{po}, \leq_{so}, W, V \rangle$ with happens before order $\leq_{hb}$ is* legal *if there is a finite "committing" sequence of sets of actions C_i and well-formed "justifying" executions $E_i = \langle A_i, P, \leq_{po_i}, \leq_{so_i}, W_i, V_i \rangle$ with happens-before $\leq_{hb_i}$, such that $C_0 = \emptyset$, $C_{i-1} \subseteq C_i$ for all $i > 0$, $\bigcup C_i = A$, and for each $i > 0$ the following rules are satisfied:*

---

[1] The *value* of an action a is $V(a)$ if a is a write, $V(W(a))$ if a is a read, or an arbitrary value otherwise.

[2] The Java Specification omits the part "$W(r) = w$", which is clearly wrong since happens-before is reflexive.

1. $C_i \subseteq A_i$.
2. $\leq_{hb_i} |_{C_i} = \leq_{hb} |_{C_i}$.
3. $\leq_{so_i} |_{C_i} = \leq_{so} |_{C_i}$.
4. $V_i|_{C_i} = V|_{C_i}$.
5. $W_i|_{C_{i-1}} = W|_{C_{i-1}}$.
6. For all reads $r \in A_i - C_{i-1}$ we have $W_i(r) \leq_{hb_i} r$.
7. For all reads $r \in C_i - C_{i-1}$ we have $W_i(r) \in C_{i-1}$ and $W(r) \in C_{i-1}$.

To get some intuition for Def. 7, we explain some examples of behaviours that the memory model tries to rule in and out, and how they are argued about. The structure of reasoning is to consider the desired outcome, and then explain how it can (or cannot) arise by some (or any) execution. When considering a possibly-legal execution, we argue that it is allowed by repeatedly extending a committing sequence with actions which could happen in some speculated justifying executions E_i. The aim is to commit the entire execution.

As a first example, consider the program on the first page and a desired execution in which the result is $r1 = r2 = 1$. To denote actions, we use $W(x, v)$ for a write of value v to variable x and $R(x)$ for a read from x. We start with C_1 being two (implicit) initialisation actions which assign the default values: $C_1 = \{W(x, 0), W(y, 0)\}$. The two reads must each see the writes of value 1, which are in opposite threads. Since writes must be committed before the reads that see them (rule 7 of legality), we next commit the writes $C_2 = C_1 \cup \{W(x, 1), W(y, 1)\}$. Finally, we can commit the reads $C_3 = C_2 \cup \{R(x), R(y)\}$. This case needs no speculation; we justify the committing sequence using only one execution, in which reads see the default writes and all the writes write 0.

Another example of a legal execution is for the first program in Fig. 2 where the read of x sees the write of x in the other thread and the read of y sees the first write of y in the first thread. We again start with $C_1 = \{W(x, 0), W(y, 0)\}$. To commit the reads, we need to commit the writes with values 42 first (rules 4 and 7). As we cannot commit x:=r2 with the value 42 yet (rule 6 and intra-thread consistency), we commit $C_2 = C_1 \cup \{W(y, 42)\}$ and justify it by an execution performing the write y:=42. Committing the read r2:=y ($C_3 = C_2 \cup \{R(y)\}$) enables this read to see the write $W(y, 42)$ (thanks to rule 5) in the corresponding justifying execution, hence we can commit the write to x with the value 42: $C_4 = C_3 \cup \{W(x, 42)\}$. Finally, committing the read r1:=x completes the committing sequence. Note that in the final execution, the instruction y:=r1 performs the write to y of 42, whereas the instruction y:=42 was used to justify it!

In contrast, the out of thin air behaviour in the second program of Fig. 2 cannot be achieved by any legal execution. To see this, suppose the contrary and consider a committing sequence. The writes of 42 must be committed before the reads (rules 4 and 7), hence when justifying the first committed of the two writes of 42 none of the reads is committed yet, thus both the reads must see the writes that happen-before them (rule 6). But the only writes that happen-before the reads are the default writes of the value 0. As a result, it is not possible to justify the first write of the value 42.

initially x = y = 0

r1 := x	r2 := y
if (r1 > 0)	x := r2
y := r1	
if (r1 == 0)	
y := 42	

initially x = y = 0

r1 := x	r2 := y
y := r1	x := r2

(allowed)   (prohibited)

Is it possible to get r1 = r2 = 42 at the end of an execution?

Fig. 2. Examples of legal and illegal executions

Definition 8 (Sequential consistency). *An execution is sequentially consistent if there is a total order consistent with the execution's program order and synchronisation order such that every read in the execution sees the most recent write in the total order.*

Definition 9 (Conflict). *An execution has a conflicting pair of actions a and b if both access the same variable and either a and b are writes, or one of them is a read and the other one is a write.*

Definition 10 (DRF). *A program is data race free if in each sequentially consistent execution of the program, for each conflicting pair of actions a and b in the execution we have either $a \leq_{hb} b$ or $b \leq_{hb} a$.*

With this definition of data race freedom, the DRF guarantee is very strong. For example, both programs below are considered data race free.

v is volatile

initially: x = y = 0		initially: x = v = 0	
r1 := x	r2 := y	x := 1	if (v == 1)
if (r1 > 0)	if (r2 > 0)	v := 1	{ x := 42
y := 1	x := 1	if (v == 2)	v := 2 }
		r := x	

The DRF guarantee ensures that in the first program [8], the reads of x and y will always see 0. In the second program, the DRF guarantees that the read r:=x can only see the write x:=42. Note that if v were not volatile, the second program would not be data race free and the read of x could see the value 1 (but not 0). Section 4 contains further discussion on the above definitions.

2.2   Notes on Relation to Informal Definitions

In our formalisation, we define several notions slightly differently to the informal specification in [1]. We define actions as an abstract data type (Def. 1) instead of a tuple containing a unique action identifier, a thread identifier, an action kind and object involved in the action. Def. 2 (execution) differs from the one of [1] by omitting the synchronises-with and happens-before orders, which are derived in terms of the program and synchronisation orders, and by giving a precise meaning to the notion of programs. Our definition of well-formed executions (Def. 6) requires the set of actions to be finite instead of just restricting the synchronisation order to an omega order. We will discuss the motivation for this change in Sect. 4. We omit action kinds irrelevant for the DRF guarantee proof – external actions and thread management actions, such as thread start, thread finish, thread spawn and thread join[3]. Compared to definition of legality in [1], we have removed rules 8 and 9 for legality as they are not important for the proof. Finally, we strengthen the notion of sequential consistency to respect mutual exclusivity of locks. See Sect. 4 for further details.

3   Proof of DRF Guarantee

Definition 11 (Well-formed program). *We say that a program P is well-formed if for all threads t and action kind-value sequences s, sequential validity of s with respect to t and P implies*

- *sequential validity of all prefixes u of s with respect to t and P (P is prefix-closed), and*
- *sequential validity of all sequences u obtained from s by changing the value of the last action-value pair to a different value with respect to t and P, provided that the last action in s is a read (P is final read agnostic).*

Lemma 1. *If $\leq_p$ is a partial order on A and $\leq_t$ is a total order on $S \subseteq A$, then $\leq_q = (\leq_p \cup \leq_t)^+$ is a partial order on A.*

Lemma 2. *For any well-formed execution of a data race free well-formed program, if each read sees a write that happens-before it, the execution is sequentially consistent.*

Proof. Using Lemma 1, $(\leq_{so} \cup \leq_{po})^+$ is a partial order. Take a topological sort $\leq_t$ on $(\leq_{so} \cup \leq_{po})^+$. Since $\leq_t$ is a total order on a finite set, it must be well-founded. We prove sequential consistency by well-founded induction on $\leq_t$.

Suppose that we have a read r and all reads $x \leq_t r$ see the most recent write. We will show that r also sees the most recent write by contradiction.

Assume that r does not see the most recent write and let w be the most recent write to the variable read by r. Let A' be $\{x \mid x \leq_t r\}$. Then the execution $E' = \langle A', P, \leq_{po} |_{A' \times A'}, \leq_{so} |_{A' \times A'}, W[r \mapsto w], V \rangle$ is a well-formed execution (see Lemma 3). From the induction hypothesis, E' is sequentially consistent (all reads in E' see the most recent write). From the well-formedness of E it cannot be the case that $W(r) \leq_{hb} w \leq_{hb} r$, i.e. either $W(r)$ and w, or w and r are a conflicting pair of actions in both E and E'.

As a result, E' is a well-formed sequentially consistent execution with a conflict. This is a contradiction with data race freedom of P.

---

[3] However, we have formalised a version that contains all these actions.

The proof of Lemma 2 is broadly similar to the informal proof in [1]. There is a minor difference in performing a topological sort on $(\leq_{so} \cup \leq_{po})^+$ instead of happens-before order. This guarantees consistency with the synchronisation order, which we use in the next lemma. A more significant difference is restricting the execution to all actions before r in $\leq_t$ order and updating $W(r)$ to see w, instead of constructing a sequentially consistent completion of the execution. The reason is that sequentially consistent completion might require to insert initialisation actions to the beginning of the execution, hence the original proof does not work as stated, because it assumes that the sequentially consistent completion only adds actions to the "end" of the execution (in terms of $\leq_t$). We discuss related issues in Sect. 4.

Lemma 3 (Cut-and-update). *Let P be a well-formed program, $\langle A, P, \leq_{po}, \leq_{so}, W, V \rangle$ a well-formed execution, $\leq_{hb}$ its happens-before order, $\leq_t$ a total order on A, $r \in A$ a read action of variable v, and $w \in A$ a write action to v such that:*

- *$\leq_t$ is consistent with $\leq_{so}$ and $\leq_{hb}$,*
- *for every read $r \in A$ we have $W(r) \leq_{hb} r$,*
- *w is the most recent write to r in $\leq t$, i.e. $w \leq_t r$ and for all writes w' to variable v either $w' \leq_t w$ or $r \leq_t w'$,*

Let A' be $\{x \mid x \leq_t r\}$. Then the execution $\langle A', P, \leq_{po} \mid_{A' \times A'}, \leq_{so} \mid_{A' \times A'}, W[r \mapsto w], V \rangle$ is a well-formed execution.

Proof. It is straightforward (although tedious) to establish all the conditions from Def. 6 for well-formedness of $\langle A', P, \leq_{po} \mid_{A' \times A'}, \leq_{so} \mid_{A' \times A'}, W[r \mapsto w], V \rangle$.

The following is our formal equivalent of Theorem 3 from [1]; ensuring this property is a key motivation behind the definitions of the JMM.

Theorem 1 (DRF guarantee). *Any legal execution E of a well-formed data race free program is sequentially consistent.*

Proof. From Lemma 2 it is sufficient to show that every read in E sees a write that happens-before it. From the legality of E we have a committing sequence $\{C_i, E_i\}$ justifying E. We will show by induction on i that all reads in C_i see writes that happens-before them.

The base case is trivial ($C_0 = \emptyset$). For the induction step, let's assume that all reads $r \in C_{i-1}$ we have $W(r) \leq_{hb} r$. We will show that for any read $r \in C_i$ we get $W(r) \leq_{hb} r$.

Note that E_i is sequentially consistent: Let $\leq_{hb_i}$ be happens-before of E_i. Using the induction hypothesis with rules 2, 5 we obtain $W(r) \leq_{hb_i} r$ for all reads $r \in C_{i-1}$. Using rule 6, for all reads $r \in A_i - C_{i-1}$ we have $W(r) \leq_{hb_i} r$. Thus, E_i is sequentially consistent by Lemma 2.

Because the program is correctly synchronised, E_i is sequentially consistent, and r and $W(r)$ are accessing the same variable, r and $W(r)$ must be ordered by $\leq_{hb_i}$ in E_i and thus in E (rules 2 and 7). From well-formedness of E we have $r \not\leq_{hb} W(r)$, so we must have $W(r) \leq_{hb} r$. This proves the induction step.

Since each read has to appear in some C_i we have proved that all reads in E see writes that happen-before them, thus E is sequentially consistent.

Note that we use rule 2 for legality ($\leq_{hb_i} |_{C_i} = \leq_{hb} |_{C_i}$) only to compare $W(r)$ and r. Rules 1, 3, 4 and the first part of rule 7 for legality (i.e. $\forall r \in C_i - C_{i-1}.r$ is read $\Rightarrow W_i(r) \in C_{i-1}$) are not used in the proof at all. Also note that rule 1 is implied by rule 2.

4   Results of the Formalisation

Our formalisation has resulted in a clarification of the JMM definitions in several areas. We have also deviated from the JMM in a few places for simplification.

The most significant changes are restricting the executions to be *finite* and *omitting default initialisation* actions because of inconsistencies in the JMM definitions. Fixing these inconsistencies introduces strange artifacts in infinite executions, which is why we confine the executions to be finite. As a side product, this also simplifies proofs without sacrificing anything important, we believe.

We have refined the memory model in several ways. We have clarified the notion of *intra-thread consistency* and identified the precise interface with the sequential part of Java. Moreover, we strengthen the DRF guarantee by considering a stronger definition of sequential consistency that requires existence of a total order consistent with program order *and synchronisation order*, making it respect mutual exclusion. In the proof itself, we fix small inconsistencies and eliminate proof by contradiction in favour of induction where possible, and we state and prove the technically challenging Cut-and-update lemma (Lemma 3).

Finally, we identify the requirements on legality that are necessary to prove the DRF guarantee. This allows us to formulate a weaker notion of legality that fixes the recently discovered bugs in the memory model.

In the following paragraphs we discuss each of the contributions in detail.

Fixing the bugs by weakening legality. The formal proof of Theorem 1(DRF guarantee) revealed that Def. 7 (legality) is unnecessarily strong. We propose (and have checked) a weaker legality requirement by omitting the rule 3 ($\leq_{so_i} |_{C_i} = \leq_{so} |_{C_i}$) and replacing rules 2 and 7 in Def 7 by the following weaker ones[4]:

2. For all reads $r \in C_i$ we have $W(r) \leq_{hb} r \iff W(r) \leq_{hb_i} r$, and $r \not\leq_{hb_i} W(r)$,

7. For all reads $r \in C_i - C_{i-1}$ we have $W(r) \in C_{i-1}$.

This fixes the counterexample to Theorem 1 of [1] discovered by Cenciarelli et al [3]. We conjecture that this fix would also enable a correct proof to be given.

While manually testing the weaker notion of legality on the documented causality tests [7], we found a previously unreported problem of the existing JMM—it violates the causality tests 17–20. Our weaker legality (revised rule 7)

---

[4] NB: we must keep rule 4, which is needed to prohibit the out of thin air behaviours.

validates these examples while properly validating the other test cases. For example, causality test case 20 says that the program below should allow the result $r1 = r2 = r3 = 42$, because optimisations may produce this (see [7] for details):

initially x = y = 0

T1	T2	T3
join T3	r2 := y	r3 := x
r1 := x	y := r2	if (r3 == 0)
y := r1		x : = 42

However, it appears that this is not legal, because when committing the write r1:=x, the write of 42 to y must be already committed, hence the read of x must see a write to x with value 42. By rules 6 and 7 of legality, this write to x must be committed and it must happen-before the read. However, there is no such write. With the weaker legality we are not constrained by rule 7.

Inconsistency for initialisation actions. The Java Memory Model requires that

> The write of the default value (zero, false, or null) to each variable synchronises-with to the first action in every thread [8]

and defines synchronises-with as an order over synchronisation actions. This is inconsistent with the definition of synchronisation actions; ordinary writes are not synchronisation actions. Moreover, the JMM does not specify the thread associated with the initialisation actions and how they are validated with respect to intra-thread consistency.

There are several solutions to this. The SC- memory model [10] suggests having a special initialisation thread and letting its termination synchronise-with first actions of other threads. In our approach, we have tried to stay close to the JMM and instead we defined a new kind of synchronisation action—an initialisation action. These actions belong to a special initialisation thread that contains only the initialisation actions for all variables accessed in the program. The initialisation actions behave like ordinary write actions except they synchronise-with the thread start action of each thread. Note that in both the SC- and our formalisation, there is no significant difference between treating initialisation actions differently from normal write actions. We have checked a second version of our formalisation which adds initialisation actions to Def. 1.

Infinite executions. The JMM does not require finiteness of well-formed executions. Instead, the synchronisation order must be an omega order. Although it is not stated explicitly in the JMM specification, the discussion of fairness in [8] implies a progress property that requires threads in finite executions to be either terminated or deadlocked. Combination of the progress with the initialisation actions introduces an unpleasant artifact. One would expect that this program:

```
while(true) { new Object() { public volatile int f; }.f++; }
```

has just one infinite execution. However, an infinite number of variables f must be initialised. These initialisations must be ordered before the start of the thread performing the loop, which violates omega-ordering of the synchronisation order. As a result, this program does not have any well-formed execution in the current JMM. A similar issue also breaks the proof of Lemma 2 in [1], as noted in the paragraph following the proof given there. In our approach we do not require the finite executions to be finished[5]. This allows us to use the Cut-and-update lemma instead of the sequentially consistent completion used in [1].

Sequential consistency. Sequential consistency in the JMM requires existence of a total order consistent with program order such that each read sees the most recent write in that total order. This definition allows the program

initially x = y = z = 0		
r1 := y	lock m	lock m
x := r1	r2 := x	y := 1
	z := 1	r3 := z
	unlock m	unlock m

to have a sequentially consistent execution resulting in $r1 = r2 = r3 = 1$, using the total order lock m, lock m, y:=1, r1:=y, x:=r1, r2:=x, z:=1, r3:=z, unlock m, unlock m. Taking the most recent writes as values of reads, this order surprisingly results in $r1 = r2 = r3 = 1$. One can check that this cannot happen in any interleaved execution respecting mutual exclusivity of locks.

To make sequential consistency compatible with the intuitive meaning of interleaved semantics, we have formalised sequential consistency by requiring existence of a total order consistent with *both* the program order and synchronisation order and proved the DRF guarantee for this case. Since our definition of sequential consistency is stricter, the definition of data race free program becomes weaker (equivalent; it turns out) and consequently the DRF guarantee in the original setting directly follows from our DRF guarantee for stronger sequential consistency.

Requirements on thread management actions. For thread management, the JMM introduces further actions for thread start, termination, spawn and join. In well-formed executions, the JMM requires certain actions to be ordered by the synchronises-with order, e.g., thread spawn must synchronise-with the corresponding thread start, thread finish synchronises-with thread join. However, it is also necessary to prohibit executions from other undesirable behaviours, such as running threads that have not been spawned.

To address this in our formalisation, we introduce a constant for application's main thread and we specify that (1) for any thread except the main thread there is a unique thread spawn action, (2) there is no thread spawn action for the main thread, (3) each thread has a unique thread start action that is ordered before all actions of that thread in the program order, (4) for each thread there is at most one thread terminate action, and there is no action ordered after the terminate action in the program order.

---

[5] We believe that this does not affect observational equivalence, since observable behaviours are finite by the definition of [1]. But we have not checked this formally.

5   Conclusion

We have formally verified the guarantee of sequential consistency for data race free programs in the Java Memory Model. We believe that this is one of the first theorem prover formalisations of the JMM and its properties; it has shown that the current JMM is still flawed, although perhaps not fatally so. The topic was an ideal target for formalisation: we started from a highly complex informal definition that is difficult to understand and for which it is hard to be certain about the claims made. Indeed, while we were working on the DRF proof (Theorem 3 of [1]), Cenciarelli et al [3] meanwhile showed a counterexample to Theorem 1 of [1] that promised legality of reordering of independent statements. We discovered another bug while justifying causality test cases [7]. The second part of the contract, the out of thin air promise, was not proved or stated in [1], and is demonstrated only on small prohibited examples so far.

In keeping with the TPHOLs recommendation for good cross-community accessibility of papers, we have avoided theorem prover-specific syntax throughout. The formalisation occupies about 4000 lines in Isabelle/Isar [11], and takes under a minute to check. Our definitions build on the standard notion of relations in Isabelle/HOL as a two-place predicate together with a set representing the domain; nevertheless we had to establish some further properties required for the proof. To explore all definitions, we had to produce multiple versions of the scripts; current theorem prover technology still makes this harder than it ought to be. For those who are interested in the Isabelle specifics, we have made our formalisation available on the web.[6]

Related Work. In the computer architecture world, there is a long history of work on weak memory models. These models usually specify allowed memory operation reorderings, which either preserve sequential consistency for data race free programs, i.e. they provide the DRF guarantee [12], or provide mechanisms for enforcing ordering (memory barriers). For a detailed survey, see [4,13].

Until recently, the programming languages community has mostly ignored the issues of memory models and relied on specifications of the underlying hardware (this is the case for, e.g., C, C++, and OCaml). But programmers write programs that execute incorrectly under memory models weaker then sequential consistency. For example, Peterson's mutual exclusion algorithm and double-checked locking are known to be incorrect for current hardware architectures [14,15]. This has encouraged recent progress on adapting the work on hardware memory models to define and explain the memory models of programming languages [16,17]. However, these techniques either violate the out of thin air property, or do not allow advanced optimisation techniques that remove dependencies. This was the reason for Java to adopt the memory model based on speculations [1,18], which has spawned semantic investigation like [3] as well as our own study.

Likewise, little work has yet been done to formalise behaviours of hardware or software memory models in formal verification community. As far as we know all

---

[6] Please see: `http://groups.inf.ed.ac.uk/request/jmmtheory/`

program logics and theorem prover based methodologies [19,20,21] for concurrent shared memory assume interleaved semantics, which implies sequential consistency. The DRF guarantee, formalised in this paper, ensures that these methods are correct for data race free programs. The data race freedom can be established inside the program logics themselves, or using dedicated type systems [22,23]. A complete framework for thread-modular verification of Java programs, including the data race freedom and atomicity verification, is currently being developed in the Mobius project [24].

More work has been done to verify properties of small programs or data structures using state exploration techniques. Huynh and Roychoudhury [14] check properties of C# programs by examining all reachable states of a program, while accounting for reorderings allowed by the CLI specification [25]. Burckhardt et al [26,27] use a SAT solver to perform bounded tests on concurrent data structures in relaxed memory models. To explore proposals for replacing the early JMM [16,28], Yang et al [29] built a flexible framework for modelling executions in memory models with complex reordering and visibility constraints. To our knowledge, the only formal verification tool for the current JMM is the data race analysis by Yang et al [30]. However, data race freedom is a relatively easy property to show—only sequentially consistent executions need to be examined. The declarative nature of the JMM and its speculative justifications make it very hard to explore all executions of the given program; the obligation to find an execution for each committed action quickly blows up the state space. Our theorem proving approach differs from state exploration in the typical way: we aim to verify general properties of the memory model rather than justify behaviour of individual programs automatically.

Future Work. The next direction for our analysis is to formalise the description and verification of the techniques used to justify optimisations in the allowed causality tests for the JMM [7]. We hope to begin this by formally checking Theorem 1 of [1] with our fix to legality.

The out of thin air guarantee is the main motivation for the JMM. Without this requirement, we could define the memory model easily by allowing all code transformations and executions that appear sequentially consistent for DRF programs [12] and leave the behaviour for programs that are not correctly synchronised unspecified. The notion of "out of thin air" is mostly example driven—we only have specific behaviours of concrete programs that should be prohibited and a general intuition that in two groups of threads, each group using disjoint sets of variables, there should not be any information leak from one group to the other, e.g., a reference allocated by a thread in the first group should not be visible to any read performed by a thread in the other group. We plan to state and prove these properties formally.

Although it is not described here, we have instantiated our framework with a simple sequential language that is sufficient to express simple examples, such as the ones in Fig. 2 or in [7]. However, the backwards style of reasoning in the JMM makes it difficult to show illegality of individual executions and we need to find better ways. Moreover, adding allocation to the language makes it impossible to verify validity of a thread trace separately, because we need to ensure freshness globally. To address this, our idea is to index locations by their allocating thread, but we have not explored the impact of this yet.

Finally, we hope that with a simplified and clear memory model, we will have a firmer basis for studying logics for concurrent programs which respect weaker memory models, which is our overall objective.

Acknowledgements. The second author is supported by a PhD studentship awarded by the UK EPSRC, grant EP/C537068. Both authors also acknowledge the support of the EU project Mobius (IST-15905).

References

1. Manson, J., Pugh, W., Adve, S.V.: The Java memory model. In: POPL '05. Proceedings of the 32nd ACM SIGPLAN-SIGACT symposium on Principles of Programming Languages, pp. 378–391. ACM Press, New York (2005)
2. Gosling, J., Joy, B., Steele, G., Bracha, G.: Memory Model. In: Java(TM) Language Specification, 3rd edn. Java Series, pp. 557–573. Addison-Wesley Professional, Reading (2005)
3. Cenciarelli, P., Knapp, A., Sibilio, E.: The Java memory model: Operationally, denotationally, axiomatically. In: 16th ESOP (2007)
4. Adve, S.V., Gharachorloo, K.: Shared memory consistency models: A tutorial. Computer 29(12), 66–76 (1996)
5. Pugh, W.: The Java memory model is fatally flawed. Concurrency - Practice and Experience 12(6), 445–455 (2000)
6. Peierls, T., Goetz, B., Bloch, J., Bowbeer, J., Lea, D., Holmes, D.: Java Concurrency in Practice. Addison-Wesley Professional, Reading (2005)
7. Pugh, W., Manson, J.: Java memory model causality test cases (2004), http://www.cs.umd.edu/~pugh/java/memoryModel/CausalityTestCases.html
8. Manson, J., Pugh, W., Adve, S.V.: The Java memory model. Special POPL Issue (submitted)
9. Lamport, L.: Time, clocks, and the ordering of events in a distributed system. Commun. ACM 21(7), 558–565 (1978)
10. Adve, S.: The SC- memory model for Java (2004), http://www.cs.uiuc.edu/~sadve/jmm
11. Wenzel, M.: The Isabelle/Isar reference manual (2005), http://isabelle.in.tum.de/doc/isar-ref.pdf
12. Adve, S.V., Aggarwal, J.K.: A unified formalization of four shared-memory models. IEEE Trans. Parallel Distrib. Syst. 4(6), 613–624 (1993)
13. Kawash, J.: Limitations and Capabilities of Weak Memory Consistency Systems. PhD thesis, The University of Calgary (2000)
14. Roychoudhury, A.: Formal reasoning about hardware and software memory models. In: George, C.W., Miao, H. (eds.) ICFEM 2002. LNCS, vol. 2495, pp. 423–434. Springer, Heidelberg (2002)
15. Bacon, D., et al.: The "double-checked locking is broken" declaration (2001), http://www.cs.umd.edu/~pugh/java/memoryModel/DoubleCheckedLocking.html
16. Maessen, J.W., Shen, X.: Improving the Java memory model using CRF. In: OOPSLA, pp. 1–12. ACM Press, New York (2000)

17. Saraswat, V., Jagadeesan, R., Michael, M., von Praun, C.: A theory of memory models. In: ACM 2007 SIGPLAN Conference on Principles and Practice of Parallel Computing, ACM, New York (2007)
18. Manson, J.: The Java memory model. PhD thesis, University of Maryland, College Park (2004)
19. Ábrahám, E., de Boer, F.S., de Roever, W.P., Steffen, M.: An assertion-based proof system for multithreaded Java. TCS 331(2-3), 251–290 (2005)
20. Flanagan, C., Freund, S.N., Qadeer, S., Seshia, S.A.: Modular verification of multithreaded programs. Theor. Comput. Sci. 338(1-3), 153–183 (2005)
21. Moore, J.S., Porter, G.: The apprentice challenge. ACM Trans. Program. Lang. Syst. 24(3), 193–216 (2002)
22. Flanagan, C., Freund, S.N.: Type-based race detection for Java. In: PLDI, pp. 219–232. ACM Press, New York (2000)
23. Boyapati, C., Rinard, M.: A parameterized type system for race-free Java programs. In: OOPSLA, pp. 56–69. ACM Press, New York (2001)
24. Huisman, M., Grigore, R., Haack, C., Hurlin, C., Kiniry, J., Petri, G., Poll, E.: Report on thread-modular verification. Mobius project deliverable D3.3 (2007), available from http://mobius.inria.fr
25. Microsoft: Standard ECMA-335 Common Language Infrastructure (CLI) (2005)
26. Burckhardt, S., Alur, R., Martin, M.M.K.: Bounded model checking of concurrent data types on relaxed memory models: A case study. In: Ball, T., Jones, R.B. (eds.) CAV 2006. LNCS, vol. 4144, pp. 489–502. Springer, Heidelberg (2006)
27. Burckhardt, S., Alur, R., Martin, M.M.K.: CheckFence: Checking consistency of concurrent data types on relaxed memory models. In: PLDI, San Diego, California, USA, ACM Press, New York (2007)
28. Manson, J., Pugh, W.: Semantics of multithreaded Java. Technical Report CS-TR-4215, Dept. of Computer Science, University of Maryland, College Park (2001)
29. Yang, Y., Gopalakrishnan, G., Lindstrom, G.: UMM: an operational memory model specification framework with integrated model checking capability: Research articles. Concurr. Comput.: Pract. Exper. 17(5-6), 465–487 (2005)
30. Yang, Y., Gopalakrishnan, G., Lindstrom, G.: Memory-model-sensitive data race analysis. In: Davies, J., Schulte, W., Barnett, M. (eds.) ICFEM 2004. LNCS, vol. 3308, pp. 30–45. Springer, Heidelberg (2004)

Finding Lexicographic Orders for Termination Proofs in Isabelle/HOL

Lukas Bulwahn, Alexander Krauss, and Tobias Nipkow

Technische Universität München, Institut für Informatik
http://www.in.tum.de/~{bulwahn,krauss,nipkow}

Abstract. We present a simple method to formally prove termination of recursive functions by searching for lexicographic combinations of size measures. Despite its simplicity, the method turns out to be powerful enough to solve a large majority of termination problems encountered in daily theorem proving practice.

1   Introduction

To justify recursive function definitions in a logic of total functions, a termination proof is usually required. Termination proofs are mainly a technical necessity imposed by the system, rather than in the primary interest of the user. It is therefore much desirable to automate them wherever possible, so that they "get in the way" less frequently. Such automation increases the overall user-friendliness of the system, especially for novice users.

Despite the general hardness of the termination problem, a large class of recursive functions occurring in practice can already be proved terminating using a lexicographic combination of size measures. One can see this class of functions as a generalization of the primitive recursive functions.

In this paper, we describe a simple method to generate termination orderings for this class of functions and construct a termination proof from these orderings. Unlike the naive enumeration of all possible lexicographic combinations, which is currently implemented in some systems, we use an algorithm by Abel and Altenkirch [3] to find the right order in polynomial time.

We subsequently show how, by a simple extension, our analysis can deal with mutual recursion, including cases where a descent is not present in every step. When analyzing the complexity of the underlying problem, it turns out that while there is a polynomial algorithm for the case of single functions, the presence of mutual recursion makes the problem NP-complete.

We implemented our analysis is Isabelle/HOL, where it can prove termination of 87% of the function definitions present in the Isabelle Distribution and the Archive of Formal Proofs [1].

K. Schneider and J. Brandt (Eds.): TPHOLs 2007, LNCS 4732, pp. 38–53, 2007.
© Springer-Verlag Berlin Heidelberg 2007

1.1 Overview of the Analysis

The analysis consists of four basic steps:

1. Assemble a set of size measures to be used for the analysis, based on the type of the function argument.
2. For each recursive call and for each measure, try to prove *local descent*, i.e. that the measure gets smaller at the call. Collect the results of the proof attempts in a matrix.
3. Operating only on the matrix from step 2, search for a combination of measures, which form a global termination ordering. This combination, if it exists, can be found in polynomial time.
4. Construct the global termination ordering and, using the proofs of local descent, show that all recursive calls decrease wrt. the global ordering.

1.2 Related Work

The field of automated termination analysis is vast, and continuously attracts researchers. Many analyses (e.g. [4,13,22]) have been proposed in the literature, and some of them are very powerful. However, these methods are often hard to integrate, as they apply to different formal frameworks (such as term rewriting), and their proofs cannot be easily checked independently.

Consequently, the state of the art in the implementations of interactive theorem provers is much less developed:

In PVS [16] and Isabelle [15], and Coq [5], no automation exists, and users must supply termination orderings manually.

HOL4 [7][1] and HOL Light [8] provide some automation by enumerating all possible lexicographic orderings. For functions with more than five or six arguments, this quickly becomes infeasible.

ACL2 [10] uses heuristics to pick a size measure of a single parameter. Lexicographic combinations must be given manually, and are expressed in terms of ordinal arithmetic.

Recently, a more powerful termination criterion has been proposed for ACL2 [14], based on a combination of the size-change principle [13] and other analyses. However, the analysis is nontrivial and only available as an axiomatic extension that must be trusted, as its soundness cannot be justified within ACL2's first-order logic.

Inspired by this approach, the second author of the present paper developed a formalization of the size-change principle in Isabelle [12], which can be used to show termination for a larger class of functions. While that approach is more powerful than the one presented here, it is also more complicated and computationally expensive.

Only HOL4 tries to guess termination orderings for mutually recursive definitions. But the algorithm is a little ad-hoc and fails on many simple examples.

---

[1] The guessing of termination orderings in HOL4 is unpublished work by Slind, extending his work on function definitions [20,21].

The algorithm we use in §3.3 to synthesize lexicographic orderings has been discovered independently but earlier by Abel and Altenkirch [2,3]. Compared to their work, we do not just check termination but construct object-level proofs in a formal framework.

2   Preliminaries

We work in the framework of classical higher-order logic (HOL). Many examples are expressed in the Isabelle's meta-logic, with universal quantification ($\bigwedge$) and implication ($\Longrightarrow$). However, the method is not specific to HOL and could easily be adapted to other frameworks, such as type theory.

2.1   Termination Proof Obligations

General recursion is provided by a function definition package [11], which transforms a definition into a non-recursive form definable by other means. Then the original recursive specification is derived from the primitive definition in an automated process.

A termination proof is needed in order to derive the unconstrained recursive equations and an induction rule. Proving termination essentially requires to show that the call relation (constructed automatically from the definition) is wellfounded. A common way of doing this is to embed the call relation in another relation already known to be wellfounded.

As an example, consider the following function implementing the merge operation in mergesort:

$$
\begin{aligned}
merge \; xs \; [] \quad &= \quad xs \\
merge \; [] \; ys \quad &= \quad ys \\
merge \; (x{\cdot}xs) \; (y{\cdot}ys) \quad &= \quad \textit{if } x \le y \textit{ then } x{\cdot}merge \; xs \; (y{\cdot}ys) \textit{ else } y{\cdot}merge \; (x{\cdot}xs) \; ys
\end{aligned}
$$

Here · denotes the Cons constructor for lists and [] is the empty list. In order to show termination of merge, we must prove the following subgoals:

1. $wf \; ?R$
2. $\bigwedge x \; xs \; y \; ys. \; x \le y \Longrightarrow ((xs, \; y{\cdot}ys), \; (x{\cdot}xs, \; y{\cdot}ys)) \in ?R$
3. $\bigwedge x \; xs \; y \; ys. \; \neg \; x \le y \Longrightarrow ((x{\cdot}xs, \; ys), \; (x{\cdot}xs, \; y{\cdot}ys)) \in ?R$

Here, $?R$ is a schematic variable which may be instantiated during the proof. Hence, we must come up with a wellfounded relation, for which the remaining subgoals can be proved. The two curried arguments of *merge* have been combined to a pair, hence we can assume that there is only one argument.

In general, if the function has n recursive calls, we get the subgoals

0. $wf \; ?R$
1. $\bigwedge v_1 \ldots v_{m_1}. \; \Gamma_1 \Longrightarrow (r_1, \; lhs_1) \in ?R$

$\vdots$

n. $\bigwedge v_1 \ldots v_{m_n}. \; \Gamma_n \Longrightarrow (r_n, \; lhs_n) \in ?R$

Here, r_i is the argument of the call, lhs_i is the argument on the left hand side of the equation, and Γ_i is the condition under which the call occurs. These terms contain the pattern variables $v_1...v_{m_i}$, which are bound in the goal.

In practice, proving the termination conditions is often straightforward, once the right relation has been found. Our approach focuses on relations of a certain form, suitable for a large class of function definitions.

2.2   A Combinator for Building Relations

Isabelle already contains various combinators for building wellfounded relations. We are going to add one more to this, which particularly suits our needs.

The *measures* combinator constructs a wellfounded relation from a list of measure functions, which map function arguments into the natural numbers. This is a straightforward generalization of the well-known *measure* combinator which takes only a single function:

measures   :: $(\alpha \Rightarrow nat)$ *list* $\Rightarrow (\alpha \times \alpha)$ *set*

measures fs $=$ *inv-image* $(lex\ less\text{-}than)$ $(\lambda a.\ map\ (\lambda f.\ f\ a)\ fs)$

While the definition with predefined combinators is a little cryptic, *measures* can be characterized by the following rules:

$$\frac{f\,x < f\,y}{(x,\ y) \in measures\ (f \cdot fs)} \qquad \text{(Measures\_Less)}$$

$$\frac{f\,x \le f\,y \qquad (x,\ y) \in measures\ fs}{(x,\ y) \in measures\ (f \cdot fs)} \qquad \text{(Measures\_Leq)}$$

And, by construction, the resulting relation is always wellfounded:

$$wf\ (measures\ fs) \qquad \text{(Measures\_WF)}$$

Our analysis will produce relations of the form *measures fs* for a suitable function list *fs*.

3   Finding Lexicographic Orderings

The overall algorithm consists of the four steps mentioned before, addressing largely orthogonal issues: Generating measure functions (by a heuristic), proving local descents (by theorem proving), finding a lexicographic combination (by combinatorics), and reconstructing the global proof (by engineering).

We will use the previously defined *merge* function as a running example.

3.1   Step 1: Generating Measure Functions

From the type τ of the function argument, we generate a set $\mathcal{M}(\tau)$ of measure functions by a simple scheme:

$$
\begin{aligned}
\mathcal{M}(T) &= \{\lambda x.\ |x|_T\} \quad \text{if } T \text{ is an inductive data type} \\
\mathcal{M}(\tau_1 \times \tau_2) &= \{m \circ \mathit{fst} \mid m \in \mathcal{M}(\tau_1)\} \cup \{m \circ \mathit{snd} \mid m \in \mathcal{M}(\tau_2)\} \\
\mathcal{M}(\tau) &= \{\} \quad \text{if } \tau \text{ is a type variable or a function type.}
\end{aligned}
$$

For inductive data types, we return the size function $|.|_T$ associated to that type. Size functions are provided automatically by the definition package for inductive data types [6]. Product types are special and treated differently, as we are mainly interested in the measures of the different components. For products, the measures for the component types are computed recursively and composed with the corresponding projections.

This scheme basically decomposes (possibly nested) tuples and creates projection functions measuring the sizes of the components. Components with a polymorphic or a function type are ignored.

For *merge*, which operates on a pair of lists, we get the two measure functions:

$$ m_1 = (\lambda x.\ |\mathit{fst}\ x|) \qquad\qquad m_2 = (\lambda x.\ |\mathit{snd}\ x|) $$

In order to handle types which are not inductive data types, the system can be extended by manually configuring one or more measure functions for them. For example, a useful measure for the integers is the function returning the absolute value.

The emphasis on size measures in this step is mainly motivated by the empirical observation that they tend to be very useful for termination proofs. In fact, the other steps do not depend on the exact nature of the measures and would work for other measures just as well.

3.2   Step 2: Proving Local Descents

A local descent is given if a given measure provably decreases at a given recursive call. For the i-th call and measure m_j, this corresponds to the following property:

$$ \bigwedge v_1 \ldots v_m.\ \Gamma_i \implies m_j\ r_i < m_j\ lhs_i $$

For each call and each measure, we try to prove this conjecture by a suitable automated method. If this fails, we try to prove the non-strict version instead:

$$ \bigwedge v_1 \ldots v_m.\ \Gamma_i \implies m_j\ r_i \le m_j\ lhs_i $$

For the proof attempts, we use Isabelle's `auto` method, which combines rewriting with classical reasoning and some arithmetic. We collect the results of the proof attempts in a matrix M with $M_{ij} \in \{<, \le, ?\}$, where $<$ and $\le$ stand for a successful proof of strict or non-strict descent, and ? denotes a failure of both proofs. The theorems resulting from successful proofs are stored for later use.

For the *merge* example, the resulting matrix is

$$M_{merge} = \begin{pmatrix} < & \leq \\ \leq & < \end{pmatrix} .$$

Using the `auto` method to solve these goals is a somewhat arbitrary decision, but it turned out that our proof obligations are routinely solved by this method, usually by unfolding the size function on constructors and using arithmetic. Again, it does not matter for the rest of the development, how these goals are proved, and other methods could be plugged in here, if needed.

If the recursive arguments contain calls to "destructor functions" (like *tail* or *delete*), lemmas about these functions are usually needed in order to prove local descent. Our method makes use of such lemmas when they are available in the theory, but discovering and proving them automatically is an orthogonal issue which we do not address. A method to do this is described by Walther [22].

3.3   Step 3: Finding Lexicographic Combinations

Recall that the rows in the matrix represent the different recursive calls and the columns represent the measures. Our problem of finding a suitable lexicographic order can now be rephrased as follows:

> *Reorder the columns in the matrix in such a way that each row starts with a (possibly empty) sequence of $\leq$-entries, followed by a $<$-entry.*

Such a permutation of the columns, denoted by a list of column indices, is called a *solution*. Usually only a prefix of this list is relevant. Formally, a solution for a matrix M is a list of indices $[c_1, \ldots, c_m]$, where for all row indices i, there is a k, such that $M_{ic_k} = <$ and for all $j < k$, $M_{ic_j} = \leq$.

The following algorithm can be used to find solutions:

1. Find a column with at least one $<$ entry and no ? entry and select it as the new front column. The search fails if no such column exists.
2. Remove all rows where the selected column contains a $<$-entry, as they can be considered "solved". Then also remove the column itself and continue the search on the resulting matrix.
3. The search is successful when the matrix is empty.

Lemma 1. *If the algorithm succeeds, the selected columns are a solution for M.*

Proof. By straightforward induction.

Note that the algorithm has a choice if more than one column could be selected in step 1. However, this does not influence the overall success, since a "wrong" choice cannot lead to a dead-end. This confluence property is illustrated by the following lemma, whose proof is obvious:

Lemma 2. *Let $\sigma = [c_1, \ldots, c_m]$ be a solution, and c a column which could also be chosen in step i of the algorithm. Then $\sigma' = [c_1, \ldots, c_{i-1}, c, c_i, \ldots, c_m]$ is also a solution.*

This confluence property eliminates the need for backtracking on failure, which is the key to making the algorithm polynomial:

Lemma 3. *For an $n \times m$-Matrix, the algorithm uses $O(n^2 m)$ comparisons.*

Although choosing an arbitrary column never makes the algorithm go wrong, it may lead to suboptimal solutions. Consider the following 10×5-matrix, where the $\leq$-entries were left out for readability:

$$
M = \begin{pmatrix}
 & < & ? & & \\
 & < & < & & \\
 & < & < & & \\
 & < & < & & \\
 & < & < & & \\
< & & < & & \\
< & & < & & \\
< & & < & & \\
 & & < & < & \\
 & & < & < & \\
\end{pmatrix}
$$

Naively proceeding from left to right will produce the solution $[1, 2, 3, 4]$, although the shorter solution $[3, 4]$ exists. In systems where proof objects are stored explicitly, their size can influence efficiency, and it might be worthwhile to invest some effort here, to keep proofs small.

As a heuristic, it might seem advantageous to always choose the column with the most $<$-entries, since this would eliminate the corresponding rows once and for all. But this greedy strategy would produce the solution $[2, 1, 5, 3, 4]$ on the above matrix, which is even bigger than with the naive strategy.

In fact, finding the shortest solution is much harder than finding just one solution:

Lemma 4. *Given a Matrix M, the optimization problem of finding a minimal solution for M is NP-hard.*

Proof. The optimization version of the NP-hard SET COVER problem [18] can easily be expressed in a matrix: For a universe $U = \{x_1, \ldots, x_n\}$ and a collection $S_1, \ldots, S_m$ of subsets of U, construct the $n \times m$-matrix M with $M_{ij} = <$ if $x_i \in S_j$ and $\leq$ otherwise. Obviously, every solution for M solves the SET COVER problem and vice-versa.

Since searching for the smallest solution can be hard, we are happy with choosing just the first suitable column in our implementation.

For our example M_{merge}, both $[1, 2]$ and $[2, 1]$ are solutions.

3.4   Step 4: Proof Reconstruction

It remains to assemble the pieces and construct a global relation and a global proof from the solution of the previous step.

From a solution $\sigma = [c_1, \ldots, c_n]$ we construct the relation

$$R = measures \, [m_{c_1}, \ldots, m_{c_n}] \, .$$

It is now straightforward to prove the termination goals with the help of the matrix M and the solution σ:

1. Instantiate the schematic variable $?R$ by the relation R.
2. Wellfoundedness is trivial by the rule MEASURES_WF.
3. For each call, inspect the matrix in M_{ic_j} for increasing j. If $M_{ic_j} = \leq$, apply rule MEASURES_LEQ and use the stored theorem from §3.2 to solve its first premise. When $M_{ic_j} = <$, apply rule MEASURES_LESS, and the stored theorem, which solves the goal.

By construction, the theorems resulting from the proofs in §3.2 exactly match the premises of MEASURES_LEQ and MEASURES_LESS, respectively.

As an example, consider the *merge* function again. We get the relation

$$R = measures \, [\lambda x. \, |fst \, x|, \, \lambda x. \, |snd \, x|]$$

After instantiating the schematic variable and solving the wellfoundedness, two subgoals remain:

1. $\bigwedge x \; xs \; y \; ys.$
    $x \leq y \implies ((xs, \, y{\cdot}ys), \, (x{\cdot}xs, \, y{\cdot}ys)) \in measures \, [\lambda x. \, |fst \, x|, \, \lambda x. \, |snd \, x|]$
2. $\bigwedge x \; xs \; y \; ys.$
    $\neg \, x \leq y \implies ((x{\cdot}xs, \, ys), \, (x{\cdot}xs, \, y{\cdot}ys)) \in measures \, [\lambda x. \, |fst \, x|, \, \lambda x. \, |snd \, x|]$

Since $M_{11} = <$, we can directly apply MEASURES_LESS to the first subgoal:

1. $\bigwedge x \; xs \; y \; ys. \; x \leq y \implies |fst \, (xs, \, y{\cdot}ys)| < |fst \, (x{\cdot}xs, \, y{\cdot}ys)|$
2. $\bigwedge x \; xs \; y \; ys.$
    $\neg \, x \leq y \implies ((x{\cdot}xs, \, ys), \, (x{\cdot}xs, \, y{\cdot}ys)) \in measures \, [\lambda x. \, |fst \, x|, \, \lambda x. \, |snd \, x|]$

Now the first subgoal is exactly what we have proved in §3.2, so we can solve it using the stored theorem.

For the remaining subgoal, we must first apply MEASURES_LEQ, since $M_{21} = \leq$:

1. $\bigwedge x \; xs \; y \; ys. \; \neg \, x \leq y \implies |fst \, (x{\cdot}xs, \, ys)| \leq |fst \, (x{\cdot}xs, \, y{\cdot}ys)|$
2. $\bigwedge x \; xs \; y \; ys. \; \neg \, x \leq y \implies ((x{\cdot}xs, \, ys), \, (x{\cdot}xs, \, y{\cdot}ys)) \in measures \, [\lambda x. \, |snd \, x|]$

Again, we solve the first subgoal using the pre-proved theorem. In one additional step, we can solve the remaining goal using MEASURES_LESS, which finishes the termination proof.

4 Mutual Recursion

For mutually recursive functions, termination generally has to be proved simultaneously. To allow for a uniform treatment, Isabelle internally converts such definitions into a definition of a single function operating on the sum type, which is a standard transformation technique (see e.g. [21]).

Consider the functions *even* and *odd*, defined by mutual recursion:

$$
\begin{aligned}
even\ 0 &= True \\
even\ (Suc\ n) &= odd\ n \\
odd\ 0 &= False \\
odd\ (Suc\ n) &= even\ n
\end{aligned}
$$

For the termination proof, the function is seen as a single function over the sum type $nat + nat$. This leads to to the following proof obligations[2]:

1. *wf ?R*
2. $\bigwedge n.\ (Inr\ n,\ Inl\ (Suc\ n)) \in\ ?R$
3. $\bigwedge n.\ (Inl\ n,\ Inr\ (Suc\ n)) \in\ ?R$

It is not hard to generalize our approach to prove termination for mutual recursions. Unfortunately, we will see that this necessarily destroys the polynomial time complexity.

4.1   Measures for Sum Types

In order to use our analysis on these problems, we must be able to generate measure functions on sum types. Thus we extend the measure generation step (§3.1) as follows:

$$\mathcal{M}(\tau_1 + \tau_2) = \{case_+\ m_1\ m_2 \mid m_1 \in \mathcal{M}(\tau_1),\ m_2 \in \mathcal{M}(\tau_2)\}$$

This means that sum measures are built by taking all combinations of the measures for the component types and combining them with the case combinator for sum types:

$$case_+ \ ::\ (\alpha \Rightarrow \gamma) \Rightarrow (\beta \Rightarrow \gamma) \Rightarrow (\alpha + \beta \Rightarrow \gamma)$$

Intuitively, each of the mutually recursive functions gets its own measure, which is applied to its arguments.

Since *even* and *odd* both get only one measure function, $case_+$ $(\lambda x.\ |x|)$ $(\lambda x.\ |x|)$ is the only combination, and with this measure the proof is indeed successful. The other parts of the analysis require no change.

4.2   Ordering the Functions

With the measures on sum types, many mutually recursive definitions can be handled without problems. But the approach fails for definition like the following:

---

[2] We denote the injection functions for sum types with *Inl* and *Inr*. If more than two functions are defined simultaneously, nested sums will occur.

$$
\begin{aligned}
f\ 0 &= 0 \\
f\ (Suc\ n) &= g\ n \\
g\ n &= Suc\ (f\ n)
\end{aligned}
$$

In the call from g to f, there is no descent, since the only argument is just passed along. The reason why this definition terminates is not that the argument decreases, but that in this call, the *function* decreases, with respect to a suitable ordering of the functions (here: $f < g$).

With our sum encoding, it is simple to capture this argument by suitable measure functions: It suffices to add measure functions which distinguish between the functions, but are otherwise constant. For f and g, we add the measure $case_+$ $(\lambda x.\ 0)$ $(\lambda x.\ 1)$. This results in the matrix

$$
M = \begin{pmatrix} < & ? \\ \leq & < \end{pmatrix}
$$

In general, it is sufficient to add measures which evaluate to 1 for one of the functions and to 0 for all others. $\mathcal{M}_{fn}(\tau)$ describes these measures formally, again depending only on the argument type τ:

$$
\begin{aligned}
\mathcal{M}_{fn}(\tau_1 + \tau_2) &= \{\,case_+\ m_1\ (\lambda x.0) \mid m_1 \in \mathcal{M}_{fn}(\tau_1)\,\} \cup \\
&\quad\ \{\,case_+\ (\lambda x.0)\ m_2 \mid m_2 \in \mathcal{M}_{fn}(\tau_2)\,\} \\
\mathcal{M}_{fn}(\tau) &= \{(\lambda x.1)\} \quad \text{if } \tau \text{ is not a sum type}
\end{aligned}
$$

It is easy to see that with these additional measures (and their lexicographic combinations, which are formed by the subsequent steps), any partial ordering between the functions can be captured.

4.3   Complexity of Mutual Recursion

Taking all combinations of measures for sum types as in §4.1 is a brute-force strategy and it destroys the polynomial runtime behaviour of the algorithm, since the number of sum measures is obviously exponential in the number of functions involved. The question arises, whether we can be a little more intelligent here.

Note in particular that we have introduced some redundancy in the proofs that are performed in step 2: In a call from f to g, it is completely irrelevant what measure we assign to h, and sum measures differing only in the components for functions other than f and g will lead to identical proofs.

It is a better strategy to look at the different calls separately: Consider a call c from f to g (written $c : f \to g$), which corresponds to a goal of the form

$$
\bigwedge v_1 \ldots v_m.\ \Gamma_i \implies (In_g\ r_i,\ In_f\ lhs_i) \in ?R
$$

Here we write In_f and In_g to abbreviate the compositions of injections corresponding to the functions f and g, respectively.

We can now generate separate sets $\mathcal{M}_f$ and $\mathcal{M}_g$ of measure functions for f and g separately and try for which choice of $m_f \in \mathcal{M}_f$ and $m_g \in \mathcal{M}_g$ the following becomes provable:

$$\bigwedge v_1 \dots v_m. \; \Gamma_i \implies m_g \; r_i < m_f \; lhs_i$$

As before, we try the $\leq$ version if the proof fails and collect the results in a matrix. This time we get one matrix M^c for each recursive call c, and the rows and columns of the matrix stand for the Elements of $\mathcal{M}_f$ and $\mathcal{M}_g$. Note that this information is still polynomial in size.

We must now construct measures on the sum type which are useful to prove termination. At least one of these sum measures must be such that it increases in none of the calls. Such a measure would be used first in the construction of the lexicographic combination.

Abstracting from functions and measures and the like, we have the following problem, which we call the COMBINATION problem:

Let A and B be finite sets and $M \subseteq A \times A \times B \times B$. Find a mapping $f : A \to B$ such that $\forall x, x' \in A. \; (x, x', f(x), f(x')) \notin M$.

The abstraction is as follows: A is the set of functions, and B is the set of basic measures, where we assume without loss of generality that the number of basic measures is the same for all functions (take the maximum!). The set M encodes the result of the proofs: $(f, g, i, j) \in M$ iff for some call $c : f \to g$, $M_{ij}^c = ?$

Is is a simple exercise to construct a set of functions from an arbitrary COMBINATION instance to see that finding sum measures is indeed required to solve this problem.

Lemma 5. *The* COMBINATION *problem is NP-complete.*

Proof. We reduce the 3-COLORING problem for graphs (see e.g. [18]) to COMBINATION. For a graph $G = (V, E)$ to be coloured, we define the problem instance

$$A = V \quad B = \{\text{Red}, \text{Green}, \text{Blue}\} \quad M = \{(v, v', c, c) \mid (v, v') \in E, \; c \in B\}.$$

Now every solution f for COMBINATION is a valid colouring: if $(v, v') \in E$ and $f(v) = c$ we have $(v, v', c, c) \in M$ and thus $f(v') \neq c$. Conversely, every colouring is clearly a valid COMBINATION. Since 3-COLORING is NP-hard, so is our problem, and since checking a given solution is trivial, it is also NP-complete.

What conclusions can be drawn from this result? First, it shows that the introduction of mutual recursion really complicates matters, leading to a search space exponential in the number of functions involved. Second, this complexity only concerns the *search* for suitable measures. The number of *proof attempts* to be performed by the theorem prover is still polynomial.

While this is interesting from a theoretic view, in practice the number of functions in a single mutually recursive definition is often quite small, which makes this approach feasible.

5   Examples

5.1   Ackermann Function

The ackermann function, defined by

$$
\begin{aligned}
ack\ 0\ m &= Suc\ m \\
ack\ (Suc\ n)\ 0 &= ack\ n\ 1 \\
ack\ (Suc\ n)\ (Suc\ m) &= ack\ n\ (ack\ (Suc\ n)\ m)
\end{aligned}
$$

is easily proved total by our tool. The generated relation is *measures* $[\lambda x.\ |fst\ x|,\ \lambda x.\ |snd\ x|]$.

5.2 Many Parameters

If the function has many parameters, enumerating lexicographic orders becomes infeasible, as the following example demonstrates. Both HOL4 and HOL Light fail to prove termination of the following function in reasonable time, while our method succeeds within a second.

$$
\begin{aligned}
blowup\ 0\ 0\ 0\ 0\ 0\ 0\ 0\ 0 &= 0 \\
blowup\ 0\ 0\ 0\ 0\ 0\ 0\ 0\ 0\ (Suc\ i) &= Suc\ (blowup\ i\ i\ i\ i\ i\ i\ i\ i) \\
blowup\ 0\ 0\ 0\ 0\ 0\ 0\ 0\ (Suc\ h)\ i &= Suc\ (blowup\ h\ h\ h\ h\ h\ h\ h\ i) \\
blowup\ 0\ 0\ 0\ 0\ 0\ 0\ (Suc\ g)\ h\ i &= Suc\ (blowup\ g\ g\ g\ g\ g\ g\ g\ h\ i) \\
blowup\ 0\ 0\ 0\ 0\ 0\ (Suc\ f)\ g\ h\ i &= Suc\ (blowup\ f\ f\ f\ f\ f\ f\ g\ h\ i) \\
blowup\ 0\ 0\ 0\ 0\ (Suc\ e)\ f\ g\ h\ i &= Suc\ (blowup\ e\ e\ e\ e\ e\ f\ g\ h\ i) \\
blowup\ 0\ 0\ 0\ (Suc\ d)\ e\ f\ g\ h\ i &= Suc\ (blowup\ d\ d\ d\ d\ e\ f\ g\ h\ i) \\
blowup\ 0\ 0\ (Suc\ c)\ d\ e\ f\ g\ h\ i &= Suc\ (blowup\ c\ c\ c\ d\ e\ f\ g\ h\ i) \\
blowup\ 0\ (Suc\ b)\ c\ d\ e\ f\ g\ h\ i &= Suc\ (blowup\ b\ b\ c\ d\ e\ f\ g\ h\ i) \\
blowup\ (Suc\ a)\ b\ c\ d\ e\ f\ g\ h\ i &= Suc\ (blowup\ a\ b\ c\ d\ e\ f\ g\ h\ i)
\end{aligned}
$$

5.3 Multiplication by Shifting and Addition

Pandya and Joseph [17] introduced a new proof rule for total correctness of mutually recursive procedures. The contribution of this proof rule is a refined method for proving termination by analysing the procedure call graph. They motivate their approach with an imperative version of the following example:

$$
\begin{aligned}
prod\ x\ y\ z &= \textbf{if } y\ mod\ 2 = 0\ \textbf{then } eprod\ x\ y\ z\ \textbf{else } oprod\ x\ y\ z \\
oprod\ x\ y\ z &= eprod\ x\ (y - 1)\ (z + x) \\
eprod\ x\ y\ z &= \textbf{if } y = 0\ \textbf{then } z\ \textbf{else } prod\ (2 * x)\ (y\ div\ 2)\ z
\end{aligned}
$$

In the calls from *oprod* and *eprod* the second argument decreases but in the calls from *prod* all arguments are unchanged. Termination is proved automatically because one can order the functions such that *oprod* and *eprod* are less than *prod*.

5.4 Pedal and Coast

Homeier and Martin [9] describe an intricate call graph analysis for which Homeier holds a US patent. Their one example is an imperative version of what they call the *bicycling* program:

$$
\begin{array}{lll}
\textit{pedal} & :: & \textit{nat} \Rightarrow \textit{nat} \Rightarrow \textit{nat} \Rightarrow \textit{nat} \\
\textit{coast} & :: & \textit{nat} \Rightarrow \textit{nat} \Rightarrow \textit{nat} \Rightarrow \textit{nat}
\end{array}
$$

$$
\begin{array}{lll}
\textit{pedal } 0 \; m \; c & = & c \\
\textit{pedal } n \; 0 \; c & = & c \\
\textit{pedal } (\textit{Suc } n) \; (\textit{Suc } m) \; c & = & \textbf{if } n < m \\
 & & \textbf{then } \textit{coast } n \; m \; (c + \textit{Suc } m) \\
 & & \textbf{else } \textit{pedal } n \; (\textit{Suc } m) \; (c + \textit{Suc } m) \\
\textit{coast } n \; m \; c & = & \textbf{if } n < m \\
 & & \textbf{then } \textit{coast } n \; (m - 1) \; (c + n) \\
 & & \textbf{else } \textit{pedal } n \; m \; (c + n)
\end{array}
$$

They claim that termination would be difficult to prove using the rule by Pandya and Joseph. With our algorithm the proof is automatic: In the call from *coast* to *pedal*, no argument decreases. But by ordering the functions such that *pedal* $<$ *coast*, the proof succeeds. In both examples, ordering the functions (see 4.2) is essential. A precise analysis of the relationship between all three termination proof methods is beyond the scope of this paper.

By the way: *prod x y z = x * y + z* and *pedal n m c = n * m + c* can be proved (the latter automatically) via the customized induction principles generated from the function definitions [11].

6   Practical Considerations and Possible Extensions

6.1   Empirical Evaluation

From the existing non-primitive recursive function definitions in the Isabelle Distribution and the Archive of Formal Proofs [1], our method can find suitable orderings for 87% of them, usually in less than a second.

The examples where it fails mainly fall in one of the following categories:

1. Definitions which use a customized size function, where some constructors are weighted more than others. This method is essentially polynomial interpretation, done manually.
2. Functions over naturals or integers, where the argument is increasing but bounded from above.
3. Examples for "difficult" functions from the documentation, where a domain specific semantic argument is used for termination.
4. Functions over more powerful set theoretic constructions like ordinals.
5. Functions that aren't total and thus require special treatment anyway.

6.2   Feedback from Failure

If our analysis fails to find a termination proof, this can have several reasons:

1. The function is indeed non-terminating.
2. The function is terminating, but the termination argument is more complicated than just lexicographic combinations of size measures.

3. Lexicographic orders are sufficient, but the automation employed to prove local descents is not sufficient to derive the required facts, although they are true.

Of course it is impossible for the system to distinguish between these three classes of errors. However, instead of just failing, we provide valuable information to the user by showing the matrix with the proof results. For example, the matrix $\begin{pmatrix} < & \leq \\ ? & \leq \end{pmatrix}$ will tell us that there must be something wrong with the second recursive call. This can be a useful debugging aid, at least if the user has a basic understanding of how the method works.

A few other enhancements help to improve feedback given to the user:

- When proving local descent, many unprovable goals get simplified to *False*. For these cases, giving the matrix the entry F instead of ? makes it clear that the $\leq$-inequality is clearly false. Apart from output, F and ? are not treated differently.
- For unsuccessful proof attempts, printing the unfinished proof states can give the user feedback on lemmas that might be necessary in order for the proof to work.
- If a row in the matrix does not have a strict descent ($<$) at all, one could highlight the corresponding recursive call because it (or its proof) needs special user attention.

6.3   Using Other Measure Functions

Our measure generation has an emphasis on size measures of data types, When working on different data, other size functions will be appropriate. We already mentioned the absolute value of an integer. User-defined types will have their own notions of structure and size, and our analysis is able to accommodate this, if users can declare their own measure functions.

Moreover, while the type based choice of measures is simple, this is not the only possible solution.

In the realm of linear arithmetic, Podelski and Rybalchenko [19] describe how to synthesize measures (which they call *ranking functions*) for simple non-nested while loops. It would be interesting to try to use such a method to generate measures for our approach, which can then be combined with others (say, from data types) to more complex termination proofs.

6.4   Incremental Operation

At the moment, the four steps of our algorithm are executed strictly sequentially. In particular, all proof attempts have to be finished and the matrix has to be complete, before the search for the lexicographic combination begins. This separation simplifies presentation and implementation, but is otherwise unnecessary.

The structure of the system could be modified in a way that the columns of the matrix are produced incrementally. Once a column "arrives", the search algorithm checks immediately, whether it can be used to solve some of the calls. Otherwise it must be stored because it could be useful in a later step.

Such an architecture allows for several immediate optimizations:

– Once an ordering is found, no more proofs about other measures have to be tried.
– If certain rows (=calls) have already been solved by previous measures, they can be ignored in subsequent proof attempts. Instead, the corresponding entries can be set immediately to ?, since they will not be used anyway.

These changes do not increase the power of the analysis, but only its efficiency. However, such a lazy strategy would allow us to increase the number of measure functions to try, without compromising the efficiency of the whole system for examples where they are not needed.

7   Conclusion

We showed how to automate termination proofs for a large class of practically relevant function definitions. Our implementation, which is already part of the Isabelle developer version, is invoked by default for all new function definitions. This makes the termination proof invisible in many cases, which helps users concentrate on their actual theorem proving tasks.

References

1. Archive of Formal Proofs, http://afp.sourceforge.net/
2. Abel, A.: foetus – termination checker for simple functional programs. Programming Lab Report (1998)
3. Abel, A., Altenkirch, T.: A predicative analysis of structural recursion. J. Functional Programming 12(1), 1–41 (2002)
4. Arts, T., Giesl, J.: Termination of term rewriting using dependency pairs. Theor. Comput. Sci. 236(1-2), 133–178 (2000)
5. Barthe, G., Forest, J., Pichardie, D., Rusu, V.: Defining and reasoning about recursive functions: a practical tool for the Coq proof assistant. In: Hagiya, M., Wadler, P. (eds.) FLOPS 2006. LNCS, vol. 3945, Springer, Heidelberg (2006)
6. Berghofer, S., Wenzel, M.: Inductive datatypes in HOL - lessons learned in formal-logic engineering. In: Bertot, Y., Dowek, G., Hirschowitz, A., Paulin, C., Théry, L. (eds.) TPHOLs 1999. LNCS, vol. 1690, pp. 19–36. Springer, Heidelberg (1999)
7. Gordon, M., Melham, T. (eds.): Introduction to HOL: A theorem proving environment for higher order logic. Cambridge University Press, Cambridge (1993)
8. Harrison, J.: The HOL Light theorem prover,
   http://www.cl.cam.ac.uk/users/jrh/hol-light
9. Homeier, P.V., Martin, D.F.: Mechanical verification of total correctness through diversion verification conditions. In: Grundy, J., Newey, M. (eds.) Theorem Proving in Higher Order Logics. LNCS, vol. 1479, pp. 189–206. Springer, Heidelberg (1998)

10. Kaufmann, M., Manolios, P., Moore, J.S.: Computer-Aided Reasoning: An Approach, June 2000. Kluwer Academic Publishers, Dordrecht (2000)

11. Krauss, A.: Partial recursive functions in higher-order logic. In: Furbach, U., Shankar, N. (eds.) IJCAR 2006. LNCS (LNAI), vol. 4130, pp. 589–603. Springer, Heidelberg (2006)

12. Krauss, A.: Certified size-change termination. In: Pfenning, F. (ed.) CADE-21. LNCS, vol. 4603, pp. 460–476. Springer, Heidelberg (to appear, 2007)

13. Lee, C.S., Jones, N.D., Ben-Amram, A.M.: The size-change principle for program termination. In: ACM SIGPLAN-SIGACT Symposium on Principles of Programming Languages, pp. 81–92. ACM Press, New York (2001)

14. Manolios, P., Vroon, D.: Termination analysis with calling context graphs. In: Ball, T., Jones, R.B. (eds.) CAV 2006. LNCS, vol. 4144, pp. 401–414. Springer, Heidelberg (2006)

15. Nipkow, T., Paulson, L.C., Wenzel, M.: Isabelle/HOL. LNCS, vol. 2283. Springer, Heidelberg (2002)

16. Owre, S., Rushby, J.M., Shankar, N.: PVS: A prototype verification system. In: Kapur, D. (ed.) Automated Deduction - CADE-11. LNCS, vol. 607, pp. 748–752. Springer, Heidelberg (1992)

17. Pandya, P., Joseph, M.: A Structure-directed Total Correctness Proof Rule for Recursive Procedure Calls. The Computer Journal 29(6), 531–537 (1986)

18. Papadimitriou, C.H.: Computational Complexity. Addison-Wesley, New York (1994)

19. Podelski, A., Rybalchenko, A.: A complete method for the synthesis of linear ranking functions. In: Steffen, B., Levi, G. (eds.) VMCAI 2004. LNCS, vol. 2937, pp. 239–251. Springer, Heidelberg (2004)

20. Slind, K.: Function definition in Higher-Order Logic. In: von Wright, J., Harrison, J., Grundy, J. (eds.) TPHOLs 1996. LNCS, vol. 1125, pp. 381–397. Springer, Heidelberg (1996)

21. Slind, K.: Reasoning About Terminating Functional Programs. PhD thesis, Institut für Informatik, TU München (1999)

22. Walther, C.: On proving the termination of algorithms by machine. Artif. Intell. 71(1), 101–157 (1994)

Formalising Generalised Substitutions

Jeremy E. Dawson[1,2]

[1] Logic and Computation Program, NICTA*
[2] Automated Reasoning Group,
Australian National University, Canberra, ACT 0200, Australia
http://users.rsise.anu.edu.au/~jeremy/

Abstract. We use the theorem prover Isabelle to formalise and machine-check results of the theory of generalised substitutions given by Dunne and used in the B method. We describe the model of computation implicit in this theory and show how this is based on a compound monad, and we contrast this model of computation and monad with those implicit in Dunne's theory of abstract commands. Subject to a qualification concerning frames, we prove, using the Isabelle/HOL theorem prover, that Dunne's results about generalised substitutions follow from the model of computation which we describe.

Keywords: general correctness, generalised substitution.

1 Introduction

In [7] Dunne gave an account of general correctness, which combines the concepts of partial correctness and total correctness, arguing for its utility in analysing the behaviour of programs. He defined a language of "abstract commands", giving several basic abstract commands and operators for joining them, for which he gave rules in terms of weakest liberal preconditions and termination conditions. In [6] we considered this abstract command language and described the operational interpretation of the abstract commands, showing how it is based on a compound monad. We used the automated theorem proving system Isabelle to prove that the operational interpretation implies the rules given by Dunne.

In [3] Chartier formalised the operations of the B method of Abrial [1] in Isabelle/HOL. He formalised generalised substitutions as an abstract type comprising the *trm* and *prd* functions and a list of variables involved in the substitution. Defining the generalised substitution operations in terms of *trm* and *prd*, he proved that these definitions are equivalent to those of Abrial's definitions in terms of the weakest precondition functions.

In [8] Dunne considered the generalised substitutions used in the B method. He developed the notion of the frame of a substitution, the variables "involved" in it, and defined generalised substitution operations in terms of frames and

* National ICT Australia is funded by the Australian Government's Dept of Communications, Information Technology and the Arts and the Australian Research Council through Backing Australia's Ability and the ICT Centre of Excellence program.

K. Schneider and J. Brandt (Eds.): TPHOLs 2007, LNCS 4732, pp. 54–69, 2007.

weakest preconditions. He then proved a number of properties of these generalised substitutions. In contrast to [7], this theory is based on total correctness.

In this paper we formalise this theory of generalised substitutions, using a similar approach to our work on abstract commands in [6], and using some of its results. That is, we develop a model of computation and define the theory in terms of it. We then find that this enables us to derive the previous definitions and results as consequences of our formulation. These results are proved using the Isabelle/HOL theorem prover, see [5]. We have also performed, in Isabelle, proofs of other results of Dunne in [8], of which details are in the Appendix.

We find that the model of computation we use is also based on a compound monad, and provides an interesting example of a distributive law for monads. Furthermore, this distributive law is also a monad morphism from the monad of [6] to the monad described in this paper.

2   The Operational Models

In [7] Dunne argued that general correctness provides a better framework for program refinement than either total or partial correctness, and its relative simplicity is supported by the results at the end of [6, §3.2]. However the theory of generalised substitutions as used in the B method is based on total correctness, so that when two generalised substitutions with the same frame are equivalent in total correctness, they are regarded as the same, although they may not be equivalent in terms of general correctness. So we need to model program (statements) in such a way that two such generalised substitutions are equal.

So we describe the two operational models. Firstly, we review the operational model of [6], which we used for *abstract commands*, based on *general correctness*. Then we describe the model, on which this paper is based, which fits the *total correctness* framework of *generalised substitutions*. We describe these models, at first without reference to frames, which we discuss in §4. Furthermore, where we state that we have proved a result of Dunne [8], this will usually refer to the result as modified by deleting reference to the frames of the substitutions.

2.1   The General Correctness Operational Model

To express that a command can either terminate in a new state or fail to terminate, in [6] we considered command *outcomes*, where an outcome is either termination in a new state or non-termination. Then we model a command as a function, of type *state → outcome set*, from states to sets of outcomes. Commands are equal if the corresponding functions are equal: that is, we have an extensional definition of equality. This model can distinguish between a command which (when executed in a particular given state) must fail to terminate from one which may or may not fail to terminate. Since Dunne's treatment of abstract commands [7] distinguished between two such commands, this model was effective in considering abstract commands. However a theory of total correctness, using weakest preconditions (which are satisfied only when a command is guaranteed to terminate), does not distinguish between two such commands.

2.2   The Total Correctness Operational Model

For the total correctness model, we model a generalised substitution as a function returning either the tag `NonTerm`, indicating possible non-termination, or `Term` S, indicating guaranteed termination in one of the states contained in the set S. Note that this implies an extensionsal definition of equality: substitutions are equal iff they are equal considered as functions of the appropriate type.

To do this we declare the Isabelle datatype

$$\texttt{datatype } \sigma \texttt{ TorN = NonTerm | Term } \sigma$$

where σ is a type variable. This means that a value of the type σ `TorN` is either the tag `NonTerm` or a member of the type σ, tagged with the tag `Term`. (Thus the type *outcome* of [6] is *state* `TorN`). We then define the type *tcres* to be *state set* `TorN`, that is, either non-termination, or termination in (one of) a set of states. (As in Isabelle, we write a type constructor after the type.)

Then we model a generalised substitution as a function of type *state* $\rightarrow$ *tcres*. For a generalised substitution C, we define $[C]$ (or *wp* C, the weakest precondition of C) for post-condition Q and initial state s, as follows. Then, from it, we define total correctness refinement $\sqsubseteq_{tc}$. By $P \longrightarrow Q$ we mean $\forall s.\ P\ s \rightarrow Q\ s$.

$$[C]\ Q\ s = \exists S.\ (\forall x \in S.\ Q\ x) \land C\ s = \textsf{Term}\ S$$
$$A \sqsubseteq_{tc} B = \forall Q.\ [A]\ Q \longrightarrow [B]\ Q$$

```
"wp_tc C Q s == EX S<=Collect Q. C s = Term S"
"ref_tc A B == ALL Q. wp_tc A Q ---> wp_tc B Q"
```

The definition makes it clear that refinement is a preorder. We then obtain a direct characterisation of refinement, and, from it, we show (as `ref_tc_antisym`) that two generalised substitutions A, B (of type *state* $\rightarrow$ *tcres*) are refinement-equivalent if and only if they are equal in our operational model. Thus refinement is a partial order. This confirms that the operational model above is appropriate for total correctness refinement and equivalence. The related result `wp_tc_inj` is useful for proving the equality of two generalised substitutions.

```
ref_tc_alt = "ref_tc A B ==
  ALL s SA. A s = Term SA --> (EX SB<=SA. B s = Term SB)"
ref_tc_antisym = "[| ref_tc A B; ref_tc B A |] ==> A = B"
wp_tc_inj = "wp_tc A = wp_tc B ==> A = B"
```

2.3   The Total Correctness Compound Monad

In [6, §3.1] we showed that the general correctness operational monad gave a monad, which we will call the *outcome set* monad. See [6, §3.1] for a brief discussion of monads, or Wadler [10] for further information. We now find that the type *tcres*, relative to the type *state*, is a monad, the *total correctness* monad.

To define a monad M, we need to define the unit and extension functions, of the types shown. The unit function models the command which does nothing (*skip*) and the extension function is used to model sequencing of commands since *ext A* models the action of command *A* on the output of a previous command. We then need to show that the unit and extension functions satisfy the following rules required for a monad.

$$unit : \alpha \to \alpha M$$
$$ext : (\alpha \to \beta M) \to (\alpha M \to \beta M)$$

$$ext\ f \circ unit = f \tag{1}$$
$$ext\ unit = unit \tag{2}$$
$$ext\ (ext\ g \circ f) = ext\ g \circ ext\ f \tag{3}$$

As a standard result (see [10]), a monad can be characterised either by the three functions *unit, map* and *join*, and seven axioms involving these functions, or the functions *unit* and *ext* and the three axioms shown above. Rule (3) lets us define sequencing of commands, $A; B$ (or *seq A B*) = $ext\ B \circ A$, and, as in [6, §3.1], the associativity of *seq* (which obviously ought to hold!) follows from (3).

We have that *tcres* = *state set* TorN. Each of the type constructors *set* and TorN with their associated unit and extension functions, is a monad. It does not follow, however, that *tcres* (relative to *state*) is a monad.

To prove that the total correctness monad is in fact a monad, we used the results of Dawson [4], which develop those of Jones & Duponcheel [9]. As in [9], we consider the composition of two monads M and N, but as in Isabelle, we write a type constructor after the type, so the compound monadic type is αNM. We write ext_{NM}, ext_M, ext_N for the extension functions of NM, M, N.

To get a compound monad, we need the function ext_{NM}, which "extends" a function f from a "smaller" domain, α, to a "larger" one, αNM. Consider, therefore, a "partial extension" function which does part of this job:

$$ext_{NM} : (\alpha \to \beta NM) \to (\alpha NM \to \beta NM)$$
$$pext : (\alpha \to \beta NM) \to (\alpha N \to \beta NM)$$

The following rules and definitions are sufficient to define a compound monad using such a function *pext*.

$$pext\ f \circ unit_N = f \tag{4}$$
$$pext\ unit_{NM} = unit_M \tag{5}$$
$$pext\ (ext_{NM}\ g \circ f) = ext_{NM}\ g \circ pext\ f \tag{6}$$
$$ext_{NM}\ g = ext_M\ (pext\ g) \tag{7}$$
$$unit_{NM} = unit_M \circ unit_N \tag{8}$$

We now give the definitions for our particular monads $N = set$ and $M = $ TorN, the suffix _*tc* indicating the total correctness monad.

$$unit\_tc : state \to tcres$$
$$prod\_tc : tcres\ set \to tcres$$
$$pext\_tc : (state \to tcres) \to state\ set \to tcres$$
$$ext\_tc : (state \to tcres) \to tcres \to tcres$$

$$unit\_tc\ s = \text{Term}\ \{s\} \tag{9}$$
$$prod\_tc\ S = \text{NonTerm} \qquad \text{if NonTerm} \in S \tag{10}$$
$$prod\_tc\ (\text{Term}'S) = \text{Term}\ (\bigcup S) \tag{11}$$
$$pext\_tc\ A\ S = prod\_tc\ (A'S) \tag{12}$$
$$ext\_tc\ A\ S = ext\_o\ (pext\_tc\ A)\ S \tag{13}$$

where ext_o is the extension function of the TorN monad (see [6]), given by

$$ext\_o\ f\ \text{NonTerm} = \text{NonTerm} \tag{14}$$
$$ext\_o\ f\ (\text{Term}\ s) = f\ s \tag{15}$$

and $f'S$ is Isabelle notation for $\{f\ s\ |\ s \in S\}$.

We have proved, in Isabelle, the following result. We did this by proving rules (4) to (6), noting that (7) and (8) follow directly from our definitions.

Theorem 1. σ set TorN *is a compound monad.*

2.4 Relation to the Outcome Set Monad

Jones & Duponcheel [9] also use a function $swap : \alpha M N \to \alpha N M$ to define a compound monad. As they show, when such a function $swap$ can be defined, satisfying certain conditions S(1) to S(4), then the compound monad $\alpha N M$ can be constructed. Equivalently, the function $swap$ is a distributive law for monads, see Barr & Wells [2, §9.2]. Jones & Duponcheel also use the function $prod$ as above, and give conditions for defining a compound monad in terms of $prod$.

In fact the total correctness monad can be defined using $swap$. In this case M is the outcome monad, and N is the set monad, and $swap$ is a function

$$swap\_tc : \sigma\ \text{TorN}\ set \to \sigma\ set\ \text{TorN}$$
$$swap\_tc\ S = \text{NonTerm} \qquad \text{if NonTerm} \in S \tag{16}$$
$$swap\_tc\ (\text{Term}'S) = \text{Term}\ S \tag{17}$$

Here, definition (16) reflects the fact that, in total correctness, a command that *may* fail to terminate is equivalent to one which *will* fail to terminate.

Our Isabelle proofs included the conditions S(1) to S(4) of [9], and so we also have shown that $swap\_tc$ is a distributive law for the monads.

The function $swap\_tc : \sigma\ \text{TorN}\ set \to \sigma\ set\ \text{TorN}$ is also a *monad morphism* from the *outcome set* monad to the *total correctness* monad. We have proved the following theorems (which characterise a monad morphism), where $unit\_os$ and ext_os are the unit and extension functions for the outcome set monad, as defined in [6, §3.1]:

$$unit\_os : state \to outcome\ set$$
$$ext\_os : (state \to outcome\ set) \to outcome\ set \to outcome\ set$$

$$unit\_tc\ a = swap\_tc\ (unit\_os\ a) \tag{18}$$
$$ext\_tc\ (swap\_tc\ \circ f)\ (swap\_tc\ x) = swap\_tc\ (ext\_os\ f\ x) \tag{19}$$

Since this monad morphism is surjective, we could use the fact that the outcome set monad satisfies the monad axioms to give an alternative proof to show that the total correctness monad also satisfies them.

Often, where two monads can be composed to form another monad, the construction depends on one of them, and the other may be arbitrary. Thus, as discussed in [6, §3.1], the TorN monad can be composed with any other monad M to give a compound monad, which gave the *outcome set* monad. In this case we have that the type σ *set* TorN is a monad (relative to σ), but it does not seem to be an example of a more general construction, in that for an arbitrary monad M, neither σ M TorN nor σ *set* M is in general a monad.

We also proved the following theorem about abstract commands. Dunne's treatment of general correctness in [7] includes a definition of total correctness refinement, which is referred to as totcref in the result below. This result also confirms that the operational model of §2.2 is appropriate for total correctness. For two abstract commands A, B (of type *state* → *outcome set*) the left-hand side says $A \sqsubseteq B$ according to the total-correctness refinement relation for abstract commands, as defined and discussed in [7] and [6, §3.2]. The right-hand side says that the refinement relation for generalised substitutions holds of the projections of A and B into the type *state* → *tcres*.

```
ref_tc_swap = "totcref A B = ref_tc (swap_tc o A) (swap_tc o B)"
```

Often in this work, we drew upon [6], using the fact that if two abstract commands are equal, then so are their projections into the total correctness monad.

3   The Generalised Substitutions

Frames. Dunne has also defined that each substitution has a *frame*. Loosely, this is the set of variables which "might" be affected. Note, however, that $frame(x := x) = \{x\}$. Also, from any command a new command may be defined which has an enlarged frame but is otherwise the same.

Stating the frame of a command does not contribute to a description of what the command, considered in isolation, does. Thus when we show, for example, that two commands behave the same way, we do so without considering their frames. Indeed, the substitution *skip* and $x := x$ behave the same way, but have different frames. Likewise, it is impossible to deduce the frame of a substitution from its behaviour. The work in this section proceeds on this basis. Therefore the results are therefore subject to the proviso that two generalised substitutions are in fact distinct if their frames differ.

On the other hand, the specified frame of a substitution does have an effect in that the parallel composition $S\|T$ depends on the frames of S and T — that is, if the frames of S or T are extended, then that changes $S\|T$.

Variables. Indeed, for many generalised substitution operations, we do not need to consider variables at all: rather, we can consider a machine state abstractly. For others, we need to consider a state as a map from variables (variable names) to values. As discussed at greater length in [6], where Q is a predicate on states, we may use the notation $Q[x := E]$ to mean Q, with occurrences of x replaced by E, when Q is written in the command language, or some similar notation. This is found in the *wp* rule for assignment, and in the related Hoare logic rule.

$$wp(x := E, Q) = Q[x := E] \qquad \{Q[x := E]\}\ (x := E)\ \{Q\}$$

In fact we could take $Q[x := E]$ to be defined as follows. Considering expression E as a function from states to values, $Q[x := E]\ s = Q\ (s[x := E\ s])$ where, for state s, $s[x := E\ s]$ means the function s, changed at the domain point x. (though using this as a *definition* makes the *wp* rule above rather trivial, since assignment will be defined to take state s to state $s[x := E\ s]$).

3.1 Meaning of Commands

skip, magic, abort. [8, §3.1, §3.3] *skip* is the command which is feasible, terminates and does nothing to the state. It is exactly the function *unit_tc*. It follows immediately from the monad laws (1) and (2) that *skip* is an identity for the binary function *seq_tc*. These are proved in Isabelle as `seq_tc_unitL/R`.

We *define magic* and *abort* in terms of the operational model, as `magic_tc_def` and `abort_tc_def`; then with these definitions, we then *prove* Dunne's definitions, as `magic_alt` and `abort_alt` (using `precon_tc` and `guard_tc`, see below).

As *abort* always fails to terminate, it fails to satisfy any post-condition. On the other hand, *magic* is always *infeasible*: while not suffering non-termination, it cannot produce any result which fails to satisfy any given post-condition, so it satisfies every post-condition. So we also prove that *magic* and *abort* are the top and bottom members in the lattice of generalised substitutions [8, §7].

```
magic_tc_def = "magic_tc s == Term {}"
abort_tc_def = "abort_tc s == NonTerm"
magic_alt = "magic_tc = guard_tc (%s. False) unit_tc"
abort_alt = "abort_tc = precon_tc (%s. False) unit_tc"
top_magic_tc = "ref_tc C magic_tc"
bot_abort_tc = "ref_tc abort_tc C"
```

preconditioned command, guarded command. [8, §3.1] The preconditioned command $P|A$ is the same as A except that, if P does not hold, then $P|A$ need not terminate. The guarded command $P \Longrightarrow A$ is the same as A if P holds, but is *infeasible* (it cannot reach any outcome, that is, it cannot run) if P does not hold. Dunne defines both of these by giving the formula for their weakest precondition. We define them using `precon_tc_def` and `guard_tc_def`, and then prove Dunne's definitions as `precon_wp_tc'` and `guard_wp_tc`.

```
precon_tc_def = "precon_tc P C s == if P s then C s else NonTerm"
guard_tc_def = "guard_tc P C s == if P s then C s else Term {}"
precon_wp_tc' = "wp_tc (precon_tc P C) Q s = (P s & wp_tc C Q s)"
guard_wp_tc = "wp_tc (guard_tc P C) Q s = (P s --> wp_tc C Q s)"
```

termination, feasibility. [8, §5] We define

```
"trm_tc C s == C s ~= NonTerm"
"fis_tc C s == C s ~= Term {}"
```

We can then prove Dunne's definition of *trm* and *fis*, and his results in [8, §5]:

```
trm_alt = "trm_tc C = wp_tc C (%s. True)"
fis_alt = "fis_tc C = Not o wp_tc C (%s. False)"
pc_trm_tc = "precon_tc (trm_tc A) A = A"
fis_guard_tc = "guard_tc (fis_tc A) A = A"
strongest_guard = "(guard_tc g A = A) = (fis_tc A ---> g)"
strongest_pc = "(precon_tc pc A = A) = (trm_tc A ---> pc)"
```

sequencing. [8, §3.1] As mentioned earlier, we define sequencing of commands using *ext_tc*, as shown in `seq_tc_def`. Dunne defines it by giving the weakest precondition of $A; B$, and we prove this result, as `seq_wp_tc`, from our definition.

```
seq_tc_def = "seq_tc A B == ext_tc B o A"
seq_wp_tc = "wp_tc (seq_tc A B) Q = wp_tc A (wp_tc B Q)"
```

choice. In [8, §3.1] Dunne defines a binary operator, $A \square B$, for *bounded choice*: $A \square B$ is a command which can choose between two commands A and B. Again, Dunne defines this by giving its weakest precondition. This is a special case of choice among an arbitrary set of commands. In the total correctness setting, where *choice_tc* C can fail to terminate if any $C \in C$ can fail to terminate, we define *choice_tc* as shown below.

As the definition is rather unintuitive, we show the types of some of its parts. Recall that if the type σ represents the machine state, then a command has type $\sigma \rightarrow \sigma$ set TorN. The definition is unintuitive perhaps because where *pext* is used (indirectly) in defining sequencing of commands, the types α and β are both the state type σ. But in the use of *pext* below, α is the type of commands.

$$choice\_tc\ C\ s = pext\ (\lambda C.\ C\ s)\ C$$
$$choice\_tc : (\sigma \rightarrow \sigma\ set\ \mathsf{TorN})\ set \rightarrow \sigma \rightarrow \sigma\ set\ \mathsf{TorN}$$
$$pext\ : (\alpha \rightarrow \beta\ set\ \mathsf{TorN}) \rightarrow \alpha\ set \rightarrow \beta\ set\ \mathsf{TorN}$$
$$\lambda C.\ C\ s : (\sigma \rightarrow \sigma\ set\ \mathsf{TorN}) \rightarrow \sigma\ set\ \mathsf{TorN}$$
$$pext\ (\lambda C.\ C\ s) : (\sigma \rightarrow \sigma\ set\ \mathsf{TorN})\ set \rightarrow \sigma\ set\ \mathsf{TorN}$$

When the definition is expanded (`choice_tc_def''` in the Isabelle proofs), it shows that if $\{C\ s \mid C \in C\}$ contains NonTerm then *choice_tc* C s = NonTerm; if $\{C\ s \mid C \in C\} = \{\mathsf{Term}\ S_C \mid C \in C\}$, then *choice_tc* C s = Term($\bigcup_{C \in C} S_C$).

We obtained the following results, relating the distribution of sequencing over choice. The theorem `seq_choice_tcL` was obtained as an easy corollary of rule (6), obtained in the course of the proofs about the total correctness monad. We also proved a result giving the weakest precondition of *choice_tc*, which is the generalisation of Dunne's definition of $A \square B$, and from which it easily follows that *choice_tc* C is the glb of the set C. Proposition 7 of [8, p288] follows.

```
seq_choice_tcL =
  "seq_tc (choice_tc Cs) B = choice_tc ((%C. seq_tc C B) ' Cs)"
seq_choice_tcR = "Cs ~= {} ==>
  seq_tc A (choice_tc Cs) = choice_tc (seq_tc A ' Cs)"
choice_wp_tc = "wp_tc (choice_tc Cs) Q s = (ALL C:Cs. wp_tc C Q s)"
choice_glb_tc = "ref_tc A (choice_tc Cs) = (ALL C:Cs. ref_tc A C)"
```

We note that for many generalised substitutions, the definition may be obtained by translation from the definitions in [6] for abstract commands. For example, for *choice_tc* we could have defined *choice_tc* $\mathcal{C}$ in terms of *choice* $\mathcal{A}$ for any set $\mathcal{A}$ of abstract commands corresponding to the set $\mathcal{C}$ of generalised substitutions. Alternatively, we can relate our definitions to the definitions of the corresponding abstract commands, where seq, precon, guard and choice are the corresponding operations on abstract commands: [6, §3.4].

```
seq_tc = "seq_tc (swap_tc o A) (swap_tc o B) = swap_tc o seq A B"
precon_tc = "precon_tc P (swap_tc o A) = swap_tc o precon P A"
guard_tc = "guard_tc P (swap_tc o A) = swap_tc o guard P A"
choice_tc = "choice_tc (op o swap_tc ' As) = swap_tc o choice As"
```

where (op o swap_tc ' As) means $\{swap\_tc \circ A \mid A \in As\}$ (We have similar results for magic_tc, abort_tc, trm_tc and fis_tc also). These results enable us to prove many results for generalised substitutions from the corresponding results for abstract commands. In some cases, such as for the theorem choice_wp_tc, this provided much simpler proofs in Isabelle.

3.2   Monotonicity

For developing a program by starting with a generalised substitution (expressing a program specification), and progressively refining it to a concrete program, it is important that the generalised substitution constructors are monotonic with respect to the refinement relation ($\sqsubseteq$). All the constructors mentioned are monotonic. We proved these results in Isabelle as (for example)

```
seq_tc_ref_mono = "[| ref_tc A1 B1; ref_tc A2 B2 |] ==>
    ref_tc (seq_tc A1 A2) (seq_tc B1 B2)"
rephat_ref_mono = "ref_tc A B ==> ref_tc (rephat A) (rephat B)"
```

3.3   Repetition and Iteration for the General Correctness Model

In [7, §7] Dunne defined $A^0 = skip$ and $A^{n+1} = A; A^n$, and we proved that $A^{n+1} = A^n; A$. From this we defined *repall* $A \ s = \bigcup_n A^n s$, that is, repall A is the (unbounded) choice of any number n of repetitions of A; it terminates iff for every n, A^n terminates (proved as repall_term).

In [7, §12] Dunne defined the *repetitive closure* A^* of A, where the outcomes of A^* are those of repall, augmented by NonTerm in the case where it is feasible to execute A infinitely many times sequentially (calling this an "infinite chain"). Thus, in [6, §3.5] we defined a function *infch*, where *infch* $A \ s$ means that it is possible to execute A infinitely many times sequentially, starting in state s.

So we had the following definition, from which we proved various results from [7], including characterisations of `repall` and `repstar` as fixpoints.

```
repstar C state == repall C state Un
            (if infch C state then {NonTerm} else {})
```

A Coinductive Definition. In [6, §3.5] we defined the concept of an infinite chain explicitly, in terms of the existence of an infinite sequence of states through which the executing program can pass. Some of these Isabelle proofs involving this definition were quite difficult.

Subsequently we used Isabelle's coinductive definition facility to give a more elegant definition of an equivalent notion: *infchs A* is the set of states from which it is possible to execute A infinitely many times sequentially. We also defined inductively a set *icnt A*, which we showed is equivalent to $\{s \mid \texttt{NonTerm} \in A^* \ s\}$.

The Isabelle definitions are:

```
coinductive "infchs A"
   intros I : "Term ns : A s ==> ns : infchs A ==> s : infchs A"

coinductive "icnt A"
   intros NTI : "NonTerm : A s ==> s : icnt A"
      icI : "Term ns : A s ==> ns : icnt A ==> s : icnt A"
```

This defines *infchs A* to be the unique maximal set satisfying

$$infchs \ A = \{s \mid \exists s'. \ \texttt{Term} \ s' \in A \ s \land s' \in infchs \ A\}$$

Then Isabelle's coinductive definition facility provides a coinduction principle:

$$\frac{a \in X \qquad \forall z. z \in X \Rightarrow \exists s'. \texttt{Term} \ s' \in A \ z \land s' \in X \cup infchs \ A}{a \in infchs \ A}$$

and similarly for *icnt*. We then proved that $s \in infchs \ A$ if and only if *infch A s* holds, and that $s \in icnt \ A$ if and only if $\texttt{NonTerm} \in A^* \ s$. This made some other proofs considerably easier than before.

3.4 Repetition and Iteration for the Total Correctness Model

For the total correctness model we used analogous definitions. We used a coinductive definition to define *infchs_tc C*, the set of states from which it is possible to execute C infinitely many times sequentially and an inductive definition for *reach_NT C*, the set of states from which `NonTerm` is reachable.

```
coinductive "infchs_tc C"     intros
"C s = Term S ==> ns : S ==> ns : infchs_tc C ==> s : infchs_tc C"

inductive "reach_NT C"
 intros "C s = NonTerm ==> s : reach_NT C"
    "C s = Term S ==> ns : S ==> ns : reach_NT C ==> s : reach_NT C"
```

Then we define *icnt_tc C*, using the same introduction rules as for *reach_NT C*, but in a coinductive definition, not an inductive definition. We then prove that *icnt_tc C = reach_NT C ∪ infchs_tc C*, and can relate *icnt_tc* to *icnt*.

```
icnt_alt = "icnt_tc C = reach_NT C Un infchs_tc C"
icnt_tc = "icnt_tc (swap_tc o A) = icnt A"
```

Also using an inductive definition, we define **treach A s** to be the set of states reachable from **s** using **A** repeatedly.

In [8, §8.2] Dunne defines the generalised substitution $C^\wedge$. He *defines* it as the least fixed point in the refinement ordering $\mu X. (C; X)\Box skip$. For us to define it in that way would require showing that the least fixed-point exists: in [8, §8.1] Dunne discusses why this result holds. Rather than proving this result in Isabelle, we *define* $C^\wedge$ using the operational interpretation (suggested in [8, §8.2]) that the result of $C^\wedge$ is the states reachable by repeating C, but with the result **NonTerm** either if **NonTerm** is reachable by repeating C or if an infinite sequence of executions of C is possible. We then *proved* that $C^\wedge$, defined thus, is in fact the least fixed-point of $\lambda X. (C; X)\Box skip$. The proofs were more difficult than the corresponding ones for abstract commands, mentioned in [6], and it was necessary to use a range of lemmas, including some of those mentioned in §2.3. We can relate the total correctness repetition constructs to those for general correctness, using *swap_tc* (for example, **rephat_star** below). We proved Dunne's examples, $magic^\wedge$ and $skip^\wedge$. We also defined a function **repall_tc**, analogously to *repall* (see §3.3), and showed that $C^\wedge$ could instead have been defined, analogously to A^*, using it. Among the following, **rephat_def** and **fprep_tc_def** are definitions.

```
rephat_def = "rephat C state ==
  if state : icnt_tc C then NonTerm else Term (treach C state)"
fprep_tc_def = "fprep_tc A X ==
  X = choice_tc {seq_tc A X, unit_tc}"
rephat_isfp = "fprep_tc A (rephat A)"
rephat_is_lfp = "fprep_tc A Y ==> ref_tc (rephat A) Y"
rephat_star = "rephat (swap_tc o A) s = swap_tc (repstar A s)"
rephat_magic = "rephat magic_tc = unit_tc"
rephat_skip = "rephat unit_tc = abort_tc"
```

Dunne then defines the *if* and *while* constructs as follows [8, §9]:

$$if\_tc \ G \ then \ S \ else \ T \ end \equiv (G \Longrightarrow S) \Box (\neg G \Longrightarrow T)$$
$$while\_tc \ G \ do \ S \ end \equiv (G \Longrightarrow S)^\wedge \, ; \, \neg G \Longrightarrow skip$$

From these we are then able to prove an alternative definition for *if* and the usual programming definition for *while*:

```
if_tc_prog = "if_tc G A B s = (if G s then A s else B s)"
ifthen_tc_prog =
  "ifthen_tc G A s = (if G s then A s else Term {s})"
while_tc_prog =
  "while_tc G A = ifthen_tc G (seq_tc A (while_tc G A))"
```

3.5 The *prd* Predicate

[8, §5] The "before-after" predicate *prd* relates the values of the variables in the frame before execution of the command to their values after the command. It is defined in [8, §5] as *prd* (*S*) ≡ ¬[*S*](*s* ≠ *s'*) where *s* = *frame*(*S*) and *s'* are new (logical) variables corresponding to the program variables *s*. Implicitly, *prd* (*S*) depends on *s'*; (*s* ≠ *s'*) is a post-condition on the values of *s* after executing *S*.

First we define `prd_tc` which assumes that the frame consists of all variables. Then, for the analysis of `prd_tc`, it is possible to treat the state as abstract.

```
"prd_tc s' C == Not o wp_tc C (%s. s ~= s')
```

where `s'`, of type *state*, represents the values *s'*. We note a difference between the definitions of [8, §6] and [7, §10]: in the former, if *S* does not terminate from state *s*, then *prd*(*S*)*s* *does* hold.

As a sort of inverse to this definition, we derived `wp_prd_tc`, an expression for *wp* in terms of *prd*, namely [*S*]*Q* = *trm S* ∧ ∀*s'*. *prd*(*S*) → *Q*. This was suggested by a similar result in [7, §10].

We also derived [8, §13, p287, Proposition 7] as `ref_tc_prdt`.

```
wp_prd_tc = "wp_tc A Q s =
  (trm_tc A s & (ALL s'. prd_tc s' A s --> Q s'))"
ref_tc_prdt = "ref_tc A B = ((trm_tc A ---> trm_tc B) &
  (ALL s'. prd_tc s' B ---> prd_tc s' A))"
```

3.6 The Least Upper Bound

[8, §7] ? In §3.1 we showed that, in the refinement ordering, the greatest lower bound of a set of commands is given by the *choice* command. To describe the least upper bound *lub S T* of *S* and *T* is more difficult. We might expect that [*lub S T*] *Q* = [*S*]*Q* ∨ [*T*]*Q* but this is not so. For if *S x* = Term {*y_S*} and *T x* = Term {*y_T*}, where *y_S* ≠ *y_T*, then (*lub S T*) *x* = Term {} and so [*lub S T*] *Q x* holds. But if neither *Q y_S* nor *Q y_T* hold, then ([*S*]*Q* ∨ [*T*]*Q*) *x* does not hold.

However in [8, §7] Dunne gives a characterisation of the least upper bound of the set of generalised substitutions on a given frame: we prove this result, applied to a set of abstract states, as `lub_tc`. As a corollary of this general result, we get `ACNF_tc`, giving Dunne's normal form, [8, §11, Proposition 4], again in terms of abstract states. These results use the functions `at_tc` and `pc_aux`. The function `at_tc` is analogous to *atd* of [6, §4.2], and is used to express Dunne's unbounded choice over a set of logical variables. The function `pc_aux_tc` is used here and in §7, and *pc_aux C s* = Term *S*, where *S* consists of those states which every *C* ∈ *C* can reach from initial state *s* (we proved this in Isabelle as `pc_aux_alt2`).

```
at_tc_def = "at_tc Ad == choice_tc (range Ad)"
pc_aux_def = "pc_aux Cs == at_tc
  (%s'. guard_tc (%s. ALL C:Cs. prd_tc s' C s) (%s. Term {s'}))"
```

```
lub_tc =
  "ref_tc (precon_tc (%s. EX C:Cs. trm_tc C s) (pc_aux Cs)) A =
    (ALL C:Cs. ref_tc C A)"
ACNF_tc = "A = precon_tc (trm_tc A)
  (at_tc (%s'. guard_tc (prd_tc s' A) (%s. Term {s'})))"
```

Having found the least upper bound of a set of generalised substitutions using the function pc_aux, we now derive an expresson for weakest precondition of
pc_aux C in terms of $\{[C] \mid C \in C\}$, using a function we called lub_pt. We then
proved that lub_pt gives the least upper bound of a set of predicate transformers, provided that they are conjunctive (and so monotonic). This is not enough
to deduce that pc_aux C is the least upper bound of C since weakest precondition functions fail to be conjunctive, where non-termination is involved. Thus
the theorem lub_tc contains the termination precondition. In §3.8 we discuss
how generalised substitutions correspond to predicate transformers satisfying
the non-empty conjunctivity condition.

Here mono_pt T means that T is monotonic. and conj_pt T Q s means
that T is conjunctive in relation to a given set Q of predicates and state s.
The results lub_pt_lub, lub_pt_ub and lub_pt_is_conj, together show that,
among conjunctive predicate transformers, lub_pt gives the least upper bound.

```
pc_aux_wp = "wp_tc (pc_aux Cs) = lub_pt (wp_tc ' Cs)"
lub_pt_def = "lub_pt Ts Q x == ALL Q':Qcs Q. EX T:Ts. T Q' x"
Qcs_def = "Qcs Q == (%y x. x ~= y) ' (- Collect Q)"
lub_pt_lub = "[| ALL Qs. conj_pt T Qs s;
  ALL U:Us. ALL Q. U Q s --> T Q s; lub_pt Us Q s |] ==> T Q s"
lub_pt_ub = "[| mono_pt T; T : Ts |] ==> T Q ---> lub_pt Ts Q"
lub_pt_is_conj = "conj_pt (lub_pt Ts) Qs s"
conj_pt_def = "conj_pt T Qs s ==
  T (%s. ALL Q:Qs. Q s) s = (ALL Q:Qs. T Q s)"
```

3.7 Parallel Composition

[8, §6] Here we describe this in the case where the frames of the commands are the
set of all program variables. This enables us to treat the machine state abstractly.
We define the parallel composition according to Dunne's informal description:
$S\|T$ can terminate in a state s only if both S and T can terminate in s (but we
define parallel composition of an arbitrary set of generalised substitutions). The
"else" part of pcomprs_tc amounts to pcomprs_tc (Term 'S) = Term ($\bigcap S$).
From this we then derive Dunne's definition, pcomp_tc_alt. We then derive the
further results given in [8, §6], and also prd_pcomp_tc, a variant of his expression
for $prd(S\|T)$ which generalises directly to give the parallel composition of an
arbitrary set of generalised substitutions.

```
pcomp_tc_def = "pcomp_tc Cs s == pcomprs_tc ((%C. C s) ' Cs)"
pcomprs_tc_def = "pcomprs_tc rs ==
  if NonTerm : rs then NonTerm else Term (Inter (sts_of_ocs rs))"
```

```
pcomp_tc_alt = "pcomp_tc Cs ==
   precon_tc (%s. ALL C:Cs. trm_tc C s) (pc_aux Cs)"
trm_pcomp_tc = "trm_tc (pcomp_tc Cs) s = (ALL C:Cs. trm_tc C s)"
prd_pcomp_tc = "prd_tc s' (pcomp_tc Cs) s =
   (trm_tc (pcomp_tc Cs) s --> (ALL C:Cs. prd_tc s' C s))"
prd_pcomp_tc2 = "prd_tc s' (pcomp_tc {A, B}) s =
   ((trm_tc B s --> prd_tc s' A s) &
    (trm_tc A s --> prd_tc s' B s))"
pcomp_choice_tc = "pcomp_tc {B, choice_tc (insert A As)} =
   choice_tc ((%a. pcomp_tc {B, a}) ' insert A As)"
```

3.8   Healthiness Conditions and Positive Conjunctivity

[8, §10.1] Dunne asks whether any choice of frame and predicate transformer gives a generalised substitution. He gives three necessary conditions, that is, properties of generalised substitutions. Of these, (GS1) is relevant only when the definitions of *frame*(S) and [S] are given at a syntactic level — they must then be well-defined at the semantic level. Here we are working at the semantic level. Condition (GS3) in effect says that a generalised substitution has no effect outside its frame. However, we look at condition (GS2) which says that a generalised substitution [S] distributes through all non-empty conjunctions (of postconditions): we prove this as wp_tc_gen_conj. Given a predicate transformer T, the result ACNF_tc enables us to determine the generalised substitution C such that, if T is a weakest precondition, then T = [C]. This gives us the definition gs_of_pt_def and the theorem gs_of_pt. We then prove (as pt_gc_gs) that if T is any predicate transformer satisfying the non-empty conjunctivity condition, then T = [gs_of_pt T]. That is, the generalised substitutions correspond to the predicate transformers satisfying the non-empty conjunctivity condition.

```
wp_tc_gen_conj = "Q : Qs ==>
   wp_tc C (%s. ALL Q:Qs. Q s) s = (ALL Q:Qs. wp_tc C Q s)"
gs_of_pt_def = "gs_of_pt T == precon_tc (T (%s. True))
   (at_tc (%s'. guard_tc (Not o T (%st. st ~= s')) (%s. Term {s'})))"
gs_of_pt = "T = wp_tc C ==> C = gs_of_pt T"
pt_gc_gs = "[| ALL Q Qs s.  Q : Qs --> conj_pt T Qs s;
   C = gs_of_pt T |] ==> T = wp_tc C"
```

3.9   Properties of Substitutions

We proved the results of Proposition 1 of [8, §10.2], and of Proposition 2 (shown).

```
trm_or_prd_tc = "trm_tc S s | prd_tc s' S s"
prd_tc_imp_fis = "prd_tc s' S ---> fis_tc S"
fis_or_wp_tc = "fis_tc S s | wp_tc S Q s"
wp_imp_trm_tc = "wp_tc S Q ---> trm_tc S"
```

Our Isabelle proofs of other results of Dunne [8] are listed in the Appendix.

4   Frames and Variable Names

So far, we have viewed a command as a function from a state to either NonTerm or a set of new states, and a condition as a predicate on states. In this treatment, the view of a state was abstract. However, as in [6, §4], we also need to discuss frames, and the values of program variables.

In our Isabelle model, as in [6, §4], the program variable names are of type 'n (eg, strings) and they take values of type 'v, where 'n and 'v are Isabelle type variables. As a state is an assignment of variables to values, we have the type definition *state* = *name* → *value*, or, in Isabelle, state = "'n => 'v".

In Dunne's formulation [7, §7], each generalised substitution comes decorated with a frame, and the frame of the new command is defined individually for each generalised substitution constructor: for example

$$frame\ (A \square B) = frame\ (A || B) = frame(A) \cup frame(B)$$

However we are unable to give an exact semantic meaning to the frame in a similar sense to the meaning we have given to commands so far. The frame may be thought of as a set of variables "potentially" set by a command, but it can be larger than the set of variables actually set by the command. The frame may be smaller than the set of variables read by the command, and two commands which have the same operational behaviour can have different frames. This means that whereas we can deduce the weakest precondition of a generalised substitution from its operational behaviour, we cannot deduce its frame. (We could confirm that it does not change variables outside its defined frame, but this seems straightforward, and we have not done it in Isabelle).

Certain of Dunne's results involving frames can be seen to follow easily from the results earlier which treat the state abstractly. Thus, to see Proposition 4 in its full generality, you consider the state as consisting of only the variables in the frame, and apply the theorem ACNF_tc. Similarly to get Dunne's characterisation of the lub of two generalised substitutions with the same frame u, you just apply lub_tc to the state consisting only of the variables in u.

We now describe how to express some of Dunne's other results involving frames, and prove them. The condition $x \setminus Q$ is defined to mean that no variable of x appears free in Q. Since we view Q semantically rather than syntactically, we defined indep x Q to be the condition that changing the value, in a state s, of a variable in x does not change Q s. In proving these results we also rely on the fact that a generalised substitution S does not change variables outside *frame(S)*. So we defined frame_tc S F to mean that F *could* be the frame of S, ie, that S does not change variables outside F. In this way we proved the frame circumscription result [8, §10.1, (GS3)], and [8, Proposition 3].

Note that $(Q \lor R)\ s \equiv Q\ s \lor R\ s$ and $(Q\ \&\&\ R)\ s \equiv Q\ s \land R\ s$.

```
GS3 = "[| frame_tc S F; indep F Q |] ==>
  wp_tc S Q s = (trm_tc S s & (fis_tc S s --> Q s))"
prop3 = "[| frame_tc S F; indep F R |] ==>
  wp_tc S (Q V R) = (wp_tc S Q V trm_tc S && R)"
```

5   Conclusion

We have formalised a computational model suggested by the notion of total correctness underlying the B method, and have proposed definitions for the generalised substitution operators in terms of this model. We have shown that this model and these definitions do in fact imply the characterisations of these operators in terms of weakest preconditions. We have proved these results in Isabelle [5], and have also proved the other results of Dunne in [8] (although not dealing explicitly with frames). Thus we have used formal verification to confirm a body of theory underlying a widely used program development methodology.

We have shown how the computational model is derived from a compound monad, and have compared this model and monad with those arising from Dunne's theory of abstract commands in [7]. We have shown how the monad arises from a distributive law, which is in fact a monad morphism.

Acknowledgements. Finally, I would like to thank Steve Dunne and some anonymous referees for some very helpful comments.

References

1. Abrial, J.-R.: The B-Book: Assigning Programs to Meanings. CUP, Cambridge (1996)
2. Barr, M., Wells, C.: Toposes, Triples and Theories. Springer, Heidelberg (1983), http://www.cwru.edu/artsci/math/wells/pub/ttt.html
3. Chartier, P.: Formalisation of B in Isabelle/HOL. In: Bert, D. (ed.) B 1998. LNCS, vol. 1393, pp. 66–83. Springer, Heidelberg (1998)
4. Dawson, J.E.: Compound Monads and the Kleisli Category (unpublished note), http://users.rsise.anu.edu.au/~jeremy/pubs/cmkc/
5. Dawson, J.E.: Isabelle files, http://users.rsise.anu.edu.au/~jeremy/isabelle/fgc/
6. Dawson, J.E.: Formalising General Correctness. In: ENTCS. Computing: The Australasian Theory Symposium, vol. 91, pp. 21–42 (2004), http://www.elsevier.com/locate/entcs
7. Dunne, S.: Abstract Commands: A Uniform Notation for Specifications and Implementations. In: ENTCS. Computing: The Australasian Theory Symposium, vol. 42, pp. 104–123 (2001), http://www.elsevier.com/locate/entcs
8. Dunne, S.: A Theory of Generalised Substitutions. In: Bert, D., Bowen, J.P., Henson, M.C., Robinson, K. (eds.) B 2002 and ZB 2002. LNCS, vol. 2272, pp. 270–290. Springer, Heidelberg (2002)
9. Jones, M.P., Duponcheel, L.: Composing Monads. Research Report YALEU/DCS/RR-1004, Yale University (December 1993)
10. Wadler, P.: The Essence of Functional Programming. In: POPL'92. Symposium on Principles of Programming Languages, pp. 1–14 (1992)

Extracting Purely Functional Contents from Logical Inductive Types

David Delahaye, Catherine Dubois,
and Jean-Frédéric Étienne

CEDRIC/CNAM-ENSIIE, Paris, France
David.Delahaye@cnam.fr, dubois@ensiie.fr,
etien_je@auditeur.cnam.fr

Abstract. We propose a method to extract purely functional contents from logical inductive types in the context of the Calculus of Inductive Constructions. This method is based on a mode consistency analysis, which verifies if a computation is possible w.r.t. the selected inputs/outputs, and the code generation itself. We prove that this extraction is sound w.r.t. the Calculus of Inductive Constructions. Finally, we present some optimizations, as well as the implementation designed in the Coq proof assistant framework.

1 Introduction

The main idea underlying extraction in proof assistants like Isabelle or Coq is to automatically produce certified programs in a correct by construction manner. More formally it means that the extracted program realizes its specification. Programs are extracted from types, functions and proofs. Roughly speaking, the extracted program only contains the computational parts of the initial specification, whereas the logical parts are skipped. In Coq, this is done by analyzing the types: types in the sort Set (or $Type$) are computationally relevant while types in sort $Prop$ are not. Consequently, inductively defined relations, implemented as Coq logical inductive types, are not considered by the extraction process because they are exclusively dedicated to logical aspects. However such constructs are widely used to describe algorithms. For example, when defining the semantics of a programming language, the evaluation relation embeds the definition of an interpreter.

Although inductive relations are not executable, they are often preferred because it is often easier to define a relational specification than its corresponding functional counterpart involving pattern-matching and recursion. For example, in Coq, it is easier to define the relation "the terms t and u unify with s as a most general unifier" than defining the function that computes the most general unifier of t and u if it exists. In this case, the difficulty is to prove the termination of the function while simultaneously defining it. Moreover, proof assistants offer many tools to reason about relational specifications (e.g. elimination, inversion tactics) and the developer may prefer the relational style rather than the

K. Schneider and J. Brandt (Eds.): TPHOLs 2007, LNCS 4732, pp. 70–85, 2007.

functional style, even though recent work (e.g. in Coq, functional induction or recursive definition) provide a better support for defining functions and reasoning about them.

Based on these observations, our aim is to translate logical inductive specifications into functional code, with an intention close to the one found in the Centaur [3] project, that is extracting tools from specifications. Another motivation for extracting code from logical inductive specifications is to get means to execute these specifications (if executable), in order to validate or test them. Better still, in a formal testing framework, the extracted code could be used as an oracle to test a program independently written from the specification.

In this paper, we propose a mechanism to extract functional programs from logical inductive types. Related work has been done on this subject around semantics of programming languages, for example [3,8,1,4,12] and [2] in a more general setting. Like [2], our work goes beyond semantic applications, even though it is a typical domain of applications for such a work. In addition, our extraction is intended to only deal with logical inductive types that can be turned into purely functional programs. This is mainly motivated by the fact that proof assistants providing an extraction mechanism generally produce code in a functional framework. Thus, we do not want to manage logical inductive specifications that would require backtracking, that is more a Prolog-like paradigm. In that sense, our work separates from Centaur [3], Petterson's RML translator [8] and Berghofer and Nipkow's approach [2]. The first one translates Typol specifications, which are inductively defined semantic relations, into Prolog programs. RML is also a formalism to describe natural semantics of programming languages, and the corresponding compiler produces C programs that may backtrack if necessary. Finally, Berghofer and Nipkow's tool produces code that can compute more than one solution, if any. We can also mention the use of Maude [12] to animate executable operational semantic specifications, where these specifications are turned into rewriting systems.

To turn an inductive relation into a function that can compute some results, we need additional information. In particular, we need to know which arguments are inputs and which arguments are outputs. This information is provided by the user using the notion of modes. Furthermore, these modes are used to determine if a functional computation is possible, in which case we say that the mode is consistent. Otherwise, the functional extraction is not possible and is rejected by our method. In order to make functional computations possible, some premises in the types of constructors may have to be reordered. The notion of mode, going back actually to attribute grammars [1], is fairly standard, especially in the logical programming community. For example, the logical and functional language Mercury [7] requires mode declarations to produce efficient code. Similar mode systems have already been described in [4,2,9].

The paper is organized as follows: first, we informally present our extraction mechanism with the help of some examples; next, we formalize the extraction method itself (in particular, the mode consistency analysis and the code generation) and prove its soundness; finally, we describe our prototype developed in the Coq proof assistant framework and discuss some optimizations.

2   Informal Presentation

In this section, we present how our functional extraction must work on some examples. For these examples, we use the Coq framework with, in particular, its syntax and OCaml [11] as one of its target languages for extraction. Our general approach is the following:

1. the user annotates his/her logical inductive type with a mode that specifies which arguments are inputs, the others being considered as outputs;
2. a mode consistency analysis is performed to determine if the extraction is possible w.r.t. the provided mode;
3. if the previous analysis is successful, the logical definition is translated into a functional program.

This process may be recursive and may call the regular extraction mechanism to extract code from functions or proofs.

A mode can be seen as the computational behavior of a logical inductive type. It is defined as a set of indices denoting the inputs of the relation. For example, let us consider the predicate add that specifies the addition of two natural numbers, i.e. given three natural numbers n, m and p, (add n m p) defines that p is the result of the addition of n and m. This predicate is defined as follows:

Inductive add : nat $\rightarrow$ nat $\rightarrow$ nat $\rightarrow$ **Prop** :=
  | addO : **forall** n, add n O n
  | addS : **forall** n m p, add n m p $\rightarrow$ add n (S m) (S p).

The mode $\{1, 2\}$ indicates that we consider n and m as inputs and we would like to compute p. The extracted function is the expected one, defined by pattern-matching on both arguments (actually only the second one is significant):

```
let rec add p0 p1 = match p0, p1 with
  | n, O → n
  | n, S m→ let p = add n m in S p
  | _ → assert false
```

We can also propose to extract a function with the mode $\{2, 3\}$. Thus, we obtain a function that performs subtraction:

```
let rec add p0 p1 = match p0, p1 with
  | n, O → n
  | S p, S m→ add p m
  | _ → assert false
```

Finally the mode $\{1, 2, 3\}$ means that the three arguments are known and that we want to produce a function that checks if the triple constitutes a possible computation or not (as a boolean result):

```
let rec add p0 p1 p2 = match p0, p1, p2 with
  | n, O, m  when n = m→ true
  | n, S m, S p→ add n m p
  | _→ false
```

However, with the mode $\{1,3\}$, the extraction is refused, not because of the mode analysis (which succeeds) but because it would produce a function with two overlapping patterns, (n,n) (obtained from the type of the first constructor addO) and (n,p) (obtained from the type of the second constructor addS). With such a configuration, more than one result might be computed and therefore the function would not be deterministic, which is incompatible with a proper notion of function. Extraction with modes involving only one input are refused for the same reason.

As a last example, let us consider a case where constraints are put on the results, e.g. in the eval_plus constructor the evaluation of a1 and a2 must map to values built from the N constructor:

Inductive Val : **Set** := N : Z → Val | ...
Inductive Expr : **Set** := V : Var → Expr | Plus : Expr → Expr → Expr.

Inductive eval : Sigma → Expr → Val → **Prop** :=
  | eval_v : **forall** (s : Sigma) (v : Var), eval s (V v) (valof s v)
  | eval_plus : **forall** (s : Sigma) (a1 a2 : Expr) (v w : Z),
        eval s a1 (N v) → eval s a2 (N w) → eval s (Plus a1 a2) (N (v +

where Sigma is an evaluation context and valof is a function looking for the value of a variable in an evaluation context.

With the mode $\{1, 2\}$, the extracted function is the following:

```
let rec eval s e = match s, e with
  | s, V v→ valof s v
  | s, Plus (a1, a2) →
  (match eval s a1 with
     | N v →
       (match eval s a2 with
          | N w→ N (zplus v w)
          | _→ assert false)
   |_→ assert false)
```

where valof and zplus are respectively the extracted functions from the definitions of valof and the addition over Z.

Regarding mode consistency analysis, detailed examples will be given in the next section.

3   Extraction of Logical Inductive Types

The extraction is made in two steps: first, the mode consistency analysis tries to find a permutation of the premises of each inductive clause, which is compatible w.r.t. the annotated mode; second, if the mode consistency analysis has been successful, the code generation produces the executable functional program. Before describing the extraction method itself, we have to specify which inductive types we consider and in particular, what we mean exactly by logical inductive types. We must also precise which restrictions we impose, either to ensure a purely functional and meaningful extraction, or to simplify the presentation of this formalization, while our implementation relaxes some of these restrictions (see Section 5).

3.1   Logical Inductive Types

The type theory we consider is the Calculus of Inductive Constructions (CIC for short; see the documentation of Coq [10] to get some references regarding the CIC), i.e. the Calculus of Constructions with inductive definitions. This theory is probably too strong for what we want to show in this paper, but it is the underlying theory of the Coq proof assistant, in which we chose to develop the corresponding implementation. An inductive definition is noted as follows (inspired by the notation used in the documentation of Coq):

$$\mathsf{Ind}(d : \tau, \Gamma_c)$$

where d is the name of the inductive definition, τ a type and Γ_c the context representing the constructors (their names together with their respective types). In this notation, two restrictions have been made: we do not deal with parameters[1] and mutual inductive definitions. Actually, these features do not involve specific technical difficulties. Omitting them allows us to greatly simplify the presentation of the extraction, as well as the soundness proof in particular. Also for simplification reasons, dependencies, higher order and propositional arguments are not allowed in the type of an inductive definition; more precisely, this means that τ has the following form:

$$\tau_1 \to \ldots \tau_n \to \mathsf{Prop}$$

where τ_i is of type Set or Type, and does not contain any product or dependent inductive type. In addition, we suppose that the types of constructors are in prenex form, with no dependency between the bounded variables and no higher order; thus, the type of a constructor is as follows:

$$\prod_{i=1}^{n} x_i : X_i.T_1 \to \ldots \to T_m \to (d\ t_1\ \ldots\ t_p)$$

where $x_i \notin X_j$, X_i is of type Set or Type, T_i is of type Prop and does not contain any product or dependent inductive type, and t_i are terms. In the following, the terms T_i will be called the premises of the constructor, whereas the term $(d\ t_1\ \ldots\ t_p)$ will be called the conclusion of the constructor. We impose the additional constraint that T_i is a fully applied logical inductive type, i.e. T_i has the following form:

---

[1] In CIC, parameters are additional arguments, which are shared by the type of the inductive definition (type τ) and the types of constructors (defined in Γ_c).

$$d_i \; t_{i1} \; \ldots \; t_{ip_i}$$

where d_i is a logical inductive type, t_{ij} are terms, and p_i is the arity of d_i.

An inductive type verifying the conditions above is called a logical inductive type. We aim to propose an extraction method for this kind of inductive types.

3.2   Mode Consistency Analysis

The purpose of the mode consistency analysis is to check whether a functional execution is possible. It is a very simple data-flow analysis of the logical inductive type. We require the user to provide a mode for the considered logical inductive type, and recursively for each logical inductive type occurring in this type.

Given a logical inductive type I, a mode md is defined as a set of indices denoting the inputs of I. The remaining arguments are the output arguments. Thus, $md \subseteq \{1, \ldots, a_I\}$, where a_I is the arity of I. Although a mode is defined as a set, the order of the inputs in the logical inductive type is relevant. They will appear in the functional translation in the same order.

In practice, it is often the case to use the extraction with, either a mode corresponding to all the arguments except one, called the computational mode, or a mode indicating that all the arguments are inputs, called the fully instantiated mode. The formalization below will essentially deal with these two modes with no loss of generality (if more than one output is necessary, we can consider that the outputs are gathered in a tuple).

In order to make functional computations possible, some premises in a constructor may have to be reordered. It will be the case when a variable appears first in a premise as an input and as an output in another premise written afterwards. For a same logical inductive type, some modes may be possible whereas some others may be considered inconsistent. Different mode declarations give different extracted functions.

Given $\mathcal{M}$, the set of modes for I and recursively for every logical inductive type occurring in I, a mode md is consistent for I w.r.t. $\mathcal{M}$ iff it is consistent for Γ_c (i.e. all the constructors of I) w.r.t. $\mathcal{M}$. A mode md is consistent for the constructor c of type $\Pi_{i=1}^n x_i : X_i.T_1 \rightarrow \ldots \rightarrow T_n \rightarrow T$ w.r.t. $\mathcal{M}$, where $T = d \; t_1 \; \ldots \; t_p$, iff there exist a permutation π and the sets of variables S_i, with $i = 0 \ldots m$, s.t.:

1. $S_0 = \mathsf{in}(md, T)$;
2. $\mathsf{in}(m_{\pi j}, T_{\pi j}) \subseteq S_{j-1}$, with $1 \leq j \leq m$ and $m_{\pi j} = \mathcal{M}(\mathsf{name}(T_{\pi j}))$;
3. $S_j = S_{j-1} \cup \mathsf{out}(m_{\pi j}, T_{\pi j})$, with $1 \leq j \leq m$ and $m_{\pi j} = \mathcal{M}(\mathsf{name}(T_{\pi j}))$;
4. $\mathsf{out}(md, T) \subseteq S_m$.

where $\mathsf{name}(t)$ is the name of the logical inductive type applied in the term t (e.g. $\mathsf{name}(add \; n \; (S \; m) \; (S \; k)) = add$), $\mathsf{in}(m, t)$ the set of variables occurring in the terms designated as inputs by the mode m in the term t (e.g. $\mathsf{in}(\{1, 2\}, (add \; n \; (S \; m) \; (S \; k))) = \{n, m\}$), and $\mathsf{out}(m, t)$ the set of variables occurring in the terms designated as outputs by the mode m in the term t (e.g. $\mathsf{out}(\{1, 2\}, (add \; n \; (S \; m) \; (S \; k))) = \{k\}$).

The permutation π denotes a suitable execution order for the premises. The set S_0 denotes the initial set of known variables and S_j the set of known variables after the execution of the πj^{th} premise (when $T_{\pi 1}$, $T_{\pi 2}$, ..., $T_{\pi j}$ have been executed in this order). The first condition states that during the execution of T (for the constructor c) with the mode md, the values of all the variables used in the terms designated as inputs have to be known. The second condition requires that the execution of a premise T_i with a mode m_i will be performed only if the input arguments designated by the mode are totally computable. It also requires that m_i is a consistent mode for the logical inductive type related to T_i (we have constrained T_i in the previous section to be a fully applied logical inductive type). According to the third condition, all the arguments of a given premise T_i are known after its execution. Finally, a mode md is said to be consistent for c w.r.t. $\mathcal{M}$ if all the arguments in the conclusion of c (i.e. T) are known after the execution of all the premises.

We have imposed some restrictions on the presence of functions in the terms appearing in the type of a constructor. To relax these conditions, such as accepting functions in the output of the premises (see Section 5), in the step j, we should verify that the function calls are computable, that is to say their arguments only involve known variables (belonging to S_{j-1}).

To illustrate the mode consistency analysis, let us consider the logical inductive type that specifies the big step semantics of a small imperative language. The evaluation of commands is represented by the relation $s \vdash_c i : s'$, which means that the execution of the command i in the store s leads to the final store s'. This relation has the type $store \rightarrow command \rightarrow store \rightarrow Prop$, where $store$ and $command$ are the corresponding types for stores and imperative commands. For example, the types of the constructors for the $while$ loop are the following:

$$while_1 : (s \vdash_e b : true) \rightarrow (s \vdash_c i : s') \rightarrow (s' \vdash_c while\ b\ do\ i : s'') \rightarrow$$
$$(s \vdash_c while\ b\ do\ i : s'')$$
$$while_2 : (s \vdash_e b : false) \rightarrow (s \vdash_c while\ b\ do\ i : s)$$

where given a store s, an expression t and a value v, $s \vdash_e t : v$ represents the evaluation of expressions, i.e. the expression t evaluates to v in the store s. For clarity reasons, we do not indicate the universally quantified variables, which are the stores s, s' and s'', the expression b and the command i.

If the mode $\{1, 2\}$ is consistent for $\vdash_e$ then the mode $\{1, 2\}$ is consistent for both $while$ constructors of $\vdash_c$. But considering the typing relation of the simply typed λ-calculus $\Gamma \vdash t : \tau$, denoting that t is of type τ in context Γ and where Γ is a typing context, t a term and τ a type, the mode $\{1, 2\}$ is not consistent for this relation. Actually, this mode is not consistent for the typing of the abstraction; the type τ_1 in the premise, considered here as an input, is not known at this step ($\tau_1 \notin S_0$):

$$abs : (\Gamma, (x : \tau_1) \vdash e : \tau_2) \rightarrow (\Gamma \vdash \lambda x.e : \tau_1 \rightarrow \tau_2)$$

In the following, we will ignore the permutation of the premises and will assume that all the premises are correctly ordered w.r.t. to the provided mode.

3.3   Code Generation

The functional language we consider as target for our extraction is defined as follows (mainly a functional core with recursion and pattern-matching):

$$
\begin{aligned}
e \quad ::= \; & x \mid c^n \mid C^n \mid \mathsf{fail} \mid \mathsf{if}\ e_1\ \mathsf{then}\ e_2\ \mathsf{else}\ e_3 \mid e_1\ e_2 \mid \mathsf{fun}\ x \rightarrow e \\
& \mid\; \mathsf{rec}\ f\ x \rightarrow e \mid \mathsf{let}\ x = e_1\ \mathsf{in}\ e_2 \mid (e_1, \ldots, e_n) \\
& \mid\; \mathsf{match}\ e\ \mathsf{with}\ \mid gpat_1 \rightarrow e_1\ \ldots \mid gpat_n \rightarrow e_n
\end{aligned}
$$

$$
gpat ::= pat \mid pat\ \mathsf{when}\ e
$$

$$
pat \quad ::= \; x \mid C^n \mid C^n\ pat \mid (pat_1, \ldots, pat_n) \mid \_
$$

where c^n is a constant of arity n, to be distinguished from C^n, a constructor of arity n. Both constants and constructors are uncurrified and fully applied. Moreover, we use the notations $e_1\ e_2\ \ldots\ e_n$ for $((e_1\ e_2)\ldots e_n)$, and $\mathsf{fun}\ x_1\ \ldots\ x_n \rightarrow e$ for $\mathsf{fun}\ x_1 \rightarrow \ldots \mathsf{fun}\ x_n \rightarrow e$ (as well as for rec functions).

Given $I = \mathsf{Ind}(d : \tau, \Gamma_c)$, a logical inductive type, well-typed in a context Γ, and $\mathcal{M}$, the set of modes for I and recursively for every logical inductive type occurring in I, we consider that each logical inductive type is ordered according to its corresponding mode (with the output, if required, at the last position), i.e. if the mode of a logical inductive type J is $\mathcal{M}(J) = \{n_1, \ldots, n_J\}$, then the n_1^{th} argument of J becomes the first one and so on until the n_J^{th} argument, which becomes the c_J^{th} one, with $c_J = \mathsf{card}(\mathcal{M}(J))$. The code generation for I, denoted by $[\![I]\!]_{\Gamma, \mathcal{M}}$, begins as follows (we do not translate the type τ of I in Γ since this information is simply skipped in the natural semantics we propose for the target functional language in Section 4):

$$
[\![I]\!]_{\Gamma, \mathcal{M}} = \begin{cases} \mathsf{fun}\ p_1\ \ldots\ p_{c_I} \rightarrow [\![\Gamma_c]\!]_{\Gamma, \mathcal{M}, P}, & \text{if } d \notin \Gamma_c, \\ \mathsf{rec}\ d\ p_1\ \ldots\ p_{c_I} \rightarrow [\![\Gamma_c]\!]_{\Gamma, \mathcal{M}, P}, & \text{otherwise} \end{cases}
$$

where $c_I = \mathsf{card}(\mathcal{M}(I))$ and $P = \{p_1, \ldots, p_{c_I}\}$.
Considering $\Gamma_c = \{c_1, \ldots, c_n\}$, the body of the function is the following:

$$
\begin{aligned}
[\![\Gamma_c]\!]_{\Gamma, \mathcal{M}, P} = \; & \mathsf{match}\ (p_1, \ldots, p_{c_I})\ \mathsf{with} \\
& \mid\; [\![c_1]\!]_{\Gamma, \mathcal{M}} \\
& \mid\; \ldots \\
& \mid\; [\![c_n]\!]_{\Gamma, \mathcal{M}} \\
& \mid\; \_ \rightarrow\ \mathsf{default}_{I, \mathcal{M}}
\end{aligned}
$$

where $\mathsf{default}_{I, \mathcal{M}}$ is defined as follows:

$$
\mathsf{default}_{I, \mathcal{M}} = \begin{cases} \mathsf{false}, & \text{if } c_I = a_I, \\ \mathsf{fail}, & \text{if } c_I = a_I - 1 \end{cases}
$$

where $c_I = \mathsf{card}(\mathcal{M}(I))$ and a_I is the arity of I.

The translation of a constructor c_i is the following (the name of c_i is skipped and only its type is used in this translation):

$$[\![c_i]\!]_{\Gamma,\mathcal{M}} = [\![\textstyle\prod_{j=1}^{n_i} x_{ij} : X_{ij}.T_{i1} \to \ldots \to T_{im_i} \to (d\ t_{i1}\ \ldots\ t_{ip_i})]\!]_{\Gamma,\mathcal{M}}$$

$$= \begin{cases} ([\![t_{i1}]\!], \ldots, [\![t_{ic_I}]\!]) \to [\![T_{i1} \to \ldots \to T_{im_i}]\!]_{\Gamma,\mathcal{M},\mathsf{cont}_{I,\mathcal{M}}}, \\ \quad \text{if } t_{i1}, \ldots, t_{ic_I} \text{ are linear,} \\ ([\![\sigma_i(t_{i1})]\!], \ldots, [\![\sigma_i(t_{ic_I})]\!]) \text{ when guard}(\sigma_i) \to \\ \quad [\![T_{i1} \to \ldots \to T_{im_i}]\!]_{\Gamma,\mathcal{M},\mathsf{cont}_{I,\mathcal{M}}}, \text{ otherwise} \end{cases}$$

where σ_i is a renaming s.t. $\sigma_i(t_{i1}), \ldots, \sigma_i(t_{ic_I})$ are linear, guard(σ_i) is the corresponding guard, of the form $x_{ij_1} = \sigma_i(x_{ij_1})$ and $\ldots$ and $x_{ij_k} = \sigma_i(x_{ij_k})$, with dom$(\sigma_i) = \{x_{ij_1}, \ldots, x_{ij_k}\}$ and $1 \le j_l \le n_i$, $l = 1 \ldots k$, and $\mathsf{cont}_{I,\mathcal{M}}$ is defined as follows:

$$\mathsf{cont}_{I,\mathcal{M}} = \begin{cases} \text{true, if } c_I = a_I, \\ [\![t_{ip_i}]\!], \text{ if } c_I = a_I - 1 \end{cases}$$

The terms $t_{i1}, \ldots, t_{ic_I}$ must only contain variables and constructors, while t_{ip_i} (if $c_I = a_I - 1$) can additionally contain symbols of functions. The corresponding translation is completely isomorphic to the structure of these terms and uses the regular extraction, presented in [6]. Moreover, we consider that the terms t_{ik} and t_{jk} are not unifiable, for $i, j = 1 \ldots n$ and $k = 1 \ldots c_I$ (otherwise, a functional extraction may not be possible, i.e. backtracking is necessary or there are several results).

The right-hand side of the pattern rules is generated with the following scheme:

$$[\![T_{ij} \to \ldots \to T_{im_i}]\!]_{\Gamma,\mathcal{M},\mathsf{cont}_{I,\mathcal{M}}} =$$
$$\begin{cases} \mathsf{cont}_{I,\mathcal{M}}, \text{ if } j > m_i, \\[4pt] \text{if } [\![d_{ij}\ t_{ij1} \ldots t_{ijc_{ij}}]\!] \text{ then } [\![T_{i(j+1)} \to \ldots \to T_{im_i}]\!]_{\Gamma,\mathcal{M},\mathsf{cont}_{I,\mathcal{M}}} \\ \text{else default}_{I,\mathcal{M}}, \text{ if } j \le m_i \text{ and } c_{ij} = a_{ij}, \\[4pt] \text{match } [\![d_{ij}\ t_{ij1} \ldots t_{ijc_{ij}}]\!] \text{ with} \\ \mid\ [\![t_{ija_{ij}}]\!] \to [\![T_{i(j+1)} \to \ldots \to T_{im_i}]\!]_{\Gamma,\mathcal{M},\mathsf{cont}_{I,\mathcal{M}}} \\ \mid\ \_ \to \text{default}_{I,\mathcal{M}}, \text{ if } j \le m_i \text{ and } c_{ij} = a_{ij} - 1 \end{cases}$$

where $T_{ij} = d_{ij}\ t_{ij1} \ldots t_{ija_{ij}}$, a_{ij} is the arity of d_{ij} and $c_{ij} = \mathsf{card}(\mathcal{M}(\Gamma(d_{ij})))$. We consider that the term $t_{ija_{ij}}$ is linear and does not contain computed variables or symbols of functions when $c_{ij} = a_{ij} - 1$ (in this way, no guard is required in the produced pattern).

4   Soundness of the Extraction

Before proving the soundness of the extraction of logical inductive types, we need to specify the semantics of the functional language we chose as a target for our extraction and presented in Section 3. To simplify, we adopt a pure Kahn style big step natural semantics (with call by value) and we introduce the following notion of value:

$$v ::= c^0 \mid C^0 \mid \Delta_C \mid \mathsf{fail} \mid <x \rightsquigarrow e, \Delta> \mid <x \rightsquigarrow e, \Delta>_{\mathsf{rec}(f)} \mid (v_1, \ldots, v_n)$$

where Δ is an evaluation context, i.e. a list of pairs (x, v), and Δ_C is a set of values of the form $C^n (v_1, \ldots, v_n)$. In addition, we introduce a set Δ_c of tuples of the form $(c^n, v_1, \ldots, v_n, v)$, with $n > 0$.

An expression e evaluates to v in an environment Δ, denoted by the judgment $\Delta \vdash e \triangleright v$, if and only if there exists a derivation of this judgment in the system of inference rules described in Appendix 6 (to save space, we do not include the corresponding error rules returning fail).

Given I, a logical inductive type, well-typed in a context Γ, and $\mathcal{M}$, the set of modes for I and recursively for every logical inductive type occurring in I, we introduce the translation (and evaluation) of the context Γ w.r.t. the logical inductive type I and the set of modes $\mathcal{M}$. A context is a set of assumptions $(x : \tau)$, definitions $(x : \tau := t)$ and inductive definitions $\mathsf{Ind}(d : \tau, \Gamma_c)$, where x and d are names, τ a type, t a term and Γ_c the set of constructors. The translation of Γ w.r.t. I and $\mathcal{M}$, denoted by $[\![\Gamma]\!]_{I,\mathcal{M}}$, consists in extracting and evaluating recursively each assumption, definition or inductive definition occurring in I (thus, this translation provides an evaluation context). For assumptions, definitions and inductive definitions which are not logical inductive types, we use the regular extraction, presented in [6]. Regarding logical inductive types, we apply the extraction described previously in Section 3.

The soundness of our extraction is expressed by the following theorem:

Theorem (Soundness). *Given $I = \mathsf{Ind}(d : \tau, \Gamma_c)$, a logical inductive type, well-typed in a context Γ, and $\mathcal{M}$, the set of modes for I and recursively for every logical inductive type occurring in I, we have the two following cases:*

- $c_I = a_I$: *if $[\![\Gamma]\!]_{I,\mathcal{M}} \vdash [\![I]\!]_{\Gamma,\mathcal{M}} [\![t_1]\!] \ldots [\![t_{c_I}]\!] \triangleright \mathsf{true}$ then the statement $\Gamma \vdash d\, t_1 \ldots t_{c_I}$ is provable;*
- $c_I = a_I - 1$: *if $[\![\Gamma]\!]_{I,\mathcal{M}} \vdash [\![I]\!]_{\Gamma,\mathcal{M}} [\![t_1]\!] \ldots [\![t_{c_I}]\!] \triangleright v \neq \mathsf{fail}$ then there exists t s.t. $[\![t]\!] = v$ and the statement $\Gamma \vdash d\, t_1 \ldots t_{c_I}\, t$ is provable.*

where $c_I = \mathsf{card}(\mathcal{M}(I))$, a_I is the arity of I, and $t_1 \ldots t_{c_I}, t$ are terms.

Proof. The theorem is proved by induction over the extraction. We suppose that $\Delta \vdash [\![I]\!]_{\Gamma,\mathcal{M}} [\![t_1]\!] \ldots [\![t_{c_I}]\!] \triangleright v$, with $\Delta = [\![\Gamma]\!]_{I,\mathcal{M}}$ and either $v = \mathsf{true}$ if $c_I = a_I$, or $v \neq \mathsf{fail}$ if $c_I = a_I - 1$. Using the definition of $[\![I]\!]_{\Gamma,\mathcal{M}}$ given in Section 3 and the rules of Appendix 6, this expression is evaluated as follows:

$$\Delta \vdash [\![I]\!]_{\Gamma,\mathcal{M}} \triangleright \begin{cases} <p_1 \ \ldots \ p_{c_I} \rightsquigarrow [\![\Gamma_c]\!]_{\Gamma,\mathcal{M},P}, \Delta>, & \text{if } d \notin \Gamma_c, \\ <p_1 \ \ldots \ p_{c_I} \rightsquigarrow [\![\Gamma_c]\!]_{\Gamma,\mathcal{M},P}, \Delta>_{\mathsf{rec}(d)} = c, & \text{otherwise} \end{cases}$$

where $P = \{p_1, \ldots, p_{c_I}\}$.

The arguments are also evaluated: $\Delta \vdash [\![t_1]\!] \triangleright v_1, \ldots, \Delta \vdash [\![t_{c_I}]\!] \triangleright v_{c_I}$. Using the definition of $[\![\Gamma_c]\!]_{\Gamma,\mathcal{M},P}$, we have the following evaluation:

$$\Delta_b \vdash \begin{pmatrix} \mathsf{match}\ (v_1, \ldots, v_{c_I})\ \mathsf{with} \\ \mid [\![c_1]\!]_{\Gamma,\mathcal{M}} \\ \mid \ldots \\ \mid [\![c_n]\!]_{\Gamma,\mathcal{M}} \\ \mid \_ \rightarrow \mathsf{default}_{I,\mathcal{M}} \end{pmatrix} \triangleright v$$

where Δ_b is defined as follows:

$$\Delta_b = \begin{cases} \Delta, (p_1, v_1), \ldots, (p_{c_I}, v_{c_I}), & \text{if } d \notin \Gamma_c, \\ \Delta, (d, c), (p_1, v_1), \ldots, (p_{c_I}, v_{c_I}), & \text{otherwise} \end{cases}$$

We know that either $v = \mathsf{true}$ or $v \neq \mathsf{fail}$ (according to c_I); this means that there exists i s.t. the pattern of $[\![c_i]\!]_{\Gamma,\mathcal{M}}$ matches the value $(v_1, \ldots, v_{c_I})$. Using the definition of $[\![c_i]\!]_{\Gamma,\mathcal{M}}$, we have to evaluate:

$$\Delta_p \vdash [\![T_{i1} \to \ldots \to T_{im_i}]\!]_{\Gamma,\mathcal{M},\mathsf{cont}_{I,\mathcal{M}}} \triangleright v \tag{1}$$

with $\Delta_p = \Delta_b, \Delta_i$, where Δ_i has the following form (by definition of $\mathsf{filter}_{\Delta_b}$):

$$\Delta_i = \begin{cases} \mathsf{mgu}_{\Delta_b}(v_t, ([\![t_{i1}]\!], \ldots, [\![t_{ic_I}]\!])), & \text{if } t_{i1}, \ldots, t_{ic_I} \text{ are linear} \\ \mathsf{mgu}_{\Delta_b}(v_t, ([\![\sigma_i(t_{i1})]\!], \ldots, [\![\sigma_i(t_{ic_I})]\!])), & \text{otherwise} \end{cases}$$

where $v_t = (v_1, \ldots, v_{c_I})$. In addition, we have $\Delta_p \vdash \mathsf{guard}(\sigma_i) \triangleright \mathsf{true}$ if $t_{i1}, \ldots, t_{ic_I}$ are not linear.

The reduction of our extraction language is weaker than the one defined for CIC; in particular, this means that we have: given $\Delta = [\![\Gamma]\!]_{I,\mathcal{M}}$, a term t and a value $v \neq \mathsf{fail}$, if $\Delta \vdash [\![t]\!] \triangleright v$ then there exists a term t' s.t. $[\![t']\!] = v$ and $\Gamma \vdash t \equiv t'$, where $\equiv$ is the convertibility relation for CIC. Moreover, considering $\Delta = [\![\Gamma]\!]_{I,\mathcal{M}}$, a term t and a value $v \neq \mathsf{fail}$, if $\sigma = \mathsf{mgu}_\Delta(v, [\![t]\!])$ then there exist t' and $\bar{\sigma}$ s.t. $[\![t']\!] = v$, $\mathsf{dom}(\bar{\sigma}) = \mathsf{dom}(\sigma)$, $[\![\bar{\sigma}(x)]\!] = \sigma(x)$ for all $x \in \mathsf{dom}(\bar{\sigma})$, and $\bar{\sigma} = \mathsf{mgu}_\Gamma(t', t)$. Using these two remarks, there exists $\bar{\Delta}_i$ as described above s.t.:

$$\Gamma \vdash \bar{\Delta}_i(d \ t_{i1} \ldots t_{ic_I}) \equiv (d \ t_1 \ldots t_{c_I}) \tag{2}$$

Note that we can consider $\Delta_b = \Delta$, since the variables p_i, $i = 1 \ldots c_I$, do not occur in I; actually, these variables are just used for the curryfication of $[\![I]\!]_{\Gamma,\mathcal{M}}$. Note also that this unification between $(d \ t_{i1} \ldots t_{ic_I})$ and $(d \ t_1 \ldots t_{c_I})$ may be total or partial according to c_I (if $c_I = a_I$ or $c_I = a_I - 1$).

Regarding the arguments of c_i, we have to consider another property: given a context Δ_a, if $\Delta_p, \Delta_a \vdash [\![T_{i1} \to \ldots \to T_{im_i}]\!]_{\Gamma,\mathcal{M},\mathsf{cont}_{I,\mathcal{M}}} \triangleright v$ then there exists a context $\Delta'_a \supseteq \Delta_a$ s.t. $\Gamma \vdash \bar{\Delta}'_a \bar{\Delta}_i T_{ij}$ is provable for $j = 1 \ldots m_i$, and $\Delta_p, \Delta'_a \vdash \mathsf{cont}_{I,\mathcal{M}} \triangleright v$. This property is proved by induction over the product type. Using the definition of $[\![T_{i1} \to \ldots \to T_{im_i}]\!]_{\Gamma,\mathcal{M}}$, we have three cases:

- $j > m_i$: $\Delta_p, \Delta_a \vdash \mathsf{cont}_{I,\mathcal{M}} \triangleright v$ and $\Delta'_a = \Delta$.
- $j \leq m_i$, $c_{ij} = a_{ij}$:

$$\Delta_p, \Delta_a \vdash \begin{pmatrix} \text{if } [\![d_{ij} \ t_{ij1} \ldots t_{ijc_{ij}}]\!] \text{ then} \\ [\![T_{i(j+1)} \to \ldots \to T_{im_i}]\!]_{\Gamma,\mathcal{M},\mathsf{cont}_{I,\mathcal{M}}} \\ \text{else default}_{I,\mathcal{M}} \end{pmatrix} \triangleright v$$

Since either $v = \mathsf{true}$ or $v \neq \mathsf{fail}$, we have $\Delta_p, \Delta_a \vdash [\![d_{ij} \ t_{ij1} \ldots t_{ijc_{ij}}]\!] \triangleright \mathsf{true}$ and the then branch is selected. By hypothesis of induction (over the soundness theorem), this means that $\Gamma \vdash \bar{\Delta}_a \bar{\Delta}_i T_{ij}$ is provable. Next, we have the evaluation $\Delta_p, \Delta_a \vdash [\![T_{i(j+1)} \to \ldots \to T_{im_i}]\!]_{\Gamma,\mathcal{M},\mathsf{cont}_{I,\mathcal{M}}} \triangleright v$ and by hypothesis of induction, there exists $\Delta'_a \supseteq \Delta_a$ s.t. $\Gamma \vdash \bar{\Delta}'_a \bar{\Delta}_i T_{ik}$ is provable for

$k = j + 1 \ldots m_i$, and $\Delta_p, \Delta'_a \vdash \mathsf{cont}_{I,\mathcal{M}} \triangleright v$. As $\Delta'_a \supseteq \Delta_a$, $\Gamma \vdash \bar{\Delta}'_a \bar{\Delta}_i T_{ij}$ is also provable.

$- j \leq m_i, c_{ij} = a_{ij} - 1$:

$$\Delta_p, \Delta_a \vdash \left(\begin{array}{l} \mathsf{match} \; [\![d_{ij} \; t_{ij1} \ldots t_{ijc_{ij}}]\!] \; \mathsf{with} \\ | \; [\![t_{ija_{ij}}]\!] \rightarrow [\![T_{i(j+1)} \rightarrow \cdots \rightarrow T_{im_i}]\!]_{\Gamma,\mathcal{M},\mathsf{cont}_{I,\mathcal{M}}} \\ | \; \_ \rightarrow \mathsf{default}_{I,\mathcal{M}} \end{array} \right) \triangleright v$$

Since either $v = \mathsf{true}$ or $v \neq \mathsf{fail}$, we have $\Delta_p, \Delta_a \vdash [\![d_{ij} \; t_{ij1} \ldots t_{ijc_{ij}}]\!] \triangleright v' \neq \mathsf{fail}$ and the pattern $[\![t_{ija_{ij}}]\!]$ matches v'. By hypothesis of induction (over the soundness theorem), this means that $\Gamma \vdash \bar{\Delta}_a \bar{\Delta}_i T_{ij}$ is provable. Next, we have the evaluation $\Delta_p, \Delta'_p \vdash [\![T_{i(j+1)} \rightarrow \cdots \rightarrow T_{im_i}]\!]_{\Gamma,\mathcal{M},\mathsf{cont}_{I,\mathcal{M}}} \triangleright v$, with $\Delta'_p = \Delta_a, \Delta_m$ and $\Delta_m = \mathsf{mgu}_{\Delta_p,\Delta_a}(v', [\![t_{ija_{ij}}]\!])$. By hypothesis of induction, there exists $\Delta'_a \supseteq \Delta'_p$ s.t. $\Gamma \vdash \bar{\Delta}'_a \bar{\Delta}_i T_{ik}$ is provable for $k = j + 1 \ldots m_i$, and $\Delta_p, \Delta'_a \vdash \mathsf{cont}_{I,\mathcal{M}} \triangleright v$. As $\Delta'_a \supseteq \Delta'_p$, $\Gamma \vdash \bar{\Delta}'_a \bar{\Delta}_i T_{ij}$ is also provable.

Using (1), (2) and the above property (with the empty context for Δ_a), there exists a context Δ'_i s.t. $\Gamma \vdash \bar{\Delta}'_i \bar{\Delta}_i T_{ij}$ is provable for $j = 1 \ldots m_i$, $\Gamma \vdash \bar{\Delta}'_i \bar{\Delta}_i (d \; t_{i1} \ldots t_{ic_I}) \equiv (d \; t_1 \ldots t_{c_I})$ and $\Delta_p, \Delta'_i \vdash \mathsf{cont}_{I,\mathcal{M}} \triangleright v$. We distinguish two cases:

- $c_I = a_I$: $\mathsf{cont}_{I,\mathcal{M}} = \mathsf{true}$ and the constructor c_i can be directly applied to prove $\Gamma \vdash d \; t_1 \ldots t_{c_I}$.
- $c_I = a_I - 1$: we have $\Delta_p, \Delta'_i \vdash [\![t_{ip_i}]\!] \triangleright v$. There exists a term t'_{ip_i} s.t. $[\![t'_{ip_i}]\!] = v$ and $\Gamma \vdash \bar{\Delta}'_i \bar{\Delta}_i t_{ip_i} \equiv t'_{ip_i}$. Thus, $\Gamma \vdash \bar{\Delta}'_i \bar{\Delta}_i (d \; t_{i1} \ldots t_{ic_I} \; t_{ip_i}) \equiv (d \; t_1 \ldots t_{c_I} \; t'_{ip_i})$ and the constructor c_i can be applied to prove $\Gamma \vdash d \; t_1 \ldots t_{c_I} \; t'_{ip_i}$.

5 Implementation and Optimizations

5.1 Implementation

A prototype has been implemented and integrated to the Coq [10] proof assistant. This implementation follows what has been described in Section 3 and is plugged into the regular extraction mechanism of Coq so that it can produce code for the same (functional) languages, i.e. OCaml, Haskell and Scheme. As an example, let us consider the addition predicate presented in Section 2 with an extraction to the OCaml language [11]:

```
Coq < Inductive add : nat → nat → nat → Prop :=
Coq <    | addO : forall n, add n O n
Coq <    | addS : forall n m p, add n m p → add n (S m) (S p).

Coq < Extraction Logical add [1 2].
(** val add : nat → nat → nat **)


let rec add p0 p1 =
  match (p0, p1) with
```

```
|  (n, O) → n
|  (n, S m) → let p = add n m in S p
|  _ → assert false
```

This implementation should be part of the forthcoming version of Coq, and currently, the development in progress is available on demand (sending a mail to the authors).

5.2   Optimizations

Conclusion inputs. In Section 3, we described the translation of a logical inductive type when rules do not overlap, that is when the types of the conclusions do not unify. However, we can implement some heuristics to overcome some of these cases. Let us consider the example of the while loop, seen in Section 3:

```
Inductive exec : store → command → store → Prop := ...
  | while1 : forall (s s1 s2 : Sigma) (b : expr) (c : command),
      (eval s b true) → (exec s c s1) → (exec s1 (while b do c) s2) →
      (exec s (while b do c) s2)
  | while2 : forall (s : Sigma) (b : expr) (c : command), (eval s b f
      (exec s (while b do c) s).
```

These two constructors overlap: the types of their conclusion are identical up to renaming. A Prolog-like execution would try to apply the first rule by computing the evaluation of the boolean expression b and matching it with the value true. If the matching fails, the execution would backtrack to the second rule. However, in this case, the execution is completely deterministic and no backtracking is necessary. In fact, we can discriminate the choice between both constructors thanks to their first premise. We introduce a heuristic to handle such cases efficiently. It requires the ability to detect common premises between both overlapping rules and to discriminate w.r.t. syntactic exclusive premises (p and $\neg p$, values constructed with different constructors of an inductive type, for example).

For the while loop example, the extracted function with the mode $\{1, 2\}$ involves only one case in the global pattern-matching to be able to handle correctly the execution:

```
let rec exec s c = match s, c with ...
  | s, while(b,c) →
    (match (eval s b) with
        | true → s
        | false →
          let s1 = exec s c in
          let s2 = exec s1 (while (b, c)) in s2)
```

Premise outputs. In the formalization, we also assumed that the outputs of the premises do not contain computed variables. Consequently, we cannot translate rules where constraints exist on these outputs, which is the case for the following constructor that describes the typing of a conditional expression in a logical inductive type named typecheck, when the mode $\{1, 2\}$ is specified:

```
Inductive typecheck : env → expr → type → Prop := ...
  | if : forall (g : env) (b, e1, e2 : expr) (t : type),
      (typecheck g b bool) → (typecheck g e1 t) → (typecheck g e2 t) →
      (typecheck g (if b then e1 else e2) t).
```

There is no difficulty to adapt the translation for such cases. Once the non-linearity between premise outputs has been detected, we use fresh variables and guards as follows:

```
let rec typecheck g e = match g, e with ...
  | g, if (b, e1, e2) →
    (match typecheck g b with
       | bool → let t = typecheck g e1 in
       (match typecheck g e2 with
          | t' when t' = t → t
          | _ → assert false)
       | _ → assert false)
```

In the same way, it is also possible to deal with nonlinearity or symbols of functions in the output of a premise.

6   Conclusion

In this paper, we have presented an extraction mechanism in the context of CIC, which allows us to derive purely functional code from relational specifications implemented as logical inductive types. The main contributions are the formalization of the extraction itself (as a translation function) and the proof of its soundness. In addition, a prototype has been implemented and integrated to the Coq proof assistant, whereas some optimizations (relaxing some limitations) are under development.

Regarding future work, we have several perspectives. First, we aim to prove the completeness of our extraction (the mode consistency analysis should be used in this proof). Concerning our implementation, the next step is to manage large scale specifications, with, for example, the extraction of an interpreter from a development of the semantics of a programming language (in Coq, there are many developments in this domain). Another perspective is to adapt our mechanism to produce Coq functions, taking benefit from the new facilities offered by Coq to define general recursive functions [10]. These new features rely on the fact that the user provides a well-founded order establishing the termination of the described function. Provided the mode and this additional information, we could extract a Coq function from a logical inductive type, at least for a large class of logical inductive types (e.g. first order unification, strongly normalizable calculi, etc). Finally, the mode consistency analysis should be completed by other analyses like determinism or termination. The logical programming community has investigated abstract interpretation to check this kind of operational properties [5]. Similar analyses could be reproduced in our case. We could also benefit from results coming from term rewriting system tools.

References

1. Attali, I., Parigot, D.: Integrating Natural Semantics and Attribute Grammars: the Minotaur System. Technical Report 2339, INRIA (1994)
2. Berghofer, S., Nipkow, T.: Executing Higher Order Logic. In: Callaghan, P., Luo, Z., McKinna, J., Pollack, R. (eds.) TYPES 2000. LNCS, vol. 2277, pp. 24–40. Springer, Heidelberg (2002)
3. Borras, P., Clément, D., Despeyroux, T., Incerpi, J., Kahn, G., Lang, B., Pascual, V.: Centaur: the System. ACM SIGSOFT/SIGPLAN Software Engineering Symposium on Practical Software Development Environments (PSDE) 24(2), 14–24 (1988)
4. Dubois, C., Gayraud, R.: Compilation de la sémantique naturelle vers ML. In: Weis, P. (ed.) Journées Francophones des Langages Applicatifs (JFLA), Morzine-Avoriaz (France) (February 1999)
5. Hermenegildo, M.V., Puebla, G., Bueno, F., López-García, P.: Integrated Program Debugging, Verification, and Optimization using Abstract Interpretation (and the Ciao System Preprocessor. Science of Computer Programming 58(1-2), 115–140 (2005)
6. Letouzey, P.: A New Extraction for Coq. In: Geuvers, H., Wiedijk, F. (eds.) TYPES 2002. LNCS, vol. 2646, pp. 200–219. Springer, Heidelberg (2003)
7. Overton, D., Somogyi, Z., Stuckey, P.J.: Constraint-based Mode Analysis of Mercury. In: Principles and Practice of Declarative Programming (PPDP), Pittsburgh (PA, USA), October 2002, pp. 109–120. ACM Press, New York (2002)
8. Pettersson, M.: A Compiler for Natural Semantics. In: Gyimóthy, T. (ed.) CC 1996. LNCS, vol. 1060, pp. 177–191. Springer, Heidelberg (1996)
9. Stärk, R.F.: Input/Output Dependencies of Normal Logic Programs. Journal of Logic and Computation 4(3), 249–262 (1994)
10. The Coq Development Team: Coq, version 8.1. INRIA (November 2006), available at: http://coq.inria.fr/
11. The Cristal Team: Objective Caml, version 3.09.3. INRIA (September 2006), available at: http://caml.inria.fr/
12. Verdejo, A., Martí-Oliet, N.: Executable Structural Operational Semantics in Maude. Journal of Logic and Algebraic Programming 67(1-2), 226–293 (2006)

Appendix A: Semantic Rules of the Extraction Language

$$\frac{(x, v) \in \Delta}{\Delta \vdash x \triangleright v} \; \mathsf{Var} \qquad\qquad\qquad \frac{}{\Delta \vdash \mathsf{fail} \triangleright \mathsf{fail}} \; \mathsf{fail}$$

$$\frac{}{\Delta \vdash c^0 \triangleright c^0} \; \mathsf{const}_0 \qquad\qquad\qquad \frac{}{\Delta \vdash C^0 \triangleright C^0} \; \mathsf{constr}_0$$

$$\frac{\Delta \vdash e_1 \triangleright v_1 \quad \ldots \quad \Delta \vdash e_n \triangleright v_n \quad (c^n, v_1, \ldots, v_n, v) \in \Delta_c}{\Delta \vdash c^n \, (e_1, \ldots, e_n) \triangleright v} \; \mathsf{const}_n$$

$$\frac{\Delta \vdash e_1 \triangleright v_1 \quad \ldots \quad \Delta \vdash e_n \triangleright v_n \quad C^n \, (v_1, \ldots, v_n) \in \Delta_C}{\Delta \vdash C^n \, (e_1, \ldots, e_n) \triangleright C^n \, (v_1, \ldots, v_n)} \; \mathsf{constr}_n$$

$$\frac{\Delta \vdash e_1 \triangleright \mathsf{true} \quad \Delta \vdash e_2 \triangleright v_2}{\Delta \vdash \mathsf{if} \; e_1 \; \mathsf{then} \; e_2 \; \mathsf{else} \; e_3 \triangleright v_2} \; \mathsf{if}_{\mathsf{true}} \qquad \frac{\Delta \vdash e_1 \triangleright \mathsf{false} \quad \Delta \vdash e_3 \triangleright v_3}{\Delta \vdash \mathsf{if} \; e_1 \; \mathsf{then} \; e_2 \; \mathsf{else} \; e_3 \triangleright v_3} \; \mathsf{if}_{\mathsf{false}}$$

$$\frac{}{\Delta \vdash \mathsf{fun} \; x \to e \triangleright {<}x \rightsquigarrow e, \Delta{>}} \; \mathsf{fun} \qquad \frac{}{\Delta \vdash \mathsf{rec} \; f \; x \to e \triangleright {<}x \rightsquigarrow e, \Delta{>}_{\mathsf{rec}(f)}} \; \mathsf{rec}$$

$$\frac{\Delta \vdash e_1 \triangleright v_1 \quad \Delta, (x, v_1) \vdash e_2 \triangleright v_2}{\Delta \vdash \mathsf{let} \; x = e_1 \; \mathsf{in} \; e_2 \triangleright v_2} \; \mathsf{let} \qquad \frac{\Delta \vdash e_1 \triangleright v_1 \quad \ldots \quad \Delta \vdash e_n \triangleright v_n}{\Delta \vdash (e_1, \ldots, e_n) \triangleright (v_1, \ldots, v_n)} \; \mathsf{Tuple}$$

$$\frac{\Delta \vdash e_1 \triangleright {<}x \rightsquigarrow e_3, \Delta{>} \quad \Delta \vdash e_2 \triangleright v_2 \quad \Delta, (x, v_2) \vdash e_3 \triangleright v_3}{\Delta \vdash e_1 \; e_2 \triangleright v_3} \; \mathsf{App}$$

$$\frac{\Delta \vdash e_1 \triangleright {<}x \rightsquigarrow e_3, \Delta{>}_{\mathsf{rec}(f)} = c \quad \Delta \vdash e_2 \triangleright v_2 \quad \Delta, (f, c), (x, v_2) \vdash e_3 \triangleright v_3}{\Delta \vdash e_1 \; e_2 \triangleright v_3} \; \mathsf{App}_{\mathsf{rec}}$$

$$\frac{\Delta \vdash e \triangleright v \quad \mathsf{filter}_\Delta(v, gpat_i) = \Delta_i \quad \mathsf{filter}_\Delta(v, gpat_j) = \mathsf{fail}, \; 1 \le j < i \quad \Delta, \Delta_i \vdash e_i \triangleright v_i}{\Delta \vdash \mathsf{match} \; e \; \mathsf{with} \; | \; gpat_1 \to e_1 \; \ldots \; | \; gpat_n \to e_n \triangleright v_i} \; \mathsf{match}$$

$$\text{with } \mathsf{filter}_\Delta(v, gpat) = \begin{cases} \Delta_p, & \text{if } gpat = pat \text{ and } \mathsf{mgu}_\Delta(v, pat) = \Delta_p, \\ \Delta_p, & \text{if } gpat = pat \text{ when } e, \; \mathsf{mgu}_\Delta(v, pat) = \Delta_p, \\ & \text{and } \Delta, \Delta_p \vdash e \triangleright \mathsf{true}, \\ \mathsf{fail}, & \text{otherwise} \end{cases}$$

A Modular Formalisation of Finite Group Theory*

Georges Gonthier[1], Assia Mahboubi[2], Laurence Rideau[3],
Enrico Tassi[4], and Laurent Théry[3]

[1] Microsoft Research
[2] Microsoft Research - Inria Joint Center
[3] INRIA
[4] University of Bologna
gonthier@microsoft.com, tassi@cs.unibo.it
{Assia.Mahboubi,Laurent.Rideau,Laurent.Thery}@inria.fr

Abstract. In this paper, we present a formalisation of elementary group theory done in COQ. This work is the first milestone of a long-term effort to formalise the Feit-Thompson theorem. As our further developments will heavily rely on this initial base, we took special care to articulate it in the most compositional way.

1 Introduction

Recent works such as [2,8,9,19] show that proof systems are getting sufficiently mature to formalise non-trivial mathematical theories. Group theory is a domain of mathematics where computer proofs could be of real added value. This domain was one of the first to publish *very long* proofs. The first and most famous example is the Feit-Thompson theorem, which states that every odd order group is solvable. Its historical proof [7] is 255 pages long. That proof has later been simplified and re-published [5,18], providing a better understanding of local parts of the proof. Yet its length remains unchanged, as well as its global architecture. Checking such a long proof with a computer would clearly increase the confidence in its correctness, and hopefully lead to a further step in the understanding of this proof. This paper addresses the ground work needed to start formalising this theorem.

There have been several attempts to formalise elementary group theory using a proof assistant. Most of them [1,12,23] stop at the Lagrange theorem. An exception is Kammüller and Paulson [13] who have formalised the first Sylow theorem. The originality of our work is that we do not use elementary group theory as a mere example but as a foundation for further formalisations. It is then crucial for our formalisation to scale up. We have therefore worked out a new development, with a strong effort in proof engineering.

First, we reuse the SSREFLECT extension of the COQ system [14] developed by Gonthier for his proof of the Four Colour theorem. This gives us a library

---

* This work was supported by the Microsoft Research - Inria Joint Center.

K. Schneider and J. Brandt (Eds.): TPHOLs 2007, LNCS 4732, pp. 86–101, 2007.
© Springer-Verlag Berlin Heidelberg 2007

and a proof language that is particularly well suited to the formalisation of finite groups. Second, we make use of many features of the CoQ proof engine (notations, implicit arguments, coercions, canonical structures) to get more readable statements and tractable proofs.

The paper is organised as follows. In Section 2, we present the SSREFLECT extension and show how it is adequate to our needs. In Section 3, we comment on some of our choices in formalising objects such as groups, quotients and morphisms. Finally, in Section 4, we present some classic results of group theory that have already been formally proved in this setting.

2 Small Scale Reflection

The SSREFLECT extension [10] offers new syntax features for the proof shell and a set of libraries making use of *small scale reflection* in various respects. This layer above the standard CoQ system provides a convenient framework for dealing with structures equipped with a decidable equality. In this section, we comment on the fundamental definitions present in the library and how modularity is carried out throughout the development.

2.1 Proof Shell

Proof scripts written with the SSREFLECT extension have a very different flavour than the ones developed using standard CoQ tactics. We are not going to present the proof shell extensively but only describe some simple features, that, we believe, have the most impact on productivity. A script is a linear structure composed of tactics. Each tactic ends with a period. An example of such a script is the following

move ⇒ x a H; **apply**: etrans (cardUI _ _).
  case: (a x); **last by rewrite** /= card0 card1.
  by rewrite [_ + x]addnC.
by rewrite {1}mem_filter /setI.

All the frequent bookkeeping operations that consists in moving, splitting, generalising formulae from (or to) the context are regrouped in a single tactic **move**. For example, the tactic **move** ⇒ x a H on the first line moves (introduces) two constants x and a and an assumption H from the goal to the context.

It is recommended practise to use indentation to display the control structure of a proof. To further structure scripts, SSREFLECT supplies a **by** tactical to explicitly close off tactics. When replaying scripts, we then have the nice property that an error immediately occurs when a closed tactic fails to prove its subgoal. When composing tactics, the two tacticals **first** and **last** let the user restrict the application of a tactic to only the first or the last subgoal generated by the previous command. This covers the frequent cases where a tactic generates two subgoals one of which can be easily disposed of. In practice, these two tacticals are so effective at increasing the linearity of our scripts that, in fact, we very rarely need more than two levels of indentation.

Finally, the **rewrite** tactic in SSREFLECT provides a concise syntax that allows a single command to perform a combination of conditional rewriting, folding and unfolding of definitions, and simplification, on selected patterns and even specific occurrences. This makes rewriting much more user-friendly and contributes to shift the proof style towards equational reasoning. In the standard library of COQ, the **rewrite** tactic is roughly used the same number of times as the **apply** tactic. In our development for group theory, **rewrite** is used three times more than **apply** — despite the fact that, on average, each SSREFLECT **rewrite** stands for three COQ **rewrites**.

2.2 Views

The COQ system is based on an intuitionistic type theory, the Calculus of Inductive Constructions [21,16]. In such a formalism, there is a distinction between logical propositions and boolean values.

On the one hand, logical propositions are objects of *sort* Prop which is the carrier of intuitionistic reasoning. Logical connectives in Prop are *types*, which give precise information on the structure of their proofs; this information is automatically exploited by COQ tactics. For example, COQ knows that a proof of A ∨ B is either a proof of A or a proof of B. The tactics **left** and **right** change the goal A ∨ B to A and B, respectively; dually, the tactic **case** reduces the goal A ∨ B ⇒ G to two subgoals A ⇒ G and B ⇒ G.

On the other hand, bool is an inductive *datatype* with two constructors true and false. Logical connectives on bool are computable *functions*, defined by their truth tables, using case analysis:

Definition $(b_1 \;||\; b_2) :=$ **if** b_1 **then** true **else** b_2.

Properties of such connectives are also established using case analysis: the tactic **by case**: b solves the goal b || ∼b = true by replacing b first by true and then by false; in either case, the resulting subgoal reduces by computation to the trivial true = true.

Thus, Prop and bool are truly complementary: the former supports robust natural deduction, the latter allows brute-force evaluation. SSREFLECT supplies a generic mechanism to have the best of the two worlds and move freely from a propositional version of a decidable predicate to its boolean version.

First, booleans are injected into propositions using the coercion mechanism:

Coercion is_true (b: bool) := b = true.

This allows any boolean formula b to be used in a context where COQ would expect a proposition, e.g., after **Lemma** ... :. It is then interpreted as (is_true b), i.e., the proposition b = true. Coercions are elided by the prettyprinter, so they are essentially transparent to the user. Then, the inductive predicate reflect is used to relate propositions and booleans

Inductive reflect (P: Prop): bool → Type :=
 | Reflect_true : P ⇒ reflect P true
 | Reflect_false : ¬P ⇒ reflect P false.

The statement (reflect P b) asserts that (is_true b) and P are logically equivalent propositions. In the following, we use the notation P $\leftrightarrow$ b for (reflect P b).

For instance, the following lemma:

Lemma andP: $\forall b_1\, b_2,\ (b_1 \wedge b_2) \leftrightarrow (b_1 \,\&\&\, b_2)$.

relates the boolean conjunction && to the logical one $\wedge$. Note that in andP, b_1 and b_2 are two boolean variables and the proposition $b_1 \wedge b_2$ hides two coercions. The conjunction of b_1 and b_2 can then be viewed as $b_1 \wedge b_2$ or as $b_1 \,\&\&\, b_2$. A naming convention in SSREFLECT is to postfix the name of view lemmas with P. For example, orP relates $\|$ and $\vee$, negP relates $\sim$ and $\neg$.

Views are integrated to the proof language. If we are to prove a goal of the form $(b_1 \wedge b_2) \Rightarrow G$, the tactic **case** $\Rightarrow E_1\, E_2$ changes the goal to G adding to the context the two assumptions $E_1: b_1$ and $E_2: b_2$. To handle a goal of the form $(b_1 \,\&\&\, b_2) \Rightarrow G$, we can simply annotate the tactic to specify an intermediate change of view: **case**/andP $\Rightarrow E_1\, E_2$.

Suppose now that our goal is $b_1 \,\&\&\, b_2$. In order to split this goal into two subgoals, we use a combination of two tactics: **apply**/andP; **split**. The first tactic performs the change of view so that the second tactic can do the splitting. Note that if we happen to have in the context an assumption H: b_1, instead of performing the splitting, the tactic **rewrite** H /=, i.e., rewriting with H followed by a simplification, can directly be used to transform the goal $b_1 \,\&\&\, b_2$ into b_2.

Views also provide a convenient way to choose between several (logical) characterisations of the same (computational) definition, by having a view lemma per interpretation. A trivial example is the ternary boolean conjunction. If we have a goal of the form $b_1 \,\&\&\, (b_2 \,\&\&\, b_3) \Rightarrow G$, applying the tactic **case**/andP leads to the goal $b_1 \Rightarrow b_2 \,\&\&\, b_3 \Rightarrow G$. We can also define an alternative view with

Inductive and3 (P Q R : Prop) : Prop := And3 of P & Q & R.

Lemma and3P: $\forall b_1\, b_2\, b_3,\ (and3\ b_1\ b_2\ b_3) \leftrightarrow (b_1 \,\&\&\, (b_2 \,\&\&\, b_3))$.

Now, the tactic **case**/and3P directly transforms the goal $b_1 \,\&\&\, (b_2 \,\&\&\, b_3) \Rightarrow G$ into $b_1 \Rightarrow b_2 \Rightarrow b_3 \Rightarrow G$.

2.3 Libraries

In our formalisation of finite groups, we reused the base libraries initially developed for the formal proof of the Four Colour theorem. These libraries build a hierarchy of structures using nested dependent record types. This technique is standard in type-theoretic formalisations of abstract algebra [3]. At the bottom of this hierarchy, the structure eqType deals with types with decidable equality.

Structure eqType : Type := EqType {
    sort :> Type;
  _ $\equiv$ _ : sort $\rightarrow$ sort $\rightarrow$ bool;
    eqP : $\forall x\, y,\ (x = y) \leftrightarrow (x \equiv y)$
}.

The :> symbol declares sort as a coercion from an eqType to its carrier type. It is the standard technique to get subtyping. If d is an object of type eqType, then an object x can have the type x : d, thanks to the sort coercion. The complete judgement is in fact x : sort d. Moreover, if x and y are of type sort d, the term $x \equiv y$ is understood as the projection of d on its second field, applied to x and y. The implicit d parameter is both inferred and hidden from the user.

In the type theory of CoQ, the only relation we can freely rewrite with is the primitive (Leibniz) equality. When another equivalence relation is the intended notion of equality on a given type, the user usually needs to use the setoid workaround [4]. Unfortunately, setoid rewriting does not have the same power as primitive rewriting. An eqType structure provides not only a computable equality $\equiv$ but also a proof eqP that this equality reflects the Leibniz one; the eqP view thus promotes $\equiv$ to a *rewritable* relation.

A non parametric inductive type can usually be turned into an eqType by choosing for $\equiv$ the function that checks structural equality. This is the case for booleans and natural numbers for which we define the two *canonical structures* bool_eqType and nat_eqType. Canonical structures are used when solving equations involving implicit arguments. Namely, if the type checker needs to infer an eqType structure with sort nat, it will automatically choose the nat_eqType structure. By enlarging the set of implicit arguments CoQ can infer, canonical structures make hierarchical structures widely applicable.

A key property of eqType structures is that they enjoy proof-irrelevance for the equality proofs of their elements: every equality proof is convertible to a reflected boolean test.

Lemma eq_irrelevance: $\forall$ (d: eqType) (x y: d) (E: x = y) (E': x = y), E = E'.

An eqType structure only defines a domain, in which sets take their elements. Sets are then represented by their characteristic function.

Definition set (d: eqType) := d → bool.

and defining set operations like $\cup$ and $\cap$ is done by providing the corresponding boolean functions.

The next step consists in building lists, elements of type seq d, whose elements belong to the parametric eqType structure d. The decidability of equality on d is needed when defining the basic operations on lists like membership $\in$ and look-up index. Then, membership is used for defining a coercion from list to set, such that (l x) is automatically coerced into $x \in l$.

Lists are the cornerstone of the definition of finite types. A finType structure provides an enumeration of its sort: a sequence in which each element of type sort occurs exactly once. Note that sort must also have an eqType structure.

Structure finType : Type := FinType {
  sort :> eqType;
  enum : seq sort;
  enumP : $\forall$x, count (set1 x) enum = 1
}.

where (set1 x) is the set that contains only x and (count f l) computes the number of elements y of the list l for which (f y) is true.

Finite sets are then sets whose domain has a finType structure. The library provides many set operations. For example, given A a finite set, (card A) represents the cardinality of A. All these operations come along with their basic properties. For example, we have:

Lemma cardUI : $\forall$ (d: finType) (A B: set d),
    card (A $\cup$ B) + card (A $\cap$ B) = card A + card B.
Lemma card_image : $\forall$ (d d': finType) (f: d $\rightarrow$ d') (A: set d),
    injective f $\Rightarrow$ card (image f A) = card A.

3   The Group Library

This section is dedicated to the formalisation of elementary group theory. We justify our definitions and explain how they relate to each other.

3.1   Graphs of Function and Intentional Sets

We use the notation f=$_1$g to indicate that two functions are extensionally equal, i.e., the fact that $\forall$x, f x = g x holds. In COQ, f=$_1$g does not imply f = g. This makes equational reasoning with objects containing functions difficult in COQ without adding extra axioms. In our case, extra axioms are not needed. The functions we manipulate have finite domains so they can be finitely represented by their graph. Given d_1 a finite type and d_2 a type with decidable equality, a graph is defined as:

Inductive fgraphType : Type :=
    Fgraph (val: seq d_2) (fgraph_sizeP: size val = card d_1): fgraphType.

It contains a list val of elements of d_2, the size of val being exactly the cardinality of d_1. Defining a function fgraph_of_fun that computes the graph associated to a function is straightforward. Conversely, a coercion fun_of_fgraph lets the user use graphs as standard functions. With graphs as functions, it is possible to prove functional extensionality:

Lemma fgraphP : $\forall$ (f g : fgraphType d_1 d_2), f =$_1$ g $\Leftrightarrow$ f = g.

Note that here f =$_1$g is understood as (fun_of_graph f) =$_1$ (fun_of_graph g).

The special case of graphs with domain d and codomain bool_eqType is denoted (setType d). We call elements of (setType d) *intentional* sets by opposition to the sets in (set d), defined by their characteristic function. We equip intentional sets with the same operations as extensional sets. {x,$E(x)$} denotes the intentional set whose characteristic function is (fun x $\rightarrow$ $E(x)$), and (f @ A) denotes the intentional set of the image of A by f.

Graphs are used to build some useful data-structures. For example, homogeneous tuples, i.e., sequences of elements of type K of fixed length n, are implemented as graphs with domain (ordinal n), the finite type {0, 1, 2,..., n−1}, and co-domain K. With this representation, the p-th element of a n-tuple t can be obtained applying t to p, as soon as p lies in the the domain of t. Also, permutations are defined as function graphs with identical domain and co-domain, whose val list does not contain any duplicate.

3.2 Groups

In the same way that eqType structures were introduced before defining sets, we introduce a notion of (finite) *group domain* which is distinct from the one of groups. It is modelled by a finGroupType record structure:

Structure finGroupType : Type := FinGroupType {
  element :> finType;
      1 : element;
     $_{-}^{-1}$: element $\rightarrow$ element;
    $_{-}$ * $_{-}$: element $\rightarrow$ element $\rightarrow$ element;
    unitP : $\forall x, 1 * x = x$;
     invP : $\forall x, x^{-1} * x = 1$;
    mulP : $\forall x_1\ x_2\ x_3, x_1 * (x_2 * x_3) = (x_1 * x_2) * x_3$
}.

It contains a carrier, a composition law and an inverse function, a unit element and the usual properties of these operations. Its first field is declared as a coercion to the carrier of the group domain, like it was the case in section 2.3. In particular, we can again define convenient global notations like $*$ or $^{-1}$ for the projections of this record type.

In the group library, a first category of lemmas is composed of properties that are valid on the whole group domain. For example:

Lemma invg_mul : $\forall x_1\ x_2, (x_2 * x_1)^{-1} = x_1^{-1} * x_2^{-1}$.

Also, we can already define operations on arbitrary sets of a group domain. If A is such a set, we can define for instance:

Definition x $\hat{\ }$ y := $y^{-1} * x * y$.
Definition A :* x := $\{y, y * x^{-1} \in A\}$. *(* right cosets *)*
Definition A :$\hat{\ }$ x := $\{y, y \hat{\ } x^{-1} \in A\}$. *(* conjugate *)*
Definition normaliser A := $\{x, (A :\hat{\ } x) \subset A\}$.

Providing a boolean predicate sometimes requires a little effort, e.g., in the definition of the *point-wise* product of two sets:

Definition A :*: B := $\{x * y, \sim(\text{disjoint } \{y, x * y \in (A :* y)\}\ B)\}$

The corresponding *view* lemma gives the natural characterisation of this object:

Lemma smulgP : $\forall A\ B\ z, (\exists x\ y, x \in A\ \&\ y \in B\ \&\ z = x * y) \leftrightarrow (z \in A :*: B)$.

Lemmas like smulgP belong to category of lemmas composed of the properties of these operations requiring only group domain *sets*.

Finally, a *group* is defined as a boolean predicate, satisfied by sets of a given group domain that contain the unit and are stable under product.

Definition group_set A := $1 \in A\ \&\&\ (A :*: A) \subset A$.

It is very convenient to give the possibility of attaching in a canonical way the proof that a set has a group structure. This is why groups are declared as structures, of type:

Structure group(elt : finGroupType) : Type := Group {
  set_of_group :> setType elt;
  set_of_groupP : group_set set_of_group
}.

The first argument of this structure is a *set*, giving the carrier of the group. Notice that we do *not* define one type per group but one type per group domain, which avoids having unnecessary injections everywhere in the development.

Finally, the last category of lemmas in the library is composed of group properties. For example, given a group H, we have the following property:

Lemma groupMl : $\forall$ x y, x $\in$ H $\Rightarrow$ (x $*$ y) $\in$ H = y $\in$ H.

In the above statement, the equality stands for CoQ standard equality between boolean values, since membership of H is a boolean predicate.

We declare a canonical group structure for the usual group constructions so that they can be displayed as their set carrier but still benefit from an automatically inferred proof of group structure when needed. For example, such canonical structure is defined for the intersection of two groups H and K that share the group domain elt :

Lemma group_setI : group_set (H $\cap$ K).
Canonical Structure setI_group := Group group_setI.

where, as in the previous section, $\cap$ stands for the *set* intersection operation.

Given a group domain elt and two groups H and K, the stability of the group law for the intersection is proved in the following way:

Lemma setI_stable : $\forall$ x y, x $\in$ (H $\cap$ K) $\Rightarrow$ y $\in$ (H $\cap$ K) $\Rightarrow$ (x $*$ y) $\in$ (H $\cap$ K).
Proof. by move $\Rightarrow$ x y H1 H2; **rewrite** groupMl. **Qed.**

The group structure on the H $\cap$ K carrier is automatically inferred from the canonical structure declaration and the **by** closing command uses the H1 and H2 assumptions to close two trivial generated goals.

This two-level definition of groups, involving group domain types and groups as first order citizens equipped with canonical structures, plays an important role in doing proofs. As a consequence, most of the theorems are stated like in a set-theoretic framework (see section 3.4 for some examples). Type inference is then used to perform the proof inference, from the database of registered canonical structures. This mechanism is used extensively throughout the development, and allows us in particular to state and use theorems in a way that follows standard mathematical practice.

3.3   Quotients

Typically, every local section of our development assumes once and for all the existence of one group domain elt to then manipulate different groups of this domain. Nevertheless, there are situations where it is necessary to build new finGroupType structures. This is the case for example for *quotients*. Let H and K be two groups in the same group universe, the quotient K/H is a group under the condition that H is *normal* in K. Of course, we could create a new group domain for each quotient, but we can be slightly smarter noticing that given a group H, all the quotients of the form K/H share the same group law, and the same unit. The idea is then to have all the quotients groups K/H in a group domain . /H.

In our finite setting, the largest possible quotient exists and is N(H)/H, where N(H) is the normaliser of H and all the other quotients are subsets of this one.

In our formalisation, normality is defined as:

Definition H ◁ K := (H ⊂ K) && (K ⊂ (normaliser H)).

If H ◁ K, H-left cosets and H-right cosets coincide for every element of K. Hence, they are just called *cosets*.

The set of cosets of an arbitrary set A is the image of the normaliser of A by the rcoset operation. Here we define the associated sigma type:

Definition coset_set (A : setType elt):= (rcoset A) @ (normaliser A).
Definition coset (A : setType elt):= eq_sig (coset_set A).

where eq_sig builds the sigma type associated to a set. This coset type can be equipped with eqType and finType canonical structures; elements of this type are intentional sets.

When H is equipped with a group structure, we define group operations on (coset H) thanks to the following properties:

Lemma cosets_unit : H ∈ (cosets H).
Lemma cosets_mul : ∀ Hx Hy : coset H, (Hx :*: Hy) ∈ (cosets H).
Lemma cosets_inv : ∀ Hx : coset H, (Hx :$^{-1}$) ∈ (cosets H).

where A :$^{-1}$ denotes the image of a set A by the inverse operation. Group properties are provable for these operations: we can define a canonical structure of group domain on coset depending on an arbitrary group object.

The quotient of two groups of the same group domain can *always* be defined:

Definition A / B := (coset_of B) @ A.

where coset_of : elt → (coset A) maps elements of the normaliser A to their coset, and the other ones to the coset unit. Hence A / B defines in fact $N_A(B)B/B$.

Every quotient G / H of two group structures is equipped with a canonical structure of *group* of the coset H group domain.

A key point in the readability of statements involving quotients is that the ./. notation is usable because it refers to a definition independent of proofs; the type inference mechanism will automatically find an associated group structure for this set when it exists.

Defining quotients has been a place where we had to rework our formalisation substantially using intentional sets instead of sets defined by their characteristic function.

A significant part of the library of finite group quotients deals with constructions of group isomorphisms. The first important results to establish are the so-called three fundamental isomorphism theorems.

Two isomorphic groups do not necessarily share the same group domain. For example, two quotients by two different groups will have distinct (dependent) types. Having sets for which function extensionality does not hold had forced us to use setoids. For theorems with types depending on setoid arguments, especially the ones stating equalities, we had to add one extensional equality condition per occurrence of such a dependent type in the statement of the theorem in order to make these theorems usable. Worse, in order to apply one of these theorems, the user had to provide specific lemmas, proved before-hand, for each equality proof. This was clearly unacceptable if quotients were to be used in further formalisations. Using intentional sets simplified everything.

3.4 Group Morphisms

Group morphisms are functions between two group domains, compatible with the group laws of their domain and co-domain. Their properties may not hold on the whole group domain, but only on a certain group of this domain. The notion of morphism is hence a local one.

We avoid the numerous difficulties introduced by formalising partial functions in type theory by embedding the domain of a morphism inside its computational definition. Any morphism candidate takes a default unit value outside the group where the morphism properties are supposed to hold. Now, we can compute back the domain of a morphism candidate from its values, identifying the kernel among the set of elements mapped to the unit:

Definition ker (f: $elt_1 \rightarrow elt_2$) := {x, $elt_1 \subset$ {y, f (x $*$ y) $\equiv$ f y}}.

This kernel can be equipped with a canonical group structure. Morphism domains are defined as:

Definition mdom (f: $elt_1 \rightarrow elt_2$) := ker f $\cup$ {x, f x $\neq$ 1}.

As a group is defined as a set plus certain properties satisfied by this set, a morphism is defined as a function, together with the properties making this function a morphism.

Structure morphism : Type := Morphism {
    mfun :> $elt_1 \rightarrow elt_2$;
    group_set_mdom : group_set (mdom mfun);
    morphM : $\forall$ x y, x $\in$ (mdom f) $\Rightarrow$ y $\in$ (mdom f) $\Rightarrow$
                    mfun (x $*$ y) = (mfun x) $*$ (mfun y)
}.

The domain mdom f of a given morphism f is hence canonically equipped with an obvious group structure.

Thanks to the use of a default unit value, the (functional) composition of two morphisms is canonically equipped with a morphism structure. Other standard constructions have a canonical morphism structure, like coset_of G as soon as G is a group.

Morphisms and quotients are involved in the universal property of morphism factorisation, also called first isomorphism theorem in the literature. We carefully stick to first order predicates to take as much benefit as possible from the canonical structure mechanism. If necessary, we embed side conditions inside definitions with a boolean test. In this way we avoid having to add pre-conditions in the properties of these predicates to ensure well-formedness. For any function between group domains, we define a quotient function by:

Definition $\text{mquo}(f : \text{elt}_1 \rightarrow \text{elt}_2)(A : \text{setType elt}_1)(Ax : \text{coset } A) :=$
   if $A \subset (\text{ker } f)$ **then** $f (\text{repr } Ax)$ **else** 1.

where repr Ax picks a representative of a coset Ax. Given any morphism, its quotient function defines an isomorphism between the quotient of its domain by its kernel and the image of the initial morphism.

Theorem first_isomorphism : $\forall H : \text{group elt}_1, \forall f : \text{morphism elt}_1 \text{ elt}_2,$
   $H \subset (\text{dom } f) \Rightarrow \text{isog } (H / (\text{ker}_H f)) (f @ H).$

An isomorphism between A and B is a morphism having a trivial kernel and mapping A to B. This localised version of the theorem builds an isomorphism between $\text{ker}_H f$, the intersection of a group H with ker f, and the image f @ H of H.

This definition of morphisms is crafted to eliminate any proof dependency which cannot be resolved by the type inference system with the help of canonical structures. A pointed out in section 3.2, statements are much more readable and formal proofs much easier.

To convince the reader of the efficiency of these canonical structure definitions, we provide hereafter a verbatim copy of the statements of the isomorphism theorems we have formally proved.

```
Theorem second_isomorphism : forall G H : group elt,
  subset G (normaliser H) -> isog (G / (G :&: H)) (G / H).

Lemma quotient_mulg : forall G H : group elt, (G :*: H) / H = G / H.

Theorem third_isomorphism  : forall G H K : group elt,
  H <| G -> K <| G -> subset K H -> isog ((G / K) / (H / K)) (G / H).
```

Here (G :&: H) is ASCII for $G \cap H$. The quotient_mulg identity follows from our design choices for the formalisation of quotients. Rewriting with quotient_mulg yields the standard statement of the second isomorphism theorem.

In the statement of third_isomorphism, the term H / K is defined as (coset_of K) @ H. Since K is a group, (coset_of K) is equipped with a canonical structure of morphism. Since H is a group, its image by a morphism has itself a canonical structure of group, hence type inference is able to find a group structure for H / K, in the group domain (coset K). Finally, this allows COQ to infer a group domain structure for coset (H / K), the domain of the isomorphism, which is (hidden) implicit parameter of the isog predicate.

4 Standard Theorems of Group Theory

In order to evaluate how practical our definitions of groups, cosets and quotients were, we have started formalising some standard results of group theory. In this section, we present three of them: the Sylow theorems, the Frobenius lemma and the Cauchy-Frobenius lemma. The Sylow theorems are central in group theory. The Frobenius lemma gives a nice property of the elements of a group of a given order. Finally the Cauchy-Frobenius lemma, also called the Burnside counting lemma, applies directly to enumeration problems. Our main source of inspiration for these proofs was some lecture notes on group theory by Constantine [6].

4.1 The Sylow Theorems

The first Sylow theorem asserts the existence of a subgroup H of K of cardinality p^n, for every prime p such that $card(K) = p^n s$ and p does not divide s. For any two groups H and K of the same group domain, we define and prove :

Definition sylow K p H := $H \subset K$ && card $H \equiv p^{\log_p(card\ K)}$.

Theorem sylow$_1$: $\forall$ K p, $\exists$ H, sylow K p H.

The first definition captures the property of H being a p-Sylow subgroup of K. The expression $\log_p$ (card K) computes the maximum value of i such that p^i divides the cardinality of K when p is prime. This theorem has already been formalised by Kammüller and Paulson [13], based a proof due to Wielandt [22]. Our proof is slightly different and intensively uses group actions on sets. Given a group domain G and a finite type S, actions are defined by the following structure:

Structure action : Type := Action {
   act_f :> S → G → S;
   act_1 : $\forall$x, act_f x 1 = x;
   act_morph : $\forall$(x y : G) z, act_f z (x * y) = act_f (act_f z x) y
}.

Note that we take advantage of our finite setting to replace the usual bijectivity of the action by the simpler property that the unit acts trivially.

A complete account of our proof is given in [20]. The proof works by induction on n showing that there exists a subgroup of order p^i for all $0 < i \leq n$. The base case is Cauchy theorem, which asserts that a group K has an element of order p for each prime divisor of the cardinality of the group K. Our proof is simpler than the combinatorial argument used in [13], which hinged on properties of the binomial. We first build the set U such that $U = \{(k_1, \ldots, k_p) \mid k_i \in$ K and $\prod_{i=1}^{i=p} k_i = 1\}$. We have that $card(U) = card(K)^{p-1}$. We then define the action of the additive group $\mathbb{Z}/p\mathbb{Z}$ that acts on U as

$$n \quad \longmapsto \quad (k_1, \ldots, k_p) \mapsto (k_{n\,mod\,p+1}, \ldots, k_{(n+p-1)\,mod\,p+1})$$

Note that defining this action is straightforward since p-tuples are graphs of functions whose domain is (ordinal p).

Now, we consider the set S_0 of the elements of U whose orbits by the action are a singleton. S_0 is composed of the elements $(k, \ldots, k)$ such that $k \in K$ and $k^p = 1$. A consequence of the orbit stabiliser theorem tells us that p divides the cardinality of S_0. As S_0 is non-empty $((1, \ldots, 1)$ belongs to $S_0)$, there exists at least one $k \neq 1$, such that $(k, \ldots, k)$ belongs to S_0. The order of k is then p.

In a similar way, in the inductive case, we suppose that there is a subgroup H of order p^i, we consider $N_K(H)/H$ the quotient of the normaliser of H in K by H. We act with H on the left cosets of H by left translation:

$$g \quad \longmapsto \quad hH \mapsto (gh)H$$

and consider the set S_0 of the left coset of H whose orbits by the action are a singleton. The elements of S_0 are exactly the elements of $N_K(H)/H$. Again, applying the orbit stabiliser theorem, we can deduce that p divides the cardinality of S_0 so there exists an element k of order p in S_0 by Cauchy theorem. If we consider H, the pre-image by the quotient operation of the cyclic group generated by k, its cardinality is p^{i+1}.

We have also formalised the second and third Sylow theorems. The second theorem states that any two p-Sylow subgroups H_1 and H_2 are conjugate. This is proved acting with H_1 on the left coset of H_2. The third theorem states that the number of p-Sylow subgroups divides the cardinality of K and is equal to 1 modulo p. The third theorem is proved by acting by conjugation on the sets of all p-Sylow subgroups.

4.2   The Frobenius Lemma

Given an element a of a group G, (cyclic a) builds the cyclic group generated by a. When proving properties of cyclic groups, we use the characteristic property of the cyclic function.

Lemma cyclicP: $\forall a\, b$, reflect $(\exists n, a\hat{\ }n \equiv b)$ (cyclic a b).

The order of an element is then defined as the cardinality of its associated cyclic group. The Frobenius lemma states that given a number n that divides the cardinality of a group K, the number of elements whose order divides n is a multiple of n. In our formalisation, this gives

Theorem frobenius: $\forall K\, n$, $n \mid (\text{card } K) \to n \mid (\text{card } \{z{:}K, (\text{orderg } z) \mid n\})$.

The proof is rather technical and has intensively tested our library on cyclic groups. For example, as we are counting the number of elements of a given order, we need to know the number of generators of a cyclic group. This is given by a theorem of our library.

Lemma $\phi\_$gen: $\forall a$, $\phi(\text{orderg } a) = \text{card (generator (cyclic a))}$.

where ϕ is the Euler function.

4.3   The Cauchy-Frobenius Lemma

Let G a group acting on a set S. For each g in G, let F_g be the set of elements in S fixed by g, and t the number of orbits of G on S, then t is equal to the average number of points left fixed by each element of G:

$$t = \frac{1}{|G|} \sum_{g \in G} |F_g|$$

To prove this lemma, we consider B, subset of the cartesian product $G \times S$ containing the pairs (g, x) such that $g(x) = x$. We use two ways to evaluate the cardinality of B, first by fixing the first component: $|B| = \sum_{g \in G} |F_g|$, then by fixing the second component: $|B| = \sum_{x \in S} |G_x|$ where G_x is the stabiliser of x in G. Then, when sorting the right hand-side of the second equality by orbits we obtain that $|B| = |Gx_1||G_{x_1}| + |Gx_2||G_{x_2}| + \cdots + |Gx_t||G_{x_t}|$ the x_i being representatives of the orbit Gx_i. Applying the Lagrange theorem on the stabiliser of x_i in G (the subgroup G_{x_i}), we obtain that for each orbit: $|Gx_i||G_{x_i}| = |G|$ and we deduce that $|B| = t|G| = \sum_{g \in G} |F_g|$.

This lemma is a special case of the powerful Pólya method, but it already has significant applications in combinatorial counting problems. To illustrate this, we have formally shown that there are 55 distinct ways of colouring with 4 colours the vertices of a square up to isometry. This is done by instantiating a more general theorem that tells that the number of ways of colouring with n colours is $(n^4 + 2n^3 + 3n^2 + 2n)/8$. This last theorem is a direct application of the Cauchy-Frobenius lemma. The encoding of the problem is the following:

Definition square := ordinal 4.
Definition colour := ordinal n.
Definition colouring := fgraphType square colour.

Vertices are represented by the set $\{0, 1, 2, 3\}$, colours by the set $\{0, 1, \ldots, n-1\}$ and colouring by functions from vertices to colours. The set of isometries is a subset of the permutations of square that preserve the geometry of the square. In our case, we use the characteristic condition that *the images of two opposite vertices remain opposite*.

Definition isometry := {p : perm square, $\forall$ i, p (opp i) = opp (p i)}.

where perm square the permutation group and opp the function that returns the opposite of a vertex. We get that the isometries is a subgroup of the permutations, since the property of conserving opposite vertices is stable by composition and the identity obviously preserve opposite vertices.

The action of an isometry p on a colouring c returns the colouring $i \mapsto c(p(i))$. Each set of identical coloured squares corresponds to an orbit of this action. To apply Cauchy-Frobenius, we first need to give an extensional definition of the isometries, i.e., there are 8 isometries: the identity, the 3 rotations of $\pi/2$, π and $3\pi/2$, the vertical symmetry, the horizontal symmetry and the 2 symmetries about the diagonals. Second, we have to count the elements left fixed by each isometry.

The proofs of the three theorems presented in this section manipulate many of the base concepts defined in our formalisation. They have been particularly important to give us feedback on how practical our definitions were.

5   Conclusion

To our knowledge, what is presented in this paper is already one of the most complete formalisations of finite group theory. We cover almost all the material that can be found in an introductory course on group theory. Very few standard results like the simplicity of the alternating group are still missing, but should be formalised very soon. The only similar effort but in set theory can be found in the Mizar system [15]. Theorems like the ones presented in Section 4 are missing from the Mizar formalisation.

We have deliberately specialised our formalisation to *finite* group theory: finite groups are *not* obtained as a sub-class of generic groups. This design choice is consistent with the usual presentation of group theory in the literature. Imposing the inheritance of finite group theory from generic group theory would be somehow artificial since they share little results, all of them being trivial ones, hence it would not help formalising proofs but create pointless delicate subtyping issues.

Getting the definitions right is one of the most difficult aspects of formalising mathematics. The problem is not much in capturing the semantics of each individual construct but rather in having all the concepts working together well. Group theory has been no exception in that respect. It took much trial and error to arrive at the definitions presented in this paper. The fact that we were able to get results like the ones presented in Section 4 relatively easily makes us confident that our base is robust enough to proceed to further formalisations.

Using SSREFLECT has been a key aspect to our formal development. Decidable types and a substantial use of rewriting for our proofs give a 'classical' flavour to our development that is more familiar to what can be found in provers like ISABELLE [17] or HOL [11] than what is usually done in CoQ. Moreover, our novel use of canonical structures allows us to reconcile the convenience of set-theoretic statements with the expressiveness of dependent types, by harnessing the automation power of type inference. We think that this combination makes the CoQ system a powerful environment for the formalisation of such algebraic theories.

An indication of the conciseness of our proof scripts is given by the following figure. The standard library of CoQ contains 7000 objects (definitions + theorems) for 93000 lines of code, this makes a ratio of 13 lines per object. The base library of SSREFLECT plus our library for groups contains 1980 objects for 14400 lines, this makes a ratio of 7 lines per object.

References

1. Arthan, R.: Some group theory, available at
   `http://www.lemma-one.com/ProofPower/examples/wrk068.pdf`
2. Avigad, J., Donnelly, K., Gray, D., Raff, P.: A Formally Verified Proof of the Prime Number Theorem. ACM Transactions on Computational Logic (to appear)
3. Bailey, A.: Representing algebra in LEGO. Master's thesis, University of Edinburgh (1993)
4. Barthe, G., Capretta, V., Pons, O.: Setoids in type theory. Journal of Functional Programming 13(2), 261–293 (2003)
5. Bender, H., Glauberman, G.: Local analysis for the Odd Order Theorem. London Mathematical Society Lecture Note Series, vol. 188. Cambridge University Press, Cambridge (1994)
6. Constantine, G.M.: Group Theory, available at
   `http://www.pitt.edu/~gmc/algsyl.html`
7. Feit, W., Thompson, J.G.: Solvability of groups of odd order. Pacific Journal of Mathematics 13(3), 775–1029 (1963)
8. Geuvers, H., Wiedijk, F., Zwanenburg, J.: A Constructive Proof of the Fundamental Theorem of Algebra without Using the Rationals. In: Callaghan, P., Luo, Z., McKinna, J., Pollack, R. (eds.) TYPES 2000. LNCS, vol. 2277, pp. 96–111. Springer, Heidelberg (2002)
9. Gonthier, G.: A computer-checked proof of the four-colour theorem, available at
   `http://research.microsoft.com/~gonthier/4colproof.pdf`
10. Gonthier, G.: Notations of the four colour theorem proof, available at
    `http://research.microsoft.com/~gonthier/4colnotations.pdf`
11. Gordon, M.J.C., Melham, T.F.: Introduction to HOL: a theorem proving environment for higher-order logic. Cambridge University Press, Cambridge (1993)
12. Gunter, E.: Doing Algebra in Simple Type Theory. Technical Report MS-CIS-89-38, University of Pennsylvania (1989)
13. Kammüller, F., Paulson, L.C.: A Formal Proof of Sylow's Theorem. Journal of Automating Reasoning 23(3-4), 235–264 (1999)
14. The Coq development team: The Coq proof assistant reference manual. LogiCal Project, Version 8.1 (2007)
15. The Mizar Home Page, `http://www.mizar.org/`
16. Paulin-Mohring, C.: Définitions Inductives en Théorie des Types d'Ordre Supérieur. Habilitation à diriger les recherches, Université Claude Bernard Lyon I (December 1996)
17. Paulson, L.C. (ed.): Isabelle. LNCS, vol. 828. Springer, Heidelberg (1994)
18. Peterfalvi, T.: Character Theory for the Odd Order Theorem. London Mathematical Society Lecture Note Series, vol. 272. Cambridge University Press, Cambridge (2000)
19. The Flyspeck Project, `http://www.math.pitt.edu/~thales/flyspeck/`
20. Rideau, L., Théry, L.: Formalising Sylow's theorems in Coq. Technical Report 0327, INRIA (2006)
21. Werner, B.: Une théorie des Constructions Inductives. PhD thesis, Paris 7 (1994)
22. Wielandt, H.: Ein beweis für die Existenz der Sylowgruppen. Archiv der Mathematik 10, 401–402 (1959)
23. Yu, Y.: Computer Proofs in Group Theory. J. Autom. Reasoning 6(3), 251–286 (1990)

Verifying Nonlinear Real Formulas Via Sums of Squares

John Harrison

Intel Corporation, JF1-13
2111 NE 25th Avenue, Hillsboro OR 97124, USA
johnh@ichips.intel.com

Abstract. Techniques based on sums of squares appear promising as a general approach to the universal theory of reals with addition and multiplication, i.e. verifying Boolean combinations of equations and inequalities. A particularly attractive feature is that suitable 'sum of squares' certificates can be found by sophisticated numerical methods such as semidefinite programming, yet the actual verification of the resulting proof is straightforward even in a highly foundational theorem prover. We will describe our experience with an implementation in HOL Light, noting some successes as well as difficulties. We also describe a new approach to the univariate case that can handle some otherwise difficult examples.

1 Verifying Nonlinear Formulas over the Reals

Over the real numbers, there are algorithms that can in principle perform quantifier elimination from arbitrary first-order formulas built up using addition, multiplication and the usual equality and inequality predicates. A classic example of such a quantifier elimination equivalence is the criterion for a quadratic equation to have a real root:

$$\forall a\ b\ c.\ (\exists x.\ ax^2 + bx + c = 0) \Leftrightarrow a = 0 \wedge (b = 0 \Rightarrow c = 0) \vee a \neq 0 \wedge b^2 \geq 4ac$$

The first quantifier elimination algorithm for this theory was developed by Tarski [32],[1] who actually demonstrated completeness and quantifier elimination just for the theory of real-closed fields, which can be characterized as ordered fields where all non-negative elements have square roots ($\forall x.\ 0 \leq x \Rightarrow \exists y.\ x = y^2$) and all non-trivial polynomials of odd degree have a root. There are several interesting models of these axioms besides the reals (e.g. the algebraic reals, the computable reals, the hyperreals) yet Tarski's result shows that these different models satisfy exactly the same properties in the first-order language under consideration.

However, Tarski's procedure is complicated and inefficient. Many alternative decision methods were subsequently proposed; two that are significantly simpler were given by Seidenberg [30] and Cohen [8], while the CAD algorithm [9], apparently the first ever to be implemented, is significantly more efficient, though relatively complicated. Cohen's ideas were recast by Hörmander [17] into a relatively simple algorithm. However, even CAD has poor worst-case complexity (doubly exponential), and the Cohen-Hörmander algorithm is generally still slower. Thus, there has been limited progress on

---

[1] Tarski actually discovered the procedure in 1930, but it remained unpublished for many years afterwards.

K. Schneider and J. Brandt (Eds.): TPHOLs 2007, LNCS 4732, pp. 102–118, 2007.
© Springer-Verlag Berlin Heidelberg 2007

applying these algorithms to problems of interest. An interesting alternative, currently unimplemented, is described in [4].

If we turn to implementation in foundational theorem provers using basic logical operations instead of complicated code, the situation is bleaker still. The Cohen-Hörmander algorithm has been implemented in Coq [23] and HOL Light [24] in a way that generates formal proofs. However, producing formal proofs induces a further significant slowdown. In practice, more successful approaches to nonlinear arithmetic tend to use heuristic approaches that work well for simple common cases like $x > 0 \wedge y > 0 \Rightarrow xy > 0$ but are incomplete (or at least impractical) in general [18,33], though in some cases they go beyond the simple algebraic operations [1].

But many important problems in practice are purely universally quantified, i.e. are of the form $\forall x_1, \ldots, x_n . P[x_1, \ldots, x_n]$ where $P[x_1, \ldots, x_n]$ is an arbitrary Boolean combination of polynomial equations and inequalities. Typical (true) examples are $\forall x\ y . x \leq y \Rightarrow x^3 \leq y^3, \forall x . 0 \leq 1 \wedge x \leq 1 \Rightarrow x^2 \leq 1$ and $\forall a\ b\ c\ x . ax^2 + bx + c = 0 \Rightarrow b^2 \geq 4ac$. For this logically restrictive but practically important case, a completely different approach is possible based on *sums of squares*.

2 Positivity and Sums of Squares

We will be concerned with the set of multivariate polynomials $\mathbb{R}[x_1, \ldots, x_n]$ over the reals, and often more specifically the subset $\mathbb{Q}[x_1, \ldots, x_n]$ with rational coefficients. The cornerstone of what follows is the relationship between a polynomial's taking nonnegative values everywhere, a.k.a. being *positive semidefinite* (PSD):

$$\forall x_1, \ldots, x_n . p(x_1, \ldots, x_n) \geq 0$$

and the existence of a decomposition into a sum of squares (SOS) of other polynomials:

$$p(x_1, \ldots, x_n) = \sum_{i=0}^{k} s_i(x_1, \ldots, x_n)^2$$

Since any square is nonnegative, the existence of a sum-of-squares decomposition implies nonnegativity everywhere. The converse is not true without restrictions — for example the following [25] is everywhere strictly positive (geometric mean $\leq$ arithmetic mean, applied to $x^2 y^4$, $x^4 y^2$ and 1), but one can show by quite elementary considerations that it is not a sum of squares in $\mathbb{R}[x, y]$.

$$1 + x^4 y^2 + x^2 y^4 - 3x^2 y^2$$

On the other hand, the positive solution of Hilbert's 17th problem [3] implies that every PSD polynomial is the sum of squares of *rational* functions. For instance, we have:

$$1 + x^4 y^2 + x^2 y^4 - 3x^2 y^2 = \left(\frac{x^2 y(x^2+y^2-2)}{x^2+y^2}\right)^2 + \left(\frac{xy^2(x^2+y^2-2)}{x^2+y^2}\right)^2 + \left(\frac{xy(x^2+y^2-2)}{x^2+y^2}\right)^2 + \left(\frac{x^2-y^2}{x^2+y^2}\right)^2$$

We will consider in what follows a liberal notion of 'sum of squares' allowing $\sum a_i s_i(\overline{x})^2$ where the a_i are nonnegative rational numbers. This amounts to no real increase in generality since every nonnegative rational can be written as a sum of four rational squares [34]. And the reasoning that $SOS \Rightarrow PSD$ is almost equally straightforward.

Direct Proof of PSD from SOS

At its simplest, we might seek to prove that a single polynomial is PSD by finding a SOS decomposition. We have seen that this approach is in general not complete. Nevertheless, in practice it often works for problems of interest, e.g. the following [12]:

$$\forall w\, x\, y\, z.\ w^6 + 2z^2w^3 + x^4 + y^4 + z^4 + 2x^2w + 2x^2z+$$
$$3x^2 + w^2 + 2zw + z^2 + 2z + 2w + 1 \geq 0$$

via the sum-of-squares decomposition:

$$w^6 + 2z^2w^3 + x^4 + y^4 + z^4 + 2x^2w + 2x^2z+$$
$$3x^2 + w^2 + 2zw + z^2 + 2z + 2w + 1 =$$
$$(y^2)^2 + (x^2 + w + z + 1)^2 + x^2 + (w^3 + z^2)^2$$

Besides its theoretical incompleteness, finding a direct SOS expansion only works for nonnegativity of a single polynomial. However, this can be generalized somewhat by a change of variables. For example, instead of proving $\forall x.\ x \geq 0 \Rightarrow p(x) \geq 0$ we can prove the equivalent $\forall x.\ p(x^2) \geq 0$. More interesting is certifying nonnegativity over a general compact interval $[a, b]$:

$$\forall x.\ a \leq x \wedge x \leq b \Rightarrow p(x) \geq 0$$

We can likewise prove this equivalent to a simple nonnegativity assertion with a change of variable. Note first that

$$x(y) = \frac{a + by^2}{1 + y^2}$$

is a surjection from $\mathbb{R}$ to $[a, b)$ with right inverse

$$y(x) = \sqrt{\frac{x - a}{b - x}}$$

and so

$$(\forall x.\ a \leq x \wedge x < b \Rightarrow p(x) \geq 0) \Leftrightarrow (\forall y \in \mathbb{R}.\ p(\frac{a + by^2}{1 + y^2}) \geq 0)$$

Moreover, because polynomials are continuous, this is equivalent to the original claim $\forall x.\ a \leq x \wedge x \leq b \Rightarrow p(x) \geq 0$. We can turn the rational function claim into purely polynomial nonnegativity by multiplying through by $(1 + y^2)^{\partial(p)}$ where $\partial(p)$ is the degree of p, since this is guaranteed to cancel all denominators:

$$(\forall x.\ a \leq x \wedge x \leq b \Rightarrow p(x) \geq 0) \Leftrightarrow (\forall y.\ (1 + y^2)^{\partial(p)} p(\frac{a + by^2}{1 + y^2}) \geq 0)$$

However, we will now consider a more general and theoretically complete approach to verifying universal formulas using SOS.

3   Important Cases of Hilbert's Theorem

A classic result due to Hilbert [16] shows that there are only a few special classes of polynomials where PSD and SOS are equivalent. We just note two of them.

Univariate Polynomials

Every PSD *univariate* polynomial is a sum of just two real squares. For the proof, observe that complex roots always occur in conjugate pairs, and any real roots must have even multiplicity, otherwise the polynomial would cross the x-axis instead of just touching it. Thus, if the roots are $a_k \pm ib_k$, we can imagine writing the polynomial as:

$$
\begin{aligned}
p(x) &= [(x - [a_1 + ib_1])(x - [a_2 + ib_2]) \cdots (x - [a_m + ib_m])] \cdot \\
&\quad [(x - [a_1 - ib_1])(x - [a_2 - ib_2]) \cdots (x - [a_m - ib_m])] \\
&= (q(x) + ir(x))(q(x) - ir(x)) \\
&= q(x)^2 + r(x)^2
\end{aligned}
$$

However, to expand a polynomial with *rational* coefficients as a sum of squares of *rational* polynomials, a more sophisticated proof is needed. For example Landau [21], building on a theorem of Hilbert, shows that every PSD univariate polynomial is the sum of 8 squares. This was subsequently sharpened by Pourchet [27] to show that 5 squares suffice, and indeed that 5 is the best possible in general. However, even the more constructive proofs of this and related results [5] do not seem to be very practical, and we will return later in this paper to finding such expansions in practice.

Quadratic Forms

Every PSD quadratic form, in any number of variables, is a sum of squares. (A *form* is a polynomial where all monomials have the same [multi-]degree, and in a quadratic form that degree is 2. So for example x^2, wz and xy are permissible monomials in a quadratic form but not 1, x or y^5.) The proof is a straightforward elaboration of the elementary technique of "completing the square" [10]. We will as usual assume a standard representation of a quadratic form

$$
f(x_1, \ldots, x_n) = \sum_{i=1}^{n} \sum_{j=1}^{n} a_{ij} x_i x_j
$$

where $a_{ij} = a_{ji}$. We are at liberty to make this symmetry assumption, for given any representation we can always choose another symmetric one by setting $a'_{ij} = a'_{ji} = (a_{ij} + a_{ji})/2$.

Theorem 1. *Given a quadratic form* $f(x_1, \ldots, x_n) = \sum_{i=1}^{n} \sum_{j=1}^{n} a_{ij} x_i x_j$ *in variables* $x_1, \ldots, x_n$ *with the coefficients* a_{ij} *rational and* $a_{ij} = a_{ji}$, *we can construct either a decomposition:*

$$
f(x_1, \ldots, x_n) = \sum_{i=1}^{n} b_i g_i(x_1, \ldots, x_n)^2
$$

where the b_i are nonnegative rational numbers and the $g_i(x_1, \ldots, x_n)$ are linear functions with rational coefficients, or particular rational numbers $u_1, \ldots, u_n$ such that $f(u_1, \ldots, u_n) < 0$.

Proof. By induction on the number of variables. If the form is zero, then it trivially has an empty SOS decomposition. Otherwise, pick the first variable x_1 (the order is unimportant), and separate the monomials into those involving x_1 and those not:

$$f(x_1, \ldots, x_n) = (a_{11}x_1^2 + \sum_{i=2}^{n} 2a_{1i}x_1x_i) + g(x_2, \ldots, x_n)$$

If $a_{11} = 0$, then there are two cases to consider. If all the a_{1i} are zero, then we effectively have a form in $n-1$ variables and so the result holds by induction; in the case of a witness of non-positive-semidefiniteness, we can assign u_1 arbitrarily. Otherwise, if any $a_{1i} \neq 0$, the form is not positive semidefinite and our witness is $u_1 = a_{ii}/2 + 1$, $u_i = -a_{1i}$ and all other $u_j = 0$; we then have $f(u_1, \ldots, u_n) = -2a_{1i}^2 < 0$ as required.

Now if $a_{11} < 0$, then again the form is not PSD, and a suitable witness is simply $u_1 = 1$ and all other $u_j = 0$, whence all monomials but $a_{11}x_1^2$ are zero and that one is negative. The more interesting case is when $a_{11} > 0$, and here we 'complete the square'. We have:

$$f(x_1, \ldots, x_n) = a_{11}(x_1 + \sum_{i=2}^{n}(a_{1i}/a_{11})x_i)^2 + \\ (g(x_2, \ldots, x_n) - \sum_{j=2}^{n}\sum_{k=2}^{n}(a_{1j}a_{1k}/a_{11})x_jx_k)$$

The second term on the right is a quadratic form in variables $x_2, \ldots, x_n$, so by the inductive hypothesis we can either find a SOS expansion or a witness of non-positive-definiteness. In the former case, we just include $a_{11}(x_1 + \sum_{i=2}^{n}(a_{1i}/a_{11})x_i)^2$ and obtain a SOS decomposition for the entire form. In the latter case, we take the witness $u_2, \ldots, u_n$ and augment it by choosing $u_1 = -\sum_{i=2}^{n}(a_{1i}/a_{11})u_i$, which makes the term $a_{11}(x_1 + \sum_{i=2}^{n}(a_{1i}/a_{11})x_i)^2$ vanish and hence gives a non-PSD witness for the whole form. QED

For example, let us apply the method to the form $6x^2 + 49y^2 + 51z^2 - 82yz + 20zx - 4xy$, with the variables in the obvious order x, y, z. We obtain a SOS decomposition as follows:

$$6x^2 + 49y^2 + 51z^2 - 82yz + 20zx - 4xy$$

$$= 6\left(x^2 - \frac{2}{3}xy + \frac{10}{3}xz\right) + (49y^2 + 51z^2 - 82yz)$$

$$= 6\left(x^2 - \frac{1}{3}y + \frac{5}{3}z\right)^2 + (49y^2 + 51z^2 - 82yz) - 6\left(-\frac{1}{3}y + \frac{5}{3}z\right)^2$$

$$= 6\left(x^2 - \frac{1}{3}y + \frac{5}{3}z\right)^2 + \left(\frac{145}{3}y^2 - \frac{226}{3}yz + \frac{78}{3}z^2\right)$$

$$= 6\left(x^2 - \frac{1}{3}y + \frac{5}{3}z\right)^2 + \frac{145}{3}\left(y^2 - \frac{226}{145}yz\right) + \frac{103}{3}z^2$$

$$= 6\left(x^2 - \frac{1}{3}y + \frac{5}{3}z\right)^2 + \frac{145}{3}\left(y - \frac{113}{145}z\right)^2 + \frac{103}{3}z^2 - \frac{12769}{435}z^2$$

$$= 6\left(x^2 - \frac{1}{3}y + \frac{5}{3}z\right)^2 + \frac{145}{3}\left(y - \frac{113}{145}z\right)^2 + \frac{722}{145}z^2$$

4 Quadratic Forms and Matrices

We can establish a correspondence between quadratic forms and matrices by writing a quadratic form in variables $x_1, \ldots, x_n$ as a vector-matrix-vector product with a vector of variables:

$$\overline{x}^T A \overline{x} = \sum_{i=1}^{n} x_i \sum_{j=1}^{n} A_{ij}x_j = \sum_{1 \leq i,j \leq n} A_{ij}x_i x_j$$

If we restrict ourselves to symmetric matrices A, then the matrix representation is unique, and the matrix elements correspond exactly to the coefficients in the standard formulation above. (In an actual implementation we may choose to use an appropriately modified upper or lower triangular matrix for efficiency reasons.)

Positive Semidefinite Matrices

Quite generally, a symmetric[2] matrix A is said to be *positive semidefinite* iff $\overline{x}^T A \overline{x} \geq 0$ for all vectors $\overline{x}$ — in other words, precisely if the associated quadratic form is positive semidefinite. Two other equivalent characterizations are:

- There is a factorization $A = L^T L$ where L is a triangular matrix and the T signifies transposition.
- All eigenvalues of A are non-negative (they are necessarily real because A is symmetric)

A proof of the former is straightforward by recasting the "completing the square" algorithm (theorem 1) in matrix terms [31]. More precisely, a factorization of the form $A = L^T L$ is obtained by Choleski decomposition. A direct translation of the 'completing the square' algorithm gives a decomposition $A = LDL^T$ where L, D and L^T are respectively lower-triangular, diagonal and upper-triangular. This has some advantages for symbolic applications because it involves only rational operations, whereas Choleski decomposition requires square roots.

5 The Universal Fragment Via SOS

The Positivstellensatz

The Artin-Schreier theorem [19] implies that every ordered integral domain can be embedded in a real-closed field called its real closure. For this reason, a *universal* formula must hold in all real-closed fields (and hence, by Tarski's completeness result, in $\mathbb{R}$) iff it holds in all ordered integral domains:

---

[2] Or Hermitian if we consider the complex case, which we will not do here.

- If it holds in all ordered integral domains, it holds in all real-closed fields, since a real-closed field is a kind of ordered integral domain.
- If it holds in all real-closed fields, it holds in the real closure of any ordered integral domain, and therefore, since quantifiers are all universal, in the substructure corresponding to that integral domain.

This already means that a valid formula can in principle be proved without using the special axioms about square roots and roots of odd-degree polynomials, based only on the axioms for an ordered integral domain. This can be put in a still sharper form. First it is instructive to look at the case of the complex numbers, where the classic *Hilbert Nullstellesatz* holds:

Theorem 2. *The polynomial equations $p_1(\overline{x}) = 0, \ldots, p_n(\overline{x}) = 0$ have no common solution in $\mathbb{C}$ iff 1 is in the ideal generated by $p_1, \ldots, p_n$, which we write as $1 \in Id \langle p_1, \ldots, p_n \rangle$.*

More explicitly, this means that the universally quantified formula $\forall \overline{x}. \, p_1(\overline{x}) = 0 \wedge \cdots p_n(\overline{x}) = 0 \Rightarrow \bot$ holds iff there are 'cofactor' polynomials $q_1(\overline{x}), \ldots, q_n(\overline{x})$ such that the following is a polynomial identity:

$$p_1(\overline{x}) \cdot q_1(\overline{x}) + \cdots + p_n(\overline{x}) \cdot q_n(\overline{x}) = 1$$

The analogous property fails over $\mathbb{R}$; for example $x^2 + 1 = 0$ alone has no solution yet 1 is not a multiple of $x^2 + 1$ (considering them as polynomials). However, in the analogous Real Nullstellensatz, sums of squares play a central role:

Theorem 3. *The polynomial equations $p_1(\overline{x}) = 0, \ldots, p_n(\overline{x}) = 0$ have no common solution in $\mathbb{R}$ iff there are polynomials $s_1(\overline{x}), \ldots, s_k(\overline{x})$ such that $s_1(\overline{x})^2 + \cdots + s_k(\overline{x})^2 + 1 \in Id \langle p_1, \ldots, p_n \rangle$.*

This can be further generalized to so-called 'Positivstellensatz' results on the inconsistency of a set of equations, inequations and inequalities.[3] Unfortunately these become a bit more intricate to state. The particular version we rely on in our implementation, following [26], can be stated as follows:

Theorem 4. *The polynomial formulas $p_1(\overline{x}) = 0, \ldots, p_n(\overline{x}) = 0, q_1(\overline{x}) \geq 0, \ldots, q_m(\overline{x}) \geq 0, r_1(\overline{x}) \neq 0, \ldots, r_p(\overline{x}) \neq 0$ are impossible in $\mathbb{R}$ iff there are polynomials P, Q, R such that $P + Q + R^2 = 0$ where $P \in Id \langle p_1, \ldots, p_n \rangle$, R is a product of powers of the r_i (we can if desired assume it's of the form $\prod_{i=1}^{p} r_i^k$) and Q is in the cone generated by the q_i, i.e. the smallest set of polynomials containing all q_i, all squares of arbitrary polynomials and closed under addition and multiplication.*

It's perhaps easier to grasp a simple example. Consider proving the universal half of the quadratic root criterion

$$\forall a \, b \, c \, x. \, ax^2 + bx + c = 0 \Rightarrow b^2 - 4ac \geq 0$$

---

[3] In principle the simple Nullstellensatz suffices to prove unsatisfiability of any unsatisfiable conjunction of atomic formulas, since in $\mathbb{R}$ we have equivalences such as $s \leq t \Leftrightarrow \exists x. \, t = s + x^2$, $s < t \Leftrightarrow \exists x. \, (t - s)x^2 = 1$ and $s \neq t \Leftrightarrow \exists x. \, (t - s)x = 1$. Indeed we could then combine a conjunction of equations into a single equation using $s = 0 \wedge t = 0 \Leftrightarrow s^2 + t^2 = 0$. However, using a general Positivstellensatz tends to be more efficient.

by showing the inconsistency of the formulas $ax^2 + bx + c = 0$ and $4ac - b^2 > 0$. We have the following polynomial identity of the form whose existence is guaranteed by the Positivstellensatz:

$$(4ac - b^2) + (2ax + b)^2 + (-4a)(ax^2 + bx + c) = 0$$

Given such a "certificate" (i.e. the additional polynomials necessary in such an equation), it's easy to verify the required result by elementary inequality reasoning: $(2ax + b)^2$ is a square and hence nonnegative, $(-4a)(ax^2 + bx + c)$ is zero since by hypothesis $ax^2 + bx + c = 0$, so $b^2 - 4ac$ must be nonnegative for the equation to hold.

Finding SOS Decompositions by Semidefinite Programming

Although the Nullstellensatz/Positivstellensatz assures us that suitable SOS certificates of infeasibility exist, the usual proofs of these results are not constructive. Lombardi [22] has proved a constructive form, showing how a refutation using Hörmander's procedure can be used to systematically construct a Nullstellensatz certificate. However, given that we know that none of the sophisticated real-closed field axioms are actually needed, we might seek a more direct approach.

Parrilo [26] pioneered the approach of using *semidefinite programming* to find SOS decompositions. Semidefinite programming is the problem of finding feasible values $u_1, \ldots, u_m$ (or more generally, maximizing some linear combination of the u_i) to make a matrix linearly parametrized by those values PSD, subject to a set of linear equational constraints on the u_i. This is a convex optimization problem, and so in principle we know it can be solved to a given accuracy in polynomial time, e.g. on the basis of the ellipsoid algorithm [2,11].[4] In practice, there are powerful semidefinite programming tools, e.g. based on primal-dual interior point algorithms or the 'spectral bundle method'. Our experiments have mostly used the system CSDP [6], which we have found to be robust and efficient.[5]

The basic idea of this reduction is to introduce new variables for the possible monomials that could appear in the squares. For example [26] to express $2x^4 + 2x^3y - x^2y^2 + 5y^4$ as a SOS, no monomials of degree > 2 can appear in the squares, since their squares would then remain uncancelled in the SOS form. With a little more care one can deduce that only the following monomials, for which we introduce the new variables z_i, need be considered:

$$z_1 = x^2, \ z_2 = y^2, \ z_3 = xy$$

Now we write the original polynomial as a quadratic form in the z_i:

$$\begin{bmatrix} z_1 \\ z_2 \\ z_3 \end{bmatrix}^T \begin{bmatrix} q_{11} & q_{12} & q_{13} \\ q_{12} & q_{22} & q_{23} \\ q_{13} & q_{23} & q_{33} \end{bmatrix} \begin{bmatrix} z_1 \\ z_2 \\ z_3 \end{bmatrix}$$

---

[4] As [29] notes, convexity rather than linearity is the fundamental property that makes optimization relatively tractable. Indeed, the first polynomial-time algorithm for linear programming [20] was based on the ellipsoid algorithm for general convex optimization, together with an argument about about the accuracy bound needed.

[5] See also the CSDP Web page https://projects.coin-or.org/Csdp/.

Comparing coefficients in the original coefficient, we obtain linear constraints on the q_{ij}:

$$q_{11} = 2$$
$$q_{22} = 5$$
$$q_{33} + 2q_{12} = -1$$
$$2q_{13} = 2$$
$$2q_{23} = 0$$

By introducing the new variables, we have returned to the case of quadratic forms, where SOS and PSD are the same. Thus, if we find q_{ij} for which the matrix is PSD, we can directly read off a sum of squares using the 'completing the square' algorithm. The price we pay is that only solutions satisfying the linear constraints above will yield an SOS expansion for the original polynomial; for our example $q_{33} = 5$ and $q_{12} = -3$ give such a solution, from which a SOS decomposition can be read off. SDP solvers can solve exactly this problem.

When just searching for a direct SOS decomposition as in the example above, we were able to place a bound on the monomials we need to consider. However, for general Positivstellensatz certificates, the only bounds known are somewhat impractical. Instead of using these, we impose relatively small limits on the degrees of the polynomials considered (in the squares and in the ideal cofactors) as well as the powers used for the product of inequations. For any particular bound, the problem reduces to semi-definite programming, and we can keep increasing the bound until it succeeds, at least in principle.

6   Implementation in HOL and Experience

We have integrated this algorithm into HOL Light, and it is freely available in the latest version (2.20) as the file `Examples/sos.ml`.

How It Works

We rely on all the existing machinery in HOL Light for eliminating various auxiliary concepts like the absolute value function, max and min, and reducing the problem to a finite set of subproblems that involve just refuting a conjunction of equations, strict and nonstrict inequalities. All this is currently used in the simple linear prover of HOL Light, and it was designed so that any other core equation/inequality refuter can be plugged in. So now the task is just to refute a conjunction of the form:

$$\bigwedge_i p_i(\overline{x}) = 0 \land \bigwedge_j q_j(\overline{x}) \geq 0 \land \bigwedge_k r_k(\overline{x}) > 0$$

We do this by systematically searching for certificates of the form guaranteed to exist by the Positivstellensatz. We use iterative deepening, so that at stage n we consider, roughly speaking, polynomials of degree n in the certificate. Symbolically, using the underlying programming language OCaml in which HOL Light is implemented, we invent parametrized polynomials for the certificate and solve the constraints that result from comparing coefficients, to obtain a semidefinite programming problem. The semidefinite programming problem is printed to a file and we call a semidefinite programming package to solve it.

Then comes a rather tricky aspect. The vector returned by the SDP solver is of floating-point numbers, and we need to translate them to rational numbers in HOL. Unfortunately if we map them to the exact rational they denote, we very often find that the resulting matrix is *not* quite PSD, because of the influence of rounding errors (e.g. 0.33333333333 instead of exactly $1/3$). So instead we postulate that the "exact" solutions probably involve rational numbers with moderate coefficients, and try rounding all the values based on common denominators $1, 2, 3, \ldots$. (Once we reach 32 we start to go up by a multiple of 2 each time.) For each attempt we test, using exact rational arithmetic in OCaml, whether the resulting matrix is PSD, using the algorithm from theorem 1. As soon as we find a case where it is, we extract the SOS decomposition and prove the resulting identity in HOL.

Generally speaking this seems to work quite well. It is interesting to note that although we only seek feasible solutions, we tend to do better when rounding if we try to optimize something (arbitrarily, we minimize the sum of the diagonal elements of the matrix). So it seems that extremal solutions tend to involve nicer rational numbers than arbitrary points. We originally attempted to find good 'simple' rational approximants to the coefficients independently, but the approach of picking a single common denominator seems to work better.

Examples

The primary interface is REAL_SOS, which attempts to prove a purely universal formula over the reals. Here is a typical user invocation:

```
# REAL_SOS
  `a1 >= &0 /\ a2 >= &0 /\
  (a1 * a1 + a2 * a2 = b1 * b1 + b2 * b2 + &2) /\
  (a1 * b1 + a2 * b2 = &0)
  ==> a1 * a2 - b1 * b2 >= &0`;;
```

and the output from HOL Light:

```
Searching with depth limit 0
Searching with depth limit 1
Searching with depth limit 2
Searching with depth limit 3
Searching with depth limit 4
Translating proof certificate to HOL
val it : thm =
  |- a1 >= &0 /\
     a2 >= &0 /\
     a1 * a1 + a2 * a2 = b1 * b1 + b2 * b2 + &2 /\
     a1 * b1 + a2 * b2 = &0
     ==> a1 * a2 - b1 * b2 >= &0
```

The informative messages indicate the iterative deepening of the bounds imposed; at each stage the semidefinite programming problem is passed to CSDP for solution. At a bound of 4 the underlying semidefinite programming problem involves a 38×38 matrix (in 8 block diagonal portions, which SDP solvers can exploit) parametrized by 143 variables. This problem is solved and HOL Light succeeds in rounding the output vector to a certificate and hence proving the original claim. The entire sequence of events takes around one second. Numerous similar instances of classic elementary inequalities can be proved efficiently, including almost all the examples in [12] and the following:

```
# REAL_SOS
  '&0 <= x /\ &0 <= y
  ==> x * y * (x + y) pow 2 <= (x pow 2 + y pow 2) pow 2';;
```

On top of REAL_SOS, we have also implemented analogous functions for $\mathbb{Z}$ and $\mathbb{N}$, which do some elimination of division and modulus followed by simple-minded and incomplete discretization (e.g. translating hypotheses of the form $x < y$ to $x \leq y - 1$) then call the real version. This is enough to solve a few not entirely trivial properties of truncating division on $\mathbb{N}$, e.g.

```
# SOS_RULE
  '!a b c d. ~(b = 0) /\ b * c < (a + 1) * d ==> c DIV d <= a DIV b';;
```

and

```
# SOS_RULE '0 < m /\ m < n  ==>  ((m * ((n * x) DIV m + 1)) DIV n = x)';;
```

Problems

This approach to verifying nonlinear inequalities, and more generally to nonlinear optimization, has much to recommend it on general grounds [26]. But in the context of a foundational theorem prover it is especially appealing, because the "difficult" part, finding the certificates, can be done using highly optimized, unverified external programs. The theorem prover merely needs to *verify* the certificate [15]. We have found it fast and powerful enough to prove many lemmas that come up in practice as part of larger proofs. Quite recently we were happy to use it for the otherwise slightly tedious lemmas $0 \leq a \wedge 0 \leq b \wedge 0 \leq c \wedge c(2a + b)^3/27 \leq x \Rightarrow ca^2b \leq x$ (1.25 seconds) and $-1 \leq t \wedge t \leq 1 \Rightarrow 0 \leq 1 + r^2 - 2rt$ (0.06 seconds). However, we have encountered two persistent problems that suggest necessary improvements.

First, sometimes our naive rounding procedure is not adequate, and even though the SDP solver seems to solve the semidefinite program fairly accurately, none of the roundings we try results in a PSD matrix. In this case, we end up in an infinite loop, exploring more complex certificates without any benefit. It would certainly be desirable to have a more intelligent approach to rounding, but at present we are not sure what the best approach is. Indeed, in principle the exact floating-point result can be platform-dependent, since the involved numerical algorithms underlying SDP have often been optimized in slightly different ways (e.g. a different order of operations when multiplying matrices).

Second, the treatment of strict inequalities in our Positivstellensatz (considering $p > 0$ as $p \geq 0$ and $p \neq 0$) means that the style of exploration of the search space depends critically on whether the inequalities are strict or non-strict. This can sometimes have tiresome consequences. For example the following example (which I got from Russell O'Connor) works quite quickly:

```
# REAL_SOS
  `a * a + a * b - b * b >= &0 /\
  &2 * a + b >= &0 /\
  c * c + c * d - d * d <= &0 /\
  d >= &0
  ==> a * d + c * b + b * d >= &0`;;
```

If we replace a few non-strict ($\geq$) inequalities in the hypotheses by strict ones ($>$), we might expect it to become *easier*. Yet because of the difference in treatment of strict inequalities, the problem is only solved at a much higher depth, and moreover at that point the rounding problem has appeared and means that we do not solve it at all!

7 Optimizing the Univariate Case

Most floating-point transcendental function implementations ultimately rely on a polynomial approximation over an interval, and we would like to verify an error bound theorem of the form $\forall x. \, a \leq x \leq b \Rightarrow |f(x) - p(x)| \leq \epsilon$ relating the function f to its polynomial approximation. By choosing a very accurate Taylor series expansion $t(x)$, one can reduce the problem to bounding a polynomial $\forall x. a \leq x \leq b \Rightarrow |t(x) - p(x)| \leq \epsilon$. This is a problem that has sometimes preoccupied the present author for some time, and formally verified solutions can be quite lengthy to compute [13,14]. The idea of proving such bounds using SOS techniques, even a direct SOS decomposition after change of variables, is very attractive.

Unfortunately, the numerical difficulties mentioned above are a serious issue here, and we have not had much success with SOS methods except on artificially simple examples. It is not hard to understand why these cases are numerically difficult. The coefficients of $p(x)$ are carefully chosen to minimize the maximum error over the interval, and are not simple rational numbers. Moreover, by design, the error bounds tend to be small relative to the coefficients. (A simple and idealized form of the same phenomenon is that the Chebyshev polynomials $T_n(x)$ are bounded by 1 over the interval $[-1, 1]$ even though their leading coefficient is 2^n.)

We therefore consider a different approach, where we adapt the simple proof that every univariate PSD polynomial is a sum of two real squares to find exact rational decompositions. This has not yet been completely automated and integrated into HOL Light, but we have a simple script that runs in PARI/GP[6] and appears to be promising. (We rely on the excellent arbitrary-precision complex root finder in PARI/GP, which implements a variant of an algorithm due to Schönhage.) We will explain the algorithm in general, as well as tracing a specific example:

$$p(x) = ((x - 1)^8 + 2(x - 2)^8 + (x - 3)^8 - 2)/4$$
$$= x^8 - 16x^7 + 126x^6 - 616x^5 + 1995x^4 - 4312x^3 + 6006x^2 - 4888x + 1768$$

---

[6] http://pari.math.u-bordeaux.fr/

Elimination of Repeated Roots

If a polynomial is ≥ 0 everywhere, then real roots must occur with even multiplicity. Therefore, we start out as in squarefree decomposition by taking $d = \gcd(p, p')$ and writing $p = d^2 q$. The remaining polynomial q must have no real roots, and hence be strictly > 0 everywhere. If we can write q as a SOS, we can just multiply inside each square by d and get a SOS for p. In our running example, this factors out one repeated root $x = 2$:

$$p = x^8 - 16x^7 + 126x^6 - 616x^5 + 1995x^4 - 4312x^3 + 6006x^2 - 4888x + 1768$$
$$p' = 8x^7 - 112x^6 + 756x^5 - 3080x^4 + 7980x^3 - 12936x^2 + 12012x - 4888$$
$$d = x - 2$$
$$q = x^6 - 12x^5 + 74x^4 - 272x^3 + 611x^2 - 780x + 442$$

Note that this step requires only rational operations and does not introduce any inaccuracy.

Perturbation

Since all polynomials of odd degree have a real root, the degree of the original p and our polynomial q must be even, say $\partial(q) = n = 2m$. Since it is *strictly* positive, there must be an $\epsilon > 0$ such that the perturbed polynomial

$$q - \epsilon(1 + x^2 + ... + x^{2m})$$

is also (strictly) positive. To find such an ϵ we just need to test if a polynomial has real roots, which we can easily do in PARI/GP; we can then search for a suitable ϵ by choosing a convenient starting value and repeatedly dividing by 2 until our goal is reached; we actually divide by 2 again to leave a little margin of safety. (Of course, there are more efficient ways of doing this.) In this case we get $\epsilon = 1/32$ and the perturbed polynomial becomes:

$$31/32x^6 - 12x^5 + 2367/32x^4 - 272x^3 + 19551/32x^2 - 780x + 14143/32$$

We have been assuming that the initial polynomial *is* indeed PSD, but if it is not, that fact will be detected at this stage by checking the $\epsilon = 0$ case.

Approximate SOS of Perturbed Polynomial

We now use the basic 'sum of two real squares' idea to obtain an approximate SOS decomposition of the perturbed polynomial r, just by using approximations of the roots, close enough to make the final step below work correctly. Now we have $r = ls^2 + lt^2 + u$ where l is the leading coefficient of r, such that the remainder u is relatively small. Using our PARI/GP script on the running example we obtain for this remainder:

$$u = 7/65536x^5 - 522851/268435456x^4 + 1527705/268435456x^3 - \\ 655717/536870912x^2 - 14239/2097152x + 1913153/536870912$$

Absorption of Remainder Term

We now have $q = ls^2 + lt^2 + \epsilon(1 + x^2 + \dots + x^{2m}) + u$, so it will suffice to express $\epsilon(1 + x^2 + \dots + x^{2m}) + u$ as a sum of squares. Note that the degree of u is $< 2m$ by construction (though the procedure to be outlined would work with minor variations even if it were exactly $2m$). Let us say $u = a_0 + a_1x + \dots + a_{2m-1}x^{2m-1}$. Note that

$$x = (x + 1/2)^2 - (x^2 + 1/4) \\ -x = (x - 1/2)^2 - (x^2 + 1/4)$$

and so for any $c \geq 0$:

$$cx^{2k+1} = c(x^{k+1} + 1/2x^k)^2 - c(x^{2k+2} + 1/4x^{2k}) \\ -cx^{2k+1} = c(x^{k+1} - 1/2x^k)^2 - c(x^{2k+2} + 1/4x^{2k})$$

Consequently we can rewrite the odd-degree terms of u as

$$a_{2k+1}x^{2k+1} = |a_{2k+1}|(x^{k+1} + \text{sgn}(a_{2k+1})/2x^k)^2 - |a_{2k+1}|(x^{2k+2} + 1/4x^{2k})$$

and so:

$$\epsilon(1 + x^2 + \dots + x^{2m}) + u = \sum_{k=0}^{m-1} |a_{2k+1}|(x^{k+1} + \text{sgn}(a_{2k+1})/2x^k)^2 + \\ \sum_{k=0}^{m}(\epsilon + a_{2k} - |a_{2k-1}| - |a_{2k+1}|/4)x^{2k}$$

where by convention $a_{-1} = a_{2m+1} = 0$. This already gives us the required SOS representation, provided each $\epsilon + a_{2k} - |a_{2k-1}| - |a_{2k+1}|/4 \geq 0$, and we can ensure this by computing the approximate SOS sufficiently accurately. In the running example, our overall expression is

$$31/32(x^3 - 25369/4096x^2 + 313/64x + 32207/4096)^2 + \\ 31/32(21757/4096x^2 - 90963/4096x + 1271/64)^2 + \\ 14239/2097152(x - 1/2)^2 + \\ 1527705/268435456(x^2 + 1/2x)^2 + \\ 7/65536(x^3 + 1/2x^2)^2 + \\ 2041/65536x^6 + \\ 1582721/67108864x^4 + \\ 23424925/1073741824x^2 + \\ 17779073/536870912$$

and we can recover a SOS decomposition for the original polynomial by incorporating the additional factor $x - 2$ into each square:

$$31/32(x^4 - 33561/4096x^3 + 35385/2048x^2 - 7857/4096x - 32207/2048)^2 +$$
$$31/32(21757/4096x^3 - 134477/4096x^2 + 131635/2048x - 1271/32)^2 +$$
$$14239/2097152(x^2 - 5/2x + 1)^2 +$$
$$1527705/268435456(x^3 - 3/2x^2 - x)^2 +$$
$$7/65536(x^4 - 3/2x^3 - x^2)^2 +$$
$$2041/65536(x^4 - 2x^3)^2 +$$
$$1582721/67108864(x^3 - 2x^2)^2 +$$
$$23424925/1073741824(x^2 - 2x)^2 +$$
$$17779073/536870912(x - 2)^2$$

8   Conclusions and Related Work

Our work so far shows that SOS is a very promising approach to this class of problem. Despite the implementation in a very foundational theorem-prover, simple problems are solved fast enough to be a real boon in practice. However, we have also noted a couple of difficulties. The rounding problem seems to be the most pressing. It could be avoided given an arbitrary-precision package for semidefinite programming. However, replacing ordinary floating-point arithmetic in a semidefinite programming engine with something like MPFR[7] would be highly non-trivial even for their designers, since they are complex programs depending on an infrastructure of linear algebra packages. Lacking a high-precision SDP solver, we need to come up with a more 'intelligent' approach to rounding, but this seems non-trivial. As an answer to our problems with strict inequalities, there are numerous possibilities, such as directly eliminating strict inequalities in terms of equations or using a different form of Positivstellensatz, even a radically different one such as Schmüdgen's [28]. We have already experimented with other valuable optimizations, e.g. exploiting symmetry and using Gröbner bases to handle equations, and these should be pursued and properly integrated into the mainstream version.

Acknowledgements

I want to thank Henri Lombardi for first taking the time to explain some of the basic theory of the Real Nullstellensatz to me, so setting me off on a long voyage of discovery. The debt to Pablo Parrilo is clear: a large part of this work is just an implementation of his key ideas. The ideas for optimizing the univariate case and its implementation in PARI/GP were worked out when I was a visitor in the Arenaire group at the ENS in Lyon. I am grateful to many people there for stimulating discussions, and in particular to Christoph Lauter for help with German translation and for some additional examples. I also benefited from the discussion at CMU when I presented SOS at a seminar organized by Jeremy Avigad and Ed Clarke. Laurent Théry, besides porting some of the work

---

[7] http://www.mpfr.org/

to Coq, persuaded me that I should write things up for publication. I'm also grateful to the anonymous referees for their constructive suggestions and for catching several errors.

References

1. Akbarpour, B., Paulson, L.C.: Towards automatic proofs of inequalities involving elementary functions. In: Cook, B., Sebastiani, R. (eds.) Proceedings of PDPAR 2006: Pragmatics of Decision Procedures in Automated Reasoning, pp. 27–37 (2006)
2. Akgül, M.: Topics in relaxation and ellipsoidal methods. Research notes in mathematics, vol. 97. Pitman (1984)
3. Artin, E.: Über die Zerlegung definiter Funktionen in Quadrate. Hamburg Abhandlung 5, 100–115 (1927)
4. Avigad, J., Friedman, H.: Combining decision procedures for the reals. Logical Methods in Computer Science (to appear), available online at http://arxiv.org/abs/cs.LO/0601134
5. Basu, S.: A constructive algorithm for 2-D spectral factorization with rational spectral factors. IEEE Transactions on Circuits and Systems–I: Fundamental Theory and Applications 47, 1309–1318 (2000)
6. Borchers, B.: CSDP: A C library for semidefinite programming. Optimization Methods and Software 11, 613–623 (1999)
7. Caviness, B.F., Johnson, J.R. (eds.): Quantifier Elimination and Cylindrical Algebraic Decomposition. Texts and monographs in symbolic computation. Springer, Heidelberg (1998)
8. Cohen, P.J.: Decision procedures for real and p-adic fields. Communications in Pure and Applied Mathematics 22, 131–151 (1969)
9. Collins, G.E.: Quantifier elimination for real closed fields by cylindrical algebraic decomposition. In: Brakhage, H. (ed.) Automata Theory and Formal Languages. LNCS, vol. 33, pp. 134–183. Springer, Heidelberg (1975)
10. Ferrar, W.L.: Algebra: a text-book of determinants, matrices, and algebraic forms, 2nd edn. Oxford University Press, Oxford (1957)
11. Grotschel, M., Lovsz, L., Schrijver, A.: Geometric algorithms and combinatorial optimization. Springer, Heidelberg (1993)
12. Guangxing, Z., Xiaoning, Z.: An effective decision method for semidefinite polynomials. Journal of Symbolic Computation 37, 83–99 (2004)
13. Harrison, J.: Verifying the accuracy of polynomial approximations in HOL. In: Gunter, E.L., Felty, A.P. (eds.) TPHOLs 1997. LNCS, vol. 1275, pp. 137–152. Springer, Heidelberg (1997)
14. Harrison, J.: Formal verification of floating point trigonometric functions. In: Johnson, S.D., Hunt Jr., W.A. (eds.) FMCAD 2000. LNCS, vol. 1954, pp. 217–233. Springer, Heidelberg (2000)
15. Harrison, J., Théry, L.: A sceptic's approach to combining HOL and Maple. Journal of Automated Reasoning 21, 279–294 (1998)
16. Hilbert, D.: Über die Darstellung definiter Formen als Summe von Formenquadraten. Mathematische Annalen 32, 342–350 (1888)
17. Hörmander, L. (ed.): The Analysis of Linear Partial Differential Operators II. Grundlehren der mathematischen Wissenschaften, vol. 257. Springer, Heidelberg (1983)
18. Hunt, W.A., Krug, R.B., Moore, J.: Linear and nonlinear arithmetic in ACL2. In: Geist, D., Tronci, E. (eds.) CHARME 2003. LNCS, vol. 2860, pp. 319–333. Springer, Heidelberg (2003)

19. Jacobson, N.: Basic Algebra II, 2nd edn. W. H. Freeman, New York (1989)
20. Khachian, L.G.: A polynomial algorithm in linear programming. Soviet Mathematics Doklady 20, 191–194 (1979)
21. Landau, E.: Über die Darstellung definiter Funktionen durch Quadrate. Mathematischen Annalen 62, 272–285 (1906)
22. Lombardi, H.: Effective real nullstellensatz and variants. In: Mora, T., Traverso, C. (eds.) Proceedings of the MEGA-90 Symposium on Effective Methods in Algebraic Geometry, Castiglioncello, Livorno, Italy. Progress in Mathematics, vol. 94, pp. 263–288. Birkhäuser Basel (1990)
23. Mahboubi, A., Pottier, L.: Elimination des quantificateurs sur les réels en Coq. In: Journées Francophones des Langages Applicatifs (JFLA) (2002), available on the Web from   `http://pauillac.inria.fr/jfla/2002/actes/index.html08-mahboubi.ps`
24. McLaughlin, S., Harrison, J.: A proof-producing decision procedure for real arithmetic. In: Nieuwenhuis, R. (ed.) Automated Deduction – CADE-20. LNCS (LNAI), vol. 3632, pp. 295–314. Springer, Heidelberg (2005)
25. Motzkin, T.S.: The arithmetic-geometric inequality. In: Shisha, O. (ed.) Inequalities, Academic Press, London (1967)
26. Parrilo, P.A.: Semidefinite programming relaxations for semialgebraic problems. Mathematical Programming 96, 293–320 (2003)
27. Pourchet, Y.: Sur la répresentation en somme de carrés des polynômes a une indeterminée sur un corps de nombres algébriques. Acta Arithmetica 19, 89–109 (1971)
28. Prestel, A., Dalzell, C.N.: Positive Polynomials: From Hilbert's 17th Problem to Real Algebra. Springer monographs in mathematics. Springer, Heidelberg (2001)
29. Rockafellar, R.T.: Lagrange multipliers and optimality. SIAM review 35, 183–283 (1993)
30. Seidenberg, A.: A new decision method for elementary algebra. Annals of Mathematics 60, 365–374 (1954)
31. Strang, G.: Linear Algebra and its Applications, 3rd edn. Brooks/Cole (1988)
32. Tarski, A.: A Decision Method for Elementary Algebra and Geometry. University of California Press (1951), Previous version published as a technical report by the RAND Corporation, J.C.C. McKinsey (1948) (reprinted in [7], pp. 24–84)
33. Tiwari, A.: An algebraic approach to the satisfiability of nonlinear constraints. In: Ong, L. (ed.) CSL 2005. LNCS, vol. 3634, pp. 248–262. Springer, Heidelberg (2005)
34. Weil, A.: Number Theory: An approach through history from Hammurapi to Legendre. Birkhäuser Basel (1983)

Verification of Expectation Properties for Discrete Random Variables in HOL

Osman Hasan and Sofiène Tahar

Dept. of Electrical & Computer Engineering, Concordia University
1455 de Maisonneuve W., Montreal, Quebec, H3G 1M8, Canada
{o_hasan,tahar}@ece.concordia.ca

Abstract. One of the most important concepts in probability theory is that of the expectation of a random variable, which basically summarizes the distribution of the random variable in a single number. In this paper, we develop the basic techniques for analyzing the expected values of discrete random variables in the HOL theorem prover. We first present a formalization of the expectation function for discrete random variables and based on this definition, the expectation properties of three commonly used discrete random variables are verified. Then, we utilize the definition of expectation in HOL to verify the linearity of expectation property, a useful characteristic to analyze the expected values of probabilistic systems involving multiple random variables. To demonstrate the usefulness of our approach, we verify the expected value of the Coupon Collector's problem within the HOL theorem prover.

1 Introduction

Probabilistic techniques are increasingly being used in the design and analysis of software and hardware systems, with applications ranging from combinatorial optimization and machine learning to communication networks and security protocols. The concept of a random variable plays a key role in probabilistic analysis. The sources of randomness associated with the system under test are modeled as random variables and then the performance issues are judged based on the properties of the associated random variables. One of the most important properties of random variables is their expectation or expected value. The expectation basically provides the average of a random variable, where each of the possible outcomes of this random variable is weighted according to its probability.

Conventional simulation techniques are not capable of conducting the probabilistic analysis in a very efficient way. In fact, simulation based techniques require enormous amounts of numerical computations to generate meaningful results and can never guarantee exact answers. On the contrary, formal methods are capable of providing exact answers in this domain, if the probabilistic behavior can be modeled using a formalized semantics and we have the means to reason about probabilistic properties within a formalized framework.

Hurd's PhD thesis [9] is a pioneering work in regards to the modeling of probabilistic behavior in higher-order-logic. It presents an extensive foundational

K. Schneider and J. Brandt (Eds.): TPHOLs 2007, LNCS 4732, pp. 119–134, 2007.

development of probability, based on the mathematical measure theory, in the higher-order-logic (HOL) theorem prover. This formalization allows us to manipulate random variables and reason about their corresponding probability distribution properties in HOL. The probability distribution properties of a random variable, such as the *Probability Mass Function* (PMF), completely characterize the behavior of their respective random variables. It is frequently desirable to summarize the distribution of a random variable by its average or expected value rather than an entire function. For example, we are more interested in finding out the expected value of the runtime of an algorithm for an NP-hard problem, rather than the probability of the event that the algorithm succeeds within a certain number of steps.

In this paper, we develop the basic techniques for analyzing the expected values of discrete random variables in the HOL theorem prover. To the best of our knowledge, this is a novelty that has not been presented in the open literature so far. We chose HOL for this purpose in order to build upon the verification framework proposed in [9]. Discrete random variables, such as the Uniform, Bernoulli, Binomial and Geometric, are widely used in a number of probabilistic analysis applications, e.g., analyzing the expected performances of algorithms [13] and efficiency of cryptographic protocols [12], etc. Most of these random variables are also *natural-valued*, i.e., they take on values only in the *natural* numbers, $\mathbb{N} = \{0, 1, 2, \cdots\}$. In order to speed up the formalization and verification process and to be able to target real life applications, we are going to concentrate in this paper on formalizing the expectation for this specific class of discrete random variables.

We first present a formal definition of expectation for *natural-valued* discrete random variables. This definition allows us to prove expectation properties for individual discrete random variables in HOL. To target the verification of expected values of probabilistic systems involving multiple random variables, we utilize our formal definition of expectation to prove the linearity of expectation property [10]. By this property, the expectation of the sum of random variables equals the sum of their individual expectations

$$Ex[\sum_{i=1}^{n} X_i] = \sum_{i=1}^{n} Ex[X_i] \tag{1}$$

where Ex denotes the expectation function. The linearity of expectation is one of the most important properties of expectation as it allows us to verify the expectation properties of random behaviors involving multiple random variables without going into the complex verification of their joint probability distribution properties. Thus, its verification is a significant step towards using the HOL theorem prover as a successful probabilistic analysis framework. In order to illustrate the practical effectiveness of the formalization presented in this paper, we analyze the expectation of the Coupon Collector's problem [13], a well know commercially used algorithm, within the HOL theorem prover. We first formalize the Coupon Collector's problem as a probabilistic algorithm using the summation of a list of Geometric random variables. Then, the linearity of expectation property is used to verify its corresponding expected value.

The rest of the paper is organized as follows: Section 2 gives a review of the related work. In Section 3, we summarize a general methodology for modeling and verification of probabilistic algorithms in the HOL theorem prover. Then, we present the formalization of the expectation function for *natural-valued* discrete random variables along with the verification of expectation properties of a few commonly used discrete distributions in Section 4. The results are found to be in good agreement with existing theoretical paper-and-pencil counterparts. Section 5 presents the verification of the linearity of expectation property. The analysis of the Coupon Collector's problem is presented in Section 6. Finally, Section 7 concludes the paper.

2   Related Work

Nędzusiak [14] and Bialas [2] were among the first ones to formalize some probability theory in higher-order-logic. Hurd [9] extended their work and developed a framework for the verification of probabilistic algorithms in HOL. He demonstrated the practical effectiveness of his formal framework by successfully verifying the sampling algorithms for four discrete probability distributions, some optimal procedures for generating dice rolls from coin flips, the symmetric simple random walk and the Miller-Rabin primality test based on the corresponding probability distribution properties. Building upon Hurd's formalization framework, we have been able to successfully verify the sampling algorithms of a few continuous random variables [7] and the classical cumulative distribution function properties [8], which play a vital role in verifying arbitrary probabilistic properties of both discrete and continuous random variables. The current paper also builds upon Hurd's framework and presents an infrastructure that can be used to verify expectation properties of *natural-valued* discrete random variables within a higher-order-logic theorem prover.

Richter [15] formalized a significant portion of the Lebesgue integration theory in higher-order-logic using Isabelle/Isar. In his PhD thesis, Richter linked the Lebesgue integration theory to probabilistic algorithms, developing upon Hurd's [9] framework, and presented the formalization of the first moment method. Due to its strong mathematical foundations, the Lebesgue integration theory can be used to formalize the expectation of most of the discrete and continuous random variables. Though, one of the limitations of this approach is the underlying complexity of the verification using interactive higher-order-logic theorem proving. It is not a straightforward task to pick a random variable and verify its expectation property using the formalized Lebesgue integration theory. Similarly, the analysis of probabilistic systems that involve multiple random variables becomes more difficult. On the other hand, our formalization approach for the expectation function, is capable of handling these kind of problems for discrete random variables, as will be demonstrated in Sections 4 and 6 of this paper, but is limited to discrete random variables only.

Expectation is one of the most useful tools in probabilistic analysis and therefore its evaluation with automated formal verification has also been explored in the probabilistic model checking community [1,16]. For instance, some probabilistic model checkers, such as PRISM [11] and VESTA [17], offer the capability of verifying expected values in a semi-formal manner. In the PRISM model checker, the basic idea is to augment probabilistic models with cost or rewards: real values associated with certain states or transitions of the model. This way, the expected value properties, related to these rewards, can be analyzed by PRISM. It is important to note that the meaning ascribed to these properties is, of course, dependent on the definitions of the rewards themselves and thus there is a significant risk of verifying false properties. On the other hand, there is no such risk involved in verifying the expectation properties using the proposed theorem proving based approach due to its inherent soundness.

Probabilistic model checking is capable of providing exact solutions to probabilistic properties in an automated way though; however, it is also limited to systems that can only be expressed as a probabilistic finite state machine. In contrast, the theorem proving based probabilistic verification is an interactive approach but is capable of handling all kinds of probabilistic systems including the *unbounded* ones. Another major limitation of the probabilistic model checking approach is the state space explosion [3], which is not an issue with the proposed theorem proving based probabilistic analysis approach.

3 Verifying Probabilistic Algorithms in HOL

This section presents the methodology, initially proposed in [9], for the formalization of probabilistic algorithms, which in turn can be used to represent random variables as well. The intent is to introduce the main ideas along with some notation that is going to be used in the next sections.

The probabilistic algorithms can be formalized in higher-order logic by thinking of them as deterministic functions with access to an infinite Boolean sequence $\mathbb{B}^\infty$; a source of infinite random bits [9]. These deterministic functions make random choices based on the result of popping the top most bit in the infinite Boolean sequence and may pop as many random bits as they need for their computation. When the algorithms terminate, they return the result along with the remaining portion of the infinite Boolean sequence to be used by other programs. Thus, a probabilistic algorithm which takes a parameter of type α and ranges over values of type β can be represented in HOL by the function

$$\mathcal{F} : \alpha \to B^\infty \to \beta \times B^\infty$$

For example, a $Bernoulli(\frac{1}{2})$ random variable that returns 1 or 0 with equal probability $\frac{1}{2}$ can be modeled as follows

$$\vdash \texttt{bit} = \lambda\texttt{s. (if shd s then 1 else 0, stl s)}$$

where s is the infinite Boolean sequence and shd and stl are the sequence equivalents of the list operation *'head'* and *'tail'*. The probabilistic programs can also be expressed in the more general state-transforming monad where states are infinite Boolean sequences.

⊢ ∀ a,s. unit a s = (a,s)
⊢ ∀ f,g,s. bind f g s = let (x,s')← f(s) ∈ g x s'

The unit operator is used to lift values to the monad, and the bind is the monadic analogue of function application. All monad laws hold for this definition, and the notation allows us to write functions without explicitly mentioning the sequence that is passed around, e.g., function bit can be defined as

⊢ bit_monad = bind sdest (λb. if b then unit 1 else unit 0)

where sdest gives the head and tail of a sequence as a pair (*shd* s, *stl* s).

The work in [9] also presents some formalization of the mathematical measure theory in HOL, which can be used to define a probability function $\mathbb{P}$ from sets of infinite Boolean sequences to *real* numbers between 0 and 1. The domain of $\mathbb{P}$ is the set $\mathcal{E}$ of events of the probability. Both $\mathbb{P}$ and $\mathcal{E}$ are defined using the Carathéodory's Extension theorem [18], which ensures that $\mathcal{E}$ is a σ-algebra: closed under complements and countable unions. The formalized $\mathbb{P}$ and $\mathcal{E}$ can be used to prove probabilistic properties for probabilistic programs such as

⊢ $\mathbb{P}$ {s | fst (bit s) = 1} = $\frac{1}{2}$

where the function fst selects the first component of a pair and $\{x|C(x)\}$ represents a set of all x that satisfy the condition C in HOL.

The measurability and independence of a probabilistic function are important concepts in probability theory. A property indep, called *strong function independence*, is introduced in [9] such that if $f \in$ indep, then f will be both measurable and independent. It has been shown in [9] that a function is guaranteed to preserve *strong function independence*, if it accesses the infinite Boolean sequence using only the unit, bind and sdest primitives. All reasonable probabilistic programs preserve *strong function independence*, and these extra properties are a great aid to verification.

The above mentioned methodology has been successfully used to verify the sampling algorithms of a few discrete random variables based on the corresponding probability distribution properties [9]. In the current paper, we further strengthen this particular higher-order-logic probabilistic analysis approach by presenting the formalization of an expectation function, which can be utilized to verify expectation properties for discrete random variables.

4   Expectation for Discrete Distributions

There are mainly two approaches that can be used to formalize the expected value of a random variable in a higher-order-logic theorem prover [10]. Since a random variable is a real-valued function defined on the sample space, S, we can formalize expectation in terms of the probability space $(S, \mathfrak{F}, P)$, where $\mathfrak{F}$ is the sigma field of subsets of S, and P is the probability measure. This approach leads to the theory of abstract Lebesgue integration. Richter [15] formalized a significant portion of the Lebesgue integration theory in higher-order-logic. Richter's formalization paves the way to manipulate expected values in a higher-order-logic theorem prover but leads to a very complex verification task when it comes to verifying expectation properties of probabilistic systems that involve multiple random variables.

An alternate approach for formalizing the expectation of a random variable is based on the fact that the probability distribution of a random variable X, defined on the real line, can be expressed in terms of the distribution function of X. As a consequence, the expected value of a *natural-valued* discrete random variable can be defined by referring to the distribution of the probability mass on the *real* line as follows

$$Ex[X] = \sum_{i=0}^{\infty} iPr(X = i) \tag{2}$$

where Pr denotes the probability. The above definition only holds if the summation, carried over all possible values of X, is convergent, i.e., $\sum_{i=0}^{\infty} |i|Pr(X = i) < \infty$.

We are going to follow the second approach. This decision not only simplifies the formalization task of expectation for discrete random variables considerably, when compared to the approach involving Lebesgue integration, but also aids in the verification of expectation properties of probabilistic systems that involve multiple random variables in a straight forward manner. The expected value of the *natural-valued* discrete random variables, given in Equation 2, can be formalized in HOL follows

Definition 1. *Expectation of natural-valued Discrete Random Variables*
$$\vdash \forall \text{ X. expec X = suminf } (\lambda \text{n. n } \mathbb{P}\{\text{s | fst(X s) = n}\})$$

where `suminf` represents the HOL formalization of the infinite summation of a *real* sequence [6]. The function `expec` accepts the random variable X with data type $B^{\infty} \to (natural \times B^{\infty})$, and returns a *real* number.

Next, we build upon the above definition of expectation to verify the expectation properties of Uniform(n), Bernoulli(p) and Geometric(p) random variables in HOL. These random variables have been chosen in such a way that each one of them ranges over a different kind of set, in order to illustrate the generality of our definition of expectation.

4.1 Uniform(n) Random Variable

The Uniform(n) random variable assigns equal probability to each element in the set $\{0, 1, \cdots, (n-1)\}$ and thus ranges over a finite number of *natural* numbers. A sampling algorithm for the Uniform(n) can be found in [9], which has been proven correct by verifying the corresponding PMF property in HOL.

$$\vdash \forall \text{ n m. m} < \text{n} \Rightarrow \mathbb{P}\{\text{s | fst(prob\_unif n s) = m}\} = \tfrac{1}{n}$$

where **prob_unif** represents the higher-order-logic function for the Uniform(n) random variable. The first step towards the verification of the expectation property of discrete random variables that range over a finite number of *natural* numbers, say k, is to transform the infinite summation of Definition 1 to a finite summation over k values. This can be done in the case of the Uniform(n) random variable by using the above PMF property to prove the fact, for all values of n greater than 0, that the Uniform(n) random variable never acquires a value greater than or equal to n.

$$\vdash \forall \texttt{ n m. (suc n)} \le \texttt{m} \Rightarrow \mathbb{P}\{\texttt{s | fst(prob\_unif (suc n) s) = m}\} = 0$$

This property allows us to rewrite the infinite summation of Definition 1, for the case of the Uniform(n) random variable, in terms of a finite summation over n values using the HOL theory of *limit of a real sequence*. The expectation property can be proved now by induction over the variable n and simplifying the subgoals using some basic finite summation properties from the HOL theory of *real* numbers along with the PMF of the Uniform(n) random variable.

Theorem 1. *Expectation of Uniform(n) Random Variable*
$$\vdash \forall \texttt{ n. expec } (\lambda \texttt{s. prob\_unif (suc n) s)} = \frac{n}{2}$$

4.2   Bernoulli(p) Random Variable

Bernoulli(p) random variable models an experiment with two outcomes; success and failure, whereas the parameter p represents the probability of success. A sampling algorithm of the Bernoulli(p) random variable has been formalized in [9] as the function **prob_bern** such that it returns *True* with probability p and *False* otherwise. It has also been verified to be correct by proving the corresponding PMF property in HOL.

$$\vdash \forall \texttt{ p. } 0 \le \texttt{p} \wedge \texttt{p} \le 1 \Rightarrow \mathbb{P}\{\texttt{s | fst(prob\_bern p s)}\} = p$$

The Bernoulli(p) random variable ranges over 2 values of *Boolean* data type. The expectation property of these kind of discrete random variables, which range over a finite number of values of a different data type than *natural* numbers, can be verified by mapping them to the *natural* line. In the case of Bernoulli(p) random variable, we redefined the function **prob_bern** such that it returns *natural* numbers 1 and 0 instead of the Boolean quantities *True* and *False* respectively, i.e., the range of the random variable was changed from *Boolean* data type to *natural* data type. It is important to note that this redefinition does not change the distribution properties of the given random variable. Now, the verification of the expectation can be handled using the same procedure used for the case of random variables that range over a finite number of *natural* numbers. In the case of Bernoulli(p) random variable, we were able replace the infinite summation of Definition 1 with the summation of the first two values of the corresponding *real* sequence using the HOL theory of *limit of a real sequence*. This substitution along with the PMF property of the Bernoulli(p) random variable and some properties from the HOL theories of *real* and *natural* numbers allowed us to verify the expectation of the Bernoulli(p) in HOL.

Theorem 2. *Expectation of Bernoulli(p) Random Variable*
$$\vdash \forall\ \mathrm{p}.\ 0 \leq \mathrm{p} \wedge \mathrm{p} \leq 1 \Rightarrow \mathtt{expec}\ (\lambda s.\ \mathtt{prob\_bernN}\ \mathrm{p}\ \mathrm{s}) = p$$

where the function `prob_bernN` represents the Bernoulli(p) random variable that ranges over the *natural* numbers 0 and 1.

4.3   Geometric(p) Random Variable

Geometric(p) random variable can be defined as the index of the first success in an infinite sequence of Bernoulli(p) trials [4]. Therefore, the Geometric(p) distribution may be sampled by extracting random bits from the function `prob_bern`, explained in the previous section, and stopping as soon as the first *False* is encountered and returning the number of trials performed till this point. Thus, the Geometric(p) random variable ranges over a countably infinite number of *natural* numbers. This fact makes it different from other random variables that we have considered so far.

Based on the above sampling algorithm, we modeled the Geometric(p) random variable using the *probabilistic while loop* [9] in HOL as follows

Definition 2. *A Sampling Algorithm for Geometric(p) Distribution*
```
⊢ ∀ p s. prob_geom_iter p s = bind (prob_bern (1-p))
              (λb. unit (b, suc (snd s)))
⊢ ∀ p. prob_geom_loop p =
          prob_while fst (prob_geom_iter p)
⊢ ∀ p. prob_geom p = bind (bind (unit (T, 1))
          (prob_geom_loop p)) (λs. unit (snd s - 1))
```

It is important to note that p, which represents the probability of success for the Geometric(p) or the probability of obtaining *False* from the Bernoulli(p) random variable, cannot be assigned a value equal to 0 as this will lead to a non-terminating while loop. We verified that the function `prob_geom` preserves *strong function independence* using the HOL theories on probability. This result may be used along with the probability and set theories in HOL to verify the PMF property of the Geometric(p) random variable.

$$\vdash \forall\ \mathrm{n}\ \mathrm{p}.\ 0 < \mathrm{p} \wedge \mathrm{p} \leq 1 \Rightarrow$$
$$\mathbb{P}\{\mathrm{s}\ |\ \mathtt{fst}(\mathtt{prob\_geom}\ \mathrm{p}\ \mathrm{s}) = (\mathtt{suc}\ \mathrm{n})\} = p(1-p)^n$$

The expectation of Geometric(p) random variable can now be verified by first plugging the above PMF value into the definition of expectation and then using the following summation identity

$$\sum_{n=1}^{\infty} n x^{n-1} = \frac{1}{(1-x)^2} \tag{3}$$

where $0 \leq x < 1$. The proof task for this summation identity was quite involved and the HOL theories of *limit of a real sequence*, *real* and *natural* numbers were mainly used. The verified expectation property of Geometric(p) random variable in HOL is give below.

Theorem 3. *Expectation of Geometric(p) Random Variable*
$$\vdash \forall\ n\ p.\ 0 < p \land p \leq 1 \Rightarrow$$
$$\text{expec}\ (\lambda s.\ \text{prob\_geom}\ p\ s)\ =\ \tfrac{1}{p}$$

5   Verification of Linearity of Expectation Property

We split the verification of linearity of expectation property in two major steps. Firstly, we verify the property for two discrete random variables and then extend the results by induction to prove the general case.

5.1   Two Random Variables

The linearity of expectation property can be defined for any two discrete random variables X and Y, according to Equation 1, as follows

$$Ex[X + Y] = Ex[X] + Ex[Y] \tag{4}$$

To prove the above relationship in HOL, we proceed by first defining a function that models the summation of two random variables.

Definition 3. *Summation of Two Random Variables*
$$\vdash \forall\ X\ Y.\ \text{sum\_two\_rv}\ X\ Y\ =$$
$$\text{bind}\ X\ (\lambda a.\ \text{bind}\ Y\ (\lambda b.\ \text{unit}\ (a + b)))$$

It is important to note that the above definition implicitly ensures that the call of the random variable Y is independent of the result of the random variable X. This is true because the infinite Boolean sequence that is used for the computation of Y is the remaining portion of the infinite Boolean sequence that has been used for the computation of X. This characteristic led us to prove that the function sum_two_rv preserves *strong function independence*, which is the most significant property in terms of verifying properties on probabilistic functions.

Theorem 4. *sum_two_rv Preserves Strong Function Independence*
$$\vdash \forall\ X\ Y.\ X \in \text{indep\_fn} \land Y \in \text{indep\_fn} \Rightarrow$$
$$(\text{sum\_two\_rv}\ X\ Y) \in \text{indep\_fn}$$

Now the linearity of expectation property for two discrete random variables can be stated using the sum_two_rv function as follows.

Theorem 5. *Linearity of Expectation for Two Discrete Random Variables*
$$\vdash \forall\ X\ Y.\ X \in \text{indep\_fn} \land Y \in \text{indep\_fn} \land$$
$$\text{summable}\ (\lambda n.\ n\ \mathbb{P}\{s \mid \text{fst}(X\ s) = n\}) \land$$
$$\text{summable}\ (\lambda n.\ n\ \mathbb{P}\{s \mid \text{fst}(Y\ s) = n\}) \Rightarrow$$
$$\text{expec}\ (\text{sum\_two\_rv}\ X\ Y)\ =\ \text{expec}\ X + \text{expec}\ Y$$

Proof: Rewriting the LHS with the definition of the functions sum_two_rv and expec and removing the monad notation, we obtain the following expression.

$$\lim_{k \to \infty} \left(\sum_{n=0}^{k} n \, \mathbb{P}\{s \mid fst(X \ s) \ + \ fst(Y \ (snd(X \ s))) \ = \ n\} \right)$$

The set in the above expression can be expressed as the countable union of a sequence of events using the HOL theory of sets.

$$\lim_{k \to \infty} \left(\sum_{n=0}^{k} n \, \mathbb{P} \bigcup_{i \leq n} \{s \mid (fst(X \ s) \ = i) \ \wedge \ (fst(Y \ (snd(X \ s))) = n - i)\} \right)$$

As all events in this sequence are mutually exclusive, the additive probability law given in the HOL theory of probability, can be used to simplify the expression as follows

$$\lim_{k \to \infty} \left(\sum_{n=0}^{k} n \, \sum_{i=0}^{n+1} \mathbb{P}\{s \mid (fst(X \ s) \ = i) \ \wedge \ (fst(Y \ (snd(X \ s))) = n - i)\} \right)$$

Using the HOL theories of limit of a real sequence, real and natural number, the above expression can be rewritten as follows

$$\lim_{k \to \infty} \left(\sum_{a=0}^{k} \sum_{b=0}^{k} (a + b) \, \mathbb{P}\{s \mid (fst(X \ s) \ = a) \ \wedge \ (fst(Y \ (snd(X \ s))) = b)\} \right)$$

Rearranging the terms based on summation properties given in the HOL theory of real numbers, we obtain the following expression.

$$\lim_{k \to \infty} \left(\sum_{a=0}^{k} \sum_{b=0}^{k} a \, \mathbb{P}\{s \mid (fst(X \ s) \ = a) \ \wedge \ (fst(Y \ (snd(X \ s))) = b)\} \right) \ +$$

$$\lim_{k \to \infty} \left(\sum_{b=0}^{k} \sum_{a=0}^{k} b \, \mathbb{P}\{s \mid (fst(X \ s) \ = a) \ \wedge \ (fst(Y \ (snd(X \ s))) = b)\} \right)$$

The two terms in the above expression can now be proved to be equal to the expectation of random variables X and Y respectively, using Theorem 4 and HOL theory of probability, sets, real and and natural numbers. $\square$

5.2 n Random Variables

The linearity of expectation property for two discrete random variables, verified in Theorem 5, can now be generalized to verify the linearity of expectation property for n discrete random variables, given in Equation 1, using induction techniques.

The first step in this regard is to define a function, similar to sum_two_rv, which models the summation of a list of n random variables.

Definition 4. *Summation of n Random Variables*
$$\vdash \text{(sum\_rv\_lst [] = unit 0)} \land$$
$$\forall \text{ h t. (sum\_rv\_lst (h::t) =}$$
$$\text{bind h } (\lambda \text{a. bind (sum\_rv\_lst t)}$$
$$\lambda \text{b. unit (a + b)))}$$

Next, we prove that the function sum_rv_lst preserves *strong function indepen-dence*, if all random variables in the given list preserve it. This property can be verified using the fact that the function sum_rv_lst accesses the infinite Boolean sequence using the unit and bind primitives only.

Theorem 6. *sum_rv_lst Preserves Strong Function Independence*
$$\vdash \forall \text{ L. } (\forall \text{ R. (mem R L) } \Rightarrow \text{ R } \in \text{ indep\_fn}) \Rightarrow$$
$$\text{(sum\_rv\_lst L) } \in \text{ indep\_fn}$$

The predicate mem in the above definition returns *True* if its first argument is an element of the list that it accepts as the second argument.

Using induction on the list argument L of the function sum_rv_lst and sim-plifying the subgoals using Theorem 5, we proved, in HOL, that the expected value of the random variable modeled by the function sum_rv_lst exists if the expectation of all individual elements of its list argument exists. Here, by the existence of the expectation we mean that the infinite summation in the expec-tation definition converges.

Theorem 7. *The Expectation of sum_rv_lst Exists*
$$\vdash \forall \text{ L. } (\forall \text{ R. (mem R L) } \Rightarrow \text{ R } \in \text{ indep\_fn } \land$$
$$\text{summable } (\lambda \text{n. n } \mathbb{P}\{\text{s } | \text{ fst(R s) = n}\})) \Rightarrow$$
$$\text{summable } (\lambda \text{n. n } \mathbb{P}\{\text{s } | \text{ fst(sum\_rv\_lst L s) = n}\})$$

The linearity of expectation property for n discrete random variables can be proved now by applying induction on the list argument of the function sum_rv_lst, and simplifying the subgoals using Theorems 5, 6 and 7.

Theorem 8. *Linearity of Expectation for n Discrete Random Variables*
$$\vdash \forall \text{ L. } (\forall \text{ R. (mem R L) } \Rightarrow \text{ R } \in \text{ indep\_fn } \land$$
$$\text{summable } (\lambda \text{n. n } \mathbb{P}\{\text{s } | \text{ fst(R s) = n}\})) \Rightarrow$$
$$\text{expec (sum\_rv\_lst L) = sum (0, length L)}$$
$$(\lambda \text{n. expec (el (length L - (n+1)) L))}$$

where the function length returns the length of its list argument and the func-tion el accepts a *natural* number, say n, and a list and returns the nth element of the given list. The term (sum(m,n) f), in the above theorem, models the summation of n values, corresponding to the arguments $m+n-1, \cdots, m+1, m$, of the real sequence f. Thus, the left-hand-side of Theorem 8 represents the expectation of the summation of a list, L, of random variables. Whereas, the right-hand-side represents the summation of the expectations of all elements in the same list, L, of random variables.

6   Coupon Collector's Problem

The Coupon Collector's problem [13] is motivated by *"collect all n coupons and win"* contests. Assuming that a coupon is drawn independently and uniformly at random from n possibilities, how many times do we need to draw new coupons until we find them all? This simple problem arises in many different scenarios. For example, suppose that packets are sent in a stream from source to destination host along a fixed path of routers. It is often the case that the destination host would like to know all routers that the stream of data has passed through. This may be done by appending the identification of each router to the packet header but this is not a practical solution as usually we do not have this much room available. An alternate way of meeting this requirement is to store the identification of only one router, uniformly selected at random between all routers on the path, in each packet header. Then, from the point of view of the destination host, determining all routers on the path is like a Coupon Collector's problem.

Our goal is to verify, using HOL, that the expected value of acquiring all n coupons is $nH(n)$, where $H(n)$ is the *harmonic number* equal to the summation $\sum_{i=1}^{n} 1/i$. The first step in this regard is to model the Coupon Collector's problem as a probabilistic algorithm in higher-order-logic. Let X be the number of trials until at least one of every type of coupon is obtained. Now, if X_i is the number of trials required to obtain the ith coupon, while we had already acquired $i-1$ different coupons, then clearly $X = \sum_{i=1}^{n} X_i$. The advantage of breaking the random variable X into the sum of n random variables $X_1, X_2 \cdots, X_n$ is that each X_i can be modeled as a Geometric random variable, which enables us to represent the Coupon Collector's problem as a sum of Geometric random variables. Furthermore, the expectation of this probabilistic algorithm can now be verified using the linearity of expectation property.

We modeled the Coupon Collector's problem in HOL by identifying the coupons with unique *natural* numbers, such that the first coupon acquired by the coupon collector is identified as number 0 and after that each different kind of a coupon acquired with subsequent numbers in numerological order. The coupon collector saves these coupons in a list of *natural* numbers. The following function accepts the number of different coupons acquired by the coupon collector and generates the corresponding coupon collector's list.

Definition 5. *Coupon Collector's List*
$$\vdash (\texttt{coupon\_lst 0 = []}) \land$$
$$\forall \texttt{ n. (coupon\_lst (suc n) = n :: (coupon\_lst n))}$$

The next step is to define a list of Geometric random variables which would model the X_i's mentioned above. It is important to note that the probability of success for each one of these Geometric random variables is different from one another and depends on the number of different coupons acquired so far. Since, every coupon is drawn independently and uniformly at random from the n possibilities and the coupons are identified with *natural* numbers, we can use the Uniform(n) random variable to model each trial of acquiring a coupon. Now we can define the probability of success for a particular Geometric random variable as the probability of the event when the Uniform(n) random variable generates a new value, i.e., a value that is not already present in the coupon collector's list. Using this probability of success, the following function generates the required list of Geometric random variables.

Definition 6. *Geometric Variable List for Coupon Collector's Problem*
$$\vdash \forall \ n. \ (\text{geom\_rv\_lst } [] \ n = [\text{prob\_geom 1}]) \ \wedge$$
$$\forall \ h \ t. \ (\text{geom\_rv\_lst } (h::t) \ n =$$
$$(\text{prob\_geom}$$
$$(\mathbb{P}\{s \mid \neg(\text{mem } (\text{fst}(\text{prob\_unif } n \ s)) \ (h::t))\})$$
$$:: \ (\text{geom\_rv\_lst } t \ n)))$$

where the functions **prob_geom** and **prob_unif** model the Geometric(p) and Uniform(n) random variables, respectively, which are given in Section 4. The function **geom_rv_lst** accepts two arguments; a list of *natural* numbers, which represents the coupon collector's list and a *natural* number, which represents the total number of coupons. It returns, a list of Geometric random variables that can be added up to model the coupon collecting process of the already acquired coupons in the given list. The base case in the above recursive definition corresponds to the condition when the coupon collector does not have any coupon and thus the probability of success, i.e., the probability of acquiring a new coupon, is 1.

Using the above definitions along with the function **sum_rv_lst**, given in Definition 4, the Coupon Collector's problem can be represented now by the following probabilistic algorithm in HOL.

Definition 7. *Probabilistic Algorithm for Coupon Collector's Problem*
$$\vdash \forall \ n. \ (\text{coupon\_collector } (\text{suc } n) =$$
$$\text{sum\_rv\_lst } (\text{geo\_rv\_lst } (\text{coupon\_lst } n) \ (\text{suc } n))$$

The function **coupon_collector** accepts a *natural* number, say k, which represents the total number of different coupons that are required to be collected and has to be greater than 0. It returns the summation of k Geometric random variables that are used to model the coupon collecting process of acquiring k coupons. The expectation property of the Coupon Collector's problem can now be stated using the function **coupon_collector** and the function **sum**, which can be used to express the summation of n values, corresponding to the arguments $m + n - 1, \cdots, m + 1, m$, of the real sequence f as **sum(m,n) f**.

Theorem 9. *Expectation of Coupon Collector's Problem*
$$\vdash \forall \ n. \ \text{expec } (\text{coupon\_collector } (\text{suc } n)) =$$
$$(\text{suc } n) \ (\text{sum } (0,(\text{suc } n)) \ (\lambda i. \ 1/(\text{suc } i)))$$

Proof: The PMF property of the Uniform(n) random variable along with the HOL theories of sets and probability can be used to verify the following probabilistic quantity

$$\forall \ n. \ \mathbb{P}\{s \mid \neg(mem \ (fst(prob\_unif \ (n+1) \ s)) \ L)\} = 1 - \frac{length \ L}{(n+1)}$$

for all lists of natural numbers, L, such that all the elements in L are less than (n+1) and none of them appears more than once. The coupon collector's list, modeled by the function `coupon_lst`, satisfies both of these characteristics for a given argument n. Therefore, the probability of succuss for a Geometric random variable that models the acquiring process of a new coupon when the coupon collectors list is exactly equal to L, in the probabilistic algorithm for the Coupon Collector's problem for (n+1) coupons, is $1 - \frac{length\ L}{(n+1)}$. The expectation of such a Geometric random variable can be verified to be equal to

$$\frac{n+1}{(n+1) - (length\ L)}$$

by the expectation property of Geometric(p) random variables, given in Theorem 3. Now, using the above result along with the linearity of expectation property and the strong function independence property of the Geometric random variables, the expectation of the sum of the list of Geometric random variables, given in the LHS of Theorem 9, can be expressed as the summation of the individual expectations of the Geometric random variables as follows

$$\sum_{i=0}^{n} \frac{(n+1)}{(n+1) - i}$$

The following summation identity, which can be proved using the HOL theory of real and natural numbers, concludes the proof.

$$\forall\ n.\ \sum_{i=0}^{n} \frac{(n+1)}{(n+1) - i} = (n+1) \sum_{i=0}^{n} \frac{1}{(i+1)} \qquad \square$$

Theorem 9 can be used as a formal argument to support the claim that the expected number of trials required to obtain all n coupons is $n \sum_{i=1}^{n} 1/i$. Also, it is worth mentioning that it was due to the linearity of expectation property that the complex task of verifying the expectation property of the Coupon Collector's problem, which involves multiple random variables, was simply proved using the expectation property of a single Geometric(p) random variable.

7   Conclusions

In this paper, we presented some techniques for verifying the expectation properties of discrete random variables in HOL. Due to the formal nature of the models and the inherent soundness of the theorem proving systems, the analysis is guaranteed to provide exact answers, a novelty, which is not supported by most of the existing probabilistic analysis tools. This feature makes the proposed approach very useful for the performance and reliability optimization of safety critical and highly sensitive engineering and scientific applications.

We presented the formalization of expectation for *natural-valued* discrete random variables. This definition was used to verify the expected values of

Uniform(n), Bernoulli(p) and Geometric(p) random variables. These random variables are used extensively in the field of probabilistic analysis and thus their expectation properties can be reused in a number of different domains. Building upon our formal definition of expectation, we also verified a generalized version of the linearity of expectation property in HOL. In order to illustrate the practical effectiveness of our work, we presented the verification of the expectation property for the Coupon Collector's problem. To the best of our knowledge, this is the first time that the Coupon Collector problem has been analyzed within a mechanized theorem prover and the results are found to be in good agreement with existing theoretical paper-and-pencil counterparts.

The HOL theories presented in this paper can be used to verify the expectation properties of a number of other *natural-valued* random variables, e.g., Binomial, Logarithmic and Poisson [10] and commercial computation problems, such as the Chinese Appetizer and the Hat-Check problems [5]. A potential case study is to analyze the two versions of the Quicksort [13] and demonstrate the distinction between the analysis of randomized algorithms and probabilistic analysis of deterministic algorithms within the HOL theorem prover. As a next step towards a complete framework for the verification of randomized algorithms, we need to formalize the concepts of variance and higher moments. These bounds are the major tool for estimating the failure probability of algorithms. We can build upon the definition of expectation given in this paper to formalize these concepts within the HOL theorem prover. A very interesting future work could be to link the formal definition of expectation, presented in this paper, with the higher-order-logic formalization of Lebesgue integration theory [15], which would further strengthen the soundness of the definitions presented in this paper.

For our verification, we utilized the HOL theories of *Boolean algebra*, *sets*, *lists*, *natural* and *real* numbers, *limit of a real sequence* and *probability*. Our results can therefore be regarded as a useful indicator of the state-of-the-art in theorem proving. Based on this experience, we can say that formalizing mathematics in a mechanical system is a tedious work that requires deep understanding of both mathematical concepts and theorem-proving. The HOL automated reasoners aid somewhat in the proof process by automatically verifying some of the first-order-logic goals but most of the times we had to guide the tool by providing the appropriate rewriting and simplification rules. On the other hand, we found theorem-proving very helpful in book keeping. Another major advantage of theorem proving is that once the proof of a theorem is established, due to the inherent soundness of the approach, it is guaranteed to be valid and the proof can be readily accessed, contrary to the case of paper-pencil proofs where we have to explore the enormous amount of mathematical literature to find proofs. Thus, it can be concluded that theorem-proving is a tedious but promising field, which can help mathematicians to cope with the explosion in mathematical knowledge and to save mathematical concepts from corruption. Also, there are areas, such as security critical software, in military or medicine applications for example, where theorem-proving will soon become a dire need.

References

1. Baier, C., Haverkort, B., Hermanns, H., Katoen, J.P.: Model Checking Algorithms for Continuous time Markov Chains. IEEE Trans. on Software Engineering 29(4), 524–541 (2003)
2. Bialas, J.: The σ-Additive Measure Theory. Journal of Formalized Mathematics 2 (1990)
3. Clarke, E.M., Grumberg, O., Peled, D.A.: Model Checking. MIT Press, Cambridge (2000)
4. DeGroot, M.: Probability and Statistics. Addison-Wesley, Reading (1989)
5. Grinstead, C.M., Snell, J.L.: Introduction to Probability. American Mathematical Society, Providence, RI (1997)
6. Harrison, J.: Theorem Proving with the Real Numbers. Springer, Heidelberg (1998)
7. Hasan, O., Tahar, S.: Formalization of the Continuous Probability Distributions. In: Conference on Automated Deduction. LNCS (LNAI), vol. 4603, pp. 3–18. Springer, Heidelberg (2007)
8. Hasan, O., Tahar, S.: Verification of Probabilistic Properties in HOL using the Cumulative Distribution Function. In: Integrated Formal Methods. LNCS, vol. 4591, pp. 333–352. Springer, Heidelberg (2007)
9. Hurd, J.: Formal Verification of Probabilistic Algorithms. PhD Thesis, University of Cambridge, Cambridge, UK (2002)
10. Khazanie, R.: Basic Probability Theory and Applications. Goodyear (1976)
11. Kwiatkowska, M., Norman, G., Parker, D.: Quantitative Analysis with the Probabilistic Model Checker PRISM. Electronic Notes in Theoretical Computer Science 153(2), 5–31 (2005)
12. Mao, W.: Modern Cryptography: Theory and Practice. Prentice-Hall, Englewood Cliffs (2003)
13. Mitzenmacher, M., Upfal, E.: Probability and Computing. Cambridge Press, Cambridge (2005)
14. Nedzusiak, A.: σ-fields and Probability. Journal of Formalized Mathematics 1 (1989)
15. Richter, S.: Formalizing Integration Theory, with an Application to Probabilistic Algorithms. Diploma Thesis, Technische Universität München, Department of Informatics, Germany (2003)
16. Rutten, J., Kwaiatkowska, M., Normal, G., Parker, D.: Mathematical Techniques for Analyzing Concurrent and Probabilisitc Systems. CRM Monograph Series, vol. 23. American Mathematical Society, Providence, RI (2004)
17. Sen, K., Viswanathan, M., Agha, G.: VESTA: A Statistical Model-Checker and Analyzer for Probabilistic Systems. In: IEEE International Conference on the Quantitative Evaluation of Systems, Washington, DC, USA, pp. 251–252. IEEE Computer Soceity Press, Los Alamitos (2005)
18. Williams, D.: Probability with Martingales. Cambridge Press, Cambridge (1991)

A Formally Verified Prover for the $\mathcal{ALC}$ Description Logic[*]

José-Antonio Alonso, Joaquín Borrego-Díaz, María-José Hidalgo,
Francisco-Jesus Martín-Mateos, and José-Luis Ruiz-Reina

Departamento de Ciencias de la Computación e Inteligencia Artificial.
Escuela Técnica Superior de Ingeniería Informática, Universidad de Sevilla
Avda. Reina Mercedes, s/n. 41012 Sevilla, Spain
{jalonso,jborrego,mjoseh,fjesus,jruiz}@us.es

Abstract. The Ontology Web Language (OWL) is a language used for the Semantic Web. OWL is based on Description Logics (DLs), a family of logical formalisms for representing and reasoning about conceptual and terminological knowledge. Among these, the logic $\mathcal{ALC}$ is a ground DL used in many practical cases. Moreover, the Semantic Web appears as a new field for the application of formal methods, that could be used to increase its reliability. A starting point could be the formal verification of satisfiability provers for DLs. In this paper, we present the PVS specification of a prover for $\mathcal{ALC}$, as well as the proofs of its termination, soundness and completeness. We also present the formalization of the well–foundedness of the multiset relation induced by a well–founded relation. This result has been used to prove the termination and the completeness of the $\mathcal{ALC}$ prover.

1 Introduction

The goal of the presented work is the formal verification of satisfiability algorithms for description logics (DLs), as a previous stage to the formal verification of DLs reasoners. In particular, we describe in this paper a formal proof of the well–known tableau algorithm for the $\mathcal{ALC}$ description logic in the PVS verification system [19].

Description Logics [5] are a family of logics which can be used to represent terminological and conceptual knowledge. Among these, the ground logic is the $\mathcal{ALC}$ logic, introduced by Schmidt–Schauß and Smolka [24], who also developed a tableau–like algorithm for testing satisfiability in it. $\mathcal{ALC}$ is the base for more expressive logics as $\mathcal{SHOIQ}$, obtained extending $\mathcal{ALC}$ in several expressive ways. The importance of $\mathcal{SHOIQ}$ stems from the fact that it and its fragments are used for reasoning in the semantic web [4]. Specifically, the fragment $\mathcal{SHOIN}$ corresponds to the ontology language OWL–DL [13,12], which was recommended by the W3C as the standard web ontology language [6]. The fragment $\mathcal{SHIQ}$ is the concept language supported by systems as FaCT++ and RACER [25,10].

---

[*] This research was partially funded by Spanish Ministry of Education and Science under grant TIN2004–03884 and Feder funds.

K. Schneider and J. Brandt (Eds.): TPHOLs 2007, LNCS 4732, pp. 135–150, 2007.

Many techniques have been proposed and investigated to obtain decision procedures for DLs reasoning. Among these, tableaux reasoning are the most successful approach so far. In fact, DLs reasoners such as FaCT++ and RACER are based on tableau algorithms.

We believe that the verification of reasoning systems for the SW poses a new challenge for the application of formal methods. In this field, our research group have carried out several works related to the formal verification of reasoning systems. Some examples are the verification of a generic framework for propositional logic reasoning algorithms [14], Knuth–Bendix based reasoning [22], Buchberger algorithm for polynomial–based logical reasoning [15,16] and conceptual processing in Formal Concept Analysis [3].

In this paper, we show a proof in PVS of correctness of the tableau algorithm for $\mathcal{ALC}$ described in theoretical papers. The hardest part of this task is the termination proof, for which we have extended the multiset library of PVS in order to include well–foundedness of the multiset order relation. We use this property and a measure function as it is described in [9] to prove the termination of the algorithm.

The paper is structured as follows. Section 2 is devoted to describe the proof of the well–foundedness of the multiset induced relation of a well–founded relation. Section 3 shows the syntax and semantics of the $\mathcal{ALC}$ logic and how we have formalized it in the PVS language specification. Also, it contains the specification in PVS of a prover for the $\mathcal{ALC}$ logic, with some details about its termination, soundness and completeness proofs. Section 4 is devoted to explain how we have constructed in PVS a concrete measure function. Finally, in the last section we draw some conclusions and suggest some lines of future work.

Since the whole formalization consists of a large collection of PVS theorems and definitions, we give an overview presenting the main results and a sketch of how the pieces fit together. We necessarily omit many details that, we expect, can be inferred from the context. We urge the interested reader to consult the whole PVS theory developed, which is widely documented and available at http://www.cs.us.es/~mjoseh/alc/.

2   Well–Founded Ordering of Multisets

Multisets (bags) over a given set T are sets that admit multiple occurrences of elements taken from T. Dershowitz and Manna [9] prove that every well–founded relation on T induces a well–founded relation on the set of finite multisets over T. They also show how the multiset ordering is used to prove the termination of production systems, programs defined in term of rewriting rules. In our work, we use this method to prove the termination and completeness of the $\mathcal{ALC}$ reasoner.

The goal of this section is to show our extension of the PVS multiset library, to include the formalization of the Dershowitz and Manna theorem. The proof formalized in the PVS system is based on the proof described by T. Nipkow [17]. It uses a characterization of well–foundedness based on the notion of well–founded part of a set, and the transitive closure of a well–founded binary relation.

2.1   An Alternative Characterization of Well–Foundedness

The definition of well–foundedness included in the PVS prelude is the usual one: a relation $<$ on T is well–founded if every non-empty subset of T has a minimal element (w.r.t. $<$). Nevertheless, the proof of well-foundedness of the multiset orderings that we have formalized is based on an alternative definition given by P. Aczel [1]. Let us start describing the PVS proof of the equivalence between Aczel's definition and the usual one.

Given a binary relation $<$ defined on a set T, the well–founded part of T with respect to $<$, denoted as $W(T, <)$, is the smallest subset of T closed under the set of rules $(\forall a \in T)[(\forall y < a)[y \in W(T, <)] \to a \in W(T, <)]$. In our PVS definition of $W(T, <)$, both the type T and the relation $<$ are introduced as theory parameters. Also, we use the support that provides PVS for constructing inductive definitions of sets or predicates.

```
[T: TYPE+, <: pred[[T,T]]]: THEORY

well_founded_part(x): INDUCTIVE bool =
  FORALL y: y < x IMPLIES well_founded_part(y)
```

This way, the above inductive definition of the well–founded part generates, automatically, the following induction axioms, which allow us to prove properties by induction on the defined set:

- Weak induction axiom for the well–founded part:

$$\frac{(\forall x)[(\forall y)[y < x \to P(y)] \to P(x)]}{(\forall x)[x \in W(T, <) \to P(x)]}$$

- Induction axiom for the well–founded part

$$\frac{(\forall x)[(\forall y)[y < x \to y \in W(T, <) \land P(y)] \to P(x)]}{(\forall x)[x \in W(T, <) \to P(x)]}$$

The following theorem characterizes the well–foundedness of a relation by means of its well–founded part.

Theorem 1. $(T, <)$ is well–founded if and only if $W(T, <) = T$.

```
well_founded_part_nsc: THEOREM
  well_founded?[T](<) IFF (FORALL x: well_founded_part(x))
```

The PVS proof of the necessary condition is carried out by induction on $(T, <)$ with respect to the predicate $x \in W(T, <)$. On the other hand, the sufficient condition is proved using the weak induction axiom for the well–founded part of T with respect to $<$.

Additionally, the PVS theory about well–foundedness that we have developed also includes alternative sufficient conditions of well–foundedness, like the following embedding lemma.

Lemma 1. If $f : (S, <') \to (T, <)$ is monotone and $(T, <)$ is well–founded, then $(S, <')$ is well–founded.

We prove it using the definition of well–foundedness based in the notion of minimal element.

2.2 Well–Foundedness of the Transitive Closure

The *transitive closure* of a binary relation on T, $<$, is the smallest relation $<^+$ such that

$$(\forall x, y \in T)[(x < y \vee (\exists z)[x <^+ z \wedge z < y]) \rightarrow x <^+ y]$$

```
tr_cl(<)(x,y): INDUCTIVE bool =
x < y OR EXISTS z: tr_cl(<)(x,z) AND z < y
```

The main result about well–foundedness and transitive closure is the following:

Theorem 2. *If $(T, <)$ is well–founded, then $(T, <^+)$ is well–founded.*

```
well_founded_cl_tr: THEOREM
  well_founded?[T](<) IMPLIES well_founded?[T](tr_cl(<))
```

To prove it, by theorem 1, it is sufficient to prove that $W(T, <) \subseteq W(T, <^+)$. We prove this in PVS using the weak induction axiom generated by the definition of $W(T, <)$.

In a similar way, the reflexive transitive closure of a relation, `rtr_cl(<)`, has been defined and their main properties have been proved in PVS.

2.3 Well–Founded Multiset Relations (in PVS)

In order to specify in PVS the multiset relations, we have used the PVS library about bags.[1] In this library, a multiset (bag) of elements in T is represented by means of a function with domain T and range $\mathbb{N}$. Let us start showing the specification of the `bag` and `finite_bag` types, and also the specifications of the basic operations `insert` and `plus`, included in it (in the following, we will denote both as $\uplus$)

```
bag: TYPE = [T -> nat]
insert(x,b): bag = (LAMBDA t: IF x = t THEN b(t) + 1 ELSE b(t) ENDIF)
plus(a,b)  : bag = (LAMBDA t: a(t) + b(t))
bag_to_set(b): set[T] = {t: T | b(t) > 0}
is_finite(b): bool = is_finite(bag_to_set(b))
finite_bag: TYPE = {b: bag | is_finite(b)}
```

Let $<$ be a relation in T and $\mathcal{M}(T)$ the set of finite multisets over T. The *multiset relation* induced by $<$ on $\mathcal{M}(T)$ is the relation $<_{mult}$ defined as: $N <_{mult} M$ if there exist multisets $M_0, K_1, K_2 \in \mathcal{M}(T)$ such that $K_1 \neq \emptyset$, $M = M_0 \uplus K_1$, $N = M_0 \uplus K_2$ and $(\forall a)[a \in K_2 \rightarrow (\exists b)[b \in K_1 \wedge a < b]]$. An alternative definition could be obtained if instead of replacing a multiset K_1 of elements in M, a

---

[1] Available at
   http://shemesh.larc.nasa.gov/fm/ftp/larc/PVS-library/pvslib.html

single element $b \in M$ were replaced by a multiset of smaller elements (w.r.t. $<$). That is, we could define the following *multiset reduction relation* denoted as $<_1$: $N <_1 M$ if there exists multisets M_0, K_2 and $b \in M$ such that $M = M_0 \uplus \{b\}$, $N = M_0 \uplus K_2$ and $(\forall a)[a \in K_2 \to a < b]$. It can be proved that if $<$ is transitive, then $<_{mult}$ is the transitive closure of $<_1$. Therefore, by theorem 2, proving the well–foundedness of $<_{mult}$ amounts to proving that $<_1$ is well–founded, provided that $<$ is transitive.

We specify the relations $<_1$ and $<_{mult}$ in PVS by less_1 and less_mult, respectively, as follows

```
less(K,a): bool = FORALL b: member(b,K) IMPLIES b < a


less_1(N,M): bool =
  EXISTS M_0,a,K: M = insert(a,M_0) AND N = plus(M_0,K) AND less(K,a)


less_mult(N,M): bool =
  EXISTS M_0,K1,K2: nonempty_bag?(K1) AND M = plus(M_0, K1) AND
                    N = plus(M_0, K2) AND
                    FORALL a: member(a,K2) IMPLIES
                              EXISTS b: member(b,K1) AND a < b
```

Then, we stablish in PVS the following result, ensuring that the relation $<_1$ is well–founded on $\mathcal{M}(T)$.

Lemma 2. *Let $<$ be a well–founded relation on T. Then $<_1$ is a well–founded relation on $\mathcal{M}(T)$.*

```
wf_less_1: THEOREM well_founded?[finite_bag[T]](less_1)
```

To prove this lemma, using theorem 1, it is sufficient to prove that $\mathcal{M}(T) \subseteq W(\mathcal{M}(T), <_1)$. The PVS proof is carried out by induction on finite multisets, according to the following scheme:

$$\frac{P(\emptyset) \wedge (\forall a)(\forall M)[P(M) \to P(M \uplus \{a\})]}{(\forall M)P(M)}$$

where the predicate $P(M)$ stands $M \in W(\mathcal{M}(T), <_1)$. Therefore, we have to prove:

1. $\emptyset \in W(\mathcal{M}(T), <_1)$ (which is true by its definition).
2. $(\forall a)[(\forall M)[M \in W(\mathcal{M}(T), <_1) \to M \uplus \{a\} \in W(\mathcal{M}(T), <_1)]]$.
   This result is proved by well–founded induction on $<$ (since it is well–founded), with the following predicate $P(a)$:

   $$(\forall M)[M \in W(\mathcal{M}(T), <_1) \to M \uplus \{a\} \in W(\mathcal{M}(T), <_1)]$$

   With this, the proof is reduced to prove $(\forall b)[b < a \to P(b)] \to P(a)$, or equivalently, to prove that if

   $$(\forall b)[b < a \to (\forall M)[M \in W(\mathcal{M}(T), <_1) \to M \uplus \{b\} \in W(\mathcal{M}(T), <_1)]]$$

then

$$(\forall M)[M \in W(\mathcal{M}(T), <_1) \to M \uplus \{a\} \in W(\mathcal{M}(T), <_1)] \tag{3}$$

We finish proving (3) using the weak induction axiom for the well–founded part $W(\mathcal{M}(T), <_1)$, with the predicate $Q(M)$:

$$M \uplus \{a\} \in W(\mathcal{M}(T), <_1) \vee M \notin W(\mathcal{M}(T), <_1).$$

Finally, as consequence of lemma 2, we obtain the main theorem of this section:

Theorem 3 (Dershowitz and Manna). *Let $<$ be a transitive and well–founded relation on T. Then the relation $<_{mult}$ is a well–founded relation on $\mathcal{M}(T)$.*

```
less_mult_is_wf: THEOREM
  transitive?[T](<) IMPLIES well_founded?[finite_bag[T]](less_mult)
```

A sketch of the proof is as follows. First, we show that the relation $<_{mult}$ is contained in $<_1^+$. Furthermore, if the relation $<$ is transitive, then $<_{mult}$ is transitive and contains the relation $<_1^+$. Then, if $<$ is transitive, $<_1^+ = <_{mult}$ and therefore, by lemma 2 and theorem 2, we conclude that $<_{mult}$ is well–founded.

3 Tableau Reasoning for $\mathcal{ALC}$–Satisfiability

In this section, we first describe the basic components of $\mathcal{ALC}$ logic, and we show below how we have formalized in PVS the tableau based algorithm for this logic, as well as the proofs of its termination, soundness and completeness.

3.1 Syntax and Semantics of the $\mathcal{ALC}$ Logic

We start presenting a brief introduction to the $\mathcal{ALC}$–logic, its syntax and its semantics, along with the corresponding description of its specification in PVS.

Let NC be a set of *concept names* and NR be a set of *role names*. The set of $\mathcal{ALC}$–*concepts* is built inductively from these names as described by the following grammar, where $A \in$ NC and $R \in$ NR

$$C ::= A \mid \neg C \mid C_1 \sqcap C_2 \mid C_1 \sqcup C_2 \mid \forall R.C \mid \exists R.C$$

The set of $\mathcal{ALC}$–concepts can be represented in PVS as a recursive datatype, using the mechanism for defining abstract datatypes [20], and specifying the constructors, the accessors and the recognizers. When a datatype is typechecked in PVS, a new theory is created providing axioms and inductions principles for this datatype. In particular, this theory contains the relation `subterm` (specifying the notion of *subconcept*) and the well–founded relation `<<`, that is useful to make recursive definitions on concepts.

To introduce the assertional knowledge, let NI be a set of *individual names*. Given individual names $x, y \in$ NI, a concept C and a role name R, the expressions $x\!:\!C$ and $(x, y)\!:\!R$ are called *assertional axioms*. An *ABox* $\mathcal{A}$ is a finite set of assertional axioms. We specify in PVS the assertional axioms by a datatype and the ABox by a type.

```
assertional_ax: DATATYPE
 BEGIN
   instanceof(left:NI, right:alc_concept) : instanceof?
   related(left:NI, role:NR, right:NI)    : related?
 END assertional_ax
```

```
ABox: TYPE = finite_set[assertional_ax]
```

The semantics of description logics is defined in terms of interpretations. An $\mathcal{ALC}$ *–interpretation* $\mathcal{I}$ is a pair $\mathcal{I} = (\Delta^{\mathcal{I}}, \cdot^{\mathcal{I}})$, where $\Delta^{\mathcal{I}}$ is a non–empty set called the *domain*, and $\cdot^{\mathcal{I}}$ is an *interpretation function* that maps every concept name A to a subset $A^{\mathcal{I}}$ of $\Delta^{\mathcal{I}}$, every role name R to a binary relation $R^{\mathcal{I}}$ over $\Delta^{\mathcal{I}}$ and every individual x to an element of $\Delta^{\mathcal{I}}$. We represent in PVS an interpretation $\mathcal{I}$ as a structure that contains the domain of $\mathcal{I}$ and the functions that define the interpretation of concept names, role names, and the individuals.

```
interpretation: NONEMPTY_TYPE =
 [# int_domain:          (nonempty?[U]),
    int_names_concept: [NC -> (powerset(int_domain))],
    int_names_roles:   [NR -> PRED[[(int_domain),(int_domain)]]],
    int_names_ind:     [NI -> (int_domain)] #]
```

It should be noted that in this specification we have used a universal type U to represent the elements of the domain. Also, we have taken advantage of the ability of PVS to deal with dependent types.

The interpretation function is extended to non-atomic concepts as follows

$$
\begin{aligned}
(\neg D)^{\mathcal{I}} &= \Delta^{\mathcal{I}} \setminus D^{\mathcal{I}} \\
(C_1 \sqcap C_2)^{\mathcal{I}} &= C_1^{\mathcal{I}} \cap C_2^{\mathcal{I}} \\
(C_1 \sqcup C_2)^{\mathcal{I}} &= C_1^{\mathcal{I}} \cup C_2^{\mathcal{I}} \\
(\forall R.D)^{\mathcal{I}} &= \{a \in \Delta^{\mathcal{I}} : (\forall b \in \Delta^{\mathcal{I}})[(a,b) \in R^{\mathcal{I}} \rightarrow b \in D^{\mathcal{I}}]\} \\
(\exists R.D)^{\mathcal{I}} &= \{a \in \Delta^{\mathcal{I}} : (\exists b \in \Delta^{\mathcal{I}})[(a,b) \in R^{\mathcal{I}} \wedge b \in D^{\mathcal{I}}]\}
\end{aligned}
$$

We have specified this notion in PVS in a natural way, by recursion on C, using the well–founded relation <<.

The interpretation $\mathcal{I}$ is a *model* of a concept C if $C^{\mathcal{I}} \neq \emptyset$. Thus, a concept C is called *satisfiable* if it has a model

```
is_model_concept(I,C): bool = nonempty?(int_concept(C,I))
concept_satisfiable?(C): bool = EXISTS I: is_model_concept(I,C)
```

The interpretation $\mathcal{I}$ *satisfies* the assertional axiom $x : C$ if $x^{\mathcal{I}} \in C^{\mathcal{I}}$ and satisfies $(x, y) : R$ if $(x^{\mathcal{I}}, y^{\mathcal{I}}) \in R^{\mathcal{I}}$. It *satisfies* the ABox $\mathcal{A}$ if it satisfies every axiom in $\mathcal{A}$. In that case, $\mathcal{A}$ is called *satisfiable* and $\mathcal{I}$ is called a *model* of $\mathcal{A}$.

We have made the PVS formalization of the above definitions using the PVS set theory and its capability of managing the existential and universal quantifiers.

The previous definitions naturally pose some standard inference problems for DLs systems, such as concept and ABox satisfiability. It can be proved, and we have done it in PVS, that concept satisfiability can be reduced to ABox satisfiability (i.e., C is satisfiable iff for all $x \in$ NI, $\{x:C\}$ is satisfiable).

3.2 Deciding Concept Satisfiability for $\mathcal{ALC}$

A tableau algorithm for $\mathcal{ALC}$ tries to prove the satisfiability of a concept C by attempting to explicitly construct a model of C. This is done considering an individual name x_0 and manipulating the initial ABox $\{x_0{:}C\}$, applying a set of completion rules. In this process, we consider concepts in negation normal form (NNF), a form in which negations appear only in front of concept names. This does not mean a restriction since it is easy to specify a PVS function such that, for each $\mathcal{ALC}$–concept computes another equivalent [2] in NNF form.

An ABox $\mathcal{A}$ contains a *clash* if, for some individual name $x \in \mathsf{NI}$ and concept name $A \in \mathsf{NC}$, $\{x{:}A, x{:}\neg A\} \subseteq \mathcal{A}$. Otherwise, $\mathcal{A}$ is called *clash–free*. To test the satisfiability of an $\mathcal{ALC}$–concept C in NNF, the $\mathcal{ALC}$–*algorithm* works starting from the initial ABox $\{x_0{:}C\}$ and iteratively applying the following *completion rules*

$\rightarrow_\sqcap$: if $x{:}C \sqcap D \in \mathcal{A}$ and $\{x{:}C, x{:}D\} \not\subseteq \mathcal{A}$
      then $\mathcal{A} \rightarrow_\sqcap \mathcal{A} \cup \{x{:}C, x{:}D\}$

$\rightarrow_\sqcup$: if $x{:}C \sqcup D \in \mathcal{A}$ and $\{x{:}C, x{:}D\} \cap \mathcal{A} = \emptyset$
      then $\mathcal{A} \rightarrow_\sqcup \mathcal{A} \cup \{x{:}E\}$ for some $E \in \{C, D\}$

$\rightarrow_\exists$: if $x{:}\exists R.D \in \mathcal{A}$ and there is no y with $\{(x, y){:}R, y{:}D\} \subseteq \mathcal{A}$
      then $\mathcal{A} \rightarrow_\exists \mathcal{A} \cup \{(x, y){:}R, y{:}D\}$ for a fresh individual y

$\rightarrow_\forall$: if $x{:}\forall R.D \in \mathcal{A}$ and there is a y with $(x, y){:}R \in \mathcal{A}$ and $y{:}D \notin \mathcal{A}$
      then $\mathcal{A} \rightarrow_\forall \mathcal{A} \cup \{y{:}D\}$

It stops when a clash has been generated or when no rule is applicable. In the last case, the ABox is *complete* and a model can be derived from it. The algorithm answers "C is satisfiable" if a complete and clash–free ABox has been generated.

These completion rules can be seen as a production system. Nevertheless, we have not formalized them in a functional way, but following a more declarative style, defining the completion rules in PVS as binary relations between ABoxes. For example, $\mathcal{A}_1 \rightarrow_\sqcap \mathcal{A}_2$ if there exists an assertional axiom $x{:}C \sqcap D$ in $\mathcal{A}_1$ such that $\{x{:}C, x{:}D\} \not\subseteq \mathcal{A}_1$ and $\mathcal{A}_2 = \mathcal{A}_1 \cup \{x{:}C, x{:}D\}$

```
and_step(AB1, AB2): bool =
 EXISTS Aa: member(Aa,AB1) AND
          instanceof?(Aa) AND
          alc_and?(right(Aa)) AND
          LET x = left(Aa), C = conc1(right(Aa)), D = conc2(right(Aa))
           IN (NOT member(instanceof(x, C), AB1) OR
              NOT member(instanceof(x, D), AB1)) AND
              AB2 = add(instanceof(x, C), add(instanceof(x, D), AB1))
```

Once the rules have been specified in this way, we define the successor relation on the ABoxes type: $\mathcal{A}_1 \rightarrow \mathcal{A}_2$ if $\mathcal{A}_1$ does not contain a clash and $\mathcal{A}_2$ is obtained from $\mathcal{A}_1$ by the application of a completion rule

---

[2] Two concepts are equivalent if they have the same models.

```
successor(AB2,AB1): bool =
  (NOT contains_clash(AB1)) AND
  (and_step(AB1,AB2)  OR or_step_1(AB1,AB2) OR or_step_2(AB1,AB2) OR
   some_step(AB1,AB2) OR all_step(AB1,AB2))
```

It should be noted that we have specified the non-deterministic rule $\to_\sqcup$ by two binary relations (`or_step_1` and `or_step_2`), one for each component.

Take into account that the completion process can be seen as a closure process, we say the ABox $\mathcal{A}_2$ is an *expansion* of the ABox $\mathcal{A}_1$ if $\mathcal{A}_1 \stackrel{*}{\to} \mathcal{A}_2$, where $\stackrel{*}{\to}$ is the reflexive and transitive closure of $\to$

```
is_expansion(AB1)(AB2): bool = rtr_cl(successor)(AB2, AB1)
```

To illustrate the completion process, the following example shows the application of some completion rules to an initial ABox $\{x_0\!:\!C\}$

Example 1. Let C be the concept $\forall R.D \sqcap (\exists R.(D \sqcup E) \sqcap \exists R.(D \sqcup F))$. Then,

$$\mathcal{A}_0 := \{x_0\!:\!\forall R.D \sqcap (\exists R.(D \sqcup E) \sqcap \exists R.(D \sqcup F))$$
$$\stackrel{*}{\to} \mathcal{A}_1 := \mathcal{A}_0 \cup \{x_0\!:\!\forall R.D, x_0\!:\!\exists R.(D \sqcup E), x_0\!:\!\exists R.(D \sqcup F)\}$$
$$\to \mathcal{A}_2 := \mathcal{A}_1 \cup \{(x_0, x_1)\!:\!R, x_1\!:\!D \sqcup E\}$$
$$\to \mathcal{A}_3 := \mathcal{A}_2 \cup \{x_1\!:\!D\}$$

Once defined the expansion relation, we use it to specify the notion of consistency: An ABox $\mathcal{A}$ is *consistent* if it has a complete and clash–free expansion. Similarly, a concept C is *consistent* if the initial ABox $\{x_0\!:\!C\}$ is consistent

```
is_consistent_abox(AB): bool =
  EXISTS AB1: is_expansion(AB)(AB1) AND complete_clash_free(AB1)

is_consistent_concept(C): bool =
  is_consistent_abox(singleton(instanceof(x_0,C)))
```

where `complete_clash_free`($\mathcal{A}$) holds if the ABox $\mathcal{A}$ is both complete and clash–free.

This definition is the PVS specification of a generic $\mathcal{ALC}$–algorithm for deciding satisfiability of $\mathcal{ALC}$–concepts. It should be pointed out the two kinds of non–determinism in it: the way in which the rule $\to_\sqcup$ is applied ("don't know" non-determinism); and the choice of which rule to apply in each step and to which axiom ("don't care" non-determinism). To prove that the algorithm is correct, we have to establish its termination, soundness and completeness. The following subsections describe the corresponding PVS proofs.

3.3 Soundness

The $\mathcal{ALC}$–algorithm is sound, that is:

```
alc_soundness: THEOREM
  is_consistent_concept(C) IMPLIES concept_satisfiable?(C)
```

The PVS proof is based on the following steps:

1. If $\mathcal{A}$ is a complete and clash–free expansion of an initial ABox $\mathcal{A}_0$, then $\mathcal{A}$ is satisfiable. We have proved this by specifying in PVS the canonical interpretation $\mathcal{I}_\mathcal{A}$ associated with $\mathcal{A}$, and proving that $\mathcal{I}_\mathcal{A}$ is a model of $\mathcal{A}$.
2. If $\mathcal{A}_1 \rightarrow \mathcal{A}_2$ and $\mathcal{A}_2$ is satisfiable, then $\mathcal{A}_1$ is satisfiable too.
3. Finally, we have proved the soundness theorem, using the induction scheme suggested by the above definition of the expansion relation (which in turn is based on the inductive definition of closure).

3.4   Termination

In order to verify the termination of the $\mathcal{ALC}$–algorithm, it suffices to prove that the successor relation, defined on the set $\mathcal{E}(C)$ of the expansions of the initial ABox $\{x_0\!:\!C\}$, is well founded

```
well_founded_successor: THEOREM
  well_founded?[expansion_abox_concept(C)](successor)
```

where by the type `expansion_abox_concept`(C), we specify the set $\mathcal{E}(C)$

```
expansion_abox_concept(C:(is_nnf?)): TYPE =
  (is_expansion(singleton(instanceof(x_0, C))))
```

The proof of the well–foundedness of the successor relation is based on the embedding lemma (Lemma 1). So, it suffices to show the existence of a type T, a well–founded relation $<$ on T, and a function

$$\mu_C : \mathcal{E}(C) \rightarrow T \tag{1}$$

such that

$$(\forall \mathcal{A}_1, \mathcal{A}_2)[\mathcal{A}_1 \rightarrow \mathcal{A}_2 \Rightarrow \mu_C(\mathcal{A}_2) < \mu_C(\mathcal{A}_1)] \tag{2}$$

Those functions with these properties are called *measure functions*.

The formalization of this proof in PVS has been carried out in two phases. In the first one, we assume the existence of a measure function, including T and $<$ in the parameters, and (1) and (2) in the body of the PVS theory,

```
[..., T: TYPE+, <: (well_founded?[T])]: THEORY

measure_concept(C): [expansion_abox_concept(C) -> T]

measure_concept_decrease_successor: AXIOM
  FORALL (AB1,AB2: expansion_abox_concept(C)):
    successor(AB2,AB1)
    IMPLIES measure_concept(C)(AB2) < measure_concept(C)(AB1)
```

and we prove that successor is well–founded on $\mathcal{E}(C)$.

In the second one, we prove the existence of measure functions. For the sake of completeness, we outline Nutt's definition of a measure function. In [18], W. Nutt constructs a measure function taking T as the type of the finite multisets of pairs of natural numbers $\mathcal{M}(\mathbb{N} \times \mathbb{N})$, and the well–founded order $<$ as the extension to $\mathcal{M}(\mathbb{N} \times \mathbb{N})$ of the lexicographic order on $\mathbb{N} \times \mathbb{N}$, that we denote by $<_{mult}$. In order to formalize in PVS that construction, it is necessary carry out two tasks:

1. To prove that the extension to $\mathcal{M}(\mathbb{N} \times \mathbb{N})$ of the lexicographic order on $\mathbb{N} \times \mathbb{N}$ is a well–founded ordering. For this, it suffices to instantiate, in theorem 3, T by $\mathbb{N} \times \mathbb{N}$ and $<$ by the lexicographic ordering on $\mathbb{N} \times \mathbb{N}$.
2. To define a function μ_C mapping each expansion $\mathcal{A} \in \mathcal{E}(C)$ to a multiset of pairs, such that $\mu_C(\mathcal{A}_2) <_{mult} \mu_C(\mathcal{A}_1)$ if $\mathcal{A}_1 \to \mathcal{A}_2$. For the sake of clarity, we devote section 4 to explain the details of its formalization.

3.5   Completeness

The last verification task is the proof of completeness of $\mathcal{ALC}$–algorithm, that is:

```
alc_completeness: THEOREM
  concept_satisfiable?(C) IMPLIES is_consistent_concept(C)
```

The PVS proof is achieved by means three subtasks in turn:

1. If $\mathcal{A}$ is a satisfiable ABox, then $\mathcal{A}$ is clash–free.
2. If $\mathcal{A}_1$ is a satisfiable and not complete ABox, then there exists a satisfiable ABox $\mathcal{A}_2$, which is successor of $\mathcal{A}_1$.
3. If $\mathcal{A} \in \mathcal{E}(C)$ is satisfiable, then there exists a complete and clash–free expansion of $\mathcal{A}$ in $\mathcal{E}(C)$ itself.

In order to carry out the second task, we have proved that for every satisfiable not complete ABox $\mathcal{A}$, for every rule r and for every axiom of $\mathcal{A}$ to which r is applied, there exists an axiom such that by adding it we obtain a satisfiable ABox. On the other hand, the last one is the key lemma for the main proof. We have proved it by well–founded induction on the successor relation.

4   Measure on $\mathcal{ALC}$–Expansion of C

In this section we show a measure function on $\mathcal{E}(C)$ verifying the monotonicity condition of section 3.4. The idea for defining the measure function μ_C is to map each expansion $\mathcal{A} \in \mathcal{E}(C)$ to a multiset of pairs, in such way that those pairs represent all possibles rules that can be applied to $\mathcal{A}$.

The first step is to define the notions of *level* and *colevel*. For this, we have used the library of graphs of PVS [7]. We define the *associated graph* to an ABox $\mathcal{A}$, $\mathcal{G}(\mathcal{A})$, as the graph whose vertices are the individuals that occur in $\mathcal{A}$, and whose edges are the subsets $\{x, y\}$, such that $(x, y) : R \in \mathcal{A}$ for some role R.

```
graph_assoc_abox(AB: ABox): graph[NI] =
  (# vert:= occur_ni(AB), edges:= dbl_assoc_abox(AB) #)
```

From this definition, we prove that if $\mathcal{A} \in \mathcal{E}(C)$, then $\mathcal{G}(\mathcal{A})$ is a tree with root x_0. This fact allows us to define the level of x in $\mathcal{A}$ as the length of the path from x_0 to x (minus 1), and the colevel of x in $\mathcal{A}$, $|x|_\mathcal{A}$, as the difference between the size of the concept C (denoted by $|C|$) and the level of x in $\mathcal{A}$.

```
level(AB)(x:(occur_ni(AB))): nat = l(path_from_root(AB)(x)) - 1
colevel(AB)(x:(occur_ni(AB))): nat = size(C) - level(AB)(x)
```

Also, we prove that the colevel of an individual in $\mathcal{A}$ remains invariant under the completion rules and that if y is a *successor* of x in $\mathcal{A}$ (i.e., $(x, y) : R \in \mathcal{A}$), then $|y|_{\mathcal{A}} = |x|_{\mathcal{A}} - 1$. Both properties are essential to prove the monotonicity of μ_C.

```
successor_preserve_colevel: LEMMA
  occur_ni(AB1)(y) AND successor(AB2,AB1)
  IMPLIES colevel(AB2)(y) = colevel(AB1)(y)

colevel_successor_related: LEMMA
  successor_related(AB)(y,x) IMPLIES colevel(AB)(y) = colevel(AB)(x) - 1
```

As we have already said, the elements of the multiset associated to an expansion $\mathcal{A}$ should represent all possibles applicable rules to $\mathcal{A}$. In some cases, the applicability of a rule is completely determined by an instance axiom of $\mathcal{A}$, but that is not the case for the $\rightarrow_\forall$ rule. Thus, in order to capture the notion of applicability of a rule, we introduce the type *activation* (`activ`), whose elements are structures consisting of an instance axiom and an individual, that made it applicable. Then, we specify when an activation is applicable in $\mathcal{A}$ and we define the *agenda* of $\mathcal{A}$, agenda($\mathcal{A}$), as the set of applicable activations in $\mathcal{A}$.

```
activ: TYPE = [# ax: (instanceof?), witness: NI #]

applicable_activ(Ac,AB): bool =
 LET Aa = ax(Ac),y = witness(Ac),x = left(Aa),D = right(Aa) IN
 member(Aa,AB) AND
 CASES D OF
   alc_a(A)      : false,
   alc_not(D1)   : false,
   alc_and(C1,C2) : x = y AND (NOT member(instanceof(x,C1),AB) OR
                               NOT member(instanceof(x,C2),AB)),
   alc_or(C1,C2)  : x = y AND NOT member(instanceof(x,C1),AB) AND
                              NOT member(instanceof(x,C2),AB),
   alc_all(R,D1)  : x /= y AND member(related(x,R,y),AB) AND
                             NOT member(instanceof(y,D1),AB),
   alc_some(R,D1) : x = y AND NOT (EXISTS y: member(related(x,R,y),AB) AND
                                           member(instanceof(y,D1),AB))
 ENDCASES

agenda(AB): finite_set[activ] = {Ac | applicable_activ(Ac, AB)}
```

To specify the function μ_C we found the following difficulty: we can not define a multiset in PVS in a declarative way, as with sets. Thus, the measure of the expansion $\mathcal{A}$, $\mu_C(\mathcal{A})$, is constructed by recursion in the agenda of $\mathcal{A}$, adding the pair $(|y|_{\mathcal{A}}, |D|)$ for each applicable activation $[x : D, y]$.

```
bag_assoc_activ(Ac, AB): finite_bag[[nat, nat]] =
  IF NOT applicable_activ(Ac, AB) THEN emptybag
```

```
ELSE LET Aa = ax(Ac), y = witness(Ac), D = right(Aa) IN
        singleton_bag((colevel(AB)(y), size(D)))
ENDIF

expansion_measure_aux(AB,(AB1: finite_set[activ])):
                    RECURSIVE finite_bag[[nat, nat]] =
 IF empty?(AB1) THEN emptybag
 ELSE plus(bag_assoc_activ(choose(AB1), AB),
           expansion_measure_aux(AB, rest(AB1)))
 ENDIF
MEASURE card(AB1)

expansion_measure(AB): finite_bag[[nat, nat]] =
  expansion_measure_aux(AB, agenda(AB))
```

We illustrate the evolution of measures through the effect of completion rules to example 1.

Example 2. The agendas and measures of the ABoxes of Example 1 are:

	agenda	measure
$\mathcal{A}_0$	$\{(x_0{:}\forall R.D \sqcap (\exists R.(D \sqcup E) \sqcap \exists R.(D \sqcup F)), x_0)\}$	$\{(15, 15)\}$
$\mathcal{A}_1$	$\{(x_0{:}\exists R.(D \sqcup E), x_0), (x_0{:}\exists R.(D \sqcup F), x_0)\}$	$\{(15, 5), (15, 5)\}$
$\mathcal{A}_2$	$\{(x_0{:}\exists R.(D \sqcup F), x_0), (x_0{:}\forall R.D, x_1), (x_1{:}D \sqcup E, x_1)\}$	$\{(14, 3), (14, 3), (15, 5)\}$
$\mathcal{A}_3$	$\{(x_0{:}\exists R.(D \sqcup F), x_0)\}$	$\{(15, 5)\}$

Finally, we prove the theorem that assures the monotony of μ_C.

Theorem 4. *Let $\mathcal{A}_1, \mathcal{A}_2 \in \mathcal{E}(C)$. If $\mathcal{A}_1 \to \mathcal{A}_2$ then $\mu_C(\mathcal{A}_2) <_{mult} \mu_C(\mathcal{A}_1)$.*

```
expansion_measure_decrease_successor: THEOREM
  successor(AB2, AB1)
  IMPLIES less_mult(expansion_measure(AB2), expansion_measure(AB1))
```

The formalization of the proof of this theorem in PVS has turned out to be more difficult than the hand proof presented in [18]. Firstly, we can observe (in Example 2) that if $\mathcal{A}_1, \mathcal{A}_2 \in \mathcal{E}(C)$ are such that $\mathcal{A}_1 \to \mathcal{A}_2$, then there exists an activation $Ac_1 = [x: D, y] \in$ agenda$(\mathcal{A}_1)$, that matches with the applied rule. In addition, $Ac_1 \notin$ agenda$(\mathcal{A}_2)$ and, for each activation Ac_2 introduced in the agenda$(\mathcal{A}_2)$ as result of the rule application, its associated pair is smaller (lexicographically) than $(|y|_\mathcal{A}, |D|)$. Indeed, one of the following cases may occur:

1. $Ac_2 = [x{:}E, z]$, being z a successor of y in $\mathcal{A}_2$. Then, $|z|_{\mathcal{A}_2} < |y|_{\mathcal{A}_2} = |y|_{\mathcal{A}_1}$. So, $(|z|_{\mathcal{A}_2}, |E|) < (|y|_{\mathcal{A}_1}, |D|)$.
2. $Ac_2 = [x{:}E, y]$, being E a subconcept of D. In this case, $|y|_{\mathcal{A}_2} = |y|_{\mathcal{A}_1}$ and $|E| < |D|$. So, $(|y|_{\mathcal{A}_2}, |E|) < (|y|_{\mathcal{A}_1}, |D|)$.

Secondly, we should note that the application of a rule can disable some activations of the agenda and, so, it can eliminate its associated pairs of the multiset.

Thus, we define in PVS the multiset $K_1 = \mu_{aux}(\mathcal{A}_1, \text{agenda}(\mathcal{A}_1) \setminus \text{agenda}(\mathcal{A}_2))$, whose elements are the pairs associated to disabled activations. Also, the multiset $K_2 = \mu_{aux}(\mathcal{A}_2, \text{agenda}(\mathcal{A}_2) \setminus \text{agenda}(\mathcal{A}_1))$ that contains the pairs associated to new enabled activations. Finally, $M_0 = \mu_{aux}(\mathcal{A}_1, \text{agenda}(\mathcal{A}_1) \cap \text{agenda}(\mathcal{A}_2))$ is the multiset whose elements are the pairs associated to the activations that remains enabled after the application of the rule. Regarding these multisets, we prove the following properties: (1) $K_1 \neq \emptyset$, (2) $\mu_C(\mathcal{A}_2) = M_0 \uplus K_2$, (3) $\mu_C(\mathcal{A}_1) = M_0 \uplus K_1$ y (4) $(\forall a \in K_2)(\exists b \in K_1)[a < b]$. Thus, we conclude that $\mu_C(\mathcal{A}_2) <_{mult} \mu_C(\mathcal{A}_1)$.

Once the measure function has been constructed, the parameters T and $<$, and the signature `measure-concept(C)` of subsection 3.4 are interpreted by the appropriated mechanism of PVS.

5   Conclusions and Future Work

We have presented a formalization of the $\mathcal{ALC}$ logic in PVS, and a formalization of a tableau–based algorithm for checking satisfiability of $\mathcal{ALC}$–concepts, proving its soundness, completeness and termination. Both for the termination proof and the completeness proof we have used the well–foundedness of the multiset relation induced by a well–founded relation, a property that we have also formally proved. This last result has been proved in a general setting. So, the parameters of the PVS theory can be instantiated in order to establish the well–foundedness of concrete relations.

It should be pointed out that the choice of PVS as our verification system has turned out to be beneficial for our formalization, since PVS provide definition of abstract datatypes, inductive sets and dependent types, as well as parameterized theories of sets, multisets and graphs.

To the best of our knowledge, it is the first work on formalizing DL reasoning, although related works (see, for example [14,11,21]) have been done for other logics. And, also, the first work in PVS about the well–foundedness of multiset relations. Others formal proofs of the well–foundedness of the multiset ordering have been carried out, in a similar way, in Coq [8] and in Isabelle. In [23], an ACL2 formalization of the same result is also presented.

Finally, we point out some possible lines for future work. We plan to continue the work following two research lines. First, we will apply type and operator refinement techniques presented in [3], in order to construct $\mathcal{ALC}$–reasoners as PVSio specifications, executable and formally verified, refining the specification of the $\mathcal{ALC}$–algorithm that we have presented here. Due to "don't care" non-determinism of the algorithm specified in PVS, its correctness will be translated to specific implementations, whose efficiency will depend of the applied optimization strategy.

Also, we are interested in extending the formalization of the $\mathcal{ALC}$ logic to other descriptive logics, incrementally approaching us to the description logic $\mathcal{SHOIN}$, which is the description logic corresponding to OWL–DL [12], by adding new constructors. The modular characteristic of the extensions of our formalization may provide the automatic synthesis of ad–hoc reasoning systems for specifics ontologies [2].

References

1. Aczel, P.: An introduction to inductive definitions. In: Barwise, J. (ed.) Handbook of Mathematical Logic, pp. 739–782. North–Holland Publishing Company, Amsterdam (1977)
2. Alonso, J.A., Borrego, J., Chávez, A.M., Martín, F.J.: Foundational challenges in automated semantic web data and ontology cleaning. IEEE Intelligent Systems 21(1), 45–52 (2006)
3. Alonso, J.A., Borrego, J., Hidalgo, M.J., Martín, F.J., Ruiz, J.L.: Verification of the Formal Concept Analysis. RACSAM (Revista de la Real Academia de Ciencias), Serie A: Matemáticas 98, 3–16 (2004)
4. Baader, F., Horrocks, I., Sattler, U.: Description logics as ontology languages for the semantic web. In: Hutter, D., Stephan, W. (eds.) Mechanizing Mathematical Reasoning. LNCS (LNAI), vol. 2605, pp. 228–248. Springer, Heidelberg (2005)
5. Baader, F., McGuiness, D., Nardi, D., Patel-Schneider, P. (eds.): The Description Logic Handbook: Theory, Implementation and Applications. Cambridge University Press, Cambridge (2003)
6. Bechhofer, S., Harmelen, F.v., Hendler, J., McGuinness, I.H.D.L., Patel-Schneider, P.F., Stein, L.A.: OWL Web Ontology Language Reference (2004), available on the Web at http://www.w3.org/TR/owl-ref
7. Butler, R.W., Sjogren, J.: A PVS graph theory library. Technical report, NASA Langley (1998)
8. Coupet-Grimal, S., Delobel, W.: An effective proof of the well–foundedness of the multiset path ordering. Applicable Algebra in Engineering, Communication and Computing 17(6), 453–469 (2006)
9. Dershowitz, N., Manna, Z.: Proving termination with multiset orderings. Communications of the ACM 22(8), 465–476 (1979)
10. Haarslev, V., Möller, R.: RACER system description. In: Goré, R.P., Leitsch, A., Nipkow, T. (eds.) IJCAR 2001. LNCS (LNAI), vol. 2083, pp. 701–705. Springer, Heidelberg (2001)
11. Harrison, J.: Formalizing basic first order model theory. In: Grundy, J., Newey, M. (eds.) Theorem Proving in Higher Order Logics. LNCS, vol. 1479, Springer, Heidelberg (1998)
12. Horrocks, I., Patel-Schneider, P.: Reducing OWL entailment to description logic satisfiability. J. of Web Semantics 1(4), 345–357 (2004)
13. Horrocks, I., Patel-Schneider, P.F., van Harmelen, F.: From $\mathcal{SHIQ}$ and RDF to OWL: The making of a Web Ontology Language. J. of Web Semantics 1(1), 7–26 (2003)
14. Martín, F.J., Alonso, J.A., Hidalgo, M.J., Ruiz, J.L.: Formal verification of a generic framework to synthesize SAT–provers. Journal of Automated Reasoning 32(4), 287–313 (2004)
15. Medina, I., Palomo, F., Alonso, J.A.: A certified polynomial-based decision procedure for propositional logic. In: Boulton, R.J., Jackson, P.B. (eds.) TPHOLs 2001. LNCS, vol. 2152, pp. 297–312. Springer, Heidelberg (2001)
16. Medina, I., Palomo, F., Alonso, J.A., Ruiz, J.L.: Verified computer algebra in ACL2. In: Buchberger, B., Campbell, J.A. (eds.) AISC 2004. LNCS (LNAI), vol. 3249, pp. 171–184. Springer, Heidelberg (2004)

17. Nipkow, T.: An inductive proof of the wellfoundedness of the multiset order. A proof due to W. Buchholz (1998), available on the Web at `http://www4.informatik.tu-muenchen.de/~nipkow/misc/multiset.ps`

18. Nutt, W.: Algorithms for constraint in deduction and knowledge representation. PhD thesis, Universität des Saarlandes (1993)

19. Owre, S., Rushby, J.M., Shankar, N.: PVS: A Prototype Verification System. In: Kapur, D. (ed.) Automated Deduction - CADE-11. LNCS, vol. 607, pp. 748–752. Springer, Heidelberg (1992)

20. Owre, S., Shankar, N.: Abstract datatype in PVS. Technical report, Computer Science Laboratory, SRI International (1997)

21. Ridge, T., Margetson, J.: A mechanically verified, sound and complete theorem prover for first order logic. In: Hurd, J., Melham, T. (eds.) TPHOLs 2005. LNCS, vol. 3603, pp. 294–309. Springer, Heidelberg (2005)

22. Ruiz, J.L., Alonso, J.A., Hidalgo, M.J., Martín, F.J.: Formal proofs about rewriting using ACL2. Ann. Math. Artif. Intell. 36(3), 239–262 (2002)

23. Ruiz, J.L., Alonso, J.A., Hidalgo, M.J., Martín, F.J.: Termination in ACL2 using multiset relation. In: Kamareddine, F.D. (ed.) Thirty Five Years of Automating Mathematics, pp. 217–245. Kluwer Academic Publishers, Dordrecht (2003)

24. Schmidt–Schauß, M., Smolka, G.: Attributive concept descriptions with complements. Artificial Intelligence 48(1), 1–26 (1991)

25. Tsarkov, D., Horrocks, I.: FaCT++ description logic reasoner: System description. In: Furbach, U., Shankar, N. (eds.) IJCAR 2006. LNCS (LNAI), vol. 4130, pp. 292–297. Springer, Heidelberg (2006)

Proof Pearl: The Termination Analysis of TERMINATOR

Joe Hurd[*]

Computing Laboratory
Oxford University
joe.hurd@comlab.ox.ac.uk

Abstract. TERMINATOR is a static analysis tool developed by Microsoft Research for proving termination of Windows device drivers written in C. This proof pearl describes a formalization in higher order logic of the program analysis employed by TERMINATOR, and verifies that if the analysis succeeds then program termination logically follows.

1 Introduction

TERMINATOR [2] is a static analysis tool developed by Microsoft Research to prove termination of Windows device drivers written in C. The device drivers are typically thousands or tens of thousands of lines of code running at the privilege level of the kernel, and an infinite loop will cause the computer to freeze.

TERMINATOR works by modifying the program to reduce the termination problem into a safety property. Given a program location l and a finite set of well-founded relations $R_1, \ldots, R_n$ on program states at location l (l-states), TERMINATOR inserts the statement

```
already_saved_state := false;
```

at the beginning of the program, and the statements

```
if (already_saved_state) {
  if ¬(R₁ state saved_state ∨ ··· ∨ Rₙ state saved_state) {
    error("possible non-termination");
  }
}
else if (*) {
  saved_state := state;
  already_saved_state := true;
}
```

just before the program location l. A static analysis tool is run on this modified program to verify that there is no execution trace leading to the error statement. In the case of TERMINATOR, this verification step is performed by the SLAM

---

[*] Supported by a Junior Research Fellowship at Magdalen College, Oxford.

K. Schneider and J. Brandt (Eds.): TPHOLs 2007, LNCS 4732, pp. 151–156, 2007.

static analysis tool [1], also developed by Microsoft Research. Since the statement
if (*) is interpreted as demonic non-deterministic choice, the error statement
being unreachable guarantees that between the ith and jth time that program
location l is reached, the l-state goes down in at least one of the well-founded
relations $R_1, \ldots, R_n$.

If for every program location there exists a set of well-founded relations that
allow this modification and check to succeed, then it is possible to conclude
that the program must always terminate [6]. It is this logical step that is formally verified in the remainder of this paper. Section 2 presents a higher order
logic formalization of programs and termination; Section 3 adds to the model
the information generated by a successful TERMINATOR analysis; and Section 4
formally verifies that it is sufficient to guarantee program termination. Finally
Section 5 extends the model to verify two optimizations that are implemented
in the TERMINATOR tool. The HOL4 theorem prover [3] was used for this proof
pearl, and all the theorems presented have been mechanically checked.[1]

Although irrelevant for the correctness proof, it is interesting to see how TER-
MINATOR automatically constructs the well-founded relations $R_1, \ldots, R_n$. The
SLAM tool called by TERMINATOR works by Counter-Example Guided Abstraction and Refinement (CEGAR), and thus in the case that the property is false
provides a concrete execution trace leading to an error statement. TERMINATOR
starts with no relations,[2] repeatedly runs SLAM to generate error traces, and
each time adds a well-founded relation that would rule it out. The well-founded
relations are heuristically generated by an external tool called RANKFINDER [5].
The hope is that eventually enough well-founded relations are chosen that the
error statement can be proven to be unreachable.

2   Formalizing Termination

Programs are formalized in higher order logic as nondeterministic state machines
equipped with a function mapping states to program locations (this captures the
intuition that the program counter is part of the state):

$$('state,'location)\ program \equiv$$
$$<|\ states : 'state \rightarrow bool;\ location : 'state \rightarrow 'location;$$
$$initial : 'state \rightarrow bool;\ transition : 'state \rightarrow 'state \rightarrow bool\ |> .$$

Note that the 'state and 'location can be any higher order logic types, and in
particular the states set can be infinite.

The set of all program locations is simply the range of the location function:

$$locations\ p \equiv image\ p.location\ p.states .$$

---

[1] The proof script can be downloaded from
http://www.cl.cam.ac.uk/~jeh1004/research/papers/terminatorScript.sml.
[2] Note that for program locations that are executed at most once, SLAM will be able
to prove the error statement is unreachable even when there are no relations.

Well-formed programs must be closed w.r.t. their set of states, and their set of program locations must be finite:[3]

> programs ≡
>> { p : ('state,'location) program |
>> finite (locations p) $\wedge$ p.initial $\subseteq$ p.states $\wedge$
>> $\forall s, s'$. p.transition $s\ s' \Rightarrow s \in p$.states $\wedge s' \in p$.states } .

A sufficient condition for a program p being terminating is that the p.transition relation is well-founded. However, this is too strong, and excludes terminating programs that have unreachable loops in their transition relation. Instead a notion of program execution traces is introduced:

> traces p ≡ { t : 'state lazy_list | $t_0 \in p$.initial $\wedge \forall t_i, t_{i+1} \in t$. p.transition $t_i\ t_{i+1}$ } .

The type α lazy_list of possibly infinite lists is already defined in the HOL4 theorem prover; this work only required some extra constants to support syntactic constructs such as the above universal quantification over adjacent elements of the list. Now a program can be defined to terminate if it has no infinite execution traces:

> terminates p ≡ $\forall t \in$ traces p. finite t .

3   The TERMINATOR Program Analysis

The previous section presented a simple formalization of programs and defined a termination predicate on them. This section completes the formalization of the main verification goal by defining what it means for a TERMINATOR program analysis to succeed.

At a particular location l of a program p, the result of a successful TERMINATOR analysis (as described in the Introduction) is formalized in higher order logic as

> terminator_property_at_location $p\ l$ ≡
>> $\exists R, n.$
>> $(\forall k \in \{0, \ldots, n-1\}.$ well_founded $(R\ k)) \wedge$
>> $\forall t \in$ traces p. $\forall x_i < x_j \in$ trace_at_location $p\ l\ t$.
>> $\exists k \in \{0, \ldots, n-1\}$. $R\ k\ x_j\ x_i$,

where trace_at_location $p\ l\ t$ filters the execution trace t leaving only the states corresponding to the location l:

> trace_at_location $p\ l\ t$ ≡ filter $(\lambda s.\ p$.location $s = l)\ t$.

The TERMINATOR analysis for a whole program succeeds if it succeeds at every location:

> terminator_property p ≡ $\forall l \in$ locations p. terminator_property_at_location $p\ l$.

---

[3] The infinite non-terminating program skip; skip; skip; $\cdots$ visits each program location precisely once and thus the TERMINATOR analysis trivially succeeds.

4 Verifying Terminator

At this point the formalization is complete, and the correctness statement for the TERMINATOR analysis can be expressed as

$$\forall p \in \text{programs. terminator\_property } p \Rightarrow \text{terminates } p \;.$$

How to prove this verification goal? The first step is to fix a program location l, and prove that no trace can visit l infinitely often.

The proof is easiest to explain by contradiction: suppose a program trace is filtered to give in an infinite list of l-states $x_0, x_1, x_2, \ldots$. The TERMINATOR analysis results in well-founded relations $R_0, \ldots, R_{n-1}$ such that for every $i < j$ there exists $0 \leq k < n$ satisfying $R_k \, x_j \, x_i$.

The proof proceeds by induction on n. If $n = 0$ then the contradiction is immediate because there is no well-founded relation available to compare x_0 and x_1. For $n > 0$ construct an undirected graph $G = (V, E)$ with vertex set $V = \mathbb{N}$ and edge relation

$$E \, i \, j = i < j \wedge R_{n-1} \, x_j \, x_i \;.$$

The next step is formalize a result of Ramsey Theory [4] that every infinite graph has an infinite subgraph that is either complete (i.e., every vertex is connected to every other) or empty (i.e., there are no edges).[4] Here is the higher order logic theorem:

$$\vdash \forall V, E. \text{ infinite } V \Rightarrow$$
$$\exists M \subseteq V. \text{ infinite } M \; \wedge$$
$$((\forall i, j \in M. \; i < j \Rightarrow E \, i \, j) \; \vee \; (\forall i, j \in M. \; i < j \Rightarrow \neg E \, i \, j)) \;.$$

What do the two cases mean for the graph G? If the infinite subgraph $G' = (M, E)$ is complete, then the subsequence of vertices in M is an R_{n-1} infinite descending sequence: a contradiction since R_{n-1} is a well-founded relation. If instead G' is empty, then the relation R_{n-1} is never used and the problem reduces to $n - 1$ well-founded relations: the contradiction is provided by the inductive hypothesis. The final theorem is

$$\vdash \forall p \in \text{programs. } \forall l \in \text{locations } p.$$
$$\text{terminator\_property\_at\_location } p \, l \Rightarrow$$
$$\forall t \in \text{traces } p. \text{ finite (trace\_at\_location } p \, l \, t) \;.$$

The final step of the verification is to deduce that if no program location is visited infinitely often then there are no infinite program traces:

$$\vdash \forall p \in \text{programs. terminator\_property } p \Rightarrow \text{terminates } p \;.$$

Note that this relies on well-formed programs having a finite set of locations.

---

[4] Formalizing Ramsey Theory in higher order logic is not novel; perhaps the earliest example is Harrison's HOL88 theory in 1994, now ported to HOL Light.

5   Optimizations

The previous section formally verified the core TERMINATOR program analysis, but the real tool also implements a number of optimizations to speed up the termination proof. In this section the verification is extended to include two of the most significant ones.

The first optimization occurs when there is only one relation that has been found (so far) at a program location l. Instead of the general program modification, TERMINATOR simply modifies the program to compare each l-state with the previous l-state, by inserting

```
already_saved_state := false;
```

at the beginning of the program, and

```
if (already_saved_state && ¬R state saved_state) {
  error("possible non-termination");
}
saved_state := state;
already_saved_state := true;
```

just before location l. The definition of a successful TERMINATOR program analysis at location l must therefore be weakened to

> terminator_property_at_location $p \ l \equiv$
>> $(\exists R.$
>>> well_founded $R \ \wedge$
>>> $\forall t \in$ traces $p. \ \forall x_i, x_{i+1} \in$ trace_at_location $p \ l \ t. \ R \ x_{i+1} \ x_i) \ \vee$
>> $[\ldots$ old definition of terminator_property_at_location $p \ l \ldots] \ .$

The second optimization that TERMINATOR implements is to skip the analysis for all but a *cut set* of program locations:

> cut_sets $p \equiv$
>> $\{L \mid L \subseteq$ locations $p \ \wedge$
>>> $\forall t \in$ traces $p.$ infinite $t \Rightarrow \exists l \in L.$ infinite (trace_at_location $p \ l \ t)\} \ .$

Intuitively, a set of program locations is a cut set if every infinite trace visits the cut set infinitely often. This is a semantic property, and in general is hard to prove.[5] In practice, TERMINATOR chooses a cut set to include all locations at the start of loops and functions that are called (mutually) recursively.

Taking both these optimizations into account, the result of a successful TERMINATOR program analysis is captured by the following augmented definition:

> terminator_property $p \equiv$
>> $\exists C \in$ cut_sets $p. \ \forall l \in C.$ terminator_property_at_location $p \ l \ .$

And the same correctness theorem is still true, requiring only modest changes to the proofs.

---

[5] Indeed, if the program is terminating, all location sets are cut sets!

6 Summary

This proof pearl presented a formal verification of the termination analysis of the TERMINATOR static analysis tool. The correctness result is not obvious (at least to the author), and the proof is an interesting application of Ramsey Theory. Naturally, the mechanized proof uses the same concepts as the original published proof [6], but was made more self-contained to simplify both formalization and presentation. The HOL4 proof script is 500 lines long (including the Ramsey Theory lemmas), and took two days to get the formalization right and then another two days to complete the verification.

The verification of the TERMINATOR optimizations in Section 5 represents a first step toward a verified practical tool, but that is a long way off. An interesting next step would be a deep embedding of structured programs, so that the TERMINATOR program modification and cut set generation could be incorporated into the verification, as well as optimizations such as ignoring program traces that leave and come back into the current loop.

Acknowledgements

Byron Cook provided the initial stimulus for this work, and it was greatly improved in discussions with both him and Andreas Podelski. Comments from the anonymous TPHOLs referees greatly improved the paper.

References

1. Ball, T., Bounimova, E., Cook, B., Levin, V., Lichtenberg, J., McGarvey, C., Ondrusek, B., Rajamani, S.K., Ustuner, A.: Thorough static analysis of device drivers. In: Proceedings of the EuroSys 2006 Conference, April 2006, pp. 73–85 (2006)
2. Cook, B., Podelski, A., Rybalchenko, A.: Terminator: Beyond safety. In: Ball, T., Jones, R.B. (eds.) CAV 2006. LNCS, vol. 4144, pp. 415–418. Springer, Heidelberg (2006)
3. Gordon, M.J.C., Melham, T.F. (eds.): Introduction to HOL (A theorem-proving environment for higher order logic). Cambridge University Press, Cambridge (1993)
4. Landman, B.M., Robertson, A.: Ramsey Theory on the Integers, February 2004. American Mathematical Society, Providence, RI (2004)
5. Podelski, A., Rybalchenko, A.: A complete method for the synthesis of linear ranking functions. In: Steffen, B., Levi, G. (eds.) VMCAI 2004. LNCS, vol. 2937, pp. 239–251. Springer, Heidelberg (2004)
6. Podelski, A., Rybalchenko, A.: Transition invariants. In: 19th IEEE Symposium on Logic in Computer Science (LICS 2004), July 2004, pp. 32–41. IEEE Computer Society Press, Los Alamitos (2004)

Improving the Usability of HOL Through Controlled Automation Tactics

Eunsuk Kang and Mark D. Aagaard

Electrical and Computer Engineering
University of Waterloo
Waterloo, ON, Canada
{ekang,maagaard}@uwaterloo.ca

Abstract. This paper introduces the concept of *controlled automation* as a balanced medium between high-level automated reasoning and low-level primitive tactics in HOL. We created a new tactic that subsumes many existing low-level tactics for logical operations and three new tactics that simplify common uses of term rewriting: definition expansion, simplification, and equational rewriting. To implement the tactics, we extended HOL with a facility to label assumptions and operate uniformly on both goals and assumptions. We select automatically and predictably which low-level tactic to apply by examining the structure of the selected assumption or goal. A simple and uniform set of hints enable users to provide the minimal information needed to guide the tactics. We performed two case studies and achieved a 60% reduction in the number of unique tactics used.

1 Introduction

HOL 4 [4] is a powerful theorem proving environment, providing a wide range of proof techniques such as tactics, term rewriting, and decision procedures. However, the vast richness of HOL can be overwhelming. A novice user often spends a significant amount of time navigating through the HOL reference manual. Even experienced HOL users occasionally encounter difficulties remembering the name or syntax of a tactic. Based on these observations, our goal was to automate common proof tasks in HOL and eliminate much of the need to search documentation when doing common reasoning. By doing so, we allow the users to focus on devising strategies to conduct the proof.

Tactics in HOL can be classified into two types. Low-level tactics are used to decompose a goal into smaller subgoals or transform it into another form through term rewriting. Most of these low-level tactics carry out one specific operation at a time, such as eliminating a conjunctive operator or expanding the definition of a constant. In comparison, high-level tactics are capable of performing multiple operations in a single step, often attempting to reduce a goal as much as possible. High-level tactics can be risky when used without careful discretion because they occasionally perform more operations than what the user wants them to do. In some other cases, they simply fail to do what the user expects. Low-level tactics provide finer control, but they are numerous and difficult to remember.

In this paper, we introduce four new tactics: ELIM_TAC, EXPAND_TAC, REDUC_TAC, and EQUATE_TAC. The purpose of our tactics is to provide a balanced medium between

K. Schneider and J. Brandt (Eds.): TPHOLs 2007, LNCS 4732, pp. 157–172, 2007.

high-level and low-level tactics. These tactics replace many of the existing low-level tactics and inference rules in HOL, significantly reducing the number of functions that the user needs to remember throughout a proof. At the same time, all of the tactics operate on the basic principle that they should perform exactly what the user instructs them to do — no more, no less — thereby giving the user the complete control of proof steps. In short, these tactics provide what we call *controlled automation*.

Each of the four tactics is specialized in terms of the types of low-level proof tasks that it automates. ELIM_TAC is intended for performing primitive logical operations, such as the elimination of a conjunctive operator. We classify term rewriting into three different categories; definitional expansion, term simplification, and equational rewriting. The three types of rewriting tasks are carried out by EXPAND_TAC, REDUC_TAC, and EQUATE_TAC, respectively.

The implementation of our tactics is based on three underlying ideas. First, we introduce a new data structure called *hints*, which allows the user to provide the minimal amount of information needed to guide our tactics. A major portion of our work focused on establishing hints as an easy-to-use, intuitive control mechanism for HOL users. Secondly, we develop a system of labelling and identifying an assumption using a string in order to allow the user to operate directly on the assumption. Lastly, we provide a precise control mechanism for the user to select between different rewriting strategies, depending on the type of the rewriting task.

We performed two case studies to evaluate the effectiveness of the new tactics in improving the usability of HOL, and solicited feedback from novice users in a graduate course on formal verification. We started with a small example where HOL is used to solve a logic puzzle from the popular novel series *Harry Potter*. We then moved on to a much larger study, where we formally proved the equivalence of several superscalar microprocessor correctness statements [1]. The statistics gathered from these studies show an approximately 60% reduction in the number of HOL functions that a user needs to use in a proof, and a 25 to 40% decrease in the size of a proof script. These results demonstrate that our work simplifies and reduces the amount of interaction between the user and the theorem prover.

In Section 2, we describe ELIM_TAC and how it replaces many of the most commonly used low-level tactics or rules in HOL. Section 3 discusses the three tactics for rewriting: EXPAND_TAC, REDUC_TAC, and EQUATE_TAC. Sections 4 and 5 contain the description of the case studies and related work, respectively.

2   Controlled Automation for Logical Operations

2.1   Problem Description

The origins of our work come from two observations that we made about typical HOL proof scripts. First, many proofs could be shortened if assumptions could be manipulated with the same logical operations that can be applied to the goal. Second, the logical operation to apply to an assumption or goal can often be predicted based on the outermost operator of the assumption or goal. From these observations, we set ourselves the goal of developing a tactic that the user would aim at the goal or an assumption and say "do the obvious thing".

Any reasonably complicated proof in HOL likely involves the manipulation of assumptions. Before the user can completely prove the goal or subgoals using automated reasoners, it is often necessary to transform assumptions into a particular form through the application of low-level tactics or inference rules. However, HOL does not contain functions that allow the user to apply a forward inference rule *directly* to a specific assumption. Instead, an assumption is either moved into the goal and modified via tactics; or is transformed into a theorem, modified via forward inference rules, and then put back onto the assumption list. There are several disadvantages to this limitation. The multi-step processes to manipulate assumptions distract the user from the main reasoning of the proof. The names of forward inference rules are often seemingly unrelated to the names of the corresponding tactic. As the number of assumptions on the goalstack increases, it becomes difficult to identify the specific assumption to be manipulated. To overcome these inconveniences, we designed ELIM_TAC to operate uniformly on both the assumptions and the goal and developed a mechanism on top of HOL to name assumptions and then identify assumptions by name.

A goal-directed proof in HOL typically involves decomposing the goal or assumptions into smaller terms. For example, conjunctive goals (e.g. P $\wedge$ Q) are decomposed into two goals, one for P and one for Q. We observed that it is often possible to guess the next logical operation to perform by examining the outermost operator of the goal or assumption. To reduce the number of tactics that the user must remember, ELIM_TAC uses simple rules to choose the tactic to apply based upon the outermost logical connective or quantifier of the identified goal or assumption.

Different tactics have different arguments for users to pass information to the tactic (e.g a witness term for the elimination of an existential quantifier). Therefore, any process to automate the low-level tactics must include an intuitive, easy-to-use method for users to pass information to the underlying tactics. Relying on heuristics to guess the requisite information would violate our intention of giving the user complete control.

The remainder of this section discusses our approaches to solving the challenge of developing robust mechanisms to:

1. Choose a particular tactic to apply based on the logical structure of a term
2. Enable users to pass requisite information to underlying tactic
3. Operate operate uniformly on a goal or an assumption
4. Ensure that tactics perform the expected operation or fail immediately.

2.2 ELIM_TAC

ELIM_TAC combines many commonly used low-level tactics. We developed it with one ultimate purpose: save users time and effort in picking out which tactic to apply. The type of ELIM_TAC is: string -> hint list -> tactic. The first argument is a label that identifies the goal or an assumption as a *target* on which the tactic will carry out its operation. The empty string " " denotes the goal.

The second argument is a list of *hints*, which serve as a control mechanism for the user to provide the tactic with the necessary information for carrying out a logical operation. The choice of hints depends on the type of the operation that is to be performed on the target expression (e.g. the nullary constructor SKOLEM instructs ELIM_TAC to

Table 1. Descriptions of data constructors for `hint`

Constructor	Type in ML	Logical Operation
ASM	string -> hint	$\Rightarrow$ elimination
MATCH	term -> hint	$\wedge$, $\vee$ elimination
INSTANCE	term -> hint	$\forall$ elimination
WITNESS	term -> hint	$\exists$ elimination
SKOLEM	hint	Skolemnization

perform skolemnization on an existential quantified term). Table 1 contains a summary of the data constructors that are applicable to ELIM_TAC. Later in this paper, we extend the definition of `hint` with additional constructors that are used in our rewrite tactics (Table 2 in Section 3.3).

Often, ELIM_TAC does not require any hints. When the logical operation to perform can be inferred from the structure of the goal or assumption, an empty list of hints suffices. In the example sequent below, the current goal is an implicative formula $P \Rightarrow Q$. Applying ELIM_TAC pushes the antecedent into the current list of assumptions (note that the string "a" on the third line represents the label for the assumption, P):

$$\vdash P \Rightarrow Q$$
By   **ELIM_TAC " " []**
a $\bullet P$
  $\vdash Q$

$\Rightarrow$ **elimination in goal**

The sequents below illustrate the other uses of ELIM_TAC for goal decomposition without hints ($\wedge$, $\vee$, and $\forall$ elimination).

$\vdash P \wedge Q$	$\vdash P \vee Q$	$\vdash \forall x.u$
By **ELIM_TAC " " []**	**By** **ELIM_TAC " " []**	**By** **ELIM_TAC " " []**
$\vdash P$ $\vdash Q$	$\vdash P$	$\vdash u[x'/x]$
$\wedge$ **elimination in goal**	$\vee$ **elimination in goal**	$\forall$ **elimination in goal**

Next, we introduce an example of a situation where the user is required to provide an extra bit of information to ELIM_TAC. In order to eliminate an existential quantifier, we specify a witness term with the WITNESS hint.

$$\vdash \exists x.t$$
By   **ELIM_TAC " " [WITNESS 'u']**
  $\vdash t[u/x]$

$\exists$ **elimination in goal**

We have already presented the use of ELIM_TAC for eliminating the disjunctive operator in a goal. By default, the tactic selects the left of the two disjuncts to spawn as the subgoal. However, if the user wishes to extract the right disjunct instead, how should this operation be specified in ELIM_TAC? The constructor MATCH accepts a higher-order pattern and attempts to match it against either one of the two disjuncts in the goal. If a match is found, it spawns the matched disjunct as a subgoal. However, if no such match is found, the tactic *immediately fails* and displays an error message, instead of arbitrarily selecting a disjunct for subgoal generation. It is important to note that this failure mechanism is a critical part of all controlled automation techniques. If an operation violates the user's intention in any way, a controlled automation tactic must halt its execution; by doing so, it prevents any further operations that might lead to undesirable results for the user.

$$\vdash P \vee Q$$

By   ELIM_TAC "" [MATCH 'Q']

$$\vdash Q$$

∨ **elimination in goal**

The sequents presented in this section encompass all of the most common logical operations that one may wish to perform on a goal. In Sections 2.3 and 2.4, we show how we extend the capabilities of ELIM_TAC in order to automate even a wider range of primitive operations in HOL.

2.3   Assumption Labelling

Black and Windley [2] discuss various ways to select one or more specific assumptions in HOL. Arguably the most straight-forward and convenient mechanism for the user is identifying assumptions by their position in the assumption list. From an informal survey of students in a graduate-level introductory course to theorem proving, we found that most of them preferred to create their own tactic that allowed them to select a specific assumption by an explicit numeric index, rather than using built-in capabilities in HOL. However, this mechanism of identification is highly undesirable since it is sensitive to changes in a proof script. In the long term, it will likely be detrimental to the maintenance of the proof script.

In order to provide a mechanism that is convenient for the user and yet insensitive to changes in a proof, we label assumptions with strings. In order to identify a target assumption or goal, the user simply passes in the label for the assumption (or the " " for the goal) to ELIM_TAC. We also provided functions to allow the user to label a newly added assumption or change the label of an existing assumption on the goalstack.

Our implementation of labelling did not involve any changes to the existing HOL code. The mapping between an assumption and a label on the goalstack is accomplished through a hash table — the key is the term that represents the assumption, and the hashed item is the string label. The one-to-one mapping between the key and the hashed item ensures that each assumption has its own unique label, thereby separating the ordering of assumptions on the goalstack from their labels. When new assumptions are added to the goalstack without explicit labels from the user, each of them is entered into the hash table with a default label. In order to create a default label for an assumption, we use simple heuristics in which we extract a representative string based on the size and the first two alphanumeric characters of the term. We designed our heuristics in such a way that it would reduce the occurrences of duplicate default labels as much as possible without requiring the user to enter tediously long labels to refer to assumptions. However, in case of duplicate default labels, all subsequent duplicate labels after the first one are suffixed with a numeric index. This operation maintains the one-to-one mapping requirement in the hash table, but also introduces the dependency of labels on the ordering in which their corresponding assumptions are added to the goalstack. Based on our experiences with ELIM_TAC, the occurrences of duplicate default labels are rare. However, in order to ensure that assumption labels stay insensitive to changes in a proof script all the time, we encourage the user to label a new assumption with a unique, more meaningful name.

2.4 Extending **ELIM_TAC** to Work with Assumptions

Given the underlying infrastructure for assumption labelling, we now describe the full capabilities of ELIM_TAC as a versatile tool for both reducing a goal and transforming an assumption into a desired form. In this section, we present sequents for uses of ELIM_TAC when operating on an assumption. We also describe how hints are used to fully specify the user's intention when more than one primitive operations may be possible.

At times, it is useful to be able to extract one specific conjunct out of a term with an arbitrary number of conjuncts. Let us assume that the user intends to perform the elimination of a conjunctive operator on an assumption `t1 ∧ t2 ∧ t3`. Applying ELIM_TAC to the assumption without any hints results in the extraction of the leftmost conjunct, `t1`.

$$
\begin{array}{ll}
\text{a} & \bullet\, t1 \wedge t2 \wedge t3 \\
& \vdash P
\end{array}
$$

By   ELIM_TAC "a" []

$$
\begin{array}{ll}
\text{a} & \bullet\, t2 \wedge t3 \\
\text{t1} & \bullet\, t1 \\
& \vdash P
\end{array}
$$

∧ **elimination in assumption**

Another common primitive task in HOL is extracting an *inner* conjunct out of an expression. Carrying this operation out by using only the built-in functions in HOL may take several steps, depending on the level of nesting for that particular conjunct. Instead, we specify a pattern that matches a particular subterm (i.e. `t2`) using the MATCH hint. The meaning of MATCH depends on the context in which ELIM_TAC is currently being used. When applied to a goal, MATCH is used for the decomposition of a disjunctive expression; when applied to an assumption, MATCH plays the role in extracting a particular conjunct out of the assumption.

a $\bullet t1 \wedge t2 \wedge t3$
     $\vdash P$
By   **ELIM_TAC "a" [MATCH `t2`]**
a $\bullet t1 \wedge t3$
t2 $\bullet t2$
     $\vdash P$

$\wedge$ elimination in assumption using MATCH

In the next example, we show how one can use ELIM_TAC to perform the modus ponens rule involving two assumptions. Given the assumptions, "a1" and "a2" in the below sequent, the intuitive next step is to match the antecedent in `t1 ==> t2` against the other assumption and obtain the goal, `t2`. The data constructor ASM indicates which assumption should be matched against the antecedent of an implicative assumption.

a1 $\bullet t1 \Rightarrow t2$
a2 $\bullet t1$
     $\vdash P$
By   **ELIM_TAC "a1" [ASM "a2"]**
a1 $\bullet t2$
a2 $\bullet t1$
     $\vdash P$

$\Rightarrow$ elimination in assumption using ASM

When applied to an existentially quantified assumption without hints, ELIM_TAC performs skolemnization. Using only the built-in tactics in HOL, the most straightforward path to skolemnization on an assumption requires four different steps. Here, using ELIM_TAC, we accomplish this operation in a single step:

a $\bullet \exists x.t$
     $\vdash P$
By   **ELIM_TAC "a" []**
a $\bullet t$
     $\vdash P$

$\exists$ elimination in assumption

When an existential quantified expression resides as a subterm within an assumption with two or more conjuncts (e.g. `t1 ∧ ?x. t2 ∧ t3`), it is sometimes desirable to perform skolemnization directly on the quantified subterm. We introduce a new constructor called SKOLEM, which instructs ELIM_TAC to search for an existentially quantified subterm and apply skolemnization directly on it.

```
a    • t1 ∧ (∃x.t2) ∧ t3
     ⊢ P
By   ELIM_TAC "a" [SKOLEM]
a    • t1 ∧ t2 ∧ t3
     ⊢ P
```

∃ elimination in assumption using SKOLEM

Lastly, eliminating the universal quantifier from an assumption involves instantiating the quantified variable with a specific constant. The user must provide this constant through the hint constructor INSTANCE:

```
a    • ∀x.t
     ⊢ P
By   ELIM_TAC "a" [INSTANCE 'u']
a    • t[u/x]
     ⊢ P
```

∀ elimination in assumption using INSTANCE

In this section, we have described the operations that a user can perform using the combination of ELIM_TAC with hints. One possible criticism against ELIM_TAC is that the user is still required to memorize the name and the syntax of the different data constructors for the type hint. In response, we have tried to keep the number of the data constructors to a minimum without compromising the robustness of ELIM_TAC in its ability to perform a wide range of primitive operations. Also, the names and the syntax of the constructors are fairly intuitive and easy to remember. An experiment with students in the graduate course in theorem proving showed that once they became familiarized with ELIM_TAC, they preferred working with our tactic over having to remember a wide range of built-in HOL tactics and inference rules.

3 Controlled Automation for Term Rewriting

3.1 Problem Description

HOL contains a wide set of rewrite tactics and as well as several hundreds of previously proven theorems that can be used "off-the-shelf" as rewrite rules. Despite the richness of rewriting capabilities available in HOL, term rewriting is not always a straightforward matter, and the learning curve is stiff for a novice user.

In this section, we identify two major challenges with term rewriting in HOL. First, we observe that it is generally difficult to control the exact location within a term to which a rewrite rule must be applied. The most commonly used rewriting tactics such as REWRITE_TAC and ONCE_REWRITE_TAC walk over the entire term in a left-to-right order and applies the rewrite rule to the first rewritable subterm that it encounters. Sometimes, these tactics fail to meet the user's expectations; they either rewrite a wrong subterm or rewrite more subterms than the user has in mind.

Secondly, HOL does not provide an efficient way to apply a rewrite rule directly to an assumption or rewrite a goal using an assumption. The former case is closely related to the discussion in Section 2.3 - that is, the lack of a built-in mechanism for identifying or directly operating on one or more specific assumptions. ASM_REWRITE_TAC attempts to rewrite the goal using all of the existing assumptions, but is not useful when the user wishes to rewrite using only a subset of them. FILTER_ASM_REWRITE_TAC improves upon the former tactic by allowing the user to select a set of assumptions as rewrite rules, but requires a condition predicate, which can be tedious to create. A simpler mechanism for rewriting using assumptions is desirable.

In the process of developing controlled automation tactics for term rewriting, we have classified common rewriting tasks into three different categories:

1. Definitional expansion
2. Term simplification
3. Other equational rewriting

Instead of creating a single tactic that performs all three types of rewriting, we designed a separate tactic for each one of them. The rationale behind the separation of tactics is that it is difficult to devise a single rewrite tactic that "does it all" without falling into the danger of violating the user's intentions. For instance, it is sometimes desirable to simplify an arithmetic expression as much as possible, whereas in other situations, the user may intend to perform a more delicate rewrite operation. In either case, it is nearly impossible to guess what the user *might* wish to do for the next step of a proof.

In Sections 3.2 and 3.3, we describe our approaches to solving the aforementioned challenges - specifying a rewritable subterm and applying rewriting operations directly to assumptions. Then, in Section 3.4, illustrate how the three rewrite tactics evolve on top of our solutions to these challenges.

3.2   Specifying the Location of Rewriting

One solution to the challenge of specifying the exact location of rewriting within a term is combining the built-in tactic GEN_REWRITE_TAC with *conversions*. A conversion in HOL is a function, with a type `term -> thm`, that takes a term t and produces a theorem $\vdash t = t'$. A composition of multiple conversions can be used to specify the search strategies for term rewriting when passed to GEN_REWRITE_TAC.

For instance, let us assume that the user wishes to rewrite the left hand side of the equation in `x - (z + y) = x - (y + z)` using the built-in theorem ADD_SYM: $\vdash \forall m\ n.\ m + n = n + m$.

The conversion RATOR_CONV applies a rewrite rule to the operator of a function application, and ONCE_DEPTH_CONV applies the rule only once to an applicable subterm; the latter conversion is necessary in order to ensure the termination of rewriting. In the following sequent, the two conversions are composed using the infix operator o and passed as an argument to the tactic.

```
      ⊢x - (z + y) = x - (y + z)
By    GEN_REWRITE_TAC (RATOR_CONV o ONCE_DEPTH_CONV) [] [ADD_SYM]
      ⊢x - (y + z) = x - (y + z)
```

We developed an alternative solution where the user simply specifies a rewritable subterm using higher-order pattern matching. The main goal of our approach is to eliminate the necessity for built-in conversions in rewriting. As a first step, we define a tactic named NEW_REWRITE_TAC with a type `hint list -> tactic`. This tactic shares the same data type `hint` as ELIM_TAC does. However, in the context of rewriting, the data constructor MATCH is used to specify the higher-order match. In addition, we add a new constructor THM : `thm -> hint`, which takes a rewrite rule as the argument. By combining these two constructors into a list, the user instructs NEW_REWRITE_TAC to rewrite only the left hand side of the equation.

```
        ⊢x - (z + y) = x - (y + z)
By    NEW_REWRITE_TAC [MATCH `z + y`, THM ADD_SYM]
      ⊢ x - (y + z) = x - (y + z)
```

As an another example, let us assume that for whatever reasons, the user wishes to rewrite the left hand side of the equation SUC (x + y) = SUC (x + y) using ADD_SYM. In this case, the original higher-order matching technique cannot be used to specify only the left hand side of the term, as any pattern would match both of the two sides. In order to ensure that our term rewriting approach is complete, we extended our matching algorithm to allow the user to point at a rewritable subterm using the underscore character ` _ `. The following sequent illustrates this example:

```
        ⊢SUC (x + y) = SUC (x + y)
By    NEW_REWRITE_TAC [MATCH `_ = a`, THM ADD_SYM]
      ⊢SUC (y + x) = SUC (x + y)
```

As a whole, the meaning of MATCH `_ = a` is equivalent to *"extract a subterm that matches the pattern provided in the hint but rewrite only the part of the subterm that is highlighted by the underscore character."* Note that since the matching algorithm used in our approach is based on higher-order pattern matching, the fragment `a` in `_ = a` matches the right hand side of the entire term (i.e. `SUC (x + y)`). This mechanism is convenient because the user does not need to spell out the entire term to provide the exact match.

3.3   Integrating Rewriting with Assumption Handling

Directly Rewriting an Assumption. In Section 2.3, we introduced the system of identifying an assumption using string labels. We now extend NEW_REWRITE_TAC to allow term rewriting on an assumption. The ML type of the tactic is also updated to:

```
    NEW_REWRITE_TAC : string -> hint list -> tactic .
```

As previously mentioned, the empty string " " denotes the goal on the current goalstack.

Rewriting a Goal using Assumptions. Since NEW_REWRITE_TAC shares the same data type `hint` as ELIM_TAC does, we take advantage of the data constructor ASM to allow the user to specify the assumption to be applied to a goal as a rewrite rule. Then, the application of the tactic

Table 2. Descriptions of complete data constructors for `hint`

Constructor	Type in ML	Logical Operation
ASM	`string -> hint`	$\Rightarrow$ elimination, modus ponens, rewrite rule
ASMS	`string list -> hint`	Rewrite rules
INSTANCE	`term -> hint`	$\forall$ elimination
MATCH	`term -> hint`	$\wedge$, $\vee$ elimination, rewrite match
SKOLEM	`hint`	Skolemnization
THM	`thm -> hint`	Rewrite rule
THMS	`thm list -> hint`	Rewrite rules
WITNESS	`term -> hint`	$\exists$ elimination

```
NEW_REWRITE_TAC "" [ASM "a1"] .
```

rewrites the goal using the assumption with the label "a1."

In some cases, it is also desirable to include multiple assumptions as rewrite rules. In order to support this capability, we introduce a new data constructor for `hint` called `ASMS`. The constructor has an ML type `string list -> hint`. Similarly, to allow the user to specify multiple built-in or previously proven theorem as rewrite rules, we extend `hint` with another constructor called `THMS`. The complete list of data constructors of `hint` and their purposes are shown in Table 2.

3.4 Controlled Rewrite Tactics

Given the supporting mechanisms for specifying a subterm and rewriting with assumptions, we finally introduce controlled automation tactics that are specialized for term rewriting. In this process, we replace NEW_REWRITE_TAC, which was discussed in the previous section, with three new tactics, EXPAND_TAC, REDUC_TAC, and EQUATE_TAC. Syntactically, these tactics share the same ML type `string -> hint list -> tactic`. We believe that the range of rewriting operations supported by our tactics is wide enough such that user will rarely need to resort to the built-in rewrite tactics in HOL.

Definitional Expansion. EXPAND_TAC performs the definitional expansion of one or more constants in a goal or an assumption. A constant is expandable if there exists a built-in or user-defined theorem $\vdash c = t$, where c is the constant itself, and t is the term that represents the definition of the constant. More generally, if c is an n-arity function, an expression equivalent to an application of c to its n parameters, $p_1, p_2, ..., p_n$ is expandable if there exists a theorem $\vdash (c\ p_1\ p_2\ ...\ p_n) = t'$, where t' is a well-typed term in the HOL-specific variant of simply typed λ-calculus. One or more of the parameters, $p_1, p_2, ..., p_n$, may be universally quantified.

When invoked without any hints, EXPAND_TAC traverses the matching subterm within the target goal or assumption in the top-down manner and unfolds the definition of the first expandable constant or expression that it encounters. Internally, unnoticed by the user, EXPAND_TAC searches through the database of existing definitions in HOL and determines whether a constant is expandable. This automatic searching capability provides convenience to the user but is not always desirable; in this case, hints act as a useful control mechanism for specifying the behaviour of the tactic.

As an alternative to specifying the rewrite rule through THM, narrowing down the scope of the subterm search by using MATCH constructor has an identical effect. For example, let us assume that two theorems, factorial and pow have already been defined.

```
factorial: |- (factorial 0 = 1) /\
               !n. factorial (SUC n) = (n + 1) * factorial n
pow: |- (!k. pow k 0 = 1) /\
         !k n. pow k (SUC n) = k * pow k n
```

As a next step, the user expands the occurrence of factorial in the left hand side of the inequality:

```
⊢ factorial (SUC n) > pow 2 (SUC n)
```
By   EXPAND_TAC "" []
```
⊢ (n + 1) * factorial n > pow 2 (SUC n)
```

However, the user changes his or her mind and decides to unfold the definition of pow instead:

```
⊢ factorial (SUC n) > pow 2 (SUC n)
```
By   EXPAND_TAC "" [THM pow]
```
⊢ factorial (SUC n) > 2 * pow 2 n
```

It is not necessarily the case that the name of the ML binder (meta-level identifier) is equal to the name of the constant (HOL term) that is currently being expanded. Alternatively, the user can specify the subterm to be rewritten using a higher-order pattern:

```
⊢ factorial (SUC n) > pow 2 (SUC n)
```
By   EXPAND_TAC "" [MATCH `a > _`]
```
⊢ factorial (SUC n) > 2 * pow 2 n
```

The latter alternative may be preferred in some cases since it eliminates the user's mandate of having to remember the name of the ML binder for a specific theorem.

Term Simplification. REDUC_TAC recursively applies a set of built-in simplification rules about numbers, lists, and propositions as well as user-provided theorems to a goal or an assumption until no rewrite rule remains applicable. In essence, REDUC_TAC is a wrapper for the built-in HOL simplifier SIMP_TAC with an external interface that gives the user greater control of where to apply simplification. REDUC_TAC is most beneficial when the user wishes to simplify only a particular subterm within a goal or an assumption. Consider the following sequent:

```
a   •c + 1 - 1 = a + b
    ⊢c + 1 - 1 = SUC (a + b - 1)
By  REDUC_TAC "" [MATCH `SUC x`]
a   •c + 1 - 1 = a + b
    ⊢c + 1 - 1 = a + b
```

Applying REDUC_TAC to the entire term would reduce `c + 1 - 1` to `c`, which, in this example, is not the desirable outcome.

Equational Rewriting. The last of the trio, EQUATE_TAC, is intended for rewriting operations that do not fall into the two other categories - definitional expansion and term simplification. EQUATE_TAC may be used to perform any equational rewriting; in this sense, its behaviour is nearly identical to GEN_REWRITE_TAC. However, the two tactics differ significantly in their user interfaces. The latter tactic accepts a set of conversions for search strategies as well as a list of rewrite rules and theorems. EQUATE_TAC achieves nearly the same level of customizability with a much simpler external interface and does not require the user to commit to memory numerous conversion functions.

4   Case Studies

In order to evaluate the effectiveness of our approach in providing controlled automation, we have carried out two separate case studies in HOL. We first begin with a small proof that is based on one of the logic puzzles in the popular novel *Harry Potter and the Sorcerer's Stone*. The details of the puzzle are irrelevant for the purpose of our discussion. The original version of the proof that we carried out is about 280 lines long in terms of the size of the proof script, and required 8 intermediate lemmas.

The original proof script served as the control subject in our case study. We then carried out the same proof from scratch, but the main difference now was that our four tactics were available for use by the human prover. It is important to note that we did not modify the general, high-level strategies for carrying out the proof between the two proof scripts. Rather, the focus of our study was to measure the effectiveness of our approach in automating low-level details in a proof. After the proof was re-done, we gathered statistics such as the size of the proof script and the number of tactics or inference rules that the user had to use in order to successfully carry out the proof.

The first row in Table 3 illustrates the statistics from the study of the Harry Potter puzzle. The data exhibit a considerable amount of reduction in the size of the proof script. We attribute this improvement mainly to our assumption handling system, which allows the user to apply an inference rule directly to an assumption in one step. Using built-in tools in HOL, the same operation would take two to three steps on average.

Perhaps more significantly, the outcome of our study in Table 3 shows a large decrease in the number of tactics or inference rules that were used during the proof; the figure "5" in the last column includes the counting of our tactics. Throughout most parts of the proof, the user was able to perform logical or rewriting operations using our controlled automation tactics. There were only a few occasions where it was necessary to resort to built-in functions in HOL.

Table 3. Reduction in the Size of Proof Scripts and Number of Functions Used

	Size (LOC)			No. Functions		
	Original	Modified	Reduction	Original	Modified	Reduction
Harry Potter	282	162	43%	13	5	62%
Microbox	2254	1678	26%	30	12	60%

We also carried out a larger case study (2200 line proof script) in which we redid the Microbox [1] proofs about correctness statements for superscalar microprocessors. The second row in Table 3 contains the statistics for the comparison between the original and the modified version of the proof script for the microprocessor correctness statements. Similar to the Harry Potter proof, we observed a significant improvement both in terms of the size of the proof script and the number of functions used. The figure "12" in the last column of the table includes all of the four controlled tactics that we have described in this paper. The remaining eight were built-in HOL functions that did not fit into our definition of controlled automation. These functions included high-level automated reasoners (e.g. PROVE_TAC) and miscellaneous facilities such as tactics for renaming assumptions or dropping unnecessary assumptions from the goalstack. Based on the case studies, we believe that our approach holds considerable promise in making theorem proving in HOL a much simpler, less time-consuming task for both novice and expert users.

5   Related Work

The purpose of our tactics is not to add expressive or deductive power to the HOL theorem prover. Rather, our goal is to enable users to quickly perform many of the common logical or rewriting operations.

Harrison compared declarative and procedural styles of theorem proving [7]. Delahaye later compared declarative, procedural, and term-based proofs (for constructive logics) [3]. Each of these different styles of proof is best suited for different types of reasoning (e.g., forward vs. backward, short proofs vs. long proofs, elegantly crafted vs. done-and-forgotten). Our work lies within the world of procedural proof, and relies upon three principal ideas: assumption labelling for simple and robust access to assumptions, hints as a uniform mechanism to pass information to tactics, and packaging low-level rewrite strategies according to user-level purposes: definition expansion, simplification and reduction, and equational substitution.

Trybulec's Mizar theorem prover has long allowed users to label proof steps [12] [10]. Harrison adapted the idea of labels to do assumption labelling in his Mizar mode for HOL [5] and in HOL-light [6]. Hickey's MetaPRL supports the labelling of proof nodes to denote the type of reasoning that led to the node (e.g. primary line of reasoning, well-formedness, or antecedent to an assertion) [8].

One of the most valuable hints in our work is MATCH, which allows the user to select a subterm to operate on. Martin and colleagues used patterns and meta-variables in the Angel tactic language to identify subterms on which to operate and to extract subterms from the program to be passed as arguments to tactics [9]. Toyn used patterns to steer tactics and to select which tactic to apply [11]. In ISAR, Wenzel uses meta-variables in proof scripts to refer to terms and includes automatic binding of standard variables, such as *???goal* [13]. All of these uses of patterns would certainly be beneficial in hints or new tactics, but some of the uses could require significant changes to the way that HOL parses terms.

6   Conclusion and Future Work

In this paper, we have presented the concept of *controlled automation* as a balanced medium between high-level automated reasoning and low-level primitive operations in the HOL theorem prover. In order to show how we achieve this type of automation, we have introduced four new HOL tactics, which we named ELIM_TAC, EXPAND_TAC, REDUC_TAC, and EQUATE_TAC. We have also described special data structures called hints, which serve as an intuitive, easy-to-use mechanism for users to provide these tactics with information for carrying out the desired operations. Two case studies that we have conducted demonstrate that our tactics significantly improve on the degree of automation in HOL by reducing the number of functions that a user needs to remember.

We have introduced these tactics (in addition to existing tactics and rules in HOL) to students who are enrolled in the introductory level course in formal verification. This year's offering is the first time that we have done so. A major assignment in the course is theorem proving using HOL, and the students are given the freedom of using our tactics. So far, an informal survey of students indicates that they prefer to use the new tactics whenever possible over the existing ones in HOL. Many students have positively expressed that they do not have to cope with the burden of remembering the names of numerous tactics and inference rules in HOL. Our current plan is to continue introducing our tactics in future offerings of the course and receive feedback from students on how we can improve our tools to better assist novice users in the process of learning interactive theorem proving.

Acknowledgements

This research was funded in part by the Natural Science and Engineering Research Council of Canada (NSERC) and Canadian Foundation for Innovation (CFI). The authors are indebted to Nancy Day and the students in CS-745: Computer-Aided Verification for their feedback on earlier versions of the tactics.

References

1. Aagaard, M.D., Day, N.A., Lou, M.: Relating multi-step and single-step microprocessor correctness statements. In: Aagaard, M.D., O'Leary, J.W. (eds.) FMCAD 2002. LNCS, vol. 2517, pp. 123–141. Springer, Heidelberg (2002)
2. Black, P.E., Windley, P.J.: Automatically synthesized term denotation predicates: A proof aid. In: Theorem Proving in Higher Order Logics, pp. 46–57. Springer, Heidelberg (1995)
3. Delahaye, D.: Free-style theorem proving. In: Carreño, V.A., Muñoz, C.A., Tahar, S. (eds.) TPHOLs 2002. LNCS, vol. 2410, pp. 164–181. Springer, Heidelberg (2002)

4. Gordon, M.J.C., Melham, T.F. (eds.): Introduction to HOL: a theorem proving environment for higher order logic. Cambridge University Press, New York (1993)

5. Harrison, J.: A Mizar mode for HOL. In: von Wright, J., Harrison, J., Grundy, J. (eds.) TPHOLs 1996. LNCS, vol. 1125, pp. 203–220. Springer, Heidelberg (1996)

6. Harrison, J.: The HOL light system reference (2006),
http://www.cl.cam.ac.uk/~jrh13/hol-light/reference_220.pdf

7. Harrison, J.R.: Proof style. In: BRA Types workshop, pp. 154–172. Springer, Heidelberg (1996)

8. Hickey, J.J.: The MetaPRL Logical Programming Environment. PhD thesis, Cornell (2001)

9. Martin, A.P., Gardiner, P.H.B., Woodcock, J.C.P.: A tactical calculus. Formal Aspects of Computing 8(4), 479–489 (1996)

10. Rudnicki, P., Trybulec, A.: On equivalents of well-foundedness. Jour. of Automated Reasoning 23(3-4), 197–234 (1999)

11. Toyn, I.: A tactic language for reasoning about z specifications. In: 3rd BCS-FACS Northern Formal Methods Workshop (September 1998)

12. Trybulec, A., Blair, H.A.: Computer assisted reasoning with MIZAR. In: Int'l Joint Conf. on Artificial Intelligence, pp. 26–28. Morgan Kaufmann, San Francisco (1985)

13. Wenzel, M.: Isar – A generic interpretative approach to readable formal proof documents. In: Bertot, Y., Dowek, G., Hirschowitz, A., Paulin, C., Théry, L. (eds.) TPHOLs 1999. LNCS, vol. 1690, pp. 167–183. Springer, Heidelberg (1999)

Verified Decision Procedures on Context-Free Grammars

Yasuhiko Minamide

Department of Computer Science
University of Tsukuba
minamide@cs.tsukuba.ac.jp

Abstract. We verify three decision procedures on context-free grammars utilized in a program analyzer for a server-side programming language. One of the procedures decides inclusion between a context-free language and a regular language. The other two decide decision problems related to the well-formedness and validity of XML documents. From its formalization, we generate executable code for a balancedness checking procedure and incorporate it into an existing program analyzer.

1 Introduction

We have been developing a program analyzer for the server-side scripting language PHP, which approximates the string output of a program with a context-free grammar [8]. We adopted and developed several advanced decision procedures on context-free grammars to check properties of a program with the analyzer [9,17]. Although the correctness of those decision procedures is often intuitively clear, their detailed proofs can be rather complicated. That motivated us to verify them by using a proof assistant.

In this paper, we verify three procedures on context-free grammars used in our analyzer in Isabelle/HOL [13]. They decide the following three problems:

- inclusion between a context-free language and a regular language;
- whether a context-free language is balanced or not;
- inclusion between a context-free language and a regular hedge language.

The second and third procedures are used to check the well-formedness and validity, respectively, of dynamically generated XML documents in the analyzer.

Of the three decision procedures, we generated executable code of the second, the balancedness checking procedure, with Isabelle's code generator. Although the formalization of the procedure is almost executable, the formalization must be revised to obtain executable code and achieve reasonable efficiency. We incorporated the generated code into the PHP string analyzer by replacing the corresponding handwritten code. The analyzer with the generated code has been applied successfully to real PHP programs.

Our formalization and verification were conducted using the development version of Isabelle. We made positive use of new features introduced in the development version, such as a new function definition package by Krauss [7] and

K. Schneider and J. Brandt (Eds.): TPHOLs 2007, LNCS 4732, pp. 173–188, 2007.
© Springer-Verlag Berlin Heidelberg 2007

the revised locale mechanism, which make it possible to write proof scripts in a more natural manner. The proof scripts of the formalization in this paper are available from `http://www.score.cs.tsukuba.ac.jp/~minamide/cfgv/`.

2   Context-Free Grammars

In this section, we formalize context-free grammars (CFGs) and several basic procedures on them. The decision procedures in this paper are based on interpretation of a CFG over a monoid. The interpretation can be naturally formalized by considering a CFG over the monoid. Thus, we extend the notion of CFGs and formalize CFGs over a monoid.

2.1   Formalization of CFGs

To simplify our formalization, we only consider a grammar in a normal form such that each production has one of the forms: $x \rightarrow a$ and $x \rightarrow yz$ where x, y, and z are nonterminals (variables) and a is a terminal. A CFG is represented with the following record type:

record $('v, 'a)$ *cfg* =
  prod1 :: $('v \times 'a)$ *set*
  prod2 :: $('v \times 'v \times 'v)$ *set*
  start :: $'v$

where $'v$ and $'a$ are the types of nonterminals and terminals, respectively. This declaration introduces a record type with three fields *prod1*, *prod2*, and *start*. The fields *prod1* and *prod2* contain productions of the form $x \rightarrow a$ and $x \rightarrow yz$, respectively. A component of a record can be accessed with the field name, *e.g.*; *prod1 r* accesses the *prod1* field of a record r. A CFG over strings is modeled with type $('v, 'a\ list)\ cfg$. Note that this type permits a production of the form $x \rightarrow w$ for any sting w. Thus, the normal form above is not as strict as Chomsky normal form.

Although a grammar itself can be given without considering a monoid operation, the operation is necessary to define the language of the grammar. The set of monoid elements generated from a nonterminal is defined as an inductively defined relation: $(x,v) \in$ *derive cfg opr* formalizes "v is derived from nonterminal x".

derive :: $[('v, 'a)\ cfg, ['a, 'a] \Rightarrow 'a] \Rightarrow ('v \times 'a)\ set$
inductive *derive cfg opr*
$(x,v) \in$ *prod1 cfg* $\Longrightarrow (x,v) \in$ *derive cfg opr*
$[\![(y,v) \in$ *derive cfg opr*; $(z,w) \in$ *derive cfg opr*; $(x,y,z) \in$ *prod2 cfg* $]\!] \Longrightarrow$
$\qquad\qquad\qquad\qquad\qquad\qquad\qquad (x, opr\ v\ w) \in$ *derive cfg opr*

For a CFG over strings, concatenation of lists, the infix operator @ in Isabelle, is used for *opr*. Although this relation is defined even if *opr* does not satisfy the laws of monoids, we only use *opr* satisfying the laws in this paper. The language of a CFG is the set of monoid elements derived from the start symbol.

  lang-of :: $[('v, 'a)\ cfg, ['a, 'a] \Rightarrow 'a] \Rightarrow 'a\ set$
  lang-of cfg opr $\equiv$ { $v.$ (*start cfg, v*) $\in$ *derive cfg opr*}

2.2   Computing the Language of a CFG over a Finite Monoid

The language of a CFG can also be characterized as a fixed point of a monotone function over $'v \Rightarrow 'a\ set$ below.

$onestep :: [('v, 'a)\ cfg, ['a,'a] \Rightarrow 'a, 'v \Rightarrow 'a\ set] \Rightarrow 'v \Rightarrow 'a\ set$
$onestep\ cfg\ opr\ m\ x \equiv m\ x \cup \{v.\ (x,v) \in prod1\ cfg\} \cup$
$\qquad \{opr\ v\ w \mid v\ w.\ \exists y\ z.\ (x,y,z) \in prod2\ cfg \wedge v \in m\ y \wedge w \in m\ z\}$

The fixed point of this function can be computed if we consider a CFG over a *finite* monoid. The procedure can be formalized as follows using the predefined *while*-combinator in Isabelle.

$compute\text{-}langs :: [('v, 'a)\ cfg, ['a, 'a] \Rightarrow 'a, 'v] \Rightarrow 'a\ set$
$compute\text{-}langs\ cfg\ opr \equiv$
$\qquad while\ (\lambda x.\ onestep\ cfg\ opr\ x \neq x)\ (onestep\ cfg\ opr)\ (\lambda x.\ \{\})$

The following equality is proved by the rule of Hoare logic for *while* formalized in Isabelle.

theorem fixes $cfg::('v::finite, 'a::finite)\ cfg$
  shows $compute\text{-}langs\ cfg\ opr\ x = \{v.\ (x,v) \in derive\ cfg\ opr\}$

To guarantee that the while loop terminates, both the sets of nonterminals and terminals must be finite. The constraints are given as the type class *finite* of $'v$ and $'a$.

2.3   Image of a Context-Free Language

An interpretation of a CFG with a monoid is considered as an image of its language under a homomorphism to the monoid.

  Let us consider a homomorphism h between monoids $'a$ and $'b$. A standard result of the theory of CFGs is that the image of a context-free language (CFL) over $'a$ under the homomorphism h is a CFL over $'b$. This is shown by constructing a grammar over $'b$ as follows:

$image\text{-}of :: [('v, 'a)\ cfg, 'a \Rightarrow 'b] \Rightarrow ('v, 'b)\ cfg$
$image\text{-}of\ cfg\ f \equiv$
$\qquad (\!|\ prod1 = prod1\ cfg \odot rel\text{-}of\ f,\ prod2 = prod2\ cfg,\ start = start\ cfg\ |\!)$

where $s \odot t$ is the composition[1] of two relations and *rel-of* converts a function into a relation.

$$s \odot t \equiv \{(x,z).\ \exists y.\ (x,y) \in s \wedge (y,z) \in t\} \qquad rel\text{-}of\ f \equiv \{(x,y).\ f\ x = y\}$$

Then, the following formalizes the result above.

theorem assumes $\forall v\ w.\ h\ (opr\ v\ w) = opr'\ (h\ v)\ (h\ w)$
  shows $lang\text{-}of\ (image\text{-}of\ cfg\ h)\ opr' = h\ `\ lang\text{-}of\ cfg\ opr$

where $h\ `\ xs$ is the image of the set xs under the function h.

---

[1] The order of the arguments is different from the standard composition operator in Isabelle/HOL.

2.4 Reachable and Generating Nonterminals

We formalize two basic procedures on CFGs: computing the set of reachable nonterminals and computing the set of generating nonterminals. The latter procedure is then extended to generate a witness for each generating nonterminal.

We say a nonterminal X is reachable if there exists a derivation $S \overset{*}{\Rightarrow} \alpha X \beta$ where α and β are strings over terminals and nonterminals, and S is the start symbol. The standard procedure to compute the set of reachable nonterminals applies depth-first search by considering production rules as a graph.

A CFG is converted into a graph with *next-rel* and, we formalize reachability based on the graph as follows.

> *next-rel cfg* $\equiv \{(x,y). \exists z. (x,y,z) \in prod2\ cfg\} \cup \{(x,z). \exists y. (x,y,z) \in prod2\ cfg\}$
> *reachable cfg xs* $\equiv$ $(next\text{-}rel\ cfg)^*$ `"` xs

where r `"` xs is the image of the set xs under the relation r.

We formalize a depth-first search to compute the set of reachable nonterminals as follows.

function
> *dfs* :: $[('v::finite, 'a)\ cfg, 'v\ list, 'v\ set] \Rightarrow 'v\ set$ **where**
> *dfs cfg* [] *ys* = *ys*
> *dfs cfg* $(x\#xs)$ *ys* =
> (*if* $x \in ys$ *then dfs cfg xs ys else dfs cfg* $(nexts\ cfg\ x@xs)$ $(insert\ x\ ys))$

The function *nexts cfg x* computes a list of nodes adjacent to x. This formalization is almost identical to a depth-first search we write in a functional programming language. It is shown that this function always terminates by a lexicographic order similar to that used by Moore in his formalization of a graph search algorithm [10]. The correctness of this procedure is verified as the following theorem.

theorem   *dfs cfg* $(nexts\ cfg\ x)$ $\{x\}$ = *reachable cfg* $\{x\}$

We say a nonterminal X is generating if $X \overset{*}{\Rightarrow} w$ where w is a terminal string. The following is a formalization of a standard algorithm to compute generating nonterminals, which is considered as a fixed-point computation.

> *genv-onestep* :: $[('v, 'a)\ cfg, 'v\ set] \Rightarrow 'v\ set$
> *genv-onestep cfg m* $\equiv m \cup \{x. \exists y\ z. (x,y,z) \in prod2\ cfg \wedge y \in m \wedge z \in m\}$

> *genv* :: $('v, 'a)\ cfg \Rightarrow 'v\ set$
> *genv cfg* $\equiv$
> *while* $(\lambda x.\ genv\text{-}onestep\ cfg\ x \neq x)$ $(genv\text{-}onestep\ cfg)$ $\{x.\ \exists v. (x,v) \in prod1\ cfg\}$

Each iteration adds the nonterminals that are shown to be generating by *genv-onestep* from the nonterminals obtained in the previous iteration. The correctness of the function is proved as follows.

lemma fixes $cfg::('v::finite, 'a)\ cfg$
>   **shows** *genv cfg* = $\{x. \exists w. (x,w) \in derive\ cfg\ opr\}$

The function *genv* is extended to obtain a map of type $s \rightharpoonup t$, which gives a witness for each generating nonterminal, *i.e.*, a string generated from it. Type $s \rightharpoonup t$ is a synonym of $s \Rightarrow t$ *option*. The extended procedure is used in the balancedness checking procedure in Section 4.

To extend *genv* naturally, we use the function *choose* defined below

$$\textit{choose xs} \equiv \textit{if xs} \neq \{\} \textit{ then Some (SOME x. x} \in \textit{xs) else None}$$

The expression *SOME x. P x* represents an arbitrary element *x* satisfying *P x*. If there is no such element, it is an arbitrary element.

We thus obtain the following function that gives a witness for each generating nonterminal.

genv-onestep' :: $[('v, {}'a) \textit{ cfg}, ['a, {}'a] \Rightarrow {}'a, {}'v \rightharpoonup {}'a] \Rightarrow {}'v \rightharpoonup {}'a$
genv-onestep' cfg opr m ≡
$(\lambda x.\ \textit{if}\ x \in \textit{dom m then m x}$
    else choose $\{\textit{opr w1 w2} \mid \textit{w1 w2.}\ \exists y\ z.\ (x,y,z) \in \textit{prod2 cfg} \wedge m\ y = \textit{Some w1} \wedge$
m z = *Some w2*$\})$

genv' :: $[('v, {}'a) \textit{ cfg}, ['a, {}'a] \Rightarrow {}'a] \Rightarrow {}'v \rightharpoonup {}'a$
genv' cfg opr ≡ *while* $(\lambda x.\ \textit{genv-onestep' cfg opr x} \neq x)\ (\textit{genv-onestep' cfg opr})$
    $(\lambda x.\ \textit{choose}\ \{v.\ (x,v) \in \textit{prod1 cfg}\})$

The structures of *genv* and *genv'* are almost identical, and thus we can easily show the following lemma.

lemma fixes $\textit{cfg}::('v::\textit{finite}, {}'a)\ \textit{cfg}$ **shows** *dom (genv' cfg opr)* = *genv cfg*

3   Decision Procedure for Inclusion Between a CFL and a Regular Language

We verify a decision procedure checking inclusion $L(G) \subseteq L(M)$ for a CFG G and a nondeterministic finite automaton M. Textbooks on formal languages usually describe a decision procedure for this problem based on product construction of a pushdown automaton and a finite automaton. On the other hand, the procedure in this section directly operates on a grammar. It is a variant of the context-free graph reachability algorithm of Reps [15]. We use Nipkow's formalization of automata in Isabelle [12].

3.1   Nipkow's Formalization of Automata

We review Nipkow's formalization of nondeterministic automata. Nipkow formalized an automaton as a triple of a start state, a transition function, and a predicate defining final states. The following is its reformulation with a record type:

record $('a, {}'s)\ \textit{na}$ =
  start :: ${}'s$

$$next :: ['a, 's] \Rightarrow 's\ set$$
$$fin :: 's \Rightarrow bool$$

where $'a$ and $'s$ are the types of an alphabet and states, respectively. The formalization itself allows the set of states to be infinite.

Then, the extended transition function *delta* over lists and the function *accepts* describing accepted strings are defined in the standard manner:

$$delta\ A\ []\quad p = \{p\}$$
$$delta\ A\ (a\#w)\ p = Union(delta\ A\ w\ `\ next\ A\ a\ p)$$

$$accepts\ A\ w \equiv \exists q \in delta\ A\ w\ (start\ A).\ fin\ A\ q$$

where the function *Union* gives the union of a set of sets and has type $'a\ set\ set \Rightarrow 'a\ set$.

3.2 Transition Monoid

The following theorem states that a regular language is characterized by a finite monoid [4].

Theorem 1. *Let Σ be a finite alphabet. The following are equivalent for $L \subseteq \Sigma^*$.*

1. *L is regular.*
2. *There exist a finite monoid $\mathcal{M}$, a homomorphism $h : \Sigma^* \to \mathcal{M}$, a subset $B \subseteq \mathcal{M}$ such that $L = h^{-1}(B)$.*

One of the easiest ways to construct the monoid, the homomorphism, and the subset in the theorem is to consider a monoid of relations over states, where the composition of relations plays the role of the monoid operation. This monoid of relations over states and the homomorphism associated with it implicitly appear in Nipkow's formalization. The function *steps* in the formalization translates a string into a relation and has the following property.

$$steps\ A\ w = \{(p,q).\ q \in delta\ A\ w\ p\}$$

This function plays the role of the homomorphism in the theorem.

In addition to Nipkow's formalization, we introduce the following function, where *final-of na* plays the role of B in the theorem for the nondeterministic automaton *na*.

$$final\text{-}of :: ('a,'s)\ na \Rightarrow ('s \times 's)\ set\ set$$
$$final\text{-}of\ na \equiv \{r.\ \exists q.\ (start\ na,\ q) \in r \wedge\ fin\ na\ q\}$$

Then, the following is a formalization of the theorem in Isabelle, which can be easily proved with the lemmas provided in Nipkow's formalization.

theorem $steps\ na\ w \in final\text{-}of\ na \longleftrightarrow accepts\ na\ w$

3.3   Decision Procedure

With the formalization of CFGs and automata, it is quite easy to formalize a decision procedure to check inclusion between the languages of a CFG and a nondeterministic finite automaton. The inclusion can be checked by interpreting a grammar with the monoid characterizing the regular language. We obtain the expression to compute the interpretation over $('s \times \, 's) \; set$ as follows.

$$(steps \; na) \, ' \, lang\text{-}of \; cfg \; (op \; @)$$
$$= lang\text{-}of \; (image\text{-}of \; cfg \; (steps \; na)) \; (op \; \odot)$$
$$= compute\text{-}langs \; (image\text{-}of \; cfg \; (steps \; na)) \; (op \; \odot) \; (start \; cfg)$$

This can then be used as the decision procedure as follows.

theorem fixes $cfg :: ('v::finite, \, 'a \; list) \; cfg$ **and** $na :: ('a, 's::finite) \; na$
  shows $lang\text{-}of \; cfg \; (op \; @) \subseteq \{w. \; accepts \; na \; w\} \; \longleftrightarrow$
  $compute\text{-}langs \; (image\text{-}of \; cfg \; (steps \; na)) \; (op \; \odot) \; (start \; cfg) \subseteq final\text{-}of \; na$

The type system of Isabelle recognizes that the type $('s \times \, 's) \; set$ is an instance of *finite* from *s::finite*. Hence, we can compute the language and decide inclusion between finite sets of type $('s \times \, 's) \; set$.

4   Balancedness Checking Procedure

We introduce a CFG over a paired alphabet and verify a balancedness checking procedure that decides whether the language of a grammar is balanced or not. The procedure was developed by Berstel and Boasson [2] and the formalization in this paper is based on [9].

4.1   Balanced Strings

For a base alphabet A, we consider a paired alphabet consisting of two sets $\acute{A}$ and $\grave{A}$:

$$\acute{A} = \{\, \acute{a} \mid a \in A \,\} \qquad \grave{A} = \{\, \grave{a} \mid a \in A \,\}$$

The elements of $\acute{A}$ and $\grave{A}$ are considered as left and right parentheses: $\acute{a}$ and $\grave{a}$ match. The fundamental notion on a string over a paired alphabet is whether it is balanced. For example, $\acute{a}\grave{b}\acute{b}\grave{c}\acute{c}\grave{a}$ and $\acute{a}\grave{a}\acute{b}\grave{b}$ are balanced, but $\acute{a}\grave{b}$ and $\acute{a}\grave{b}\acute{b}$ are not. We call the set of all balanced strings the Dyck set [1]. A language L is balanced if all $\phi \in L$ are balanced.

We formalize strings over a paired alphabet as lists over the following data type.

datatype $'a \; balphabet \; = L \; 'a \mid R \; 'a$

Then, the set of balanced strings, the Dyck set, is formalized as the following inductively defined set.

$dyckset :: \, 'a \; balphabet \; list \; set$
inductive $dyckset$
  $[] \in dyckset$
  $xs \in dyckset \Longrightarrow [L \; x]@xs@[R \; x] \in dyckset$
  $[\![xs \in dyckset; \; ys \in dyckset \,]\!] \Longrightarrow \; xs@ys \in dyckset$

4.2   Monoid for Balancedness Checking

The Dyck set is not regular and thus cannot be characterized with a finite monoid. However, there is an infinite monoid, that makes it possible to decide whether the language of a CFG is balanced or not.

We say a string ϕ is *partially balanced* if it is a substring of some balanced string. Each partially balanced ϕ can be uniquely factorized into the following form:

$$\phi = \phi_1 \grave{a}_1 \phi_2 \grave{a}_2 \ldots \phi_n \grave{a}_n \varphi \acute{b}_m \psi_m \cdots \acute{b}_2 \psi_2 \acute{b}_1 \psi_1$$

where ϕ_i, ψ_i, and φ are all balanced. We say $\grave{a}_1 \grave{a}_2 \ldots \grave{a}_n \acute{b}_m \cdots \acute{b}_2 \acute{b}_1$ the reduced form of the string and write $\rho(\phi)$ for it. The set of reduced forms $\grave{A}^* \acute{A}^*$ with $\perp$ constitute a monoid, where $\perp$ represents the reduced form of unbalanced strings. The balancedness checking procedure is developed based on this monoid.

We formalize the monoid over $\grave{A}^* \acute{A}^* \cup \{\, \perp \,\}$ with the following data type:

datatype $'a\ bmonoid\ =\quad B\ 'a\ list\ 'a\ list\ |\ Bot$

where $B\ [a_1, a_2, \ldots, a_n]\ [b_1, b_2, \ldots, b_m]$ represents $\grave{a}_1 \grave{a}_2 \ldots \grave{a}_n \acute{b}_m \cdots \acute{b}_2 \acute{b}_1$, and $B\ []$ $[]$ is the unit of the monoid.

Let ϕ and ψ be partially balanced strings. The monoid operation between their reduced forms is defined by considering that of their concatenation $\phi\psi$. It is formalized as follows.

function
$concat :: ['a\ bmonoid,\ 'a\ bmonoid] \Rightarrow 'a\ bmonoid$ (**infixr** $\diamond$ 65) **where**
$B\ cs1\ []\ \diamond\ B\ cs2\ ss2\ =\ B\ (cs1 @ cs2)\ ss2$
$B\ cs1\ ss1\ \diamond\ B\ []\ ss2\ =\ B\ cs1\ (ss2 @ ss1)$
$B\ cs1\ (s \# ss1)\ \diamond\ B\ (c \# cs2)\ ss2\ =\ (if\ s = c\ then\ B\ cs1\ ss1\ \diamond\ B\ cs2\ ss2\ else\ Bot)$
$Bot\ \diamond\ y\ =\ Bot$
$x\ \diamond\ Bot\ =\ Bot$

Intuitively, it is clear that this operation is associative. On the other hand, the proof of this is not straightforward. We derive an equivalent definition of the function using the prefix relation of lists and prove associativity based on the definition.

With the monoid laws of $'a\ bmonoid$, it is straightforward to show that h defined below is a homomorphism from lists over a paired alphabet to the monoid.

$hom\text{-}of :: ['a \Rightarrow 'b\ bmonoid,\ 'a\ list] \Rightarrow 'b\ bmonoid$
$hom\text{-}of\ h\ []\ =\ B\ []\ []$
$hom\text{-}of\ h\ (x \# xs)\ =\ h\ x\ \diamond\ hom\text{-}of\ h\ xs$

$h \equiv hom\text{-}of\ (\lambda x.\ case\ x\ of\ L\ x \Rightarrow B\ []\ [x]\ |\ R\ x \Rightarrow B\ [x]\ [])$

Finally, we show that the Dyck set is characterized by this monoid.

theorem $xs \in dyckset \longleftrightarrow h\ xs = B\ []\ []$

The implication from left to right is easily proved by induction on the derivation of $xs \in dyckset$. The other direction is rather difficult to prove. We introduce a notion similar to the partially balanced string as an inductively defined set and prove: $xs \notin dyckset \longrightarrow h\ xs \neq B\ []\ []$.

For balancedness checking, we also introduce an ordering over reduced forms, which was used to improve the time complexity of a balancedness checking procedure in [9]. The ordering is defined as follows.

$$\grave{a}_1 \cdots \grave{a}_n \acute{c}_m \cdots \acute{c}_1 \leq \grave{a}_1 \cdots \grave{a}_n \grave{b}_1 \cdots \grave{b}_j \acute{b}_j \cdots \acute{b}_1 \acute{c}_m \cdots \acute{c}_1$$

This is formalized as the following order over *bmonoid*.

$$b1 \leq b2 \equiv (\exists\ cs\ ss\ zs.\ b1 = B\ cs\ ss \wedge b2 = B\ (cs@zs)\ (ss@zs))$$
$$\vee\ (b1 = Bot \wedge b2 = Bot)$$

4.3   Decision Procedure

Because the monoid introduced in the previous subsection is infinite, it does not directly give rise to a balancedness checking procedure. However, it is shown that balancedness can be checked by generating the monoid elements derived from each nonterminal to some bound.

In this section, we assume that a CFG is reduced. This means that every nonterminal is accessible from the start symbol and every nonterminal produces at least one terminal string. This condition is expressed with the following conditions on *cfg* in Isabelle.

$$\forall\ x.\ x \in reachable\ cfg\ \{start\ cfg\} \qquad \forall\ x.\ \exists\ w.\ (x,\ w) \in derive\ cfg\ opr$$

Because we assume that a grammar is reduced, for each nonterminal X, we can find terminal strings ϕ_1 and ϕ_2 such that $S \overset{*}{\Rightarrow} \phi_1 X \phi_2$. We then have $S \overset{*}{\Rightarrow} \phi_1 \psi \phi_2$ for any ψ such that $X \overset{*}{\Rightarrow} \psi$. For $\phi_1 \psi \phi_2$ to be balanced, the reduced forms of ϕ_1 and ϕ_2 must be the following forms: $\rho(\phi_1) = \acute{a}_n \ldots \acute{a}_1$ and $\rho(\phi_2) = \grave{b}_1 \cdots \grave{b}_m$. Furthermore, we have $\rho(\psi) \leq \grave{a}_n \ldots \grave{a}_1 \grave{b}_1 \cdots \grave{b}_m$. This observation is formalized as the following lemmas for *bmonoid*.

lemma assumes $b1 \diamond b2 \diamond b3 = B\ []\ []$
       shows $(\exists\ ss.\ b1 = B\ []\ ss) \wedge (\exists\ cs.\ b3 = B\ cs\ [])$

lemma assumes $B\ []\ ss \diamond b \diamond B\ cs\ [] = B\ []\ []$ **shows** $b \leq B\ ss\ cs$

These properties enable us to use $\grave{a}_n \ldots \grave{a}_1 \grave{b}_1 \cdots \grave{b}_m$ above as a bound when we check the balancedness of the language of a grammar.

We have the following decision procedure based on the observation so far by considering the interpretation of a CFG over the monoid.

1. Compute ϕ_1 and ϕ_2 such that $S \overset{*}{\Rightarrow} \phi_1 X \phi_2$ for each nonterminal X.
2. Generate the monoid elements derived from each nonterminal to the bound determined by ϕ_1 and ϕ_2.
3. If the bound is exceeded for some nonterminal, then the language is not balanced. Otherwise, the language is balanced iff the start symbol only generates the unit element, *i.e.*, $B\ []\ []$ in Isabelle.

The first step of the procedure is based on the procedures to compute reachable and generating nonterminals. First, we must compute a witness for each generating nonterminal by the procedure in Section 2.4. Then, we apply a depth-first search procedure to compute ϕ_1 and ϕ_2 above. Then, from ϕ_1 and ϕ_2, the bound is constructed by the following function.

$mkbound\ (B\ []\ ss,\ B\ cs\ []) = B\ ss\ cs$

The depth-first search procedure computes paths from the start symbol to all the reachable nonterminals, where a path corresponds to a pair ϕ_1 and ϕ_2 above. Please refer to the proof script for details.

The second step of the procedure is easily formalized as follows, where the bound is given as a function *bounds*.

$compute\text{-}langs'\ ::\ [('v,\ 'a)\ cfg,\ ['a,\ 'a]\ \Rightarrow\ 'a,\ 'v\ \Rightarrow\ 'a\ set,\ 'v]\ \Rightarrow\ 'a\ set$
$compute\text{-}langs'\ cfg\ opr\ bounds\ \equiv$
    $while\ (\lambda m.\ onestep\ cfg\ opr\ m \neq m \wedge (\forall x.\ m\ x \subseteq bounds\ x))$
        $(onestep\ cfg\ opr)\ (\lambda x.\ \{\})$

If *bounds* x is finite for all x, the function terminates.

The following is the formalization of the whole decision procedure, where *mkcon* is the depth-first search procedure and finds a bound, a pair of ϕ_1 and ϕ_2 above, for each nonterminal by using a function *gf* giving a generated monoid element for each nonterminal.

$bcheck\ cfg\ \equiv$
$(let\ gf\ =\ \lambda x.\ the\ (genv'\ cfg\ (op\ \Diamond)\ x);$
    $con\ =\ \lambda x.\ the\ (mkcon\ (op\ \Diamond)\ (B\ []\ [])\ cfg\ gf\ (start\ cfg)\ x)\ in$
$(\forall x.\ \exists ss\ cs.\ con\ x\ =\ (B\ []\ ss,\ B\ cs\ []))\ \wedge$
$(let\ bounds\ =\ \lambda x.\ \{b.\ b \leq mkbound\ (con\ x)\};$
    $result\ =\ compute\text{-}langs'\ cfg\ (op\ \Diamond)\ bounds\ in$
$\forall x.\ result\ x \leq bounds\ x \wedge result\ (start\ cfg) = \{B\ []\ []\}))$

The correctness of this procedure is verified in the following sense.

theorem fixes $cfg::('v::finite,\ 'a\ balphabet\ list)\ cfg$
  assumes $\forall x.\ \exists w.\ (x,\ w) \in derive\ cfg\ (op\ @)$
        $\forall x.\ x \in reachable\ cfg\ \{start\ cfg\}$
  shows $bcheck\ (image\text{-}of\ cfg\ h)\ \longleftrightarrow\ lang\text{-}of\ cfg\ (op\ @) \subseteq dyckset$

5   Decision Procedure for Inclusion Between a Context-Free Language and a Regular Hedge Language

We formalize a decision procedure deciding inclusion between a context-free language and a regular hedge language [11]. The procedure can be considered as a combination of the previous two decision procedures, and was developed by Minamide and Tozawa [9].

5.1   Hedges and Balanced Strings

We call a sequence of trees over the unranked alphabet Σ a hedge. The sets of trees and hedges denoted by t and h are defined as follows:

$$t ::= a\langle h\rangle$$
$$h ::= \epsilon \mid t\,h$$

where $a \in \Sigma$. We write $\mathcal{H}(\Sigma)$ for the set of hedges over Σ. By expanding t in the definition of hedges, hedges can also be defined as follows.

$$h ::= \epsilon \mid a\langle h\rangle h$$

We formalize this definition as the following datatype in Isabelle.

datatype $'a\ hedge = Empty \mid Br\ 'a\ 'a\ hedge\ 'a\ hedge$

Hedges can be considered as balanced strings by the following function.

$hedge2word :: 'a\ hedge \Rightarrow 'a\ balphabet\ list$
$hedge2word\ Empty = []$
$hedge2word\ (Br\ a\ xs\ ys) = [L\ a]@hedge2word\ xs@[R\ a]@hedge2word\ ys$

It is shown that this function is injective and its range is the set of balanced strings. The key to proving these properties is the following property of balanced strings. It is proved by using the monoid in Section 4.

lemma assumes $[L\ a]@xs1@[R\ a]@xs2 = [L\ a]@ys1@[R\ a]@ys2$
$\qquad\qquad xs1 \in dyckset\ ys1 \in dyckset$
$\quad$**shows** $xs1=ys1 \wedge xs2 = ys2$

5.2   Regular Hedge Grammars and Binoids

A regular hedge grammar (RHG) is a grammar over hedges with production rules of the following forms.

$$X \to \epsilon \qquad\qquad X \to a\langle Y\rangle Z$$

The set of hedges generated by a RHG is called a regular hedge language (RHL). It is basically a regular tree language over an unranked alphabet.

RHGs are formalized with the following record type as CFGs, and the derivation and the language of a RHG are formalized in the same manner as those of CFGs.

record $('v,\ 'a)\ rhg =$
$\quad prod1 :: 'v\ set$
$\quad prod2 :: ('v \times 'a \times 'v \times 'v)\ set$
$\quad start :: 'v$

Pair and Quere showed that a RHL is characterized with an algebra called binoid [14]. A binoid $\mathcal{B}$ over Σ is a monoid with the following additional operation.

$$\hat{\ }(\_) : \Sigma \times \mathcal{B} \to \mathcal{B}$$

For example, the set of hedges itself constitutes a binoid, where the monoid operation is the concatenation of two hedges and the additional operation above is one that builds $a\langle h \rangle$ from a and h.

The following shows that a RHL can be characterized with a *finite* binoid.

Theorem 2. *The following are equivalent for a set of hedges $L \subseteq \mathcal{H}(\Sigma)$.*

1. *L is regular.*
2. *There exist a finite binoid $\mathcal{B}$, a homomorphism $h : \mathcal{H}(\Sigma) \to \mathcal{B}$, a subset $B \subseteq \mathcal{B}$ such that $L = h^{-1}(B)$.*

The binoid satisfying the theorem above can be obtained by considering a monoid of relations over nonterminals. The additional operation $\hat{\ }(\_)$ is defined as *up rhg a b* for a and b below.

$up :: [('v, 'a) \; rhg, \; 'a, \; ('v \times 'v) \; set] \Rightarrow ('v \times 'v) \; set$
$up \; rhg \; a \; b \equiv \{(x,y) \mid x \; y. \; \exists (z, f) \in \; b. \; f \in prod1 \; rhg \wedge (x,a,z,y) \in prod2 \; rhg\}$

Although this binoid is used in the decision procedure for CFL-RHL inclusion, any binoid that satisfies the theorem is also suitable for the procedure. Thus, we introduce the locale *binoid* below and describe the main part of the procedure in the locale. Finally, we obtain our decision procedure by instantiating it to the binoid above.

locale *binoid* =
  fixes *up* :: $['a, \; 'b] \Rightarrow 'b$
  fixes *prod* :: $['b, \; 'b] \Rightarrow 'b$ (**infixr** $\Diamond$ *70*)
  fixes *unit* :: $'b$
  assumes *assoc*: $(x \; \Diamond \; y) \; \Diamond \; z = x \; \Diamond \; y \; \Diamond \; z$
  assumes *unitl*: $unit \; \Diamond \; x = x$
  assumes *unitr*: $x \; \Diamond \; unit = x$

5.3   Monoid for CFL-RHL Inclusion

Let us assume that a RHL is characterized with a binoid $\mathcal{B}$, a homomorphism $\_^{\circ}$, and a set B. The idea of the decision procedure is to interpret a set of strings generated from each nonterminal by using elements of the $\mathcal{B}$. However, each string ϕ such that $X \stackrel{*}{\Rightarrow} \phi$ is not necessarily balanced, but rather partially balanced. Therefore, we again use the factorization of ϕ:

$$\phi = \phi_1 \grave{a}_1 \phi_2 \grave{a}_2 \ldots \phi_n \grave{a}_n \varphi \acute{b}_m \psi_m \cdots \acute{b}_2 \psi_2 \acute{b}_1 \psi_1$$

where ϕ_i, ψ_i, and φ are all balanced. Then, we interpret ϕ with an element of $(\mathcal{B}\Sigma)^* \mathcal{B}(\Sigma \mathcal{B})^*$ as follows:

$$\phi_1^{\circ} \grave{a}_1 \phi_2^{\circ} \grave{a}_2 \ldots \phi_n^{\circ} \grave{a}_n \varphi^{\circ} \acute{b}_m \psi_m^{\circ} \cdots \acute{b}_2 \psi_2^{\circ} \acute{b}_1 \psi_1^{\circ}$$

where $\_^{\circ}$ is applied to balanced strings by considering them hedges. This is the ideas of the decision procedure.

The elements of the set $(\mathcal{B}\Sigma)^* \mathcal{B}(\Sigma \mathcal{B})^* \cup \{\bot\}$ constitute a monoid, and it is represented by the following datatype:

datatype $('b, 'a)$ *bmonoid* $= B \ ('b \times 'a) \ list \ 'b \ ('b \times 'a) \ list \ | \ Bot$

where $'b$ and $'a$ are the types for $\mathcal{B}$ and Σ, respectively.

Then, by using the locale *binoid* we formalize the monoid operation with the following function, where *concat x y z* is written as $x \triangleleft y \triangleright z$ with Isabelle's mixfix annotation.

function (in *binoid***)**
$concat :: [('b, 'a) \ bmonoid, 'b, ('b, 'a) \ bmonoid] \ \Rightarrow \ ('b, 'a) \ bmonoid$ **where**
$B \ cs1 \ b1 \ [] \ \triangleleft x \triangleright \ B \ [] \ b2 \ ss2 = B \ cs1 \ (b1 \Diamond x \Diamond b2) \ ss2$
$B \ cs1 \ b1 \ [] \ \triangleleft x \triangleright \ B \ ((cb2,c2)\#cs2) \ b2 \ ss2 = B \ (cs1@(b1 \Diamond x \Diamond cb2,c2)\#cs2) \ b2 \ ss2$
$B \ cs1 \ b1 \ ((sb1,s1)\#ss1) \ \triangleleft x \triangleright \ B \ [] \ b2 \ ss2 = B \ cs1 \ b1 \ (ss2@(sb1 \Diamond x \Diamond b2,s1)\#ss1)$
$B \ cs1 \ b1 \ ((sb1,s)\#ss1) \ \triangleleft x \ \triangleright \ B \ ((cb2,c)\#cs2) \ b2 \ ss2 =$
$(if \ s = c \ then \ B \ cs1 \ b1 \ ss1 \ \triangleleft \ up \ s \ (sb1 \Diamond x \Diamond cb2) \ \triangleright \ B \ cs2 \ b2 \ ss2 \ \ else \ Bot)$
$Bot \ \triangleleft x \triangleright \ b = Bot$
$b \ \triangleleft x \triangleright \ Bot = Bot$

The monoid operation is then $\lambda xy.x \triangleleft unit \triangleright y$, where *unit* is the unit of the binoid.

The rest of the decision procedure is quite similar to the balancedness checking procedure and is formalized in the same manner.

6   Executing a Verified Decision Procedure

We generated executable code of the balancedness checking procedure from our formalization with Isabelle's code-generating facility [6]. The generated procedure was incorporated into the PHP string analyzer [8] by replacing the corresponding handwritten procedure. The analyzer checks whether a PHP program always generates a well-formed XHTML document with the procedure. The revised analyzer was tested on real PHP programs. We describe issues that arose during this experiment.

The formalization of the balancedness checking procedure we have described is almost executable, but still requires some revisions to obtain executable code. We have formalized decision procedures as abstractly as possible by using *set* and $s \rightharpoonup t$ instead of concrete data structures. They are barriers to generating code and making it efficient.

Isabelle has the library *ExecutableSet*, which allows us to generate code for finite sets using lists. We generated executable code for sets with this library, but some revisions of the formalization and an extension of the library were required. We explain the issues with the procedure for computing the set of generating nonterminals with a witness.

$genv\text{-}onestep' \ cfg \ opr \ m \ \equiv$
$(\lambda x. \ if \ x \in dom \ m \ then \ m \ x$
$\quad else \ choose \ \{opr \ w1 \ w2 \ | \ w1 \ w2. \ \exists y \ z. \ (x,y,z) \in prod2 \ cfg \ \wedge \ m \ y = Some \ w1 \ \wedge$
$m \ z = Some \ w2\})$

$genv' \ cfg \ opr \ \equiv while \ (\lambda x. \ genv\text{-}onestep' \ cfg \ opr \ x \neq x) \ (genv\text{-}onestep' \ cfg \ opr)$
$(\lambda x. \ choose \ \{v. \ (x,v) \in prod1 \ cfg\})$

The first issue is the set comprehension in the formalization. The definition includes the following set comprehension: $\{v. \ (x,v) \in prod1 \ cfg\}$. Although this set is finite if $prod1$ is finite, this is not explicit in the expression and executable code cannot be directly generated from it. To obtain executable code, we must revise the formalization by using the following property.

$$\{v. \ (x, \ v) \in prod1 \ cfg\} \ = \bigcup (x', \ v) \in prod1 \ cfg. \ if \ x = \ x' \ then \ \{v\} \ else \ \{\}$$

The second problem concerns the *choose* function in the definition. The definition of *choose* uses *SOME*, *i.e.*, Hilbert's ϵ, for which code generation is not supported by the library. Furthermore, it appears that the code of *choose* cannot be implemented faithfully with lists. If *choose* is implemented with *choosel* over a list, then *choosel xs* = *choosel ys* should hold for lists xs and ys representing the same set. This property cannot be satisfied without any additional structure on its elements. To overcome this issue, we revised our formalization so that *choose* is used only for sets over types that are instances of *linorder*. The definition of *choose* was also revised so that it chooses the minimum element in a set.

We could generate code with these revisions. However, to obtain code with reasonable efficiency, more revisions were required. In our experiments, we represented nonterminals with type `int` in the ML side. Because the set of elements of `int` is finite and linearly ordered, the type satisfies the required conditions to use it as the type of nonterminals. However, the following two issues arise.

We verified the correctness of our decision procedures under the assumption that all nonterminals are generating and reachable. This simplified our verification, but it is not reasonable to assume it when we represent nonterminals with type `int` in ML. Thus, we revised our formalization so that the procedures assume that only the nonterminals used in a CFG are generating and reachable.

Finally, the evaluation strategy of functional programming languages becomes an issue for efficient execution: they do not evaluate the expression inside a lambda abstraction. In the decision procedure, type $s \rightharpoonup t$ is used to represent finite maps. The type is actually a function type to *option* type. Then, all the computation related to a map is delayed until the map is applied to an argument. That caused an exponential blowup of execution time. To avoid this blowup, we insert the function *reduce-fun* with the following type into the places where evaluation inside a lambda abstraction is desirable.

$$reduce\text{-}fun \ :: \ ['a{::}\{finite, linorder\} \ set, \ 'a \Rightarrow \ 'b] \Rightarrow 'a \Rightarrow \ 'b$$

An expression *reduce-fun f s* forces the evaluation of f for the values in the set s and reconstructs the function. For the definition of the function, please refer to the proof script.

By applying these revisions, we could run the analyzer with the code generated by Isabelle for real PHP programs. We tested it on two PHP programs, for which the analyzer generated CFGs with 170 and 70 production rules. With the handwritten code, the balancedness can be checked very quickly, taking 0.016 and 0.003 seconds for the two programs. On the other hand, the generated code was quite slow, taking 32.6 and 16.7 seconds. We checked execution times for each part of the procedure and found that the depth-first search is efficient, but the fixed-point computations used in *genv'* and *compute-langs'* are very slow. We think that this is because the formalization of depth-first search is very close to a standard implementation, but the formalization of the fixed-point computation is rather abstract. It will be necessary to revise its formalization and adopt a more efficient data structure to represent finite maps to obtain more efficient code.

7   Related Work

Our formalization is strongly influenced by Nipkow's formalization of automata, which formalizes automata and regular expressions, and verifies a lexical analyzer obtained from a regular expression [12]. There have been several other attempts to formalize the theory of formal languages in a proof assistant. Courant and Filliâtre formalized regular and context-free languages in Coq [3]. The formalization includes some standard theory of context-free languages such as transformation between a context-free grammar and a pushdown automaton. Rival and Goubault-Larrecq formalized tree automata in Coq [16] and executed some procedures on tree automata in Coq.

We have described several issues in obtaining an (efficient) executable balancedness checking procedure in Section 6. The importance of obtaining efficient executable code from an elegant formalization is recognized in the context of ACL2. Greve et al. reviewed issues there and described the features in ACL2 to support it [5]. This will be good guide to obtain really efficient executable code for our decision procedures.

8   Conclusion

We have verified three precision procedures on context-free grammars. The formalization and verification of the procedures went smoothly and took me about non-intensive two months. On the other hand, the revisions to generate executable code for the balancedness checking procedure required more time than we expected.

We plan to generate code for the other two procedures. Although code will be generated in the same manner as the balancedness checking procedure, we expect a more severe problem with efficiency. It is because the relations over states or nonterminals used there will become too large if `int` are used in the ML side.

References

1. Berstel, J.: Transductions and Context-Free Languages. Teubner Studienbucher (1979)
2. Berstel, J., Boasson, L.: Formal properties of XML grammars and languages. Acta Informatica 38(9), 649–671 (2002)
3. Courant, J., Filliâtre, J.-C.: Beginning of formal language theory (1993), http://coq.inria.fr/contribs-eng.html

4. Eilenberg, S.: Automata, Languages, and Machines. ch. 3, Academic Press, London (1974)
5. Greve, D.A., Kaufmann, M., et al.: Efficient execution in an automated reasoning environment. Journal of Functional Programming (to appear, 2007)
6. Haftmann, F.: Code generation from Isabelle/HOL theories, available in the Isabelle distribution (2007)
7. Krauss, A.: Partial recursive functions in higher-order logic. In: Furbach, U., Shankar, N. (eds.) IJCAR 2006. LNCS (LNAI), vol. 4130, pp. 589–603. Springer, Heidelberg (2006)
8. Minamide, Y.: Static approximation of dynamically generated Web pages. In: Proceedings of the 14th International World Wide Web Conference, pp. 432–441. ACM Press, New York (2005)
9. Minamide, Y., Tozawa, A.: XML validation for context-free grammars. In: Kobayashi, N. (ed.) APLAS 2006. LNCS, vol. 4279, pp. 357–373. Springer, Heidelberg (2006)
10. Strother Moore, J.: An exercise in graph theory. In: Kaufmann, M., Manolios, P., Strother Moore, J. (eds.) Computer-Aided Reasoning: ACL2 Case Studies, ch. 5, pp. 41–74. Kluwer Academic Publishers, Dordrecht (2000)
11. Murata, M.: Hedge automata: a formal model for XML schemata (1999), http://www.xml.gr.jp/relax/hedge_nice.html
12. Nipkow, T.: Verified lexical analysis. In: Grundy, J., Newey, M. (eds.) Theorem Proving in Higher Order Logics. LNCS, vol. 1479, pp. 1–15. Springer, Heidelberg (1998)
13. Nipkow, T., Paulson, L.C., Wenzel, M.: Isabelle/HOL. LNCS, vol. 2283. Springer, Heidelberg (2002)
14. Pair, C., Quere, A.: Définition et étude des bilangages réguliers. Information and Control 13(6), 565–593 (1968)
15. Reps, T.: Program analysis via graph reachability. Information and Software Technology 40(11–12), 701–726 (2000)
16. Rival, X., Goubault-Larrecq, J.: Experiments with finite tree automata in Coq. In: Boulton, R.J., Jackson, P.B. (eds.) TPHOLs 2001. LNCS, vol. 2152, pp. 362–377. Springer, Heidelberg (2001)
17. Tozawa, A., Minamide, Y.: Complexity results on balanced context-free languages. In: Proc. of Tenth International Conference on Foundations of Software Science and Computation Structures. LNCS, vol. 4423, pp. 346–360. Springer, Heidelberg (2007)

Using XCAP to Certify Realistic Systems Code: Machine Context Management

Zhaozhong Ni[1], Dachuan Yu[2], and Zhong Shao[3]

[1] Microsoft Research, One Microsoft Way, Redmond, WA 98052, U.S.A.
zhaozhong.ni@microsoft.com
[2] DoCoMo Communications Laboratories USA, Inc, Palo Alto, CA 94304, U.S.A.
yu@docomolabs-usa.com
[3] Department of Computer Science, Yale University, New Haven, CT 06520, U.S.A.
shao@cs.yale.edu

Abstract. Formal, modular, and mechanized verification of realistic systems code is desirable but challenging. Verification of machine context management (a basis of multi-tasking) is one representative example. With context operations occurring hundreds to thousands of times per second on every computer, their correctness deserves careful examination. Given the small and stable code bases, it is a common misunderstanding that the context management code is suitable for informal scrutiny and testing. Unfortunately, after being extensively studied and used for decades, it still proves to be a common source of bugs and confusion. Yet its verification remains difficult due to the machine-level detail, irregular patterns of control flows, and rich application scenarios.

This paper reports our experience applying XCAP—a recent theoretical verification framework—to certify a realistic x86 implementation of machine context management. XCAP supports expressive and modular logical specifications, but has only previously been applied on simple idealized machine and code. By applying the XCAP theory to an x86 machine model, building libraries of common proof tactics and lemmas, composing specifications for the context data structures and routines, and proving that the code behave accordingly, we achieved the first formal, modular, and mechanized verification of realistic x86 context management code. Our proofs are fully mechanized in the Coq proof assistant. Our certified library code runs on stock hardware and can be linked with other certified systems and application code. Our technique applies to other variants or extensions of context management (*e.g.*, more complex context, different platforms), provides a solid basis for further verification of thread implementation and concurrent programs, and illustrates how to achieve formal, modular, and mechanized verification of realistic systems code.

1 Introduction

Formally establishing safety and correctness properties of realistic systems code in a modular and machine-checkable fashion is a highly desirable but extremely

K. Schneider and J. Brandt (Eds.): TPHOLs 2007, LNCS 4732, pp. 189–206, 2007.

challenging goal. Among various systems code libraries, machine context management, the basis of multi-tasking and an essential feature of modern system software, is one representative example. We use the following 19-line x86 machine-context switching routine (omitting floating-point and special registers) to illustrate our point.

```
swapcontext:
    mov eax, [esp+4]        |  mov eax, [esp+8]
    mov [eax+_eax], 0       |  mov esp, [eax+_esp]
    mov [eax+_ebx], ebx     |  mov ebp, [eax+_ebp]
    mov [eax+_ecx], ecx     |  mov edi, [eax+_edi]
    mov [eax+_edx], edx     |  mov esi, [eax+_esi]
    mov [eax+_esi], esi     |  mov edx, [eax+_edx]
    mov [eax+_edi], edi     |  mov ecx, [eax+_ecx]
    mov [eax+_ebp], ebp     |  mov ebx, [eax+_ebx]
    mov [eax+_esp], esp     |  mov eax, [eax+_eax]
                            |  ret
```

The left half of the code saves the current machine context, whereas the right half loads the new machine context and resumes the program control from there. Although conceptually easy to recognize, context switching is hard to reason about even at the meta-level—it involves program counters, register files, stacks, private and shared heaps, function calls/returns, higher-order control-flows, *etc.*

Because context switching occurs so frequently—hundreds to thousands of times per second on every computer—code sequences similar to the above one deserve the most careful examination. Their safety and correctness are crucial to all multi-tasking software built on top of them. A common misunderstanding is that such code is so stable and small in size that it is more suitable for informal scrutiny and testing. Unfortunately, despite having been extensively studied and used for decades, this code still proves to be a common source of bugs and confusion. A quick web search reveals many reports and discussions of bugs in context management code [8,20,11,7,17,19] even today. Thus, it should be a focus of formal methods and mechanized verifications. Yet to the authors' knowledge, there has been no formal proof, either manual or mechanized, of the safety and correctness of code similar to the above one.

Recently, formal studies on systems code for operating system kernels have attracted growing interest. One example is the Singularity project [5], which aims to build a highly reliable OS using a type-safe language (C#) and other techniques. Another example is the Verisoft project [3], which uses computer-aided logical proofs to obtain the correctness of critical systems including OS kernels. Unfortunately, both fall short at the above 19-line code: Singularity trusts unsafe assembly code for doing context switching; Verisoft uses an abstract model of user process that hides the context switching details. Moreover, without a full verification of context management, existing work on concurrent verification is prevented from being integrated with the verification of systems code, as it relies on the correctness of concurrency primitives.

This paper reports our experience on applying XCAP [12], a recent assembly code verification framework, to an x86 machine model, and certifying a realistic machine context implementation with it. XCAP allows expressive and modular logical specifications of safety and correctness, but has been applied previously only on a simple idealized machine model and application code. Starting with the code for context management, we show in this paper how to build the implementation infrastructure and carry out the verification. We first applied the XCAP theory to an x86 machine model, which required some changes to the inference rules for program reasoning. To support practical verification, we built libraries of proof tactics and lemmas. We then specified the context data structures and routines using the XCAP logic-based specifications, and proved that the code behaves accordingly.

Our library code and proof can be linked with other systems code and application code, as well as their corresponding proofs. The code runs on stock hardware. Our approach is applicable to other variants of context management (such as more complex contexts, different hardware platforms, *etc.*). It provides a solid basis for further verification of concurrent programs. Besides achieving the first formal, modular, and mechanized verification of x86 context management code, our experience also illustrates how verification of realistic systems code can be done in general.

In particular, we want to point out the following features in our case study.

- As shown by *swapcontext*(), our code is representative and realistic, and runs on stock hardware. Its verification does not require a change of programming style or the abandonment of legacy code. There are no performance penalties or compatibility issues.
- Without compromising soundness, our machine model supports realistic features such as variable-length instruction decoding, finite machine-word, word-aligned byte-addressed memory, conditional flags, stack push/pop, and function call/return.
- Our specifications are modular and expressive. For example, the private local data that belongs to a context can be of arbitrary shape and size. The approach is not specialized to a particular kind of multi-tasking implementation, thus our method will likely support other possible usages of machine contexts.
- Everything—the code, machine model, adapted XCAP meta theory (including soundness), proof tactics and lemmas, and code specification and proof—is fully mechanized using the Coq proof assistant, thus leaving a tiny trusted computing base.

The paper is organized as follows. We start in Section 2 by discussing our machine context implementation. In Section 3 we show how to apply XCAP to an x86 machine model. We then specify and verify the context code in Section 4. Section 5 discusses our Coq implementation. Finally, we compare with related work and conclude in Section 6.

2   Machine Context Management

Context refers to the local (private) data of a computation task. It is a widely used concept in software and programming. It is crucial to multi-tasking, as the latter is eventually carried out by doing a context switch. Depending on its application and abstraction level, a context may contain program counters, register files, stacks, private heap, thread control blocks, process control blocks, *etc.* Common context management operations include context creation, restoring, and switching.

Context data structures. The x86 machine context implementation in this paper is at the same level as those found in typical Windows, Unix, and Linux systems. To simplify the problem and focus on the most critical part, we ignore orthogonal features such as floating point and special registers. The machine context structure mctx_st contains the eight general purpose registers of an x86 processor (including a stack pointer register, which should point to a stack with a valid return address on top). The corresponding pointer type is mctx_t. Below are the definitions in C.

```
typedef struct mctx_st *mctx_t;
struct mctx_st {int eax, int ebx, int ecx, int edx,
                int esi, int edi, int ebp, int esp};
```

Context creation. The *makecontext*() function initializes a new context with its arguments: location of context, new stack pointer, return link, address of target function, and argument for target function. It is basis of and analogous to the creation of a new thread. The new stack pointer points to a stack frame prepared for the target function. Notice here *func*() is a **higher-order function pointer**, and *lnk* is also a **higher-order continuation pointer**. When the newly created context gets first switched to, *func*() will start execution. When it finishes, *func*() should return to *lnk*.

```
void makecontext (mctx_t mctx, char *sp, void *lnk, void *func, void *arg);
  mov eax, [esp+4]     // load address of the context
  mov ecx, [esp+8]     // load stack top pointer for the new stack frame
  mov edx, [esp+20]    // load the function's argument
  mov [ecx-4], edx     // push it onto new stack
  mov edx, [esp+12]    // load the function's return link
  mov [ecx-8], edx     // push it onto new stack
  mov edx, [esp+16]    // load the function address
  mov [ecx-12], edx    // push it as return IP onto new stack
  sub ecx, 12
  mov [eax+_esp], ecx // all useful info for fresh context is on new stack
  ret
```

Context switching. The *swapcontext*() function saves the current old context and loads a new one for further execution. Because the stack pointer is changed to the new context's, instead of returning to its direct caller in the old context, it returns to its previous caller in the new context. (Alternatively, the first time a new context gets switched to, it "returns" to the function pointer $func()$, as supplied upon its creation.) Because its code was presented in the beginning of the paper, we only present its interface below.

```
void swapcontext (mctx_t old, mctx_t new);
```

Context loading. The *loadcontext*() function loads a new context and continues execution from there. It is essentially the second half of *swapcontext*(), with a slight difference in the location of context pointers. Technically speaking, it is not a "function" since it never returns to its caller.

```
void loadcontext (mctx_t mctx);
  mov eax, [esp+8]      // load address of the new context
  mov esp, [eax+_esp]   // load the new stack pointer
  mov ebp, [eax+_ebp]   // load the new registers
  mov edi, [eax+_edi]
  mov esi, [eax+_esi]
  mov edx, [eax+_edx]
  mov ecx, [eax+_ecx]
  mov ebx, [eax+_ebx]
  mov eax, [eax+_eax]
  ret                   // invoke the new context
```

Why traditional methods are insufficient? One may be tempted to think that traditional type systems or program logics should be sufficient to verify the safety and correctness of this "simple" code. After all, it is only 3 functions and 40 assembly instructions. However, as will become apparent in the detailed discussion in the next few sections, a general verification of this code requires at least the following features: 1) polymorphism over arbitrary shape of program data; 2) explicit multiple stacks with flexible stack handling (such as one context manipulating other contexts' stacks); 3) separation-logic-like strong-update style of memory model (*i.e.*, context data should not be managed by garbage collectors, as is in the real-world scenario); 4) general embedded code pointers (not merely higher-order functions, but also higher-order continuations, *e.g.*, see the discussion of $func$ and lnk for *makecontext*() earlier); 5) support of partial correctness. Traditional type systems such as Typed Assembly Languages (TAL) [9] typically have problems with (1), (2), (3), and (5). Traditional program logics, including Hoare Logic [4] and Separation Logic [16] often fail on (4), as explained in [12]. The very recent index-based semantic model approach for Foundational Proof-Carrying Code [1] does not support (5). Only with recent hybrid type/logic systems such as XCAP [12], can all of these features be supported simultaneously.

3   Applying XCAP to x86 Machine Model

Our verification is carried out following XCAP [12], a logic-based verification framework that facilitates modular reasoning in the presence of embedded code

$$
\begin{array}{llll}
(Prog) & \mathbb{P} ::= (\mathbb{S}, pc) & (Word) & \mathtt{w} ::= i \ (uint32) \\
(State) & \mathbb{S} ::= (\mathbb{H}, \mathbb{R}, \mathbb{F}) & (CdLbl) & \mathtt{f} ::= i \ (uint32) \\
(Mem) & \mathbb{H} ::= \{1_1 \rightsquigarrow \mathtt{w}_1, \ldots, 1_n \rightsquigarrow \mathtt{w}_n\} & (Label) & \mathtt{l} ::= i \ (i\%4=0) \\
(Rfile) & \mathbb{R} ::= \{\mathsf{eax} \rightsquigarrow \mathtt{w}_1, \ldots, \mathsf{esp} \rightsquigarrow \mathtt{w}_8\} & (Bool) & \mathtt{b} ::= tt \mid ff \\
(FReg) & \mathbb{F} ::= \{\mathsf{cf} \rightsquigarrow \mathtt{b}_1, \mathsf{zf} \rightsquigarrow \mathtt{b}_2\} & (Addr) & \mathtt{d} ::= i \mid \mathtt{r}{\pm}i \\
(Cond) & cc ::= \mathsf{a} \mid \mathsf{ae} \mid \mathsf{b} \mid \mathsf{be} \mid \mathsf{e} \mid \mathsf{ne} & (Opr) & \mathtt{o} ::= i \mid \mathtt{r}
\end{array}
$$

$(Reg) \quad \mathtt{r} ::= \mathsf{eax} \mid \mathsf{ebx} \mid \mathsf{ecx} \mid \mathsf{edx} \mid \mathsf{esi} \mid \mathsf{edi} \mid \mathsf{ebp} \mid \mathsf{esp}$

$(Instr) \quad \mathtt{c} ::= \mathsf{add}\ \mathtt{r}, \mathtt{o} \mid \mathsf{sub}\ \mathtt{r}, \mathtt{o} \mid \mathsf{mov}\ \mathtt{r}, \mathtt{o} \mid \mathsf{mov}\ \mathtt{r}, [\mathtt{d}] \mid \mathsf{mov}\ [\mathtt{d}], \mathtt{o} \mid \mathsf{cmp}\ \mathtt{r}, \mathtt{o} \mid \mathsf{jcc}\ \mathtt{f} \mid \mathsf{jmp}\ \mathtt{o}$
$\qquad\qquad \mid \mathsf{push}\ \mathtt{o} \mid \mathsf{pop}\ \mathtt{r} \mid \mathsf{call}\ \mathtt{o} \mid \mathsf{ret}$

Fig. 1. Syntax of the x86 machine model

pointers and other higher-order features. In [12], XCAP is applied to an idealized RISC-like toy machine and simple user-level code. When applying XCAP to x86, we had to make practical adaptations and build useful abstractions, particularly for the machine-level details and the handling of the stack and function calls. In this section we first briefly present our adaptation steps and then show how to carry out the verification in general. Interested readers are referred to [12] and the technical report [15] for more details.

Machine model. We formalized a subset of x86 as the machine model for XCAP, as presented in Fig. 1. The execution environment consists of a memory, a register file of general-purpose registers, a flags register made up of a carry bit and a zero bit, and a program counter. The memory appears as a single continuous address space, where both code and data (static and dynamic) reside in. The data part of the memory, the register file, and the flags register form the machine state. We support common instructions for arithmetic, data movement, comparison, control flow transfer, and stack manipulation, as well as realistic x86 features such as variable-length instruction decoding, finite machine-word, word-aligned byte-addressed memory, conditional flags, stack push/pop, and function call/return. Operational semantics for the x86 machine model can be found in the TR [15] . In the rest of this paper, $\mathbb{I}$ represents a sequence of instructions; and $\mathsf{Next_c}$ denotes a function that computes the resulting state of executing instruction $\mathtt{c}$.

Basic reasoning. The basic idea of XCAP follows Hoare logic—a program point can be associated with an assertion which documents its requirement on the machine state. The readers can assume that an assertion is simply a logical predicate on machine state.

A program can be viewed as a collection of code blocks (instruction sequences) connected together with control-flow instructions such as jmp and call. Every code block has an associated assertion as its precondition, which is put together in a *code heap specification* Ψ (think of this as a header file). The verification is carried out by finding appropriate intermediate assertions for all program points, following inference rules.

To verify that a code block $\mathsf{add}\ \mathsf{r},\mathsf{o};\mathbb{I}$ is *well-formed* (*i.e.*, correct with respect to the specification) under pre-condition a, which can be thought of as a predicate of type $State \to Prop$, we must find an intermediate assertion a' to serve both as the post-condition of $\mathsf{add}\ \mathsf{r},\mathsf{o}$ and as the pre-condition of $\mathbb{I}$. More specifically, we must establish: (1) if a holds on a machine state, then a' holds on the updated machine state after executing $\mathsf{add}\ \mathsf{r},\mathsf{o}$; (2) $\mathbb{I}$ is well-formed under pre-condition a'. Below is the corresponding inference rule ($\Rightarrow$ and $\circ$ stand for assertion implication and function composition).

$$\frac{\mathsf{a} \Rightarrow (\mathsf{a}' \circ \mathsf{Next_{add\ r,o}}) \qquad \Psi \vdash \{\mathsf{a}'\}\,\mathbb{I}}{\Psi \vdash \{\mathsf{a}\}\,\mathsf{add}\ \mathsf{r},\mathsf{o};\mathbb{I}}\ (\text{ADD})$$

Reasoning about memory. The reasoning on memory (data heap and stack) operations is carried out following separation logic [16]. In particular, the primitives of separation logic are defined as shorthands using the primitives of the underlying assertion logic in XCAP via a shallow embedding. Some representative cases are given as follows.

$$\begin{aligned}
\mathsf{emp} &\triangleq \lambda\mathbb{H}.\,\mathbb{H} = \{\} \\
\mathsf{l} \mapsto \mathsf{w} &\triangleq \lambda\mathbb{H}.\,\mathsf{l} \neq \mathsf{NULL} \wedge \mathbb{H} = \{\mathsf{l} \rightsquigarrow \mathsf{w}\} \\
\mathsf{l} \mapsto \_ &\triangleq \lambda\mathbb{H}.\,\exists\mathsf{w}.\,(\mathsf{l} \mapsto \mathsf{w}\ \mathbb{H}) \\
\mathsf{a_1} * \mathsf{a_2} &\triangleq \lambda\mathbb{H}.\,\exists\mathbb{H}_1,\mathbb{H}_2.\,\mathbb{H}_1 \uplus \mathbb{H}_2 = \mathbb{H} \wedge \mathsf{a_1}\ \mathbb{H}_1 \wedge \mathsf{a_2}\ \mathbb{H}_2 \\
\mathsf{l} \mapsto \mathsf{w_1},\dots,\mathsf{w}_n &\triangleq \mathsf{l} \mapsto \mathsf{w_1} * \mathsf{l}{+}4 \mapsto \mathsf{w_2} * \dots * \mathsf{l}{+}4(n{-}1) \mapsto \mathsf{w}_n \\
\mathsf{l} \mapsto [n] &\triangleq \mathsf{l} \mapsto \_,\dots,\_ \qquad \textit{(the number of \_ is } n/4\textit{)}
\end{aligned}$$

Reasoning about control-flow transfer. Direct control transfers are simple—when transferring control to code at label f, one should establish the pre-condition of f as required by the code heap specification. This is illustrated with the following rule:

$$\frac{\mathsf{a} \Rightarrow \Psi(\mathsf{f}) \qquad \mathsf{f} \in \mathsf{dom}(\Psi)}{\Psi \vdash \{\mathsf{a}\}\,\mathsf{jmp}\ \mathsf{f}}\ (\text{JMPI})$$

A distinguishing feature of XCAP compared to other program logics is the special support for embedded code pointers. It introduces a syntactic construct $\mathsf{cptr}(\mathsf{f},\mathsf{a})$ to serve as an assertion of "f points to code with pre-condition a". For an indirect jump, the verification only uses the information enclosed in the cptr assertion. Modularity is achieved by not referring to the actual target address or the local code heap specification.

$$\frac{\mathsf{a} \Rightarrow (\lambda(\mathbb{H},\mathbb{R}).\,\mathsf{a}'\ (\mathbb{H},\mathbb{R}) \wedge \mathsf{cptr}(\mathbb{R}(\mathsf{r}),\mathsf{a}'))}{\Psi \vdash \{\mathsf{a}\}\,\mathsf{jmp}\ \mathsf{r}}\ (\text{JMPR})$$

The above rule claims that it is safe to jump to register r under assertion a, if r contains a code pointer with a pre-condition a' that is weaker than a. Interested readers are referred to [12] for more details on cptr and the new assertion language, *PropX*. For this paper, please keep in mind that assertions are actually of type $State \to PropX$.

The function call and return instructions are supported as in the following new rules:

$$\frac{a \Rightarrow (\Psi(\mathtt{f}) \circ \mathsf{Next}_{\mathsf{push}\ \mathtt{f}_{ret}}) \qquad \mathtt{f} \in \mathsf{dom}(\Psi)}{\Psi \vdash \{a\}\,\mathsf{call}\ \mathtt{f};[\mathtt{f}_{ret}]} \quad \text{(CALLI)}$$

$$\frac{a \Rightarrow \lambda(\mathbb{H},\mathbb{R},\mathbb{F}).\,\mathsf{cptr}(\mathbb{H}(\mathbb{R}(esp)), a') \qquad a \Rightarrow (a' \circ \mathsf{Next}_{\mathsf{pop}})}{\Psi \vdash \{a\}\,\mathsf{ret}} \quad \text{(RET)}$$

A call instruction pushes a return address onto the stack and transfers control to the target code. In our actual implementation, the return address is calculated from the *pc*. To avoid obfuscating the presentation, we use an explicit $[\mathtt{f}_{ret}]$ in the above Rule CALLI. This rule says, if a holds on the current state, then $\Psi(\mathtt{f})$ holds on the updated state after executing the stack push. The rule RET says, the top of the stack is a code pointer with pre-condition a' and, if a holds on the current state, a' holds on the updated state after executing the stack pop (of the return address). It is worth noting that Rule CALLI does not enforce the validity of the return address. This allows some "fake" function calls that never return, a pattern indeed used in *loadcontext*().

Stack and calling convention. The support for call and return instructions is one of the many adaptations made for x86. Besides specializing XCAP for the machine model, we also built key abstractions to help manage the complexity of the reasoning, such as the handling of the stack and calling convention. The calling convention is illustrated in Fig. 2. It is convenient to build a specification template reflecting this convention.

For a function with n arguments $a_1 \ldots a_n$, we write its specification (*i.e.*, a pre-condition in the form of an assertion) as:

$$\mathsf{Fn}\ \ a_1, \ldots, a_n\ \{\mathsf{Aux}: x_1, \ldots, x_m;\ \mathsf{Local}: [fs];\ \mathsf{Pre}: \mathsf{a}_{pre};\ \mathsf{Post}: \mathsf{a}_{post}\}$$

The intention of this macro is that $x_1, \ldots, x_m$ are "auxiliary variables" commonly used in Hoare-logic style reasoning, fs is the size of required free space on the stack, and a_{pre} and a_{post} are the pre- and post-conditions of the function. This macro is defined as:

$$\exists a_1, \ldots, a_n, cs, sp, ss, ret, x_1, \ldots, x_m, \mathsf{a}_{prv}.$$
$$\mathsf{reg}(cs, sp) \wedge ss \geq fs$$
$$\wedge\ \mathsf{stack}(sp, ss, ret, a_1, \ldots, a_n) \quad * \ \mathsf{a}_{prv} * \mathsf{a}_{pre}$$
$$\wedge\ \mathsf{cptr}(ret, \exists retv.\ \mathsf{reg}(cs, sp{+}4) \wedge \mathsf{eax} = retv$$
$$\wedge\ \mathsf{stack}(sp{+}4, ss{+}4, a_1, \ldots, a_n) * \mathsf{a}_{prv} * \mathsf{a}_{post})$$

The first line of this definition quantifies over the values of (1) function arguments $a_1, \ldots, a_n$, (2) callee-save registers cs (a 4-tuple), (3) the stack pointer sp, (4) the size of available space on stack ss, (5) the return address ret, (6) auxiliary variables $x_1, \ldots, x_m$, and (7) some hidden private data expressed as the predicate a_{prv}.

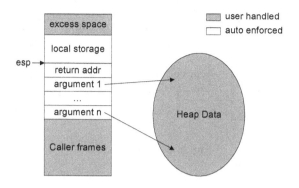

Fig. 2. Function calling convention

The second line relates the register file with the callee-save values cs (4-tuple) and the stack pointer sp and makes sure that there is enough space available on the stack.

$$\mathsf{reg}(ebx, esi, edi, ebp, esp) \triangleq \mathsf{ebx} = ebx \wedge \mathsf{esi} = esi \wedge \mathsf{edi} = edi \wedge \mathsf{ebp} = ebp \wedge \mathsf{esp} = esp$$

The third line describes (1) the stack frame upon entering the function using the macro below, (2) the private data hidden from the function, and (3) the user customized pre-condition a_{pre}, which does not directly talk about register files and the current stack frame, because they are already handled by the calling convention.

$$\mathsf{stack}(sp, ss, w_1, \ldots, w_n) \triangleq sp - ss \mapsto [ss] * sp \mapsto w_1, \ldots, w_n.$$

The last two lines of the Fn definition specify the return address ret as an embedded code pointer using cptr. When a function returns, the callee-save registers, stack frame, and private data must all be preserved, and the post-condition a_{post} must be established. Note that (1) eax may contain a return value $retv$, and (2) the return instruction automatically increases the stack pointer by 4.

4 Formal Verification of Machine Context Management

What is a machine context? Although the C specification in Section 2 appears to indicate that a context is merely eight words, the actual assumptions underlying it are rather complex. As illustrated in Figure 3, the eight words represent a return value $retv$, six registers referred to collectively as cs, and a stack pointer sp. sp points to a return address ret found on top of a stack frame. The saved registers may point to some private data. There may also be some environment data shared with external code. Eventually, a context is consumed when being invoked. A correct invocation of jumping to the return address ret requires (1) the saved register contents be restored into the register file, (2) the stack and private data be preserved, and (3) the shared environment be available.

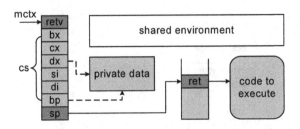

Fig. 3. Machine context

All these requirements make it challenging to specify the invariants on contexts. Because of the expressiveness of XCAP, we can define a heap predicate mctx_t($a_{env}, mctx$) for the context data structure, parametric to the environment described as a_{env},

$$\exists retv, cs, sp, ret, a_{prv}. \qquad\qquad mctx \mapsto retv, cs, sp * sp \mapsto ret * a_{prv}$$
$$\wedge \mathsf{cptr}(ret, \mathsf{reg}_6(cs, sp+4)) \wedge \mathsf{eax} = retv \wedge a_{env} * mctx \mapsto retv, cs, sp * sp \mapsto ret * a_{prv})$$

where a_{prv} describes the private data, and reg_6 is defined similarly to reg with 6-tuple.

Context switching. The *swapcontext*() function take two pointers (one to the old context and another to the new context) and performs three tasks: saves registers to the old context, loads registers from the new context, and transfers control to the new context. From the implementation, *swapcontext*() gets called by one client and "returns" to another. However, this is entirely transparent to the clients—when *swapcontext*() returns, the stack and private data of that client are kept intact.

We present the specification and proof outline of *swapcontext*() in Fig. 4. It uses a macro Fn$_6$, a variant of Fn obtained by replacing reg with reg_6 and changing cs to refer to 6 registers. Fn$_6$ automatically manages the preservation of the stack and private data. In addition, the pre-condition specifies three pieces of memory: (1) the old context pointed to by *old*—at the beginning of the routine it is simply 32 bytes of memory available for use, (2) the shared data a_{env}, and (3) the new context pointed to by *new*.

The new context is specified with the help of the macro mctx_t. The environment parameter of this macro consists of two parts: the shared data a_{env} and another mctx_t macro, describing the old context. This is because the old context will be properly set up by the routine before switching to the new one. One tricky point is that the old context will be expecting an (existentially quantified) **new shared environment** a_{newenv}. Although one may expect the new environment to be simply the old one, a_{env}, together with the new context at *new*, this may not necessarily be the case. For instance, the new context may be dead already and de-allocated when the old context regains control.

The post-condition of *swapcontext*() is relatively simple: the space for the old context will still be available, together with the new shared data a_{newenv}. An

Fn₆ old,new { Aux: a_{newenv}; Local: [0];
  Pre: $old \mapsto [32] * a_{env} * mctx\_t(mctx\_t(a_{newenv}, old) * a_{env}, new)$;
  Post: $old \mapsto [32] * a_{newenv} \wedge eax = 0$ }

`swapcontext:`   // void swapcontext (mctx_t old, mctx_t new);

$reg_6(cs, sp) \quad \wedge ss \geq 0 \quad \wedge stack(sp, ss, ret, old, new) \quad * old \mapsto [32] \quad * a_{prv} * a_{env}$
$*mctx\_t(mctx\_t(a_{newenv}, old) * a_{env}, new)$
$\wedge cptr(ret, reg_6(cs, sp+4) \wedge eax = 0 \wedge stack(sp+4, ss+4, old, new) * old \mapsto [32] \quad * a_{prv} * a_{newenv})$

          `mov eax, [esp+4]`   // load address of the context data structure we save in
          `...`   // save old context
          `mov eax, [esp+8]`   // load address of the context data structure we have to load

$eax = new \quad \wedge ss \geq 0 \quad \wedge stack(sp, ss, ret, old, new) \quad * old \mapsto 0, cs, sp * a_{prv} * a_{env}$
$*mctx\_t(mctx\_t(a_{newenv}, old) * a_{env}, new)$
$\wedge cptr(ret, reg_6(cs, sp+4) \wedge eax = 0 \wedge stack(sp+4, ss+4, old, new) * old \mapsto [32] \quad * a_{prv} * a_{newenv})$

                          // shuffle and cast

$eax = new \wedge \qquad old \mapsto 0, cs, sp * sp \mapsto ret * stack(sp, ss) * sp+4 \mapsto old, new * a_{prv}$
$\wedge cptr(ret, reg_6(cs, sp+4)$
$\qquad \wedge eax = 0 \wedge a_{newenv} * old \mapsto 0, cs, sp * sp \mapsto ret * stack(sp, ss) * sp+4 \mapsto old, new * a_{prv})$
$\qquad\qquad\qquad * a_{env} * mctx\_t(mctx\_t(a_{newenv}, old) * a_{env}, new)$

                          // pack old context

$eax = new \wedge mctx\_t(a_{newenv}, old) * a_{env} * mctx\_t(mctx\_t(a_{newenv}, old) * a_{env}, new)$

                          // unpack new context

$eax = new \wedge mctx\_t(a_{newenv}, old) * a_{env} * new \mapsto retv', cs', sp' * sp' \mapsto ret' * a_{newprv}$
$\wedge cptr(ret', reg_6(cs', sp'+4)$
$\qquad \wedge eax = retv' \wedge mctx\_t(a_{newenv}, old) * a_{env} * new \mapsto retv', cs', sp' * sp' \mapsto ret' * a_{newprv})$

          `mov esp, [eax+_esp]` // load the new stack pointer.
          `...`   // load the new context

$reg_6(cs', sp') \wedge eax = retv' \wedge mctx\_t(a_{newenv}, old) * a_{env} * new \mapsto retv', cs', sp' * sp' \mapsto ret' * a_{newprv}$
$\wedge cptr(ret', reg_6(cs', sp'+4)$
$\qquad \wedge eax = retv' \wedge mctx\_t(a_{newenv}, old) * a_{env} * new \mapsto retv', cs', sp' * sp' \mapsto ret' * a_{newprv})$

          `ret`

Fig. 4. Verification of machine context switching

interesting proof step in Fig. 4 is the one after the old context is packed but
before the new one is unpacked. At that point, there is no direct notion of stack
or function. The relevant machine state essentially comprises of two contexts
and one environment:

$$eax = new \wedge \ mctx\_t(a_{newenv}, old) * a_{env} \ * mctx\_t(mctx\_t(a_{newenv}, old) * a_{env}, new)$$

Intuitively, it should be safe to load the new context from eax and then switch
to it.

Context creation. We present the specification and proof outline of *makecontext()*
in Figure 5. The intermediate assertions are also organized using Fn. For conciseness, we omitted common parts of these macros, thus emphasizing only the change-
able parts.

  The pre-condition of the routine specifies (1) an empty context at *mctx*, (2)
a stack *nsp* with available space of size *nss*, (3) some private data of the target

Fn $mctx, nsp, lnk, func, arg$ { Aux: a_{env}; Local: [0];
  Pre: $mctx \mapsto [32] * \mathsf{stack}(nsp, nss) * \mathsf{a}_{prv} \wedge nss \geq 12$
         $\wedge \mathsf{cptr}(lnk, \mathsf{esp} = nsp - 4 \wedge \mathsf{stack}(nsp-4, nss-4, arg) * \mathsf{a}_{ret})$
         $\wedge \mathsf{cptr}(func, \mathsf{Fn}\ arg'$ { Local: $nss - 8$;
                   Pre: $sp' = nsp - 8 \wedge arg' = arg \wedge \mathsf{a}_{env} * mctx \mapsto [32] * \mathsf{a}_{prv}$;
                   Post: a_{ret} });
  Post: $\mathsf{mctx\_t}(\mathsf{a}_{env}, mctx)$ }

`makecontext:`   // *void makecontext (mctx_t mctx, char *sp, void *lnk, void *func, void *arg);*

Local: [0]; Pre: $mctx \mapsto [32] * \mathsf{stack}(nsp, nss) * \mathsf{a}_{prv} \wedge nss \geq 12$
         $\wedge \mathsf{cptr}(lnk, \mathsf{esp} = nsp - 4 \wedge \mathsf{stack}(nsp-4, nss-4, arg) * \mathsf{a}_{ret})$
         $\wedge \mathsf{cptr}(func, \mathsf{Fn}\ arg'$ { Local: $nss - 8$;
                   Pre: $sp' = nsp - 8 \wedge arg' = arg \wedge \mathsf{a}_{env} * mctx \mapsto [32] * \mathsf{a}_{prv}$;
                   Post: a_{ret} });

```
        mov eax, [esp+4]        // load address of the context data structure.
        ...                     // initialize the new context
        mov [eax+_esp], ecx     // only the stack pointer matters for a fresh new context
```

Local: [0]; Pre: $mctx \mapsto [28], nsp - 12 * \mathsf{stack}(nsp-12, nss-12, func, lnk, arg) * \mathsf{a}_{prv}$
         $\wedge \mathsf{cptr}(lnk, \mathsf{esp} = nsp - 4 \wedge \mathsf{stack}(nsp-4, nss-4, arg) * \mathsf{a}_{ret})$
         $\wedge \mathsf{cptr}(func, \mathsf{Fn}\ arg'$ { Local: $nss - 8$;
                   Pre: $sp' = nsp - 8 \wedge arg' = arg \wedge \mathsf{a}_{env} * mctx \mapsto [32] * \mathsf{a}_{prv}$;
                   Post: a_{ret} });

        // *unfold, shuffle, and cast*

Local: [0]; Pre: $mctx \mapsto retv', cs', nsp - 12 * nsp - 12 \mapsto func$
        $* \mathsf{stack}(nsp-12, nss-12) * nsp - 8 \mapsto lnk, arg * \mathsf{a}_{prv}$
        $\wedge \mathsf{cptr}(lnk, \mathsf{esp} = nsp - 4 \wedge \mathsf{stack}(nsp-4, nss-4, arg) * \mathsf{a}_{ret})$
$\wedge \mathsf{cptr}(func, \mathsf{reg}_6(cs', nsp - 8) \wedge \mathsf{eax} = retv' \wedge \mathsf{a}_{env} * mctx \mapsto retv', cs', nsp - 12 * nsp - 12 \mapsto func$
        $* \mathsf{stack}(nsp-12, nss-12) * nsp - 8 \mapsto lnk, arg * \mathsf{a}_{prv}$
        $\wedge \mathsf{cptr}(lnk, \mathsf{esp} = nsp - 4 \wedge \mathsf{stack}(nsp-4, nss-4, arg) * \mathsf{a}_{ret}))$;

        // *pack the fresh context*

Local: [0]; Pre: $\mathsf{mctx\_t}(\mathsf{a}_{env}, mctx)$;

```
        ret
```

Fig. 5. Verification of machine context creation

context (potentially accessible from the argument arg of the function $func()$ of the target context, (4) a link (return address) lnk to be used when the target context finishes execution, and (5) a function pointer $func()$ for the code to be executed in the target context. It also specifies the exact requirements on the code at pointers lnk and $func$: (1) a_{ret} occurs both in the post-condition of $func()$ and in the pre-condition of lnk, indicating that the code at the return address lnk may expect some results from the context function $func()$; (2) the stack should be properly maintained upon returning to lnk. The post-condition of the routine simply states that, when $makecontext()$ returns, $mctx$ will point to a proper context which expects a shared environment of a_{env}.

Our interface of $makecontext()$ is faithful to the Unix/Linux implementations. The heavy usage of function and continuation pointers shows how crucial

```
loadcontext:                    // void loadcontext (mctx_t mctx);
```

$\mathsf{reg}(cs, sp) \wedge \mathsf{stack}(sp, ss, ret, mctx) * \mathsf{a}_{env} * \mathsf{mctx\_t}(\mathsf{stack}(sp, ss, ret, mctx) * \mathsf{a}_{env}, mctx)$

```
        mov eax, [esp+4]
```

$eax = mctx \wedge \mathsf{stack}(sp, ss, ret, mctx) * \mathsf{a}_{env} * \mathsf{mctx\_t}(\mathsf{stack}(sp, ss, ret, mctx) * \mathsf{a}_{env}, mctx)$

// unpack context

$eax = mctx \qquad\qquad \wedge \mathsf{a}_{newenv} * \mathsf{mctx\_t}(\mathsf{a}_{newenv}, mctx)$

// unpack context

$eax = mctx \qquad\qquad \wedge \mathsf{a}_{newenv} * mctx \mapsto retv', cs', sp' * sp' \mapsto ret' * \mathsf{a}_{prv}$
$\wedge \mathsf{cptr}(ret', \mathsf{reg}_6(cs', sp'+4) \wedge eax = retv' \wedge \mathsf{a}_{newenv} * mctx \mapsto retv', cs', sp' * sp' \mapsto ret' * \mathsf{a}_{prv})$

```
        mov esp, [eax+_esp] // load the new stack pointer.
        mov ebp, [eax+_ebp]
        mov edi, [eax+_edi]
        mov esi, [eax+_esi]
        mov edx, [eax+_edx]
        mov ecx, [eax+_ecx]
        mov ebx, [eax+_ebx]
        mov eax, [eax+_eax]
```

$\mathsf{reg}_6(cs', sp'+4) \wedge eax = retv' \wedge \mathsf{a}_{newenv} * mctx \mapsto retv', cs', sp' * sp' \mapsto ret' * \mathsf{a}_{prv}$
$\wedge \mathsf{cptr}(ret', \mathsf{reg}_6(cs', sp'+4) \wedge eax = retv' \wedge \mathsf{a}_{newenv} * mctx \mapsto retv', cs', sp' * sp' \mapsto ret' * \mathsf{a}_{prv})$

```
        ret
```

Fig. 6. Verification of machine context loading

XCAP's support of embedded code pointers is. As the proof shows, the most complex step is on transforming code pointers' pre-conditions and packing all the resources into a context.

Context loading. loadcontext() essentially performs the second half of the task of *swapcontext()*, with some differences in the stack layout. Although we refer to it as a "function", it actually never returns and does not require the stack top to contain a valid return address. We present the verification of *loadcontext()* in Figure 6.

5   The Coq Implementation

We have mechanized everything in this paper using the Coq proof assistant [18]. By everything we mean the machine model, XCAP and its meta theory (including soundness proof), separation logic, and specification and proof of the context implementation.

Proof details. Our Coq implementation (downloadable at [14]) consists of approximately 17,000 lines of Coq code. Figure 7 presents a break down of individual components in the implementation. The full compilation of our implementation in Coq (proof-script checking and proof-binary generation) takes about 52

Implementation component	Line of code	Compile time
Safe extension to Coq on extensional equality on functions	9 Loc	1s
Math lemmas	384 Loc	1s
Set level mapping	220 Loc	1s
Type level mapping	218 Loc	1s
Type list	103 Loc	1s
Target machine (TM)	441 Loc	10s
PropX meta theory (independent of XCAP meta theory)	4,504 Loc	6m
PropX lemmas (independent of XCAP meta theory)	258 Loc	3s
Separation-logic style memory assertions	74 Loc	1s
Common data-structure related lemmas (independent of XCAP meta theory)	1,171 Loc	10s
XCAP (x86 version)	755 Loc	3s
XCAP common definitions and lemmas	297 Loc	3s
Machine context module: code, data structure, and specification	144 Loc	1s
Proof for loadcontext() function	753 Loc	15s
Proof for swapcontext() function	4,917 Loc	3m
Proof for makecontext() function	2,372 Loc	40m
Total (on Intel Core 2 Duo T7200 2GHz / 4MB L2 / 2GB Ram)	16,620 Loc	52m

Fig. 7. Break-down of Coq implementation

minutes under Windows Vista on an Intel Core 2 Duo T7200 2GHz CPU with 4MB L2 cache and 2GB memory.

The proof for lemmas and the context code is typically on implications from one assertion to another, either on the same machine state (casting), or on two consecutive states before and after the execution of an instruction. Proof steps mostly adjust the shape of the assertions to match, split implications into smaller ones, and track the changed parts down to the basic data units. Coq's proof searching ability is useful, but often too weak for the reasoning about memory and resources.

Coq has many built-in proof tactics for intuitive handling of proofs of *Prop* sort, such as *intro, split, left, right, exists, cut, auto, etc.* Following them, we defined a similar set of proof tactics for *PropX*, such as *introx, splitx, leftx, rightx, existsx, cutx, autox, etc.* Each of these new *PropX* tactics can be used similarly to the *Prop* ones, which increases the productivity when working with *PropX* for experienced Coq users.

To make *PropX* formulas more readable, we defined some pretty-printing notations. For example, one can directly write the following formula:

```
All x, <<even x>> .\/ Ex y, z. <<x = y + z>> ./\ <<prime y /\ prime z>>
```

and write a function specification in the same style as used in our paper presentation:

```
Fn ... {Aux : ...; Local: [...]; Pre: ... ; Post: ...}
```

```
Definition mctx_t L aenv mctx : Heap -> PropX L := fun H =>
Ex retv, bx, cx, dx, si, di, bp, sp, ret.
 star (ptolist _ mctx (retv::bx::cx::dx::si::di::bp::sp::nil))
(star (pto _ sp ret)
      (fun H => extv _ _ (eq_rect _ _
        (Lift _ _ (var t0 _ H)
     ./\ codeptr _ ret
        (fun S' => match S' with ((H',R'),F') in
           reg6 _ bx cx dx si di bp (sp+4) R' ./\ << R' eax = retv>>
        ./\ star (fun H => Shift _ _
                           (eq_rect _ _ (aenv H) _ (app_nil_eq _)) _)
           (star (ptolist _ mctx (retv::bx::cx::dx::si::di::bp::sp::nil))
           (star (pto _ sp ret)
                (fun H => Lift _ _ (var t0 _ H)))) H'
      end))                         _ (nil_app_eq _))))            H.
```

Fig. 8. Coq encoding of mctx_t

Development time. The development of the proof took about three person-months. There are several reasons for the large proof size and development time. First of all, this is the first time we did this kind of realistic proof, so a lot of infrastructure code and experience needed to be developed and learned. For example, about half of the 17,000 lines of code is independent of machine context verification; such code can be reused for other verification purposes. The first procedure we certified, *swapcontext*(), took one person-month and 5,000 lines of code. We believe these numbers would be at least halved if we did it again. Second, there is much redundancy due to the relatively low level of proof reuse. The third reason is the complexity of the machine model, which needs features such as finite integers that are not supported well in Coq. Nevertheless, the biggest reason, we believe, is the complexity of reasoning about the actual code.

As an example, the machine context data type in the previous section is implemented as in Figure 8, which is far more complex than what its meta presentation looks like. Part of the complexity is due to the de Bruijn representation of impredicative quantifiers. Further improved pretty printing notations can help simplify the presentation. Still, there is the inherent complexity surrounding a machine context data structure that can not be omitted or avoided by any formal reasoning about it.

Discussion on the proof size. The large size of the proof naturally raises practicality concerns. However, when making comparisons with other verification methods, there are several aspects of our method that need to be taken into consideration.

For comparison with abstraction-based verification methods, we believe that while they provide insights on the invariants of the algorithms and high-level programs, for low-level systems code such as context management, working at an abstract level will not have an actual advantage. As explained in the beginning of this paper, it is the level it works at and the complexity of this code that are most interesting.

For comparison with analysis- and test-based verification methods, the important question to ask is what kind of guarantee one can deliver. Many of these tools can automatically find bugs, but only in a "best-effort" fashion—false negatives are expected. In our case, we want to completely exclude certain categories of bugs, as guaranteed by the language-based approach in general.

For comparison with other language-based methods, such as type systems, the important question to ask is what kind of code is supported. There have been efforts to use higher-level safe languages for systems programming, all with trade-offs in efficiency and/or compatibility, some even with significant changes in programming style. In our case, we require no change to the existing systems programming style and code base, and thus we expect no performance or compatibility issues. In general, we believe that systems and application code requires different level of safety guarantees, thus their verification will naturally result in different levels of productivity. For example, it is feasible to automatically generate proofs for TAL programs in XCAP [13] and link them with the certified context routines in this paper following methods in [13] or [2].

6   Related Work and Conclusion

Hoare-logic style systems have been widely used in program verification. They support formal reasoning using assertions and inference rules based on expressive program logics. Nonetheless, there has been no work in the literature on the logical specification and verification of machine context management. The challenge there, based on our experience, largely lies in working with embedded code pointers. For example, among the efforts applying Hoare-logic-based verification to machine code, an earlier work, Yu *et al* [21], is able to do mechanized verification of MC68020 object code. However, as explained in [12], they cannot support embedded code pointers and they encountered the problem of "functional parameters". Recently, Myreen *et al* [10] support verification of realistic ARM code, but support of embedded code pointers is missing.

Separation logic [16,6] provides a helpful abstraction for working with memory. Our verification makes use of a shallow embedding of separation logic in the assertion language to reason about the machine state.

The Singularity OS [5] uses a mixture of C# and assembly code to implement threading. Whereas most parts of the code enjoy type safety, context switching is written in unsafe assembly code. Furthermore, threading and context data structures are specified using managed data pointers, which belong to the *weak update* memory model (ML-like reference types also belong to it). It is significantly different from the separation-logic style unmanaged *strong update* memory model used in this paper, as well as in Unix/Windows kernel. One disadvantage for using *weak update* for certified systems programming is that its memory management relies on garbage collection, which may not be appropriate for some systems programs.

The verification of context switching in this paper addresses the actual implementation details, including those hidden behind the implementation of continuations and storage management. The code we verified is at the same level as the actual executable running on a real machine. The trusted computing base is extremely small. Besides the obvious progress/preservation property, because our verification is based on logical assertions, it conveys a more expressive safety policy: the run-time states of the machine should satisfy the corresponding assertions as written in the specification.

Conclusion. We have presented the first formal, modular, and mechanized verification of machine context management code and showed how to build a verification infrastructure for certifying realistic low-level systems code. In particular, we applied the XCAP framework to an x86 machine model, developed new proof-tactics and lemma libraries, and used it to certify the code and data structures in an x86 machine-context implementation. Everything has been mechanized in the Coq proof assistant. Our approach is applicable to other variants of context, provides a solid basis for further verification of thread implementations, and illustrates the formal, modular, and mechanized verification of realistic systems code in general.

By following better engineering practices and building smarter domain-specific proof-searching tools, especially those for separation logic and program logics, we believe that the automation in systems code specification and verification can be gradually increased to a level where it is practical to apply to the building of provably correct software.

Acknowledgment. We thank David Tarditi and anonymous referees for suggestions and comments on the draft of this paper. A large part of this research was done when the first author was at Yale University and supported in part by gifts from Intel and Microsoft, and NSF grant CCR-0524545. Any opinions, findings, and conclusions contained in this document are those of the authors and do not reflect the views of these agencies.

References

1. Appel, A.W., Mellies, P.-A., Richards, C.D., Vouillon, J.: A very modal model of a modern, major, general type system. In: Proc. 34th ACM Symp. on Principles of Prog. Lang., January 2007, ACM Press, New York (2007)
2. Feng, X., Ni, Z., Shao, Z., Guo, Y.: An open framework for foundational proof-carrying code. In: Proc. Workshop on Types in Language Design and Implementation (January 2007)
3. Gargano, M., Hillebrand, M., Leinenbach, D., Paul, W.: On the correctness of operating system kernels. In: Hurd, J., Melham, T. (eds.) TPHOLs 2005. LNCS, vol. 3603, pp. 2–16. Springer, Heidelberg (2005)
4. Hoare, C.A.R.: An axiomatic basis for computer programming. Communications of the ACM (October 1969)

5. Hunt, G.C., Larus, J.R., Abadi, M., Aiken, M., Barham, P., Fahndrich, M., Hawblitzel, C., Hodson, O., Levi, S., Murphy, N., Steensgaard, B., Tarditi, D., Wobber, T., Zill, B.: An overview of the Singularity project. Technical Report MSR-TR-2005-135, Microsoft Research, Redmond, WA (October 2005)

6. Ishtiaq, S.S., O'Hearn, P.W.: BI as an assertion language for mutable data structures. In: Proc. 28th ACM Symp. on Principles of Prog. Lang., pp. 14–26. ACM Press, New York (2001)

7. Jabber software development list: Jabberd crash in swapcontext() via _mio_raw_connect() (2001),
   http://mailman.jabber.org/pipermail/jdev/2001-March/005655.html

8. Libc for alpha systems mailing list: {make,set,swap}context broken on powerpc32 (2006),
   http://www.archivesat.com/Libc_for_alpha_systems/thread2267226.htm

9. Morrisett, G., Walker, D., Crary, K., Glew, N.: From System F to typed assembly language. In: Proc. 25th ACM Symp. on Principles of Prog. Lang., January 1998, pp. 85–97. ACM Press, New York (1998)

10. Myreen, M.O., Gordon, M.J.C.: Hoare logic for realistically modelled machine code. In: Proc. 13th International Conference on Tools and Algorithms for Construction and Analysis of Systems (2007)

11. NetBSD port-amd64 mailing list: swapcontext(3) does not work? (2004),
    http://mail-index.netbsd.org/port-amd64/2004/11/30/0003.html

12. Ni, Z., Shao, Z.: Certified assembly programming with embedded code pointers. In: Proc. 33rd ACM Symp. on Principles of Prog. Lang., January 2006, ACM Press, New York (2006)

13. Ni, Z., Shao, Z.: A translation from typed assembly languages to certified assembly programming (October 2006),
    flint.cs.yale.edu/flint/publications/talcap.html

14. Ni, Z., Yu, D., Shao, Z.: Coq code for using xcap to certify realistic systems code: Machine context management (March 2007),
    http://flint.cs.yale.edu/flint/publications/mctx.html

15. Ni, Z., Yu, D., Shao, Z.: Technical report for using xcap to certify realistic systems code: machine context management (June 2007),
    http://flint.cs.yale.edu/flint/publications/mctx.html

16. Reynolds, J.: Separation logic: a logic for shared mutable data structures. In: Proc. 17th Symp. on Logic in Computer Science (2002)

17. SecurityTracker.com: Solaris 10 x64 kernel setcontext() bug lets local users deny service (2006),
    http://securitytracker.com/alerts/2006/Feb/1015557.html

18. The Coq Development Team: The Coq proof assistant reference manual (v8.0) (2004)

19. The glibc-bugs mailing list: [bug libc/357] new: getcontext() on ppc32 destroys saved parameter 1 in caller's frame (2004),
    http://sourceware.org/ml/glibc-bugs/2004-08/msg00201.html

20. The glibc-bugs mailing list: [bug libc/612] new: makecontext broken on powerpc-linux (2004),
    http://sources.redhat.com/ml/glibc-bugs/2004-12/msg00102.html

21. Yu, Y.: Automated Proofs of Object Code For A Widely Used Microprocessor. PhD thesis, The University of Texas at Austin (1992)

Proof Pearl: De Bruijn Terms Really Do Work

Michael Norrish[1] and René Vestergaard[2]

[1] Canberra Research Lab, Nicta
Michael.Norrish@nicta.com.au
[2] School of Information Science, JAIST, Ishikawa, Japan
vester@jaist.ac.jp

Abstract. Placing our result in a web of related mechanised results, we give a direct proof that the de Bruijn λ-calculus (à la Huet, Nipkow and Shankar) is isomorphic to an α-quotiented λ-calculus. In order to establish the link, we introduce an "index-carrying" abstraction mechanism over de Bruijn terms, and consider it alongside a simplified substitution mechanism. Relating the new notions to those of the α-quotiented and the proper de Bruijn formalisms draws on techniques from the theory of nominal sets.

1   Introduction

Implementors and theorists alike have long been in de Bruijn's debt [4]. Representing λ-terms without names is a relatively straightforward way of implementing binders internally in, e.g., theorem-proving systems such as Isabelle and HOL4. Complementing this, the same idea has made it possible to formalise a great many results about syntax that features binders.

However, we believe that the state-of-the-art for formalisation has moved on. Implementors may well keep de Bruijn terms in their systems' internals, but it does now seem as if it is possible to mechanise important results about syntax without needing to prove "painful" and "non-obvious" lemmas about indices [11]. The emerging formalisation technologies are appealing for a range of reasons, but here we focus on just two: i) it is now possible to check that multiple formalisations do actually correspond and ii) "non-obvious" lemmas about indices turn out to be related to general nominal properties of de Bruijn terms.

In particular, we can confirm that de Bruijn terms are a model for the λ-calculus, and can do so in an elegant way. By way of contrast, see for example Appendix C of Barendregt [2], where the proofs are given as "implicit in de Bruijn [4]"; or the pioneering work by Shankar [15], where mechanised proofs of complex theorems establish a connection between *unquotiented* λ-terms and de Bruijn terms.

In fact, there are a number of isomorphism results already extant in the literature. In this paper, we summarise these, and provide a new link between de Bruijn terms and what we hope will be an ever-expanding web of results, and body of understanding.

K. Schneider and J. Brandt (Eds.): TPHOLs 2007, LNCS 4732, pp. 207–222, 2007.

2 Formalising Binding

In this section, we position our result in the space of relationships between ten different formalisations of the λ-calculus, following Figure 1. λ^C is Curry's unquotiented λ-terms using variable names and fresh-naming substitution [3] (plus explicit α [7]). λ_α^{Hi}, due to Hindley [7], is a quotient construction saying that an equivalence class reduces to another if there are two syntactic terms that witness the reduction, in this case in λ^C. λ^V is similar to λ^C but uses renaming-free substitution (and explicit α), as studied in Vestergaard [17]. λ_α^V is the "Hindley-quotient" of λ^V. λ_α^{Ho} is a quotient of Curry's set-up but with substitution rather than reduction lifted from the syntactic to the quotient type, as studied in Homeier [8]. dB_2 is the set of well-formed, two-sorted de Bruijn terms in Gordon [5]. λ_α^G is the type derived from this, in Gordon and Melham [6]. λ_α^N is a quotient of the first order syntax, with substitution defined directly on the quotiented level, as in Norrish [12]. dB is the type of pure de Bruijn terms (with indices representing free and bound variables), as mechanised in Shankar [15], Huet [9] and Nipkow [11]. Finally, dB' is an intermediate formalism that we define here. It uses constructors that are not injective, hence the oval node: conceptually, dB' is syntactic sugar for dB that looks like λ_α^N.

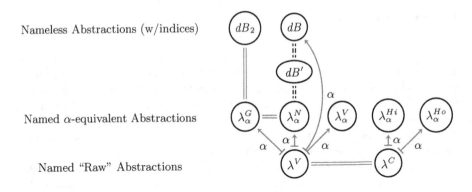

Fig. 1. λ-calculus formalisations and their directly-proved relationships; dashed, dark lines are the results in this paper. Double lines are isomorphisms; arrows α-quotienting.

2.1 Named Abstraction

We use Λ^{var} to refer to the "raw" syntax of the λ-calculus, that is the free algebra generated by the recursion equation

$$\Lambda^{\mathrm{var}} \cong V + \Lambda^{\mathrm{var}} \times \Lambda^{\mathrm{var}} + V \times \Lambda^{\mathrm{var}} \qquad (1)$$

with V some countably-infinite set of variable names. We use Λ_α to refer to the quotient of Λ^{var} with respect to α-equivalence. The various λ_α^X are reduction systems defined over Λ_α, while λ^V and λ^C are defined directly over Λ^{var}.

Table 1. Signatures for formalisms with named abstraction, see Figure 1. The α-collapsed types below a dashed line are bootstrapped from the preceding "raw" type (λ^V/λ^C). For λ_α^G, substitution is bootstrapped from dB_2. See the text for the [proofs: ...]-comments.

λ^V [proofs: $=_{\Lambda^{\text{var}}}$]	substitution: $\Lambda^{\text{var}} \times V \times \Lambda^{\text{var}} \to \Lambda^{\text{var}}$ reduction: $\quad \Lambda^{\text{var}} \times \Lambda^{\text{var}}$
λ_α^V	reduction: $\quad \Lambda_\alpha \times \Lambda_\alpha$
λ^C [proofs: $=_\alpha$]	substitution: $\Lambda^{\text{var}} \times V \times \Lambda^{\text{var}} \to \Lambda^{\text{var}}$ reduction: $\quad \Lambda^{\text{var}} \times \Lambda^{\text{var}}$
λ_α^{Hi}	reduction: $\quad \Lambda_\alpha \times \Lambda_\alpha$
λ_α^{Ho}	substitution: $\Lambda_\alpha \times V \times \Lambda_\alpha \to \Lambda_\alpha$ reduction: $\quad \Lambda_\alpha \times \Lambda_\alpha$
λ_α^G	substitution: $\begin{cases} (dB_2 \times V \times dB_2 \to dB_2) \\ \Lambda_\alpha \times V \times \Lambda_\alpha \to \Lambda_\alpha \end{cases}$ reduction: $\quad \Lambda_\alpha \times \Lambda_\alpha$
λ_α^N	substitution: $\Lambda_\alpha \times V \times \Lambda_\alpha \to \Lambda_\alpha$ reduction: $\quad \Lambda_\alpha \times \Lambda_\alpha$

There are seven different types identified in Figure 1 that use names under abstractions. Though intuition (and, as we shall see, mechanised results) assure us that they are all the "same", their constructions are all different to varying degrees. The differences are most clearly seen in the types' definitions of substitution, see Table 1. At the "raw" level, λ^V defines substitution to be "renaming free", as used to be the tradition in logic books: where a substitution would cause a free variable to become captured, the substitution is instead defined to be the identity function, with the implicit (and satisfiable) requirement that actual uses avoid such situations. This approach finesses many of the problems of λ^C, where an everywhere-correct capture-avoiding substitution mandates fresh-naming (via either simultaneous substitution, as in Homeier [8], or by well-founded recursion on term sizes) and, thus, only allows us to reason "up to α" for most properties [7]. Alternatively, and with substitution defined for Λ^{var}, the type itself can be α-quotiented. In the case of λ_α^{Ho}, Homeier lifts the substitution function and proceeds to define β-reduction at the quotiented type. In the case of λ_α^{Hi} and λ_α^V, Hindley and Vestergaard lift β-reductions from Λ^{var} [7,17].

In λ_α^G, substitution is defined with reference to the substitution function in dB_2. In λ_α^N, substitution is defined directly on Λ_α, using its "native" notion of primitive recursion, as in Norrish [12] and Pitts [14].

2.2   De Bruijn's Anonymous Abstraction, Using Indices

The type of de Bruijn terms is the free algebra generated by the recursion equation

$$dB \cong \mathbb{N} + dB \times dB + dB \tag{2}$$

We will use constructors dV, dAPP, and dABS to correspond to the three cases in the equation above, with the idea that, e.g., dABS (dV 0) is the *identity* function: "$\lambda x.x$", and dABS (dABS (dAPP (dV 1) (dV 0))) is *apply*: "$\lambda f.\lambda x.f\ x$". We will use t, u, z to range over values in dB, while M, N will range over values in Λ_α.

Nipkow [11] (following Huet [9]) defines two functions by primitive recursion over this type (see Figure 2). The first is lift, which adds one to the value of all free indices that are at least equal to the provided bound. (Shankar [15] calls his version of this function BUMP; it is slightly different because he has the first bound index of an abstraction be 1, not 0.)

```
lift (dV i) k        = if i < k then dV i
                       else dV (i + 1)
lift (dAPP t u) k    = dAPP (lift t k) (lift u k)
lift (dABS t) k      = dABS (lift t (k + 1))

nsub z k (dV i)      = if k < i then dV (i - 1)
                       else if i = k then z
                       else dV i
nsub z k (dAPP t u)  = dAPP (nsub z k t) (nsub z k u)
nsub z k (dABS t)    = dABS (nsub (lift z 0) (k + 1) t)
```

Fig. 2. Functions from Nipkow's formalisation of de Bruijn terms [11]

Second is substitution, which we call nsub here.[1] In order to make their proofs simpler, Nipkow, Huet and Shankar all define a notion of substitution that simultaneously performs a substitution and decrements the indices of the other free variables that appear in the term in which the substitution is occurring. This reflects the fact that the substitution is intended to be used for defining β-contraction, where a dABS constructor disappears in the process. As usual, the considered β-reduction relation is given as β-contraction plus congruence rules.

Definition 1 (Nipkow [11]). $\rightarrow_d$ *is the least relation satisfying the following rules:*

$$\overline{dAPP\ (dABS\ t)\ u\ \ \rightarrow_d\ nsub\ u\ 0\ t}$$

$$\frac{t\ \rightarrow_d\ u}{dAPP\ t\ z\ \rightarrow_d\ dAPP\ u\ z} \qquad \frac{t\ \rightarrow_d\ u}{dAPP\ z\ t\ \rightarrow_d\ dAPP\ z\ u}$$

$$\frac{t\ \rightarrow_d\ u}{dABS\ t\ \rightarrow_d\ dABS\ u}$$

---

[1] We have altered the order of arguments to be compatible with the other mechanisations: the value being substituted comes first, followed by the index being substituted out, followed by the term in which the substitution is occurring.

2.3 Existing Results

We say that two types of the form we consider, e.g., $\langle X, \rightarrow_x \rangle$, $\langle Y, \rightarrow_y \rangle$, are isomorphic if there exists a bijection, $f : X \longrightarrow Y$, that is homomorphic

$$\forall x_1, x_2 . x_1 \rightarrow_x x_2 \Leftrightarrow f(x_1) \rightarrow_y f(x_2) \tag{3}$$

In the case of α-quotients, the mappings between the types are surjective and have the same kernels. By the appropriate adaptation of the First Isomorphism Theorem of Algebra,[2] this means that the various range types of each "raw" type are pairwise isomorphic. Once it has been established that the α-equivalences of λ^V and λ^C coincide, this means that the isomorphism of λ^V and λ^C implies that all the range types, i.e., dB and the λ_α^X, are pairwise isomorphic. (In [13], we further show that a broad class of properties is also shared between the elements of the "raw" syntax and the range types.)

As noted, the λ^V-to-λ_α^V and λ^C-to-λ_α^{Hi} α-quotients of the figure are underpinned by an epimorphism (i.e., (3) plus surjectivity) by construction [7,17]. In the remaining "raw-to-quotient" cases, property (3) plus surjectivity have been verified by Norrish [12] (λ^V-to-λ_α^G, λ^V-to-λ_α^N) and Homeier [8] (λ^C-to-λ_α^{Ho}, implicitly).

Vestergaard has mechanised the isomorphism at the base of the figure, between λ^V and λ^C (including their respective α-relations), in Coq. This follows the proof in Vestergaard [17].

The isomorphism at the named α-equivalent abstractions level between λ_α^G and λ_α^N is between the Gordon-Melham terms and the terms formed by quotienting the raw syntax (Λ^{var}). This isomorphism is uninteresting (and implicitly demonstrated in [12]) because the constructors and definitions in each type are immediate images of each other.

The isomorphism between dB_2 and λ_α^G is between the well-formed terms in Gordon's two-sorted de Bruijn type [5], and the terms of Gordon and Melham's subsequent paper [6]. This connection is a bijection by construction: the latter type is established using the HOL principle of type definition, which permits new types to be defined isomorphic to non-empty subsets of old types. Further, the bijection is behaviour-respecting because substitution in the new type is defined by following the bijection back to the old type, performing the substitution there and then returning.

The result most similar to that in this paper is Shankar's link between dB and λ^V [15]. (Strictly speaking Shankar's λ^V is not quite the same as the one used by Vestergaard [17]: where Vestergaard's substitution will go wrong, it returns the term being substituted into unchanged; in the same situation, Shankar returns the result of a recursive descent with free variables incorrectly captured. In neither case does this detail matter: references to both substitution functions are set about with side conditions ensuring they are applied only in situations that make sense.)

Shankar represents the bijection between the two types with a function from λ^V to dB (called TRANSLATE) and a function UNTRANS for the opposite direction.

---

[2] The result has been verified in Coq by Vestergaard.

Neither of these can work directly on the values from the types, but need to be accompanied by contextual information. For example, the statement that TRANSLATE undoes an UNTRANS is given as

```
117. Theorem.  UNTRANS-TRANS (rewrite):
     (IMPLIES (AND (TERMP X) (LEQ (FIND-M X N) M))
             (EQUAL (TRANSLATE (UNTRANS X M N)
                               (BINDINGS M N))
                    X))
```

The other identity is even more complicated, partly because the equality is actually α-equivalence. The subsequent statements that β-reductions in each type match up are similarly complex. (They are used to good effect: the Church-Rosser result for dB is transferred back to λ^V.)

As we shall see, our own directly-established connection can be expressed more naturally because we build an isomorphism to λ^N_α instead of λ^V. We also provide an isomorphism result for η-reduction (in Section 4.4).

3 Nominal Reasoning

In this section we provide a brief introduction to the nominal technology that has an important rôle to play in the isomorphism proofs to come. (For more on this, see for example, Pitts [14].)

Permutations. Nominal reasoning proceeds over sets that support a permutation action satisfying certain conditions. We call such sets, *nominal sets*.[3] At the "base level" permutations are defined in terms of their effect on strings.

Definition 2 (Permutations Applied to Strings). *A permutation (written π, π_1 etc) is a bijection on strings that is the identity on all but finitely many strings. We represent a permutation as a list of pairs of strings, and define the action of a permutation π on a string s (written $\pi(s)$) by primitive recursion on the structure of the list:*

$$[\,]\,(s) = s$$
$$((x,y) :: \pi)\,(s) = \text{if } x = \pi(s) \text{ then } y \text{ else if } y = \pi(s) \text{ then } x$$
$$\text{else } \pi(s)$$

If permutation π is the singleton list $[(x, y)]$, then π is also written $(x\,y)$.

For a type other than strings to be a nominal set, the type must support a permutation action (written $\pi \cdot x$, for x in the putative nominal set) satisfying the following conditions:

$$[\,] \cdot t = t$$
$$\pi_1 \cdot (\pi_2 \cdot t) = (\pi_1 \circ \pi_2) \cdot t \tag{4}$$
$$(\forall s.\ \pi_1(s) = \pi_2(s)) \Rightarrow \pi_1 \cdot t = \pi_2 \cdot t$$

---

[3] Pitts only calls sets nominal if each element also has *finite support*, for which see below.

As our permutations are actually lists, permutation composition ($\pi_1 \circ \pi_2$ in the second condition) is actually list concatenation. This is also the reason why the third condition tests for extensional equality (over strings) on the permutations π_1 and π_2.

Examples

- The natural numbers and the booleans are both nominal sets, with a permutation action that is everywhere the identity.
- If A is a nominal set, then so too are lists of values drawn from A. The permutation action over a list value is the permutation of each element.
- If A and B are nominal sets, then so too are functions from A to B. The permutation action is defined to be

$$\pi \cdot (f : A \to B) \;=\; \lambda(x : A). \; \pi \cdot (f \; (\pi^{-1} \cdot x))$$

It follows that $\pi \cdot (f(x)) = (\pi \cdot f)(\pi \cdot x)$

Support. With a permutation action defined, a nominal set immediately gives rise to a notion of "support".

Definition 3. *We say that the set A supports a value t if*

$$\forall x\, y \notin A. \; (x\, y) \cdot t = t$$

If there is a finite set that supports a value t, then there is a smallest such supporting set, which we refer to as the support of t (written $\mathsf{supp}(t)$). For types such as λ-calculus terms, support corresponds to the free variables of the term.

When a value has empty support, it follows that $(x\, y) \cdot t = t$ for all possible x and y. When the value is a function, this gives us a nice result about the distribution of permutations over applications:

$$(x\, y) \cdot (f(v)) \;=\; ((x\, y) \cdot f)((x\, y) \cdot v) \;=\; f((x\, y) \cdot v)$$

This result extends to arbitrary permutations, so that $\pi \cdot f(x) = f(\pi \cdot x)$. Better yet, if the function is actually a relation or predicate (a function whose range is the boolean type), then the outer π disappears and we have that $R \; (\pi \cdot x_1) \ldots (\pi \cdot x_n) \Leftrightarrow R\, x_1 \ldots x_n$. Such a predicate or relation is said to be *equivariant*.

4   Isomorphisms and De Bruijn Terms

Our goal is to show that dB is isomorphic to λ_α^N, *i.e.*, a formalism where reductions occur between α-equivalence classes of the raw syntax. The mechanisation was performed by Norrish using the HOL4 proof assistant.

At the base level, a bijection between the terms of the quotiented λ-calculus (Λ_α) and dB requires a bijection between strings and natural numbers because the existing mechanisation of Λ_α uses strings for its variables. Though occasionally awkward, the fact that the two sorts of variables are of different types is a useful sanity check when proofs are being performed. In what follows, s, s', v and v' will range over strings, and i, j and k over natural numbers. The bijections between the types will be written with a hat, so that $\hat{i}$ is the string corresponding to number i, while $\hat{s}$ is the number corresponding to string s.

4.1   An Intermediate Formalism: dB'

We define dB' to match λ_α^N, both in its construction and in its reduction relations. In particular, abstraction in dB' will involve an identifier in the style of "λ2.2" (for the *identity* function). This new constructor is necessarily not injective (as, otherwise, we would distinguish, e.g., "λ2.2" and "λ1.1"). Abstraction in λ_α^N is also not injective but, whereas the λ_α^N-construction is based on a quotient of Λ^{var}, the non-injectivity of the new λ-constructor in dB' follows directly from its definition as syntactic sugar for the existing dABS constructor in dB. Though a separate oval in Figure 1, dB' is based on the same underlying HOL type as dB. The difference arises from its use of different constructors to "cover" the type, and a different reduction relation.

We begin by defining dB-substitution without the index-decrementing used in nsub. We shall see that this function is isomorphic to substitution over Λ_α, while nsub has no natural reading in Λ_α.

Definition 4 (A clean notion of substitution for dB).

$$\mathrm{sub}\ z\ k\ (\mathrm{dV}\ i) \ = \ \mathrm{if}\ i = k\ \mathrm{then}\ z\ \mathrm{else}\ \mathrm{dV}\ i$$
$$\mathrm{sub}\ z\ k\ (\mathrm{dAPP}\ t\ u) \ = \ \mathrm{dAPP}\ (\mathrm{sub}\ z\ k\ t)\ (\mathrm{sub}\ z\ k\ u)$$
$$\mathrm{sub}\ z\ k\ (\mathrm{dABS}\ t) \ = \ \mathrm{dABS}\ (\mathrm{sub}\ (\mathrm{lift}\ z\ 0)\ (k+1)\ t)$$

The (non-injective) dLAM-function that performs abstraction over a particular index can now be defined as follows.

Definition 5 (Abstraction over an index).

$$\mathrm{dLAM}\ i\ t = \mathrm{dABS}\ (\mathrm{sub}\ (\mathrm{dV}\ 0)\ (i+1)\ (\mathrm{lift}\ t\ 0))$$

All dABS terms can be seen as abstractions over an arbitrary fresh index.

Lemma 6 (dABS terms as dLAM terms). *If i is not among the free indices of dABS t, then there exists a t_0 such that dABS $t =$ dLAM i t_0. By the definition of dLAM and the injectivity of dABS we further know that*

$$t = \mathrm{sub}\ (\mathrm{dV}\ 0)\ (i+1)\ (\mathrm{lift}\ t_0\ 0)$$

Proof. Prove by structural induction on t that there exists a t_0 such that $t = \mathrm{sub}\ (\mathrm{dV}\ n)\ i\ (\mathrm{lift}\ t_0\ n)$, where i is again suitably fresh.   □

Now we define $\to_{d'}$, the β-reduction relation for dB'. It mimics the traditional statement in the λ-calculus for both contraction and congruence rules.

Definition 7 (dB' β-reduction).

$$\overline{\mathsf{dAPP}\,(\mathsf{dLAM}\,i\,t)\,u\ \to_{d'}\ \mathsf{sub}\,u\,i\,t}$$

$$\frac{t\ \to_{d'}\ u}{\mathsf{dAPP}\,t\,z\ \to_{d'}\ \mathsf{dAPP}\,u\,z}\qquad\frac{t\ \to_{d'}\ u}{\mathsf{dAPP}\,z\,t\ \to_{d'}\ \mathsf{dAPP}\,z\,u}$$

$$\frac{t\ \to_{d'}\ u}{\mathsf{dLAM}\,i\,t\ \to_{d'}\ \mathsf{dLAM}\,i\,u}$$

4.2 dB' *vs* λ_α^N: Nominal Reasoning with Indices

Thus far we have been working entirely with the dB type, where functions are trivial to define by primitive recursion. Now we are faced with a choice: to define a function from dB into Λ_α, or *vice versa*. The former choice is less appealing because a choice of arbitrary fresh name would need to be made in the recursive dABS-clause. One might imagine writing something like

$$f\,(\mathsf{dABS}\,t) = \mathsf{LAM}\,(\mathsf{fresh}(t))\,(f\,(\mathsf{sub}\,(\mathsf{fresh}(t))\,0\,t))$$

where $\mathsf{fresh}(t)$ generates an index fresh for t. But this clause is not primitive recursive, so one would, e.g., have to write an f that took an additional environment parameter specifying how the bound variables encountered so far should be replaced. Instead, we take as our objective a bijective $f : \Lambda_\alpha \to \mathsf{dB}$, satisfying the following equations

$$\begin{aligned} f\,(\mathsf{VAR}\,v) &= \mathsf{dV}\,\hat{v}\\ f\,(\mathsf{APP}\,M\,N) &= \mathsf{dAPP}\,(f\,M)\,(f\,N)\\ f\,(\mathsf{LAM}\,v\,M) &= \mathsf{dLAM}\,\hat{v}\,(f\,M) \end{aligned} \tag{5}$$

The existence of such an f is not immediate because Λ_α is not a free algebra (LAM is not injective). However, suitable recursion principles for this type do exist, as shown in Pitts [14].

de Bruijn Terms are a Nominal Set. In order to use recursion principles for Λ_α, it remains to be shown that the range of the desired function is a *nominal set*, as in Section 3. A subtlety derives from the fact that we (necessarily must) send free variables to suitably free indices. Permutation on free variables therefore must be reflected on free indices. Conversely, bound indices are what they are and must be left untouched.

Thus we are required to define a permutation action for de Bruijn terms, and it can not be a trivial one (everywhere the identity, say). Inevitably, the complexity arises in the dABS clause of the definition. When a permutation passes through an abstraction, the free variables it is acting on are now at different index positions, which means that the permutation has to be similarly adjusted.

Definition 8 (Permutation for dB). *Let inc ("increment") over permutations be*

$$inc \, [] = []$$
$$inc \, ((s_1, s_2) :: tl) = (\widehat{s_1 + 1}, \widehat{s_2 + 1}) :: inc \, tl$$

The action of a permutation π on a term in dB (written $\pi \cdot t$) is

$$\pi \cdot (dV \, i) = dV \, (\widehat{\pi(\hat{i})})$$
$$\pi \cdot (dAPP \, t \, u) = dAPP \, (\pi \cdot t) \, (\pi \cdot u)$$
$$\pi \cdot (dABS \, t) = dABS \, (inc(\pi) \cdot t)$$

It is straightforward to show that this definition satisfies the requirements to make dB a nominal set. The support for a value in type dB is as one might expect: its set of free indices converted into strings *via* the hat-isomorphism.

Relating dLAM and Permutation. In order to admit (5), we must also characterise the relationship between dLAM (which appears on the RHS of (5)), and dB-permutation. As dLAM is defined in terms of lift and sub, analogous results are required of these constants.

We first characterise the relationship between lift and permutation. This requires the definition of an *inc* that is parameterised by the index below which variables should not be touched, with the already-defined *inc* being *inc$_0$* and with *inc$_i$* being the obvious generalisation.

Lemma 9 (Permutations and lift).

$$lift \, (\pi \cdot t) \, n = (inc_n(\pi)) \cdot (lift \, t \, n)$$

Proof. By induction on the structure of t. The result first needs

$$inc_0 \, (inc_n \, \pi) = inc_{n+1}(inc_0 \, \pi)$$

to be shown. This latter is just the sort of tedious result that the POPLmark authors inveigh against so convincingly in [1]. (Note that it is also an equality on the representing lists of pairs, not just extensionally in terms of the permutations' effect on strings.) $\square$

This lemma leads to important results about sub, dLAM and $\rightarrow_{d'}$:

Theorem 10 (sub and dLAM have empty support; $\rightarrow_{d'}$ is equivariant).

$$\pi \cdot (sub \, t \, j \, u) \quad = \quad sub \, (\pi \cdot t) \, (\widehat{\pi(\hat{j})}) \, (\pi \cdot u)$$
$$\pi \cdot (dLAM \, i \, t) \quad = \quad dLAM \, (\widehat{\pi(\hat{i})}) \, (\pi \cdot t)$$
$$\pi \cdot t \; \rightarrow_{d'} \; \pi \cdot u \quad \Leftrightarrow \quad t \; \rightarrow_{d'} \; u$$

See Lemma 17 below for the contrast with nsub.

Proof. The substitution result follows from a structural induction on t. The result for dLAM is then immediate. The result for $\rightarrow_{d'}$ follows from a rule induction showing that $t \rightarrow_{d'} u \Rightarrow \pi \cdot t \rightarrow_{d'} \pi \cdot u$. The fact that all permutations have inverses gives the other direction of the if-and-only-if. □

Theorem 11 (dB is in bijection with Λ_α). *There exists a bijective* $f : \Lambda_\alpha \rightarrow$ dB *with defining equations as in (5).*

Proof. The existence of f now follows once dB is established as a nominal set, and it is shown that

$$\mathsf{supp}(\mathsf{dLAM}\ i\ t) = \mathsf{supp}(t)\backslash\{\hat{\imath}\}$$

This in turn relies on results specifying the free variables (or support) of sub and lift (the latter is from Nipkow).

Injectivity of f follows from a structural induction, and standard properties of substitution. Surjectivity of f follows from a complete induction on the size of the dB term onto which a value in Λ_α maps.[4] □

The Homomorphism between dB' and λ_α^N. Given its construction, it is not surprising that dB with relation $\rightarrow_{d'}$ is isomorphic to Λ_α and relation $\rightarrow_\beta$

Theorem 12.
$$M \rightarrow_\beta N \Leftrightarrow f(M) \rightarrow_{d'} f(N)$$

Proof. Two straightforward rule inductions, one for each direction. Both results rely on the fact that

$$f\ (M[v := N])\ =\ \mathsf{sub}\ (f\ N)\ \hat{v}\ (f\ M)$$

which is proved by "BVC-compatible" structural induction (see [12]) on M. □

4.3   The Homomorphism Between dB and dB'

Now we must grasp the nettle, and get to grips with Nipkow's definition of $\rightarrow_d$, and the accompanying nsub function. We will establish that $\rightarrow_d$ and $\rightarrow_{d'}$ are in fact the same relation, giving us the identity as a homomorphism between dB and dB'.

We begin by proving the following:

Lemma 13.
$$n \leq i \Rightarrow$$
$$\mathsf{sub}\ u\ i\ t = \mathsf{nsub}\ u\ n\ (\mathsf{sub}\ (\mathsf{dV}\ n)\ (i+1)\ (\mathsf{lift}\ t\ n))$$

Proof. By structural induction on t. □

---

[4] Complete induction allows us to assume the induction hypothesis for all smaller terms, not just those of size one smaller.

Using this, we can show that

$$\mathsf{dAPP}\,(\mathsf{dLAM}\,i\,t)\,u \;\to_d\; \mathsf{sub}\,u\,i\,t$$

which is to say that Nipkow's relation $\to_d$ does indeed reduce $\to_{d'}$-redexes in the correct way. If we expand the definition of dLAM on the LHS, we see that the redex is

$$\mathsf{dAPP}\,(\mathsf{dABS}\,(\mathsf{sub}\,(\mathsf{dV}\,0)\,(i+1)\,(\mathsf{lift}\,t\,0))\,u)$$

Using Lemma 13 with $n = 0$ we get the desired identity. The same lemma is used to show the "converse" relation, that

$$\mathsf{dAPP}\,(\mathsf{dABS}\,t)\,u \;\to_{d'}\; \mathsf{nsub}\,u\,0\,t$$

The congruence rules for dAPP are the same in both relations, so our remaining task is to show that the different congruence rules for dABS and dLAM match up.

Abstraction Congruences Correspond. One of the two correspondences is to show that

$$t \to_{d'} u \;\Rightarrow\; \mathsf{dABS}\,t \to_{d'} \mathsf{dABS}\,u$$

In order to apply the abstraction rule for $\to_{d'}$, we must show that the dABS terms correspond to dLAM terms. Using Lemma 6, we can pick a suitably fresh i, and show the existence of t_0 and u_0 such that

$$\mathsf{dABS}\,t = \mathsf{dLAM}\,i\,t_0$$
$$\mathsf{dABS}\,u = \mathsf{dLAM}\,i\,u_0$$
$$t = \mathsf{sub}\,(\mathsf{dV}\,0)\,(i+1)\,(\mathsf{lift}\,t_0\,0)$$
$$u = \mathsf{sub}\,(\mathsf{dV}\,0)\,(i+1)\,(\mathsf{lift}\,u_0\,0)$$

We have $t \to_{d'} u$, and want $t_0 \to_{d'} u_0$, from which the abstraction rule for $\to_{d'}$ would give us $\mathsf{dABS}\,t \to_{d'} \mathsf{dABS}\,u$. The problem here is that our assumption is about a large, complicated term, and we want to conclude that the reduction occurs between sub-terms (t_0 and u_0). Standard proofs by rule induction would handle the reverse situation well (results of the form $t \to u \Rightarrow \mathsf{sub}\,w\,i\,t \to \mathsf{sub}\,w\,i\,u$), but our goal looks like the converse.

The Nominal "Aha!". The solution to our problem is to realise that both the substitution and the lifting that occur in terms t and u are no more than variable permutations, and that they are in fact the same permutation applied to t_0 and u_0. Then, we will express our assumption $t \to_{d'} u$ as $\pi \cdot t_0 \to_{d'} \pi \cdot u_0$ for some permutation π. Because $\to_{d'}$ is equivariant (Theorem 10), this gives $t_0 \to_{d'} u_0$ as desired.

That a substitution of a fresh variable into a term is a permutation is an easy induction. The interest comes in showing that a lifting is also a permutation. First we define a function *lift-pm* that constructs a "lifting permutation". Given a lower bound ℓ and an upper bound m, *lift-pm*(ℓ, m) constructs the permutation that maps $\hat{\imath}$ to $\widehat{i+1}$ if $\ell \le i \le m$, maps $\widehat{m+1}$ back to $\hat{\ell}$, and preserves the values of all other arguments.

Lemma 14 (Lifting is a permutation). *If n is at least as large as the largest free index in t, then*

$$\texttt{lift } t \; m = (\textit{lift-pm}(m, n)) \cdot t$$

Proof. By structural induction on t. The dABS case requires another tedious result about index-maneuvering, namely that

$$\textit{inc}_0(\textit{lift-pm}(m, n)) = \textit{lift-pm}(m + 1, n + 1)$$

Thankfully, the result does not need to be generalised to cover the behaviour of $\textit{inc}_i$.   □

We can now prove that abstraction congruences for any equivariant reduction relation must correspond:

Theorem 15 (Abstraction Congruences Correspond). *If R is equivariant, that is $R\,(\pi \cdot t)\,(\pi \cdot u) \Leftrightarrow R\,t\,u$, then*

$$\frac{R\,t\,u}{R\,(\texttt{dABS } t)\,(\texttt{dABS } u)} \qquad \Leftrightarrow \qquad \frac{R\,t\,u}{R\,(\texttt{dLAM } i\;t)\,(\texttt{dLAM } i\;u)}$$

where one can read each inference rule as an implication universally quantified (over t, u and i) at the top level. The generality of the result is useful when we consider η-reduction.

Proof. Immediate, given Lemma 14, and Lemma 6.   □

Lemma 16 ($\rightarrow_d \subseteq \rightarrow_{d'}$).

$$t \rightarrow_d u \;\Rightarrow\; t \rightarrow_{d'} u$$

Proof. A rule induction over the definition of $\rightarrow_d$. The redex case is handled by Lemma 13 (as already discussed). The dAPP congruence cases are immediate; the dABS congruence case is as just discussed (by Lemma 14, and Theorem 10).   □

The Other Inclusion. Showing $\rightarrow_{d'} \subseteq \rightarrow_d$, we know that $\rightarrow_d$ can perform both $\rightarrow_{d'}$'s redex-reductions (from Lemma 13), and the application congruences. To show the abstraction congruence case, we need to show that $\rightarrow_d$ is equivariant in order to apply Theorem 15.

But the definition of $\rightarrow_d$ involves nsub, so we have to characterise how nsub behaves when it interacts with a permutation. This prompts a rather incomprehensible lemma (note the odd way in which the permutation π does not affect the index i):

Lemma 17.

$$\pi \cdot (\texttt{nsub } t\;i\;u) = \texttt{nsub } (\pi \cdot t)\;i\;(\textit{inc}_i(\pi) \cdot u)$$

Proof. By structural induction on u. The dV case requires a number of splits on the ordering possibilities $(<, =, >)$ between the index of the variable and i. The dABS case uses Lemma 9.   □

Now we can conclude that $\rightarrow_d$ is equivariant (by rule induction), and follow immediately with

Lemma 18 ($\rightarrow_{d'} \subseteq \rightarrow_d$).

$$t \rightarrow_{d'} u \Rightarrow t \rightarrow_d u$$

Theorem 19 (Relations $\rightarrow_d$ and $\rightarrow_{d'}$ Coincide).

$$t \rightarrow_{d'} u \Leftrightarrow t \rightarrow_d u$$

Proof. Combining Lemmas 16 and 18.   □

Theorem 20 (Isomorphism). *The types dB and λ_α^N, with their respective reduction relations, $\rightarrow_d$ and $\rightarrow_\beta$, are isomorphic, as witnessed by the bijective f:*

$$M \rightarrow_\beta N \Leftrightarrow f(M) \rightarrow_d f(N)$$

Proof. From Theorems 12 and 19.   □

4.4   Bonus: η-Reduction

Nipkow [11] also defines a notion of η-reduction for his terms. The congruence rules are standard. Writing $\rightarrow_{ne}$ for "Nipkow's η", the redex rule is

$$\frac{0 \notin \text{dFV}(t)}{\text{dABS (dAPP } t \text{ (dV 0))} \rightarrow_{ne} \text{nsub } u\, 0\, t}$$

where the choice of u is immaterial. (Because 0 is not a free index of t, nsub is used only to decrement the free indices of t, which is required as t moves out from underneath an abstraction.)

Using exactly the same techniques as before, it is easy to define a notion of reduction that better emulates the definition in the λ-calculus. This relation (written $\rightarrow_e$), has contraction rule

$$\frac{i \notin \text{dFV}(t)}{\text{dLAM } i \text{ (dAPP } t \text{ (dV } i\text{))} \rightarrow_e t}$$

It is straightforward to show that $\rightarrow_e$ corresponds to the η-reduction rule in Λ_α. Thanks to Theorem 15, showing that $\rightarrow_{ne}$ and $\rightarrow_e$ correspond only requires us to show the equivalence of the redex rules, and that $\rightarrow_{ne}$ and $\rightarrow_e$ are equivariant. These proofs are mainly straightforward. We use some of the lemmas stated in Nipkow, among them

$$\text{nsub } u\, n\, (\text{lift } t\, n) = t$$

We also state and prove the similar

$$n \notin \text{dFV}(t) \Rightarrow \text{lift (nsub } u\, n\, t)\, n = t$$

5   Conclusion

We have proved what everyone knew (or hoped) to be true from the outset. However, the proofs we have described are not entirely trivial, suggesting that they were indeed worth doing. In fact, the proofs are only made in the least palatable by using insights from the theory of nominal sets.

This theory helps in two important ways: it makes it possible to define the bijection f from Λ_α to dB in a natural style; and it helps us perform many of the resulting proofs. In particular, the proofs are helped greatly by the realisation that lift is a permutation. To best exploit this, we needed to prove that our reduction relations $\to_d$ and $\to_{d'}$ were equivariant, which in turn prompted the curious Lemma 17.

We hope that this work encourages others to extend the web of equivalence results in Figure 1, which we believe to be a valuable summary of existing work in its own right. In the near future, we hope to consider, for example, the two-sorted calculus of McKinna and Pollack [10], and the weak HOAS style construction of the λ-calculus in Urban and Tasson [16].

Finally, we hope this work will go some way towards bringing about the day when reasoning about de Bruijn terms is never again necessary.

Acknowledgements. NICTA is funded by the Australian Government's *Backing Australia's Ability* initiative, in part through the Australian Research Council. We would like to thank James Cheney for valuable discussions in this area, and comments on this paper in particular.

Availability. The sources mechanising this paper's proofs are distributed as part of the HOL4 system, available from `http://hol.sourceforge.net`. (The proofs for β are part of the latest public release (January 2007); the η proofs are in the publicly accessible CVS repository.)

References

1. Aydemir, B.E., Bohannon, A., Fairbairn, M., Nathan Foster, J., Pierce, B.C., Sewell, P., Vytiniotis, D., Washburn, G., Weirich, S., Zdancewic, S.: Mechanized metatheory for the masses: the POPLMARK. In: Hurd, J., Melham, T. (eds.) TPHOLs 2005. LNCS, vol. 3603, Springer, Heidelberg (2005)
2. Barendregt, H.P.: The Lambda Calculus: its Syntax and Semantics. Studies in Logic and the Foundations of Mathematics, vol. 103. revised edn. Elsevier, Amsterdam (1984)
3. Curry, H.B., Feys, R.: Combinatory Logic. North-Holland, Amsterdam (1958)
4. de Bruijn, N.G.: Lambda calculus notation with nameless dummies, a tool for automatic formula manipulation, with application to the Church-Rosser Theorem. Indag. Math. 34, 381–392 (1972)
5. Gordon, A.D.: A mechanisation of name-carrying syntax up to alpha-conversion. In: Joyce, J.J., Seger, C.-J.H. (eds.) HUG 1993. LNCS, vol. 780, pp. 413–425. Springer, Heidelberg (1994)

6. Gordon, A.D., Melham, T.: Five axioms of alpha conversion. In: von Wright, J., Harrison, J., Grundy, J. (eds.) TPHOLs 1996. LNCS, vol. 1125, pp. 173–190. Springer, Heidelberg (1996)
7. Roger Hindley, J.: The Church-Rosser Property and a Result in Combinatory Logic. PhD thesis, University of Newcastle upon Tyne (1964)
8. Homeier, P.: A proof of the Church-Rosser theorem for the lambda calculus in higher order logic. In: Boulton, R.J., Jackson, P.B. (eds.) TPHOLs 2001. LNCS, vol. 2152, pp. 207–222. Springer, Heidelberg (2001)
9. Huet, G.P.: Residual theory in lambda-calculus: a formal development. Journal of Functional Programming 4(3), 371–394 (1994)
10. McKinna, J., Pollack, R.: Some lambda calculus and type theory formalized. Journal of Automated Reasoning 23(3–4), 373–409 (1999)
11. Nipkow, T.: More Church-Rosser proofs (in Isabelle/HOL). Journal of Automated Reasoning 26, 51–66 (2001)
12. Norrish, M.: Mechanising λ-calculus using a classical first order theory of terms with permutations. Higher-Order and Symbolic Computation 19, 169–195 (2006)
13. Norrish, M., Vestergaard, R.: Structural preservation and reflection of diagrams. Technical Report IS-RR-2006-011, JAIST (2006)
14. Pitts, A.M.: Alpha-structural recursion and induction. Journal of the ACM 53(3), 459–506 (2006)
15. Shankar, N.: A mechanical proof of the Church-Rosser theorem. Journal of the ACM 35(3), 475–522 (1988)
16. Urban, C., Tasson, C.: Nominal techniques in Isabelle/HOL. In: Nieuwenhuis, R. (ed.) Automated Deduction – CADE-20. LNCS (LNAI), vol. 3632, pp. 38–53. Springer, Heidelberg (2005)
17. Vestergaard, R.: The Primitive Proof Theory of the λ-Calculus. PhD thesis, School of Mathematical and Computer Sciences, Heriot-Watt University (2003)

Proof Pearl: Looping Around the Orbit

Steven Obua

Technische Universität München
D-85748 Garching, Boltzmannstr. 3, Germany
obua@in.tum.de
http://www4.in.tum.de/~obua

Abstract. We reexamine the *While* combinator of higher-order logic (HOL) and introduce the *For* combinator. We argue that both combinators should be part of the toolbox of any HOL practitioner, not only because they make efficient computations within HOL possible, but also because they facilitate elegant inductive reasoning about loops. We present two examples that support this argument.

1 Introduction

Higher-order logic (HOL), as implemented for example in the theorem proving assistant Isabelle, is a logic of total functions. Despite that it is also possible to reason about partial functions in HOL, an issue that crops up quickly when the functions under consideration originate from functional programs [2]. In this paper we are concerned with those partial HOL functions which correspond to *while* and *for loops* in imperative languages like C. We present a methodology for reasoning about and computing with them that rests on treating these functions as parameterizations of two combinators, the *While* and the *For* combinator. The *For* combinator is a derivation of the *While* combinator so that the termination relevant part of the state of the computation can be treated separately.

The *While* combinator itself is well-known in the HOL community [2,3,4]. Nevertheless, the same community shuns its direct use whenever possible. This is due to the fact that it is widely believed that reasoning about the *While* combinator must be done using a rather awkward Hoare-style rule which mingles termination and partial correctness issues. That this is not so can be shown by specializing also well-known techniques for dealing with partial functions [1,2] to the *While* combinator case. In doing so, the notion of the *orbit* of a map finds a natural application. It allows to settle the termination issue in a concrete enough fashion to deal with simple loops, so that one can concentrate on solving the partial correctness issue using ordinary inductive reasoning.

We illustrate this point by reexamining the example of a *find* function from [3,4]. We then proceed to the example that actually inspired this paper; it deals with the calculation of simple properties of planar graphs that are represented as hypermaps. The later example also illustrates how valuable loops are for calculations on concrete data.

K. Schneider and J. Brandt (Eds.): TPHOLs 2007, LNCS 4732, pp. 223–231, 2007.
© Springer-Verlag Berlin Heidelberg 2007

2 The *While* Combinator

Here is a prototypical code snippet in the programming language C which employs a *while* loop:

```
s = s0;
while (Continue(s))
    s = f(s);
s1 = s;
```

The variable s is initialized with the value of s0; then, as long as the condition Continue(s) is met, s is updated with f(s). Upon exiting the loop the resulting value s is written to the variable s1. If the loop does not terminate, the line s1 = s will never be executed.

The *While* combinator models the above loop in HOL. Its signature is

$$While :: (\alpha \to bool) \to (\alpha \to \alpha) \to \alpha \to \alpha, \tag{1}$$

and its relation to the above code snippet is given by

$$s_1 = While\ continue\ f\ s_0. \tag{2}$$

There is a catch, though; like all HOL functions, *While* is total. Therefore it must return *some* value, even if the loop does not terminate. This problem is usually solved by returning *arbitrary* in the nonterminating case, where *arbitrary* is a polymorphic constant without any definition.

We will not concern ourselves with the details of defining the *While* combinator. We used the *function* package for defining partial functions by Krauss [1] which he has recently extended to deal with tail-recursive functions in a special way. Two theorems characterize the *While* combinator. The first theorem is well-known and describes *While* as a tail-recursive function:

$$While\ continue\ f\ s = \textbf{if}\ continue\ s\ \textbf{then}\ While\ continue\ f\ (f\ s)\ \textbf{else}\ s. \tag{3}$$

It is generated automatically by the *function* package. The second one allows to reason inductively about *While*. In order to state it, we first introduce the notion of the orbit of a function at a given point,

$$Orbit\ f\ s = \{f^n\ s\,|\,n \in \mathbb{N}\} = \{s, f\ s, f(f\ s), \ldots\}, \tag{4}$$

and use it to define the predicate *terminates*:

$$terminates\ (continue, f, s) = \exists t.\ t \in Orbit\ f\ s \wedge \neg(continue\ t) \tag{5}$$

We can now state the induction rule:

$$\frac{terminates\ (continue, f, s) \qquad \forall x.\ (terminates\ (continue, f, x) \wedge (continue\ x \longrightarrow P\ (f\ x))) \longrightarrow P\ x}{P\ s} \tag{6}$$

This rule is proven by improving on the induction rule which is generated by the *function* package; most importantly, we replace the abstract domain *While-dom* which is defined as the accessible part of the call-graph relation by the simpler and more concrete *terminates* predicate.

A more compact, but still quite useful induction rule can be derived from (6):

$$\frac{terminates \text{ (continue, f, s)} \qquad \forall x. \text{ (continue x} \longrightarrow P \text{ (f x))} \longrightarrow P \text{ x}}{P \text{ s}} \tag{7}$$

Rule (7) indicates even more clearly how the issues of termination and partial correctness can be treated separately when reasoning about *While*.

Compare these two pretty induction rules with the following Hoare-style total correctness rule, which is usually used for reasoning about *While*:

$$\frac{\begin{array}{ll} A \text{ s} & \forall x. \text{ A x} \longrightarrow \text{ continue x} \longrightarrow A \text{ (f x)} \\ \forall x. \text{ A x} \longrightarrow \neg \text{ (continue x)} \longrightarrow B \text{ x} \\ R \text{ is well-founded} & \forall x. \text{ A x} \longrightarrow \text{ continue x} \longrightarrow (f \text{ x, x)} \in R \end{array}}{B \text{ (While continue f s)}} \tag{8}$$

This rule mingles termination and partial correctness issues, and is therefore often more difficult to handle. No wonder it is introduced in [3] with the warning

...termination rears its ugly head again.

Note that (8) is easily derived from (7) by setting

$$P \text{ s} = (A \text{ s} \longrightarrow B \text{ (While continue f s)}). \tag{9}$$

3   Example: Finding a Fixpoint

A simple example of the usage of *While* is the *find* function which searches for a fixpoint of a function f by repeatedly applying f. It should obey the equation

$$find \text{ f x} = \textbf{if } \text{ f x} = \text{ x } \textbf{then } \text{ x } \textbf{else } find \text{ f (f x)}. \tag{10}$$

We use the *While* combinator to define *find*:

$$find \text{ f x} = While \text{ } (\lambda x. \text{ f x} \neq x) \text{ f x}. \tag{11}$$

A trivial observation is that above definition can be written in shorter notation:

$$find \text{ f} = While \text{ } (\lambda x. \text{ f x} \neq x) \text{ f}. \tag{12}$$

The point is: If you *cannot* rewrite your loop in this shorter notation that does not mention the loop state explicitly, then you are probably in trouble and you should rethink your definition, as problems may arise later when reasoning about your loop by induction.

Equation (10) follows directly and automatically from (3) and (11). It can be used for calculations on concrete data, for example to show the following theorem:

$$\frac{\text{f 0} = 1 \qquad \text{f 1} = 2 \qquad \text{f 2} = 2}{find \text{ f 0} = 2} \tag{13}$$

In case of termination, we expect the result of *find* f x to be a fixpoint of f:

$$\frac{terminates\ (\lambda x.\, f\, x \neq x,\ f,\ x)}{f\ (find\ f\ x) = find\ f\ x} \tag{14}$$

We prove (14) by using the induction rule (7), where

$$P\ s = (f\ (find\ f\ s) = find\ f\ s). \tag{15}$$

Because we assume termination in (14), we only need to show the second assumption in (7): for any x, show P x, given that

$$continue\ x\ implies\ P\ (f\ x). \tag{16}$$

We do this by case distinction:

- If continue x does not hold, then we have f x = x by just using the definition of continue in the *find* case. Using (10), we obtain *find* f x = x. Therefore P x rewrites to f x = x, which we assumed to be true in this branch of our case distinction.
- If continue x does hold, we can again use (10), obtaining *find* f x = *find* f (f x). Rewriting P x with this identity yields P (f x), which we know to be true because of (16).

It is hard to imagine a simpler and more straightforward proof of (14) than the above one. Compare this to the presentation in [3, 183-186], where the direct definition of *find* via the *While* combinator is regarded a necessary evil to achieve executability. Also, the correctness result obtained there has a much stronger termination assumption than our theorem. We did not need to think at all about the termination assumption of our theorem: after all, we *know* when a loop terminates, and this knowledge is encoded once and for all in the definition of the *terminates* predicate.

From a computational point of view, the correctness result (14) is not very useful: Using (13) together with (14) (and ignoring the termination assumption, which makes matters only worse), we obtain the theorem

$$\frac{f\ 0 = 1 \qquad f\ 1 = 2 \qquad f\ 2 = 2}{f\ 2 = 2} \tag{17}$$

which is probably not the most useful of theorems.

The computational perspective will brighten up with our next example. But first, we will introduce a useful specialization of the *While* combinator.

4   The *For* Combinator

Look at the following code snippet in the programming language C:

```
for (i = i0, a = a0; Continue(i); i = f(i))
    a = A(i, a);
a1 = a;
```

Here the state of the loop is split into two variables, the loop index i and the accumulator a. After the initialization of i and a the loop iterates as long as the condition $\texttt{Continue(i)}$ holds. After each loop step a is updated with $\texttt{A(i, a)}$ and i with $\texttt{f(i)}$, respectively. Upon exiting the loop the loop index is discarded and the accumulator stored in $\texttt{a1}$.

We call the combinator that models the above loop the *For* combinator. Its signature is

$$\textit{For} :: (\alpha \to \textit{bool}) \to (\alpha \to \alpha) \to (\alpha \to \beta \to \beta) \to \alpha \to \beta \to \beta, \tag{18}$$

and its relation to the above code snippet is given by

$$a_1 = \textit{For} \text{ continue f A } i_0 \text{ } a_0. \tag{19}$$

It can be defined directly using the *While* combinator:

$$\begin{aligned}
&\textit{For} \text{ continue f A } i_0 \text{ } a_0 = \\
&\quad \textit{fst} \ (\textit{While} \ (\lambda \, (a,i).\ \text{continue } i) \ (\lambda \, (a,i).\ (A \text{ } i \text{ } a, f \text{ } i)) \ (a_0, i_0)).
\end{aligned} \tag{20}$$

Of course, this definition should never be used except for proving the simplification and induction rules of *For*. Here is the simplification rule:

$$\begin{aligned}
&\textit{For} \text{ continue f A } i \text{ } a = \\
&\quad \textbf{if } \text{continue } i \textbf{ then } \textit{For} \text{ continue f A } (f \text{ } i) \ (A \text{ } i \text{ } a) \textbf{ else } a.
\end{aligned} \tag{21}$$

Its proof is immediate using the simplification rule (3) for the *While* combinator.

Why is the *For* combinator useful? Could we not just use *While* instead? The answer should be obvious: It often simplifies reasoning about the termination of the loop because it splits the loop state into two components, one which is relevant for termination, the loop index, and one which is not, the accumulator. This becomes apparent when looking at its induction rule:

$$\frac{\textit{terminates} \ (\text{continue}, f, j) \qquad \forall i\, a.\ (\textit{terminates}\,(\text{continue}, f, i) \wedge (\text{continue}\, i \longrightarrow P\,(f\,i)\,(A\,i\,a))) \longrightarrow P\,i\,a}{P\,j\,b} \tag{22}$$

Note that the *terminates* predicate only mentions the loop index, but not the accumulator. The proof of the induction rule follows from (6) and the theorem

$$\begin{aligned}
&\textit{terminates} \ (\lambda\,(a,i).\ \text{continue } i, \lambda\,(a,i).\ (A \text{ } i \text{ } a, f \text{ } i), (a, i)) = \\
&\qquad\qquad \textit{terminates} \ (\text{continue}, f, i).
\end{aligned} \tag{23}$$

Again, there is a more compact form of the above rule:

$$\frac{\textit{terminates} \ (\text{continue}, f, j) \qquad \forall i\, a.\ \text{continue}\, i \longrightarrow P\,(f\,i)\,(A\,i\,a) \longrightarrow P\,i\,a}{P\,j\,b} \tag{24}$$

Now we are equipped to deal with our next (and last) example.

5   Example: Planar Graphs

Recently, planar graphs have received attention for being at the heart of two large-scale verification efforts, the completed proof of the Four Color Theorem by Gonthier [5], and the ongoing Flyspeck Project [7], which aims at formalizing Hales's proof of the Kepler Conjecture [8]. An important part of the Flyspeck Project has already been completed by Nipkow and Bauer [6], the enumeration of all tame graphs, which are special planar graphs. As a planar graph consists of nodes, edges and faces, one possibility to represent a planar graph would be a list of faces, where each face is again a list of nodes, leaving the representation of the edges implicit in the arrangement of nodes. This is the representation used in [6]. Gonthier instead favors the *hypermap* representation. It builds on the notion of *dart*. Darts can be viewed as the oriented edges of a graph (Gonthier chooses a different, but equivalent, point of view; he sees them as angles between incident edges of the same face). Let us assume that we are given three permutations e, n and f of a finite set D of darts. Two darts α and β are called equivalent with respect to a permutation p of D iff $\exists n.\ \alpha = p^n\,\beta$ holds. The such induced relation on darts is an equivalence relation, and we write $|p|$ for its number of equivalence classes. If now the given three permutations fulfill the equations

$$e = e^{-1} = n \circ f \quad \text{and} \quad 2\,|e| = |D| \quad \text{and} \quad |e| + |f| + |n| = |D| + 2, \qquad (25)$$

then we can construct a connected planar graph in the following way:

1. The nodes, edges and faces are the equivalence classes of n, e and f.
2. An edge $E = \{\delta_1, \delta_2\}$ consists therefore of the two oriented edges δ_1 and δ_2.
3. There is an oriented edge δ from node N_1 to node N_2 iff $\delta \in N_1$ and $e\,\delta \in N_2$.
4. An oriented edge δ belongs to a face F iff $\delta \in F$.

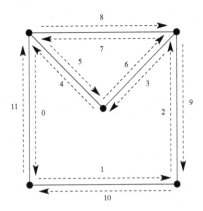

Fig. 1. A planar graph

Consider the planar graph in Fig. 1. Each dart is denoted by a number, and we have $D = \{0, 1, 2, \ldots, 11\}$. The permutations are given by

$$
\begin{aligned}
f &= (0 \mapsto 1 \mapsto 2 \mapsto 3 \mapsto 4, \ 5 \mapsto 6 \mapsto 7, \ 8 \mapsto 9 \mapsto 10 \mapsto 11), \\
e &= (0 \mapsto 11, \ 1 \mapsto 10, \ 2 \mapsto 9, \ 3 \mapsto 6, \ 4 \mapsto 5, \ 7 \mapsto 8), \\
n &= (0 \mapsto 5 \mapsto 8, \ 1 \mapsto 11, \ 2 \mapsto 10, \ 3 \mapsto 9 \mapsto 7, \ 4 \mapsto 6).
\end{aligned}
\tag{26}
$$

It might be instructive to check the equations (25).

Darts are also viewed as faces, nodes and edges. For example, there are three faces, face 0, face 5, and face 8 (to see why there are three faces, not two, imagine how the graph looks when drawn on a sphere instead of in the plane); and face 7 is the same as face 5.

Each one of the three permutations can be expressed in HOL as function of type $nat \rightarrow nat$. Given such representations $face$, the face permutation, and $node$, the node permutation, we are interested in two simple calculations:

- Given a dart representing a node, calculate the number of edges that are incident with the node.
- Given a dart representing a face, calculate the number of edges that border the face.

Both calculations amount to the same task:

Given a function $h :: \alpha \rightarrow \alpha$ and a value $x :: \alpha$, calculate $|Orbit\ h\ x|$.

We can express this calculation as a *for* loop,

$$
card\text{-}orbit\ h\ x \ = \ For\ (\lambda\, y.\ y \neq x)\ h\ (\lambda\, y\ a.\ a + 1)\ (h\ x)\ 1,
\tag{27}
$$

and calculate/prove in HOL

$$
card\text{-}orbit\ face\ 0 = 5 \quad \text{and} \quad card\text{-}orbit\ node\ 0 = 3,
\tag{28}
$$

therefore we expect face 0 to be bordered by 5 edges, and node 0 to be incident with 3 edges. To show that these expectations are justified, we need to prove

$$
terminates\ (\lambda\, y.\ y \neq x,\ h,\ h\ x) \ \longrightarrow \ card\text{-}orbit\ h\ x \ = \ |Orbit\ h\ x|.
\tag{29}
$$

So, how do we prove this? A direct reasoning by induction is problematic for two reasons.

First, we cannot "curry away" the loop state in (27), as we could do for our previous example by moving from (11) to (12). We can remedy this by introducing a more general loop:

$$
card\text{-}section\ continue\ h\ y\ a \ = \ For\ continue\ h\ (\lambda\, y\ a.\ a + 1)\ y\ a.
\tag{30}
$$

Note that we not only generalized the loop state, but also the continuation condition. This is not really necessary, in principle you could just as well work with the concrete continuation condition.

Second, the reason why (29) is correct cannot be seen by going from one loop iteration to the next, as the loop accumulator is just a counter. The reason why incrementing the loop accumulator is the right action to take is that the current loop index is different from all other loop indices that have been encountered before. But this loop invariant cannot be expressed in terms of the loop state, and is therefore lost for a proof by induction that aims at proving (29) directly. We remedy this by also "generalizing" the accumulator from a number to a set:

$$\textit{section continue h y A} \;=\; \textit{For continue h } (\lambda\, y\, A.\ A \cup \{y\})\ y\ A. \qquad (31)$$

To state and prove the correctness of *section*, we need a more general concept than what *Orbit* provides. We define:

$$\textit{Section continue h y} \;=\; \{f^n\, y \mid n \in \mathbb{N} \ \wedge\ \forall\, m \le n.\ \textit{continue } (f^m\, y)\}. \qquad (32)$$

An easy loop induction (that is, an induction based on (24)) yields:

$$\frac{\textit{terminates (continue, h, y)}}{\textit{section continue h y A} \;=\; A\ \cup\ \textit{Section continue h y}} \qquad (33)$$

Basic considerations lead to the theorem

$$\{x\}\ \cup\ \textit{Section } (\lambda\, y.\ y \ne x)\ h\ (h\, x) \;=\; \textit{Orbit h x}, \qquad (34)$$

and together with (33) we arrive at

$$\frac{\textit{terminates } (\lambda\, y.\ y \ne x,\ h,\ h\, x)}{\textit{section } (\lambda\, y.\ y \ne x)\ h\ (h\, x)\ \{x\} \;=\; \textit{Orbit h x}} \qquad (35)$$

All we need to do now is to connect *card-section* with *section*, and we would be done with the proof of (29)! The following theorem does exactly that:

$$\frac{\textit{terminates (continue, h, y)} \qquad \textit{finite A}}{\textit{card-section continue h y } |A| \;= \; |\textit{section continue h y A}| + |A\ \cap\ \textit{Section continue h y}|} \qquad (36)$$

Its proof is again straightforward by loop induction, this time based on (22) instead of (24). Here the strength of the *For* combinator shows, because it emphasizes the similarities of *section* and *card-section* which are different only in the accumulator they use, but equal with respect to termination issues.

We are returning now to the computational point of view, as earlier promised. How can we use (29) for computations on concrete data within HOL? Well, this is obvious enough; combining for example (28) with (29) we obtain the theorem

$$\frac{\textit{terminates } (\lambda\, y.\ y \ne 0,\ \textit{face},\ 1) \qquad \textit{terminates } (\lambda\, y.\ y \ne 0,\ \textit{node},\ 5)}{|\textit{Orbit face 0}| = 5 \quad \wedge \quad |\textit{Orbit node 0}| = 3} \qquad (37)$$

This looks already pretty useful, but we can do even better. Note that the termination conditions can be calculated themselves! This is possible because the *terminates* predicate is governed by the general recursion equation

terminates (continue, h, x) =
> **if** continue x **then** *terminates* (continue, h, h x) **else** *True*.   (38)

"Calculating away" the termination conditions in (37) leaves us with

$$|Orbit\ face\ 0| = 5 \quad \land \quad |Orbit\ node\ 0| = 3.$$ (39)

6 Conclusion

We showed that both *While* and *For* are natural, computational useful and elegant tools for defining and reasoning about loops. *Natural*, because every programmer knows intuitively how to handle them, *computational useful*, because they allow for computing with partial functions on concrete data in HOL without worrying about termination if the concrete data induces termination, and *elegant*, because they come with clean induction rules.

Their main advantage over current automated tools for defining partial functions like the *function* package [1] is that the termination conditions of the loops defined by them can be automatically derived as simple parameterizations of the termination conditions of the respective combinator. Especially the *For* combinator shines here. Consider for example the functions *card-section* and *section*: They would have been assigned different termination domains *card-section-dom* and *section-dom* by the *function* package, although they obviously have the same termination behaviour.

All theorems and proofs of this paper have been formalized in Isabelle/HOL [3], and can be obtained from [9].

Acknowledgement. Thanks to Alexander Krauss for explaining the details of his *function* package and numerous issues concerning partial functions in HOL. Also thanks to Norbert Schirmer for illuminating the Hoare-logic point of view.

References

1. Krauss, A.: Partial Recursive Functions in Higher-Order Logic. In: Furbach, U., Shankar, N. (eds.) IJCAR 2006. LNCS (LNAI), vol. 4130, Springer, Heidelberg (2006)
2. Owens, S., Slind, K.: Adapting Functional Programs to Higher-Order Logic (submitted)
3. Nipkow, T., Paulson, L.C., Wenzel, M.: Isabelle/HOL: A Proof Assistant for Higher-Order Logic. Springer, Heidelberg (2002)
4. Berghofer, S., Nipkow, T.: Executing Higher-Order Logic. In: Callaghan, P., Luo, Z., McKinna, J., Pollack, R. (eds.) TYPES 2000. LNCS, vol. 2277, Springer, Heidelberg (2002)
5. Gonthier, G.: A computer-checked proof of the Four Color Theorem, http://research.microsoft.com/ gonthier/4colproof.pdf
6. Nipkow, T., Bauer, G., Schultz, P.: Flyspeck I: Tame Graphs. In: Furbach, U., Shankar, N. (eds.) IJCAR 2006. LNCS (LNAI), vol. 4130, Springer, Heidelberg (2006)
7. Hales, T.: The Flyspeck Project, http://www.math.pitt.edu/~thales/flyspeck/
8. Hales, T.: A proof of the Kepler conjecture. Annals of Mathematics 162, 1065–1185
9. Looping around the Orbit, http://www4.in.tum.de/~obua/looping/

Source-Level Proof Reconstruction for Interactive Theorem Proving

Lawrence C. Paulson and Kong Woei Susanto

Computer Laboratory, University of Cambridge, England
LP15@cam.ac.uk, kongwoei@gmail.com

Abstract. Interactive proof assistants should verify the proofs they receive from automatic theorem provers. Normally this proof reconstruction takes place internally, forming part of the integration between the two tools. We have implemented source-level proof reconstruction: resolution proofs are automatically translated to Isabelle proof scripts. Users can insert this text into their proof development or (if they wish) examine it manually. Each step of a proof is justified by calling Hurd's Metis prover, which we have ported to Isabelle. A recurrent issue in this project is the treatment of Isabelle's axiomatic type classes.

1 Introduction

Interactive theorem proving is notoriously labour intensive. Researchers are actively developing many verification technologies that are fully automatic, such as model checkers and SMT solvers. However, interactive theorem provers are unrivalled for their rich assertion languages that support quantifiers, recursive definitions and set notation. Interactive theorem provers also excel at managing elaborate hierarchies of formal developments. Much recent work concerns adding automation to interactive theorem provers to increase their users' productivity.

Correctness is paramount when external tools are coupled to interactive theorem provers. Although most verification tools appear to be highly reliable, errors can easily be introduced in the interface code, which translates problems from the interactive prover to the automatic tool. The translations themselves can be unsound: Meng and Paulson [9] show that using a compact translation improves the external tool's success rate, but admits the possibility of unsound proofs. Finally, many interactive provers adhere to the LCF philosophy [2] that all inferences must be checked by a small proof kernel. For all of these reasons, the interactive prover must check the automatic tool's output.

This paper concerns proof reconstruction at the source level. Rather than checking the proof behind the scenes, we deliver an actual piece of proof script. Source-level reconstruction is particularly appropriate when the external tool needs large computational resources: the user can write the proof script with the help of a powerful, multi-core workstation, and later replay it on an elderly laptop. A visible proof script also gives the highest possible confidence of correctness, as the reasoning is broken down into small steps that can be examined by hand.

K. Schneider and J. Brandt (Eds.): TPHOLs 2007, LNCS 4732, pp. 232–245, 2007.

Our particular interest lies in automatic theorem provers (ATPs) for first-order logic. We have elsewhere described [11] an interface between Isabelle and resolution theorem provers. Until now, we have been able to call external provers from Isabelle but could not do much with the result. We can now perform proof reconstruction by parsing the output of any ATP that delivers proofs in TSTP format [21]. Each inference is justified by a call to Hurd's Metis prover [5].

Paper outline. We begin (§2) by presenting the background material: Isabelle and our project to link it with automatic theorem provers. We then describe our experience of porting Metis to Isabelle (§3). There follows a lengthy presentation of how we generate single-step proof scripts (§4), with additional examples (§5). We finally give brief conclusions (§6).

2 Background

Isabelle/HOL [14] is an interactive theorem prover for higher-order logic, built upon the Isabelle logical framework [16]. (Henceforth, we shall use Isabelle and Isabelle/HOL synonymously.) Isabelle has been used for countless projects, such as the mechanization of the prime number theorem by Avigad et al. [1]. Isabelle's version of higher-order logic has many similarities with that used in HOL4 [15] and HOL Light [3]. All are based on polymorphic simple type theory, without subtyping or dependent types. Polymorphism is expressed by free type variables with implicit universal quantification, so a theorem like `rev (rev xs) = xs` is universally quantified both in the list `xs` and in the anonymous type of its elements. None of these tools offer explicit quantification over type variables [7].

2.1 Order-Sorted Polymorphism

Order-sorted polymorphism [12] distinguishes Isabelle's version of higher-order logic from other versions. In Isabelle, a type may belong to any finite number of *type classes.* This idea, which gives a controlled treatment of overloading, originates with Wadler and Blott [22]. It is particularly powerful in an interactive theorem prover, where type classes can be specified using axioms [24]. Finite types, for example, can be characterized by an axiom stating that there exists a list enumerating all of the type's elements. We can then prove individual types to be finite by exhibiting such lists. We can even prove that certain type constructors, such as Cartesian product, preserve the property of finiteness; the proof requires exhibiting a construction that enumerates the elements of the product given enumerations of its component types.

Orderings provide other examples of type classes. The class `order` of partial orderings consists of all types equipped with a reflexive, anti-symmetric and transitive relation $\leq$. The class `linorder` of linear orderings extends `order` with the axiom $x \leq y \lor y \leq x$. To prove that the type of integers belongs to class `linorder`, we define a suitable instance of $\leq$ and prove suitable instances of the four axioms. The definition of $\leq$ on lists can refer to $\leq$ on list elements. The lexicographic ordering on lists yields a partial order if the list elements are partially ordered and a linear order if they are linearly ordered. We declare such facts to Isabelle as follows:

```
instance list :: (order) order
   ...

instance list :: (linorder) linorder
   ...
```

Here, ... designates the proofs of the type class axioms, which typically refer to the corresponding properties of the element type. Paulson has shown how axiomatic type classes allow the various numeric types such as the integers, rationals and reals to be formalized without proving separate instances of algebraic properties for each type [17].

Axiomatic type classes are powerful, but they complicate the task of using external verification tools to prove Isabelle subgoals. For one thing, we must ensure that the automatic tools can reason with type classes as well as Isabelle can. Isabelle automatically applies its database of `instance` declarations to specific cases; for example, it can automatically recognize that lists of lists of integers belong to class `linorder`. Also, Isabelle automatically applies forgetful inclusions, for example that `linorder` is a subclass of `order`.

Incorrect treatment of type classes compromises soundness. Hurd [5] reports that types can be ignored entirely when integrating HOL4 with an automatic theorem prover. He describes a potential unsoundness by exhibiting a polymorphic "Russell constant" R such that $RR = \neg(RR)$ if types are ignored. (With types, the fatal equation cannot even be written.) He uses proof reconstruction to detect unsoundness, which he says "occurs in less than 1% of all HOL subgoals". Omitting type information is unthinkable in the presence of axiomatic type classes. They govern the properties that may be assumed of Isabelle's numerous overloaded functions, such as orderings and the arithmetic operators. Type information is necessary to stop the ATP from assuming, for example, that the subset relation is a linear ordering. Such errors are far more likely than the automatic discovery of Russell's paradox. Although unsound proofs cannot survive proof reconstruction, they can prevent sound proofs from being found.

We have described our first-order formalization of type information elsewhere [11].

- Types are first-order terms. A type operator taking n operands is simply an n-ary function symbol, while type variables are first-order variables. For example, the type of lists of integers might be `tc_list(tc_int)`.
- Type classes are first-order predicates. For example, the claim that the type of booleans is finite might be `class_finite(tc_bool)`. To express an `instance` declaration, for example that the Cartesian product of two finite types is itself finite, we use the obvious implication.
- Type class inclusions, such as that every linear ordering is a partial ordering, are formalized as implications between two atomic formulas.

As we are using resolution theorem provers, we use *clause form*: disjunctions of possibly negated atomic formulas. The formalization of the type class hierarchy is close to clause form already, as it consists of implications between atomic formulas. Since resolution uses proof by contradiction, the conjecture to be proved is negated before it is translated into clauses; existing theorems being used as lemmas are also translated. In both cases, we have to formalize class constraints on the type variables appearing in a clause. (For examples, see §4.2 below.)

- Because the conjecture has been negated, the implicit universal quantification over its type variables becomes existential. Type variables in the conjecture are Skolemized, yielding new constants. Class constraints on these type variables become additional facts, such as `class_finite(t_a)`.
- Type variables in a lemma remain universally quantified. Type constraints in a clause take the form of additional negative literals, with the intuitive meaning such as "if `class_finite(T)` then ...".

Although this formalization is straightforward, it complicates the translations between higher-order logic and first-order logic. Proof reconstruction has to take first-order clauses that contain minimal type information and somehow recover as much of it as possible. The parts of the proof that relate to the type system must then be deleted, as they represent reasoning that Isabelle carries out implicitly. References to specific literals in a clause must be adjusted to account for such deletions.

2.2   The Interface Between Isabelle and ATPs

The Isabelle-ATP interface is designed to give users push-button assistance. When invoked, it examines its entire database of approximately 7000 theorems, selecting several hundred that appear to be relevant to the problem [10]. If the problem contains higher-order features such as functions or booleans being passed as arguments, then it is translated into a first-order form [9]. An automatic theorem prover is then invoked: currently, either E [19], SPASS [23] or Vampire [18]. The prover is given a considerable amount of processor time, perhaps 60 seconds per subgoal. Because this is much longer than users may want to wait, the prover runs in the background, allowing the user to continue working interactively. Responses from the ATP, whether successful or not, are reported when they appear.

The first working version of this system [11] could occasionally reconstruct Isabelle proofs, but it was problematical. It worked by reading the output of SPASS and emulating each SPASS inference rule in Isabelle. SPASS used many inference rules that differed slightly from one another. The information it delivered was incomplete, omitting details such as which subterm of which literal had been rewritten. Finally, SPASS re-ordered the literals in the clauses it was given.

In view of these difficulties, we decided instead to base proof reconstruction on Hurd's Metis prover, described below. We would parse an ATP's output merely to extract the names of the lemmas used; then, we would deliver that list of lemmas to Metis. This was a sensible division of labour: leading ATPs can cope with problems that contain hundreds of clauses; Metis is relatively easy to integrate with interactive theorem provers.

However, we foresaw that Metis alone would often be insufficient. We performed extensive experiments [8] with 285 first-order problems. We were able to put nearly all of these problems into a minimal form by using an ATP to identify the necessary axioms. These minimal problems were similar to those that Metis would have to prove if we relied on it for proof reconstruction. Metis was unable to prove 8% of them in 10 seconds[1] and even given 60 seconds failed to prove 5%. It is a shame to let proof reconstruction fail for so many problems, especially as they are likely to be the most difficult ones. Another objection is that it is wasteful to use an ATP merely as a relevance filter when it delivers full proofs. We decided to parse these proofs and reconstruct them line by line, but instead of emulating an ATP's specific inference rules, we would justify each line by calling Metis. That project is the main subject of this paper.

3   Porting Metis to Isabelle

Hurd has written his Metis prover [5] in order to add further automation to HOL4. He has already shown [4] how difficult it is to harness existing ATPs for this purpose: ambiguities in their output complicate proof reconstruction. Although Metis cannot compete with the best ATPs, it includes a full implementation of the superposition calculus, and its performance is respectable [6].

Metis expresses proofs using five simple inference rules, designed for easy emulation in any interactive proof assistant for higher-order logic.[2]

$$\frac{}{A_1 \bigvee \ldots \bigvee A_n} \text{ axiom } [A_1, \ldots, A_n]$$

The *axiom* rule constructs an axiom. It takes as its argument a list of literals and returns their disjunction. The corresponding theorem must already be known to the proof assistant; axioms in the resolution proof correspond to uses of existing theorems as lemmas.

$$\frac{}{L \bigvee \neg L} \text{ assume } L$$

The *assume* rule takes as argument a literal L and returns the theorem $L \bigvee \neg L$.

$$\frac{A_1 \bigvee \ldots \bigvee A_n}{A_1[\sigma] \bigvee \ldots \bigvee A_n[\sigma]} \text{ instantiate } \sigma$$

The instantiate rule instantiates free variables. It takes two arguments, a substitution and a theorem, returning the appropriate instance of the theorem.

$$\frac{A_1 \bigvee \ldots \bigvee L \bigvee \ldots \bigvee A_m \quad B_1 \bigvee \ldots \bigvee \neg L \bigvee \ldots \bigvee B_n}{A_1 \bigvee \ldots \bigvee A_m \bigvee B_1 \bigvee \ldots \bigvee B_n} \text{ resolve } L$$

---

[1] On a 2.8GHz Intel Xeon processor.

[2] While we were revising this paper, Hurd released Metis 2.0. The set of inference rules in this version is simpler than its predecessor; we describe the new version.

The *resolve* rule takes a literal L and two theorems. The resulting theorem contains all literals of the first theorem other than L and all literals of the second theorem other than $\neg L$.

$$\frac{}{\neg(s = t) \bigvee \neg L \bigvee L[t]} \quad \text{equality } (L, p, t)$$

The *equality* rule takes a literal L, a path p and a term t. Writing s for the term denoted by path p and $L[t]$ for the result of replacing this occurrence by t, it yields a theorem stating that if $s = t$ and L then $L[t]$.

Unification is not required: all substitutions are supplied explicitly using the instantiate rule. The idea is that the Metis performs the unifications and proof reconstruction merely has to perform the supplied instantiations. This description makes it sound like integration with Isabelle ought to be easy, but we encountered some difficulties.

We began by modifying the Metis sources to compile with Isabelle. We then did the easy half of the integration: allowing Isabelle to call Metis, passing Isabelle theorems as axioms. We then turned to the difficult half, proof reconstruction, using the rules above. Most of the rules were straightforward; the difficult one was instantiate, and ironically we would have preferred to do our own unifications. Reconstructing type information missing from the resolution proof requires us to ignore any supplied instantiations that do relate to types, instead performing type inference to generate the correct type instantiations.

Converting Metis terms into Isabelle terms required type inference and proved to be surprisingly complicated. We finally got proof reconstruction working for first-order problems without types. Adding translations for higher-order problems and a treatment of types and type classes required another five months before proof reconstruction became robust. Among our problems was the need to adjust path quantifiers to account for the deletion of type literals. We also discovered several bugs (none affecting soundness) in Isabelle's forward proof mechanisms. A major difference between Isabelle and HOL4 is that Isabelle works almost entirely by backward proof, while HOL4 ultimately reduces everything to forward proof.

4   Producing Single-Step Proofs

The Metis proof method gives us a new way to reconstruct resolution proofs generated by another ATP. As in our first attempt [11], we translate each clause in the resolution proof to an Isabelle formula. Rather than emulate the ATP's specific inference rules, however, we prove each clause by calling Metis, passing it the inference rule's premises. Rather than parse the output of SPASS, we parse TSTP format [21], a recently introduced language for proof communication. TSTP format is easy to parse and is precisely documented.[3] E can output TSTP format and we have reason to hope that SPASS and Vampire will support it eventually.

---

[3] http://www.cs.miami.edu/~tptp/TPTP/SyntaxBNF.html

4.1   TSTP Format

TSTP (Thousands of Solutions from Theorem Provers) format defines a language for communicating proofs. A resolution prover typically produces a list of proof lines, each containing a clause and a justification referring to previous lines. The final line contains a contradiction. A proof line in TSTP format has the following syntax:

`cnf(<name>,<formula_role>,<cnf_formula><annotations>).`

Here is a description of these items:

- The `<name>` is a symbol identifying the formula. Although identifiers are permitted, all ATPs that we know of use positive integers.
- The `<formula_role>` is `axiom` for an axiom clause or `negated_conjecture` for clauses arising (even indirectly) from the negation of the conjecture.
- The `<cnf_formula>` is the formula itself. As we use clause form, it is a disjunction of literals. The disjunction symbol is | and the empty clause explicitly contains the literal `$false`.
- Any number of `<annotations>` may follow. These describe the provenance of the formula, for example as a named clause in a given file or proved from previous lines. Proof justifications can vary from one ATP to the next, but we only need to identify references to previous proof lines.

4.2   A Small Example

Let us examine the proof of a simple goal, one of our standard test problems. It arises in the middle of an interactive proof; the remaining goal is to prove $0 \leq f(x) + (-lb(x))$ from the two assumptions

$$\forall y.\, lb(y) \leq f(y) \quad \text{and} \quad \forall y.\, f(y) \leq lb(y) + g(y).$$

The proof is trivial. Ignore the second assumption and in the first one instantiate y by x; then, move $lb(x)$ across the inequality. Given the equivalent clause form, E immediately generates a 22-line resolution proof. Below we present about half of these lines to illustrate some issues involved in the translation. We have reformatted the lines and shortened some names to improve clarity.

The proof refers to specific axioms from the input file. The first axiom is $X - X = 0$.

```
cnf(216,axiom,
    (c_minus(X,X,X3)=c_HOL_Ozero(X3) |
     ~class_OrderedGroup_Oab__group__add(X3)),
    file('BigO__bigo_bounded2_1', cls_right__minus__eq_1)).
```

The variable $X3$ ranges over types, and the second literal restricts type $X3$ to belong to the class *OrderedGroup.ab_group_add* (Abelian groups). This type class was implicit in the original problem through its use of overloaded operators such as addition. As subtraction (c_minus) and zero (c_HOL_Ozero) are polymorphic, they carry type information as an additional argument. We have to undo this translation to obtain an Isabelle formula.

The next two axioms express inclusions between type classes. They state that elements of Ring_and_Field.ordered_idom (ordered integral domains) also belong to the classes OrderedGroup.ab_group_add (Abelian groups) and OrderedGroup. pordered_ab_group_add (partially ordered Abelian groups). These axioms cannot be expressed in Isabelle, so references to them must be deleted from proofs.

```
cnf(343,axiom,
    (class_OrderedGroup_Opordered__ab__group__add(X3) |
     ~class_Ring__and__Field_Oordered__idom(X3)),
    file('BigO__bigo_bounded2_1', clsrel_Ring__and__Field_123)).
cnf(350,axiom,
    (class_OrderedGroup_Oab__group__add(X3) |
     ~class_Ring__and__Field_Oordered__idom(X3)),
    file('BigO__bigo_bounded2_1', clsrel_Ring__and__Field_923)).
```

Negating the test problem generates an additional conjecture clause: one asserting type information about the type variable 'b, which is implicit in the subgoal. As remarked above in §2.1, negating a polymorphic subgoal creates an existentially quantified type variable that turns into a Skolem constant. This type, t_b, belongs to the class of ordered integral domains. The other conjecture clause shown refers to the assumption $\forall y. lb(y) \leq f(y)$.

```
cnf(335,negated_conjecture,
    (class_Ring__and__Field_Oordered__idom(t_b)),
    file('BigO__bigo_bounded2_1', tfree_tcs)).
cnf(336,negated_conjecture,
    (c_lessequals(v_lb(X3),v_f(X3),t_b)),
    file('BigO__bigo_bounded2_1', cls_conjecture_0)).
```

Now the proof begins. The first two lines follow type class inclusions, deducing that the type variable 'b belongs to the class of Abelian groups. During the translation, such proof steps must be deleted.

```
cnf(366,negated_conjecture,
    (class_OrderedGroup_Opordered__ab__group__add(t_b)),
    inference(spm,[status(thm)],[343,335,theory(equality)])).
cnf(367,negated_conjecture,
    (class_OrderedGroup_Oab__group__add(t_b)),
    inference(spm,[status(thm)],[350,335,theory(equality)])).
```

The next proof step creates an instance of $X - X = 0$ for type 'b, deleting the second literal. As this step still concerns type information, it too must be deleted.

```
cnf(1968,negated_conjecture,
    (c_minus(X,X,t_b)=c_HOL_Ozero(t_b)),
    inference(spm,[status(thm)],[216,367,theory(equality)])).
```

After several steps, omitted here, E nears the conclusion. E takes its time: the last three steps each express contradiction. Naturally such repeated steps must be deleted.

```
cnf(4421,negated_conjecture,
    ($false | $false),
    inference(rw,[status(thm)],
        [inference(rw,[status(thm)],[4420,2575,theory(equality)]),
                    336,theory(equality)]])).
cnf(4422,negated_conjecture,
    ($false),
    inference(cn,[status(thm)],[4421,theory(equality)]])).
cnf(4423,negated_conjecture,
    ($false),
    4422,['proof']).
```

4.3   The Translation Method

Our system translates a TSTP file into an Isabelle proof by parsing it, reconstructing type information, removing redundancy and discarding steps that have no place in Isabelle's inference system. If the original subgoal contained higher-order features such as function variables, then its first-order counterpart will contain an explicit "apply" operator and "is-true" predicate [9]; these must also be removed.

We represent abstract syntax by a data structure for n-ary trees with integers in the leaves and strings labelling the branch nodes. Here is the corresponding ML datatype declaration:

```
datatype stree = Int of int | Br of string * stree list;
```

Isabelle provides top-down parsing primitives that we use to parse CNF lines. We have written additional code to translate TSTP identifiers (which must be strictly alphanumeric) back to the Isabelle ones from whence they came. For example, _O in a TSTP identifier corresponds to a full stop (.) in an Isabelle identifier. We first remove the prefix indicating what class of identifier it is: c_ for constant, tc_ for type constructor, T_ for type variable, etc. If the ATP generates its own variables, such as X3, then we have to guess what they stand for. Note that variables in a resolution proof always start with a capital letter.

Next, we identify type information. Although type class information must be deleted from proofs, it must be noted so that the Isabelle terms we generate are well-typed. Polymorphic constants must be reconstructed. Given a constant, we look up its definition. If its type scheme contains n type variables, then its last n arguments represent types. Type literals in a clause help us by specifying the type classes of some type variables.

```
cnf(2542,negated_conjecture,
    (c_plus(c_HOL_Ozero(t_b),X3,t_b)=X3 |
     ~class_OrderedGroup_Oab__group__add(t_b)),
    inference(spm,[status(thm)],[147,1968,theory(equality)]])).
```

For example, the type variable $'b$ in the clause above belongs to the type class `OrderedGroup.ab_group_add`; this determines the types of the constants 0 and + in the clause. In other clauses, the type class of $'b$ is `Ring_and_Field.ordered_idom`.

Having type class constraints for all type variables allows us to generate the corresponding instances of constants, which in turn should allow us to reconstruct terms correctly. Our experience confirms this, even with 100-step proofs involving many type classes.

For each clause, we separate the type literals from the others. The remaining literals, those meaningful to Isabelle, are formed into a disjunction. Type inference is then performed using the stored type class information. The disjunction is finally generalized over its free variables. If no "real" literals are present, then the clause contains type information only; we represent it differently from an empty clause, which represents contradiction.

In order to re-assemble the proof, we examine the supplied annotations, extracting all the integers they contain. With E, all integers in annotations refer to previous proof lines. (If an ATP used integers for other purposes, then we would need to identify and delete them.) We go through three phases.

1. Axiom references are deleted. Axioms represent either type information or known Isabelle theorems. The latter can be designated by their Isabelle identifiers, so it would be pointless to include them as proof lines. At this stage we also eliminate duplicate proofs of an assertion; these typically differ in type literals only.
2. The proof is then purged of chains of reasoning relating to types. This step is repeated until the deletions stop.
3. Finally, some proof lines are removed in order to reduce the proof length. Removal of a line involves replacing all references to it by references to its antecedents. The proof tree becomes shorter but bushier.

The user can control the factor by which proof lines are combined to shorten the proof. If the factor is n, then only every nth line is retained. Polymorphic lines must be removed because Isabelle does not have type quantifiers; such lines typically involve instantiating a polymorphic lemma to other polymorphic types. After removing all polymorphic lines, we still have a proof because the final line is monomorphic: it is simply `False` and has type `bool`.

We output the proof as an Isar structured script [13] of a simple form: a series of assertions and justifications. The script begins with the proof method `neg_clausify`, which negates the subgoal and converts it into clauses. All assertions must be explicit in Isar proofs, so the conjecture clauses that are used must be introduced explicitly using Isar `assume` declarations. Each intermediate clause of the proof is introduced using a `have` declaration and proved by calling Metis with its antecedents. Isar requires the final line to be declared using `show`; the assertion is always `False`.

```
proof (neg_clausify)
fix x
assume 0: "∧y. lb y ≤ f y"
assume 1: "¬ (0::'b) ≤ f x + - lb x"
have 2: "∧X3. (0::'b) + X3 = X3"
  by (metis diff_eq_eq right_minus_eq)
have 3: "¬ (0::'b) ≤ f x - lb x"
  by (metis 1 compare_rls(1))
have 4: "¬ (0::'b) + lb x ≤ f x"
  by (metis 3 le_diff_eq)
show "False"
  by (metis 4 2 0)
qed
```

Note that E's line numbers, which ranged into the thousands, have been renumbered starting from zero. References to axiom clauses are replaced by the corresponding Isabelle theorem references, such as le_diff_eq or compare_rls(1).

As of this writing, the default output contains a huge amount of type information, most of which is redundant. We have switched this off for our examples in order to improve readability. Some problems require type information, but we should generate no more than is necessary. This merely requires some bookkeeping to ensure that (variable, type) and (type variable, class) pairs only appear once.

```
proof (neg_clausify)
fix x
assume 0: "Y ⊆ X ∨ X = Y ∪ Z"
assume 1: "Z ⊆ X ∨ X = Y ∪ Z"
assume 2: "(¬ Y ⊆ X ∨ ¬ Z ⊆ X ∨ Y ⊆ x) ∨ X ≠ Y ∪ Z"
assume 3: "(¬ Y ⊆ X ∨ ¬ Z ⊆ X ∨ Z ⊆ x) ∨ X ≠ Y ∪ Z"
assume 4: "(¬ Y ⊆ X ∨ ¬ Z ⊆ X ∨ ¬ X ⊆ x) ∨ X ≠ Y ∪ Z"
assume 5: "∧V. ((¬ Y ⊆ V ∨ ¬ Z ⊆ V) ∨ X ⊆ V) ∨ X = Y ∪ Z"
have 6: "LOrder.sup Y Z ≠ X ∨ ¬ X ⊆ x ∨ ¬ Y ⊆ X ∨ ¬ Z ⊆ X"
  by (metis 4 sup_set_eq)
have 7: "Z ⊆ x ∨ LOrder.sup Y Z ≠ X ∨ ¬ Y ⊆ X"
  by (metis 3 sup_set_eq Un_upper2 sup_set_eq 1 sup_set_eq)
have 8: "Z ⊆ x ∨ LOrder.sup Y Z ≠ X"
  by (metis 7 Un_upper1 sup_set_eq 0 sup_set_eq)
have 9: "LOrder.sup Y Z = X ∨ ¬ Z ⊆ X ∨ ¬ Y ⊆ X"
  by (metis equalityI 5 sup_set_eq Un_upper2 sup_set_eq Un_upper1 sup_set_eq
Un_least sup_set_eq)
have 10: "Y ⊆ x"
  by (metis 2 sup_set_eq Un_upper2 sup_set_eq 1 sup_set_eq Un_upper1 sup_set_eq
0 sup_set_eq 9 Un_upper2 sup_set_eq 1 sup_set_eq Un_upper1 sup_set_eq 0 sup_set_eq)
have 11: "X ⊆ x"
  by (metis Un_least sup_set_eq 9 Un_upper2 sup_set_eq 1 sup_set_eq Un_upper1
sup_set_eq 0 sup_set_eq 8 9 Un_upper2 sup_set_eq 1 sup_set_eq Un_upper1 sup_set_eq
0 sup_set_eq 10)
show "False"
  by (metis 11 6 Un_upper2 sup_set_eq 1 sup_set_eq Un_upper1 sup_set_eq 0 sup_set_eq
9 Un_upper2 sup_set_eq 1 sup_set_eq Un_upper1 sup_set_eq 0 sup_set_eq)
qed
```

Fig. 1. Proof of First Example

5   Two Larger Examples

The example presented above was trivial. Here, we consider two examples that involve lengthy proofs. These illustrate the appearance of non-trivial proofs and the effect of the reduction factor.

Our first example involves proving a logical equivalence:

$$X = Y \cup Z \iff Y \subseteq X \wedge Z \subseteq X \wedge (\forall V.\, Y \subseteq V \wedge Z \subseteq V \to X \subseteq V)$$

E produces a TSTP proof consisting of 53 lines. These include 6 conjecture clauses. The resulting single-step proof contains a further 26 steps. Increasing the reduction factor to 4 results in a proof consisting of 6 steps (Fig. 1). The series of claims is almost legible, especially if we note that `LOrder.sup` is equivalent to union.

```
proof (neg_clausify)
fix c x
assume 0: "⋀X1. |h X1| ≤ c * |f X1|"
assume 1: "c ≠ (0::'a)"
assume 2: "¬ |h x| ≤ |c| * |f x|"
have 3: "⋀X3. |0::'a| = |X3| * (0::'a) ∨ ¬ (0::'a) ≤ (0::'a)"
  by (metis abs_mult_pos mult_cancel_right1)
have 4: "|(1::'a) * (0::'a)| = - ((1::'a) * (0::'a))"
  by (metis abs_of_nonpos mult_le_cancel_right2 max.f_below_strict_below.below_refl
max.f_below_strict_below.below_refl)
have 5: "c = (0::'a) ∨ c < (0::'a)"
  by (metis linorder_antisym_conv2 2 abs_of_nonneg linorder_linear 0)
have 6: "(0::'a) ≤ (1::'a)"
  by (metis zero_le_square AC_mult.f.commute mult_cancel_left1)
have 7: "⋀X3. (0::'a) = |X3| ∨ X3 ≠ (0::'a)"
  by (metis abs_minus_cancel neg_equal_iff_equal 4 mult_cancel_right1 3 mult_cancel_right1
max.f_below_strict_below.below_refl mult_cancel_right1 minus_equation_iff 3
mult_cancel_right1 max.f_below_strict_below.below_refl)
have 8: "⋀X1 X3. (0::'a) * |X1| = |X3 * X1| ∨ X3 ≠ (0::'a)"
  by (metis abs_mult 7)
have 9: "⋀X1 X3. X3 * X1 = (0::'a) ∨ X3 ≠ (0::'a)"
  by (metis zero_less_abs_iff 8 mult_cancel_left1 abs_not_less_zero 3 mult_cancel_right1
max.f_below_strict_below.below_refl)
have 10: "⋀X3. X3 * (1::'a) = (0::'a) ∨ |X3| ≠ (0::'a) ∨ ¬ (0::'a) ≤ (1::'a)"
  by (metis abs_eq_0 abs_mult_pos mult_cancel_right1 AC_mult.f.commute)
have 11: "⋀X3. ¬ |X3| < (0::'a) ∨ ¬ (0::'a) ≤ (1::'a)"
  by (metis abs_not_less_zero abs_mult_pos mult_cancel_right1 AC_mult.f.commute)
have 12: "⋀X3. X3 = (0::'a) ∨ ¬ |X3| ≤ (0::'a) ∨ ¬ (0::'a) ≤ (1::'a)"
  by (metis abs_le_zero_iff abs_mult_pos mult_cancel_right1 AC_mult.f.commute
mult_cancel_right1 AC_mult.f.commute)
have 13: "⋀X3. X3 * X3 = (0::'a) ∨ ¬ X3 ≤ (0::'a) ∨ ¬ (0::'a) ≤ X3"
  by (metis 12 6 abs_mult abs_mult_self AC_mult.f.commute mult_le_0_iff)
have 14: "⋀X3. |h X3| ≤ |f X3| ≤ (0::'a)"
  by (metis 0 10 mult_cancel_right1 AC_mult.f.commute 6 abs_mult AC_mult.f.commute
9 mult_eq_0_iff abs_mult_self 13 abs_ge_zero abs_mult_pos mult_cancel_right1
AC_mult.f.commute 6)
have 15: "⋀X3. |h X3| < (0::'a) ∨ ¬ c < (0::'a) ∨ ¬ (0::'a) < |f X3|"
  by (metis order_le_less_trans 0 mult_less_0_iff)
show "False"
  by (metis 15 5 1 11 6 2 abs_of_nonpos 2 abs_of_nonneg linorder_linear 0 7
mult_cancel_right1 14 linorder_not_le 12 6 linorder_not_le)
qed
```

Fig. 2. Proof of Second Example

Our second example involves proving $|h(x)| \leq |c| \times |f(x)|$ from the assumptions $\forall x. |h(x)| \leq c \times |f(x)|$ and $c \neq 0$. The original hand proof is six lines long, and involves first proving the lemma $c \times |f(x)| \leq |c| \times |f(x)|$ using the monotonicity of multiplication. However, E produces a 303-step proof. The single-step Isabelle proof contains 61 steps (including 3 conjecture clauses), which decreases to 16 steps if we set the reduction factor to 4 (Fig. 2). It is clear that this proof could be further simplified. For example, claim 6 proves $0 \leq 1$, which is already a theorem in Isabelle. We should process these proofs to make them as simple and as natural as possible.

6   Conclusions

Translating the output of an automatic theorem prover into a fragment of proof script has many advantages. Correctness can be checked automatically, but the script is also open to manual inspection. User can insert these scripts into their proof developments, eliminating the need to run ATPs a second time. There are some rough edges at present, but the system reliably translates proofs that are hundreds of lines long.

We have ported Hurd's Metis prover to Isabelle to use as the basis of these proof scripts. In most cases, a single call to Metis suffices to reproduce the proof. Sometimes, however, Metis fails or a more detailed proof description is required. We have therefore implemented a translation from the TSTP output format to Isar structured proof scripts. E produces TSTP output and we expect other ATPs to follow suit. The work can similarly be ported to other interactive provers, since the Isar scripts we generate are simple sequences of assertions justified by Metis calls.

The idea of an interactive prover generating its own proof scripts is promising. It opens up many new avenues for research.

Acknowledgements. The research was funded by the EPSRC grant GR/S57198/01 *Automation for Interactive Proof.* The first implementation of proof reconstruction in our system is due to Claire Quigley. Jia Meng also made many contributions to our work. Joe Hurd offered much advice on Metis. The TPHOLs referees made many valuable comments.

References

1. Avigad, J., Donnelly, K., Gray, D., Raff, P.: A formally verified proof of the prime number theorem. ACM Transactions on Computational Logic (in press)
2. Gordon, M., Wadsworth, C.P., Milner, R.: Edinburgh LCF. LNCS, vol. 78. Springer, Heidelberg (1979)
3. Harrison, J.: HOL Light: A tutorial introduction. In: Srivas, M., Camilleri, A. (eds.) FMCAD 1996. LNCS, vol. 1166, pp. 265–269. Springer, Heidelberg (1996)
4. Hurd, J.: Integrating Gandalf and HOL. In: Bertot, Y., Dowek, G., Hirschowitz, A., Paulin, C., Théry, L. (eds.) TPHOLs 1999. LNCS, vol. 1690, pp. 311–321. Springer, Heidelberg (1999)

5. Hurd, J.: First-order proof tactics in higher-order logic theorem provers. In: Archer, M., Di Vito, B., Muñoz, C. (eds.) Design and Application of Strategies/Tactics in Higher Order Logics, number NASA/CP-2003-212448 in NASA Technical Reports, pp. 56–68 (September 2003)
6. Hurd, J.: Metis performance benchmarks (2004), http://gilith.com/software/metis/performance.html
7. Melham, T.F.: The HOL logic extended with quantification over type variables. Formal Methods in System Design 3(1-2), 7–24 (1994)
8. Meng, J., Paulson, L.C.: Lightweight relevance filtering for machine-generated resolution problems. In: Sutcliffe, G., Schmidt, R., Schulz, S. (eds.) FLoC'06 Workshop on Empirically Successful Computerized Reasoning. CEUR Workshop Proceedings, vol. 192, pp. 53–69 (2006)
9. Meng, J., Paulson, L.C.: Translating higher-order problems to first-order clauses. In: Sutcliffe, G., Schmidt, R., Schulz, S. (eds.) FLoC'06 Workshop on Empirically Successful Computerized Reasoning. CEUR Workshop Proceedings, vol. 192, pp. 70–80 (2006)
10. Meng, J., Paulson, L.C.: Lightweight relevance filtering for machine-generated resolution problems. Journal of Applied Logic (in press)
11. Meng, J., Quigley, C., Paulson, L.C.: Automation for interactive proof: First prototype. Information and Computation 204(10), 1575–1596 (2006)
12. Nipkow, T.: Order-sorted polymorphism in Isabelle. In: Huet, G., Plotkin, G. (eds.) Logical Environments, pp. 164–188. Cambridge University Press, Cambridge (1993)
13. Nipkow, T.: Structured Proofs in Isar/HOL. In: Geuvers, H., Wiedijk, F. (eds.) TYPES 2002. LNCS, vol. 2646, pp. 259–278. Springer, Heidelberg (2003)
14. Nipkow, T., Paulson, L.C., Wenzel, M.: Isabelle/HOL. LNCS, vol. 2283. Springer, Heidelberg (2002)
15. Norrish, M., Slind, K.: The HOL system description (2007), On the Internet at http://hol.sourceforge.net/
16. Paulson, L.C.: The foundation of a generic theorem prover. Journal of Automated Reasoning 5(3), 363–397 (1989)
17. Paulson, L.C.: Organizing numerical theories using axiomatic type classes. Journal of Automated Reasoning 33(1), 29–49 (2004)
18. Riazanov, A., Voronkov, A.: The design and implementation of VAMPIRE. AI Communications 15(2), 91–110 (2002)
19. Schulz, S.: System description: E 0.81. In: Basin, D., Rusinowitch, M. (eds.) IJCAR 2004. LNCS (LNAI), vol. 3097, pp. 223–228. Springer, Heidelberg (2004)
20. Sutcliffe, G., Schmidt, R., Schulz, S. (eds.): FLoC'06 Workshop on Empirically Successful Computerized Reasoning. CEUR Workshop Proceedings, vol. 192 (2006)
21. Sutcliffe, G., Zimmer, J., Schulz, S.: TSTP data-exchange formats for automated theorem proving tools. In: Zhang, W., Sorge, V. (eds.) Distributed Constraint Problem Solving and Reasoning in Multi-Agent Systems. Frontiers in Artificial Intelligence and Applications, vol. 112, pp. 201–215. IOS Press, Amsterdam (2004)
22. Wadler, P., Blott, S.: How to make ad-hoc polymorphism less ad hoc. In: 16th AnnualSymposium on Principles of Programming Languages, pp. 60–76. ACM Press, New York (1989)
23. Weidenbach, C.: Combining superposition, sorts and splitting. In: Robinson, A., Voronkov, A. (eds.) Handbook of Automated Reasoning, ch. 27, vol. II, pp. 1965–2013. Elsevier Science, Amsterdam (2001)
24. Wenzel, M.: Type classes and overloading in higher-order logic. In: Gunter, E.L., Felty, A.P. (eds.) TPHOLs 1997. LNCS, vol. 1275, pp. 307–322. Springer, Heidelberg (1997)

Proof Pearl: The Power of Higher-Order Encodings in the Logical Framework LF

Brigitte Pientka

School of Computer Science
McGill University
bpientka@cs.mcgill.ca

Abstract. In this proof pearl, we demonstrate the power of higher-order encodings in the logical framework Twelf[PS99] by investigating proofs about an algorithmic specification of bounded subtype polymorphism, a problem from the POPLmark challenge [ABF+05]. Our encoding and representation of the problem plays to the strengths of the logical framework LF. Higher-order abstract syntax is used to deal with issues of bound variables. More importantly, we exploit the full advantage of parametric and higher-order judgments. As a key benefit we get a tedious narrowing lemma, which must normally be proven separately, for free. Consequently, we obtain an extremely compact and elegant encoding of the admissibility of general transitivity and other meta-theoretic properties.

1 Introduction

Stimulated by the POPLmark challenge [ABF+05], there have been many discussions over the last two years about what support current proof assistants provide for specifying programming languages and proofs about them. In this paper we present an implementation of bounded subtype polymorphism within the logical framework Twelf [PS99], inspired by the first problems in the POPLmark challenge[ABF+05]. The logical framework LF [HHP93] provides an elegant meta-language for the specification of deductive systems together with the proofs about them. It has been particularly successful in encoding the meta-theory of programming languages. Encodings in LF typically rely on ideas of higher-order abstract syntax where object variables and binders are implemented by variables and binders in the meta-language (i.e. logical framework). One of the key benefits behind higher-order abstract syntax representations is that one can avoid implementing common and tricky routines dealing with variables, such as capture-avoiding substitution, renaming and fresh name generation.

However concentrating on encoding object variables and binders by variables and binders in the meta-language only utilizes part of the power of higher-order encodings. One important and often neglected aspect of higher-order encodings is the direct support for implementing hypothetical and parametric judgments via higher-order functions. This has two important consequences: 1) A context or environment to keep track of assumptions is unnecessary. This eliminates the

K. Schneider and J. Brandt (Eds.): TPHOLs 2007, LNCS 4732, pp. 246–261, 2007.
© Springer-Verlag Berlin Heidelberg 2007

need of building up a context and managing it explicitly. More importantly, it eliminates the need to explicitly reason about the properties of the context such as weakening, exchange, or strengthening. 2) Since we can view hypothetical judgments as functions, applying a substitution lemma amounts to function application. As a consequence tedious substitution lemmas need not be proven separately. Encodings within the logical framework LF usually try to exploit both properties extensively. This approach typically greatly reduces the size of the final proofs. Moreover, the meta-theoretic development scales better when we extend the language by including new constructors.

In this proof pearl we play to the strengths of logical frameworks, and we follow in spirit the philosophy expressed by Bob Harper's comments subsequent to posting our solution to the POPLmark mailing list:

> " You have to listen to the logical framework, as it were, and take its advice in guiding you towards a better way to formulate your system. We learned this lesson many years ago when we first invented LF — the exercise of formalizing a logic in LF does wonders for the logic." (Bob Harper's post to the POPLmark-list 2 May 2006).

In other words, the representation of our problem determines our success or failure to prove properties about it. Hence, we start by taking a close look at the original problem posed in the POPLmark challenge, and explain our choice of representation in the logical framework LF to take full advantage of the logical framework LF. The pay-off will be substantial, compared to other solutions which follow the problem specification more literally. We use not only higher-order abstract syntax to encode bound variables in our object language, but we model parametric and hypothetical judgments as higher-oder functions thereby eliminating the need to prove substitution and narrowing lemmas separately. Our reasoning is purely structural and does not require any extra arguments to reason explicitly about the size of arguments and derivations. And finally, our solutions unlike others does not require tedious explicit proofs to show that certain cases are impossible. As we will demonstrate our proof of admissibility of transitivity is remarkably short and fits on less than a page.

Organization of the paper

The paper is organized as follows: We first introduce our algorithmic subtyping relation for bounded polymorphism, and comment on the difference between this formulation and the original challenge in [ABF+05]. Next, we will discuss its encoding in the logical framework Twelf, develop the proof that transitivity is admissible and show its implementation in Twelf. Finally, we will compare and discuss other POPLmark challenge solutions to this problem.

2   Bounded Polymorphic Subtyping

In this section, we will briefly introduce bounded subtype polymorphism and the basic meta-theory of System F_{sub} (see also Ch. 26 [Pie02b]). In this system, we enrich polymorphic types such as $\forall \alpha.T$ with a subtype relation and refine the universal quantifier to carry a subtyping constraint. The syntax of types can be defined as follows:

$$\text{Types} \quad T ::= \text{top} \mid \alpha \mid T_1 \Rightarrow T_2 \mid \forall \alpha \leq T_1.T_2$$
$$\text{Context } \Gamma ::= \cdot \mid \Gamma, w{:}\alpha \leq T$$

In $\forall \alpha \leq T_1.T_2$, the type variable α only binds occurrences of α in T_2. We will use small Greek letters such as α, β etc. to denote type variables. The typing context Γ keeps track of constraints such as $\alpha \leq T$. A context $\Gamma, w{:}\alpha \leq T$ is well-formed if T is a well-formed type in the context Γ and there exists no other assumption $\alpha \leq S$ in Γ, i.e. there is a unique constraint $\alpha \leq T$ for each type variable. Next, we describe a subtyping algorithm using the judgment:

$$\Gamma \vdash T \leq S \qquad \text{Type } T \text{ is a subtype of } S \text{ in the context } \Gamma$$

$$\frac{}{\Gamma \vdash T \leq \text{top}} \text{ sa-top} \qquad \frac{\alpha \leq T \in \Gamma}{\Gamma \vdash \alpha \leq T} \text{ sa-hyp} \qquad \frac{}{\Gamma \vdash \alpha \leq \alpha} \text{ sa-ref-tvar}$$

$$\frac{\Gamma \vdash T_1 \leq S_1 \quad \Gamma \vdash S_2 \leq T_2}{\Gamma \vdash S_1 \Rightarrow S_2 \leq T_1 \Rightarrow T_2} \text{ sa-arr} \qquad \frac{\Gamma \vdash \alpha \leq U \quad \Gamma \vdash U \leq T}{\Gamma \vdash \alpha \leq T} \text{ sa-tr-tvar}$$

$$\frac{\Gamma \vdash T_1 \leq S_1 \quad \Gamma, w{:}\alpha \leq T_1 \vdash S_2 \leq T_2}{\Gamma \vdash \forall \alpha \leq S_1.S_2 \leq \forall \alpha \leq T_1.T_2} \text{ sa-all}^{\alpha,w}$$

The description is algorithmic in the sense that general rules for reflexivity and transitivity are admissible, and for each type constructor, top, $\forall$ and $\Rightarrow$ there is one rule which can be applied. Following standard design principles found in many logics, we allow hypothetical reasoning, i.e. given an assumption $\alpha \leq T$ we can directly conclude $\alpha \leq T$. While the resulting algorithm is syntax directed, it does not eliminate all non-determinism, if viewed as a bottom-up search algorithm. In the rule sa-tr-tvar for example we still need to guess the type U. To illustrate how a proof can be derived, consider the following example:

$$\frac{\dfrac{}{w{:}\alpha \leq \text{top}, v{:}\beta \leq \alpha \vdash \alpha \leq \alpha} \text{ sa-ref-tvar} \quad \dfrac{}{w{:}\alpha \leq \text{top}, v{:}\beta \leq \alpha \vdash \beta \leq \alpha} \text{ sa-hyp}}{\dfrac{w{:}\alpha \leq \text{top}, v{:}\beta \leq \alpha \vdash (\alpha \Rightarrow \beta) \leq (\alpha \Rightarrow \alpha)}{\dfrac{w{:}\alpha \leq \text{top} \vdash (\forall \beta \leq \alpha.\alpha \Rightarrow \beta) \leq (\forall \beta \leq \alpha.\alpha \Rightarrow \alpha)}{\cdot \vdash (\forall \alpha \leq \text{top}.\forall \beta \leq \alpha.\alpha \Rightarrow \beta) \leq (\forall \alpha \leq \text{top}.\forall \beta \leq \alpha.\alpha \Rightarrow \alpha)} \text{ sa-all}^{\alpha,w}} \text{ sa-all}^{\beta,v}} \text{ sa-arr}}$$

We note that the formulation of the transitivity rule given here is different from the challenge problem stated in [ABF$^+$05]. Instead of the sa-hyp and the sa-tr-tvar rule, we typically find the following specialized transitivity rule:

$$\frac{(\alpha \leq U) \in \Gamma \quad \Gamma \vdash U \leq T}{\Gamma \vdash \alpha \leq T} \text{ sa-tr'}$$

In contrast to the rule sa-tr-tvar, there is no need to guess U. Clearly, the rule sa-tr' is a derived rule in the system we stated. In other words, the system we consider is slightly more general. The lack of a general hypothesis rule is compensated by using sa-tr' together with reflexivity. For example to prove $w{:}\alpha \leq \beta \vdash \alpha \leq \beta$, we will use first transitivity to look up $\alpha \leq \beta$ in the context, and then prove that $\beta \leq \beta$ by reflexivity. As we will show, our logically motivated algorithmic description of subtyping will lead to a much cleaner meta-theoretic development and is a nice example how the original problem specification influences the proofs about it.

3   Representing Bounded Polymorphism Using HOAS

In this section, we encode bounded polymorphic types together with the algorithmic subtyping system in the Twelf system, which is an implementation of the logical framework LF. Twelf supports the specification of deductive systems, given via axioms and inference rules, together with the proofs about them, and is hence ideally suited for this task. The LF language, a dependently typed lambda-calculus, can be briefly described as follows:

$$
\begin{aligned}
\text{Kinds } K \quad &::= \text{type} \mid \Pi x{:}A.K\\
\text{Types } A \quad &::= a\ M_1 \ldots M_n \mid A_1 \to A_2 \mid \Pi x : A_1.A_2\\
\text{Objects } M &::= x \mid c \mid M_1\ M_2 \mid \lambda x{:}A.M
\end{aligned}
$$

Objects provided by the logical framework LF include lambda-abstraction, application, constants and variables. The type label at the lambda-abstraction can be omitted in practice. Types classify objects, and range over type constants a which may be indexed by objects $M_1 \ldots M_n$, as well as non-dependent and dependent function types. Viewing types as propositions, LF types can be interpreted as logical propositions. The atomic type $a\ M_1 \ldots M_n$ corresponds to an atomic proposition, the non-dependent function type $A_1 \to A_2$ corresponds to an implication, and the dependent function type $\Pi x{:}A.B$ can be interpreted as the universal quantifier. We will use types and formulas interchangeably. Kinds classify types. For a thorough introduction to LF including the typing rules and meta-theoretic development we refer the reader to [Pfe97]. Here we focus on how to use the full power of LF to formalize the example of bounded polymorphism and proofs about it.

3.1   Encoding Bounded Polymorphic Types

To represent the previous system describing bounded subtype polymorphism, we start with representing the language of types as objects in LF. The first obvious question is how to represent the polymorphic type $\forall \alpha \leq T_1.T_2$, in particular how to represent type variables α and the fact that any occurrence of the type variable α in the type T_2 is bound by the universal quantifier. Encodings in the logical framework LF are typically based on higher-order abstract syntax where we represent variables in the object language (i.e. the type variables α in

$\forall \alpha \leq T_1.T_2)$ with variables in the meta-language (i.e. bound variables in LF). In other words, type variables α bound by $\forall$ in the object-language will be bound by λ-abstraction in the meta-language. With this representation the framework provides α-conversion and substitution for the object language.

To clarify the translation between object-level types and their representation in LF, we introduce the following function $\ulcorner \cdot \urcorner$ which maps object-level types to their representation in the logical framework LF. On the left, we show how to translate object-level types to their representation into LF, and on the right we show the definition of the constructors in LF.

Encoding object-level types to LF objects   Data-type definition in LF

```
                                            tp : type.
```

$$
\begin{aligned}
\ulcorner \alpha \urcorner &= \alpha \\
\ulcorner \text{top} \urcorner &= \text{top} \\
\ulcorner T_1 \Rightarrow T_2 \urcorner &= \text{arr } \ulcorner T_1 \urcorner \ulcorner T_2 \urcorner \\
\ulcorner \forall \alpha \leq T_1.T_2 \urcorner &= \text{all } \ulcorner T_1 \urcorner \lambda \alpha. \ulcorner T_2 \urcorner
\end{aligned}
$$

```
                                            top : tp.
                                            arr : tp -> tp -> tp.
                                            all : tp -> (tp -> tp) -> tp.
```

On the right, we define an LF type called `tp`, with the constructors `top`, `arr`, and `all`. The type for the constructor `all` takes in two arguments, an argument of type `tp` and another argument of function type (`tp -> tp`). Intuitively, the first argument stands for the bound, while the second argument represents the body of the forall-expression. The key idea to note is that in the type $\forall \alpha \leq T_1.T_2$ the type variable α is a binding occurrence with scope T_2 and is not allowed to occur in T_1. Variables α in the object-level are represented by variables α in the meta-level. To illustrate the encoding of a concrete type, consider the following examples.

Object-level type	LF object
$\forall \alpha \leq \text{top}.\alpha \Rightarrow \alpha$	`all top (`$\lambda \alpha.$` arr `α` `α`)`
$\forall \alpha \leq \text{top}.\forall \beta \leq \alpha.\beta \Rightarrow \alpha$	`all top (`$\lambda \alpha.$` all `α` (`$\lambda \beta.$` arr `β` `α`))`

To prove the adequacy of this encoding we need to show that there is a bijection between the types represented in our object-language and the types described in the logical framework LF. This follows standard principles which are extensively discussed for example in [HL06]. We need to prove that every object-level type T which may contain the free type variables $\alpha_1, \ldots, \alpha_n$ has a representation as an LF object T of type `tp` in an LF context $a_1:\text{tp}, \ldots,$ $a_n:\text{tp}$, and vice versa. Here we will highlight only the role of the LF context, since Twelf provides us with the ability to specify the shape of it and check that indeed every LF object of type `tp` will be generated in this context. This is done by the following combination of block and world declarations

```
%block g : block a:tp.
%worlds (g) (tp).
```

The block and world declaration states that the LF context is essentially of the form $a_1:\text{tp}, \ldots, a_n:\text{tp}$. This guarantees that every valid LF object of type `tp` is either generated by a constant from the signature or by an assumption in the LF context.

3.2   Encoding Subtyping Relation

A succinct feature of higher-order abstract syntax encodings is that we do not represent variables as a syntactic category explicitly, but variables are implicit. This will play a important role when we encode the subtyping relation described in the previous section. Recall that the algorithmic description is syntactically defined by cases for each possible type. Moreover there are two rules, sa-ref-tvar and sa-tr-tvar, which are specifically restricted to type variables. A direct immediate encoding seems problematic since trying to distinguish on variables as syntactic entities is inherently against the idea of higher-order abstract syntax! The benefit of HOAS is that it eliminates the need for object level variables, but the price is that we now cannot directly access them and we cannot even state a generic rule for variables.

There are different approaches to solve this problem – for example one could introduce a separate judgment to check if a given object is in fact a type variable. This approach has been followed in the implementation by Ashley-Rollman, Crary, and Harper [MARH]. However, this has also some disadvantages. In particular, we have to prove substitution and narrowing lemmas separately, as well as various lemmas about impossible cases. Here we will take a different approach: Instead of a general variable rule, we will add *rules for reflexivity and transitivity for each type variable*. In other words, every time we introduce a type variable α, we also introduce the corresponding reflexive and transitive properties such as $\alpha \leq \alpha$ and an assumption which says for all U and V, if $\alpha \leq U$ and $U \leq V$ then $\alpha \leq V$. Taking full advantage of the power of our meta-language, we allow not only atomic assumptions such as $\alpha \leq T$ or $\alpha \leq \alpha$, but we also allow more complex assumptions which from a meta-logic point of view can be described using universal quantifiers and implications in the meta-logic. So "for all U and V, if $\alpha \leq U$ and $U \leq V$ then $\alpha \leq V$" is represented as $\Pi U.\Pi V.\alpha \leq U \to U \leq V \to \alpha \leq V$. Now we can rewrite our formal algorithmic system given in the previous section.

$$\frac{}{\Gamma \vdash T \leq \text{top}} \text{ sa-top} \qquad \frac{\alpha \leq T \in \Gamma}{\Gamma \vdash \alpha \leq T} \text{ sa-hyp} \qquad \frac{\Gamma \vdash T_1 \leq S_1 \quad \Gamma \vdash S_2 \leq T_2}{\Gamma \vdash S_1 \Rightarrow S_2 \leq T_1 \Rightarrow T_2} \text{ sa-arr}$$

$$\frac{\Gamma \vdash T_1 \leq S_1 \qquad \begin{array}{c} \Gamma, \ tr{:}\Pi U.\Pi V.\alpha \leq U \to U \leq V \to \alpha \leq V \\ w{:}\alpha \leq T_1, \ ref{:}\alpha \leq \alpha \vdash S_2 \leq T_2 \end{array}}{\Gamma \vdash \forall \alpha \leq S_1.S_2 \leq \forall \alpha \leq T_1.T_2} \text{ sa-all}$$

It is worth keeping in mind that in order to use a universally quantified assumption $\Pi U.\Pi V.\alpha \leq U \to U \leq V \to \alpha \leq V$ we first must instantiate U and V appropriately.

We are now ready to show the encoding of these subtyping rules in LF. We first define the constant **sub** which describes the subtyping relation. Next, we represent each inference rule in the object-language as a clause consisting of nested universal quantifiers and implications. Upper-case letters denote logic variables which are implicitly bound by a Π-quantifier at the outside.

```
sub : tp -> tp -> type.
sa_top : sub S top.
sa_arr : sub S2 T2 -> sub T1 S1
              -> sub (arr S1 S2) (arr T1 T2) .
sa_all : (Πa:tp.
              (ΠU.ΠV.sub U V ->  sub a U -> sub a V) ->
              sub a T1 -> sub a a ->
              sub (S2 a) (T2 a))
           -> sub T1 S1
           -> sub (all S1 (λv.(S2 v))) (all T1 (λv.(T2 v))).
```

```
%block 10 :
some {T:tp}
block {a:tp} {tr:ΠU.ΠV. sub U V -> sub a U -> sub a V}
     {w: sub a T}{ref: sub a a}.
%worlds (10) (sub _ _).
```

Using a higher-order logic programming interpretation, we can read the clause sa_arr as follows: To prove the goal sub (S1 => S2) (T1 => T2), we must prove sub T1 S1 and then sub S2 T2. Similarly we can read the clause sa_all: To prove sub (all S1 (λv.(S2 v))) (all T1 (λv.(T2 v))), we need to prove first sub T1 S1, and then assuming tr: ΠU.ΠV. sub U V -> sub a U -> sub a V, w:sub a T1, and ref:sub a a, prove that sub (S2 a) (T2 a) is true where a is a new parameter of type tp.

LF objects belonging to the type sub T S are derivations showing that indeed T is a subtype of S. All derivations for sub T S (i.e. all LF objects belonging to the type sub T S) are generated either by a constant in the signature or by an element in the LF context which assert the following four assumptions:a:tp, tr:ΠU.ΠV.sub U V->sub a U->sub a V, w:sub a T, ref:sub a a. The block declaration describes the shape of the LF context, and the world declaration verifies that these are the only LF contexts constructed. Next we show the derivation for the example considered earlier encoded as an LF object:

```
ex1 : sub (all top (λa. all a (λ b.arr a b)))
          (all top (λa. all a (λ b.arr a a))) =
sa_all
   (λa:tp. λtr_a:ΠU:tp.ΠV:tp.sub U V -> sub a U -> sub a V.
    λw:sub a top. λref_a:sub a a.
      sa_all
        (λb:tp.λtr_b:ΠU:tp.Π.V:tp.sub U V -> sub b U -> sub b V
         λv:sub b a.λref_b:sub b b. sa_arr v ref_a) ref_a)
   sa_top.
```

3.3   Encoding Admissibility of Transitivity

Finally, we can turn our attention to encoding the proof for transitivity.

Theorem 1 (Admissibility of transitivity).
If $\Gamma \vdash S \leq Q$ and $\Gamma \vdash Q \leq T$ then $\Gamma \vdash S \leq T$.

Typically, this requires the proof of the following narrowing lemma which needs to be proven simultaneously.

Lemma 1 (Narrowing).
If $\Gamma, w{:}\alpha \leq Q \vdash J$ and $\Gamma \vdash T \leq Q$ then $\Gamma, v{:}\alpha \leq T \vdash J$.

However, in our setting, since we localized all rules involving type variables, we will see this is unnecessary. Following the general LF philosophy, we now encode the proof that transitivity is admissible as a relation between derivations. The implementation of the proof is shown in Figure 1.

```
% Transitivity proof:
trans: ΠQ:tp.sub S Q -> sub Q T -> sub S T -> type.
%mode trans +Q +D +E -F.

tr-top: trans T D sa_top sa_top.

tr-ar: trans Q2 D2 E2 F2 ->
       trans Q1 E1 D1 F1 ->
       trans (arr Q1 Q2) (sa_arr D2 D1) (sa_arr E2 E1) (sa_arr F2 F1).

tr-all:
(Πa:tpΠv:sub a T1.Πref: sub a a
 Πtr:ΠU.ΠV.sub a U -> sub U V -> sub a V.
% Assumption v
(ΠP:tp.ΠE:sub T1 P.trans T1 v E (tr T1 P v E)) ->
(% Reflexivity
ΠP:tp.ΠE:sub a P. trans a ref E E) ->
(% Transitivity
ΠT':tp.ΠS':tp.ΠU':tp.ΠD':sub a U'.ΠD'':sub U' T'.
ΠE':sub T' S'.ΠF':sub U' S'.
trans T' D'' E' F' ->
trans T' (tr U' T' D' D'') E' (tr U' S' D' F')) ->
% i.h. on D2' and E2
trans (Q2 a) (D2 a (tr _ _ v E1) ref tr) (E2 a v ref tr) (F2 a v ref tr)) ->
% i.h. on E1 and D1
trans Q1 E1 D1 F1 ->
trans (all Q1 Q2) (sa_all D2 D1) (sa_all E2 E1) (sa_all F2 F1).
```

Fig. 1. Admissibility of transitivity implemented in Twelf

We begin by defining a type family, which may be thought of as a meta-predicate corresponding to our lemma that transitivity is admissible as follows:

```
trans: ΠQ.sub S Q -> sub Q T -> sub S T -> type.
%mode +P +D +E -F.
```

Twelf binds implicitly variables S and T at the outside via Π-quantifier and reconstructs their appropriate types. We will however quantify explicitly over the variable Q, since our induction will proceed on the structure of the type Q and the first derivation sub S Q. The meta-predicate trans specifies how to translate the derivation D:sub S Q and E:sub Q T to a derivation F:sub S T. In other words, given D:sub S Q and E:sub Q T we aim to construct a derivation F:sub S T. This translation must be total, i.e. it must be defined on all possible inputs. While the theoretical foundation underlying the logical framework guarantees that only valid derivations are constructed, we must verify separately that all cases are covered and all appeals to the induction hypothesis are valid, relying on external checkers such as mode, coverage, termination and totality. The mode declaration specifies that the first two derivations together with the type Q are viewed as inputs. The last derivation sub S T is viewed as an output. To verify totality we need to show that every appeal to the induction hypothesis is valid. The induction will proceed simultaneously on the type Q and the derivation D = sub S Q, and we can apply the induction hypothesis if either Q is smaller or if Q stays the same, the derivation D is decreasing. Because of this we explicitly reason about the the type Q and we explicitly quantify over it at the beginning. Each case in the proof will correspond to a clause in our meta-program. Next, we will consider each case in the proof individually.

Case. First, we consider a generic case for top.

$$\mathcal{D} = \frac{}{\Gamma \vdash S \leq Q} \quad \text{and} \quad \mathcal{E} = \frac{}{\Gamma \vdash Q \leq \text{top}} \text{ sa-top}$$

Clearly, there exists a derivation $\mathcal{F} : \Gamma \vdash S \leq \text{top}$ by using the rule sa-top. This is represented as a clause in our meta-program as follows:

```
tr_top : trans Q D (sa_top) (sa_top).
```

Case. $\mathcal{D} = \dfrac{\begin{array}{cc} \mathcal{D}_1 & \mathcal{D}_2 \\ \Gamma \vdash Q_1 \leq S_1 & \Gamma \vdash S_2 \leq Q_2 \end{array}}{\Gamma \vdash S_1 \Rightarrow S_2 \leq Q_1 \Rightarrow Q_2}$ sa-arr

This derivation is represented as sa_arr D2 D1.

$\mathcal{E} = \dfrac{\begin{array}{cc} \mathcal{E}_1 & \mathcal{E}_2 \\ \Gamma \vdash T_1 \leq Q_1 & \Gamma \vdash Q_2 \leq T_2 \end{array}}{\Gamma \vdash Q_1 \Rightarrow Q_2 \leq T_1 \Rightarrow T_2}$ sa-arr

This derivation is represented as sa_arr E2 E1.

$\mathcal{F}_1 : \Gamma \vdash T_1 \leq S_1$ by i.h. on $\mathcal{E}_1$ and $\mathcal{D}_1$
$\mathcal{F}_2 : \Gamma \vdash S_2 \leq T_2$ by i.h. on $\mathcal{D}_2$ and $\mathcal{E}_2$
$\mathcal{F} : \Gamma \vdash (S_1 \Rightarrow S_2) \leq (T_1 \Rightarrow T_2)$ by rule sa-arr using $\mathcal{F}_1$ and $\mathcal{F}_2$

The appeal to the induction hypothesis corresponds to recursively applying the meta-predicate **trans** to sub-derivations E1 and D1 and D2 and E2 respectively. This case corresponds to the following case in the implementation of the proof.

```
tr-ar:
trans Q2 D2 E2 F2 ->
trans Q1 E1 D1 F1 ->
trans (arr Q1 Q2) (sa_arr D2 D1) (sa_arr E2 E1) (sa_arr F2 F1).
```

The most interesting case is the case for sa-all.

Case. In the case for sa-all we have the following:

$$\mathcal{D} = \Gamma \vdash \forall \alpha \leq S_1.S_2 \leq \forall \alpha \leq Q_1.Q_2 \qquad \mathcal{E} = \Gamma \vdash \forall \alpha \leq Q_1.Q_2 \leq \forall \alpha \leq T_1.T_2$$

By inversion on $\mathcal{D}$ we get:

$\mathcal{D}_1 : \Gamma \vdash Q_1 \leq S_1$ and
$\mathcal{D}_2 : \Gamma, \ tr{:}\Pi U.\Pi V.\alpha \leq U \rightarrow U \leq V \rightarrow \alpha \leq V, \ w{:}\alpha \leq Q_1, \ ref{:}\alpha \leq \alpha \vdash S_2 \leq Q_2.$

We note that $\mathcal{D}_2$ is parametric in α and hypothetical in the three assumptions tr, w, and ref. This parametric and hypothetical derivation is encoded as a function in Twelf. The LF object describing the derivation $\mathcal{D}$ is described by the following term:

```
(sa_all (λa:tp.λtr:ΠU.ΠV.sub U V -> sub a U -> sub a V.
         λw:sub a Q1.λref:sub a a.D2 a tr w ref)
        D1)
```

By inversion on $\mathcal{E}$ we get:

$\mathcal{E}_1 : \Gamma \vdash T_1 \leq Q_1$ and
$\mathcal{E}_2 : \Gamma, \ tr{:}\Pi U.\Pi V.\alpha \leq U \rightarrow U \leq V \rightarrow \alpha \leq V, \ v{:}\alpha \leq T_1, \ ref{:}\alpha \leq \alpha \vdash Q_2 \leq T_2.$

This is described by the derivation

```
(sa_all (λa:tp.λtr:ΠU.ΠV.sub U V -> sub a U -> sub a V.
         λv:sub a T1.λref:sub a a. E2 a tr v ref)
        E1)
```

To prove that there exists a derivation for $\mathcal{F} = \Gamma \vdash \forall \alpha \leq S_1.S_2 \leq \forall \alpha \leq T_1.T_2$ we first appeal to the induction hypothesis on $\mathcal{E}_1$ and $\mathcal{D}_1$ to obtain a derivation

$$\mathcal{F}_1 = \Gamma \vdash T_1 \leq S_1$$

This can be represented in Twelf as **trans Q1 E1 D1 F1**. If we now could derive some derivation

$$\mathcal{F}_2 : \Gamma, \ tr{:}\forall U \forall T.\alpha \leq U \rightarrow U \leq T \rightarrow \alpha \leq T, \ v{:}\alpha \leq T_1, \ ref{:}\alpha \leq \alpha \vdash S_2 \leq T_2$$

then we could simply assemble a derivation $\mathcal{F}$ using the sa-all rule together with $\mathcal{F}_1$ and $\mathcal{F}_2$. However applying the induction hypothesis on $\mathcal{D}_2$ and $\mathcal{E}_2$ to obtain such a $\mathcal{F}_2$ will not work because $\mathcal{D}_2$ depends on the assumption $w{:}a \leq Q_1$ while $\mathcal{E}_2$ depends on the assumption $v{:}\alpha \leq T_1$. We need to first create a derivation $\mathcal{D}_2'$ which depends on $v{:}\alpha \leq T_1$! How can this be done? – This is the place where typically we must appeal to the narrowing lemma which allows us to replace the assumption $w{:}a \leq Q_1$ with the assumption $v{:}a \leq T_1$ since $T_1 \leq Q_1$. Here, we will take however a different view.

Recall $\mathcal{D}_2$ is a parametric and hypothetical derivation which can be viewed as a function which expects as inputs $tr{:}\Pi U.\Pi V.\alpha \leq U \to U \leq V \to \alpha \leq V$, an object of type $\alpha \leq Q_1$, and $ref{:}\alpha \leq \alpha$. In other words, we need to turn a function which expects an object of type $\alpha \leq Q_1$ into a function which expects an object v of type $\alpha \leq T_1$. The idea is to substitute a derivation $\mathcal{W}$ which depends on $v{:}\alpha \leq T_1$ for any use of $w{:}\alpha \leq Q_1$. We can construct such a derivation $\mathcal{W}$ as follows:

$$
\mathcal{W}^{\alpha,v} = \cfrac{\cfrac{}{\alpha \leq T_1}\,v \qquad \cfrac{\mathcal{E}_1}{T_1 \leq Q_1}}{\alpha \leq Q_1}\,tr
$$

Note that the derivation $\mathcal{W}$ is parametric in α and hypothetical in $v{:}\alpha \leq T_1$. By substituting $\mathcal{W}$ for any use of w in the hypothetical derivation $\mathcal{D}_2$, we obtain a derivation $\mathcal{D}_2'^{\,\alpha,v}$ which is parametric in α and hypothetical in $v{:}\alpha \leq T_1$. Now we are able to appeal to the i.h. on $\mathcal{D}_2'^{\,\alpha,v}$ and $E_2^{\,\alpha,v}$, and obtain

$$
\mathcal{F}_2 : \Gamma,\ tr{:}\forall U \forall T.\alpha \leq U \to U \leq T \to \alpha \leq T,\ v{:}\alpha \leq T_1,\ ref{:}\alpha \leq \alpha \vdash S_2 \leq T_2
$$

This derivation $\mathcal{W}$ can be represented as an object (tr T1 Q1 v E1) in LF. To obtain a derivation $\mathcal{D}_2'$ from $\mathcal{D}_2$ we simply apply $\mathcal{D}_2$ to a, (tr T1 Q1 v E1), ref, and tr. This will be encoded by the following line in the proof

```
    trans (Q2 a)
       (D2 a tr (tr T1 Q1 v E1) ref) (E2 a tr v ref) (F2 a tr v ref))
```

We are not done yet with the case for sa-all. Since our context keeps track of local rules for reflexivity and transitivity, our proof must also account for these cases locally. In particular the appeal to the i.h. on $\mathcal{D}_2'$ and E_2 takes place in a context where we have the assumptions tr, v, and ref. These cases will be part of the encoding of of the case for sa_all. We will consider each of the local assumptions next and show the encoding for each of them, before we assemble all the pieces into the encoding for the case of sa-all. We emphasize that these cases correspond to the local assumptions by writing the name of the rule in question in type-writer font. Note that these proofs about local assumptions take place in the context where we have in fact the local assumptions tr, v, and ref. Hence, we are free to use some of these assumptions in our proof.

Case. Given $\mathcal{D} = \cfrac{}{\Gamma \vdash \alpha \leq T_1}\,$ v and $\mathcal{E} = \Gamma \vdash T_1 \leq P$

we must construct a derivation $\mathcal{F} = \Gamma \vdash \alpha \leq P$.

First, we note that we must prove this case for any type P and for any derivation $\mathcal{E}{:}\Gamma \vdash T_1 \leq P$, if we have a derivation $\mathcal{D}{:}\Gamma \vdash \alpha \leq T_1$ and a derivation $\mathcal{E}$ we can construct a derivation $\Gamma \vdash \alpha \leq P$. How can this be achieved? This is done by instantiating the transitivity rule tr with T_1 and P and using $\mathcal{D}$ and $\mathcal{E}$ to fill in the premises. Since all proofs are done in an LF context where we have the assumption tr denoting the transitivity rule for type variables, this is feasible. Therefore this case will be represented as

> (ΠP:tp.Π.E:sub T1 P.trans T1 v E (tr T1 P v E))

We explicitly quantify universally over P and E to emphasize the fact that this translation holds universally.

Case. Given $\mathcal{D} = \dfrac{}{\Gamma \vdash \alpha \leq \alpha}$ ref and $\mathcal{E} = \Gamma \vdash \alpha \leq P$,

we must construct a derivation $\mathcal{F} = \Gamma \vdash \alpha \leq P$, but this is simply achieved by providing $\mathcal{E}$. Again, this must be proven for all types P and all derivations $\mathcal{E}$, and we explicitly quantify universally over P and E to emphasize the fact that this translation holds universally. Therefore this case is represented as :

> (ΠP:tp.ΠE:sub a P.trans a ref E E)

Case. Given $\mathcal{D} = \dfrac{\overset{\displaystyle \mathcal{D}'}{\Gamma \vdash \alpha \leq U'} \qquad \overset{\displaystyle \mathcal{D}''}{\Gamma \vdash U' \leq T'}}{\Gamma \vdash \alpha \leq T'}$ tr and $\mathcal{E}' = \Gamma \vdash T' \leq S'$

we must show that there exists a derivation $\mathcal{F} = \Gamma \vdash \alpha \leq S'$.

$\mathcal{F}' : \Gamma \vdash U' \leq S'$ by i.h. on $\mathcal{D}''$ and $\mathcal{E}'$
$\mathcal{F} : \Gamma \vdash \alpha \leq S'$ by tr rule using $\mathcal{D}'$ and $\mathcal{F}'$.

This case will be represented as:

> ΠT':tp.ΠS':tp.ΠU':tp.
> ΠD':sub a U'.ΠD'': sub U' T'.ΠE':sub T' S'.ΠF':sub U' S'.
> trans T' D'' E' F' ->   % appeal to i.h. on D'' and E'
> trans T' (tr U' T' D' D'') E' (tr U' S' D' F'))

Again we explicitly quantify over the type variables T', S', U', and the derivations involved in this case to emphasize that we prove this statement for all types T', S', and U', and all derivations D', D'', and E'.

Finally, we can assemble all the pieces to represent the polymorphic case which is described in Figure 1.

Checking modes, termination, coverage. To verify that the encoding indeed constitutes a proof, meta-theoretic properties such as coverage and termination need to be established separetely. Coverage guarantees that all cases have been covered, and termination guarantees that all appeals to the induction hypothesis are valid. In Twelf, the user must declare specifically which checkers are to be

```
%block 1 :
some  {T1:tp}
block {a:tp}
      {tr:ΠU:tp.ΠT:tp.sub U T -> sub a U -> sub a T}
      {w:sub a T1}
      {ref:sub a a}
      {tr-w  :ΠU:tp.ΠE:sub T1 U.trans T1 w E (tr T1 U E w)}
      {tr-ref:ΠU:tp.ΠE:sub a U.trans a ref E E}
      {tr-tr :(ΠT':tp.ΠS':tp.ΠU':tp.
                ΠD':sub a U'.ΠD'':sub U' T'.
                ΠE':sub T' S'.ΠF':sub U' S'.
                trans T' D'' E' F' ->
                trans T' (tr U' T' D'' D') E' (tr U' S' F' D'))}.
%worlds (1)  (trans Q D E F).
%covers trans +Q +D +E -F.
%terminates {Q D} (trans Q D E F).
%total {Q D} (trans Q D E F).
```

Fig. 2. Checking totality of the **trans** encoding

used. This is shown in Figure 2. The mode declaration %mode trans +Q +D +E -F specifies inputs and outputs of the defined meta-predicate, and directly corresponds to what we assume in the statement of transitivity and what we need to prove. The mode checker [RP96] verifies that all inputs are known when the predicate is called and all output arguments are known after successful execution of the predicate. To guide the coverage checker [SP03], we must declare the context we prove the theorem in. This block and world declaration must include all the dynamic parameters and dynamic hypothesis. Then the coverage declaration %covers trans +Q +D +E -F verifies that we have covered all cases for the inputs Q and D in the proof for trans, i.e. either there is a case for objects generated by the signature or there is a case which arises due to our dynamic parameters and assumptions. The declaration %terminates {Q D} (trans Q D E F). verifies that in all appeals to the induction hypothesis either the type Q was decreasing or if Q stayed the same the derivation D decreased in size [Pie05b]. Finally, the totality declaration verifies that our proof is total relying on mode, coverage and termination.[1]

Remark 1. In addition to the proof for admissibility of transitivity, we have also encoded the proof that reflexivity is admissible, and showed that the algorithm described here is a correct implementation of the declarative description of bounded subtype polymorphism where we have general reflexivity and transitivity rules. To use the admissibility lemmas, we were required to weaken the worlds of some of the lemmas such that they all shared a common world. This is an artifact of Twelf's world checker. The full implementation is available

---

[1] Technically, we can only specify total, but we found it cleaner to specify the declarations corresponding to the different parts of the totality checker separately.

at `http://www.cs.mcgill.ca/~bpientka/code/pearl` and is an interesting example of higher-order judgments in the logical framework and their power.

Remark 2. In addition to reasoning about a formal specification it is interesting to investigate whether we can execute and test our specification. This is important since it allows the developer to generate sample behavior and animate a given specification. In our view, whether a given specification can be directly executed is to a large extent determined by the underlying operational semantics used. Using the types-as-formulas paradigm, we can assign types a higher-order logic programming interpretation [Pfe91] which allows us to execute specification. The encoding provided for subtyping is, maybe surprisingly, executable, although at first sight, it may seem we did not gain an algorithm since there is some non-deterministic left; however, this non-determinism is very limited to the specialized transitivity rules. A simple loop detection mechanism as provided by the tabled higher-order logic programming engine [Pie02a,Pie05a] in Twelf is able to handle the remaining non-determinism in the transitivity rule.

4 Conclusion

We have presented a higher-order encoding of subtyping algorithm for bounded polymorphism, one of the challenge problems from the POPLmark challenge. We not only use higher-order abstract syntax for implementing the types but exploit the full power of parametric and higher-order judgments. As a key benefit we get the narrowing lemma for free. This makes the encoding of the proof that general transitivity is admissible is extremely compact. Our reasoning is purely structural and does not require any extra size argument. Finally, unlike other encodings based on higher-order abstract syntax ours does not require proofs showing that some cases are impossible. It is remarkable that the proof for admissibility of transitivity fits on less than a page, and it is by far the shortest one so far submitted. We believe our development illustrates nicely how the problem formulation does wonders for the subsequent meta-theoretic development.

As mentioned, our case study is inspired by one of the POPLmark challenge problems, and there have been several solutions submitted exploring a wide range of possible variable encodings. We can categorize the solutions into several categories: encoding variables via de Bruijn indices, encoding variables via concrete names, encoding variables in a nameless approach, and giving an encoding using nominal types. All these solutions must prove the narrowing lemma and often various other properties about variables separately. Closest to our solution is the one by Ashley-Rollman, Crary, and Harper within the logical framework Twelf. While their proposal uses higher-order abstract syntax for encoding bound type variables, it does not exploit the full power of higher-order functions to implement hypothetical judgments. Our solution differs from their solution in that we push the power of hypothetical and parametric judgments and it demonstrates what is possible if we design the specification following the LF methodology.

We believe this case study provides interesting insights in how higher-order encodings can yield extremely compact implementations. The key behind this encoding is to think about derivations as higher-order functions, and compose higher-order functions to create new derivation. Due to the compactness of our encoding we also believe it is easier to scale. For example, to add new type constructors for cross products we simply add the corresponding cases in the subtyping algorithm and in the transitivity proof. However, we do not need to prove any additional lemmas.

In the future, it would be interesting to investigate whether our approach can be replicated in other systems which support higher-order abstract syntax and hypothetical and parametric judgments. For example, Momigliano and Ambler [MA03] propose an extension to Hybrid which supports meta-reasoning with higher-order abstract syntax in Isabelle HOL. In Coq, Felty has developed a two-level meta-logic to facilitate hypothetical and parametric reasoning [Fel02]. Another meta-logic capable of replicating our proof idea is $FO\lambda^{\triangledown\mathbb{N}}$ by McDowell and Miller [MM02]. Replicating the meta-theoretic development in this paper in other systems would provide valuable insights into how well the methodology scales to other systems. It also would allow a direct comparison between these systems concerning their philosophy, automatic proof support, and complexity of encoding.

Acknowledgment

I would like to thank Chad E. Brown, Stefan Monnier, David Xi Li, and Amy Felty for listening and commenting on the implementation.

References

ABF+05.   Aydemir, B., Bohannon, A., Fairbairn, M., Foster, J., Pierce, B., Sewell, P., Vytiniotis, D., Washburn, G., Weirich, S., Zdancewic, S.: Mechanized metatheory for the masses: The POPLmark challenge. In: Hurd, J., Melham, T. (eds.) TPHOLs 2005. LNCS, vol. 3603, pp. 50–65. Springer, Heidelberg (2005)

Fel02.   Felty, A.P.: Two-level meta-reasoning in Coq. In: Carreño, V.A., Muñoz, C.A., Tahar, S. (eds.) TPHOLs 2002. LNCS, vol. 2410, pp. 198–213. Springer, Heidelberg (2002)

HHP93.   Harper, R., Honsell, F., Plotkin, G.: A framework for defining logics. Journal of the Association for Computing Machinery 40(1), 143–184 (1993)

HL06.   Harper, R., Licata, D.: Mechanizing metatheory in a logical framework (submitted for publication)

MA03.   Momigliano, A., Ambler, S.J.: Multi-level meta-reasoning with higher-order abstract syntax. In: Gordon, A.D. (ed.) ETAPS 2003 and FOSSACS 2003. LNCS, vol. 2620, pp. 375–391. Springer, Heidelberg (2003)

MARH.   Crary, K., Ashley-Rollman, M., Harper, R.: Twelf solution to POPLmark challenge, electronically available at
http://fling-l.seas.upenn.edu/~plclub/cgi-bin/poplmark/

MM02.   McDowell, R.C., Miller, D.A.: Reasoning with higher-order abstract syntax in a logical framework. ACM Transactions on Computational Logic 3(1), 80–136 (2002)

Pfe91.   Pfenning, F.: Logic programming in the LF logical framework. In: Huet, G., Plotkin, G. (eds.) Logical Frameworks, pp. 149–181. Cambridge University Press, Cambridge (1991)

Pfe97.   Pfenning, F.: Computation and deduction (1997)

Pie02a.   Pientka, B.: A proof-theoretic foundation for tabled higher-order logic programming. In: Stuckey, P.J. (ed.) ICLP 2002. LNCS, vol. 2401, pp. 271–286. Springer, Heidelberg (2002)

Pie02b.   Pierce, B.C.: Types and Programming Languages. MIT Press, Cambridge (2002)

Pie05a.   Pientka, B.: Tabling for higher-order logic programming. In: Nieuwenhuis, R. (ed.) Automated Deduction – CADE-20. LNCS (LNAI), vol. 3632, pp. 54–68. Springer, Heidelberg (2005)

Pie05b.   Pientka, B.: Verifying termination and reduction properties about higher-order logic programs. Journal of Automated Reasoning 34(2), 179–207 (2005)

PS99.   Pfenning, F., Schürmann, C.: System description: Twelf — a meta-logical framework for deductive systems. In: Ganzinger, H. (ed.) Automated Deduction - CADE-16. LNCS (LNAI), vol. 1632, pp. 202–206. Springer, Heidelberg (1999)

RP96.   Rohwedder, E., Pfenning, F.: Mode and termination checking for higher-order logic programs. In: Nielson, H.R. (ed.) ESOP 1996. LNCS, vol. 1058, pp. 296–310. Springer, Heidelberg (1996)

SP03.   Schürmann, C., Pfenning, F.: A coverage checking algorithm for LF. In: Basin, D., Wolff, B. (eds.) TPHOLs 2003. LNCS, vol. 2758, pp. 120–135. Springer, Heidelberg (2003)

Automatically Translating Type and Function Definitions from HOL to ACL2

James Reynolds

University of Cambridge
jr291@cam.ac.uk
http://www.cl.cam.ac.uk/

Abstract. We describe an automatic, semantics preserving translation between HOL, the higher-order logic supported by the HOL4 theorem proving environment, and a deep embedding of the first order logic supported by ACL2. An implementation of this translation allows ACL2 to be used as a symbolic execution engine for functions defined in HOL.

1 Introduction and Previous Work

A deep embedding of the ACL2 universe of *s-expressions* was given in the earlier paper [1], this embedding allowed the formulation of relationships between theorems in HOL and theorems in ACL2 using a small section of trusted printing code. Using this formulation the basic axioms of ACL2 were imported into HOL and proved consistent using the HOL4 theorem prover.

Previously, if one wished to export HOL definitions to ACL2 these would have to be proven interactively to be equivalent to definitions in the embedding of *s-expressions*. In this paper we present an *automatic system* for translating functions and values from HOL into the embedded language of *s-expressions*, henceforth `sexp`, and therefore ACL2. This allows us to use ACL2 as a symbolic execution engine for HOL, or to use HOL as a specification language for a development in ACL2, as well as a number of other possibilities [2]. This builds on the previous work by providing automation from the original definition in HOL to the specification in ACL2.

The previous work also refers to other systems designed to translate HOL to Boyer-Moore style theorem provers, however, it was noted that the translation of formulae using these tools may be unsound. The work described here attempts to alleviate this criticism by using a proof driven translation from HOL to the deep embedding, so the full translation only relies on a very small body of trusted code.

The ideas behind the automatic translation will be introduced first via a number of concrete examples, after which the general translation will be given.

1.1 Translating Binary Trees

The type of numbered binary trees may be defined in HOL using the datatype definition:

$$bintree = \mathsf{Node}\ of\ bintree \to bintree\ |\ \mathsf{Leaf}\ of\ num$$

K. Schneider and J. Brandt (Eds.): TPHOLs 2007, LNCS 4732, pp. 262–277, 2007.

From this definition the translation described later will automatically create an ACL2 predicate, `bintreep`, which recognises *s-expressions* corresponding to translations of HOL binary trees:

```
(defun bintreep (s)
  (if (consp s)
      (if (equal 0 (car s))
          (if (consp (cdr s))
              (if (bintreep (cadr s)) (bintreep (cddr s)) nil)
              nil)
          (if (equal 1 (car s)) (natp (cdr s)) nil))
      nil))
```

The flatten function takes a binary tree and produces a list of its leaves in depth-first search order:

$$\vdash (\forall a\ b.\ \mathsf{flatten}\ (\mathsf{Node}\ a\ b) = \mathsf{app}\ (\mathsf{flatten}\ a)\ (\mathsf{flatten}\ b)) \land$$
$$(\mathsf{flatten}\ (\mathsf{Leaf}\ x) = \mathsf{Cons}\ x\ nil)$$

This function is automatically translated to the embedding of *s-expressions* and then pretty-printed to the following ACL2 `defun`:

```
(defun acl2_flatten (a)
  (if (bintreep a)
      (if (equal (car a) 0)
          (binary-append (acl2_flatten (cadr a))
                         (acl2_flatten (cddr a)))
          (cons (cdr a) nil))
      nil))
```

Finally, using the automatically generated translation function, $\mathcal{E}$, that translates HOL types to *s-expressions*, the translation will also return a theorem of semantic equivalence:

$$\vdash \mathcal{E}\ (\mathsf{flatten}\ tree) = \mathtt{acl2\_flatten}\ (\mathcal{E}\ tree)$$

Translating values from HOL to the `sexp` universe requires creating functions from HOL types to `sexp` and their inverses, as well as generating a *recogniser* predicate in `sexp` that can be exported to ACL2. In order to prove semantic equivalence these functions must be proven to be bijections between the set denoted by the HOL type and the set defined by the recogniser predicate.

The translation of functions from HOL to `sexp` requires converting from a form in which clauses pattern match constructors to a single clause which uses destructor functions. The translation will also need to match the domain of the HOL function to that of the function over the untyped universe `sexp`. This will involve restrictions requiring the recogniser predicate as well as dealing with functions which are not fully specified.

1.2   Tabulating Primes - An Example

The *Sieve of Eratosthenes* is a simple algorithm for tabulating all the primes up to a specified natural number. This algorithm creates a list of numbers from two to n, then repeatedly reads off the head of the list as prime and removes multiples of this from the rest of the list.

The following four HOL functions implement this algorithm to find primes up to n:

$$\vdash (\forall a.\ \mathsf{nlist}\ 0\ a = a)\ \wedge$$
$$(\forall n\ a.\ \mathsf{nlist}\ (\mathsf{Suc}\ n)\ a = \mathsf{nlist}\ n\ (\mathsf{Cons}\ (\mathsf{Suc}\ n)\ a))$$

$$\vdash \forall h\ l.\ \mathsf{tail}\ (\mathsf{Cons}\ h\ l) = l$$

$$\vdash (\forall n.\ \mathsf{flist}\ n\ \mathsf{Nil} = \mathsf{Nil})\ \wedge$$
$$(\forall n\ x\ xs.\ \mathsf{flist}\ n\ (\mathsf{Cons}\ x\ xs) =$$
$$if\ \mathsf{divides}\ n\ x$$
$$then\ \mathsf{flist}\ n\ xs$$
$$else\ \mathsf{Cons}\ x\ (\mathsf{flist}\ n\ xs))$$

$$\vdash (\mathsf{plist}\ \mathsf{Nil} = \mathsf{Nil})\ \wedge$$
$$(\forall x\ xs.\ \mathsf{plist}\ (\mathsf{Cons}\ x\ xs) = \mathsf{Cons}\ x\ \mathsf{plist}\ (\mathsf{flist}\ x\ xs))$$

$$\vdash \forall n.\ \mathsf{primes}\ n = \mathsf{plist}\ (\mathsf{tail}\ (\mathsf{nlist}\ n\ \mathsf{Nil}))$$

In the above code nlist creates the list of numbers, flist removes multiples of a number n and plist performs the iterative step to produce the list of primes.

The terms 0 and Suc represent the constructors for num, the type of the natural numbers, and the terms Cons and Nil are the constructors for lists of natural numbers. Running this code in HOL using the built in evaluator EVAL it is possible to generate primes up to 1000 in just under six minutes.

1.3   The Sexp Universe

The sexp universe consists of four basic constructors: for named symbols, characters, strings and complex rational numbers, and is closed under a pairing operator cons. The sexp universe is an untyped one, hence, in order to reason about the translation of HOL types predicates are used to partition the universe into sets corresponding to types in HOL.

1.4   Translating Lists of Natural Numbers

The datatype declaration $numlist$ describes the constructors for lists of natural numbers, num. The declaration specifies an empty list constructor, Nil and a Cons constructor that adds natural numbers to the front of the list:

$$numlist = \mathsf{Nil}\ |\ \mathsf{Cons}\ of\ num \rightarrow numlist$$

In order to translate values from the HOL type $numlist$ to the sexp universe, a function $\mathcal{E}_{numlist}$ is created that translates values of type $numlist$ to values of type sexp. This function, to be defined later, labels the constructors using a natural number representing their position in the type declaration, hence Nil $\mapsto 0$ and Cons $\mapsto 1$. Each constructor is translated by forming pairs (using cons) of the translations of each argument to that constructor. In the following definition the form $'n$ is used to indicate the complex number $n + 0i$ in the sexp universe and $\mathcal{E}_{num}$ denotes the corresponding translation function for the *num* type:

$$\vdash (\mathcal{E}_{numlist} \ \mathsf{Nil} = \mathsf{cons} \ '0 \ '0)$$
$$(\forall a \ b. \ \mathcal{E}_{numlist} \ (\mathsf{Cons} \ a \ b) = \mathsf{cons} \ '1 \ (\mathsf{cons} \ (\mathcal{E}_{num} \ a) \ (\mathcal{E}_{numlist} \ b)))$$

The translation is simplified by ensuring that all translations, including those for empty constructors, are pairs, hence Nil is translated as cons $'0 \ '0$.

In order to prove the *semantic equivalence* of any encoded function two other definitions are required: the inverse of the function $\mathcal{E}_{numlist}$; $\mathcal{D}_{numlist}$ and a predicate that recognises translated values, $\mathcal{P}_{numlist}$.

As well as defining the sexp universe the embedding also provides a base set of defined constants, referred to as $\mathcal{F}$. The constants relevant to the encoding of the *numlist* type are as follows:

Constant	Function	HOL Type
if_{sexp}	if-then-else constructor	$: sexp \rightarrow sexp \rightarrow sexp \rightarrow sexp$
$=_{sexp}$	equality operator	$: sexp \rightarrow sexp \rightarrow sexp$
t, nil	true and false	$: sexp$
car	first element of a cons	$: sexp \rightarrow sexp$
car	second element of a cons	$: sexp \rightarrow sexp$
consp	predicate for cons	$: sexp \rightarrow sexp$
natp	predicate for a natural number	$: sexp \rightarrow sexp$

Using this set of functions it is easy to define a function $\mathcal{D}_{numlist}$ and predicate $\mathcal{P}_{numlist}$. The latter of which must be constructed entirely using constructs from the base set, $\mathcal{F}$, as it will eventually be exported to ACL2. In the following definition of numlistp, $p \ \wedge_{sexp} \ q$ and $p \ \vee_{sexp} \ q$ are shorthand for $\mathsf{if}_{sexp} \ p \ q$ nil and $\mathsf{if}_{sexp} \ p \ \mathsf{t} \ q$:

$$\vdash \forall s. \ (\mathsf{numlistp} : sexp \rightarrow sexp) \ s =$$
$$(\mathsf{consp} \ s) \ \wedge_{sexp} \ (=_{sexp} \ '0 \ (\mathsf{car} \ s)) \ \wedge_{sexp} \ (=_{sexp} \ '0 \ (\mathsf{cdr} \ s)) \ \vee_{sexp}$$
$$(\mathsf{consp} \ s) \ \wedge_{sexp} \ (=_{sexp} \ '1 \ (\mathsf{car} \ s)) \ \wedge_{sexp} \ (\mathsf{consp} \ (\mathsf{cdr} \ s)) \wedge_{sexp}$$
$$(\mathsf{natp} \ (\mathsf{car} \ (\mathsf{cdr} \ s))) \ \wedge_{sexp} \ (\mathsf{numlistp} \ (\mathsf{cdr} \ (\mathsf{cdr} \ s)))$$

1.5 Translation from Clause Form

Function definitions in ACL2 are not given in the clause form commonly seen in definitions in HOL. For this reason, before translation can take place the functions must be converted into a single clause form that does not perform pattern matching. This procedure replaces pattern matching on constructors with functions that detect the constructor used and call appropriate *destructors*.

Since the constructors of *numlist* were translated as labeled products it is a simple matter to generate functions that correspond to this type's destructors. The destructors for the *numlist* type will be the two functions, hd and tl, that act as follows:

$$\vdash \forall a \ b. \ \mathsf{hd} \ (\mathsf{Cons} \ a \ b) = a$$
$$\vdash \forall a \ b. \ \mathsf{tl} \ (\mathsf{Cons} \ a \ b) = b$$

These functions could be defined using primitive recursion, however, to ease further translation they are instead created by translating, selecting the appropriate member of the product, then performing the inverse translation:

$$\vdash \forall x.\ \mathsf{hd}\ x = \quad \mathcal{D}_{num}\ (\mathsf{cadr}\ (\mathcal{E}_{numlist}\ x))$$
$$\vdash \forall x.\ \mathsf{tl}\ \ x = \mathcal{D}_{numlist}\ (\mathsf{cddr}\ (\mathcal{E}_{numlist}\ x))$$

Here the functions cadr x and cddr x are built-in abbreviations for the compositions car (cdr x) and cdr (cdr x).

As well as these functions, a function that returns the constructor number is created by decoding the label at the left of the product:

$$\vdash \forall x.\ \mathsf{Label}\ x = \mathcal{D}_{num}\ (\mathsf{car}\ (\mathcal{E}_{numlist}\ x))$$

and the following theorem is generated:

$$\vdash \forall x.\ (\mathsf{Label}\ x\ = 1) \Rightarrow (x = \mathsf{Cons}\ (\mathsf{hd}\ x)\ (\mathsf{tl}\ x))$$

With these three functions it is possible to convert the functions used in the sieve from forms using clauses to a forms more suitable for conversion, e.g:

$$\vdash \forall n\ l.\ \mathsf{flist}\ n\ l =$$
$$if\ \mathsf{Label}\ l = 1\ then\ \mathsf{Nil}$$
$$else\ if\ \mathsf{divides}\ (\mathsf{hd}\ l)\ n$$
$$then\ \mathsf{flist}\ n\ (\mathsf{tl}\ l)$$
$$else\ \mathsf{Cons}\ (\mathsf{hd}\ l)\ (\mathsf{flist}\ n\ (\mathsf{tl}\ l))$$

1.6   Definition of Flist$_{sexp}$

In order to preserve semantic equivalence the function flist$_{sexp}$ is defined in such a way that it will only operate on the **sexp** equivalent of values of the *num* and *numlist* types. This is achieved by defining flist$_{sexp}$ as a guarded call to the function flist with translated values:

$$\vdash \forall n\ l.\ \mathsf{flist}_{sexp}\ n\ l =$$
$$if_{sexp}\ (if_{sexp}\ (\mathsf{natp}\ n)\ (\mathsf{numlistp}\ l)\ \mathsf{nil})$$
$$\mathcal{E}_{numlist}(\mathsf{flist}\ (\mathcal{D}_{num}\ n)(\mathcal{D}_{numlist}\ l))$$
$$\mathsf{cons}\ '0\ '0$$

In the event that flist$_{sexp}$ is called with the incorrect types of values, the encoding of the empty list, cons $'0\ '0$, will be returned.

During the encoding of the *numlist* type the following relationships are automatically proved:

$$\vdash \forall x.\ \mathcal{D}_{numlist}(\mathcal{E}_{numlist}\ x) = x$$
$$\vdash \forall x.\ \models \mathsf{numlistp}\ x \Rightarrow (\mathcal{E}_{numlist}(\mathcal{D}_{numlist}\ x) = x)$$
$$\vdash \forall x.\ \models \mathsf{numlistp}\ (\mathcal{E}_{numlist}\ x)$$

here the $\models$ operator converts the **sexp** notion of truth to the HOL boolean values, T and F:

$$\vdash \forall x.\ \models x = \neg(x = \mathsf{nil})$$

Using these and the corresponding theorems for the num type it is trivial to convert the definition of flist_{sexp} to get the semantic equivalence theorem:

$$\vdash \forall n\ l.\ \mathcal{E}_{numlist}\ (\mathsf{flist}\ n\ l) = \mathsf{flist}_{sexp}\ (\mathcal{E}_{num}\ n)\ (\mathcal{E}_{numlist}\ l) \qquad (1)$$

1.7   The Recursive Form of Flist_{Sexp}

The last stage in the translation process is to convert the definition of flist_{sexp} to one which only uses functions over sexp. This is achieved by rewriting the term $\mathsf{flist}\ (\mathcal{D}_{num}\ n)\ (\mathcal{D}_{numlist}\ l)$, in the definition with the body of flist given in 1.5, then rewriting any recursive calls with the following theorem derived from the semantic equivalence theorem (1):

$$\vdash \forall n\ l.\ \mathsf{flist}\ n\ l = \mathcal{D}_{numlist}\ (\mathsf{flist}_{sexp}\ (\mathcal{E}_{num}\ n)\ (\mathcal{E}_{numlist}\ l))$$

This results in the recursive theorem:

$$
\begin{aligned}
\vdash \forall n\ l.\ &\mathsf{flist}_{sexp}\ n\ l = \\
&\mathsf{if}_{sexp}\ (\mathsf{if}_{sexp}\ (\mathsf{natp}\ n)\ (\mathsf{numlistp}\ l)\ \mathsf{nil}) \\
&\quad\quad \mathcal{E}_{numlist}(if\,(\mathsf{Label}\ (\mathcal{D}_{numlist}\ l)) = 1 \\
&\quad\quad\quad\quad\quad\quad then\ \mathsf{Nil} \\
&\quad\quad\quad\quad\quad\quad else\ if\ \mathsf{divides}\ (\mathsf{hd}\ (\mathcal{D}_{numlist}\ l))\ (\mathcal{D}_{num}\ n) \\
&\quad\quad\quad\quad\quad\quad\quad\quad then\ \mathcal{D}_{numlist}\ (\mathsf{flist}_{sexp}\ (\mathcal{E}_{num}\ (\mathcal{D}_{num}\ n)) \\
&\quad\quad\quad\quad\quad\quad\quad\quad\quad\quad\quad\quad (\mathcal{E}_{numlist}\ (\mathsf{tl}\ (\mathcal{D}_{numlist}\ l)))) \\
&\quad\quad\quad\quad\quad\quad\quad\quad else\ \mathsf{Cons}\ (\mathsf{hd}\ l) \\
&\quad\quad\quad\quad\quad\quad\quad\quad\quad\quad \mathcal{D}_{numlist}\ (\mathsf{flist}_{sexp}\ (\mathcal{E}_{num}(\mathcal{D}_{num}\ n)) \\
&\quad\quad\quad\quad\quad\quad\quad\quad\quad\quad\quad\quad (\mathcal{E}_{numlist}\ (\mathsf{tl}\ (\mathcal{D}_{numlist}\ l))))) \\
&\quad\quad\mathsf{cons}\ '0\ '0
\end{aligned}
$$

The final stage in the translation involves *pushing* the function $\mathcal{E}_{numlist}$ over the HOL functions to get:

$$
\begin{aligned}
\vdash \forall n\ l.\ &\mathsf{flist}_{sexp}\ n\ l = \\
&(\mathsf{if}_{sexp}\ (\mathsf{if}_{sexp}\ (\mathsf{natp}\ n)\ (\mathsf{numlistp}\ l)\ \mathsf{nil}) \\
&\quad\quad (\mathsf{if}_{sexp}\ (=_{sexp}\ (\mathsf{car}\ l)\ '1) \\
&\quad\quad\quad\quad \mathsf{cons}\ '0\ '0 \\
&\quad\quad\quad\quad (\mathsf{if}_{sexp}\ (\mathsf{divides}_{sexp}\ (\mathsf{cadr}\ l)\ n) \\
&\quad\quad\quad\quad\quad\quad (\mathsf{flist}_{sexp}\ n\ (\mathsf{cddr}\ l)) \\
&\quad\quad\quad\quad\quad\quad (\mathsf{cons}\ '1\ (\mathsf{cons}\ (\mathsf{cadr}\ l)\ (\mathsf{flist}_{sexp}\ n\ (\mathsf{cddr}\ l)))))))) \\
&\quad\quad\mathsf{cons}\ '0\ '0
\end{aligned}
$$

The destructors and label functions will always be translated at the following stages:

$$
\begin{aligned}
&\mathcal{E}_{num}\ (\mathsf{Label}\ (\mathcal{D}_{numlist}\ x)) \\
&\mathcal{E}_{num}\ (\mathsf{hd}\ (\mathcal{D}_{numlist}\ y)) \\
&\mathcal{E}_{numlist}\ (\mathsf{tl}\ (\mathcal{D}_{numlist}\ z))
\end{aligned}
$$

In the case of Label this can be reduced to $\mathsf{car}\ x$ if the theorem $\vdash \mathsf{numlistp}\ x$ can be proven at that point. The hd and tl functions may be reduced to $\mathsf{cadr}\ y$

and cddr z respectively, but only if the theorems $\vdash$ numlistp x *and* $\vdash$ car $x =$ '1 can be proven. This means that during the translation process the predicates relating to the variables must be handled very carefully.

1.8   The Finished Translation

The first step in exporting the translated definitions to ACL2 is to export the definition for the predicate numlistp. The other *sieve* functions are translated as follows:

$\vdash \forall l.$ tail$_{sexp}$ $l =$
  (if$_{sexp}$ (if$_{sexp}$ (numlistp l) (=$_{sexp}$ (car l) '1) nil)
      (cddr l)
      (cons '0 '0))

$\vdash \forall n$ $a.$ nlist$_{sexp}$ n $a =$
  (if$_{sexp}$ (if$_{sexp}$ (numlistp a) (natp n) nil)
      (if$_{sexp}$ (=$_{sexp}$ n '0)
          a
          (nlist$_{sexp}$ (+$_{sexp}$ n (−$_{sexp}$ '1)) (cons '1 (cons n a))))
      (cons '0 '0))

$\vdash \forall l.$ plist$_{sexp}$ $l =$
  (if$_{sexp}$ (numlistp l)
      (if$_{sexp}$ (=$_{sexp}$ (car l) '0)
          (cons '0 '0)
          (cons '1 (cons (cadr l)
                    (plist$_{sexp}$ (flist$_{sexp}$ (cadr l) (cddr l))))))
      (cons '0 '0))

$\vdash \forall n.$ primes$_{sexp}$ $n =$
  (if$_{sexp}$ (natp n)
      (plist$_{sexp}$ (tail$_{sexp}$ (nlist$_{sexp}$ n (cons '0 '0))))
      (cons '0 '0))

The recursive definition of tail$_{sexp}$ has an extra *guard*, (=$_{sexp}$ (car l) '1) this is because the tail function is not specified for the empty list.

Once these definitions were exported to ACL2 the compiled program computes primes up to 1000 in 0.82s and could even tabulate the primes up to 10,000 in just over two minutes. The final theorem of semantic equivalence is stated as:

$$\vdash \forall n \; l. \; \mathcal{E}_{numlist} \; (\text{primes } n) = \text{primes}_{sexp} \; (\mathcal{E}_{num} \; n)$$

2   The General Translation

The HOL universe is strictly typed with a type τ donating a set of values, Ω_τ, by contrast, the universe of *s-expressions* is an untyped one; ACL2 uses predicates to partition the universe into types. To relate HOL typed values to elements in the universe of *s-expressions*, Ω_{sexp}, for each type τ a function $\mathcal{E}_\tau : \Omega_\tau \rightarrow \Omega_{sexp}$ must be constructed and a predicate, $\mathcal{P}_\tau$, defined to denote the corresponding subset of Ω_{sexp}:

$$\mathcal{E}_\tau : \Omega_\tau \rightarrow \{x \mid \mathcal{P}_\tau \ x\} \subseteq \Omega_{sexp}$$

A function in HOL, $f : \tau_0 \rightarrow \ldots \rightarrow \tau_n \rightarrow \tau$ may be viewed as a function over sets; $\Omega_{\tau_0 \times \ldots \times \tau_n} \rightarrow \Omega_\tau$. All functions in HOL are total, as such any function, f_{sexp} over *s-expressions* must be seen as a function: $\Omega_{sexp} \rightarrow \Omega_{sexp}$. This translation therefore relates functions using a *default value* for each type τ, donated $V_\tau \in \Omega_{sexp}$, so that functions can be constrained to be:

$$f_{sexp} \in (\{x \mid \mathcal{P}_{\tau_0 \times \ldots \times \tau_n} \ x\} \rightarrow \{x \mid \mathcal{P}_\tau \ x\}) \bigcup (\{x \mid \neg \mathcal{P}_{\tau_0 \times \ldots \times \tau_n} \ x\} \rightarrow \{V_\tau\})$$

The value V_τ is selected to be in the set $\{x \mid \mathcal{P}_\tau \ x\}$, this enables us to easily prove $\vdash \forall x. \ \mathcal{P}_\tau \ (f_{sexp} \ x)$ which simplifies the translation process. The relationship between the functions f and f_{sexp} is embodied in HOL as a theorem of equivalence that represents the commutativity of translating the result of f and applying f_{sexp} to translated arguments:

$$
\begin{array}{ccc}
f \ x & \xrightarrow{\ evaluate\ } & result \in \Omega_\tau \\[4pt]
\Big\downarrow {\scriptstyle translate} & & {\scriptstyle translate} \Big\downarrow \\[4pt]
f_{sexp} \ x_{sexp} & \xrightarrow{\ evaluate\ } & result_{sexp} \in \Omega_{sexp}
\end{array}
$$

If a function recurses using the function r, e.g. $f \ x = g \ (f \ (r \ x))$, then since HOL is strictly typed it is obvious that: $\vdash \forall \ x. \ x \in \Omega_\tau \Rightarrow (r \ x) \in \Omega_\tau$. In the sexp world however this fact must be proven from the definition of r, hence as part of the translation each function r used to recurse must be proven to preserve the property $\mathcal{P}_\tau$;

$$\vdash \forall x_{sexp}. \ \models \mathcal{P}_\tau \ x_{sexp} \Rightarrow \models \mathcal{P}_\tau \ (r_{sexp} \ x_{sexp})$$

3 Compound Types

The HOL system has a number of methods for describing types, however, the most common, and most amenable to automatic procedures is the system of constructing *compound types* from a set of previously defined types. In the example given in 1.2 the list of natural numbers type, *num list*, is a compound type formed by defining the constructors $\mathsf{Cons} : \Omega_{num} \rightarrow \Omega_{num \ list} \rightarrow \Omega_{num \ list}$ and $\mathsf{Nil} : \Omega_{num \ list}$.

A compound type may be viewed as a *tree* where each node represents a constructor and edges represent the values given to the constructor. A mutually recursive compound type with free type variables $\{\alpha_0, \ldots, \alpha_n\}$ is created from a specification of the form:

$$(\alpha_0, \ldots, \alpha_n) \ \tau_0 \ = \ \mathsf{C}_{00} \ of \ \overrightarrow{\tau_{00}} \mid \ldots \mid \mathsf{C}_{i0} \ of \ \overrightarrow{\tau_{i0}}$$

$$\ldots$$

$$(\alpha_0, \ldots, \alpha_n) \ \tau_j \ = \ \mathsf{C}_{0j} \ of \ \overrightarrow{\tau_{0j}} \mid \ldots \mid \mathsf{C}_{ij} \ of \ \overrightarrow{\tau_{ij}}$$

where $\overrightarrow{\tau_{00}} \dots \overrightarrow{\tau_{ij}}$ are vectors of types whose elements can be either a pre-defined type τ or any of $\alpha_0, \dots, \alpha_n, \tau_0 \dots \tau_n$.

Since all compound types may be viewed as trees, algorithms can be designed to work in the same way on all compound types, this class of algorithms is called polytypic[4]. The translation given in this paper uses a polytypic algorithm to generate definitions for the functions $\mathcal{E}_\tau : \Omega_\tau \to \Omega_{sexp}$, their inverses; $\mathcal{D}_\tau : \Omega_{sexp} \to \Omega_\tau$, and the predicates $\mathcal{P}_\tau$.

The algorithm operates by mapping each constructor, or node, to the encoding of a labeled product of its arguments. The inverse mapping simply inverts this procedure and the predicate is similarly defined. This reduces the problem of translating compound types to translating products and certain base types.

3.1   Translating Labeled Products

Both HOL and ACL2, and hence sexp, have simple product constructors, infix comma $(,)$ and cons respectively. In HOL the product constructor forms the Cartesian product of two types, written $\tau_0 \times \tau_1$, which donates the Cartesian product of the associated sets: $\Omega_{\tau_0} \times \Omega_{\tau_1}$. The cons constructor, in contrast, actually defines the set Ω_{sexp} as being closed under the operator cons and four basic constructors for symbols, characters, strings and complex rational numbers.

Since the comma operator in HOL is polymorphic, e.g. it constructs products for any τ_0 and τ_1, the translation of products requires use of higher order functions. Each function (or predicate) involved in the translation of $\tau_0 \times \tau_1$ will rely on the corresponding functions (or predicates) for τ_0 and τ_1. The function:

$$\mathcal{E}_{\tau_0 \times \tau_1} : (\Omega_{\tau_0} \to \Omega_{sexp}) \to (\Omega_{\tau_1} \to \Omega_{sexp}) \to \Omega_{\tau_0} \times \Omega_{\tau_1} \to \Omega_{sexp}$$

is simply defined as:

$$\vdash \forall f\ g\ a\ b.\ \mathcal{E}_{\tau_0 \times \tau_1}\ f\ g\ (a,b) = \mathsf{cons}\ (f\ a)\ (g\ b)$$

where f and g are the corresponding functions for τ_0 and τ_1.

The inverse operation and predicate are defined similarly:

$$\vdash \forall f\ g\ a\ b.\ \mathcal{D}_{\tau_0 \times \tau_1}\ f\ g\ (\mathsf{cons}\ a\ b) = (f\ a, g\ b)$$
$$\vdash \forall f\ g\ a\ b.\ \mathcal{P}_{\tau_0 \times \tau_1}\ f\ g\ (\mathsf{cons}\ a\ b) = \mathsf{if}_{sexp}\ (f\ a)\ (g\ b)\ \mathsf{nil}$$

The relationships between the functions may be formally written:

$$\vdash \forall x.\ \mathcal{D}_\tau\ (\mathcal{E}_\tau\ x) = x \tag{2}$$
$$\vdash \forall x.\ \models \mathcal{P}_\tau\ x \Rightarrow \mathcal{E}_\tau (\mathcal{D}_\tau\ x) = x \tag{3}$$
$$\vdash \forall x.\ \models \mathcal{P}_\tau\ (\mathcal{E}_\tau\ x) \tag{4}$$

and in the case of products are easily proved using their definitions.

An arbitrary sized product, written $\tau_0 \times \dots \times \tau_n$, may be encoded using $n-1$ instantiations of $\mathcal{E}_{\tau_x \times \tau_y}$, in future this will be abbreviated as follows:

$$\vdash \forall f_0\ \dots\ f_n.\ \mathcal{E}_{\tau_0 \times \dots \times \tau_n}\ f_0\ \dots\ f_n = \mathcal{E}_{\tau_0 \times \tau_1 \dots \tau_n}\ f_0\ (\mathcal{E}_{\tau_1 \times \tau_2 \dots \tau_n}\ f_1\ \dots\ f_n) \dots)$$

Similar abbreviations will be used for $\mathcal{D}_{\tau_0 \times \ldots \times \tau_n}$ and $\mathcal{P}_{\tau_0 \times \ldots \times \tau_n}$. Labeled products are easily defined by using the complex number constructor to produce the natural numbers, the function $\mathcal{E}_{num} : \mathbb{N} \to \Omega_{sexp}$ will be used to represent this operation with the type num representing the naturals; $\Omega_{num} = \mathbb{N}$.

Example 1. **The α List type**

The α *List* datatype can be written using the recursive form given previously as:

$$\alpha \; List = \mathsf{Nil} \mid \mathsf{Cons} \; of \; \alpha \to \alpha \; List$$

which results in a set consisting of Nil and closed under the operation Cons:

$$\vdash \mathsf{Nil} \in \Omega_{\alpha List}$$
$$\vdash \forall a \; b. \; a \in \Omega_{\alpha List} \wedge b \in \Omega_\alpha \Rightarrow \mathsf{Cons} \; a \; b \in \Omega_{\alpha List}$$

The α *List* type may easily be translated using labeled products as follows:

$$\vdash (\forall f. \; \mathcal{E}_{\alpha List} \; f \; \mathsf{Nil} = \mathcal{E}_{num \times num} \; \mathcal{E}_{num} \; \mathcal{E}_{num} \; (\mathbf{0}, \mathbf{0})) \wedge$$
$$(\forall f \; a \; b. \; \mathcal{E}_{\alpha List} \; f \; (\mathsf{Cons} \; a \; b) = \mathcal{E}_{num \times \alpha \times \alpha List} \; \mathcal{E}_{num} \; f \; (\mathcal{E}_{\alpha List} \; f) \; (\mathbf{1}, a, b))$$

Since the translation process requires labeled products, empty constructors, such as Nil, are given an arbitrary second element, in this case the encoding of the label $\mathbf{0}$.

The $\mathcal{D}_{\alpha List}$ function is defined in a similar way, but must check whether the label is $\mathbf{0}$ or $\mathbf{1}$ to determine which product function to call. In order to do this an identity translation function is used which simply acts as $\vdash \forall a. \; I \; a = a$, it can be used to translate part of the product, leaving the rest of the product available for future translation. In the following example the *let* $(x, y) = a$ *in* b syntax is shorthand for the paired-lambda abstraction: $(\lambda(x, y). \; b) \; a$.

$$\vdash \forall f. \; \mathcal{D}_{\alpha List} \; f \; x =$$
$$let \; (l, r) = \mathcal{D}_{num \times \tau} \; \mathcal{D}_{num} \; I \; x$$
$$in \; if \; l = 0 \; then \; \mathsf{Nil}$$
$$else \; if \; l = 1 \; then \; (let \; (a, b) = \mathcal{D}_{\alpha \times \alpha List} \; f \; (\mathcal{D}_{\alpha List} \; f) \; r \; in \; \mathsf{Cons} \; a \; b)$$
$$else \; \mathbf{ARB}$$

The HOL term **ARB** is a constant defined in every type about which only reflection may be proven, it is used here to reinforce the concept that if $\mathcal{P}_\tau \; x$ is false then $\mathcal{D}_\tau \; x$ is not specified.

The predicates, $\mathcal{P}_\tau$, are defined similarly, except that truth values are used instead of constructors.

Example 2. **The $RoseTree$ type, nested mutual recursion**

The $RoseTree$ datatype defines an arbitrarily branching tree using the α *List* type described previously:

$$RoseTree = \mathsf{Branch} \; of RoseTree \; List$$

which results in a set of trees:

$$\vdash \forall a.\ a \in \Omega_{RoseTree\ List} \Rightarrow \mathsf{Branch}\ a \in \Omega_{RoseTree}$$

The definition is more easily viewed as a *mutually recursive* definition, where *RoseTree* and *RoseTreeList*, distinct from *RoseTree List*, are described in the same declaration:

$$RoseTree = \mathsf{Branch}\ of\,RoseTreeList;$$
$$RoseTreeList = \mathsf{Nil}\mid\mathsf{Cons}\ of\ RoseTree \to RoseTreeList$$

The translation functions for the *RoseTree* type are easily *stated* as simple extensions of the functions for *List*:

$$\vdash \forall a.\ \mathcal{E}_{RoseTree}\ (\mathsf{Branch}\ a) = \mathcal{E}_{RoseTree\ List}\ \mathcal{E}_{RoseTree}\ a$$
$$\vdash \forall a.\ \mathcal{D}_{RoseTree}\ (\mathsf{Branch}\ a) = \mathcal{D}_{RoseTree\ List}\ \mathcal{D}_{RoseTree}\ a$$
$$\vdash \forall a.\ \mathcal{P}_{RoseTree}\ (\mathsf{Branch}\ a) = \mathcal{P}_{RoseTree\ List}\ \mathcal{P}_{RoseTree}\ a$$

However, HOL requires all functions defined to be total, hence they must all be proven to terminate, as such the definition of the above functions cannot take place without reference to the corresponding functions $\mathcal{E}_{\alpha List}$, $\mathcal{D}_{\alpha List}$ and $\mathcal{P}_{\alpha List}$. This is resolved by defining the *RoseTree* type *as if* it had been defined as a mutually recursive type using a *placeholder* function X then removing X by proving it equivalent to $\mathcal{E}_{RoseTree\ List}\ \mathcal{E}_{RoseTree}$ using a simple induction on the type *List*:

$$\vdash (\forall a.\ \mathcal{E}_{RoseTree}\ (\mathsf{Branch}\ a) = X\ a) \land$$
$$(X\ \mathsf{Nil} = \mathcal{E}_{num\times num}\ \mathcal{E}_{num}\ \mathcal{E}_{num}\ (0,0)) \land$$
$$(\forall a\ b.\ X\ (\mathsf{Cons}\ a\ b) =$$
$$\mathcal{E}_{num\times RoseTree\times RoseTree\ List}\ \mathcal{E}_{num}\ \mathcal{E}_{RoseTree}\ X(1,a,b))$$

The other translation functions are defined in a similar manner.

4   Converting Functions

As well as an embedding of the **sexp** universe in HOL, the theories defined in [1] also provide **sexp** equivalents of various ACL2 low level functions. These functions were proven by hand to be equivalent, up to translation, to similar functions defined in HOL. For each function f which has an equivalent defined for the **sexp** universe the following equivalence was proven in the form of a *rewrite* theorem:

$$\vdash \forall a_0\ \ldots a_n.\ \mathcal{E}_\tau\ (f\ a_0\ \ldots\ a_n) = f_{sexp}\ (\mathcal{E}_{\tau_0}\ a_0)\ \ldots\ (\mathcal{E}_{\tau_n}\ a_n)$$

This set of base functions, $\mathcal{F}$, serves as a starting point for the translation process, once a function is translated, it is added to the set in the rewrite form above and can then be used by further translations.

The translation given here maintains semantic equivalence by defining the function $f_{sexp} : \Omega_{sexp} \to \Omega_{sexp}$ as the function:

$$\vdash \forall x.\; f_{sexp}\; x = if_{sexp}\; (\mathcal{P}_\tau\; x)\; (\mathcal{E}_{\tau'}\; (f\; (\mathcal{D}_\tau\; x)))\; V_{\tau'}$$

Using the relationships 2, 3 and 4 it is easy to show that this definition implies that:

$$\vdash \forall x.\; f\; x = \mathcal{D}_{\tau_{result}}\; (f_{sexp}\; (\mathcal{E}_{\tau_{argument}} x)) \tag{5}$$

Once f_{sexp} is defined it must be expressed in a form that uses only functions found in $\mathcal{F}$.

4.1 Functions in Clause Form

A recursive function in HOL is given as a number of *clauses* that each match a particular constructor:

$$\vdash (\forall \overrightarrow{a_0}.\; f\; (\mathsf{C}_0\; \overrightarrow{a_0}) = A\; \overrightarrow{a_0}) \wedge$$
$$\cdots$$
$$(\forall \overrightarrow{a_n}.\; f\; (\mathsf{C}_n\; \overrightarrow{a_n}) = A\; \overrightarrow{a_n}) \wedge$$

Definitions in ACL2 however do not use this form; an ACL2 definition can be viewed as an equivalence between a function term and its body, e.g:

$$\forall \overrightarrow{a}.\; f\; \overrightarrow{a} = A\; \overrightarrow{a}$$

The first step in translating a function from HOL to sexp then is to translate the clause definition to one suitable for translation to ACL2, this involves replacing the clause definitions with a function that can determine which constructor was used and call an appropriate *destructor*.

The *destructor* for the argument m of constructor n is the function D_{mn} that satisfies:

$$\vdash \forall \overrightarrow{a_m}.\; \mathsf{D}_{mn}\; (\mathsf{C}_m\; \overrightarrow{a_m}) = \overrightarrow{a_m}(n).$$

If a labeling function is specified such that:

$$\vdash \forall m\; \overrightarrow{a_m}.\; \mathsf{Label}\; (\mathsf{C}_m\; \overrightarrow{a_m}) = m$$

then the translation can replace pattern matching of constructed arguments with a statement that uses Label and the destructor functions $D_{00} \ldots D_{ij}$.

As described in section 1.5, the destructor functions are defined by translating the value, selecting the appropriate member of the product then performing the inverse translation:

$$\mathsf{D}_{mn}\; x = \mathcal{D}_{\overrightarrow{\tau_m}(n)}\; (\mathsf{select}\; n\; (\mathcal{E}_{\tau_m}\; x))$$

The select construct is an abbreviation for a term constructed from car and cdr to select the appropriate element in the product. The label function is defined similarly except that the label is known to be of type *num* and at the left of the product:

$$\mathsf{Label}\; x = \mathcal{D}_{num}\; (\mathsf{car}\; (\mathcal{E}_{\tau_m}\; x))$$

Example 3. **The Append function;** app

The append function can be defined in HOL as:

$$\vdash (\forall c.\ \text{app Nil}\ c = c) \land$$
$$(\forall a\ b\ c.\ \text{app (Cons}\ a\ b)\ c = \text{Cons}\ a\ (\text{app}\ b\ c))$$

and may be modified to a single function clause using the list destructors: Like the *numlist* type given earlier, destructors for Cons are constructed by selecting the appropriate product:

$$\vdash \forall a\ b.\mathcal{D}_\alpha\ (\text{cadr}\ (\mathcal{E}_{\alpha List}\ (\text{Cons}\ a\ b))) = a$$
$$\vdash \forall a\ b.\mathcal{D}_\alpha\ (\text{cddr}\ (\mathcal{E}_{\alpha List}\ (\text{Cons}\ a\ b))) = b$$

and the label function is defined by decoding the left of the product:

$$\vdash \forall a.\ (\mathcal{D}_{num}\ (\text{car}\ (\mathcal{E}_{\alpha List}\ \text{Nil})) = 0) \land (\mathcal{D}_{num}\ (\text{car}\ (\mathcal{E}_{\alpha List}\ (\text{Cons}\ a\ b))) = 1)$$

Using these functions it is a simple matter to prove the append function has the equivalent definition:

$$\vdash \forall x\ y.\ \text{app}\ x\ y =$$
$$if\ (\mathcal{D}_{num}\ (\text{car}\ (\mathcal{E}_{\alpha List}\ \text{Nil})) = 0)$$
$$then\ y$$
$$else\ \text{Cons}\ (\mathcal{D}_\alpha\ (\text{cadr}\ (\mathcal{E}_{\alpha List}\ x)))$$
$$(\text{app}\ (\mathcal{D}_\alpha\ (\text{cddr}\ (\mathcal{E}_{\alpha List}\ x)))\ y)$$

4.2   Rewriting

The second stage of the translation process is to convert the function f_{sexp} in the form given earlier to a recursive definition that uses only functions in $\mathcal{F}$. This is achieved by rewriting $f\ x$ in the definition of f_{sexp} with its body, and then replacing any recursive calls to f using equation 5. This results in a recursive definition of f_{sexp} which may be completed by rewriting terms using the translations for the functions found in $\mathcal{F}$. However, this process must also form rewrites for the destructor and labeling constructs.

The rewriting stage involves pushing $\mathcal{E}_\tau$ functions over terms, so the destructor functions will be translated from: $\mathcal{E}_{\overrightarrow{Tm}(n)}\ (\mathcal{D}_{\overrightarrow{Tm}(n)}\ (\text{select}\ n\ x))$, using equation3 this can be reduced to:

$$\vdash \forall x.\ \models \mathcal{P}_{\overrightarrow{Tm}(n)}\ (\text{select}\ n\ x) \Rightarrow (\mathcal{E}_{\overrightarrow{Tm}(n)}\ (\mathcal{D}_{\overrightarrow{Tm}(n)}\ (\text{select}\ n\ x))) = \text{select}\ n\ x$$

In order to resolve the antecedent theorems of the form:

$$\vdash \forall x.\ (\models \mathcal{P}_{\tau_m}\ x) \land (\mathcal{D}_{num}\ (\text{car}\ x) = n) \Rightarrow \models \mathcal{P}_{\overrightarrow{Tm}(n)}\ (\text{select}\ n\ x)$$

are constructed when the type is first processed. The rewriting process then keeps track of which type predicates and constructor predicates have been encountered in *if* statements and uses these to resolve the antecedents.

Example 4. **Translating a guarded statement**

The following term may be encountered when processing a list function, the check on the label was inserted by the translation process and as such has a standard form:

$$\mathcal{E}_{\alpha List} \ (if \ (\mathcal{D}_{num} \ (\mathsf{car} \ x) = 1) \ then \ (\mathcal{D}_{\alpha List} \ (\mathsf{cddr} \ x)) \ else \ \mathsf{Nil}$$

The rewrite would progress by *pushing* the encoding function over the *if* statement to get a term of the form:

$$if_{sexp} \ (\mathcal{E}_{bool} \ (\mathcal{D}_{num} \ (\mathsf{car} \ x) = 1)) \ (\mathcal{E}_{\alpha List} \ (\mathcal{D}_{\alpha List} \ (\mathsf{cddr} \ x))) \ (\mathcal{E}_{\alpha List} \ \mathsf{Nil})$$

Before this is translated any further the branches of the *if* statement will be encoded, the first of which will result in the term:

$$\vdash (\models \mathcal{P}_{\alpha List} \ (\mathsf{cddr} \ x)) \Rightarrow (\mathcal{E}_{\alpha List} \ (\mathcal{D}_{\alpha List} \ (\mathsf{cddr} \ x)) = \mathsf{cddr} \ x)$$

which will be reduced to:

$$\vdash (\models \mathcal{P}_{\alpha List} \ x) \wedge (\mathcal{D}_{num}(\mathsf{car} \ x) = 1) \Rightarrow (\mathcal{E}_{\alpha List} \ (\mathcal{D}_{\alpha List} \ (\mathsf{cddr} \ x)) = \mathsf{cddr} \ x)$$

Since the second of these terms is included in the predicate of the *if* statement the rewriter can then reduce the entire expression to:

$$\vdash (\models \mathcal{P}_{\alpha List} \ x) \Rightarrow (\ldots = if_{sexp}(\mathsf{car} \ x =' 1)(\mathsf{cddr} \ x)(\mathsf{cons} \ '0 \ '0))$$

The final antecedent will be removed later as the whole function would have been guarded with a $\mathcal{P}_{\alpha List} \ x$ term.

4.3 Incomplete Specifications

As well as the domain of a function in HOL being limited by its type, it is also possible for functions to have their domain limited further at the time of specification using the HOL **ARB** construct. Since it is not possible to prove anything about a clause whose value is **ARB** it is not possible, at that point in the domain, to relate f to f_{sexp}.

This translation solves this by allowing the user to supply a predicate X to limit the domain of the translation to avoid the areas for which the result of f is **ARB** . The values of f_{sexp} are hence defined to be V_τ, and the theorem stating the commutativity of the translation is then dependent upon X.

As was mentioned earlier, it is important to also be able to prove that the function preserves this restriction on the domain, in the case of incomplete specifications the user must supply this theorem:

$$\vdash \forall \overrightarrow{x}. \ X \ \overrightarrow{x} \Rightarrow P \ \overrightarrow{x} \Rightarrow X \ (r \ \overrightarrow{x})$$

where P represents conditional statements between the original function and the recursive call.

The equivalent theorem in `sexp` is produced automatically.

Example 5. **The last function**

Like many list functions, the last function is an example of a function which is often implemented with an incomplete specification. The function last may be implemented in HOL as follows:

$$\vdash (\forall a. \; \mathsf{last} \; (\mathsf{Cons} \; a \; \mathsf{Nil}) = a)$$
$$(\forall a \; b \; c. \; \mathsf{last} \; (\mathsf{Cons} \; a \; (\mathsf{Cons} \; b \; c)) = \mathsf{last} \; (\mathsf{Cons} \; b \; c))$$

The function may be translated using the label functions and destructors to:

$$\vdash \forall a. \; \mathsf{last} \; a =$$
$$if \; (\mathcal{D}_{num} \; (\mathsf{car} \; (\mathcal{E}_{\alpha List}(\mathcal{D}_\alpha \; (\mathsf{cddr} \; (\mathcal{E}_{\alpha List} \; a)))))) = 1)$$
$$then \; (\mathcal{D}_\alpha \; (\mathsf{cadr} \; (\mathcal{E}_{\alpha List} \; (\mathcal{D}_\alpha \; (\mathsf{cddr} \; (\mathcal{E}_{\alpha List} \; a))))))$$
$$else \; (\mathcal{D}_\alpha \; (\mathsf{cddr} \; (\mathcal{E}_{\alpha List} \; (\mathcal{D}_\alpha \; (\mathsf{cddr} \; (\mathcal{E}_{\alpha List} \; a))))))$$

The last_{sexp} function would then be defined using the predicate $\neg(\mathsf{null} \; a)$:

$$\vdash \forall a. \; \mathsf{last}_{sexp} \; a =$$
$$if \; \mathcal{E}_{bool}(\neg(\mathsf{null} \; a)) \wedge \mathcal{P}_{\alpha List} \; a$$
$$then \; \mathcal{E}_{\alpha List} \; \mathcal{E}_\alpha \; (\mathsf{last} \; (\mathcal{D}_{\alpha List} \; \mathcal{D}_\alpha \; a))$$
$$else \; \mathcal{E}_{num \times num} \; \mathcal{E}_{num} \; \mathcal{E}_{num} \; (0,0)$$

The user would also have to supply a theorem to prove that when the recursive call to last is made using the second matched constructor the tail of the list will not be empty:

$$\vdash \forall a. \; \neg(\mathsf{null} \; a) \Rightarrow (\exists \; a \; b \; c. \; (\mathsf{Cons} \; a \; (\mathsf{Cons} \; b \; c))) \Rightarrow \neg(\mathsf{null} \; (\mathsf{tl} \; a))$$

4.4   Using Higher Level ACL2 Constructs

Constants defined in ACL2 can make use of constructs that operate outside of the ACL2 logic to lower execution times, these constructs have no effect on the semantics of the function they only affect the method of execution. When defining the base set of constants, $\mathcal{F}$, it is advantageous to use high level ACL2 functions, however this often requires translating types in a manner that deviates from the automatic translation. For example, the $\alpha \; List$ translation given in example 1 differs from the ACL2 notion of lists; a string of cons pairs terminated using nil. In these cases hand-proven translation functions are used that correspond closely to the definitions used in ACL2, this allows $\mathcal{F}$ to contain high level constants such as len and last.

ACL2 also has a Single Threaded Object construct, which allows imperative style execution using destructive updates. Work is ongoing to allow the automatic translation of monadic HOL functions to use these objects.

5   Conclusions

The translation presented in this paper allows first-order functions defined using compound types composed of a base set of hand-proven types to be exported to

ACL2 in a logically consistent manner, and has been extended to automatically translate first-order instantiations of maps and folds. So far, other first order constructs available in HOL, such as inductive rule definitions, may only be translated after their equivalence to a functional form has been proven.

This method may also be applied to other target domains, some success has already been made in this area; translations to functions over lists of booleans have been performed using rules given to a general mechanism.

The translation has already been successfully applied to the type and associated functions of Red-Black trees as well as an implementation of IEEE floating point arithmetic used in the ARM Vector Floating Point unit [3]. The following table compares the timings of evaluating powers of e, it neatly demonstrates the gains in efficiency the translation provides in symbolic execution:

Precision:		Iterations:	HOL time:	ACL2 time:
Single	32 bit	5	7.72s	0.01s
		10	16.2s	0.02s
Double	64 bit	5	13.7s	0.04s
		10	27.4s	0.07s
Extended	80 bit	5	17.5s	1.08s
		10	35.2s	2.12s

In the future we aim to use this translation to translate the VFP model and ARM model together in order to efficiently evaluate whole floating point programs.

References

1. Gordon, M.J.C., Reynolds, J., Hunt, W.A., Kaufmann, M.: An integration of hol and acl2. fmcad 0, 153–160 (2006)
2. Gordon, M.J.C., Hunt, W.A., Kaufmann, M., Reynolds, J.: An embedding of the acl2 logic in hol. ACL2 Workshop 0, 40–46 (2006)
3. Reynolds, J.: A hol implementation of the arm fp co-processor programmer's model. In: Hurd, J., Melham, T. (eds.) TPHOLs 2005. LNCS, vol. 3603, Springer, Heidelberg (2005)
4. Slind, K., Hurd, J.: Applications of polytypism in theorem proving. In: Basin, D., Wolff, B. (eds.) TPHOLs 2003. LNCS, vol. 2758, pp. 103–119. Springer, Heidelberg (2003)

Operational Reasoning for Concurrent Caml Programs and Weak Memory Models

Tom Ridge

University of Cambridge

Abstract. This paper concerns the formal semantics of programming languages, and the specification and verification of software. We are interested in the verification of real programs, written in real programming languages, running on machines with real memory models. To this end, we verify a Caml implementation of a concurrent algorithm, Peterson's mutual exclusion algorithm, down to the operational semantics. The implementation makes use of Caml features such as higher order parameters, state, concurrency and nested general recursion. Our Caml model includes a datatype of expressions, and a small step reduction relation for programs (a Caml expression together with a store). We also develop a new proof of correctness for a modified version of Peterson's algorithm, designed to run on a machine with a weak memory.

1 Introduction

Program verification has a long and venerable history, from the pioneering work of Turing [MJ84], through to recent work such as the mechanized verification of the Four Colour Theorem [Gon05]. However, there are problems with existing approaches.

- The languages and programs are typically highly idealized, and far removed from the real languages people actually use. Attempts to address real languages are typically not foundational.
- With the advent of multicore processors, assumptions about how to model memory are no longer justified, and existing proofs are typically invalid in the case that the algorithm is running on a machine with a weak memory.

We explore the issues involved by conducting two verifications: for the first, we verify a non-trivial concurrent Caml program, Peterson's algorithm for mutual exclusion [Pet81], down to the operational semantics; for the second we verify Peterson's algorithm with a weak memory model.

The Caml code we verify appears in Fig. 1 and can be compiled and run with recent versions of OCaml[1] (for readers not familiar with Caml syntax, we describe a standard pseudocode version in Sect. 2). We formalize a semantics for Caml in Sect. 3 and the proof in Sect. 4. The complexity that arises in the proofs stems from the size of individual states (Caml expressions that occupy

---

[1] http://caml.inria.fr

K. Schneider and J. Brandt (Eds.): TPHOLs 2007, LNCS 4732, pp. 278–293, 2007.

```
let turn = ref false in
let trys =
  let try_f = ref false in
  let try_t = ref false in
    fun x -> if x then try_t else try_f in
let rec loop = fun id ->
  (trys id := true)                              (* set trying flag *)
  ; (turn := not id)                             (* set turn flag   *)
  ; (let rec test = fun _ ->
      if !turn = id || not !(trys (not id)) then () else test ()
      in test ())                                (* looping in test *)
  ; ()                                           (* critical region *)
  ; (trys id := false)                           (* exit crit       *)
  ; loop id
in
(Thread.create loop false, Thread.create loop true)
```

Fig. 1. Peterson's algorithm, Caml code

several pages), the large number of reachable states for each thread , and the consequent intricacy of the interleavings of the two threads. Reasoning directly about the operational semantics requires clever proof techniques to mitigate these complexities. We briefly outline these techniques, which we describe in greater detail in Sect. 4.

- We factor the proof into an abstract part and an operational part. We isolate the core interleavings of the threads by constructing an abstract model of Peterson's algorithm. The Caml implementation is a refinement of this abstract model.
- The Caml part of the proof is an invariant proof. We use the theorem prover to symbolically execute along paths of the system, proving the invariant along the way.
- We employ a strong induction hypothesis, which makes use of a notion of "recurrent states". We consider paths starting from these recurrent states, and whenever we encounter another recurrent state, we apply the induction hypothesis, and so terminate symbolic execution along that particular branch. The induction scheme, with the notion of recurrent states, is useful even for non-concurrent, infinite state systems.
- To reduce the complexity of the state space of the parallel composition of the two threads, $T_1|T_2$, we replace a thread, T_2 say, with an invariant I_2, which represents possible interference of T_2, but is much easier to work with. We also consider $I_1|T_2$. This is similar to rely-guarantee reasoning [Jon81], and allows us to perform a thread-modular verification. The rely-guarantee style reasoning extends smoothly to multiple threads.
- In order for the induction to work smoothly we eliminate the interleaving between T_1 and I_2, so that T_1 is always making progress. We construct a

thread-like object T_1', that executes roughly as T_1, but incorporates possible interference from I_2 into each T_1 step. It is the system T_1' that we symbolically execute.

These techniques allow us to reduce the Caml proof to little more than simplification, which we use to symbolically execute the thread-like objects, and to check the invariant at each stage. In fact, the proof could be entirely automated. *Moreover, the techniques apply directly to similar algorithms such as Simpson's 4-slot for which we already have abstract proofs [Rid].* We claim that our approach is reproducible and can be applied to many other algorithms: given an abstract proof of an algorithm, proving the connection to a Caml (or other) implementation can often be reduced to little more than symbolic execution using the theorem prover's simplifier.

To address the second problem, we demonstrate reasoning about Peterson's algorithm at an abstract level with a very weak memory model. This requires us to formalize a model of weak memory (Sect. 6), modify Peterson's algorithm, and to develop a new proof of correctness (Sect. 7). In essence, the proof of Peterson's algorithm with a weak memory model follows the outline of the original abstract proof, but includes proof patches to cope with the additional complexities. We include background information on weak memory models in Sect. 5.

Mechanization of these proofs is vital, especially as we move towards verification of realistic full scale languages: the reachable states of the operational semantics are simply too complex for informal proof. Moreover, reasoning about concurrent algorithms even without weak memory models is considered difficult. With the additional complexity of weak memory models, we found mechanization to be invaluable. For example, the process of constructing the proof revealed several possible execution paths that we were not aware of, and which required us to alter our proofs.

Our contributions are:

- We develop a mechanized verification of a Caml implementation of Peterson's algorithm, down to the operational semantics.
- The Caml implementation is a refinement of an abstract model of Peterson's algorithm. *This is important because there are many abstract verifications which we would like to reuse for more complex program models.*
- We develop some novel proof techniques which we have sketched above, and which we describe more fully in Sect. 4.
- We develop a mechanized proof of correctness for a version of Peterson's algorithm, with a weak memory model.

Small-step operational semantics are the most successful means of language specification available. In principle, it is clear that operational reasoning is sufficient to prove the correctness of programs. If the language and programs are specified by means of operational semantics, the *most direct form of proof is by using operational reasoning*. The motivation of this work is to promote operational reasoning as a means of program verification.

Basic definitions. Given an underlying set of states S, a *state transition system* or *sts* on S is a pair consisting of a set of *start states* $\subseteq S$, and a *transition relation* $\subseteq S \times S$. Given an sts L, a *sequence* p is a function from $\mathbb{N}$ to S, such that adjacent points $p\,n, p\,(n+1)$ are related by the transition relation of L. A *path* is a sequence that starts in a start state. A state a is *reachable* if there is a path p, and position n, such that $p\,n = a$. If L and K are defined on the same set of underlying states S, the *parallel composition* of L and K is the sts formed by taking the union of the start states, and the union of the transition relations. An *abstraction relation* R from an sts L to an sts K relates each start state of L to some start state of K, and if a is reachable by L, and related to b, and L makes a transition from a to a', then K can make a transition from b to b', and moreover a' and b' are also related by R. The key fact about an abstraction relation is that for every path of L, there is a path of K such that corresponding positions in the paths are related. Abstraction relations are a form of simulation relations.

Isabelle/HOL. The mechanizations described here were conducted in the Isabelle/HOL theorem prover. List cons is represented in Isabelle syntax by an infix #, and updating a function f at argument a with value v is written $f(a := v)$. Isabelle also has two implications, $\longrightarrow$ and $\Longrightarrow$. For the purposes of this paper, they may be considered equivalent. Apart from that, Isabelle's syntax is close to informal mathematics.

2   Background on Peterson's Algorithm

In this section, we describe Peterson's algorithm informally using pseudocode, give a formal model of the abstract algorithm in HOL, give the key lemmas needed to prove the mutual exclusion property, and state the mutual exclusion property itself.

In Fig. 1 we give the Caml version of Peterson's algorithm that we verify. By way of introduction, we here present an informal pseudocode version, Fig. 2, and explain how it works. The algorithm uses two variables, `trys` (an array

```
trys[0]   = 0
trys[1]   = 0
turn      = 0

P0: trys[0] = 1                     P1: trys[1] = 1
    turn = 1                            turn = 0
    while( trys[1] && turn == 1 );      while( trys[0] && turn == 0 );
            // do nothing                       // do nothing
    // critical section                // critical section
    ...                                ...
    // end of critical section         // end of critical section
    trys[0] = 0                         trys[1] = 0
```

Fig. 2. Peterson's algorithm, informal pseudocode

peterson-trans i s s′ ≡

(* *j is the other process* *)
let *j* = ¬ *i in*

(* *extract parts of the state* *)
let ((*turn,trys*),*pcs*) = *s in*
let ((*turn′,trys′*),*pcs′*) = *s′ in*
let (*itry,ipc*) = (*trys i, pcs i*) *in*
let (*itry′,ipc′*) = (*trys′ i, pcs′ i*) *in*
let (*jtry, jpc*) = (*trys j, pcs j*) *in*
let (*jtry′, jpc′*) = (*trys′ j, pcs′ j*) *in*

(* *nothing happens to j* *)
(*jpc′* = *jpc* ∧ *jtry′* = *jtry*)

(* *process i takes a step* *)
∧ (

(* *looping in any state* *)
((*ipc′,itry′,turn′*) = (*ipc,itry,turn*))

∨ ((*ipc,ipc′*) = (*NonCrit,SetTry*)
∧ (*itry′,turn′*) = (*itry,turn*))

∨ ((*ipc,ipc′*) = (*SetTry,SetTurn*)
∧ (*itry′,turn′*) = (*True,turn*))

∨ ((*ipc,ipc′*) = (*SetTurn,Test*)
∧ (*itry′,turn′*) = (*itry,j*))

∨ ((*ipc,ipc′*) = (*Test,Crit*)
∧ ((*jtry* = *False*) ∨ (*turn* = *i*))
∧ (*itry′,turn′*) = (*itry,turn*))

∨ ((*ipc,ipc′*) = (*Crit,Exit*)
∧ (*itry′,turn′*) = (*itry,turn*))

∨ ((*ipc,ipc′*) = (*Exit,NonCrit*)
∧ (*itry′,turn′*) = (*False,turn*)))

Fig. 3. Thread transitions for Peterson's algorithm, in HOL

of booleans) and `turn`. A `trys[0]` value of 1 indicates that thread P0 wants to enter the critical section, similarly `trys[1]` = 1 indicates that P1 wants to enter the critical section. The variable `turn` holds the id of the thread whose turn it is. Entrance to the critical section is granted for P0 if P1 does not want to enter its critical section or if P1 has given priority to P0 by setting `turn` to 0. The algorithm guarantees that the two threads are never executing their critical sections simultaneously.

It is straightforward to formalize an abstract state transition system for Peterson's algorithm. For each thread, the *program counter*, or *pc*, is either non-critical, about to set the try variable, about to set the turn variable, testing the turn variable and the other thread's try variable, in the critical section, or exiting the critical section by unsetting the try variable.

datatype *pc* = *NonCrit* | *SetTry* | *SetTurn* | *Test* | *Crit* | *Exit*

We identify *thread id* with a boolean rather than an integer. The *turn* and *try* variables are booleans (*try* is indexed by thread id). The system state is a tuple consisting of the turn and try variables, and the program counters for each thread. The transition relation for a thread is parameterised on the thread id.

types *thread-id = bool*   **types** *turn = thread-id*   **types** *trys = (thread-id ⇒ bool)*
types *pcs = (thread-id ⇒ pc)*   **types** *peterson-state = (turn * trys) * pcs*

constdefs *peterson-trans :: thread-id ⇒ peterson-state ⇒ peterson-state ⇒ bool*

We define the transitions in Fig. 3. Each thread starts in its non-critical state, with all variables initialised to false. The state transition system is a parallel composition of the two threads.

constdefs *peterson-starts :: peterson-state set*
  peterson-starts ≡ {((False,λ x. False),λ x. NonCrit)}

constdefs *peterson-sts :: peterson-state sts*
  peterson-sts ≡
  par (peterson-starts, peterson-trans False) (peterson-starts, peterson-trans True)

We first characterise the thread states where the try variable is set, following Lemma 10.5.1 in [Lyn96]. The key lemma, *lemma-10-5-2*, is proved by induction on n. Mutual exclusion follows directly, since *turn* cannot be both i and j.

lemma *lemma-10-5-2*:
  ∀ *i p. is-path peterson-sts p*
  ⟶ (∀ *n.*
  let ((turn,trys),pcs) = p n in
  let (itry,ipc) = (trys i, pcs i) in
  let j = ¬i in
  let (jtry,jpc) = (trys j, pcs j) in
  ipc = Crit ∧ jpc ∈ {Test,Crit}
  ⟶ (*turn = i*))

lemma *mutual-exclusion*:
  ∀ *p. is-path peterson-sts p*
  ⟶ (∀ *n i.*
  let ((turn,trys),pcs) = p n in
  let (itry,ipc) = (trys i, pcs i) in
  let j = ¬i in
  let (jtry,jpc) = (trys j, pcs j) in
  ¬ (*ipc = Crit ∧ jpc = Crit*))

3   Caml Formalization

In this section we give the datatype of Caml expressions, describe the small-step operational semantics for Caml, and give the state transition system for the Caml implementation of Peterson's algorithm.

If we examine the code in Fig. 1, we see that we need to model several features of Caml: general recursion, nested recursion, state, higher order parameters, and concurrency. We do not model features, such as modules, that are not required for our example. Adding additional features would not essentially alter the proof, however, which rests largely on symbolic evaluation of the code.

We declare a datatype of Caml expressions in Isabelle/HOL. This includes the usual functional core (including *let*), constants (including *fix*), state (assignment, reference, dereference, and locations) and concurrency (*Par*). A trace expression is not part of the standard Caml syntax. It is semantically neutral (i.e. *Trace(a,e)* behaves as *e*), and it removes the need to quote Caml expressions explicitly.

datatype *'a exp =*

    Var var
    | *Lam 'a lambda*
    | *App 'a exp * 'a exp*
    | *LetVal 'a exp * 'a lambda*

    | *Const const*

    | *Assign 'a exp * 'a exp*
    | *Deref 'a exp*
    | *Ref 'a exp*
    | *Loc loc*

    | *Par 'a exp * 'a exp*

    | *Trace 'a * 'a exp*

                and *'a lambda = Lambda var * 'a exp*

We use the `-dparsetree` OCaml compiler switch to obtain an abstract syntax tree of the Caml code, which we import into Isabelle/HOL, modulo some pretty printing of the thread pair as a *Par*. We first modify the Caml code by tagging subexpressions with trace information, in particular, we modify the () expression in the critical section to `Trace("Crit",())`.

constdefs *peterson* :: *string exp*
  peterson ≡
  LetVal(Trace("turn",Ref (Const FFalse)),Lambda("turn",LetVal(Trace("trys",...

We need to model how Caml expressions evaluate or reduce. Expressions reduce in the context of a store. Our store is a pair (n, w) where n is the next free location in the store w, a map from locations to expressions. Our reduction relation is then a relation between (n, w, e), the current store and expression, with (n', w', e'), the store and expression at the next step. To make symbolic evaluation easier, we phrase this as a function *reduce'* from (n, w, e) to a list of possible next states, which we later lift to a relation *rreduce*. We give an excerpt from this definition, illustrating that variables and lambdas do not reduce, and the reduction of a function value (lambda expression) e_1 applied to a value e_2 is by substituting *e2* in the body of the function.

primrec
  reduce' n w (Var v) = []
  reduce' n w (Lam l) = []
  reduce' n w (App e1e2) = reduce'-3 n w e1e2
  reduce'-3 n w (e1,e2) = (
    if is-value e1 then (
      if is-value e2 then (
        if is-Lam e1 then [(n,w,subst-lambda e2 (dest-Lam e1))]
        else ...)))

We combine the Caml definition of Peterson's algorithm with the Caml reduction relation to get a state transition system for the Caml implementation of Peterson's algorithm.

types *caml = loc * (loc ⇒ string exp) * string exp*

constdefs *peterson-starts* :: *caml set*
  peterson-starts ≡ {(*loc-counter*, λ *x*. *null-exp*, *peterson*)}

constdefs *peterson-sts* :: *caml sts*
  peterson-sts ≡ (*peterson-starts*, *rreduce*)

4 Proof of Correctness

In this section, we outline the proof of correctness. The difficulty of the proof arises from the complexity of the state space. For example, in the abstract model, we can show a property is invariant by case splitting on a thread's program counter.For the Caml thread, which is represented as a Caml expression, case splitting does not make sense, and we have to find some other way to characterise the possible states the thread might take.

Given that we have added trace information to identify the critical section, our statement of correctness informally says that it is not the case that the Caml expression is a *Par* of two threads executing in their critical section. A thread is represented as a Caml sequence of the current expression, and the remaining expressions to execute. A sequence is just a *let* of the current expression, and the rest of the sequence as the body of the *let*. This gives rise to the following statement of correctness.

lemma *mutual-exclusion*:
  ∀ *p n*. *is-path peterson-sts p* ⟶ ¬ (∃ *e1 l1 e2 l2*. *let* (*n*,*w*,*e*) = *p n in*
  e = *Par* (*LetVal* (*Trace* ("*Crit*",*e1*),*l1*), *LetVal* (*Trace* ("*Crit*",*e2*),*l2*)))

The proof proceeds by constructing an abstraction relation from the Caml sts to the abstract sts.

lemma *is-abstraction*: *is-abstraction PetersonML.sts Peterson2.peterson-sts R*

The abstraction relates Caml states matching *Trace*("*Crit*", *e*) to abstract states with program counter *Crit*. If the Caml threads were both in their critical section, then by the main property of abstraction relations, so too would the two abstract threads. Since we have shown that this is impossible, we get mutual exclusion for the Caml implementation. To show that *R* is indeed an abstraction relation, we have to show that, for reachable states of the Caml system, transitions can be matched by transitions of the abstract system. That is, we have to show an invariant of all reachable states.

The main barrier to this approach is the complexity of the reachable states of the Caml implementation. Intermediate program expressions can grow substantially larger than the original program (because *let rec* duplicates a body of code, and we have nested use of *let rec*, and we also have two thread subexpressions which duplicate the outer loop code). Individual instructions, which execute in a single step in the abstract model, can take many steps to execute in the concrete model, especially as many features are defined on top of the relatively small core. For example, the Caml code corresponding to the *Test* instructions can take more than 40 steps to execute. This in turn influences the interleavings that can occur. These factors combine to cause a blowup in the complexity of the state space.

Although intermediate states are extremely large, the state space is still finite. This means it is at least theoretically possible to enumerate all the reachable states and prove mutual exclusion this way. This would not tell us anything about proving general programs correct with an operational semantics. We therefore resolve to develop general techniques that do not take any advantage of the finiteness of the state space.

Let the two Caml thread transition systems be T_i, T_j, where $\{i, j\} = \{true, false\}$. By definition of *reachable*, we must prove $\forall p \, \forall n \, (is\text{-}path \, (par \, T_i \, T_j) \, p \rightarrow I \, (p \, n))$ where I states that if T_i takes a step, then so too can the abstract model of T_i, all respecting the abstraction relation (we also prove the equivalent for T_j). We attempt to prove this by cases on n. If $n = 0$, then we prove $I(p \, 0)$, else if $n = 1$ we prove $I(p \, 1) \ldots$, at each stage using the knowledge of the previous state to determine the next state (using the definition of Caml reduction). Where reduction may result in several alternatives, for example when reading the value of an undetermined variable (we symbolically execute parametric expressions), we have a branch in the proof. In this way, the machine keeps track of the possible Caml expression at each stage. This allows us to avoid spelling out which states are reachable.

Eventually, the path will loop back to a state already seen. Rather than paths, we consider sequences p which may start in one of these recurrent states. Instead of proving $\forall p \, \forall n \, (\ldots \rightarrow I(p \, n))$ we prove the equivalent $\forall n \, \forall p \, (\ldots \rightarrow I(p \, n))$, by complete induction on n (then cases on n, as above). The induction statement contains quantification over a higher-order object, the function p, which makes it a relatively strong use of induction. Suppose $n > 30$, and $(p \, 30)$ is a recurrent state (not necessarily occurring elsewhere on p). Then consider $n' = n - 30$, and $p' = drop \, 30 \, p$, i.e. p' is the subsequence of p starting at position 30. We can invoke the induction hypothesis on n' (since $n' < n$) with p' as the path (which starts in a recurrent state) to show $I(p' \, n')$, i.e. $I(p \, n)$ and we have finished the proof. This technique does not require the state space to be finite, or for computations to terminate, indeed our threads never terminate. To preempt possible mis-readings, we emphasize that the recurrent states are not necessarily states that have been seen previously on the path.

We wish to avoid considering the interleavings of each thread, so we use a form of rely-guarantee style reasoning [Jon81]. Our system is a parallel composition of two threads T_i, T_j. Write this as $T_i|T_j$. The lemma we want to prove is that if T_i takes a step, so too can the abstract model. Then we replace the state of T_j with some arbitrary (but reachable for $T_i|T_j$) state of T_j, and replace the transitions of T_j with I_j where I_j represents the invariant guaranteed by (an arbitrary number of steps of) T_j. In our case, I_j simply states that the *trys j* and *turn* variables in the Caml state are either *Const TTrue* or *Const FFalse*, and the *trys i* variable is preserved. A key point is that the reachability of $T_i|I_j$

is at least that of $T_i|T_j$. This technique extends smoothly to cope with more than two threads.

At every step we have to consider that I_j may make a transition, in which case we invoke the induction hypothesis, since the state of T_j is unchanged. This leads to lengthy proofs. We can reduce the proof size by half in the following way. Instead of considering transitions of $T_i|I_j$, we consider transitions of T_i', where $(T_i'\ x\ x') \leftrightarrow \exists y\ (T_i\ x\ y \wedge I_j\ y\ x')$. In effect, our transitions include steps of T_i together with interference from I_j. The key point, again, is that the reachability of T_i' is at least that of $T_i|I_j$, and therefore at least that of $T_i|T_j$. Note that we have now modularised the proof, since we are considering an sts T_i' which is very close to the sts for our original single thread T_i. Again, this technique extends smoothly to cope with more than two threads.

We have reduced the problem to examining paths of a single "thread" sts T_i' that looks similar to T_i. The proofs consist of little more than simplification to execute the reduction steps, and to check abstract transitions match concrete transitions, and some manual instantiation of the induction hypothesis when reaching a recurrent state. So the parts of the proof which are specific to Peterson's algorithm are reduced to simplification, whilst the techniques described above can be captured in general lemmas, and reused in other settings. This concludes our discussion of the Caml verification.

5   Background on Weak Memory Models

Programmers usually understand concurrent programs based on a notion of "sequential consistency" [Kaw00], i.e. there is some sequential execution of the program which validates the observed behaviour. For example, suppose two concurrent threads T_r, T_w execute as follows. All variables are initialized to 0. T_w writes 1 to location x, then 2 to location y. T_r reads 2 from location y, then 0 from location x.

$$T_w :\ x \leftarrow 1;\ y \leftarrow 2;$$
$$T_r :\ y \rightarrow 2;\ x \rightarrow 0;$$

With a sequentially consistent memory, such an execution would be impossible. $y \rightarrow 2$ must occur after $y \leftarrow 2$, and so after $x \leftarrow 1$, in which case $x \rightarrow 0$ should be $x \rightarrow 1$. Although this type of reasoning is usually valid on single processor machines, it is costly to provide such behaviour in multiprocessor machines, so most multicore systems provide weaker guarantees about the order in which reads and writes are seen. In a weak memory model, where no guarantee is provided about the order of reads and writes to *different* memory locations, the execution above might be perfectly feasible. However, most algorithms are verified with a sequentially consistent model of memory. In the presence of weak memory models, existing algorithms must be modified (or new algorithms invented), along with new proofs of correctness. Practical experience bears out these claims. For example, Holzmann [HB06] describes how a standard implementation of Peterson's algorithm was observed to fail when executing on the Intel Pentium D processor.

Weak memory models are difficult to program against. Indeed, it is known [Kaw00] that problems such as mutual exclusion are impossible to solve, even with relatively strong memory models, without explicit synchronization primitives, such as a "memory barrier" instruction. A memory barrier ensures that all writes on all processors are flushed to main memory. Although these operations can provide the guarantees programmers need, they are typically very expensive to execute, so that there is a desire to reduce their use as much as possible.

In general there is a three-way trade off, between the strength of the synchronization primitive, the extent to which the primitive is used in an algorithm, and the strength of the memory model. In this work, we fix our synchronization primitive as a per location memory barrier. We must now choose between a strong algorithm (many memory barriers) coupled to a weak memory model, or a weak algorithm with a strong memory model. We choose a strong algorithm, i.e. we emphasize portability between memory models over efficiency of the algorithm. We modify Peterson's algorithm slightly to work with a weak memory. With reference to the original pseudocode, Fig. 2, we include memory barriers after the first write of each thread to their **try** variables, and after writes to the **turn** variable.

6   Weak Memory Model Formalization

Compared to the previous abstract formalization, the model is more complex. Reads and writes no longer refer directly to memory. Memory locations must be reified in the model, so that we can talk about a write to a particular memory location. We model the history of writes by maintaining a list, *pending-writes*, which is updated every time a thread writes to memory.

types *thread-id* $= bool$ **datatype** *loc* $= Turn \mid Try\ thread\text{-}id$

datatype $pc = NonCrit \mid SetTry \mid Barrier\ loc \mid SetTurn \mid Test \mid Crit \mid Exit$

types $val = bool$ **types** $memory = loc \Rightarrow val$
types $pending\text{-}writes = (thread\text{-}id * loc * val)\ list$
types $pcs = thread\text{-}id \Rightarrow pc$ **types** $peterson\text{-}state = memory * pending\text{-}writes * pcs$

pending-writes is a purely logical construct that reflects the history of the trace into the current state, allowing easier invariant proofs. It is *not* intended that a real implementation maintain a cache of pending writes. The *memory*, a map from locations to values, is also a logical construct. The interpretation of the *memory* at location *loc* will turn out to be the following: *if there have been no writes by any thread to loc since the last memory barrier, then two threads reading from loc agree on the value, which is (memory loc)*. Our proofs are valid for any memory model where the memory barrier satisfies this property.

On executing a memory barrier for a location *loc*, if there is some pending write for *loc*, then the memory is updated by taking the last write that some thread made to *loc*. The thread that is chosen need not be the thread executing

$\vee\ ((ipc,ipc') = (Barrier\ Turn, Test)$
$\quad \wedge\ barrier\ Turn\ (memory,pws)\ (memory',pws'))$

$\vee\ ((ipc,ipc') = (Test, Crit)$
$\quad \wedge\ (read\ memory\ pws\ (i, Try\ j, False) \vee read\ memory\ pws\ (i, Turn, i))$
$\quad \wedge\ (memory',pws') = (memory,pws))$

Fig. 4. Peterson's algorithm, modified for weak memory, excerpt

the memory barrier instruction. All pending writes for *loc* are then dropped from the list of pending writes. If there are no pending writes, memory remains unaltered.

constdefs *barrier* :: *loc* ⇒ *memory* ∗ *pending-writes* ⇒ *memory* ∗ *pending-writes* ⇒ *bool*

In accordance with our logical interpretation of pending writes, the *write* operation simply appends the write to the list of pending writes. Since we aim to keep our memory model as weak as possible, we declare but do not define the *read* operation. We will later constrain *read* with properties that are required for the correctness proof. The transitions are phrased in a similar style to before, and we give an excerpt only, Fig. 4.

constdefs *write* :: (*thread-id* ∗ *loc* ∗ *val*) ⇒ *pending-writes* ⇒ *pending-writes*
$\quad$*write tidlocv pws* ≡ *tidlocv#pws*

consts *read* :: *memory* ⇒ *pending-writes* ⇒ (*thread-id* ∗ *loc* ∗ *val*) ⇒ *bool*

7   Proof of Correctness

The weak memory proof follows the outline of the previous abstract proof. The read operation depends on the memory and the pending writes. Our first task is to characterise the pending writes to each location, given the state of a thread. For example, in the following lemma, invariant P shows that if thread i is in the non-critical state, then the pending writes to i's try variable are either empty, or contain a single write by i, setting the try variable to false. The lemma is named because it logically precedes Lemma 10.5.1; it does not appear in [Lyn96].

lemma *lemma-10-5-0*:
$\quad$**defines** *P-def*: $P \equiv \lambda\ i\ memory\ pws\ pcs\ ipc.$
$\quad$*let pws-Try-i = filter* (λ (*tid,loc,v*). *loc* = *Try i*) *pws in*
$\quad$*if ipc* ∈ {*NonCrit,SetTry*} *then pws-Try-i* ∈ {[],[(*i, Try i,False*)]}
$\quad$*else if ipc* = *Barrier* (*Try i*) *then pws-Try-i* ∈ {[(*i, Try i, True*)], [(*i, Try i, True*),(*i, Try i,False*)]}
$\quad$*else pws-Try-i* = []
$\quad$**defines** *R-def*: $R \equiv \lambda\ i\ memory\ pws\ pcs\ ipc.$
$\quad$*let pws-i-Turn = filter* (λ (*tid,loc,v*). *tid* = *i* ∧ *loc* = *Turn*) *pws in*

if ipc = Barrier Turn then pws-i-Turn $\in$ {[(i, Turn,¬i)],[]}
else pws-i-Turn = []
shows $\forall$ *p. is-path peterson-sts p*
$\longrightarrow$ ($\forall$ *n i.*
let (memory,pws,pcs) = p n in
let ipc = pcs i in
P i memory pws pcs ipc
$\land$ *R i memory pws pcs ipc*)

One might imagine that placing a memory barrier after every write to a location is sufficient to ensure correctness. This is not correct for our model of memory, because it is still possible to read from a location with a pending write, in which case the read is unconstrained. Another subtlety is the interaction of the memory barriers. For example, thread i may have written to variable *turn*, and be on the point of doing a memory barrier to force the write to memory. In the meantime, the other thread j may also write to *turn*, and complete the subsequent memory barrier. In this case, i will execute the memory barrier but i's pending write will have been discarded by j's memory barrier. This case can be seen in the characterisation of the pending writes, since if i's *pc* is *Barrier Turn*, the pending writes to the turn variable may be the empty list. In this scenario, i's write may never reach memory at all.

With *lemma-10-5-0*, we can prove the equivalent of *lemma-10-5-1*, i.e. that if thread i's program counter lies in the range *SetTurn* to *Exit*, and thread j reads i's try variable to be v, then v must be true. The proof requires a restriction on the behaviour of the *read* operation: if there have been no writes to a location since the last memory barrier for that location, and two threads read that location, then they read the same value. It is easiest to express this as the existence of a function *memory* from locations to values, which gives the common value that threads must read in case there are no pending writes. We use a *locale* to capture this assumption, and the proof is conducted within this locale, in the scope of the assumption.

locale l = **assumes** a:
$\forall$ *memory pws tid loc v. filter* (λ (*tid,loc',v*). *loc' = loc*) *pws = []*
$\longrightarrow$ (*read memory pws (tid,loc,v) = (memory loc = v)*)

We can now prove the equivalent of *lemma-10-5-2*, property Q in the following lemma statement. We require an auxiliary fact to handle the case that a thread's write to the *turn* variable has been discarded by the memory barrier of the other thread. For example, it is conceivable that j writes to *turn*, i writes to *turn*, i performs a memory barrier, and subsequently enters the critical section. j then performs a memory barrier (but there are no pending writes), reads i's write to *turn* which gives priority to j, and so enters the critical section. However, if i enters the critical section, then i's memory barrier must have committed j's pending write to the *turn* variable. In which case, j is prevented from entering the critical section. Some work is required to phrase this reasoning as the invariant P. As before, our final correctness theorem follows directly from Q, since *memory Turn* cannot be both i and j simultaneously.

lemma (in l) *lemma-10-5-2*:
  defines *P-def*:
  $P \equiv \lambda\ i\ ipc\ jpc\ memory\ pws.$
  $ipc = Crit$
  $\wedge\ jpc = Barrier\ Turn$
  $\wedge\ filter\ (\lambda(tid,loc,c).\ loc = Turn)\ pws = []$
  $\longrightarrow\ memory\ Turn = i$
  defines *Q-def*:
  $Q \equiv \lambda\ i\ ipc\ jpc\ memory\ pws.$
  $ipc = Crit$
  $\wedge\ jpc \in \{\,Test,Crit\}$
  $\longrightarrow\ memory\ Turn = i$

shows
  $\forall\ p.\ is\text{-}path\ peterson\text{-}sts\ p$
  $\longrightarrow (\forall\ n\ i.$
  let $(memory,pws,pcs) = p\ n\ in$
  let $ipc = pcs\ i\ in$
  let $j = \neg\ i\ in$
  let $jpc = pcs\ j\ in$
  $P\ i\ ipc\ jpc\ memory\ pws$
  $\wedge\ Q\ i\ ipc\ jpc\ memory\ pws)$

8 Related Work

A substantial amount of program verification has used Hoare logics [Hoa69]. A state of the art example of mechanized Hoare reasoning for while-programs with state is [MN05]. The language treated is significantly simpler than that here. The work of Homeier [HM95] also treats a very simple language. This work includes a verification condition generator, essentially a tool that constructs a syntax-directed proof for the program (augmented with user hints and invariants), and returns the steps that could not be proven automatically as "verification conditions".

Our work uses operational reasoning directly above an operational semantics. Operational reasoning is much more flexible then Hoare logic, since any technique allowed by the meta-logic (in our case higher-order logic) is directly usable. On the other hand, we know of no essential advantages of Hoare logic over operational reasoning. Strother Moore has also followed this course. The detail of the operational models mandate mechanical support, but current theorem provers are more than up to the task. Indeed, Strother Moore states[2] "had there been decent theorem provers in the 1960s, Floyd and Hoare would never have had to invent Floyd-Hoare semantics!" His work [LM04] focuses on operational Java program verification. However, he first compiles the Java to bytecode, and then verifies this. Correctness properties are phrased as properties of the bytecode, and reasoning occurs above the bytecode, not above the original Java program. The examples treated, such as an "add one" program, and a Java function that implements factorial, are significantly simpler than the work presented here. Concurrency, and the problem of the state space explosion in interleaving between threads, is also not tackled. A very rare example of operational reasoning applied to a high-level language is the work of

---

[2] http://www.cs.utexas.edu/users/moore/best-ideas/vcg/index.html

Compton [Com05] who verifies a version of Stenning's protocol for a restricted model of Caml and UDP. This work is similar, but again much simpler, than that presented here.

Of course, where concurrency is involved, all these examples assume a sequentially consistent memory model. There has been much work on weak memory models. The PhD of Kawash [Kaw00] provides good references into the literature. Mechanization usually takes the form of model checking. Examples include [MLP04], where the authors tackle the problem by analysing dependencies between reads and writes; and [BAM06], where the authors use a constraint based approach based on the SAT encoding method in [GYS04]. As far as interactive mechanization goes, Mike Gordon has some early unpublished work[3] on memory models of the Alpha processor.

For weak memory models, model checking offers a tractable approach to many of the main problems. However, model checking is not always an option. The thrust of our work is to see if traditional reasoning techniques, employed when *designing* algorithms such as Peterson's, can scale to the weak memory case. Our experience leads us to believe that they can, but that the effort is great, and mechanical assistance seemingly mandatory. Put simply, it is very hard for humans to design concurrent algorithms if they are restricted to reasoning about the interleaving of thread transitions. Weak memory models add even more complexity. However, new ways of thinking (and proving facts) about weak memory may alleviate the problem.

9   Conclusion

We presented the verification of a Caml implementation of Peterson's algorithm, down to the operational semantics. The proofs were non-trivial, and we spent considerable effort phrasing the lemmas and shaping the induction statements, as described in Sect. 4. However, once the overall structure of the proof was in place, the actual body of the proof was mostly symbolic execution. The lemmas, induction schemes, and proof techniques are general, and have the potential to scale to real programs in real languages, so that future verifications will benefit from the experience described here. We also addressed the problem of weak memory models by verifying a version of Peterson's algorithm running on a weak memory model.

Our model of Caml included all the features necessary to support the example of Peterson's algorithm. However, we are interested in verifying other programs which use more Caml features. To this end, we are working with several others on a highly realistic model of Caml, using the Ott tool [SNO+] to state our definitions. We intend to develop metatheory for this model, and operational proofs of program correctness for other Caml programs. The next program we intend to verify is a Caml implementation of a fully automatic theorem prover for first order logic [RM05].

---

[3] See http://www.cl.cam.ac.uk/research/hvg/FTP/FTP.html

References

[BAM06] Burckhardt, S., Alur, R., Martin, M.M.K.: Bounded model checking of concurrent data types on relaxed memory models: A case study. In: Ball, T., Jones, R.B. (eds.) CAV 2006. LNCS, vol. 4144, pp. 489–502. Springer, Heidelberg (2006)

[Com05] Compton, M.: Stenning's protocol implemented in UDP and verified in Isabelle. In: Atkinson, M.D., Dehne, F.K.H.A. (eds.) CATS. CRPIT, vol. 41, pp. 21–30. Australian Computer Society (2005)

[Gon05] Gonthier, G.: A computer-checked proof of the Four Colour Theorem (2005), http://research.microsoft.com/~gonthier/4colproof.pdf

[GYS04] Gopalakrishnan, G., Yang, Y., Sivaraj, H.: An efficient execution verification tool for memory orderings. In: Alur, R., Peled, D.A. (eds.) CAV 2004. LNCS, vol. 3114, pp. 401–413. Springer, Heidelberg (2004)

[HB06] Holzmann, G.J., Bosnacki, D.: The design of a multi-core extension of the Spin Model Checker. In: FMCAD. Formal Methods in Computer Aided Design (November 2006)

[HM95] Homeier, P.V., Martin, D.F.: A mechanically verified verification condition generator. Comput. J. 38(2), 131–141 (1995)

[Hoa69] Hoare, C.A.R.: An axiomatic basis for computer programming. Communications of the ACM, 12 (1969)

[Jon81] Jones, C.B.: Development methods for computer programs including a notion of interference. Technical Report PRG-25, Programming Research Group, Oxford University Computing Laboratory (1981)

[Kaw00] Kawash, J.Y.: Limitations and capabilities of weak memory consistency systems. PhD thesis, Computer Science, University of Calgary (2000)

[LM04] Liu, H., Moore, J.S.: Java program verification via a JVM deep embedding in ACL2. In: Slind, K., Bunker, A., Gopalakrishnan, G.C. (eds.) TPHOLs 2004. LNCS, vol. 3223, pp. 184–200. Springer, Heidelberg (2004)

[Lyn96] Lynch, N.A.: Distributed Algorithms. Morgan Kaufmann, San Francisco (1996)

[MJ84] Morris, F.L., Jones, C.B.: An early program proof by Alan Turing. Annals of the History of Computing 6(2), 143–193 (1984)

[MLP04] Midkiff, S.P., Lee, J., Padua, D.A.: A compiler for multiple memory models. Concurrency and Computation: Practice and Experience 16(2-3), 197–220 (2004)

[MN05] Mehta, F., Nipkow, T.: Proving pointer programs in higher-order logic. Information and Computation 199, 200–227 (2005)

[Pet81] Peterson, G.L.: Myths about the mutual exclusion problem. Information Processing Letters 12(3), 115–116 (1981)

[Rid] Ridge, T.: Simpson's four slot algorithm in Isabelle/HOL, available online, at http://www.cl.cam.ac.uk/~tjr22

[RM05] Ridge, T., Margetson, J.: A mechanically verified, sound and complete theorem prover for FOL. In: Hurd, J., Melham, T. (eds.) TPHOLs 2005. LNCS, vol. 3603, Springer, Heidelberg (2005)

[SNO+] Sewell, P., Nardelli, F.Z., Owens, S., Peskine, G., Ridge, T., Sarkar, S., Strniša, R.: Ott: Effective tool support for the working semanticist. In: ICFP 2007. The 12th ACM SIGPLAN International Conference on Functional Programming (accepted, 2007)

Proof Pearl:
Wellfounded Induction on the Ordinals Up to ε_0

Matt Kaufmann[1] and Konrad Slind[2]

[1] Department of Computer Sciences, University of Texas, Austin
kaufmann@cs.utexas.edu
[2] School of Computing, University of Utah
slind@cs.utah.edu

Abstract. We discuss a proof of the wellfounded induction theorem for the ordinals up to ε_0. The proof is performed on the embedding of ACL2 in HOL-4, thus providing logical justification for that embedding and supporting the claim that the ACL2 logic has a model.

1 Introduction

A formalization of the ACL2 logic in higher order logic is described in [5,6]. The formalization involved defining the type of s-expressions, defining the primitive functions of ACL2, and stating the logical axioms used by ACL2. The formal *soundness* of the ACL2 logic has been pursued by doing a theory interpretation: if each of the ACL2 axioms can be proved as a theorem, then ACL2 has a model. The main motivation for doing this proof was to ensure that the embedding is logically sound. More specifically, we want to know that if a theorem, ϕ, is proved in a given ACL2 theory, $\mathcal{T}$, then the translation of ϕ to SEXP (the ACL2 theory in HOL) is provable in HOL from the translation of $\mathcal{T}$ into SEXP. Thus, ACL2 theorems can be safely imported into HOL, allowing principled access to the ACL2 proof engine (which includes its evaluator) from HOL. In the work reported in [5,6] all of the axioms identified for ACL2 were proved in HOL, except for those sanctioning the use of induction and recursion. This note finishes the task.[1]

Induction and recursion in ACL2 are important sources of reasoning power. In this paper, we show how the wellfounded induction and recursion theorems already proved in HOL-4 can be instantiated to obtain the induction and recursion theorems used in ACL2. The essential lemma is that a particular order relation ($<_o$) on the ordinals up to ε_0 is wellfounded.

---

[1] Hanbing Liu and Robert Krug [email communications] have subsequently discovered first-order axioms that are not made explicit in the list of axioms distributed with ACL2, and hence have not been proved in HOL. All such missing axioms need to be made explicit and then proved in order truly to finish the task, but addressing that deficiency is potential future work beyond the scope of this paper.

K. Schneider and J. Brandt (Eds.): TPHOLs 2007, LNCS 4732, pp. 294–301, 2007.
© Springer-Verlag Berlin Heidelberg 2007

2   Ordinal Notation for ε_0

An *ordinal notation* gives a syntactic representation for the ordinals, and thus supports computation over entities capable of representing a wide variety of infinite sets. The main use of the ordinals in ACL2 is to provide a basis for the termination proofs required to install recursive definitions in the logic and to justify induction schemes. However, there are other uses as well; for example, an ACL2 formalization of algorithms implementing ordinal arithmetic may be found in [9].

Different notations capture different initial segments of the countable ordinals. One important notation captures the ordinals up to ε_0. In the following, we will present this notation as an exercise in datatypes and inductive definitions in higher order logic and, as well, provide the ACL2 definitions actually used in the proof. A point worth noting is that we are not ascribing any semantics at all to the notation; a separate proof would be needed to show that indeed the following definitions do correspond to the ordinals up to ε_0. A good basis for such work would be Huffman's formalization of the countable ordinals in Isabelle/HOL [7].

Definition 1 (Raw syntax of ordinals). *The raw syntax of ordinals is captured by the following ML-style datatype definition:*

```
osyntax = End of num
        | Plus of (osyntax * num) * osyntax
```

We will occasionally write Plus *as infix* $+$, *and will also treat* Plus *as being curried rather than taking a pair of arguments.*

As can be seen, an osyntax element is essentially a list of *exponent* $\times$ *coefficient* pairs, ending in a natural number. The intuition is that the syntax $(\mathsf{Plus}(\alpha, k)\ t)$ represents the ordinal $\omega^\alpha \cdot k + t$, but a few more definitions are necessary to ensure this. On the raw syntax we first define some basic functions and the notion of rank. The *rank* of an ordinal x is a natural number describing the height of the tower of exponents in the first term of x.

Definition 2 (osyntax operations).

$$\mathsf{finp}(\mathsf{End}\ \_) = \mathsf{T} \qquad\qquad \mathsf{tail}(\mathsf{Plus}\ \_\ t) = t$$
$$\mathsf{finp}(\mathsf{Plus}\ \_\ \_) = \mathsf{F}$$

$$\mathsf{expt}(\mathsf{End}\ \_) = \mathsf{End}(0) \qquad\qquad \mathsf{coeff}(\mathsf{End}\ x) = x$$
$$\mathsf{expt}(\mathsf{Plus}(e, k)\ t) = e \qquad\qquad \mathsf{coeff}(\mathsf{Plus}(e, k)\ t) = k$$

$$\mathsf{rank}(\mathsf{End}\ \_) = 0$$
$$\mathsf{rank}(\mathsf{Plus}(e, k)\ t) = 1 + \mathsf{rank}\ e$$

The order relation $<_o$ is defined with an inductive definition.

Definition 3 ($<_o$).

$$\frac{x < y}{\mathsf{End}(x) <_o \mathsf{End}(y)} \qquad\qquad \overline{\mathsf{End}(x) <_o \mathsf{Plus}(e, k)\, t}$$

$$\frac{e_1 <_o e_2}{\mathsf{Plus}(e_1, k_1)\, t_1 <_o \mathsf{Plus}(e_2, k_2)\, t_2} \qquad\qquad \frac{e_1 = e_2 \qquad k_1 < k_2}{\mathsf{Plus}(e_1, k_1)\, t_1 <_o \mathsf{Plus}(e_2, k_2)\, t_2}$$

$$\frac{e_1 = e_2 \qquad k_1 = k_2 \qquad t_1 <_o t_2}{\mathsf{Plus}(e_1, k_1)\, t_1 <_o \mathsf{Plus}(e_2, k_2)\, t_2}$$

The ordinals less than ε_0 are then the subset of the raw syntax elements meeting the following inductively defined predicate.

Definition 4 (Cantor Normal Form).

$$\frac{}{\mathsf{ord}(\mathsf{End}\, x)} \qquad \frac{\mathsf{ord}(e) \qquad e \neq \mathsf{End}(0) \qquad 0 < k \qquad \mathsf{ord}(t) \qquad \mathsf{expt}(t) <_o e}{\mathsf{ord}(\mathsf{Plus}(e, k)\, t)}$$

Thus, if $\mathsf{ord}(x)$ holds, x has the form

$$w^{\alpha_1} \cdot k_1 + w^{\alpha_2} \cdot k_2 + \cdots + w^{\alpha_n} \cdot k_n + p$$

and successive exponents strictly decrease, *i.e.*, $\alpha_n <_o \cdots <_o \alpha_2 <_o \alpha_1$. Also, exponents and coefficients must be non-zero.

2.1   ACL2 Definitions

The above definitions are for essentially presentational purposes, as our verification must use the actual definitions used by ACL2 (as represented in the HOL-4 theory SEXP). Since ACL2 does not have the strict type system of HOL, and also requires total functions, the definitions have to take care over default cases. We will use a shorthand from [6] for bridging the gap from s-expressions to the booleans used by HOL. In ACL2, a statement is false if it is equal to the symbol nil; otherwise it is true.

Definition 5. $\models x = (x \neq \mathsf{nil})$

In the following collection of definitions, an atom is anything that is not a cons; less is the usual (strict) order on numbers; nat injects a natural number into the complex rationals used by ACL2; and natp is true if its argument is a natural number. Finally, sharp-eyed readers will note that rank delivers a HOL natural number and not an s-expression, unlike the other definitions. This provided a small convenience in the proof (by induction) of the main lemma.

Definition 6 (ACL2 formalization).

finp x = atom x
tail x = cdr x
expt x = if $\models$ finp x then (nat 0) else car(car x)
coeff x = if $\models$ finp x then x else cdr(car x)
rank x = if $\models$ finp x then 0 else $1 +$ rank(expt x)

oless x y =
    if $\models$ finp x then (if $\models$ not(finp y) then not(finp y) else less x y) else
    if $\models$ finp y then nil else
    if $\models$ not(equal (expt x) (expt y)) then oless (expt x) (expt y) else
    if $\models$ not(equal(coeff x) (coeff y)) then less (coeff x) (coeff y)
    else oless (tail x) (tail y)

ord x =
    if $\models$ finp x then (natp x) else
    if $\models$ consp(car x) then
    if $\models$ ord(expt x) then
    if $\models$ not(equal (nat 0) (expt x)) then
    if $\models$ posp(coeff x) then
    if $\models$ ord(tail x) then oless (expt(tail x) (expt x))
    else nil else nil else nil else nil else nil

For readability we give a definition describing an ordinal with rank no greater than n.

Definition 7. ordn n x = ord(x) $\wedge$ rank $x \leq n$

The reader may think that the proof we are about to conduct is made more difficult by these apparently more complex definitions; however, the true complexity of the proof lies at a more abstract level and the differences between styles of definition are lost in the noise.

3   The Proof

The final theorem is a simple consequence of the following lemma.[2]

Theorem 1 (Main Lemma). *Every set having at least one ordinal of rank $\leq n$ has an $<_o$-minimal element.*

$$\forall n. \ \forall P. \ (\exists x. \ P \ x \wedge \text{ordn} \ n \ x) \supset$$
$$\exists x. \ P \ x \wedge \text{ordn} \ n \ x \wedge \forall y. \ \text{ordn} \ n \ y \wedge y <_o x \supset \neg P \ y$$

---

[2] After developing the proof, we were surprised to recall a similar, informal proof in the ACL2 online documentation under the heading *Proof-of-well-foundedness*. Of course, the theorem is second-order and therefore cannot be stated within ACL2, let alone proved in that system.

Proof. A proof by complete induction is perhaps simpler, but we originally obtained the proof by mathematical induction, and there is no essential difference. We will be perhaps painfully pedantic in the following proof; the reason for this is that we want to provide enough detail that this can be a useful pedagogical example.

We can restrict our attention to non-empty sets of ordinals of rank $\leq n$ since adding non-ordinals or ordinals of rank $> n$ to the set P makes no difference to the existence of an $<_o$-minimal element.

Base Case. *Every non-empty set of ordinals of rank ≤ 0 is a set of natural numbers, so has a minimal (in fact least) element by the well-ordering property, and this is an $<_o$-minimal element since natural numbers are smaller than any other kind of ordinal.*

Step Case. *Assume the IH. We want to show that every non-empty set of ordinals of rank $\leq n + 1$ has an $<_o$-minimal element. So assume we are given a non-empty set of ordinals of rank $\leq n + 1$. Either some element of the set has rank $\leq n$, or every element has rank exactly $n + 1$. In the former case, we can immediately use the IH to get an $<_o$-minimal element.*

Otherwise, we can refine our goal to that of showing that every non-empty set of ordinals of rank $= n + 1$ has a minimal element. We then proceed by contradiction, namely we assume there exists a non-empty set of ordinals, each of rank $n + 1$, where for each element in the set, there exists an $<_o$-smaller element also in the set. That means that there exists a non-empty set of such sets:[3]

$$\exists S. \, (\exists s_i. \, s_i \in S) \, \wedge$$
$$(\forall s_i. \, s_i \in S = (\exists x. \, x \in s_i) \wedge$$
$$(\forall x \in s_i. \, \mathsf{ord}(x) \wedge (\mathsf{rank} \, x = n + 1) \wedge \exists y. \, y \in s_i \wedge y <_o x))$$

From that we know that the set of first exponents of ordinals occurring anywhere in S is non-empty.

$$\exists E. \, (\exists e. \, e \in E) \wedge \forall e. \, e \in E = \exists s_i \, x. \, s_i \in S \wedge x \in s_i \wedge e = \mathsf{expt} \, x$$

Moreover, every element of E has rank n, so the IH applies, and E has a minimal element α_1. Now consider some $s_j \in S$ such that α_1 is the first exponent of some element of s_j:

$$\exists s_j \, x. \, s_j \in S \wedge x \in s_j \wedge \alpha_1 = \mathsf{expt} \, x$$

We are going to work inside s_j from now on. Consider s_{α_1}, the subset of s_j consisting of all ordinals with first exponent α_1; this is a non-empty set. Now $\{\mathsf{coeff}(x) \mid x \in s_{\alpha_1}\}$, the set of first coefficients of elements of s_{α_1}, is a non-empty set of numbers, so has a minimal element k_1. This yields s_{α_1,k_1}, a non-empty subset of s_{α_1} where each element has first exponent k_1.

$$\exists s_{\alpha_1,k_1}. \, (\exists a. \, a \in s_{\alpha_1,k_1}) \wedge (\forall b. \, b \in s_{\alpha_1,k_1} = b \in s_{\alpha_1} \wedge \mathsf{coeff}(b) = k_1)$$

---

[3] This is the crucial use of higher order in the proof, moving from a set having a property to a set of sets, each having that property.

We have $s_{\alpha_1,k_1} \subseteq s_{\alpha_1} \subseteq s_j \in S$. At this point, we have in effect constructed the first term in a minimal witness $\omega^{\alpha_1} \cdot k_1 + \ldots$, which will result in our desired contradiction. We could continue to find α_2 and k_2 and so on. The following steps make this 'and so on' precise.

Consider the set of all tails of elements in s_{α_1,k_1}. This is non-empty.

$$\exists \mathsf{Tails}.\ (\exists b.\ b \in \mathsf{Tails}) \wedge \forall c.\ c \in \mathsf{Tails} = \exists b.\ b \in s_{\alpha_1,k_1} \wedge c = \mathsf{tail}\ b$$

Now we do a case split on whether there is an element in Tails with rank $\leq n$. If there is, we may use the IH to obtain a minimal element $t \in \mathsf{Tails}$, and use this to obtain $\omega^{\alpha_1} \cdot k_1 + t$, an element of s_j with no element of s_j being, by construction, $<_o$-smaller than it. This contradicts $s_j \in S$.

Otherwise, every element in Tails has rank $n+1$. Now consider whether Tails has a $<_o$-minimal element. If it does, then we again build a minimal element of s_j and obtain a contradiction. Otherwise, Tails is a non-empty set of ordinals, each of rank $n + 1$, with no minimal element. So $\mathsf{Tails} \in S$. The smallest first exponent of any element of Tails must be $<_o$-smaller than α_1; however, recall that α_1 was chosen to be the smallest first exponent of any element in any set in S. So $\mathsf{Tails} \notin S$. Contradiction.

Theorem 2 (Corollary). *Every set with at least one ordinal has an $<_o$-minimal element.*

$$\forall P.\ (\exists x.\ P\ x \wedge \mathsf{ord}\ x) \supset \exists x.\ P\ x \wedge \mathsf{ord}\ x \wedge \forall y.\ \mathsf{ord}\ y \wedge y <_o x \supset \neg P\ y$$

Proof. By instantiating n in the main lemma to $\mathsf{rank}\ x$. *In other words, the induction of the Main Lemma is essentially on the rank of x.*

We now recall the formal definition of wellfoundedness. A relation R is well-founded if every non-empty set has an R-minimal element:

Definition 8 (Wellfoundedness).

$$\mathsf{WF}(R) \equiv \forall P.\ (\exists w.\ P\ w) \supset \exists min.\ P\ min \wedge \forall b.\ R\ b\ min \supset \neg P\ b.$$

Then if we define $<_{ord} \equiv \lambda x\ y.\ \mathsf{ord}\ x \wedge \mathsf{ord}\ y \wedge x <_o y$, which just requires that the arguments of $<_o$ be in Cantor Normal form, it is trivial to prove $\mathsf{WF}(<_{ord})$. Now we are ready to directly use the general theorem for induction already available in HOL-4:

$$\mathsf{WF}(R) \supset (\forall x.\ (\forall y.\ R\ y\ x \supset P\ y) \supset P\ x) \supset \forall x.\ P\ x\ .$$

The desired induction theorem is a simple instantiation, given the fact that measure functions into wellfounded sets yield wellfounded sets.

Theorem 3 (ε_0-Induction).

$$(\forall x.\ (\forall y.\ m(y) <_{ord} m(x) \supset P\ y) \supset P\ x) \supset \forall x.\ P\ x$$

3.1   Recursion

The wellfounded recursion theorem in HOL-4 is formulated as

$$\mathsf{WF}(R) \supset \exists! f. \ \forall x. \ f(x) = M \ (f \,|\, R, x) \ x$$

where the notation $(f \,|\, R, x)$ restricts f to be applied only to elements that are R-less than x. A corresponding recursion theorem for the ordinals up to ε_0 is again a simple instantiation.

Theorem 4 (ε_0-Recursion).

$$\exists! f. \ \forall x. \ f(x) = M \ (f \,|\, (\lambda x y. \ m(x) <_{ord} m(y)), x) \ x$$

Although this recursion theorem is appealingly succinct, it is not used to justify recursive definitions in ACL2 [8]. Instead, a primitive recursive interpreter-based definition (with a "clock") can in principle be defined to build a function satisfying a specified recursive equation. The interpreter-based definition always terminates (given a large enough clock) because of the well-foundedness of $<_{ord}$. The relationship of the existing approach in ACL2 and the ε_0-recursion theorem may be interesting to explore.

4   Discussion

We have formally proved ε_0-induction in higher order logic, thus helping finalize an embedding of ACL2 in HOL-4 [5,6]; the whole development may be found in the `examples/acl2/ml` directory in the HOL-4 distribution. The presentation of the proof of the Main Lemma is informal but it follows the formal proof quite closely, e.g., important formulas occurring in the proof have been faithfully transcribed. In particular, after the induction on rank, the backbone of the proof is the existence of the sets S, E, s_j, s_{α_1}, s_{α_1, k_1}, and *Tails*. We do not claim that the proof given here is original or unsurpassably beautiful—although we like it—but it has been presented in detail so that others can follow and adapt it.

The ordinal ε_0, originally defined by Cantor, is very important in the history of logic and set theory. Gentzen used PRA (Primitive Recursive Arithmetic, a subsystem of PA, Peano Arithmetic) plus ε_0-induction to prove the consistency of PA [2]. Hence, by Goedel's second incompleteness theorem, ε_0-induction is not provable in PA. (Of course, ε_0-induction is not even a formula of PA, so some work needs to be done to give this statement some force.) Gentzen showed how to derive ε_0-induction in [3], by means of proof theory, in contrast to our set-theoretic proof. An accessible discussion on the use of ordinals in proof theory, especially for PA and related systems, may be found in [1].

Although the main point of our formal proof of ε_0-induction is to help check the axiomatization of ACL2 it may be that—in analogy to Goodstein's entertaining theorem [4] which can be stated in PA, but the proof of which needs ε_0-induction—useful theorems emerge which are not provable in ACL2. In that case, it may be possible to transfer the statement to the ACL2 embedding in HOL, and prove it there, justifying its subsequent use in ACL2.

Acknowledgements

This material is based upon work supported by DARPA and the National Science Foundation under Grant No. CNS-0429591.

References

1. Franzen, T.: Inexhaustibility, a non-exhaustive treatment. Lecture Notes in Logic, vol. 16. A.K. Peters (2004)
2. Gentzen, G.: The consistency of elementary number theory. In: Szabo, M.E. (ed.) The Collected Papers of Gerhard Gentzen. Studies in Logic and the Foundations of Mathematics, North Holland, Amsterdam (1969)
3. Gentzen, G.: Provabillity and nonprovability of restricted transfinite induction in elementary number theory. In: Szabo, M.E. (ed.) The Collected Papers of Gerhard Gentzen. Studies in Logic and the Foundations of Mathematics, North Holland, Amsterdam (1969)
4. Goodstein, R.: On the restricted ordinal theorem. Journal of Symbolic Logic 9, 33–41 (1944)
5. Gordon, M.J.C., Hunt, W.A., Kaufmann, M., Reynolds, J.: An embedding of the ACL2 logic in HOL. In: Proceedings of ACL2 2006. ACM International Conference Proceeding Series, vol. 205, pp. 40–46. ACM Press, New York (2006)
6. Gordon, M.J.C., Hunt, W.A., Kaufmann, M., Reynolds, J.: An integration of HOL and ACL2. In: Proceedings of FMCAD 2006, pp. 153–160. IEEE Computer Society Press, Los Alamitos (2006)
7. Huffman, B.: Countable ordinals. Isabelle Archive of Formal Proofs (November 2005)
8. Kaufmann, M., Moore, J.S.: Structured theory development for a mechanized logic. Journal of Automated Reasoning 26(2), 161–203 (2001)
9. Manolios, P., Vroon, D.: Ordinal arithmetic: Algorithms and mechanization. Journal of Automated Reasoning, 1–37 (2006)

A Monad-Based Modeling and Verification Toolbox with Application to Security Protocols*

Christoph Sprenger and David Basin

Department of Computer Science, ETH Zurich, Switzerland
{sprenger,basin}@inf.ethz.ch

Abstract. We present an advanced modeling and verification toolbox for functional programs with state and exceptions. The toolbox integrates an extensible, monad-based, component model, a monad-based Hoare logic and weakest precondition calculus, and proof systems for temporal logic and bisimilarity. It is implemented in Isabelle/HOL using shallow embeddings and incorporates as much modeling and reasoning power as possible from Isabelle/HOL. We have validated the toolbox's usefulness in a substantial security protocol verification project.

1 Introduction

The choice of a specification formalism with supporting verification methods and tools is critical to the success of substantial verification projects. In order to obtain manageable proofs, models and their properties must be formulated at an appropriate level of abstraction and verification methods and tools must be available for reasoning at that abstraction level. In this paper, we present a comprehensive formalism providing such abstractions for the specification and verification of functional programs with non-pure features, namely state and exceptions. It consists of the following elements: (1) a modeling language capturing the computational structure of the systems under study, (2) a notion of component for structuring models, (3) a notion of component abstraction, including a proof method to establish an abstraction relation between two components, and (4) property specification languages and proof methods. We have implemented this toolbox in Isabelle/HOL [18]. Our aim is to provide a set of practically useful tools rather than to develop meta-theoretical studies about programming languages and logics. Therefore, we work with shallow embeddings and exploit Isabelle/HOL's expressive specification language (for 1–2) and powerful reasoning tools (for 3–4) as much as possible. We now discuss (1)–(4) in turn.

Ad 1. Modeling state and exception handling directly in HOL results in models that are cluttered with additional state parameters and error-handling branches. This situation calls for an additional layer of abstraction, which can be elegantly modeled using monads [15]. In our case, the monad of choice is a deterministic state-exception monad, which extends HOL with operations for sequential composition, state manipulation, and exception handling. All other control structures, such as pattern matching, if-then-else

---

* This work was partially supported by the Zurich Information Security Center. It represents the views of the authors.

K. Schneider and J. Brandt (Eds.): TPHOLs 2007, LNCS 4732, pp. 302–318, 2007.

and function definitions, are borrowed directly from Isabelle/HOL. We would like to stress that most of our method and tools can be easily adapted to other monads.

Ad 2. We take a simple view of components as modules encapsulating a state with interface functions that manipulate this state. We represent the state in an object-oriented style as an extensible record and component composition as record extension and function composition. Using extensible records allows the extended component to automatically inherit properties proved for the base component.

Ad 3. We compare (abstract or refine) components using bisimilarity. Two components are bisimilar if all pairs of equally named interface functions are bisimilar. To show this, we have developed a compositional proof system to establish the bisimilarity of programs. Its judgments and rules resemble those of Hoare logic except that pre- and post-conditions are relations between pairs of states of two programs.

Ad 4. In order to state and prove properties about components, we have embedded several logics in Isabelle/HOL: a weakest pre-condition (WP) calculus, a Hoare logic, and linear-time temporal logic (LTL). All these logics rely on HOL's set theory as their underlying assertion language. The WP calculus is derived from Pitts' evaluation logic [20] and provides the basis for the definition of the Hoare logic. Both of these are tailored to the state-exception monad, whereas the temporal logic is interpreted over standard transition systems. The benefit of embedding these logics in Isabelle/HOL is that this enables the use of the corresponding, well-established proof methods. We reduce the verification of temporal properties to pre-/post-condition and assertional reasoning using standard proof rules [14]. The resulting Hoare triples are proved using a combination of Hoare logic and the underlying WP calculus. While Hoare logic provides the full flexibility of interactive proofs, we may unfold Hoare triples at any point during a proof and invoke the WP calculus, using Isabelle's efficient simplifier to automatically reduce the resulting weakest pre-conditions into simpler HOL assertions.

Our contribution is two-fold. First, we show how to leverage the rich modeling and reasoning infrastructure provided by a theorem prover like Isabelle/HOL for semantic embeddings of various modeling, specification, and verification concepts. This allows us to model, specify and reason at an adequate level of abstraction. We adapt and integrate well-known techniques with less standard and new ones to build a unique, comprehensive, and modular modeling and verification toolbox. Second, we provide a ready-to-use verification toolbox with a wide scope of application. This toolbox has proved its effectiveness in a substantial cryptographic protocol verification project [21]. For a rough idea of the size of the theories involved, our development spans more than 22k lines of Isabelle/HOL sources, organized into more than 50 theories. The toolbox accounts for about 20% of these figures. In particular, the combination of Hoare logic and the WP calculus offers a good degree of proof automation, which was crucial to the successful completion of the sizable verification effort involved. We use examples from our project [21] to illustrate the application of the concepts presented in this paper.

2   Background

Isabelle/HOL notation. In Isabelle/HOL, $t :: T$ denotes a term t of type T. The expression $c\ x \equiv t$ defines the constant c with the parameter x as the term t. Definitions constitute the principal mechanism for producing conservative extensions of HOL. Type variables are denoted by lowercase Greek letters. Given types α and β, $\alpha \Rightarrow \beta$ is the type of (total) functions from α to β, $\alpha \times \beta$ is the product type, and α *set* is the type of sets of elements of type α. The type *unit* contains a single element. There are several mechanisms to define new types. A datatype declaration introduces an inductive data type. For example, the polymorphic option type is defined by datatype α *option* = *None* | *Some* α. Functions of type $\alpha \Rightarrow \beta$ *option* are used to model partial functions from α to β. The declaration types $T_1 = T_2$ merely introduces a new name for the type T_2, possibly with parameters, as in types $\alpha \rightharpoonup \beta = \alpha \Rightarrow \beta$ *option*.

Application: Cryptographically Sound Protocol Verification. In our security protocol verification project [21], we work with the protocol model proposed by Backes, Pfitzmann, and Waidner [2], henceforth called the *BPW model*. This model is substantially more complex than standard Dolev-Yao models (e.g., [19]), but has the advantage of being cryptographically sound, which means that properties proven of protocols hold with respect to standard cryptographic definitions of security (defined in probabilistic and complexity-theoretic terms). Roughly speaking, the BPW model can be viewed as a centralized cryptographic library component: it has an encapsulated state, where it tracks which principals know which messages, and a collection of interface functions for constructing, decomposing, and transmitting messages. Principals (and the attacker) use the interface functions when executing (respectively attacking) protocols. We model not only the BPW model, but also protocols defined on top of it, as components. We have constructed a second formalization of the BPW model, which abstracts the representation of protocol messages from DAGs to inductive terms, and we have proved its bisimulation equivalence with the first formalization. Finally, we have modeled the Needham-Schroeder-Lowe authentication protocol [12] on top of the second formalization and proved various security (secrecy and authentication) properties.

We refer the interested reader to [21] for more details about this application as well as for a detailed comparison with related work on security protocol verification.

3   Monads and Components

In this section, we describe a monad-based hierarchical component model. Components are formalized as an encapsulated state manipulated by a set of interface functions. Our formalization of components is extensible, whereby properties proved for a given component remain valid for all extensions.

3.1   State-Exception Monad

Monads are a concept from category theory introduced in programming language semantics by Moggi [15] to model different computational phenomena in a functional setting, including exceptions, state, non-determinism, and input/output. From a programming perspective, a monad is a type constructor with a unit and a binding operation enjoying unit and associativity properties. In our case, we are working with a state-exception monad with just a single type of exception:

```
datatype α result = Exception | Value α          -- result type
types (α, σ) S = σ ⇒ α result × σ                -- monad type

return :: α ⇒ (α, σ) S                           -- monad unit
return a ≡ λs. (Value a, s)

bind :: (α, σ) S ⇒ (α ⇒ (β, σ) S) ⇒ (β, σ) S     -- monad bind
bind m k ≡ λs. let (a, t) = m s in
                 case a of Exception ⇒ (Exception, t) | Value x ⇒ k x t
```

A term of type (α, σ) S is called a *computation*. Computations act on a state of type σ and either result in an exception or a result value of type α. The monad unit, which we call return, embeds a value into a computation. Binding acts as sequential composition with value passing in the style of a let-binding. We write do $x \leftarrow m$; $k\ x$ for *bind m k*. The monad unit and associativity laws are easily proved in Isabelle/HOL:

```
lemma bind_left_unit: do x ← return a; k x = k a
lemma bind_right_unit: do x ← m; return x = m
lemma bind_assoc: do y ← (do x ← m; k x); h y = do x ← m; (do y ← k x; h y)
```

The monad-specific operations are concerned with state transformations and exception handling. State extraction and update are handled by the functions *distill* and *xform*, respectively.

```
distill :: (σ ⇒ α) ⇒ (α, σ) S                    -- return transformed state
distill f ≡ λs. return (f s) s

xform :: (σ ⇒ σ) ⇒ (unit, σ) S                   -- set transformed state as new state
xform f ≡ do t ← distill f; λs. return () t
```

Exception handling is achieved by the functions throw and try_catch, which are duals of return and *bind* with respect to the type of result.

```
throw :: unit ⇒ (α, σ) S
throw x ≡ λs. (Exception, s)

try_catch :: (α, σ) S ⇒ (α, σ) S ⇒ (α, σ) S
try_catch k h ≡ λs. let (r, t) = k s in
                      case r of Exception ⇒ h t | Value b ⇒ (Value b, t)
```

We write try k catch h instead of try_catch k h and we call h the exception handler. Exception handling can easily be generalized to handle multiple types of exceptions. In this case, the exception would be passed to the exception handler h.

We borrow control structures such as if -then- else and pattern matching (case) from the Isabelle/HOL meta-language. We do not need iteration and recursion in our application, but these can also be borrowed from Isabelle/HOL to a certain extent, which we discuss below. Summarizing, we use the state-exception monad to add a layer of abstraction to Isabelle/HOL that is appropriate to specify our models.

Generality of our approach. Ideally, we would like to define monads and the monad laws abstractly and instantiate them to the concrete monads of interest. This could be achieved by using axiomatic constructor classes in the style of Haskell, but Isabelle's type system only supports the less axiomatic *type* classes. The latter do not support type constructors and the axioms may only contain a single free type variable. Thus, we can only define concrete monads. There are also restrictions concerning the definition of recursive functions. Only terminating functions can be defined and the corresponding Isabelle/HOL packages are pushed to their limits when termination not only depends on the explicit function arguments, but also on the implicit state argument of the monad. One possible solution is to define and prove specialized fixed point theorems as in [11].

A different, more elaborate solution to both problems above is proposed by Huffman, Matthews, and White [6]. They formalize axiomatic constructor classes in Isabelle/ HOLCF, an extension of Isabelle/HOL with domain theory. By a clever construction, they are able to represent HOLCF domains in a universal domain and reflect representable domains as values and type constructors as continuous functions. This allows them to define axiomatic constructor classes in terms of axiomatic type classes and apply them to realize an abstract definition of monads. Moreover, in the domain-theoretic context, fixed points can be used to define recursive functions given any continuous functional. However, for our toolbox, we have chosen to live with the restrictions imposed by the simpler, direct formalization of concrete monads in Isabelle/HOL.

3.2 Hierarchical Component Model

Our components consist of a state that is manipulated by a set of *interface functions*. For reasons that will become clear shortly, we model a state as a record and consider its individual fields to be the state variables. For example, record *point* $= x :: nat \; y :: nat$ defines a record type for points, of which the record $(|x=1, \; y=2|)$ is an element.

Example 1 (BPW model). We start by briefly describing the BPW model and refer the reader to [2] for full details. The BPW model constitutes a library of cryptographic operations, which keeps track of, and controls access to, the messages known by each party. The BPW model provides *local functions* for operating on messages and *send functions* for exchanging them between an arbitrary, but fixed, number N of honest users and the adversary (which we identify with the network). The state of our abstract formalization of the BPW model is defined as:

record δ *mLibState* $= knowsM :: party \Rightarrow hnd \rightharpoonup \delta \; msg$

There is a single state variable called *knowsM*, which defines for each party a partial function mapping handles to protocol messages. Here, the type δ of payload data is polymorphic, since it depends on the concrete protocol built on top of the BPW model.

The interface functions refer to messages indirectly using *handles*, which are a form of pointer required for reasons of cryptographic soundness. As an example of an interface function, we show here the function for generating fresh nonces.

gen_nonceM $:: party \Rightarrow (hnd, (\delta, \sigma) \; mLibState\_scheme) \; S$
gen_nonceM $u \equiv$ do $n \leftarrow distill \; (\lambda s. \; freshTagM \; s); \; newmsgM \; u \; (mNonce \; n)$

The function *freshTagM* returns a fresh tag, which has not been used so far, i.e. is not part of any known message. Then *newmsgM* $u \; (mNonce \; n)$ creates a fresh handle h and updates the knowledge map *knowsM* for user u with the new mapping $h \mapsto mNonce \; n$.

For hierarchical model construction and proofs we rely on record extensibility: record *cpoint* = *point* + *c* :: *color* extends points with a color field. Behind the scenes, the definition of a record type *r* creates a *record scheme* α *r_scheme*, which extends the declared type *r* with a polymorphic field *more* of type α. The type *r* is derived as *unit r_scheme*. Record extensibility is based on the instantiation of the record scheme parameter α with additional fields, which induces a subtyping relation between record schemes and their instantiations [16]. For example, *point* and *cpoint* are both subtypes of α *point_scheme* (but *cpoint* is not a subtype of *point*).

We exploit record subtyping to construct new components from existing ones. Given an existing component C with a state of type, say, *C_scheme*, we construct a new component D by extending the state of C with additional variables and defining a new set of interface functions. This construction has the advantage that any invariant I (in fact, any property) we have proved for component C still holds when C's interface functions operate on the extended state; since the latter is just an instance of *C_scheme*, there is no need for an explicit proof of this fact. This explains why the function *gen_nonce* in Example 1 operates on the record scheme (δ, σ) *mLibState_scheme* instead of the plain record δ *mLibState*. Moreover, if the component D only uses C's interface functions to manipulate C's part of the state (as sound engineering practice dictates), then a straightforward proof shows that the invariant I lifts to D.

Observe that record extension is linear and neither associative nor commutative. Therefore, this is a hierarchical method rather than a compositional one. Although this is adequate in our case, it may be too restrictive for other applications. Without using record subtyping, we would have to explicitly embed the state of each component into a global system state and prove that properties of individual components can be lifted to the composed system. The benefit of such additional work would be a compositional method, where properties of individual components can be proved separately.

Example 2 (Generic protocols). Security protocols are modeled on top of the BPW model. Each user A runs a protocol component P_A, which maintains its own local state and provides a user and a network handler, which respond to input from the user and the network, respectively. The local state of each user is modeled as an extension of the state of the BPW model with a new polymorphic field *loc* type *user* $\Rightarrow \sigma$. The type variable σ will be instantiated by concrete protocols.

record (δ, σ) *globState* = δ *mLibState* +
   loc :: *user* $\Rightarrow \sigma$ -- local state of each protocol machine

The protocol handlers invoke the local BPW functions to parse and construct protocol messages. The output of either handler may go to the user or the network (i.e., the adversary). A protocol component is a record type, whose fields are the two protocol handlers. A protocol is a function assigning a protocol component to each honest user. Concrete protocols inhabit instances of the type $(\iota, o, \delta, \sigma)$ *protocol*, where ι and o are the types of user input and output.

datatype *o proto_out* = *pToUser o* | *pToNet netmsg*

record $(\iota, o, \delta, \sigma)$ *proto_component* =
   proto_user_handler :: $\iota \Rightarrow (o$ *proto_out*, (δ, σ) *globState*) S
   proto_net_handler :: *user* $\Rightarrow$ *hnd* $\Rightarrow (o$ *proto_out*, (δ, σ) *globState*) S

types $(\iota, o, \delta, \sigma)$ *protocol* = *user* $\Rightarrow$ $(\iota, o, \delta, \sigma)$ *proto_component*

The complete protocol system provides (1) local BPW model functions used by the adversary to parse and construct messages and (2) system-level user and network handlers, which are parametrized by the protocol. These handlers connect the protocol-level handlers to the BPW-model send functions in order to exchange messages with the adversary. A message transfer corresponds to updating the recipient's knowledge map.

Example 3 (NSL protocol). We now give an instance of the above protocol type: the Needham-Schroeder-Lowe (NSL) protocol [12], a well-studied, three-step protocol for mutual authentication. In our setting, the local state of each protocol component consists of a variable *nonces*, which is a function mapping each user to a set of nonce handles that were created in protocol sessions with that user. Below, we show the protocol user handler in some detail, but we only sketch the protocol network handler.

record *ustate* = *nonces* :: *user* $\Rightarrow$ *hnd set*

NeedhamSchroederLowe :: $(user, user, user, ustate)$ *protocol*
NeedhamSchroederLowe A $\equiv$ (|
   proto_user_handler = λB.   −− construct the first NSL message
      do *na* $\leftarrow$ *gen_nonce (User A)*; do *z* $\leftarrow$ *add_nonce A B na*;
      do *nameA* $\leftarrow$ *store (User A) A*; do *m* $\leftarrow$ *pair (User A) (na, nameA)*
      do *em* $\leftarrow$ *encrypt (User A) (pke (User A) B) m*;
      return $(pToNet (A, B, em))$

   proto_net_handler = $\lambda B\ m$.   −− respond to incoming NSL messages
      do *pm* $\leftarrow$ *parse_msg A B m*;
   case *pm* of
      msg1 nb nameB $\Rightarrow$*mk_msg2 A B nb*
    | *msg2 na nb nameB* $\Rightarrow$*mk_msg3 A B nb*
    | *msg3 nb* $\Rightarrow$ return $(pToUser B)$
|)

The protocol user handler for user A initiates the protocol with another user B by constructing, stepwise, the first protocol message (whose form is $\{N_A, A\}_{K(B)}$, i.e., the public-key encryption of a nonce and user name) using the interface functions of the BPW model. The auxiliary function *add_nonce* adds the freshly generated nonce handle *na* to the set of nonces that A has created in runs with B (stored in variable *nonces*). The protocol network handler receives a message (at handle m), parses it, and, depending on the result, reacts by constructing a reply message (*mk_msg2* or *mk_msg3*) or returning to the user at the end of the protocol run (the third case).

Component behavior. We give an operational semantics to components in terms of a derived transition system. A transition system σ *trsys* is a record with two fields: the set *init* of initial states of type σ *set* and the transition relation *trans* :: $(\sigma \times \sigma)$ *set*. A computation m gives rise to a transition relation *tr* $m \equiv \{(s, snd (m\ s)) \mid s.\ True\}$. The transition relation of a component is the union of the transition relations of its interface functions. By adding a set of initial states, we obtain the transition system associated with a component. The runs of a transition system are defined as infinite sequences of states, σ *run* = *nat* $\Rightarrow$ σ, starting in an initial state and where successive states are related by transitions. The runs will serve as models for LTL formulas.

4 Program and Temporal Logics

In this section, we describe the weakest pre-condition calculus and the Hoare logic, which we use for pre-/post-condition reasoning, and the linear-time temporal logic used for temporal reasoning. All these logics use HOL sets (of states) as their basic assertions and set operations as boolean connectives. Hence, when we say that a state s satisfies a basic assertion P, we mean $s \in P$. The WP calculus and the Hoare logic are both tailored to our state-exception monad, whereas the temporal logic is interpreted over standard transition systems and linked to the other logics via gluing lemmas. We first present the logics and then illustrate their combined application in Section 4.4.

4.1 Weakest Pre-condition Calculus

Our weakest pre-condition calculus is inspired by Pitts' evaluation logic [20], which generalizes first-order dynamic logic by interpreting it over monads. We present a semantic embedding of a variant of evaluation logic, instantiated to the state-exception monad. We have two box modalities: $[x \leftarrow m]Q\,x$ for normal termination and $[@\,m]Q$ for exceptional termination. These correspond to the weakest pre-condition of the computation m with respect to the post-condition Q. We do not need the dual diamond modalities for our purposes (these could be defined directly or using set complement).

$$[x \leftarrow m]Q\,x \equiv \{s.\ \forall x\ t.\ (m\,s) = (Value\ x,\ t) \longrightarrow t \in Q\,x\}$$
$$[@\,m]Q \equiv \{s.\ \forall t.\ (m\,s) = (Exception,\ t) \longrightarrow t \in Q\}$$

Note the dependence of the assertion Q on the result value x in $[x \leftarrow m]Q\,x$. The following general properties of the WP calculus follow directly from the definition.

lemma *BoxN_true*: $[x \leftarrow p]\ true = true$
lemma *BoxN_conj*: $[x \leftarrow p]((P\,x) \cap (Q\,x)) = [x \leftarrow p](P\,x) \cap [x \leftarrow p](Q\,x)$
lemma *BoxN_monotone*: $\forall x.\ P\,x \subseteq Q\,x \Longrightarrow [x \leftarrow p]\ P\,x \subseteq [x \leftarrow p]\ Q\,x$

Analogous results can be shown for the exception modality $[@\,p]$. We also prove properties related to the monad operations. For the basic monad operations we have:

lemma *BoxN_return*: $[x \leftarrow \mathsf{return}\ a]\ Q\,x = Q\,a$
lemma *BoxE_return*: $[@\ \mathsf{return}\ a]\ P = true$

lemma *BoxN_bind*: $[y \leftarrow (\mathsf{do}\ x \leftarrow p; q\,x)]\ Q\,y = [x \leftarrow p][y \leftarrow q\,x]\ Q\,y$
lemma *BoxE_bind*: $[@\ \mathsf{do}\ x \leftarrow p; q\,x]\ Q = [x \leftarrow p][@\ q\,x]\ Q \cap [@\,p]\ Q$

The first lemma reflects the fact that the return value a is bound to x and the state remains unchanged. The second lemma expresses that return never produces an exception. The third lemma decomposes the modality for the binding operator into two modalities. The fourth lemma states that the weakest pre-condition of do $x \leftarrow p; q\,x$ with respect to exceptions and Q is composed of two conditions: (1) if p terminates with value x and $(q\,x)$ results in an exception then the resulting state satisfies Q, and (2) whenever p directly produces an exception then the resulting state also satisfies Q.

Similar equations hold for the exception operations, where throw and try_catch are dual (with respect to the type of result) to the cases for return and *bind*, respectively.

lemma *BoxN_throw*: $[z \leftarrow$ throw $()](P\ z) = true$
lemma *BoxE_throw*: $[@$ throw $()]P = P$

lemma *BoxN_try_catch*: $[x \leftarrow$ try p catch $q](P\ x) = [x \leftarrow p](P\ x) \cap [@\ p][x \leftarrow q](P\ x)$
lemma *BoxE_try_catch*: $[@$ try p catch $q]Q = [@\ p][@\ q]Q$

The weakest pre-conditions of the state-manipulation operations satisfy the following equations. The cases for exceptions equal *true* and are therefore not shown.

lemma *BoxN_distill*: $[x \leftarrow$ distill $f](P\ x) = \{s.\ s \in P\ (f\ s)\}$
lemma *BoxN_xform*: $[z \leftarrow$ xform $f](P\ z) = f^{-1}\ (P\ ())$

The first equation describes that *distill f* returns the result of applying f to the current state, but does not modify the state itself. The second equation states the weakest pre-condition for state update consists of exactly those states that are elements of $P\ ()$ under f, where f^{-1} denotes the inverse image of f.

4.2 Hoare Logic

We construct our Hoare logic on top of the WP calculus. This is reflected in the following definitions of Hoare triples:

$$\{P\}\ m\ \{> Q\} \equiv P \subseteq [x \leftarrow m](Q\ x) \qquad \{P\}\ m\ \{@\ Q\} \equiv P \subseteq [@\ m]Q$$

Again, we have one type of triple for each kind of termination, where the assertion Q in $\{P\}\ m\ \{> Q\}$ depends on the value returned by computation m.

By defining the Hoare triples in terms of the WP calculus, we can switch from Hoare logic to the WP calculus at any point simply by unfolding the definition of Hoare triples. Typically, we start non-trivial proofs using the rules of Hoare logic. Later, we switch to the WP calculus and automatically rewrite the resulting goals into assertions of HOL's set theory, using the equations of Section 4.1. The resulting assertions are often automatically solved using standard reasoning tools provided by Isabelle/HOL.

Next, we present the set of proof rules of our Hoare logic. In a deep embedding of Hoare logic in HOL, we would inductively define a derivability relation (and a program syntax) as in [17]. Here, we are working with a shallow embedding and therefore we represent proof rules semantically as Isabelle/HOL rules. Deriving these rules in Isabelle corresponds to proving their soundness. The two rules for return follow directly from the WP calculus by unfolding the definitions of Hoare triples.

$$\frac{}{\{P\ x\}\ \text{return}\ x\ \{> P\}}\ returnN \qquad \frac{}{\{P\}\ \text{return}\ x\ \{@\ Q\}}\ returnE$$

The first rule expresses that the state and the value x are invariant in return x. The second rule captures the fact that the return statement never produces an exception and therefore vacuously establishes an arbitrary post-condition (including *false*).

The two rules for *bind* are proved using the lemma *BoxN_monotone* above.

$$\frac{\{P\}\ p\ \{> Q\} \qquad \bigwedge x.\ \{Q\ x\}\ q\ x\ \{> R\}}{\{P\}\ \text{do}\ x \leftarrow p;\ q\ x\ \{> R\}}\ bindN$$

$$\frac{\{P\}\ p\ \{@\ R\} \qquad \{P\}\ p\ \{> Q\} \qquad \bigwedge x.\ \{Q\ x\}\ q\ x\ \{@\ R\}}{\{P\}\ \text{do}\ x \leftarrow p;\ q\ x\ \{@\ R\}}\ bindE$$

In the last premise of these rules, the symbol $\bigwedge$ denotes the universal quantifier of Isabelle's meta-logic. Thus, the corresponding Hoare triple must hold for all possible inputs to computation q. In the rule *bindE*, we distinguish two cases: the first premise covers the case where computation p terminates with an exception, while the other two deal with the case where p terminates with a value x, but q x results in an exception.

The proof rules for the try_catch construct are dual to the rules for *bind* and can be proved using the lemma *BoxE_monotone*:

$$\frac{\{P\}\, p\, \{> R\} \qquad \{P\}\, p\, \{@\, Q\} \qquad \{Q\}\, q\, \{> R\}}{\{P\}\, \text{try } p \text{ catch } q\, \{>\ R\}}\ try\_catchN$$

$$\frac{\{P\}\, p\, \{> Q\} \qquad \{Q\}\, q\, \{@\, R\}}{\{P\}\, \text{try } p\, \text{catch } q\, \{@\, R\}}\ try\_catchE$$

The rules for the state manipulation functions *distill* and *xform* directly reflect their WP calculus characterization in the lemmas *BoxN_distill* and *BoxN_xform*.

$$\frac{\cdot}{\{\{t.\ t \in P(f\, t)\}\}\, distill\, f\, \{> P\}}\ distillN \qquad \frac{\cdot}{\{f^{-1}(P\, ())\}\, xform\, f\, \{> P\}}\ xformN$$

Finally, we have proved various additional rules, such as the consequence rule of Hoare logic, which is used to strengthen preconditions and weaken postconditions.

Following the classical argument (e.g., [23]), we have proved the completeness of our Hoare logic rules relative to the HOL assertion language in Isabelle/HOL. The core of the argument is an induction on computations m, which establishes the derivability of $\{[x \leftarrow m]Q\, x\}\, m\, \{> Q\}$, for all Q. Since we are working with a shallow embedding, we have not formalized the program syntax, so we prove each case of the induction separately. Additionally, we must ensure that $[x \leftarrow m]Q\, x$ can be expressed in our assertion language (HOL set theory), which is the case by construction in our setting.

4.3 Linear-Time Temporal Logic

We now briefly sketch our embedding of LTL with past operators in Isabelle/HOL. We have chosen to keep this embedding independent of monads, so that it can be reused independently in different contexts. We interpret LTL formulas over runs and transition systems, in the standard way (see, e.g., [14]). Hence, we restrict ourselves to a summarized account.

We have formalized the syntax of LTL formulas in Isabelle/HOL as an inductive data type σ *ltl* parametrized by a type of states σ. Here we deviated from our principle of working with shallow embeddings. Since LTL does not have binding operators, the overhead associated with a deep embedding was small and allowed us to prove some meta-theoretical results about LTL by induction on the syntax. We note however that a shallow embedding would have also been sufficient for our work. LTL formulas are interpreted in the standard way at positions of runs: $(r,\ i) \models f$ means that formula f holds at position i of run r. A transition system T satisfies a formula if all of its runs at position 0 do, which is written $T \models f$. A component, in the sense of Section 3.2, satisfies a LTL formula if its derived transition system does.

Proof rules. Following the approach of [14], we derive a set of proof rules to reduce temporal reasoning to pre-/post-condition reasoning. The most important rule that we have derived is the following one for establishing an invariant P of a transition system T using an inductive invariant I and a previously proved auxiliary invariant J.

$$\frac{T \models \Box J \qquad (\mathit{init}\ T) \subseteq I \qquad I \cap J \subseteq P \qquad \{I \cap J\}\ (\mathit{trans}\ T)\ \{I\}}{T \models \Box P}\ INV$$

The Hoare triple appearing in this rule is defined over a transition relation.

$$\{P\}\ \mathit{tran}\ \{Q\} \equiv \forall s\ t.\ s \in P \wedge (s,t) \in \mathit{tran} \rightarrow t : Q$$

To enable structured reasoning about components in our Hoare logic, we prove a gluing lemma for each component that reduces Hoare triples about the component's transition relation to a set of Hoare triples over the component's interface functions. Here is an example of such a gluing lemma.

Example 4 (Hoare triples for protocol system). We define a notion of Hoare triple for the global protocol system component and link it to the Hoare triples for the transition relation derived from that component. The definition overloads the notation $\{\_\}\ \_\ \{\_\}$ and uses $\{P\}\ m\ \{\&\ Q\}$ for the conjunction of $\{P\}\ m\ \{> \lambda x.\ Q\}$ and $\{P\}\ m\ \{@\ Q\}$.

$\{P\}\ \mathit{proto}\ \{Q\} \equiv \forall h\ \mathit{im}\ \mathit{nm}\ \mathit{pkh}\ \mathit{skh}\ u\ \dots\ .$
  $\{P\}\ \mathit{sys\_user\_handler}\ \mathit{proto}\ u\ \mathit{im}\ \{\&\ Q\} \wedge$
  $\{P\}\ \mathit{sys\_net\_handler}\ \mathit{proto}\ \mathit{nm}\ \{\&\ Q\} \wedge$
  $\{P\}\ \mathit{gen\_nonce}M\ \mathit{Adv}\ \{\&\ Q\} \wedge \{P\}\ \mathit{encrypt}M\ \mathit{Adv}\ \mathit{pkh}\ h\ \{\&\ Q\} \wedge$
  $\{P\}\ \mathit{decrypt}M\ \mathit{Adv}\ \mathit{skh}\ h\ \{\&\ Q\} \wedge \dots$

lemma *HoareSys_decomposition*: $\{P\}\ (\mathit{glob\_trans}\ \mathit{proto})\ \{Q\} = \{P\}\ \mathit{proto}\ \{Q\}$

The relation *glob_trans proto* denotes the transition relation derived from the entire protocol system. Triples of the form $\{P\}\ (\mathit{glob\_trans}\ \mathit{proto})\ \{Q\}$ arise as subgoals, when rule *INV* is applied to prove protocol invariants. Using the above lemma, these are rewritten to a set of Hoare triples over the protocol system interface functions.

4.4   Example: Nonce Secrecy Invariant for the NSL Protocol

To illustrate the use of our reasoning tools, we state and prove an invariant of the NSL protocol: the nonces created in sessions between two honest users remain secret.

nonceSecrecy $\equiv \{s.\ \forall A\ B\ n.$
  $n \in \mathit{Nonces}\ s\ A\ B \longrightarrow \mathit{secret}\ s\ (m\mathit{Nonce}\ n)\ \{\mathit{User}\ A,\ \mathit{User}\ B\}\ \}$

theorem *nonceSecrecy_invariant*: $NSLtrsys \models \Box nonceSecrecy$

Here, *Nonces s A B* is the set of nonces that A has created in runs with B (these are accessible via the handles in the set *nonces s A B*). The predicate *secret s m U* expresses that in state s message m can be derived by at most the parties $A \in U$ from their knowledge in *knowsM s A*. The theorem states that *nonceSecrecy* is an invariant of the transition system derived from the NSL protocol system ($\Box$ denotes "always" in LTL). The proof proceeds in several stages.

1. Apply rule *INV* and lemma *HoareSys_decomposition* to reduce the temporal statement to a set of preservation lemmas over the NSL system interface functions.
2. Prove the preservation of the invariant by each BPW model interface function. Here, we automate most proofs using the WP calculus.
3. Lift the previous preservation results to the NSL protocol level by automatically applying Hoare logic rules to "pull" the invariant through the protocol handlers.
4. Lift these results to the system level by applying Hoare logic rules interactively with user-supplied assertions.

We provide an example of the last point. At the NSL system level, the main cases concern the system user and network handlers. Roughly speaking, these compose the respective protocol-level handler with the user send function, which transmits network messages to the adversary. The user send function requires an additional pre-condition to preserve the invariant, which simply states that adding the sent message to the adversary knowledge does not compromise nonce secrecy. We manually apply the *bindN* rule, which separates the respective protocol handler from the user send function. As the intermediate assertion Q, we use the conjunction of the invariants (main and auxiliary) with a previously established strong post-condition of the respective protocol handler, which states that the relevant nonces are fresh and encrypted and thus inaccessible to the adversary. Since these postconditions imply the pre-condition of the user send function, we use the consequence rule to complete the proof.

5   Bisimulation

Abstracting components (e.g. the state representation) can substantially improve proof automation. When doing this, we must ensure that the behavior of the abstracted component is equivalent to the original one. We use bisimilarity as our notion of equivalence. We first define bisimulation in the context of the state-exception monad and then give compositional proof rules for establishing the bisimilarity of two components. Finally, we present an example from our formalization of the BPW model.

5.1   Bisimilar Components

The state-exception monad is deterministic. Therefore, two computations m_1 and m_2 are bisimilar, with respect to a witnessing relation R, if they produce a (unique) pair of bisimilar states and identical results, whenever started in a pair of bisimilar states.

> *bisim* $R \, m_1 \, m_2 \equiv \forall s \, t \, s' \, t' \, x \, y.$
> $(s, \ t) \in R \land m_1 \, s = (x, s') \land m_2 \, t = (y, t') \ \longrightarrow$
> $(\exists \, v. \ x = \textit{Value } v \land y = \textit{Value } v \land (s', \ t') \in R)$
> $\lor \ (x = \textit{Exception } \land y = \textit{Exception } \land (s', \ t') \in R)$

This notion is lifted pointwise to functions and afterwards to components by requiring that corresponding pairs of functions in both components match up[1]. Note that, since we are working with shallow embeddings of components and bisimulation, the notion

---

[1] This definition can be seen as an instantiation of the coalgebraic definition of bisimulation [10] when the component is viewed as a coalgebra [9].

of bisimilar components is not formalized itself in Isabelle/HOL. Instead, the proof that two components C and C' are bisimilar consists of a collection of lemmas of the form *bisim* $R\ f\ f'$, one for each pair of associated interface functions f of C and f' of C'.

We would like to prove such judgments compositionally by following the structure of the computations m_1 and m_2. The idea is to consider the statement *bisim* $R\ m_1\ m_2$ as a Hoare-like tuple of the form $\{R\}\ m_1\ m_2\ \{R\}$, where the bisimulation relation R acts as both the pre- and postcondition. For compositional proofs, we need to generalize these judgments, as we can neither expect that intermediate pairs of states arising from program decomposition are in the bisimulation relation nor that intermediate outputs are identical. Therefore, we obtain the definition of *bisim* $R\ m_1\ m_2$ as an instance of a generalized notion of a *bisimulation tuple*:

$$\{R\}\ m_1\ m_2\ \{\lambda\,a\,b.\ S\,a\,b\,|\,T\} \equiv \forall s\ t\ s'\ t'\ x\ y.$$
$$(s,\ t) \in R \wedge m_1\ s = (x, s')\ \wedge m_2\ t = (y, t')\ \longrightarrow$$
$$(\exists\,a\,b.\ x = Value\ a \wedge y = Value\ b \wedge (s',\ t') \in S\,a\,b)$$
$$|\ (x = Exception \wedge y = Exception \wedge (s',\ t') \in T)$$

$$bisim\ R\ m_1\ m_2 \equiv \{R\}\ m_1\ m_2\ \{(\lambda\,a\,b.\ \{p.\ a = b\} \cap R)\,|\,R\}$$

Bisimulation tuples have two postconditions. The first postcondition is a parametrized relation $S\,a\,b$, required to hold whenever the computation m_1 returns the value a and m_2 returns the value b. The second postcondition T covers the case where both computations terminate with an exception. Note that $\{R\}\ m_1\ m_2\ \{\lambda a\,b.\ true\,|\,true\}$ expresses the property that both computations terminate with the same type of result. We call this property *equi-termination*.

5.2   Compositional Proof Rules for Bisimulation

Since proving a bisimulation tuple $\{R\}\ m_1\ m_2\ \{S\,|T\}$ requires compositional reasoning about two computations simultaneously, we need $\mathcal{O}(n^2)$ proof rules to cover all cases, where n is the number of constructs of our "programming language". We can distinguish rules for pairs of computations with (1) identical top-level constructors from (2) those with different ones. As for (2), many combinations are only bisimilar in restricted or trivial cases. For instance, return and throw are only bisimilar, if the precondition is equivalent to *false*. A simple example of (1) is the return rule.

$$\frac{R \subseteq Sn\ a\ b}{\{R\}\ (\text{return } a)\ (\text{return } b)\ \{Sn\ |\ Se\}}\ bisim\_return$$

More interesting are the rules for composed computations. The basic rule for the case where both computations are sequential compositions is stated as follows.

$$\frac{\{R\}\ m_1\ m_2\ \{Sn\ |\ Te\} \qquad \bigwedge a\,b.\ \{Sn\ a\ b\}\ (k_1\ a)\ (k_2\ b)\ \{Tn\ |\ Te\}}{\{R\}\ (\text{do } a \leftarrow m_1;\ k_1\ a)\ (\text{do } b \leftarrow m_2;\ k_2\ b)\ \{Tn\ |\ Te\}}\ bind\_sym$$

This rule only covers the well-behaved case where the first parts of both sequential compositions equi-terminate. This situation is depicted in Figure 1, where computations are shown above the arrow and their results below. The rule *bind_sym* does not cover the case where m_1 and m_2 do not equi-terminate or where the second computation has

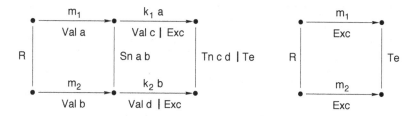

Fig. 1. Bisimulation for *bind*, symmetric case

a different structure. For such asymmetric cases, we derive the rule *bind_left* (below) and *bind_right* (symmetric, not shown).

$$\frac{\{R\}\ m_1\ m_2\ \{\lambda a\,b.\ false \mid Te\}}{\{R\}\ (\text{do}\ a \leftarrow m_1;\ k_1\ a)\ m_2\ \{Tn \mid Te\}}\ bind\_left$$

When read backwards, this rule allows us to cut off the second part k_1 of a sequential composition with m_1, which is never invoked, in case both m_1 and m_2 always equi-terminate with an exception (and establish Te).

In general, when we prove a subgoal whose form matches the conclusion of rule *bind_sym* we must partition the relation R into two relations Ra and Rb, according to whether or not m_1 and m_2 equi-terminate on a pair of states in R. We then apply rule *bind_sym* in the former case and rules *bind_left* and *bind_right* in the latter case.

We have derived similar rules for the exception handling constructs. Again, all other control flow constructs including recursion are borrowed directly from HOL. All rules are sound by construction. Their completeness has not yet been investigated.

Using component invariants. In non-trivial bisimulation proofs we usually need invariants of both components to strengthen the bisimulation relation. We have derived a specialized rule for sequential composition from rule *bind_sym*, which allows us to use invariants in bisimulation proofs.

$$\frac{\{R \cap I \times J\}\ m_1\ m_2\ \{Sn \mid Te\} \quad \bigwedge a\,b.\ \{Sn\ a\,b \cap I \times J\}\ (k_1\ a)\ (k_2\ b)\ \{Tn \mid Te\} \quad \{I\}\ m_1\ \{> \lambda z.\ I\} \quad \{J\}\ m_2\ \{> \lambda z.\ J\}}{\{R \cap I \times J\}\ (\text{do}\ a \leftarrow m_1;\ k_1\ a)\ (\text{do}\ b \leftarrow m_2;\ k_2\ b)\ \{Tn \mid Te\}}\ bind\_sym\_inv$$

The Hoare triples in premises 3 and 4 express that I and J are indeed invariants of m_1 and m_2, respectively. This rule allows us to "pull" the invariants over sequential compositions and carry them along in the proof.

Example 5 (Bisimulation of BPW model interface functions). Recall from the introduction that we have formalized two versions of the BPW model: a first one with DAG-based messages and a second one, where these messages are abstracted into inductively defined terms. In order to allow us to work with the more abstract second formalization for concrete protocol verification, we have proved its bisimilarity with the first one. The state of the DAG-based version is a record containing a knowledge map *knowsI* of type *user* $\Rightarrow$ *hnd* $\rightharpoonup$ *ind*, which maps handles to indices for each user, and a table *db* of type *ind* $\Rightarrow$ '*d entry*, which maps indices to message entries. The latter correspond to message constructors, which may contain indices themselves. The bisimulation relation *I2M* expresses that for a given user and handle, the DAG-based message i in *knowsI* is abstracted to the message term m in *knowsM*.

> *I2M* $\equiv$ { (s, t). ($\forall u$. *dom* (*knowsI s u*) = *dom* (*knowsM t u*)) $\wedge$
> ($\forall u h i m$. *knowsI s u h* = *Some i* $\wedge$ *knowsM t u h* = *Some m* $\longrightarrow$ *message s i m*) }

We prove bisimilarity for each pair of matching BPW model interface functions. Let us consider the case of the length query function. There we must show that the bisimulation relation is preserved and that both versions return the same message length. We obtain the subgoal below after unfolding the definitions of the length query functions.

> {*I2M Int* (*finiteKnowsI Int lengthInv*) $\times$ *finiteKnowsM*}
> (do (i, e) $\leftarrow$ *lookupI u h*; return (*len e*))
> (do m $\leftarrow$ *lookupM u h*; return (*len_ofM m*))
> {$\lambda la\ lb$. {p. $la = lb$} *Int I2M* | *I2M*}

Note the auxiliary invariants in the pre-condition of the bisimulation tuple. In particular, the invariant *lengthInv* of the DAG-based formalization states that a concrete message i and its abstract counterpart m (related by *message s i m*) have identical lengths. We apply the rule *bisim_sym_inv* to separate the message lookup operation from the return statements. The intermediate relation *Sn* in this rule is instantiated to the following relation, which states that the index i pointing to entry e as returned by *lookupI* is abstracted to the term-based message m returned by *lookupM*.

> $\lambda(i, e)$ m. *I2M* $\bigcap$ {(s, t). *knowsI s u h* = *Some i* $\wedge$ *db s i* = e $\wedge$ *message s i m*}

The first premise of the rule *bisim_sym_inv* is covered by a previously proved lemma about the lookup functions. Thanks to the intermediate relation above, we can easily derive the second premise using the rule *bisim_return* and the invariant *lengthInv*. The remaining premises are discharged by previously proved invariant preservation results.

In summary, the rules allow compositional bisimulation proofs. They capture repetitive reasoning patterns and thus help us to concentrate on the essential aspects of the proofs, namely the invariants and intermediate relations.

6   Conclusions and Related Work

We have presented a general-purpose toolbox for modeling state-based components using monads, for reasoning about their properties using program and temporal logics, and for reasoning about their equivalence using a compositional proof system for bisimulation. Since our principal motivation was pragmatic rather than meta-theoretical, we have used shallow embeddings and introduced new concepts and proof rules only where we deemed them necessary to raise the level of abstraction. This allows us to exploit Isabelle/HOL's specification language, its extensive libraries, and its reasoning tools as much as possible. For example, we have only formalized sequential composition and exception handling, while all further control structures are borrowed from HOL. Our experience in a substantial case study showed that this provides appropriate abstraction in modeling component-based systems and in proving complex theorems about them.

Related Work. Filiâtre [5] appears to be the first to use monads to formalize an ML-like imperative language in the proof assistant Coq. He gives a functional translation of this language and generates proof obligations from pre-/post-condition annotations. Krstić and Matthews [11] interpret BDD algorithms written in C in a state-exception monad isomorphic to ours. They verify the functional correctness of these algorithms directly in Isabelle/HOL without additional program logics. In fact, they state that the complexity of the BDD programs forced them to use the monadic approach as a more flexible alternative to Hoare logic. However, our work shows that monads and Hoare logic can be combined to take advantage of features of both.

There is a sizable body of work on modeling Java(-like) languages and associated Hoare logics, including the Bali [22] and the LOOP [7] projects. The latter is most closely related to our work. They have formalized a coalgebraic semantics of Java and a corresponding Hoare logic in PVS. These handle non-termination, normal termination, and several forms of abrupt termination. In [9], the connection to monads is investigated. We do not model partiality, but we treat normal termination and exceptions similarly. Jacobs [8] develops WP calculi to improve proof automation and implements two of them as new PVS commands. In contrast, our Hoare logic is directly formulated in terms of the WP calculus and we use the standard Isabelle simplifier to rewrite WP expressions. Our approach is simpler, but does not admit alternative search strategies.

Nipkow has formalized Hoare logics for a family of while-languages and proved soundness and completeness results for each of them [17]. He models exceptions by adding an error flag to the state. As a consequence, most proof rules require preconditions depending on this flag. In contrast, in the state-exception monad, exceptions are more akin to values, which makes the rules for exception handling duals of those for return and *bind* and leads to a more abstract and modular treatment.

There exist several shallow embeddings of temporal logics in HOL. Långbacka has formalized the temporal logic of actions (TLA) in the HOL prover [13]. The Isabelle distribution [1] contains an axiomatization of TLA in HOL by Merz and a formalization of a temporal logic for I/O automata by Müller in HOLCF.

Benton [3] has proposed a relational Hoare logic (RHL) related to our bisimulation proof system to prove the correctness of optimizing program transformations for a while-language. He shows how to embed standard Hoare logic, as well as other logics, into RHL. We have chosen to follow a pragmatic approach and integrate our separate Hoare logic into the bisimulation proof system, which allows us to use the underlying WP calculus for automating proofs.

Future Work. One direction for future work is to extend the modeling language, e.g. by adding object-oriented features such as inheritance, overriding and late binding along the lines of [16, 4] or by lifting the limitations on the definition of monad-based general recursive functions. Another interesting topic is the completeness of the bisimulation proof system and the possibility of adapting it to different kinds of monads.

References

[1] Isabelle home page (2007), http://isabelle.in.tum.de
[2] Backes, M., Pfitzmann, B., Waidner, M.: A universally composable cryptographic library. IACR Cryptology ePrint Archive 2003/015 (January 2003)

[3] Benton, N.: Simple relational correctness proofs for static analyses and program transformations. In: Proc. of Principles of Programming Languages (POPL) (2004)

[4] Brucker, A., Wolff, B.: A package for extensible object-oriented data models with an application to IMP++. In: International Verification Workshop (VERIFY) (August 2006)

[5] Filliâtre, J.-C.: Proof of imperative programs in type theory. In: Altenkirch, T., Naraschewski, W., Reus, B. (eds.) TYPES 1998. LNCS, vol. 1657, Springer, Heidelberg (1999)

[6] Huffman, B., Matthews, J., White, P.: Axiomatic constructor classes in Isabelle/HOLCF. In: Hurd, J., Melham, T. (eds.) TPHOLs 2005. LNCS, vol. 3603, pp. 147–162. Springer, Heidelberg (2005)

[7] Huisman, M., Jacobs, B.: Java program verification via a Hoare logic with abrupt termination. In: Maibaum, T.S.E. (ed.) ETAPS 2000 and FASE 2000. LNCS, vol. 1783, pp. 284–303. Springer, Heidelberg (2000)

[8] Jacobs, B.: Weakest precondition reasoning for Java programs with JML annotations. Journal of Logic and Algebraic Programming 58, 61–88 (2004)

[9] Jacobs, B., Poll, E.: Coalgebras and monads in the semantics of Java. Theoretical Computer Science 291(3), 329–349 (2003)

[10] Jacobs, B., Rutten, J.: A tutorial on (co)algebras and (co)induction. EATCS Bulletin 6, 222–259 (1997)

[11] Krstić, S., Matthews, J.: Verifying BDD algorithms through monadic interpretation. In: Cortesi, A. (ed.) VMCAI 2002. LNCS, vol. 2294, pp. 182–195. Springer, Heidelberg (2002)

[12] Lowe, G.: Breaking and Fixing the Needham-Schroeder Public-Key Protocol Using FDR. Software - Concepts and Tools 17, 93–102 (1996)

[13] Långbacka, T.: A HOL formalisation of the temporal logic of actions. In: Melham, T.F., Camilleri, J. (eds.) Higher Order Logic Theorem Proving and Its Applications. LNCS, vol. 859, pp. 332–345. Springer, Heidelberg (1994)

[14] Manna, Z., Pnueli, A.: Completing the temporal picture. Theoretical Computer Science 83(1), 97–139 (1991)

[15] Moggi, E.: Notions of computation and monads. Information and Computation 93, 55–92 (1991)

[16] Naraschewski, W., Wenzel, M.: Object-oriented verification based on record subtyping in higher-order logic. In: Grundy, J., Newey, M. (eds.) Theorem Proving in Higher Order Logics. LNCS, vol. 1479, pp. 349–366. Springer, Heidelberg (1998)

[17] Nipkow, T.: Hoare logics in Isabelle/HOL. In: Schwichtenberg, H., Steinbrüggen, R. (eds.) Proof and System-Reliability, pp. 341–367. Kluwer, Dordrecht (2002)

[18] Nipkow, T., Paulson, L.C., Wenzel, M.: Isabelle/HOL. LNCS, vol. 2283. Springer, Heidelberg (2002)

[19] Paulson, L.: The inductive approach to verifying cryptographic protocols. J. Computer Security 6, 85–128 (1998)

[20] Pitts, A.M.: Evaluation logic. In: Birtwistle, G. (ed.) IVth Higher Order Workshop, Banff 1990. Workshops in Computing, pp. 162–189. Springer, Heidelberg (1991)

[21] Sprenger, C., Backes, M., Basin, D., Pfitzmann, B., Waidner, M.: Cryptographically sound theorem proving. In: 19th IEEE Computer Security Foundations Workshop, Venice, Italy, July 2006, pp. 153–166. IEEE Computer Society, July (2006)

[22] von Oheimb, D., Nipkow, T.: Hoare logic for NanoJava: Auxiliary variables, side effects and virtual methods revisited. In: Eriksson, L.-H., Lindsay, P.A. (eds.) FME 2002. LNCS, vol. 2391, pp. 89–105. Springer, Heidelberg (2002)

[23] Winskel, G.: The Formal Semantics of Programming Languages. MIT Press, Cambridge (1993)

Primality Proving with Elliptic Curves

Laurent Théry and Guillaume Hanrot

INRIA, France
{Laurent.Thery,Guillaume.Hanrot}@inria.fr

Abstract. Elliptic curves are fascinating mathematical objects. In this paper, we present the way they have been represented inside the COQ system, and how we have proved that the classical composition law on the points is internal and gives them a group structure. We then describe how having elliptic curves inside a prover makes it possible to derive a checker for proving the primality of natural numbers.

1 Introduction

Elliptic curves are a very classical topic of interest in number theory and algebraic geometry, and the basis for a very large body of theory, with lots of far-fetched generalisations. Their most famous application is, without any doubt, the proof of Fermat's last theorem. They are also commonly used in algorithmic number theory since the mid 80's for factoring integers [15] or proving primality [8], but have also made their way more recently in cryptography, see e.g. [5].

It is then natural to try formalising them inside a proof system. In this work, the main property we are interested in is their group structure. The difficult part of the formalisation is in proving associativity. In our formal proof, we follow an elementary algebraic approach that is particularly suited to proof systems. Our main source of inspiration has been the proof proposed by Stefan Friedl [7]. The proof is very technical and consists in massaging equalities over an abstract field under various conditions. Some of these equalities (exactly 3) are so huge that they cannot be reasonably handled by a human being. In his paper, Stefan Friedl advocates the use of a computer algebra like COCOA [4] to check these equalities. Reflecting these computations inside the proof system is the main difficulty of the formal proof. In this paper, we explain how this has been done inside the proof system COQ [22].

Once the group structure has been established, we can use elliptic curves in a very effective way to prove the primality of some natural numbers. For this, we use *prime certificates*: various primality proving algorithms provide the user with a compact output, a *certificate*, with the property that it can be easily checked, whereas generating it is usually cpu-intensive.

We have already played with the idea of prime certificates and in particular of Pocklington certificates in [9,10]. This allows us to prove the primality of some large numbers like the millennium prime (a prime number with exactly 2000 digits discovered by John Cosgrave) or the 27th Mersenne prime $2^{44497} - 1$. The only drawback of the certificates we have been using so far is that they only apply

K. Schneider and J. Brandt (Eds.): TPHOLs 2007, LNCS 4732, pp. 319–333, 2007.

to a restricted class of prime numbers. For example, a Pocklington certificate can be generated for N if $N - 1$ can be factored; in particular, we are not able to generate a Pocklington certificate in the case where $(N-1)/2$ turns out not to be prime (this can be shown by compositeness tests) but it is impossible to factor it, which is a typical case as soon as N grows large. In contrast, under some deep (typically Crámer's conjecture) conjectures of analytic number theory, elliptic curve certificates exist for any prime and can be found in polynomial time. At the moment, the largest prime for which an elliptic certificate has been generated has 20562 decimal digits. Ten days are needed to verify its certificate [18].

The paper is organised as follows. In Section 2, we recall what elliptic curves are and explain how their group structure has been formally established. In Section 3, we focus on prime certificate and show how it is possible to formally derive a checker for elliptic curve certificates.

2 Elliptic Curves and Group Structure

In algebraic geometry, an elliptic curve is defined as follows.

Definition. Let K be a commutative field. An elliptic curve $E(K)$ is a pair (C, P) where C is a (complete) algebraic curve of genus 1 defined over $\mathbb{C}$ and P a point of $C(K)$.

This definition is not very tractable in practice, and the following characterization, which follows easily from the Riemann-Roch Theorem [21], is rather used as a definition.

Proposition. Every elliptic curve over K admits an affine plane model of the form

$$y^2 + a_1 xy + a_3 y = x^3 + a_2 x^2 + a_4 x + a_6, \tag{1}$$

where the distinguished point of the definition is the projective point $(0 : 1 : 0)$, i.e. the direction $y \to \infty$. If the characteristic of K is greater than 5, the equation further simplifies to

$$y^2 = x^3 + Ax + B. \tag{2}$$

Conversely, a nonsingular curve of the form (1) – or (2) if the characteristic is greater than 5 – defines an elliptic curve. For (2) the non-singularity assumption is equivalent to $4A^3 + 27B^2 \neq 0$.

Most of the interest for elliptic curves stems from the fact that they come with a natural group structure. A composition law $(P, Q) \mapsto P + Q$ over $E(K)$ can be constructed as follows:

- The neuter element is the point at infinity;
- Let (PQ) be the line through P and Q (the tangent to the curve at P if $P = Q$).
- Let R be the third point of intersection of (PQ) and K.
- The point $P + Q$ is the symmetrical of R with respect to the line $y = 0$.

An alternative way of seeing the composition law is that three aligned points add up to zero, which is the point at infinity.

Theorem 1. $(E(K), +)$ *is a group.*

The only difficult part is associativity. Classically, there are two roads for proving this. The "low road" uses either computer algebra (the one that we shall carefully take later on) or elementary but subtle geometric considerations. The "high road" instead defines a group by taking the quotient of the free abelian group over $E(K)$ by a subgroup of relations (generated by the relations "three aligned points add up to zero"), and proceeds to prove that each class contains one and only one representative consisting of a single point (so that the underlying set is in bijection with $E(K)$) and that the operation is the same as $+$. All these are consequences of the (non-trivial) Riemann-Roch Theorem.

In our formalisation, we start from (2). We take an arbitrary field K of characteristic other than 2 (this is the only assumption that is needed to prove the group structure) and two elements A and B such that $4A^3 + 27B^2 \neq 0$. The type elt that represents the elements of the curve is defined as follows

```
Inductive elt: Set :=
  inf_elt: elt
| curve_elt (x: K) (y: K) (H: y^2 = x^3 + A * x + B):  elt.
```

An element of type elt is either 0 (inf_elt) or an element of the curve (curve_elt) that contains an x, a y and a proof H that the point (x, y) is on the curve.

For the operations on the curve, we need to define the opposite and the addition. Given a point p of the curve, we define $-p$ as

- If $p = 0$ then $-p = 0$
- If $p = (x, y)$ then $-p = (x, -y)$

Given two points p_1 and p_2 on the curve, we define $p_1 + p_2$ as

- If $p_1 = 0$ then $p_1 + p_2 = p_2$
- If $p_2 = 0$ then $p_1 + p_2 = p_1$
- If $p_1 = -p_2$ then $p_1 + p_2 = 0$
- If $p_1 = p_2 = (x, y)$ and $y \neq 0$ then
      let $l = (3x^2 + A)/2y$ and $x_1 = l^2 - 2x$ in
      $p_1 + p_2 = (x_1, -y - l(x_1 - x))$.
- If $p_1 = (x_1, y_1)$ and $p_2 = (x_2, y_2)$ and $x_1 \neq x_2$ then
      let $l = (y_2 - y_1)/(x_2 - x_1)$ and $x_3 = l^2 - x_1 - x_2$ in
      $p_1 + p_2 = (x_3, -y_1 - l(x_3 - x_1))$.

We also use $p_1 - p_2$ as a shortcut for $p_1 + (-p_2)$. Note that, as points of the curve contain a proof that they belong to the curve, the definition of these operations must also incorporate a proof that these operations are internal. For example, the opposite is represented by a function **opp** whose type is elt $\rightarrow$ elt and its definition is

```
Definition opp p :=
   match p with
     inf_elt => inf_elt
   | curve_elt x y H => curve_elt x (-y) opp_lem
   end.
```

where `opp_lem` represents the proof that if we know that $y^2 = x^3 + Ax + B$ (this is H) then we have $(-y)^2 = x^3 + Ax + B$.

We get that 0 is the neuter element, $-p$ is the opposite of p, and the addition is commutative directly from the definitions. Proving associativity is rather technical. A detailed description of the formal proof is given in [23]. Here, we only sketch the proof and discuss the most interesting issues.

As the definition of addition contains five cases, the proof heavily relies on case analysis. The addition $p_1 + p_2$ is trivial if $p_1 = 0$ or $p_2 = 0$ or $p_1 = -p_2$. When the addition is non-trivial we use the notation $p_1 \oplus p_2$. In turn, this addition can correspond to the tangent case, $p_1 \oplus_t p_2$, where $p_1 = p_2$ or the general case, $p_1 \oplus_g p_2$, where $p_1 \neq p_2$. For associativity, it is easy to discharge the trivial cases and what remains to be proved is then that $p_1 \oplus (p_2 \oplus p_3) = (p_1 \oplus p_2) \oplus p_3$. Each of these additions can be tangent or general, this can be further reduced to four main cases:

1. $p_1 \oplus_g (p_2 \oplus_g p_3) = (p_1 \oplus_g p_2) \oplus_g p_3$.
2. $p_1 \oplus_g (p_2 \oplus_t p_2) = (p_1 \oplus_g p_2) \oplus_g p_2$.
3. $p_1 \oplus_g (p_1 \oplus_g (p_1 \oplus_t p_1)) = (p_1 \oplus_t p_1) \oplus_t (p_1 \oplus_t p_1)$
4. $p_1 \oplus_g (p_2 \oplus_g (p_1 \oplus_g p_2)) = (p_1 \oplus_g p_2) \oplus_t (p_1 \oplus_g p_2)$

The first three cases are discharged using explicit computations while the last case is derived using auxiliary properties such as the cancellation law, i.e. if $p + p_1 = p + p_2$ then $p_1 = p_2$. To understand what it means to perform cases $1-3$ by explicit computations, let us consider the first case. If we take the x component of equation 1 and unfold the definition of addition, we get the conditional equation to be satisfied given in Figure 1. We can now transform this equation into a polynomial one and then use Buchberger algorithm [3] to check that the equation is satisfied. This is where the computer algebra system comes into play. Integrating Buchberger algorithm in a safe way inside a prover is possible and has already been done [6,13], but cases $1-3$ can be decided by a much simpler strategy. To illustrate this strategy, let us consider a more elementary example, i.e. the proof that the addition is internal in the tangent case. It amounts to proving that

$$
\begin{aligned}
y^2 &= x^3 + Ax + B \quad \wedge \\
l &= (3x^2 + A)/2y \quad \wedge \\
x_1 &= l^2 - 2x \quad \quad \wedge \\
y_1 &= -y - l(x_1 - x) \wedge \\
\Rightarrow y_1^2 &= x_1^3 + Ax_1 + B
\end{aligned}
$$

The first step is to get rid of division by normalising the equation into an expression of the form $N/D = 0$ where N and D are two polynomial expressions.

$$x_1 - x_2 \neq 0 \qquad \wedge$$
$$x_4 - x_3 \neq 0 \qquad \wedge$$
$$x_2 - x_3 \neq 0 \qquad \wedge$$
$$x_5 - x_1 \neq 0 \qquad \wedge$$
$$y_1^2 = x_1^3 + Ax_1 + B \qquad \wedge$$
$$y_2^2 = x_2^3 + Ax_2 + B \qquad \wedge$$
$$y_3^2 = x_3^3 + Ax_3 + B \qquad \wedge$$
$$x_4 = (y_1 - y_2)^2/(x_1 - x_2)^2 - x_1 - x_2 \qquad \wedge$$
$$y_4 = -(y_1 - y_2)/(x_1 - x_2)(x_4 - x_1) - y_1 \wedge$$
$$x_6 = (y_4 - y_3)^2/(x_4 - x_3)^2 - x_4 - x_3 \qquad \wedge$$
$$y_6 = -(y_4 - y_3)/(x_4 - x_3)(x_6 - x_3) - y_3 \wedge$$
$$x_5 = (y_2 - y_3)^2/(x_2 - x_3)^2 - x_2 - x_3 \qquad \wedge$$
$$y_5 = -(y_2 - y_3)/(x_2 - x_3)(x_5 - x_2) - y_2 \wedge$$
$$x_7 = (y_5 - y_1)^2/(x_5 - x_1)^2 - x_5 - x_1 \qquad \wedge$$
$$y_7 = -(y_5 - y_1)/(x_5 - x_1)(x_7 - x_1) - y_1$$
$$\Rightarrow x_6 - x_7 = 0$$

where

$$(x_4, y_4) = p_1 \oplus_g p_2, \ (x_5, y_5) = p_2 \oplus_g p_3,$$
$$(x_6, y_6) = (p_1 \oplus_g p_2) \oplus_g p_3 \text{ and } (x_7, y_7) = p_1 \oplus_g (p_2 \oplus_g p_3)$$

Fig. 1. Condition for the x component of the first case

We are then left with proving that $N = 0$. In our example, a naive normalisation gives

$$2^{10}y^8 - 2^{10}y^6x^3 - 2^{10}Ay^6x - 2^{10}By^6 = 0$$

The second step is to replace all the occurrences of y^2 by $x^3 + Ax + B$.

$$2^{10}(x^3 + Ax + B)^4 - 2^{10}(x^3 + Ax + B)^3x^3 - 2^{10}A(x^3 + Ax + B)^3x - 2^{10}B(x^3 + Ax + B)^3 = 0$$

The final step is to use distributivity, associativity, commutativity and collect equal monomials so that everything cancels out.

Note that even a dedicated computer algebra system like Maple may fail, by using the general Gröbner machinery, to prove such a large identity. The remedy, like here, is to perform "by hand" the reductions modulo the ideal $< y_1^2 - x_1^3 - Ax_1 - B, y_2^2 - x_2^3 - Ax_2 - B >$, by using the fact that the basis given for this ideal is already a Gröbner basis for the lex ordering $y_1 > y_2 > x_1 > x_2$.

To sum up, three ingredients are needed to automate the proof of the three lemmas corresponding to cases $1-3$: a procedure to normalise polynomial expressions (last step), a procedure to rewrite polynomial expressions (second step) and a procedure to normalise rational expressions (first step).

The procedure to normalise polynomial expressions was already present in COQ and is described in [11]. Its main characteristic is to use an internal representation of polynomials in Horner form. This representation is unique up to variable ordering. Given a polynomial P and a variable x, we write P as $P_1 + x^i Q_1$ where x does not occur in P_1 and is not a common factor in Q_1 and we proceed on P_1 and Q_1 recursively. The normal form is further simplified writing 0 for $m0$ and P for $0 + P$ and $P + 0$. For example

$$2^{10}y^8 - 2^{10}y^6x^3 - 2^{10}Ay^6x - 2^{10}By^6$$

is represented as

$$y^6((B(-2^{10}) + x(A(-2^{10}) + x^2(-2^{10}))) + y^2 2^{10})$$

for the ordering $y > x > A > B$. Once the procedures to add and multiply polynomials in Horner form have been defined, the normal form of a polynomial P is obtained by a simple structural traversal of P. As described in [11], this leads to a very effective way of proving ring equalities by just checking that the normal form of the left side of the equality is structurally equal to the normal form of the right side of the equality.

Rewriting has been implemented in a naive way on Horner representation. It uses a simple procedure that, given a monomial m, splits a polynomial P in a pair (P_1, Q_1) in such a way that $P = P_1 + mQ_1$. Now rewriting once with the equation $m = R$ is performed by building the polynomial $P_1 + RQ_1$. For example, if we want to rewrite the previous polynomial with the equation $y^2x^2 = z + t$, we first split the polynomial

$$y^6((B(-2^{10}) + x(A(-2^{10}) + x^2(-2^{10}))) + y^2 2^{10})$$

into

$$(\, y^6((B(-2^{10}) + x(A(-2^{10}))) + y^2 2^{10}) \,,\, y^4x(-2^{10}) \,)$$

We then build

$$(y^6((B(-2^{10}) + x(A(-2^{10}))) + y^2 2^{10})) + (z+t)(y^4x(-2^{10}))$$

and normalise it. For rewriting with respect to a list of equations, we just iterate the single rewriting operation for all the equations in a fair way. Note that in our specific case we are always rewriting with equations of the type $y_i^2 = x_i^3 + Ax_i + B$, so we take a special care in choosing a variable ordering for the Horner representation such that the y_i are privileged. By doing so, the splitting procedure has only to visit a small part of the polynomial.

Normalising rational equalities is not as simple as for polynomial expressions. When reducing the initial expression to a common denominator, the expressions for the numerator and the denominator can grow very quickly. Our experiments with the proofs of cases $1-3$ have shown that getting a normalised numerator of a reasonable size was mandatory in order to be able to complete the following rewriting phase. So, when normalising, some reductions are needed. For example, when normalising $P_1/Q_1 + P_2/Q_2$ we can do much better than building the naive fraction $(P_1Q_2 + P_2Q_1)/Q_1Q_2$. Unfortunately, gcd algorithms for multivariate polynomials are far more complex to implement than the simple Euclidean algorithm for univariate polynomials. So, we have just implemented a syntactic heuristic. Our heuristic factorises the products that are in common between Q_1

and Q_2 by a simple structural traversal of the lists of products that compose Q_1 and Q_2. For example, normalising $1/x + 1/xy + 1/y = 0$ gives $y + 1 + x = 0$.

The three procedures (polynomial normaliser, rewriter and rational normaliser) are put together in a single tactic `field`. This tactic works on arbitrary field structures. Given F a rational expression, calling the tactic `field[H₁ H₂]` attempts to solve the goal $F = 0$ using the rewriting rules `H₁` and `H₂`. The three procedures have been defined inside the COQ logic using the two-level approach [1]. Their correctness can then be stated inside the proof system and formally proved. This ensures once and for all applications that the `field` tactic only performs valid simplifications. A key aspect of this tactic is its efficiency. Proving the group law requires non-trivial computation. Having a relatively efficient procedure is mandatory to be able to complete the proof. On an Intel Xeon (2.66 GHz) with 2Gb of RAM, compiling the definition of elliptic curves up to associativity takes one minute and twenty seconds in COQ.

3   Prime Certificate

The group structure on $E(\mathbb{Z}/p\mathbb{Z})$ is used in the same way as the group structure on $(\mathbb{Z}/p\mathbb{Z})^*$ is used in Pocklington's $p - 1$ test, which we recall:

Proposition 1 (Pocklington). *Let N be an integer. Assume that there exists a coprime to N and s such that*

- *$a^s = 1 \bmod N$;*
- *for all prime divisor p of s, one has $\gcd(a^{s/p} - 1, N) = 1$.*

Then, for any prime $q|N$, one has $q = 1 \bmod s$, so that if $s \geq \sqrt{N}$, N is prime.

The main drawback of Pocklington's test is the fact that if one is not able to factor $N - 1$ to some extent (a little thought shows that the first condition implies, if N is actually prime, $s|N - 1$, since the conditions stated imply that s is the order of $a \bmod N$), then there is no way one can apply the theorem.

The following theorem is thus much more versatile, the main point being that, under reasonable conjectures, we are always able to find, in polynomial time, a curve over $\mathbb{Z}/N\mathbb{Z}$ with cardinality which can be factored.

We make use of points in projective coordinates, which is required to give a meaningful statement. This allows to give formulas without division for the group law, which thus remain meaningful in any ring – since $\mathbb{Z}/N\mathbb{Z}$ can be assumed to be a field only after N has been proved prime...

Proposition 2 (Goldwasser-Kilian). *Let N be an integer. Assume that there exist an elliptic curve $y^2 = x^3 + Ax + B$ with $A, B \in \mathbb{Z}$ and $\gcd(4A^3 + 27B^2, N) = 1$, a point $P = (x_P : y_P : 1)$ such that $y_P^2 = x_P^3 + Ax_P + B \bmod N$, and an integer s such that*

- *$s.P = (0 : 1 : 0) \bmod N$;*
- *for all prime $p|s$, $(s/p).P = (x_p : y_p : z_p) \bmod N$ with $\gcd(z_p, N) = 1$.*

Then, for all prime $q|N$, we have the number of points of $E(\mathbb{Z}/q\mathbb{Z})$ is such that $\#E(\mathbb{Z}/q\mathbb{Z}) = 0 \bmod s$.

In view of the Hasse-Weil bound [21], which states that for all prime q and elliptic curve E over $\mathbb{Z}/q\mathbb{Z}$, one has $\#E(\mathbb{Z}/q\mathbb{Z}) \leq (\sqrt{q} + 1)^2$, we see that N is prime as soon as $s > \sqrt{q} + 1$. In the sequel, we shall use the slightly weaker but much easier bound $\#E(\mathbb{Z}/q\mathbb{Z}) \leq 2q + 1$, which shows that N is prime as soon as $s > \sqrt{2q + 1}$.

An elliptic curve certificate is thus defined recursively by:

$$C_N := (N, A, B, x_P, y_P, s, (q_1, C_{q_1}), \ldots, (q_k, C_{q_k})),$$

where the q_i are the prime factors of s, and checking the certificate amounts to checking the hypotheses of the theorem, hence modular arithmetic.

Computing a certificate is a much harder problem. The most efficient way is to use the theory of complex multiplication, after Atkin and Morain. For a more extensive bibliography, the interested reader can refer to the nice survey of primality proving by Morain [19].

The idea behind the formal proof of Proposition 2 is to relate computations with projective coordinates done in $\mathbb{Z}/N\mathbb{Z}$ with the same computations with standard coordinates done in $\mathbb{Z}/q\mathbb{Z}$ when q is a prime divisor of N. We use a non-standard definition of projective coordinates where we still single out the zero. A point is either 0 or a triplet $(x : y : z)$. We also define the projection t_q as $t_q(0) = 0$ and $t_q((x : y : z)) = (x \bmod q/z \bmod q, y \bmod q/z \bmod q)$. Note that the projection in the second case is possible only if $z \bmod q$ has effectively an inverse in $\mathbb{Z}/q\mathbb{Z}$ for prime divisor q of N, so only if $gcd(n, N) = 1$. In the following, we write the property of n having an inverse as $inv_N(n)$.

We have to be careful when computing in $\mathbb{Z}/N\mathbb{Z}$ since we want the computation in $\mathbb{Z}/N\mathbb{Z}$ to project faithfully to the same computation in $\mathbb{Z}/q\mathbb{Z}$. Suppose that we test to zero a variable n. Obviously if we have $n = 0$, we also have $n \bmod q = 0$, but the converse may not be true: $n \neq 0$ does not imply that $n \bmod q \neq 0$. So every time we have a test to zero on a variable n, we have to check the extra condition that $inv_N(n)$ to ensure that the computation on $\mathbb{Z}/q\mathbb{Z}$ would take the same branch. For this reason, all the functions that we have defined for $\mathbb{Z}/N\mathbb{Z}$ take an extra argument that represents the side conditions so far and return a pair composed of the result plus the new side conditions. We encode all the side conditions in a single number using the property that $inv_N(mn)$ implies $inv_N(m)$ and $inv_N(n)$.

A result (p_1, sc_1) of a computation can be correctly interpreted only if we have $inv_N(sc_1)$ when $p_1 = 0$ or $inv_N(z_1 sc_1)$ when $p_1 = (x_1 : y_1 : z_1)$. In the following, we use the notation $\lceil p_1, sc_1 \rceil$ to indicate that this property holds. To give a concrete example, consider the function *double* that doubles a point p_1 under the initial side condition sc_1. Its definition is

$double(p_1, sc_1) =$
    if $p_1 = 0$ then $(0, \ sc_1)$ else
    let $(x_1 : y_1 : z_1) = p_1$ in

if $y_1 = 0$ then $(0, z_1 sc_1)$ else
let $m = 3x_1^2 + Az_1^2$ and $l = 2y_1z_1$ in
let $l_2 = l^2$ and $x_2 = m^2 z_1 - 2x_1 l_2$ in
$((x_2 l : l_2(x_1 m - y_1 l) - x_2 m : z_1 l_2 l), \ sc_1)$

and its correctness is stated as

$$\forall p_1 \ sc_1 \ p_2 \ sc_2, \ \texttt{let} \ (p_2, sc_2) = double(p_1, sc_1) \ \texttt{in} \ \lceil p_2, sc_2 \rceil \Rightarrow t_q(p_2) = 2.t_q(p_1)$$

Another key property is that the final side condition includes the initial one

$$\forall p_1 \ sc_1 \ p_2 \ sc_2, \ \texttt{let}(p_2, sc_2) = double(p_1, sc_1) \ \texttt{in} \ \lceil p_2, sc_2 \rceil \Rightarrow \lceil p_1, sc_1 \rceil$$

Knowing that these two properties must hold, we can now explain how the side conditions have been generated in the body of the function $double$. When p_1 is zero, no condition has to be added. When p_1 is $(x_1 : 0 : z_1)$, the result is zero so we include the final side condition that z_1 must be invertible. Finally, when p_1 is $(x_1 : y_1 : z_1)$ with $y_1 \neq 0$, a defensive final side conditions would be $y_1 z_1 sc_1$ to insure that y_1 and z_1 are invertible but this is not necessary since if we look at the z component, $z_1 l_2 l$, of the resulting point, that contains already the product $y_1 z_1$.

The function add that adds two points is defined in a similar way. With the two functions $double$ and add, we can define the function $scal$ that adds n times the point p_1 under the side condition sc_1:

$scal(n, p_1, sc_1) =$
    if $n = 1$ then (p_1, sc_1) else
    if n is even then let $(p_2, sc_2) = double(p_1, sc_1)$ in $scal(n/2, p_2, sc_2)$ else
    let $(p_2, sc_2) = double(p_1, sc_1)$ in
    let $(p_3, sc_3) = scal((n-1)/2, p_2, sc_2)$ in
    $add(p_1, p_3, sc_3)$

and its correctness is stated as

$$\forall n \ p_1 \ sc_1, \ p_2 \ sc_2, \ \texttt{let} \ (p_2, sc_2) = scal(n, p_1 sc_1) \ \texttt{in} \ \lceil p_2, sc_2 \rceil \Rightarrow t_p(p_2) = n.t_p(p_1)$$

Given a list $l = [(q_1, \alpha_1), \ldots, (q_n, \alpha_n)]$ such that $s = q_1^{\alpha_1} \ldots q_n^{\alpha_n}$, checking that $s.a = 0$ and $(s/q_i).a \neq 0$ for $1 \leq i \leq n$ is done by factorising computations as much as possible. We first compute $p_1 = (s/(q_1 \ldots q_n)).a$. The function $scalL$ that, given a point p_1 and a list l such that $l = [q_1, \ldots, q_n]$ and a side condition sc_1, verifies that $(q_1 \ldots q_n).p_1 = 0$ and $(q_1 \ldots q_n/q_i).p_1 \neq 0$ for every q_i is defined as follows

$scalL(l, p_1, sc_1) =$
    if $length(l) = 0$ then (p_1, sc_1) else
    let $(p_2, sc_2) = scal(hd(l), p_1, sc_1)$ in
    let $(p_3, sc_3) = scal\_list(tl(l), p_1, sc_2)$ in
        if $p_3 = 0$ then $(0, 0)$ else
        let $(x_3, y_3, z_3) = p_3$ in $scalL(tl(l), p_2, z_3 sc_3)$

where the functions hd and tl return the head element and the tail of a list respectively and the function $scal\_list$ applied to l and p_1, where $l = [q_i, \ldots, q_n]$, computes $(q_i \ldots q_n).p_1$. In every recursive call of the function $scalL$, p_3 represents one of the $(q_1 \ldots q_n/q_i).p_1$. If p_3 is 0, we put 0 in the side condition in order to invalidate the final result. If p_3 is not 0, $t_p(p_3)$ must also be non-zero so we add its z component into the side condition.

The actual representation of COQ certificates is a list of elementary certificates rather than a tree. This list must be well-founded in the sense that the primality of a number that is needed by an elementary certificate at position i is justified by another certificate at position $j > i$. An elementary certificate is either an immediate certificate, a Pocklington certificate or an elliptic certificate. An immediate certificate is for numbers whose primality is given by a predefined theorem. In our library there are predefined theorems for the first 5000 prime numbers. Our elliptic certificates slightly differ from the standard ones to accommodate the certificates produced by the tool PRIMO [17]. An elliptic certificate is composed of seven elements: $\{N, A, B, x_1, y_1, n_0, [(q_1, \alpha_1), \ldots, (q_n, \alpha_n)]\}$:

- N is the number to be proved prime;
- A and B are the parameters of the elliptic curve $y^2 = x^3 + Ax + B$;
- x_1 and y_1 are the coordinates of the initial point, in projective coordinates the initial point is $p_0 = (x_1 : y_1 : 1)$;
- n_0 is an initial scalar, so the point whose order is checked is $n_0.p_0$.
- $[(q_1, \alpha_1), \ldots, (q_n, \alpha_n)]$ is a complete factorisation of the order s of $n_0.p_0$, i.e. $s = q_1^{\alpha_1} \ldots q_n^{\alpha_n}$ where all the q_i are prime.

An example of such a certificate is

```
{
   329719147332060395689499,
   −94080,
   9834496,
   0,
   3136,
   8209062,
   [(40165264598163841, 1)]
}
```

It allows to assess the primality of 329719147332060395689499 knowing that 40165264598163841 is prime with the curve $y^2 = x^3 - 94080x + 9834496$ and the point $8209062.(0, 3136)$ whose order is 40165264598163841.

The function $testCertif$ that checks an elliptic certificate c is defined as follows:

$testCertif(c) =$
$\quad$ let $(N, A, B, x_1, y_1, n, l) = c$ in
$\quad$ let $p_0 = (x_1, y_1, 1)$ in
$\quad$ let $sc_0 = 4A^3 + 27B^2$ in
$\quad$ let $(p_1, sc_1) = scal(n, p_0, sc_0)$ in
$\quad$ let $s = mull(l)$ in

let $(n', l') = split(l)$ in
let $(p_2, sc_2) = scal(n', p_1, sc_1)$ in
let $(p_3, sc_3) = scalL(l', p_2, sc_2)$ in
$N > 1$ and $odd(N)$ and $4N < (s - 1)^2$ and
$\quad y_1^2 \bmod N = (x_1^3 + Ax_1 + B) \bmod N$ and
$\quad p_3 = 0$ and $gcd(sc3, N) = 1$

where, if $l = [(q_1, \alpha_1), \ldots, (q_n, \alpha_n)]$, the function $mull$ applied to l returns $q_1^{\alpha_1} \ldots q_n^{\alpha_n}$ and the function $split$ applied to l returns $(q_1^{\alpha_1 - 1} \ldots q_n^{\alpha_n - 1}, [q_1, \ldots, q_n])$. The correctness of the function $testCertif$ is stated as

$$\forall c, (testCertif(c) = true \land (\forall q\, \alpha, (q, \alpha) \in getL(c) \Rightarrow prime(q))) \Rightarrow prime(getN(c))$$

where $getN$ and $getL$ are the accessor functions for the first component and the last component of the certificate respectively.

Proving the correctness of the function $testCertif$ is straightforward. It is standard program verification. Getting the side conditions right was the only tricky part. Note that it would be very difficult to detect a missing side condition just by testing. The program only returns a boolean value and it is mainly applied to certificates for which a positive answer is expected. Missing a side condition never invalidates valid certificates. Compared to standard checkers, we had to compromise with the bound on the order s of an element over $\mathbb{Z}/q\mathbb{Z}$. We use the naive bound $4N < (s - 1)^2$ that is easy to establish. Standard checkers use the sharper Hasse-Weil bound. Getting this bound formally is a challenge on its own.

4   Some Benchmarks

Figure 2 shows some benchmarks on prime numbers from 25 to 250 decimal digits. These benchmarks have been done on a processor Intel Xeon (2.66 GHz) with 2Gb of RAM. For each number length, there are nine examples. We generate the ith example of length n by starting with the digit i and repetitively incrementing the previous digit by 1 modulo 10 to get the next digit. Once we have n digits, we just take the first prime number above this number. For example, the nine prime numbers with 25 digits are:

1234567890123456789012353,	2345678901234567890123567,
3456789012345678901234573,	4567890123456789012345689,
5678901234567890123456797,	6789012345678901234567903,
7890123456789012345678973,	8901234567890123456789017,
9012345678901234567890149	

To generate certificates, we automatically convert the ones produced by the program PRIMO. For each example, we give the number of Pocklington certificates and elliptic certificates that compose the overall certificate and the time in seconds that COQ needs to verify the certificate. Out of the 1538 elliptic certificates generated by the standard version of PRIMO only two could not be proved inside

		25	50	75	100	125	150	175	200	225	250
	$n-1$	1	0	4	2	3	5	5	2	6	7
1	ell	1	4	8	13	14	17	20	26	28	28
	time	0.2	8	36	105	297	523	865	1570	2353	3018
	$n-1$	0	5	3	3	2	3	4	4	3	6
2	ell	2	1	7	10	19	21	24	24	27	35
	time	0.9	4	26	105	333	569	1007	1704	2462	3573
	$n-1$	2	0	1	4	4	1*	4	3	5	7
3	ell	2	1	7	10	19	19*	24	25	27	35
	time	0.1	11	42	132	288	515*	1277	1774	2477	2960
	$n-1$	2	3	4	0	4	6	3	3	7	5
4	ell	2	4	7	12	12	9	22	27	30	40
	time	1.1	11	49	130	257	339	948	1754	2275	4688
	$n-1$	1	3	3	5	3	5	8	3	4	3
5	ell	1	2	6	9	11	20	20	29	33	37
	time	0.7	3	36	143	264	514	1092	1859	2882	4090
	$n-1$	1	2	4	3*	4	2	7	4	2	1
6	ell	0	3	8	14*	14	19	21	22	34	33
	time	0.1	6	39	189*	223	479	977	1317	2811	3727
	$n-1$	0	1	5	2	1	2	4	5	7	3
7	ell	2	4	10	14	16	19	27	27	28	34
	time	0.8	11	54	148	329	453	1259	1514	2498	3327
	$n-1$	2	2	3	7	4	5	2	7	2	1
8	ell	0	4	7	6	17	20	28	31	34	40
	time	0.1	6	44	91	310	489	1442	2252	2817	3721
	$n-1$	2	2	3	5	7	4	5	7	5	5
9	ell	1	4	10	13	9	20	27	26	29	33
	time	0.4	7	46	139	194	549	1229	2061	2509	3645

Fig. 2. Checking certificates for numbers from 25 to 250 digits

Coq. They are indicated by a star in Figure 2. This comes from the fact that our condition $4N < (s-1)^2$ is stronger than the usual bound given by Hasse Theorem. The first certificate that fails is for $N = 896191029759386718510467381341$ and $s = 1501356318335977$, the second one for $N = 13524493647665641984723$ and $s = 95147824089$. To let us prove these primes correct, Marcel Martin, the developer of PRIMO, has added an extra option to PRIMO so to make the search for certificates "less aggressive" and only generate certificates that can be checked using the modified Hasse bound. The two certificates indicated by a star in Figure 2 have been generated using this extra option.

All the examples and the code are available at

http://coqprime.gforge.inria.fr/

They compile with the current version 8.1 of the Coq system. The time to check a certificate grows quickly with the number of digits, for example we need one hour to check a number with 250 decimal digits. Note that the theory predicts that the worst-case complexity for checking a certificate for N with an underlying quadratic multiprecision arithmetic is $O((\log N)^4)$, which more or less corresponds to what we observe. Note also that it would be easy to gain a small constant factor in the current implementation by optimizing our function *scal*, eg. by using sliding window methods and/or addition-substraction chains.

In order to be able to check larger numbers, we would need two main improvements in the COQ system. First, all our computations are done inside COQ with user-defined data-structures, i.e. we use the modular arithmetic defined in [10] based on a datatype composed of 256 constructors that simulates an 8-bit arithmetic. We would need a direct access to the machine 32-bit arithmetic instead. In [10], some tests for Pocklington certificates with a native 32-bits arithmetic exhibit a speed-up of 80. Such speed-up would make it possible, in our case, to verify a 250-digit number in less than a minute. We have also experienced with extracting our code to OCAML [16] and linking it with the arbitrary-precision integer library BIGNUM [20]. We got in this case an even bigger speed-up since checking one of our 250-digit numbers only takes 0.2 second and we were capable to check in 36 seconds the millennium prime, a prime with 2000 decimal digits whose certificate generated by PRIMO contains 245 elliptic certificates and 8 Pocklington ones.

Second, we are in a purely functional setting and a large amount of time is thus spent in allocating memory for new numbers. Computations should use constant memory to be really efficient. For this, we would need COQ to accommodate destructive datastructures as proposed for ACL2 in [2] with a monadic approach.

5   Conclusion

We believe that what is presented in this paper is a very nice illustration of a key aspect of formal verification. Defining prime numbers from scratch is very simple in a proof assistant. It is done with five definitions in COQ: one for the natural numbers, one for the addition, one for the multiplication, one for the divisibility and finally one for the primality. All these definitions are straightforward, so it is easy to get convinced that the notion of primality has been correctly captured in the proof system. Then, the fact that there exists a formal proof for each of the numbers of Figure 2 ensures that the primality of these numbers follows logically from these five definitions. For the actual proofs, we are free to use any elaborate devices like in our case elliptic certificates. Of course, this is true only if the proof system is sound. It is then crucial to keep the trusted base of the prover as small as possible. This is what we have done here, reflecting the symbolic manipulations and internally checking the prime certificates generated by PRIMO.

Another aspect that this example illustrates is how important is for a proof system not only to reason right but also to compute right. Our initial attempts in proving cases $1-3$ have clearly indicated that we were on the fringe of what was actually possible to prove inside COQ: the parser had problems to handle the huge terms we were generating and using the standard rewriting tactic of

COQ was generating titanic proof terms. Reflecting symbolic manipulation was the key point that made everything possible. All we have developed was generic enough to be integrated into the COQ system. Nevertheless, a way to look at what we have done is to consider that we have just been reflecting a specific rewriting strategy. It would be interesting to investigate how we could reflect a generic rewriting strategy instead and get back our symbolic manipulation by simple instantiation.

Finally, the initial motivation that has lead to this work was to see how far we could go in proving primality inside a proof system. With elliptic certificates, we have reached the current state of the art. We can now prove the primality of any number with less than 300 decimal digits. We believe that, with the future improvement of numerical evaluation inside COQ, this limit will quickly increase. Anyway, the infrastructure is there. In particular, this is, to our knowledge, the first time that associativity has been formally proved inside a proof system. We hope that this initial effort will motivate deeper mathematical formalisations with elliptic curves inside proof systems.

Acknowledgments

Many people made this work possible. Joe Hurd was the first to draw our attention to formalising elliptic curves inside a prover [14]. After unsuccessful attempts, John Harrison revitalised our interest showing us that he could automatically solve the equation of the x component of the generic case in less than 3 minutes inside HOLLIGHT [12] with his integrated version of Buchberger algorithm. Bruno Barras and Benjamin Grégoire helped us with their expertise in integrating the `field` tactic into COQ. Finally, Marcel Martin has very kindly added extra options to the PRIMO system to fit our needs.

References

1. Boutin, S.: Using Reflection to Build Efficient and Certified Decision Procedures. In: Ito, T., Abadi, M. (eds.) TACS 1997. LNCS, vol. 1281, pp. 515–529. Springer, Heidelberg (1997)
2. Boyer, R.S., Moore, J.S.: Single-threaded objects in ACL2. In: Ramakrishnan, I.V. (ed.) PADL 2001. LNCS, vol. 1990, pp. 9–27. Springer, Heidelberg (2001)
3. Buchberger, B.: Introduction to Gröbner Bases. In: Buchberger, B., Winkler, F. (eds.) Gröbner Bases and Applications, pp. 3–31. Cambridge University Press, Cambridge (1998)
4. Capani, A., Niesi, G., Robbiano, L.: Cocoa: Computations in commutative algebra, available at http://cocoa.dima.unige.it/
5. Cohen, H., Frey, G.: Handbook of Elliptic and Hyperelliptic Curve Cryptography. Discrete Mathematics and Its Applications. Chapman & Hall / CRC (2005)
6. Créci, J., Pottier, L.: Gb: une procédure de décision pour le système Coq. In: JFLA'2004, pp. 83–90 (2004)
7. Friedl, S.: An elementary proof of the group law for elliptic curves. Excerpt from undergraduate thesis, Regensburg (1998), available at
http://www.labmath.uqam.ca/~friedl/papers/AAELLIPTIC.PDF

8. Goldwasser, S., Kilian, J.: Almost all primes can be quickly certified. In: Proceedings of the 18th STOC, pp. 316–329 (1986)
9. Grégoire, B., Théry, L.: A Purely Functional Library for Modular Arithmetic and its Application to Certifying Large Prime Numbers. In: Furbach, U., Shankar, N. (eds.) IJCAR 2006. LNCS (LNAI), vol. 4130, pp. 423–437. Springer, Heidelberg (2006)
10. Grégoire, B., Théry, L., Werner, B.: A Computational Approach to Pocklington Certificates in Type Theory. In: Hagiya, M., Wadler, P. (eds.) FLOPS 2006. LNCS, vol. 3945, pp. 97–113. Springer, Heidelberg (2006)
11. Grégoire, B., Mahboubi, A.: Proving ring equalities done right in Coq. In: Hurd, J., Melham, T. (eds.) TPHOLs 2005. LNCS, vol. 3603, pp. 98–113. Springer, Heidelberg (2005)
12. Harrison, J.: HOL light: A tutorial introduction. In: Srivas, M., Camilleri, A. (eds.) FMCAD 1996. LNCS, vol. 1166, pp. 265–269. Springer, Heidelberg (1996)
13. Harrison, J.: Complex quantifier elimination in HOL. In: Boulton, R.J., Jackson, P.B. (eds.) TPHOLs 2001. LNCS, vol. 2152, pp. 159–174. Springer, Heidelberg (2001)
14. Hurd, J.: Formalized elliptic curve cryptography, available at `http://www.cl.cam.ac.uk/~jeh1004/research/talks/elliptic-talk.pdf`
15. Lenstra Jr., H.W.: Factoring integers with elliptic curves. Ann. Math. 126, 649–673 (1987)
16. Leroy, X.: Objective Caml (1997), available at `http://pauillac.inria.fr/ocaml/`
17. Martin, M.: PRIMO - primality proving, available at `http://www.ellipsa.net/`
18. Morain, F.: Certificate for $(((((((((2^3 + 3)^3 + 30)^3 + 6)^3 + 80)^3 + 12)^3 + 450)^3 + 894)^3 + 3636)^3 + 70756)^3 + 97220$, available at `http://www.lix.polytechnique.fr/Labo/Francois.Morain`
19. Morain, F.: La primalité en temps polynomial, d'après Adleman, Huang; Agrawal, Kayal, Saxena. Séminaire Bourbaki, 3(55) (2002)
20. Ménissier-Morain, V.: The CAML Numbers Reference Manual. Technical Report 141, INRIA (1992)
21. Silverman, J.H.: The Arithmetic of Elliptic Curves. Springer, Heidelberg (1986)
22. The COQ development team: The Coq Proof Assistant Reference Manual v7.2. Technical Report 255, INRIA (2002), available at `http://coq.inria.fr/doc`
23. Théry, L.: Proving the group law for elliptic curves formally. Technical Report 330, INRIA (2007)

HOL2P - A System of Classical Higher Order Logic with Second Order Polymorphism

Norbert Völker

University of Essex, England
http://cswww.essex.ac.uk/staff/norbert

Abstract. This paper introduces the logical system HOL2P that extends classical higher order logic (HOL) with type operator variables and universal types. HOL2P has explicit term operations for type abstraction and type application. The formation of type application terms $t\,[T]$ is restricted to small types T that do not contain any universal types. This constraint ensures the existence of a set-theoretic model and thus consistency.

The expressiveness of HOL2P allows category-theoretic concepts such as natural transformations and initial algebras to be applied at the level of polymorphic HOL functions. The parameterisation of terms with type operators adds genericity to theorems. Type variable quantification can also be expressed.

A prototype of HOL2P has been implemented on top of HOL-Light. Type inference is semi-automatic, and some type annotations are necessary. Reasoning is supported by appropriate tactics. The implementation has been used to check some sample derivations.

1 Introduction

Classical higher order logic (HOL) is one of the most successful logics in mechanised theorem proving. Theorem proving assistants based on it include the original HOL system [7], and its various descendants such as HOL4, Proof-Power and HOL-Light [9]. In these systems, the logic is coupled with a simply-typed polymorphic λ-calculus, that was extended with type classes in case of Isabelle/HOL [15].

The design of HOL theorem provers has been influenced by functional programming languages and their type systems. In the latter domain, there has been a lot of research into systems that go beyond simply-typed polymorphism, see for example extensions of Haskell in the Glasgow Haskell Compiler (GHC) [12]. An important driving force for these developments has been the wish to support generic programming [2,1].

The research described in this paper is an experiment in extending higher order logic beyond simply-typed polymorphism. The aim is to support more generic theorems that can be instantiated to particular polymorphic functions and type constructors. The inspiration comes from the way category-theoretic notions [13] have been applied in generic programming. In addition, the system should allow quantification over type variables as introduced by T. Melham [14].

K. Schneider and J. Brandt (Eds.): TPHOLs 2007, LNCS 4732, pp. 334–351, 2007.
© Springer-Verlag Berlin Heidelberg 2007

2 A Recap of Higher Order Logic

It is assumed that the reader has a working understanding of higher-order logic. The following section provides a brief recap as a basis for discussing the HOL2P extensions. The details of the presentation follow HOL-Light.

The HOL syntax is that of a simply-typed polymorphic lambda calculus. Every term belongs to exactly one type. HOL types are either type variables, or type constructor applications:

$$T ::= \alpha \qquad\qquad \text{type variable}$$
$$|\ (T_1, \ldots, T_n)\, \tau \quad \text{type constructor application } (n \geq 0)$$

Type constructors are identified by their name and have a fixed arity. Primitive HOL type constructors are the 0-ary *bool*, a type of individuals *ind* and the binary function type operator *fun*. The latter is usually written in infix form using the "$\to$" symbol. New type constructors can be defined via a bijection to a non-empty subset of an existing type. In particular, the type *num* of natural numbers is defined as isomorphic to a subset of *ind*.

Types containing type variables are called polymorphic. Type substitution replaces type variables in a type with other types. The type resulting from a substitution is also called an instance of the original type.

HOL terms are either variables, constants, applications or abstractions.

$$t ::= v : T \qquad\quad \text{variable}$$
$$|\ \ c : T \qquad\quad \text{constant}$$
$$|\ \ t\, t \qquad\qquad \text{application}$$
$$|\ \ \lambda\,(v : T).\, t \quad \text{abstraction}$$

Constants are uniquely identified by their name. Polymorphic constants can have differently typed instances, and each constant occurrence in a term is annotated with its type. Variables are identified by their name and HOL type. Variables with the same name but a different HOL type are unrelated. In particular, a λ-abstraction with a bound variable v does not bind variables in the abstraction body with the same name as v but a different type.

An explicit specification of all types in a term would be extremely cumbersome. Like in functional languages, HOL gets around this problem by an automated type inference process that starts off with an untyped HOL term and adds types to the constants and variables occurring in the term.

In HOL-Light, the only primitive constants are equality and Hilbert's choice operator. New constants can be introduced as abbreviations for expressions that are build up from existing constants.

Term instantiation replaces variables in a term with other terms. Unlike type variables, term variables can be bound, so instantiation only applies to the free variables.

HOL theorems take the form of sequents $(n \geq 0)$:

$$P_1, \ldots, P_n \vdash P$$

where the hypotheses P_i as well as the conclusion P are terms of type *bool*. Theorems can be generated by various inference rules. In HOL-Light, there are ten primitive inference rules. The following rules are of most interest here:

— Rule ABS says that in order to show equality of two λ-abstractions with identical bound variables, it is sufficient to show the equality of the abstraction bodies. The rule has the side condition that the bound variable x does not occur free in any of the assumptions Γ:

$$\frac{\Gamma \vdash s = t}{\Gamma \vdash \lambda x.\, s = \lambda x.\, t} \tag{ABS}$$

— Rule MK_COMB says that in order to show equality of two applications, it is sufficient to show equality of the operators and the operands.

$$\frac{\Gamma_1 \vdash f = g \qquad \Gamma_2 \vdash x = y}{\Gamma_1 \cup \Gamma_2 \vdash f\, x = g\, y} \tag{MK\_COMB}$$

— Rule BETA is the trivial case of β-conversion from typed λ-calculus. The general case can be derived from this by applying the instantiation rule INST which is described later.

$$\frac{}{\Gamma \vdash (\lambda x.\, t)x = t} \tag{BETA}$$

— Rule INST_TYPE describes the fact that type variables are schematic, which means that the substitution of types variables in a theorem results in a new theorem. Note that instantiation applies to both hypotheses and the conclusion.

$$\frac{\Gamma[\alpha_1, \ldots, \alpha_n] \vdash p[\alpha_1, \ldots, \alpha_n]}{\Gamma[T_1, \ldots, T_n] \vdash p[T_1, \ldots, T_n]} \tag{INST\_TYPE}$$

— Rule INST is analogous but describes the instantiation of variables by terms of the same type.

$$\frac{\Gamma[x_1, \ldots, x_n] \vdash p[x_1, \ldots, x_n]}{\Gamma[t_1, \ldots, t_n] \vdash p[t_1, \ldots, t_n]} \tag{INST}$$

HOL also has type and term definition principles. These yield theorems that connect the new type constructors to non-empty subsets of existing types, and the new term constants to existing terms. In both cases, the extended theory can be shown to have the same set-theoretic semantic model as the original one. Lastly, in case of HOL-Light, there are just three axioms: eta-conversion from λ-calculus, an axiom for Hilbert's choice which make the logic classical, and an axiom expressing infinity of type *ind*.

HOL theorem proving systems have earned a reputation as being extremely trustworthy. This stems to a significant degree from their clean system architecture that follows the LCF approach [6], as well as the combination of a small number of basic inference rules and axioms with a few definitional extension principles that are logically safe.

Limitations of Simply-Typed Polymorphism

A lot of theorem proving can be done within the simply-typed HOL polymorphic framework. However, there are some cases where its limitations do bite. Generic Programming is a calculus that allows programs to be parameterised with type operators. While there has been some research on formalising this framework in HOL [5], the simple-type restriction does not allow to apply it at the level of polymorphic HOL functions.

As an example, consider a predicate *functor* which asserts that a HOL function ϕ is a functor from the category of HOL functions to itself. According to its mathematical definition, this means that ϕ should preserve the identity ($id = \lambda x.\ x$) and function composition:

$$\phi\ id = id \tag{1}$$

$$\phi\ (f \circ g) = \phi\ f \circ \phi\ g \tag{2}$$

A typical example for such a function ϕ is the map operation on lists:

$$
\begin{aligned}
&map\_list\ ::\ (\alpha \to \beta) \to \alpha\ list \to \beta\ list \\
&map\_list\ f\ [\,] &&= [\,] \\
&map\_list\ f\ (cons\ x\ xs) &&= cons\ (f\ x)\ (map\_list\ f\ xs) \\
&map\_list\ id &&= id \\
&map\_list\ (f \circ g) &&= map\_list\ f \circ map\_list\ g
\end{aligned}
$$

There are two problems if one tries to define a general HOL predicate *functor* that characterises those functions ϕ that satisfy rules (1, 2):

1. From abstracting the type constructor *list* in the *map_list* example, one would expect *functor* to be parameterised with a unary type operator variable. There are no type operator variables in HOL.
2. In general, the three occurrences of ϕ in equation (2) all have different types. It is not possible to have differently typed instances of one variable in HOL.

The conclusion is that simply-typed polymorphic higher order logic is not expressive enough for the formalisation of such a *functor* predicate on polymorphic HOL functions. Similar problems arise with the application of other category-theoretic concepts such as natural transformations or initial algebras.

3   The Logic HOL2P

3.1   HOL2P Types

The type system of HOL2P extends simply typed HOL with:

- Universal types ($\Pi \alpha.\ T$) which bind a type variable α in a type T.
- Type variables with an arity greater than zero. These will normally be referred to as "type operator variables" in order to distinguish them from the usual 0-ary type variables.

Universal types are known from the polymorphic λ-calculus ("System F") [4]. By supporting nested type quantification, they make it possible to define functions with "truly polymorphic" arguments that can be instantiated with different types. Type operator variables have been used in some programming language type systems [16].
The syntax of HOL2P types is as follows ($n \geq 0$):

$$
\begin{array}{lll}
T ::= & (\alpha :: rank) & \text{type variable (rank} = large \text{ or rank} = small) \\
\mid & (T_1, \ldots, T_n)\ \tau & \text{type constructor application} \\
\mid & (T_1, \ldots, T_n)\ \theta & \text{type operator variable application} \\
\mid & \Pi\,(\alpha :: small).\ T & \text{universal type}
\end{array}
$$

For an n-fold universal type, there is the usual abbreviated notation:

$$\Pi\,\alpha_1 \ldots \alpha_n.\ T = \Pi\,\alpha_1.\ (\ \ldots(\Pi\,\alpha_n.\ T))$$

The *rank* of a type variable is either *large* or *small*. A type will be called *small* if it does not contain any large type variables and no universal types. The instantiation of small type variables is restricted to small types. Small HOL2P types that do not contain any type operator variables correspond to the normal HOL types.
    The introduction of universal types that bind type variables leads to a distinction between *free* and *bound type* type variables in a type. A bound type variable is always small. Type operator variables can not be bound in HOL2P and are thus always free. A type is called *closed* if it has no free type variables and no type operator variables. Two types are α-*convertible* if they can be made identical by a replacement of bound type variables with fresh new type variables. There is no β-conversion of types, as the HOL2P type system does not have a corresponding application operation.
    When writing down HOL2P formulas and types, all free type variables are assumed by default to be large, while the bound type variables are small. With this convention in mind, the explicit indication of the rank of type variables can usually be omitted. As an example, here is a HOL2P type for the *functor* predicate from above:

$$functor :: (\Pi\,\alpha\ \beta.\ (\alpha\ \rightarrow \beta) \rightarrow \alpha\ \theta \rightarrow \beta\ \theta)\ \rightarrow\ bool \qquad (3)$$

The definition of type substitution in HOL2P has to take bindings of type variables into account. Only free type variables can be instantiated. Also, the capture of type variables needs to be avoided. The latter can be ensured as usual by performing α-conversions that introduce fresh bound type variables as necessary. Lastly, as mentioned above, a small type variable may only be instantiated with a small type.

The substitution of an n-ary type operator variable θ can take two forms.

- The replacement is an n-ary type constructor τ. In this case, the replacement of an occurrence $(T_1 \ldots T_n)\,\theta$ is simply the type $(T_1, \ldots, T_n)\,\tau$.
- The replacement can be an n-ary type operator that is specified using the universal type syntax $(\Pi\,\alpha_1 \ldots \alpha_n.\ T)$ with T a small type. In this case, the replacement of $(T_1 \ldots T_n)\,\theta$ is the type T with occurrences of each variable α_i replaced by the corresponding argument type T_i.

As an example for a type substitution, consider the type of predicate $\widetilde{functor}(3)$. Replacing the 1-ary type variable θ with the type constructor *list* yields:

$$(\Pi\,\alpha\ \beta.\ (\alpha\ \to\ \beta) \to \alpha\ list \to \beta\ list)\ \to\ bool$$

while a substitution of θ with the 1-ary type operator specified by $(\Pi\,\alpha.\ (\alpha\ list)\ list)$ gives the following instance:

$$(\Pi\,\alpha\ \beta.\ (\alpha\ \to\ \beta) \to (\alpha\ list)list \to (\beta\ list)list)\ \to\ bool$$

HOL2P has the same primitive type constructors as HOL, and new type constructors can be introduced that are isomorphic to non-empty subsets of existing types. Such type definitions will be restricted to small types, as this allows the simple syntactic characterisation of small types given above.

3.2   HOL2P Terms

HOL2P extends the terms of HOL with type abstractions and type applications. This gives the following syntax of terms:

$$
\begin{array}{lll}
t ::= & (v : T) & \text{variable} \\
\mid & (c : T) & \text{constant} \\
\mid & t\,t & \text{application} \\
\mid & \lambda\,(v : T).\,t & \text{abstraction} \\
\mid & \Lambda\,\alpha.\,t & \text{type abstraction} \\
\mid & t\,[T] & \text{type application}
\end{array}
$$

There are two important restrictions on the formation of terms:

(R1) As in System F, the formation of a type abstraction term $\Lambda\,\alpha.\,t$ has the side condition that the type variable α must not occur freely in the type of any free variable of t.

(R2) In a type application term $t\,[T]$, T must be a small type.

The typing rules for HOL2P variables, constants, applications and abstractions are as in HOL. For type abstractions and type application terms, we have:

$$\Lambda\alpha.\,(t:T) \qquad : \Pi\alpha.\,T$$
$$(t:\Pi\alpha.\,S)\,[T] : S[T\backslash\alpha]$$

It follows that the type variable α in a type abstraction term $(\Lambda\alpha.\,t)$ as well as all type variables within the argument type T of a type application $(t\,[T])$ must be small. This will be assumed whenever a HOL2P term is written down.

With the exception of type operator variables, the types and terms of HOL2P are a subset of those of System F. The typing rules of HOL2P agree with those in System F, apart from an implicit "type β-reduction" that needs to be applied to the System F type of a type application term so as to obtain the corresponding HOL2P type.

Type membership in HOL2P is unique modulo α-equivalence of types. In particular, if T and T' are two α-convertible types and t is a term, then $t:T$ holds if and only if $t:T'$.

Having both term and type variable bindings in HOL2P terms means that α-equivalence needs to allow for a renaming of either kind of bound variables. It also gives rise to a β-conversion of type abstraction/application combinations discussed in Section 3.3.

Because of restriction (R1) on the formation of type abstractions, the free variables in a type abstraction $\Lambda\alpha.\,t$ or application $t\,[T]$ are the same as the free variables of the base term t. This implies that the two new term formation operations do not interfere with term substitutions, i.e. for a term variable v and a replacement term r of the same type as v, we have:

$$(\Lambda\alpha.\,t)\,[r\backslash v] = \Lambda\alpha.\,t\,[r\backslash v]$$
$$(t\,[T])\,[r\backslash v] = (t\,[r\backslash v])\,[T]$$

For type instantiations of HOL2P terms, the possible capture of type variables in type abstractions needs to be taken into account. This can be solved as usual by α-conversions that introduce fresh bound type variables.

In the area of theorem proving, universal types are well known from systems based on intuitionistic logic such as COQ [17]. For classical higher order logic, there is the problem that its combination with the full polymorphic λ-calculus is inconsistent [3]. In HOL2P, this is avoided by permitting only a subset of polymorphic λ-calculus terms - (R2) restricts HOL2P terms such that only type abstractions over small types can occur.

HOL2P is also restricted in the sense that the formation of universal types is limited to 0-ary type variables, despite the presence of type operator variables in the system. Because of these restrictions, the term "second order polymorphism" seems appropriate for HOL2P.

3.3   Rules

All HOL inference rules also apply in HOL2P. As an example, the inference rule
REFL

$$\overline{\Gamma \vdash t = t} \tag{REFL}$$

expresses the reflexivity of equality on HOL2P terms. In case of rule INST_TYPE, HOL2P extends the HOL version with type operator variable instantiation, and the instantiation of type (operator) variables has to preserve the smallness of types.

HOL2P has three additional inference rules compared to HOL. These support equational reasoning with type abstractions and applications.

- The congruence rule for type variable abstraction is analogous to the HOL congruence rule ABS for term abstractions. It also has a similar side condition in that the type variable α must not occur freely in the assumption list Γ:

$$\frac{\Gamma \vdash s = t}{\Gamma \vdash \Lambda \alpha.\, s = \Lambda \alpha.\, t} \tag{TYABS}$$

- The congruence rule for type application is reminiscent of the HOL rule MK_CONG, but the assumption about equality of the argument terms is replaced by a side condition that the two argument types S and T have to be α-equivalent.

$$\frac{\Gamma \vdash s = t}{\Gamma \vdash s\,[S] = t\,[T]} \tag{TYAPP}$$

- There is also a β-conversion rule for combinations of type abstraction and applications terms. This is similar to the HOL rule BETA. Again, the general case of this rule can be derived from the special case by suitable instantiations.

$$\overline{\Gamma \vdash (\Lambda \alpha.\, t)\,[\alpha] = t} \tag{TYBETA}$$

Lastly, the three HOL axioms and the type and term definition principles also carry over to HOL2P. As already explained, there is a pragmatic restriction in that type definitions are not allowed to involve universal types, as this avoids the need to annotate type constructors with a small/large label.

4   Outline of HOL2P Semantics

Simple-typed higher order logic has a set-theoretic semantics due to A. Pitts [8]. Recently, J. Harrison [10] has proof checked a variation of this semantics in HOL-Light. Our presentation takes some inspiration from the latter source. In particular, we follow its lead by constructing only a standard model for the three primitive HOL type constructors *bool*, *ind* and function space. It is straightforward (but somewhat tedious) to extend the approach so as to cater for other HOL type constructors introduced by type definitions.

The HOL2P semantics will be given in four steps:

1. A recap of the standard semantics for HOL types and terms.
2. The construction of a universe for HOL2P types.
3. The semantics of HOL2P types.
4. The semantics of HOL2P terms.

4.1   The Semantics of HOL Terms

According to the well-known semantics of simple-typed HOL [8], there exists a universe $\mathcal{U}_0$ of sets such that each *monomorphic* HOL type T is modelled by a set $[\![T]\!] \in \mathcal{U}_0$. In addition, it can be assumed that the interpretation is standard:

- the model of type *bool* is a special two-element set `boolset`,
- the model of type *ind* is a special infinite set `indset` and
- the model of a function type $A \to B$ is the set theoretic function space between the models of A and B:

$$[\![A \to B]\!] = [\![A]\!] \to_{set} [\![B]\!]$$

The subscript *set* in $\to_{set}$ is used to distinguish the set theoretic function space from the HOL function space.

The semantics $[\![T]\!]_\rho$ of a general, possibly *polymorphic*, HOL type T is parameterised with a valuation function ρ which associates each type variable with an element of $\mathcal{U}_0$.

The meaning $[\![t]\!]_{\sigma,\rho}$ of a HOL term t is additionally parameterised with a valuation σ that associates each variable with an element of some set in $\mathcal{U}_0$.

The term model has to be consistent with the type model:

$$[\![t : T]\!]_{\sigma,\rho} \in [\![T]\!]_\rho$$

4.2   A Universe for HOL2P Types

Because of restriction (R2), the type variable α in a HOL2P universal type $\Pi\,\alpha.\ T$ can only be instantiated with a small HOL2P type. Ignoring type operator variables for the moment, small HOL2P types correspond to types of HOL, and thus can be interpreted as U_0 elements. This suggests that HOL2P universal types can be modelled as products over U_0. This observation leads us to a introduce a new set-theoretic universe $\mathcal{U}_1$ with the following properties:

- $\mathcal{U}_1$ extends $\mathcal{U}_0$: $\mathcal{U}_0 \subseteq \mathcal{U}_1$
- $\mathcal{U}_1$ is closed with respect to the function space operator: $A \in \mathcal{U}_1 \wedge B \in \mathcal{U}_1 \to A \to_{set} B \in \mathcal{U}_1$
- $\mathcal{U}_1$ is closed with respect to the formation of set theoretic products indexed by $\mathcal{U}_0$, i.e. for $f : \mathcal{U}_0 \to \mathcal{U}_1$ we have $\Pi_{u \in \mathcal{U}_0} f\ u \in \mathcal{U}_1$.

Similar to the case of $\mathcal{U}_0$, such a set $\mathcal{U}_1$ can be constructed iteratively by starting from the base set $\mathcal{U}_0$ and adding in iteration $(n + 1)$ all the sets that can be formed from the elements of iteration n by applying either the function space operator or products indexed over $\mathcal{U}_0$.

4.3   The Semantics of HOL2P Types

The interpretation of HOL2P types has to take type operator variables of arity $n > 0$ into account. These will be modelled as n-ary functions of type $\mathcal{U}_1^n \to \mathcal{U}_1$. This means that the semantics $[\![\, T \,]\!]_\rho$ of a HOL2P type T is parameterised with a valuation function ρ which maps each type (operator) variable of arity $n \geq 0$ to an element of $\mathcal{U}_1^n \to \mathcal{U}_1$.

Small HOL2P types should be modelled as elements of the $\mathcal{U}_0$ subset of $\mathcal{U}_1$. This is ensured by imposing two restrictions on the valuation functions ρ used in HOL2P type interpretations. Firstly, they have to respect smallness of type variables, e.g. small type variables must be mapped to elements of $\mathcal{U}_0$:

$$\rho\,(\alpha :: small) \in \mathcal{U}_0$$

Secondly, because type operator variable applications preserve the smallness of types, the valuation $\rho\,\theta$ of a type operator variable must be a function that preserves the $\mathcal{U}_0$ subset of $\mathcal{U}_1$:

$$u_1 \in \mathcal{U}_0 \wedge \ldots 0 \wedge u_n \in \mathcal{U}_0 \Rightarrow (\rho\,\theta)\,(u_1,\ldots,u_n) \in \mathcal{U}_0$$

The definition of $[\![\, T \,]\!]_\rho$ is by primitive recursion over the structure of T:

$$
\begin{aligned}
[\![\, bool \,]\!]_\rho &= \texttt{boolset} \\
[\![\, ind \,]\!]_\rho &= \texttt{indset} \\
[\![\, A \to B \,]\!]_\rho &= [\![\, A \,]\!]_\rho \to_{set} [\![\, B \,]\!]_\rho \\
[\![\, \alpha \,]\!]_\rho &= \rho\,\alpha \\
[\![\, (T_1,\ldots,T_n)\,\theta \,]\!]_\rho &= (\rho\,\theta)\,([\![\, T_1 \,]\!]_\rho,\ldots,[\![\, T_n \,]\!]_\rho) \\
[\![\, \Pi\,\alpha.\,T \,]\!]_\rho &= \Pi_{u \in \mathcal{U}_0}[\![\, T \,]\!]_{\rho[\alpha \mapsto u]}
\end{aligned}
$$

The first four equations above define the semantics of small HOL2P types without type operator variables. This definition agrees with the normal HOL type semantics.

4.4   The Semantics of HOL2P Terms

For variable, constant, application and abstraction terms in HOL2P, the meaning $[\![\, t \,]\!]_{\sigma,\rho}$ of t with respect to valuations σ and ρ can be defined in the same way as in HOL [10]. For the two HOL2P specific term operations, we have:

$$
\begin{aligned}
[\![\, \Lambda\,\alpha.\,t \,]\!]_{\sigma,\rho} &= \lambda_{set}\,(u \in \mathcal{U}_0).\,[\![\, t \,]\!]_{\sigma,\rho[\alpha \mapsto u]} \\
[\![\, t\,[T] \,]\!]_{\sigma,\rho} &= [\![\, t \,]\!]_{\sigma,\rho}\,[\![\, T \,]\!]_\rho
\end{aligned}
$$

By induction over the term structure, it can be shown that the meaning of HOL2P terms is consistent with that of HOL2P types, e.g.:

$$[\![\, t : T \,]\!]_{\sigma,\rho} \in [\![\, T \,]\!]_\rho$$

The reader might wonder where the construction of a semantics would break down if we allowed terms ranging over the full polymorphic λ-calculus in our system. The crucial property is that in case of HOL2P, the model of a universal type is a product indexed by the fixed set $\mathcal{U}_0$. This allows the iterative construction of a universe $\mathcal{U}_1$ with the required properties in a countable number of steps.

Lastly, the three inference rules specific to HOL2P express congruence properties of type abstractions and applications as well as β-reduction. The validity of these rules in the model follows directly from the corresponding properties of set theoretic functions and their applications.

5   Application Examples

Type Quantification

As a first application, we show that HOL2P can express type quantification terms [14]. For a predicate p and a type variable α, we define $\forall \alpha.\, p$ and $\exists \alpha.\, p$ to be abbreviations for the following *boolean* HOL2P terms:

$$\forall \alpha.\, p \ \equiv\ ((\Lambda \alpha.\, p) = (\Lambda \alpha.\, \mathit{True})) \tag{4}$$

$$\exists \alpha.\, p \ \equiv\ ((\Lambda \alpha.\, p) \neq (\Lambda \alpha.\, \mathit{False})) \tag{5}$$

As usual, a multiple universal quantification can be written in a shorter form:

$$\forall \alpha_1 \ldots \alpha_n.\, p \ \equiv\ \forall \alpha_1.\ \ldots \forall \alpha_n.\, p$$

The introduction rule for universal quantification over types follows directly from its definition and the HOL2P TYABS rule. It is subject to the usual side condition that α is not free in the assumption list Γ:

$$\frac{\Gamma \vdash p}{\Gamma \vdash \forall \alpha.\, p} \tag{TYALL-I}$$

The elimination rule for universal quantification over types follows directly from the HOL2P TYAPP rule and the "type-β" conversion for type application/type abstraction combinations (e.g. the general case of TYBETA):

$$\frac{\Gamma \vdash \forall \alpha.\, p}{\Gamma \vdash p[T \backslash \alpha]} \tag{TYALL-E}$$

There are similar rules for existential quantification over types which can be derived either from its definition above or by rewriting it in form of a negated universal type quantification:

$$\exists \alpha.\, p \ \equiv\ \neg(\forall \alpha.\, \neg\, p) \tag{6}$$

As an example for a derivation, consider the statement that there exists a HOL2P type which is a terminal object in the category of HOL2P functions:

$$\exists \alpha.\, \forall f\, g.\, f = (g : \beta \to \alpha)$$

The proof of this statement is by contradiction using the fact that the unit type 1 is a witness, e.g. it is such a terminal object:

$\exists \alpha.\ \forall f\ g.\ f = (g : \beta \rightarrow \alpha)$

$\Leftrightarrow$ { Equation (6), negation rules }

$\forall \alpha.\ \neg(\forall f\ g.\ f = (g : \beta \rightarrow \alpha)) \vdash False$

$\Leftarrow$ { Forward reasoning from assumption by TYALL-E with $T = 1$ }

$\neg(\forall f\ g.\ f = (g : \beta \rightarrow 1)) \vdash False$

$\Leftrightarrow$ { property of unit type 1 }

$True$

Notions from Category Theory

The predicate *functor* discussed in Section 2 applies to universally type-quantified functions ϕ:

$$\phi : \Pi\,\alpha\,\beta.\ (\alpha \rightarrow \beta) \rightarrow (\alpha\ \theta \rightarrow \beta\ \theta) \tag{7}$$

It is defined in HOL2P as follows (compare with equations (1, 2) above):

$functor\ \phi = \ (\forall \alpha.\ \phi\,[\alpha]\,[\alpha] = (id : \alpha\ \theta \rightarrow \ \alpha\ \theta))$
$\qquad\qquad \land\ \forall \alpha\ \beta\ \gamma.\ \forall (f : \ \alpha \rightarrow \beta)(g : \beta \rightarrow \gamma).\ \phi\ (g \circ f) = \phi\ g \circ \phi\ f$

For example, the fact that *map_list* is a functor is expressed by the proposition:

$functor\ (\Lambda\,\alpha\,\beta.\ (map\_list : (\alpha \rightarrow \beta) \rightarrow (\alpha\ list \rightarrow \beta\ list))$

This shows one of the costs of working in HOL2P - the definition of the *map_list* constant is given in a form that has free type variables α and β, and these type variables have to be bound if we want to use *map_list* as an argument to *functor* or similar functions that operate on polymorphic arguments.

The definition of predicate *functor* is parameterised with a free one-ary type operator variable θ. This is instantiated whenever the constant *functor* is applied to a function ϕ, e.g. we have $\theta = list$ in case of $\phi = map\_list$.

Natural transformations are a key concept of category theory [13]. Given two functors ϕ and ψ between categories C and D, a natural transformation associates every object X in C with a "morphism" $\eta_X : \phi\ X \rightarrow \psi\ X$ subject to a commutativity rule:

$$\psi(f) \circ \eta_X = \eta_Y \circ \phi(f)$$

In our application of category theory to polymorphic HOL functions embedded within HOL2P, natural transformations are simply polymorphic functions which are compatible with two "functor" functions ϕ and ψ of a type as in (7). This leads to the definition of a three-argument predicate *ntrf* as follows:

$ntrf \qquad :: (\Pi\,\alpha\,\beta.\ (\alpha \rightarrow \beta) \rightarrow (\alpha\ \phi \rightarrow \beta\ \phi))$
$\qquad\qquad \rightarrow (\Pi\,\alpha\,\beta.\ (\alpha \rightarrow \beta) \rightarrow (\alpha\ \psi \rightarrow \beta\ \psi))$
$\qquad\qquad \rightarrow (\Pi\,\alpha.\ \alpha\ \phi\ \rightarrow\ \alpha\ \psi)\ \rightarrow bool$
$ntrf\ \phi\ \psi\ \eta = \forall \alpha\ \beta.\ \forall\ (f : \alpha \rightarrow \beta).\ \psi\ f \circ \eta\ = \eta \circ \phi\ f$

Since HOL2P functions are total, the predicate *ntrf* can be applied to any functions ϕ and ψ that are of the right type, not just functors.

Many polymorphic functions are natural transformations between "type functors". In fact, this statement is just a rephrasal of the "theorem for free" [20] one can infer (under certain provisos) from the type of a function. As a simple example, consider the function *rev* which reverses the order of elements in a list:

$$rev\,[\,] \qquad = [\,]$$
$$rev\,(cons\ h\ t) = append\,(rev\ t)\,[h]$$

It is a "natural transformation from lists to lists", or to be more precise, from the *map_list* functor to the *map_list* functor:

$$ntrf \quad (\Lambda\alpha\ \beta.\,(map\_list:(\alpha \to \beta) \to (\alpha\ list \to \beta\ list)))$$
$$(\Lambda\alpha\ \beta.\,(map\_list:(\alpha \to \beta) \to (\alpha\ list \to \beta\ list)))$$
$$(\Lambda\alpha.\,(rev:\alpha\ list \to\ \alpha\ list))$$

After unfolding definitions, it becomes apparent that this statement is equivalent to the following better known proposition:

$$rev\,(map\_list\ f\ x) = map\_list\ f\,(rev\ x)$$

Category theory defines a "horizontal" and a "vertical" composition of natural transformations, as well as compositions with functors. It is straightforward to translate these operations so that they apply to the HOL2P natural transformations defined above, and to show that the results of the operations are again natural transformations. Formal proofs can be found in the HOL2P example files. These also contain some further derivations related to homomorphisms, initial algebras and catamorphisms.

6   Implementation

It would be possible to implement a HOL2P proof assistant in a green-field software development project, starting from scratch. However, because the logic is an extension of HOL, and given the availability of several high quality HOL implementations, it makes more sense to built such a system by trying to reuse at least parts of existing provers.

For the prototype HOL2P implementation described in this paper, HOL-Light was chosen as the starting point. This decision was made because of its compactness and clean design which helps to keep the implementation of an extension more manageable. Having identified the base system, a fundamental question about the new HOL2P prover arises: should it aim to stay compatible with the existing HOL-Light prover and its associated libraries or should its design reflect the extended logic as much as possible?

In order to simplify the reuse of the existing HOL-Light libraries, it was decided to try and keep the number of modifications to a minimum. This was achieved by taking an iterative development approach. Starting off with the existing HOL-Light system, one by one, modules were replaced with a new HOL2P version. Whenever a new module was completed, a test was carried out to ensure that the whole system was still a functioning theorem proving environment. In particular, interfaces were only ever extended, and not modified in any other way. Similarly, all functions kept their original signature, although the functionality they provide now applies to the more general case of HOL2P types and terms.

A typical example of this conservative development philosophy is the basic *hol_type* datatype that represents HOL/HOL2P types. In HOL-Light, this type is defined as:

$$hol\_type = Tyvar \ of \ string \mid Tyapp \ of \ string \ * \ hol\_type \ list$$

In principle, there are several possible options for the design of a corresponding HOL2P *hol_type* datatype. Having both type variables and type operator variables in the logic suggests a generalisation of *Tyvar* so that it takes a second arity argument, as well as introducing a type application operator similar to System F. Disregarding universal types for the moment, this might lead to a type declaration such as the following:

$$hol\_type = Tycon \ of \ string \mid Tyvar \ of \ string * rank * int$$
$$\mid Tyapp \ of \ hol\_type \ * \ hol\_type \ list \mid \ ...$$

While perfectly acceptable for a new design, this definition was rejected. The rationale was that some HOL-Light libraries make use of the visibility of *hol_type* in order to define functions by pattern matching. Changing the existing constructors would thus have implied changes to such libraries. Instead, the definition of *hol_type* in HOL2P keeps the existing constructors and simply adds a new constructor for universal types [1]

$$hol\_type = Tyvar \ of \ string \mid Tyapp \ of \ string \ * \ hol\_type \ list$$
$$\mid Utype \ of \ hol\_type \ * \ hol\_type$$

This declaration raises the question how small and large type variables are distinguished. This is done on a purely syntactic basis. Small type variables are recognised by starting with an apostrophe character. Similarly, type operator variables are distinguished from type constructors by starting with an underscore character.

The reward of this conservative development philosophy is a high degree of backward compatibility of the new HOL2P system with HOL-Light, and it is possible to run at least the main HOL-Light theory developments without any changes.

---

[1] The reader might be surprised that the first argument of the *Utype* constructor is not simply a *string*, e.g. the type variable name. It was done in order to ease reuse by keeping the representation in line with the HOL-Light treatment of term level abstractions. The latter employs a constructor *Abs* that takes a *term* as first argument, and not just a variable name.

A brief summary of some major implementation aspects is given below. The reader interested in details is referred to the system source files and accompanying documentation [18].

- The main challenge in the implementation of the logical core was the presence of type variable bindings in HOL2P. In particular, this makes the type and term substitution code more complex as well as requiring a notion of α-equivalence of types. In order to achieve a uniform treatment of instantiations, type operator variables, constant names and replacement type operators are all represented as *hol_type* elements.
- For the implementation of derived logical operations, the main difficulty is the matching of types in the presence of type operator variables. Similar to normal "higher order" term matching with function variables, it is possible to have more than one match. For example, trying to solve:

$$?F(?x) = (nat\ list)\ list$$

there are several possible solutions, i.e.

(1) $?F = \Lambda\,\alpha.\ \alpha$ $?x = (nat\ list)\ list$
(2) $?F = list$ $?x = (nat\ list)$
(3) $?F = \Lambda\,\alpha.\ \alpha\ list\ list$ $?x = nat$
(4) $?F = \Lambda\,\alpha.\ nat\ list\ list$ $?x$ can be any HOL type

In the current HOL2P implementation, a rather simple approach was chosen - the algorithm will only match type operator variables against a type constructor or another type operator variable. This means that only solution (2) is allowed. In order to return other solutions, an explicit instantiation of the type operator variable has to be performed by the user, e.g. by adding it in the statement of a goal or by instantiating a theorem before using it in a proof step. For example, after applying the instantiation $?F = \Lambda\,\alpha.\ \alpha$, the first solution will be returned, while setting $?F = \Lambda\,\alpha.\ (\alpha\ ?G)\ ?H$ will result in solution (3).
- In the implementation of type inference, the presence of type operator variables poses the same problem for the unification algorithm as for the matching algorithm above, and the same approach of restricting the number of solutions was chosen. In order to reduce the amount of explicit type annotations, user can explicitly declare the type of a variable. This information will then be used during the parsing of later goal statements and other terms input by the user. Unfortunately, despite this facility, a fair number of explicit type annotations and type instantiations can be necessary, see for example the category theory derivation source files. Additionally, the way type applications terms are handled in the parser makes it necessary to explicitly specify both the original type of a term as well as the type resulting from performing the operation.
- Boolean type quantification terms as described in Section 5 are treated simply as syntactic sugar, e.g. they are parsed into normal HOL2P terms according to the defining equations (4) and (5).

– Reasoning about terms containing type abstractions and type applications is supported by appropriate tactics. In particular there are tactics that perform the introduction and elimination of universal type quantification terms as described by rules (TYALL-I) and (TYALL-E) above. There is also a conversion that will perform a "type-β-reduction", e.g. simplifying a type abstraction/type application combination by performing the corresponding type instantiation on the abstraction body term.

7   Conclusions and Further Work

HOL2P is a new logical system that extends classical higher order logic with type operator variables and universal types, albeit in a restricted form in order to ensure consistency. The paper shows that the logic is capable of expressing boolean type quantification terms, as well as allowing the application of basic category-theoretic notions on the level of polymorphic HOL functions.

HOL2P has been implemented as a modification of HOL-Light using a conservative approach which respects existing module interfaces and other visible module features. This has resulted in a proof assistant that is to a high degree backwards compatible with HOL-Light, and in particular it is possible to run the standard theories that come with that system.

The implementation of the logical core of the HOL2P was relatively straightforward by transferring techniques for dealing with bound term variables to the type level. The presence of type operator variables poses a a major challenge when solving type equations occurring during matching of terms or when unification is required by type inference. In the current HOL2P implementation, a simple approach was taken which restricts the number of automatically found solutions to at most one. In situations where another solution is required, users need to give explicit type instantiations or annotations, e.g. when stating goals or when specifying theorems that are to be applied during a proof.

Further work is necessary in order to investigate the practical value of HOL2P. For example, one could imagine more category-theory inspired datatype definition packages. These could make use of the extra expressiveness of HOL2P in order to derive theorems by instantiation from their generic counterparts, with the aim of reducing the amount of work done at the ML programming level. Similarly, one could consider recasting recursive function definition packages so that they operate on hylomorphisms [11] with the aim of simplifying further reasoning by making use of fusion properties. The use of monads [21] and the application of generic programming concepts might lead to more structure in the definition of functions and more calculational proofs. Other potential applications include model-theoretic reasoning where it can be useful to have a predicate that expresses the existence of a type.

HOL2P was conceived as a minimal extension of HOL that supports reasoning about HOL types and polymorphic HOL functions, with free type operator variables for genericity. It should be possible to extend the approach to arbitrary higher-rank polymorphism, provided one adds appropriate restrictions in the type/term formation rules so as to avoid the impredicativity inherent in full System F. Another plausible extension would be the introduction of universal types that bind type operator variables.

With regards to the HOL2P implementation, further work should revisit the algorithms used for type matching, unification and type inference so as to reduce the amount of explicit type annotations required from the user. This work might benefit from recent advances in type inference research for higher-rank types [12,19]. Because of the complexity of HOL2P, it would be appropriate to mechanically check the semantics given in this paper, and ideally also some of the algorithms used in the implementation of the logical core, similar to the verification work done for HOL-Light [10].

Acknowledgements

The author would like to thank Ray Turner who suggested the idea of extending HOL with a second type layer, and who provided moral support. The anonymous TPHOLs reviewers deserve credit for their helpful comments.

References

1. Backhouse, R., Jansson, P., Jeuring, J., Meertens, L.: Generic programming - an introduction. In: Swierstra, S.D., Oliveira, J.N. (eds.) AFP 1998. LNCS, vol. 1608, Springer, Heidelberg (1999)
2. Bird, R.S., de Moor, O.: Algebra of Programming. Prentice-Hall, Englewood Cliffs (1997)
3. Coquand, T.: A new paradox in type theory. In: Prawitz, D., Skyrms, B., Westerståhl, D. (eds.) Proceedings 9th Int. Congress of Logic, Methodology and Philosophy of Science, pp. 555–570. North-Holland, Amsterdam (1994)
4. Girard, J.-Y., Lafont, Y., Taylor, P.: Proofs and Types. Cambridge Tracts in Theoretical Computer Science, vol. 7. Cambridge University Press, Cambridge (1989)
5. Glimming, J.: Logic and Automation for Algebra of Programming. PhD thesis, MSc Thesis, University of Oxford (2001)
6. Gordon, M., Wadsworth, C.P., Milner, R.: Edinburgh LCF. LNCS, vol. 78. Springer, Heidelberg (1979)
7. Gordon, M.J.C., Melham, T.F.: Introduction to HOL. Cambridge University Press, Cambridge (1993)
8. Gordon, M.J.C., Pitts, A.: The HOL Logic and System. In: Bowen, J. (ed.) Towards Verified Systems. Real-Time Safety Critical Systems Series, vol. 2, Elsevier, Amsterdam (1994)
9. Harrison, J.: The HOL Light System Reference – Version 2.20 (2006), http://www.cl.cam.ac.uk/ jrh13/hol-light
10. Harrison, J.: Towards self-verification in HOL-Light. In: Furbach, U., Shankar, N. (eds.) IJCAR 2006. LNCS (LNAI), vol. 4130, Springer, Heidelberg (2006)
11. Hu, Z., Iwasaki, H., Takeichi, M.: Deriving structural hylomorphisms from recursive definitions. In: ICFP, pp. 73–82 (1996)
12. Jones, S.P., Vytiniotis, D., Weirich, S., Shields, M.: Practical type inference for arbitrary-rank types. Journal of Functional Programming 17(1) (2007)

13. Mac Lane, S.: Categories for the Working Mathematician. Springer, Heidelberg (1971)
14. Melham, T.F.: The HOL logic extended with quantification over type variables. Formal Methods in System Design 3(1–2), 7–24 (1994)
15. Nipkow, T., Paulson, L.C., Wenzel, M.: Isabelle/HOL. LNCS, vol. 2283. Springer, Heidelberg (2002)
16. Pierce, B.C.: Types and Programming Languages. MIT Press, Cambridge (2002)
17. The Coq Development Team. The Coq Proof Assistant Reference Manual – Version V8.0 (2004), `http://coq.inria.fr`
18. Völker, N.: HOL2P Prototype Implementation (2007), `http://cswww.essex.ac.uk/staff/norbert/hol2p`
19. Vytiniotis, D., Weirich, S., Jones, S.P.: Boxy types: inference for higher-rank types and impredicativity. ACM SIGPLAN Notices 41(9), 251–262 (2006)
20. Wadler, P.: Theorems for free? In: Functional Programming Languages and Computer Architecture, Springer, Heidelberg (1989)
21. Wadler, P.: The essence of functional programming. In: POPL, pp. 1–14 (1992)

Building Formal Method Tools in the Isabelle/Isar Framework

Makarius Wenzel[1,*] and Burkhart Wolff[2]

[1] Technische Universität München, Institut für Informatik,
http://www.in.tum.de/~wenzelm/
[2] ETH Zürich, Information Security,
http://www.infsec.ethz.ch/people/wolffb

Abstract. We present the generic system framework of Isabelle/Isar underlying recent versions of Isabelle. Among other things, Isar provides an infrastructure for Isabelle plug-ins, comprising extensible state components and extensible syntax that can be bound to tactical ML programs. Thus the Isabelle/Isar architecture may be understood as an extension and refinement of the traditional "LCF approach", with explicit infrastructure for building derivative systems. To demonstrate the technical potential of the framework, we apply it to a concrete formal methods tool: the HOL-Z 3.0 environment, which is geared towards the analysis of Z specifications and formal proof of forward-refinements.

1 Introduction

Nearly 15 years ago, Paulson concluded his handbook article on theorem prover design [18] with the "final advice":

> Don't write a theorem prover. Try to use someone else's.

Even today, reuse of existing prover technology is still not common practice — many recent research projects are still based upon attempts to start from scratch, in particular if formal methods are implemented. This has mostly three reasons: Besides (1) general ignorance over or scepticism about the logical framework approach and (2) concerns about efficiency, it is believed that (3) the overhead to represent a particular formal method in a generic system is in fact too large.

There is a remarkable body of literature addressing (1) and (2); various forms of *logical embeddings* have been studied and applied to a wide range of logics or specification languages. Furthermore, a wide range of techniques to *integrate decision procedures* have been developed. Here the usual alternatives are fully expansive tactics, or procedures generating checkable proof objects or external implementations integrated via an oracle-mechanism into the LCF proof engine.

In this paper, we want to address (3) and explore the much less known fact that underlying the most recent versions of Isabelle (which Paulson had in mind

---

* Supported by BMBF project "Verisoft".

K. Schneider and J. Brandt (Eds.): TPHOLs 2007, LNCS 4732, pp. 352–367, 2007.

in the above quote) there is a generic system framework called Isabelle/Isar that can be compared in a rough analogy to the Eclipse programming system framework. Some key aspects of Isabelle/Isar are

1. hierarchical organization of theory documents,
2. *incremental* document processing for interactive theory and proof development (with unlimited undo),
3. batch-mode processing for high-quality document preparation (LaTeX),
4. extensible syntax for toplevel commands, embedded methods and attributes, and the inner term language,
5. type-safe programming interfaces for generic user data within the logical environment,
6. LCF-style programming interfaces for derived rules, tactics etc.

This framework has been applied to build a family of *formal method tools*. With this category we refer to a class of tools that provide support for a software specification formalism and a pragmatics or formalized "method" to use it for software analysis. Examples of such FM tools implemented as Isabelle/Isar "plugins" are the test-case generation system HOL-TestGen [11, 2], the environment for object-oriented modeling HOL-OCL [4, 10], or the proof-environment for refinement-oriented system development HOL-Z 3.0 [5]. In the present paper we take the latter as a running example, since the logical embedding [16] and the proof-support [9] have been described earlier, the overall plug-in is still relatively small (12000 lines of code if the Java-based front-end is included), and since there exists a "monolithic" implementation [3] of an environment for Z based on a HOL theorem prover offering the potential of a fair comparison.

The analysis method of HOL-Z 3.0 (built on top of HOL within Isabelle2005) is based on the idea that a designer writes a specification document in the specification language Z. This can be done completely independent from Isabelle in an Emacs/ZETA environment providing type-checking and elementary animation of Z formulae [1]. In a further step, the designer might want to state a number of conjectures on his model. In particular, these may be *analytical statements* such as "A is refined by B" or "spec A is consistent" in order to describe the task to proof engineers. Depending on the underlying method, such statements were compiled to *proof-obligations* (PO), i.e. formulas to be proven at the end by the proof-engineer using interactive or automated proof techniques.

The paper proceeds as follows. In §2 we introduce the HOL-Z 3.0 tool as it appears to end-users. In §3 we outline the main aspects of the Isabelle/Isar architecture that are relevant for building formal method tools. In §4 we report on the implementation of HOL-Z 3.0 within the Isabelle/Isar framework. In §5 we compare our Isabelle/HOL-Z system with the more monolithic ProofPower.

2   A Guided Tour Through HOL-Z

2.1   The HOL-Z 3.0 System Architecture

As shown in Figure 1, the model development process with Isabelle/HOL-Z is divided into two phases. In the modeling phase, the designer concentrates his attention on describing a model of the system in Z. The model (a LATEX document) is type-checked by ZETA [1] and passed to the verification phase. In the latter, the proof engineer can prove proof obligations — e. g. stemming from an interactive refinement — using proof commands. The theorem proving process is recorded in proof documents. Both ZETA as well as HOL-Z support "literate specifications", where formal specifications and proofs are mixed with informal explanations and the system generates a final document after checking all proofs. Technically, Isabelle/HOL-Z consists of a shallow embed-

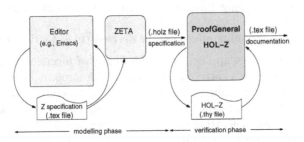

Fig. 1. The HOL-Z system architecture perspective

ding of the Z language constructs, a library called the *mathematical toolkit*, a compiler converting ZETA-output into the logical representation, a number of generic proof-procedures providing automatic support for Z-specific constructs like *schemas* (sets of records), or the *schema calculus* with its own quantifier and logical connectives. HOL-Z also provides proof-obligation management instantiated with a concrete method, namely the forward refinement method for Z as described in Spivey's book [19]. A complete HOL-Z spec and proof documentation for Spivey's "BirthdayBook" example, a toy data-base system presented in an abstract and a concrete version and related via refinement proofs, can be downloaded as "standard example" via the HOL-Z home page [5]. There are also references to substantial case-studies that have been done with the system.

2.2   The HOL-Z 3.0 Workflow

The proof document can be processed interactively via Proof General [6]. Subsequently, we highlight the main steps taken when verifying the birthday book example; the reader interested in the details is referred to the complete download of the "standard example". We start by loading the output of ZETA when type-checking the model of the designer:

```
1    load_holz "BBSpec"
```

This results in an environment holding all definitions and various automatically derived simplification rules. In particular, this includes the state invariants for the abstract state *BirthdayBook* and the concrete *BirthdayBook1*, the abstract insertion operation *AddBirthday* and its concrete counterpart *AddBirthday1* and the abstraction relation *Abs*. In the BirthdayBook example, all these definitions are presented in the Z idiom as schemas. By typing

```
set_abs "Abs" [functional]
```

we inform the refinement package that the *Abs* schema represents the abstraction relation and set the system in a mode for functional refinement (i. e. it will generate simplified POs). This setting will also generate a PO requiring that *Abs* actually represents a function, i. e. any concrete state is in fact related to a unique abstract state. After the statement:

```
refine_op AddBirthday Addbirthday1
```

we will have two new POs (we will show the second below) in the proof obligation database, which can be listed and inspected by the user. The concrete instance for the second PO resulting from the statement above can be referenced via a PO name. For example, if we *discharge* this PO, we can refer to it by:

```
po "BBSpec_functional.fw_refinementOp_AddBirthday"
```

The system reacts by displaying this well-known condition of forward-simulation. In more detail, this means that whenever the concrete system transition relation *AddBirthday1* relates a concrete state in *BirthdayBook1* to a state in *BirthdayBook1'* and whenever an abstract state *BirthdayBook* can be related via *Abs* to a state in *BirthdayBook1*, then *AddBirthday* must allow a transition to the abstract state *BirthdayBook'* which is an abstraction of *BirthdayBook1'*:

$$\forall\, BirthdayBook \,\bullet\, \forall\, BirthdayBook' \,\bullet\, \forall\, BirthdayBook1 \,\bullet\, \forall\, BirthdayBook1' \,\bullet$$
$$(\forall\, date? : DATE.\, \forall\, name? : NAME.$$
$$preAddBirthday \wedge Abs \wedge AddBirthday1 \wedge Abs' \Rightarrow AddBirthday)$$

Recall that in the above Z formula *BirthdayBook* etc. refer to schemas, which implies that there are implicit parameters (occasionally decorated by ′). The Z specific binding structure is suppressed in pretty-printing. The `po` command initializes the proof state, which may now be refined by a sequence of regular Isabelle proof commands [21] (such as `apply`) that refer to proof methods from generic Isabelle/HOL or specific ones from HOL-Z.

After reaching the final proof state, one can state

```
discharged
```

whereby this PO will be erased from the proof obligation database.

3   Internals: The Isabelle/Isar System Architecture

The system architecture of Isabelle/Isar [22] extends the original "LCF approach". We briefly review the latter, before explaining our additional concepts.

3.1   The "LCF Approach"

The "LCF approach" was pioneered by the original LCF system due to Robin
Milner [14]. LCF means "Logic of Computable Functions", but the underlying
logic is not really relevant for the architecture. The same principles have been
transferred later to the HOL family [13, 12], and some traces are also present in
Coq [7]. The main idea of the "LCF approach" is twofold:

1. A full functional programming language acts as "meta language" (ML),
   which allows arbitrary manipulations of term entities represented as values.
   ML is *not* part of the logic, but provides access to its implementation.
2. The strong type-discipline of ML ensures "correctness-by-construction", as
   all critical information is wrapped into abstract datatypes. In particular, an
   abstract type *thm* guarantees that any value of that type is in fact derivable,
   relative to a small kernel implementing the primitive inferences of the logic.

Figure 2 illustrates the main ML types of a typical "LCF-style" system. In this
diagram a solid line means structural containment (reading downwards, e. g. a
term is contained in a *thm*), while dashed lines link operand-operation pairs (e. g.
a *tactic* operates on a *goal*). The three columns categorize entities according to
their typical use: basic values (manipulated directly), state information (handled
implicitly), and the main "active" operations invoked by the user.

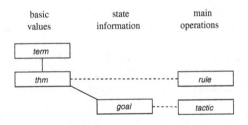

Fig. 2. The original "LCF approach"

The concrete datatype *term* provides a syntactic model of λ-terms (consisting of free/bound variables, abstraction, application), with the usual operations
(substitution, reduction etc.). Terms are annotated by explicit type-information,
which may have to be re-checked explicitly for critical operations (this is usually
easy due to the restriction to simple types).

The abstract type *thm* implements primitive inference objects of the underlying logic (e. g. HOL). Since ML enforces type-safety, the *thm* type does not need
to store any explicit information about the inferences that lead to a particular
theorem. Some systems provide an explicit proof trace as an option, but this
typically increases space requirements by several orders of magnitude.

Type *rule* covers functions that produce theorems, e. g. unary $thm \to thm$,
binary $thm \to thm \to thm$, or parameterized ones $term \to thm \to thm$. General rules programmed in ML need to replay the constituent inferences for every

application at run-time. An important special class of *immediate derived rules* may be implemented more efficiently, using auxiliary theorems that internalize the rule as a statement of the logic; this technique essentially exploits the Deduction Theorem. In Isabelle, derived rules are internalized by default, using the $\bigwedge$ quantifier and $\Longrightarrow$ connective of the Pure logical framework to represent Natural Deduction schemes [17]. Note that in conclusions, the outermost prefix of $\bigwedge x$ quantifiers is turned into schematic variables $?x$ of Isabelle.

Beyond primitive inferences, the LCF approach includes some minimal infrastructure for tactical theorem proving, which supports backwards reasoning from a *goal* by a sequence of *tactic* applications. In Isabelle, a *goal* is again a *thm* stating that the sub-goals entail the main conclusion, and a *tactic* is a lazy function $goal \rightarrow goal^{**}$ that enumerates possible follow-up goals [17]. The tactical layer of the LCF approach imposes a particular discipline of goal-oriented reasoning, which has turned out quite successful very early [14]: the art of representing problems as goals (including auxiliary facts within the statement) and complex manipulations as tactics has thrived over several decades.

Beyond programming tactics, people have also managed to build advanced specification mechanisms that turn high-level user input into primitive definitions and proven theorems. This approach has been employed many times to implement inductive sets and datatypes, recursive functions etc. on top of the core logic implementation. E. g. see [15] or [8] for techniques of bootstrapping higher specification concepts in HOL.

Limitations. Despite this success in building complex logical environments from basic principles, there has traditionally been very little general system infrastructure to support this task systematically. Consequently, "LCF system programming" has often a flavor of working on bare-metal. Moreover, implementors of particular extensions often re-invent auxiliary infrastructure, which duplicates work and tends to result in a diversity of incompatible features.

To illustrate the limitations of raw LCF, consider the problem of combining advanced tactics in classic Isabelle. Given tactic *simp* (the Simplifier, implemented by N.) that depends on a private rule collection, which is represented by type *simpset* and maintained by *addsimp*, *delsimp*: $thm \rightarrow simpset \rightarrow simpset$; given another family of tactics *fast*, *blast* etc. (the Classical Reasoner, implemented by P.) that depend on a *claset* with similar operations; then a combined tactic *force* (implemented by O.) depends on $clasimpset = claset \times simpset$. This is slightly awkward, since declarations on the individual components (*addsimp* on *simpset* etc.) need to be lifted to the tupled container, and users need to know which container type is passed to which tactic exactly. Even worse, this technique requires the participant tactic families and corresponding container types to be known in advance. So this naive composition does not scale well.

Our refined LCF approach addresses such issues by a generic environment that assimilates arbitrary data in a type-safe fashion. So all tactics may depend on a uniform *context*, which is maintained by declarations on the same type.

3.2   The Isabelle/Isar Framework

Although the original motivation for Isabelle/Isar is to support human-readable proof texts [20], the internal system organization has been quite generic from early on, continuing the original idea of Isabelle as a "logical framework" [17] in a broader sense. Consequently, the mechanisms for structured proofs are merely another application of considerably more general infrastructure, which may be re-used in completely different applications as well. Figure 3 gives an overview of the main constituents of the Isabelle/Isar framework. In this diagram, a solid or dashed line means the same as in Figure 2, while an arrow means a backwards reference that may mutate in a monotonic fashion (as explained below).

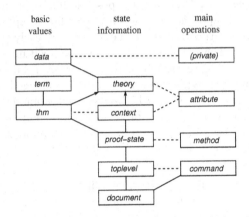

Fig. 3. Main concepts of Isabelle/Isar

Here the original entities of the "LCF approach" are still present, although some have been elevated to more sophisticated concepts.

Generic *data*, which can be modeled by the user as arbitrary ML types, is organized explicitly within a *theory* or *context*. Operations on *data* are private to the particular module implementation; access is mediated by higher elements, notably *attribute*, *method*, or *command*.

A *term* is exactly the same as in raw LCF, but a *thm* holds an additional reference to the enclosing *theory* as an explicit certificate. A *context* is certified against its background *theory* in the same way. An *attribute* covers primitive operations on theorems, as well as declarations to the *theory* or *context*.

An Isar *proof-state* wraps the raw LCF *goal* into a rich block-structured configuration, with an explicit *context* at each position. A *method* supersedes *tactic* as the main goal refinement mechanism, depending on additional structure from the *context* and immediate theorems presented in the proof text.

The Isar *toplevel* integrates the main state components, and encapsulates all operations by a transaction concept that supports recovery from errors and unlimited undo. The Isar toplevel loop replaces the bare-bones ML toplevel of LCF: end-users are no longer exposed to the underlying programming environment.

A *document* consists of a *command* sequence, interleaved with the resulting *toplevel* state at each position. This allows to generate output for LATEX type-setting, involving both the original sources and pretty printed output of logical entities (using "antiquotations" for *term* and *thm* in the text).

We shall now take a closer look at the key concepts required for building formal reasoning tools within the Isabelle/Isar framework.

Logical Environments. Our central concepts of *theory* and *context* are motivated by certain aspects of the underlying calculus. Derivations in Isabelle/Pure [17] (and the HOL family in general [13]) can be described as a judgment $\Gamma \vdash_\Theta \varphi$, meaning that proposition φ is derivable from assumptions Γ, within theory Θ. Both Θ and Γ act as a *logical environment*, but have different characteristics: Θ holds global declarations of polymorphic type constructors, term constants, and axioms; Γ covers locally fixed type variables, term variables, and hypotheses. The following main principles operate on Γ and Θ wrt. the conclusion φ:

- Transfer: due to monotonicity of derivations, results may be transferred into a *larger* environment, i. e. $\Gamma \vdash_\Theta \varphi$ implies $\Gamma' \vdash_{\Theta'} \varphi$ for $\Theta' \supseteq \Theta$ and $\Gamma' \supseteq \Gamma$.
- Export: by discharging assumptions, results may be exported into a *smaller* environment, i. e. $\Gamma' \vdash_\Theta \varphi$ implies $\Gamma \vdash_\Theta \Delta \implies \varphi$ where $\Gamma' \supseteq \Gamma$ and $\Delta = \Gamma' - \Gamma$. Note that Θ remains unchanged here, discharge of theory content is not directly supported.

Isabelle/Isar elevates raw Θ to a *theory* and Γ to a *context*, both supporting arbitrarily typed data, being introduced by the user at compile time.

Theories. A *theory* is a named data container with a unique identifier. Theories are related by a nominal sub-theory relation, which corresponds to the dependency graph of the original construction; each theory is derived from a certain sub-graph of ancestor theories. Locally, a theory is updated in a strictly linear discipline, which reduces the total number of theory identifiers. This organization is able to support large-scale logical environments efficiently.

The operation *merge*: *theory* × *theory* → *theory* builds the least upper bound of two theories, which is trivial for nominally related theories. The operation *begin*: *name* → *theory** → *theory* starts a new theory by importing several parent theories and entering a special *draft* mode, which is sustained until the final operation *end*: *theory* → *theory*, where the theory is named and identified for permanent storage. An intermediate draft theory acts like a linear type, where updates invalidate earlier versions. The operation *checkpoint*: *theory* → *theory* produces an intermediate stepping stone that will survive the next update: both the original and the changed theory remain valid and are related by the sub-theory relation. Checkpointing essentially recovers pure theory values, at the expense of extra bookkeeping. The operation *copy*: *theory* → *theory* produces an auxiliary version with the same content, but detached from the original.

Theory data. may refer to destructive entities, which are maintained in direct correspondence to the globally graph-structured and locally linear evolution of theory values, including explicit copies of impure data. A theory data declaration needs to implement the following ML specification:

type T	representation
val $empty: T$	initial value
val $copy: T \rightarrow T$	refresh impure data
val $extend: T \rightarrow T$	re-initialize on import
val $merge: T \times T \rightarrow T$	join on import

A *theory reference* maintains a live link to an evolving theory: updates on drafts are propagated automatically. Derived entities (notably *thm* or *context*) store a theory reference in order to indicate the enclosing logical environment. Soundness substantially depends on monotonicity of the underlying calculus, as the referenced theory may grow spontaneously.

Contexts. A *context* is a pure data container with a back-reference to the enclosing *theory*. The operation *init*: *theory* → *context* creates an empty context from a given theory. Modifications to draft theories are propagated to the context as explained above. The actual context data does not require any special bookkeeping, thanks to the lack of destructive features at this point.

Although contexts may be manipulated arbitrarily (analogous to *thm* values), the common discipline is to follow block structure: a given context is extended consecutively, and results are exported back into the original context. Note that an Isar *proof-state* models block-structure explicitly (using a stack).

Context data is declared by implementing the following ML specification:

type T	representation
val $init: theory \rightarrow T$	initial value

Generic *theory* and *context* data is used in Isabelle/Pure from the very beginning of bootstrapping the system. Even the inference kernel itself depends on types, constants, and axioms being maintained as theory data. If we liken the original LCF approach to a "micro-kernel" architecture, we may understand the Isabelle/Isar data management facility as a "nano-kernel".

After having boot-strapped the basic functionality of Isabelle/Pure, with many layers of theory and context data, the same principle is continued in object-logics like Isabelle/HOL. This includes data for reasoning tools (Simplifier, Classical Reasoner etc.) and derived specification mechanisms (inductive sets, recursive functions etc.). There is no reason to stop here, of course (cf. §4).

Attributes. An *attribute* covers any immediate operation on a theorem or the data within the underlying environment (*theory* or *context*):

global-attribute = *theory* → *thm* → *thm*	global rule
| *thm* → *theory* → *theory*	global declaration
local-attribute = *context* → *thm* → *thm*	local rule
| *thm* → *context* → *context*	local declaration

Practically speaking, attributes model various kinds of ad-hoc transformations and marginal declarations. Attributes may be adjoined to theorems wherever these occur in other Isar elements, using postfix notation *thm* [*attribute*]. For example, *thm* [*simp*] is a declaration that corresponds to the primitive *addsimp* (cf. §3.1), but operates directly on *theory* or *context*. Another example is *thm* [*symmetric*] which concludes a symmetric version of the given theorem, using a suitable symmetry rule picked from the environment.

Proof States and Methods. A *proof-state* is a stack over *context* × *goal*$^?$, together with some additional information to model the linguistic structure of an Isar proof text [20]. Unstructured proof scripts are incorporated into this model as a trivial case, by ignoring part of this structure.

A *method* operates on the *goal* field of a *proof-state*, depending on the proof *context* and immediate facts stemming from previous reasoning; the result is an enumeration of possible successive *goal* configurations, with optional *case* declarations to augment the context of the subsequent proof body:

$$method = context \rightarrow thm^* \rightarrow goal \rightarrow (case^* \times goal)^{**}$$

Non-empty cases only occur in the most advanced methods, notably *cases* and *induct* [21]. Moreover, many methods merely insert the indicated list of theorems into the goal as local premises, and then continue in the plain-old tactical sense. Thus the following simplified version suffices for most situations (recall that *tactic* = *goal* → *goal***):

$$simple\text{-}method = context \rightarrow tactic$$

In other words, a simple method is a plain tactic that refers to the proof context explicitly, retrieving arbitrary data as required (*simp* rules etc.). In order to combine such methods, each constituent part merely needs to pass-on the *context* it has received, such that every component will be able select its own data.

Toplevel Commands. The Isar toplevel maintains an implicit state that is transformed by a sequence of commands, either interactively or in batch-mode. In interactive mode, toplevel state transitions are encapsulated as safe transactions, such that both failure and undo are handled conveniently, without destroying the underlying draft theory. In batch mode, transitions operate in a strictly linear fashion, so an error will abort the present attempt to process the input.

A *toplevel* state consists of a history over *empty* | *theory* | *proof-state*. Special control commands may revert to previous states (**undo**), or abort the present theory or proof construction (**kill**). Regular commands operate on the topmost history entry, transforming the current *theory* or *proof-state*. The following typed interfaces allow to compose such toplevel commands:

$$
\begin{aligned}
&Toplevel.theory &&: (theory \rightarrow theory) \rightarrow transformer \\
&Toplevel.begin\text{-}proof &&: (theory \rightarrow proof\text{-}state) \rightarrow transformer \\
&Toplevel.proof &&: (proof\text{-}state \rightarrow proof\text{-}state^{**}) \rightarrow transformer \\
&Toplevel.end\text{-}proof &&: (proof\text{-}state \rightarrow theory) \rightarrow transformer
\end{aligned}
$$

Here are some example Isabelle/Isar commands [21] that are based on these.

Toplevel.theory   : **types, consts, axioms, defs,** . . .
Toplevel.begin-proof : **lemma, theorem, typedef,** . . .
Toplevel.proof   : **apply, proof, fix, assume, show,** . . .
Toplevel.end-proof   : **done, qed, sorry,** . . .

Both *Toplevel.theory* and *Toplevel.begin-proof* may be understood as theory specification elements, the latter with a separate proof obligation; variations on these are regularly introduced by add-on tools. In contrast, *Toplevel.proof* and *Toplevel.end-proof* refer to the Isar proof language [20], which is not so easily extended beyond the predefined elements: deeper insight into the proof engine is required. In practice, it is usually sufficient to plug additional proof tools into the restricted interface for proof methods.

3.3 Syntax

As an "LCF-style" system, Isabelle/Isar works directly with *semantic* entities, modeled as abstract types in ML. Concrete syntax is adjoined superficially between the core system and the end-user, such that theory sources may be presented as plain text. There are essentially three syntax layers in Isabelle/Isar:

1. outer syntax: toplevel commands,
2. embedded syntax: attributes and methods,
3. inner syntax: terms and types.

In particular, a command definition includes a parser function to turn a certain portion of input source into a semantic toplevel transaction. Similar parser functions may be installed for attributes and methods. Term syntax depends on an unrestricted context-free grammar maintained within the theory; new grammar productions may be added by mixfix annotations for constants.

The vertical relationship between abstract system concepts and superficial user syntax may be represented e. g. for type *term* as the pair of functions *read*: *context* → *string* → *term* and *print*: *context* → *term* → *string*. Internally, all components communicate directly in a horizontal manner, bypassing concrete syntax altogether. This works uniformly for pre-defined primitives and add-on tools alike. Taking the detour via generated sources is not recommended: both efficiency and robustness would suffer due to the full round-trip through various (extensible!) syntax layers. This also means that decent tools are obliged to provide proper internal interfaces by default, not just concrete syntax for end-users. Otherwise, the tool development chain would be broken here.

4   Application: Implementing HOL-Z 3.0

We now present concrete instances for the generic slots outlined above.

4.1   Theory Data: Z Environment

HOL-Z requires its own state capturing specific data for parsing and theorem proving, called the Z-environment (of ML type `Zenv`). For example, schema identifiers must have an internal signature ("schema signature") assigning to local names their type and type constraint. This signature is necessary to construct the binding structure of a schema-logical expression. As an example for proof support, there is a set of type-constraint information ("f is a partial function": $f \in A \nrightarrow B$) that is used to eliminate side-conditions of this form which occur in many situations throughout proofs. The data-base of currently unproven proof-obligations is also part of `Zenv`. Our theory data declaration looks like this:

```
structure ZEnv_Data = TheoryDataFun
 (type T = ZEnv.Zenv
  val empty = ZEnv.mt_zenv
  fun copy T = T
  fun extend T = T
  val merge = ZEnv.merge)
```

The core definitions of the `Zenv` type (not shown here) are passed to the functor `TheoryDataFun`, which extends the theory container by an additional data entry in a type-safe way. This results in access primitives `ZEnv_Data.get: theory -> Zenv` and `ZEnv_Data.map: (Zenv -> Zenv) -> theory -> theory`, which we keep private to our module; only some high-level user operations will be exposed later.

Unlike an immediate implementation of such a state component by a global ML reference variable, official theory data is subject to toplevel **undo** operations performed interactively by the user (as part of the Proof General protocol).

4.2   Toplevel Commands

A common scheme of tool interaction is a facility allowing the import of the results of a predecessor in the tool-chain. Instead of ad-hoc attempts to generate Isabelle theory documents indirectly as a text file, we strongly suggest to base such a facility on the internal Isabelle `term`-structure and the type-checker. This way, problems with ambiguous syntax trees can be avoided. Moreover, the parser for the inner term language is designed for flexibility and power, not for efficiency! Such an import mechanism is `load_holz: string -> theory -> theory` (not further discussed here), which will be bound by the subsequent invocation to a new toplevel command of the same name:

```
OuterSyntax.add_parsers
 [OuterSyntax.command "load_holz"
   OuterKeyword.thy_script
   (OuterParse.name >> (Toplevel.theory o load_holz))]
```

The construction re-uses a number of combinators from various libraries such as the parsing combinator library where *parsers* are functions that map a prefix in an input stream into a function representing the *meaning* of this prefix; here, this meaning is a transition function on the theory. There are elementary parsers like

`OuterParse.name`, or infix combinators like `>>`, which pipes the meaning of the previously parsed prefix into another function. Summing up, this gives a parser for `load_holz "<holz-file-name>"` which results in a transition from a theory into another one, where the definitions contained in the output file from ZETA were added. The hint of `OuterKeyword.thy_script` tells Proof General [6] about the type of command defined here.

Similarly, the toplevel command `zlemma` (for the toplevel statement with syntax `zlemma <thm-name>: "<goal-text>"`) is defined; in contrast to the standard command `lemma` for starting a proof, `zlemma` uses the HOL-Z parser for Z formulas that can make the implicit binding structure in a schema expression explicit.

4.3   Methods and Attributes

Syntactically, *methods* are embedded into existing toplevel proof commands, such as `apply` or `by`. We bind the specialized tactic `intro_sch_all_tac` for the introduction of the universal schema quantifier is passed to the method `zintro_sch_all`:[1]

```
Method.add_methods [...
  ("zintro_sch_all",
    nat_arg (tac2meth_unary intro_sch_all_tac),
    "intro␣schema␣all␣quantifier"),
  ...]
```

Analogously, *attributes* can be introduced that provide forward reasoning elements into a domain-specific Isar language extension. By a similar piece of setup-code, the attribute syntax *thm* [zstrip] can be defined which applies a rule in the sense of §3.1 of type `context -> thm -> thm` to some theorem. In our example, this transformer applies a number of destructive operations on schema-operators (similar to `intro_sch_all_tac`), which lead to a HOL-ified version of a Z-etish definition. Such adoptions are a prerequisite for Isabelle's automated proof methods (*simp*, *blast*, *auto* etc.), such as `apply (simp add: thm [zstrip])`.

4.4   Operator Syntax for Z

The so-called *inner syntax* of Isabelle/Isar is used for denoting terms (occurring in definitions, lemmas, proofs etc.) Inner syntax is usually wrapped inside quotes `"..."`. The grammar rules are derived from mixfix annotations in constant declarations — probably the syntax mechanism that is best-known to end-users.

Z favors the conciseness of mathematical notation to an usual degree; a lot of effort in the language design has been put in inventing mathematical symbols and shortcuts for many operations. The Z standard offers several representations of the "lexems" of the language. HOL-Z takes this into account and supports several of these formats. For example, the operator providing the set of partial functions is declared by an (internal) operator symbol having a standard denotation in the

---

[1] For various reasons, this rule cannot be represented by one single `thm`. Rather, universal schema introduction in Z is a rule scheme that has to be instantiated on the fly for a given goal; see [9] for details.

email-format (allowing keyboard shortcuts at the GUI level in Proof General). Moreover, there is a mapping of the internal operator symbol to the *xsymbols-format*, which is inspired by the LATEX format of the Z standard.

```
consts
    partial_func  ::"['a␣set,'b␣set]␣=>␣('a␣<=>␣'b)␣set"
             ("_␣-|->␣_"    [54,53]  53)

5  syntax (xsymbols)
    partial_func  ::"['a␣set,'b␣set]␣=>␣('a␣<=>␣'b)␣set"
             ("_␣\<pfun>␣_"    [54,53]  53)
```

It is possible to configure Proof General to associate with the xsymbols-format a specific font that allows this concise notation to be directly used on screen during proof work. Furthermore, it is also possible to configure LATEX style files in a way that LATEX macros for these symbols are used during the batch-mode document generation; then \<pfun> is really shown as ↦.

5 A Comparison to ProofPower

It is instructive to compare HOL-Z to ProofPower [3]. The latter has been built on top of HOL88 in a collaborative project, which ran from 1990 through to the end of 1992. It is free software with the exception of a component for specifying and verifying Ada programs (excluded from our comparison).

ProofPower comprises a developer kit (even providing its own parser generator), an X11/Motif front-end, a HOL prover kernel as well as the key component, a Z specification and proof development system including libraries and customized proof procedures.

ProofPower and HOL-Z have been both used in substantial case studies and possess a similar architecture; it is therefore possible to compare the systems in order to highlight the potential of the generic technologies of Isabelle. The comparison in Figure 4 deliberately excludes generic code from Isabelle/Isar or Isabelle/HOL. Under "document generation" we summarize only the LATEX style

	HOL-Z	ProofPower
LATEX-Frontend with Type-Checker	10340 lines (Java)	not available
document generation	1200 lines	2400 lines
user interface	100	14000 lines (C)
emb. + lib. + tactics	1521+7150+3543 lines	329965 lines
build process	165 lines	4700 lines

Fig. 4. Statistics on the two implementations

files; for HOL-Z, the generation mechanism itself is generic. Under "user interface", we summarize the code for the Motif frontend, which is roughly equivalent to Proof General. The main difference comes in position "logical embedding +

library + tactic support": for ProofPower, we essentially count all document files (.doc) of the system comprising the own HOL-system, HOL-libraries already geared to Z, Z libraries, and the overall proof-technical environment. On the HOL-Z side, we just consider the embedding in HOL (not Isabelle/HOL itself), the Z library, and specialized tactics for proof support and methodological support (Proof-Obligation Management for consistency and refinement, which is lacking on the ProofPower side). In our view, the proof-scripts are notably more concise; this is due to the Isar proof language as well as more automated proof procedures available in Isabelle.

One could object that counting lines of literate specification .doc files punishes ProofPower for its excellent documentation. However, even if taking this into account by a very conservative factor 3, the code size of ProofPower is still an order of magnitude larger than HOL-Z. Another objection is that a monolithic development strategy can build sometimes on better components (e.g. Proof General/Emacs is not really a show-case in GUI design). Further, a generic development strategy has also costs in terms of work not reflected in code sizes: namely, from time to time, new versions of Isabelle are released requiring adoptions to modified interfaces; it takes some effort to share the work of others. Still, we believe that the advantages outweigh these costs by far.

6   Conclusion

Presenting Isabelle/Isar as a framework for building formal method tools might appear as a bit of a surprise at first sight: the Pure logical framework of Isabelle [17] was originally conceived as a playground for experimenting with various versions of constructive type theory; the Isar layer [20] was mainly motivated by human readable proof texts. None of this is directly relevant to HOL-Z 3.0.

On the other hand, Isabelle has been conceived as a platform for a broad range of applications from early on. Strictly speaking, this idea is already present in the original LCF/HOL family, but Isabelle has also managed to reduce the dependency of a specific logic. This "generic-everything" attitude has been emphasized even further when revising the key system concepts for Isar.

Thus the Isabelle/Isar framework (as of Isabelle2005) already comprises a solid basis for building advanced applications such as Isabelle/HOL, and HOL-Z as presented here. Nevertheless, this only marks an intermediate stage in further development, both of the framework and its applications. For example, in post-Isabelle2005 versions the notions of *theory* and *context* are refined further into a *local-theory*, which will support very general notions of derived theory specifications, relative to local parameters and assumptions.

A more practical limit for the systematic re-use of existing system infrastructure is that of documentation and education. There is plenty of folklore wisdom and oral tradition, which is not easily available in a systematized form. The present paper — together with an ongoing effort to clean up the actual implementation and provide up-to-date manuals for implementors — is intended as an initiative to communicate concepts of the framework at a higher level.

Acknowledgment. Achim Brucker made valuable suggestions for the design of the proof-obligation manager and provided many valuable comments.

References

[1] ZeTa system (August 1997), http://uebb.cs.tu-berlin.de/zeta/

[2] HOL-TestGen (January 2005), http://www.brucker.ch/projects/hol-testgen/

[3] ProofPower (January 2005), http://www.lemma-one.com/ProofPower/index/

[4] Isabelle/HOL-OCL (March 2006), http://www.brucker.ch/projects/hol-ocl/

[5] Isabelle/HOL-Z (January 2007), http://www.brucker.ch/projects/hol-z/

[6] Aspinall, D.: Proof General: A generic tool for proof development. In: Schwartzbach, M.I., Graf, S. (eds.) ETAPS 2000 and TACAS 2000. LNCS, vol. 1785, Springer, Heidelberg (2000)

[7] Barras, B., et al.: The Coq Proof Assistant Reference Manual, v. 8. INRIA (2006)

[8] Berghofer, S., Wenzel, M.: Inductive datatypes in HOL — lessons learned in Formal-Logic Engineering. In: Bertot, Y., Dowek, G., Hirschowitz, A., Paulin, C., Théry, L. (eds.) TPHOLs 1999. LNCS, vol. 1690, Springer, Heidelberg (1999)

[9] Brucker, A.D., Rittinger, F., Wolff, B.: HOL-Z 2.0: A proof environment for Z-specifications. Journal of Universal Computer Science 9(2), 152–172 (2003)

[10] Brucker, A.D., Wolff, B.: The HOL-OCL book. Technical Report 525, ETH Zürich (2006)

[11] Brucker, A.D., Wolff, B.: Using HOL-TestGen for test-sequence generation with an application to firewall testing. In: Meyer, B., Gurevich, Y. (eds.) TAP 2007: Tests And Proofs. LNCS, Springer, Heidelberg (2007)

[12] Gordon, M.J.C.: From LCF to HOL: a short history. In: Plotkin, G., Stirling, C., Tofte, M. (eds.) Proof, Language, and Interaction: Essays in Honour of Robin Milner, MIT Press, Cambridge (2000)

[13] Gordon, M.J.C., Melham, T.F. (eds.): Introduction to HOL: A theorem proving environment for higher order logic. Cambridge University Press, Cambridge (1993)

[14] Gordon, M., Wadsworth, C.P., Milner, R.: Edinburgh LCF. LNCS, vol. 78. Springer, Heidelberg (1979)

[15] Harrison, J.: Hol light: A tutorial introduction. In: Srivas, M., Camilleri, A. (eds.) FMCAD 1996. LNCS, vol. 1166, Springer, Heidelberg (1996)

[16] Kolyang, Santen, T., Wolff, B.: A structure preserving encoding of Z in Isabelle/HOL. In: von Wright, J., Harrison, J., Grundy, J. (eds.) TPHOLs 1996. LNCS, vol. 1125, Springer, Heidelberg (1996)

[17] Paulson, L.C.: Isabelle: the next 700 theorem provers. In: Odifreddi, P. (ed.) Logic and Computer Science, Academic Press, London (1990)

[18] Paulson, L.C.: Handbook of Logic in Computer Science. In: Designing a Theorem Prover, vol. 2, pp. 415–475. Clarendon Press, Oxford (1992)

[19] Spivey, J.M.: The Z Notation: A Reference Manual, 2nd edn. Prentice Hall International Series in Computer Science (1992)

[20] Wenzel, M.: Isar — a generic interpretative approach to readable formal proof documents. In: Bertot, Y., Dowek, G., Hirschowitz, A., Paulin, C., Théry, L. (eds.) TPHOLs 1999. LNCS, vol. 1690, Springer, Heidelberg (1999)

[21] Wenzel, M.: The Isabelle/Isar Reference Manual, Part of Isabelle2005 (2005)

[22] Wenzel, M., Paulson, L.C.: Isabelle/Isar. In: Wiedijk, F. (ed.) The Seventeen Provers of the World. LNCS (LNAI), vol. 3600, Springer, Heidelberg (2006)

Simple Types in Type Theory: Deep and Shallow Encodings

François Garillot[1] and Benjamin Werner[2,*]

[1] École Normale Supéieure
45 rue d'Ulm, Paris, France
and INRIA-Futurs at
LIX, École Polytechnique, Palaiseau, France
francois.garillot@ens.fr
[2] INRIA-Futurs at
LIX, École Polytechnique, Palaiseau, France
Benjamin.Werner@inria.fr

Abstract. We present a formal treatment of normalization by evaluation in type theory. The involved semantics of simply-typed λ-calculus is exactly the simply typed fragment of the type theory. This means we have constructed and proved correct a decompilation function which recovers the syntax of a program, provided it belongs to the simply typed fragment. The development runs and is checked in Coq. Possible applications include the formal treatment of languages with binders.

1 General Setting

1.1 Deep vs. Shallow

The denomination "normalization by evaluation" is now well-established and designates a class of techniques dealing with functional programs. However, depending upon the framework these techniques are used in, the aim can vary greatly. In all cases, the idea is to translate functional programs (λ-terms) from one level of language to another. This is precisely what we do here. In type theory, a λ-term can exist under very different forms. Let us consider the term $\lambda x.\lambda y.x$. Given any type X of the type theory, we can build the corresponding program; in Coq syntax it will be `fun (x:X)(y:X) => x`. This is what is generally called the *shallow* embedding.

We can however also go for the deep embedding. This involves defining a data-type describing λ-terms. Again in Coq we can take:

```
Inductive term : Type :=
 Var : id -> term | Lam : id -> term -> term
  | App : term -> term -> term.
```

where `id` is a well-chosen datatype. The same term is then represented as the object `Lam x (Lam y (Var x))` of type `term`.

---

* This work was partly supported by the The Microsoft Research-INRIA Joint Centre.

K. Schneider and J. Brandt (Eds.): TPHOLs 2007, LNCS 4732, pp. 368–382, 2007.
© Springer-Verlag Berlin Heidelberg 2007

Given a λ-term, each of the representations has its advantages and shortcomings. Advantages of the deep embedding representation include:

- We "know" the code of the term, for instance we can print it, compute its length, etc.
- Correspondingly, we can reason by induction over the structure of the λ-term.
- We can define properties of λ-terms (typing, reduction...) by induction or by recursion over the term's structure.

All these things are, at first, impossible with the shallow encoding. On the other hand, there are tasks where the latter has its advantages:

- With the shallow representation, we do not "know" the code, but we can run it. Furthermore, the λ-terms are logically identified modulo β-conversion.
- With the deep encoding, one has to make the dreaded choice between de Bruijn indexes and named variables; both coming with their own, well-known, difficulties (explicit lifting functions with de Bruijn, treatment of α-conversion with named variables). With the shallow encoding, this is basically subcontracted to the proof-system's implementation.

It is therefore an interesting question to what extent one can switch between the two representations and recover one from the other. It is this question we try to address in this work.

Terminology. Since the shallow encoding corresponds to an executable, but not readable, representation, we will speak of the *compiled representation*. On the other hand, the deep encoding's representation we will call the *decompiled* or *source level* representation.

1.2 Normalization by Evaluation

The more difficult translation is going from the compiled to the source code. On the compiled level, the inner code of functions cannot be accessed: given a function, the only possible operation is to apply an argument to it, evaluate and examine the result. We can think of fuctions as being represented as closures in an abstract machine. Opening these closures and reconstructing the original code is precisely what *Normalization by Evaluation* (NbE) is about.

The result of this decompilation process is always in normal form. This is, of course, the reason for the terminology "normalization by evaluation" which was coined by Ulrich Berger. To be precise, the result of the decompilation is in *strong* normal form, which means that code under binders is also in normal form. A consequence is that NbE is used in practice for partial evaluation of functional programs.

The content of this work can thus roughly be summed up as being a formal treatment of a particular kind of NbE in Coq. Dependent type theories, like Coq, are a very interesting framework for using NbE for several reasons:

- The decompilation function takes an argument whose type will vary. When working in a conventional language like ML, one needs, for instance, to insert an additional layer (like HOAS in [10]) in order to accommodate this. Using dependent types, the decompilation is naturally typed.
- Functional programs are, by essence, objects of type theory (compiled form). But in many cases, for instance when doing metatheory, they are also objects of study inside the type theory. One will then want to reason about the syntax of programs, thus using the decompiled form. NbE is precisely the way to switch from the first encoding to the second.
- Finally, since type-theories are a framework where one can, at the same time, do computations and proofs, we can not only write the NbE routines, but also specify and certify their behavior.

1.3   The General Idea

We outline the framework by recalling the basic ideas in the case of a functional programming language with side-effects. We therefore use Caml syntax in this section.

We write programs performing NbE over simply typed λ-terms. The routines use type information in an essential way. We thus first need a data-type for representing simple types as well as one representing the terms:

```
type st = Iota | Arr of st*st ;;
```

```
type term = Var of string | Lam of string*term
               | App of term * term ;;
```

It is well-known that an important point is being able to produce fresh variables. In this first rough description, we "cheat" by relying on side-effects: we use a gensym function returning a new string each time it is called.

We then can program the decomp decompilation function; as usual it is defined simultaneously with a function "compiling" values. We here call this function long since it builds a η-long form of variables. Both functions are known under various names in the literature (reify, value...).

```
let rec decomp t = function
  | Iota        -> t
  | Arr(u1,u2) -> let x = gensym() in
      Lam(x,(decomp (t (long (Var(x)) u1)) u2))

and long t = function
  | Iota        -> t
  | Arr(u1,u2) -> fun x->(long (App(t,(decomp x u1))) u2);;
```

The type of the argument t of decomp, as well as the type of the result of long, depend on their second argument and the programs are therefore not typable in this form. However, if we locally switch off the type-checker, we can see, for instance, that the evaluation of (decomp (Arr Iota Iota) (fun x->x)) indeed returns something of the form Lam(s,Var(s)) where s corresponds to the current state of gensym.

1.4   Syntax vs. Semantics Point of View

Looking at what is going on through the lenses of the Curry-Howard isomorphism, one obtains another interesting explanation: typed λ-terms standing for proofs, the deep encoding corresponds to the syntactical notion of provability. The compiled/shallow encoding, on the other hand, is semantical: it is a translation of the logic of simple types into the type theoretical framework. Having understood this, it appears that NbE corresponds to a *completeness result*, since it lifts results from the semantics back into the syntax. This remark is enlightening even if it is less central in the present work than in the ones of Catarina Coquand and Jean-Louis Krivine.

1.5   Related Work

We are not aware of too many actually implemented formal treatments of NbE. The main one is indeed Catarina Coquand's pioneering work [8] which we saw first presented at the 1992 European Types meeting; a later version can today be found in [9]. The motivation however is not exactly the same, and in consequence we can list some technical differences:

- As mentioned above, Catarina Coquand's point of view is more on the logical side and the result is understood as a completeness result. The compiled level is understood as a semantics. Thus, semantics are always defined with respect to a context; which we will try to avoid. Also, she uses dependent types in a much more intensive way than what we do.
- The main technical difference however is the type of the semantics. She uses a Kripke-style typing of the compiled terms, which is useful for stating and proving completeness. On the other hand, it makes the actual compiled/semantical code more complex, which is what we try to avoid.

The Kripke-style typing of the semantics can also be found, among others, in the work by Altenkirch et al. [1], which extends NbE the sum types.

Even closer to us is the line of work initiated by Ulrich Berger and Helmut Schwichtenberg [2,4,6,5]. However, and even if their constructions are precisely described, the only actual implementation is not exactly NbE, but a formalization of Tait's strong normalization proof [3]. Ulrich Berger also showed that Tait's proof is actually what underlies NbE algorithms; but this analogy is not explicit in the formalization. Technically, if we leave the issue of formalization aside, the main difference with Berger's NbE is due to the fact that again we use a (slightly) simpler typing of the compiled terms. We have to sacrifice the efficiency of the normalization algorithm for that, whereas efficiency was precisely his main motivation.

A lot of very detailed work has, of course, been devoted to NbE by Olivier Danvy. He does not set his work in type theory, but his ideas are obviously influential in this and the related works. Since his original motivation was partial evaluation, the same technique is called *type directed partial evaluation* in his work. Finally, as mentioned above, Jean-Louis Krivine's work [14] on the completeness theorem, although very different bears also some relations with ours.

1.6   About the Formal Coq Development

In what follows, we indicate the Coq name of the definitions and lemmas, so one can relate the article with the formal proof.[1]

2   The Syntax of Simply Typed λ-Calculus

The first data-type we need is a representation of simple types. In the present case, we only use one atomic type we will call Iota in reference to Church. It seems obvious however that the whole development could accommodate several atomic types without too much effort. We thus have an inductive type with two constructors; in Coq syntax:

```
Inductive ST : Set := Iota : ST | Arr : ST -> ST -> ST.
```

From now on, except for short Coq verbatim, we write $\Rightarrow$ for Arr and ι for Iota. Thus $\iota \Rightarrow \iota \Rightarrow \iota$ stands for (Arr Iota (Arr Iota Iota)). When studying simply-typed λ-calculus, it is often convenient to have the type of the variable be part of its name (or identifier), because it precludes the use of context for defining typing. We thus take:

```
Record id : Type := mkid {idx : nat ; idT : ST}.
```

In the present description we write x^A for (mkid x A), except in Coq verbatim.
We can now define the syntax of the language:

```
Inductive term : Type :=
 Var : id -> term | Lam : id -> term -> term
  | App : term -> term -> term.
```

We stress that the natural number component of the identifiers should really be understood as a "name" and not as anything even remotely related to de Bruijn indexes. This is reflected in the type of the LAM constructor, and in the definition of the list of free variables (representing the finite set of their identifiers), as the recursive function verifying the following equations:

$$\mathrm{FV}(\mathsf{Var}\ x) \equiv \{x\}$$
$$\mathrm{FV}(\mathsf{App}\ t\ u) \equiv \mathrm{FV}(t) \cup \mathrm{FV}(u)$$
$$\mathrm{FV}(\mathsf{Lam}\ x) \equiv \mathrm{FV}(t) \setminus \{x\}$$

---

[1] The formal development is available on the web at
http://www.lix.polytechnique.fr/Labo/Benjamin.Werner/

We also define a function generating a fresh identifier, that is, given a type, an identifier of this type which does not belong to a given finite set:

$$\text{fresh} : (\text{set id}) \rightarrow \text{ST} \rightarrow \text{id}$$
$$\text{fresh } l \ T \equiv j^T \text{ where } j = max\{i, i^T \in l\} + 1$$

3   Decompilation

We now have to make the most important choice in this development. Namely the type of the objects on the compiled side. What differentiates our work with previous ones is that we here take, from the start, the simplest possible translation described by the following equations :

$$\text{tr}(\iota) \equiv \text{term}$$
$$\text{tr}(A \Rightarrow B) \equiv \text{tr}(A) \rightarrow \text{tr}(B)$$

This means that we want to define decompilation such that :

$$\text{decomp} : \forall T : \text{ST}, \text{tr}(T) \rightarrow \text{term}$$
$$\text{long} : \text{term} \rightarrow \forall T : \text{ST}, \text{tr}(T)$$

Note that this means that decomp will return a term even when applied to a "pathological" object (for instance a function $f : \text{term} \rightarrow \text{term}$ which discriminates between β-convertible terms). The "well-behaved" objects, for which the decompilation result is meaningful, are characterized in section 6.

We are now back at the question of fresh variables: when decompiling a function $f : \text{tr}(A) \rightarrow \text{tr}(B)$, we have to "guess" what free variables are "hidden" inside it. What are the possible options ?

- Berger deals with the problem by having the program to be decompiled computing not only its own normal form, but also the variables that were used in order to decompile it. This results in a very efficient normalization function, but in the definition of tr, term has to be replaced by $\text{nat} \rightarrow \text{term}$. The main negative consequence is that terms which originally contain free variables are more delicate to deal with.
- If we want to emulate the behavior of the imperative *gensym* used in the introduction, we run into a similar problem. We would need to perform a state-passing-style transformation over the program. Not only the decomp program, but also the program f we want to decompile; which means again changing the definition of tr.

We here explore another possibility, in which we sacrifice efficiency to salvage the simplicity of tr: we compute the set of free variables inside f by first decompiling f after applying a "dummy" variable to it. We then can find a fresh variable and decompile it again. Our definition thus reads:

$$\text{decomp } \iota \ t \equiv t$$
$$\text{decomp } A \Rightarrow B \ f \equiv \text{let } x = \text{fresh } (\text{FV}(\text{decomp } B \ (f \ (\text{long Var(dum) } A)))) \ A$$
$$\text{in } \quad \text{Lam}(x, \text{decomp } B \ (f \ (\text{long } x \ A)))$$

where dum is a particular identifier chosen for this purpose.

Of course, since it uses two recursive calls instead of one, the algorithm is exponentially slower than the "reasonable" options above. The advantage is that it is easy to build terms on the semantical side. For example decompiling Lam x ($Var\ y^{\iota}$) will return the constant function fun a=>Var t^{ι}.

One technicality here is the issue of the freshness of the dummy itself. When given a term f (long Var(dum) A), there is no obvious way to tell whether Var(dum) itself is indeed free in (the term corresponding to) f. The idea here is that the β-conversion relation is such that simply observing the *structure* of a β-normal object obtained from the application of a "dummy" to a term will allow us to infer the free variables of this term.

This is made precise in our development, in which the following lemma comes up as a requirement:

Lemma 1 (fvc).

$$\forall x\ t\ u,\ (\mathsf{App}\ t\ (\mathsf{Var}\ x) =_{\beta\eta} u \land y \notin FV(u)) \Rightarrow \exists v, (t =_{\beta\eta} v \land y \notin FV(v))$$

This lemma is essentially about untyped λ-calculus. Its proof is quite intricate when going into the details of α-conversion. The formalization involves a number of technical results about β-conversion in a named setting. We provide a formal proof, admitting two well-known properties of the untyped β-reduction : the postponability of α-conversion, and the Church-Rosser property.

4   Basic Syntactic Definitions

4.1   Typing

As we have seen, decompilation can be defined independently of typing, reduction and the usual basic notions about λ-terms. These definitions are however obviously necessary for going on. We describe a practical definition of typing. Typing is a binary relation between a term and a type. We can, of course use the inductive predicate corresponding to the usual rules:

$$\frac{}{n^{T}:T} \qquad \frac{t:T}{\mathsf{Lam}\ n^{U}t:U \Rightarrow T} \qquad \frac{t:U \Rightarrow T \quad u:U}{\mathsf{App}\ t\ u:T}$$

It is then possible to show that it is decidable whether a term bears a type or not. In practice, it appears convenient to proceed the other way around starting with the inference function and then using it to define well-typedness.

$$
\begin{aligned}
\mathsf{infer}(\mathsf{Var}(x^{A})) &\equiv \mathsf{Some}(A) \\
\mathsf{infer}(\mathsf{Lam}(x^{A},t)) &\equiv \mathsf{None} & &\text{if } \mathsf{infer}(t) = \mathsf{None} \\
\mathsf{infer}(\mathsf{Lam}(x^{A},t)) &\equiv \mathsf{Some}(A \Rightarrow B) & &\text{if } \mathsf{infer}(t) = \mathsf{Some}(B) \\
\mathsf{infer}(\mathsf{App}(t,u)) &\equiv \mathsf{Some}(B) & &\text{if } \mathsf{infer}(t) = \mathsf{Some}(A \Rightarrow B) \\
& & &\text{and } \mathsf{infer}(u) = \mathsf{Some}(A) \\
\mathsf{infer}(\mathsf{App}(t,u)) &\equiv \mathsf{None} & &\text{in the other cases}
\end{aligned}
$$

It is then easy to define well-typedness :

- A term t is well-typed iff infer$(t) \neq$ None
- the term t is of type T iff infer$(t) =$ Some(T)

A technical point which is useful for the actual feasibility of the development is that since equality is (obviously) decidable over ST, the equalities above are *booleans* (which can when necessary be coerced to propositions). Together with Georges Gonthier's SSR proof tactic package [13], this makes many proofs shorter and easier. We come back to this in section 5.

Proving equivalence between the two formulations of typing is easy (10 lines).

4.2 Substitution

Because of the necessary renaming operations, the primitive substitution operation needs to be defined over several variables. A substitution is a list of pairs (x, t) meaning that the variables of identifier x are to be substituted by the term t. The recursive substitution function is defined by the following equations:

$$(\mathsf{App}\ t\ u)[\sigma] \equiv \mathsf{App}\ t[\sigma]\ u[\sigma]$$
$$(\mathsf{Var}\ x)[\sigma] \equiv \mathsf{Var}\ x \quad \text{if no } (x, u) \text{ occurs in } \sigma$$
$$(\mathsf{Var}\ x)[\sigma] \equiv u \quad \quad \text{if } (x, u) \text{ is the first occurrence of } x \text{ in } \sigma$$
$$(\mathsf{Lam}\ x\ t)[\sigma] \equiv \mathsf{Lam}\ x'\ t[(x, \mathsf{Var}\ x') :: \sigma]$$
$$\text{where } x' = \mathsf{fresh}\left(\bigcup\nolimits_{z \in \mathrm{FV}(t) \setminus \{x\}} FV(\mathsf{Var}\ z[\sigma])\right)$$

Subsitution is primitively defined as handling several variables simultaneously. This allows us to define substitution through structural recursion over the substituted term rather than over its size and considerably simplifies proofs.

Moreover, when applying a substitution, we systematically rename all bound variables in a uniform manner, using fresh, a deterministic choice function defined up to the set of variables it takes as an argument. This set is chosen such that is exactly characterizes the free variables of the substituted term, i.e.:

Lemma 2 (eFVS_FV). $\bigcup_{z \in FV(t) \setminus \{x\}} FV(\mathsf{Var}\ z[\sigma]) = FV(t[\sigma])$

Following the method described by A. Stoughton [17], this provides us with a way to normalize terms w.r.t. alpha-conversion when applying substitution. We indeed prove the following lemma:

Lemma 3 (alpha_norm). *If $t =_\alpha u$, then $\forall \sigma, t[\sigma] = u[\sigma]$*

We can then simply treat alpha-conversion as the equality on terms w.r.t. a substitution in the rest of the formalization, a simplification that was pivotal in making the treatment of alpha-convertibility manageable in this named setting.

Since the identifiers carry their type, it is straightforward to define what it means for a substitution to be well-typed. One then easily shows that such well-typed substitutions preserve typing.

4.3   Conversion and Normal Forms

Since we do not deal with strong normalization here, we can avoid the pain to define the oriented reduction relation. We just define conversion as an inductive equivalence relation.

Definition 1 (conv, normal, atomic). *Conversion, written $=_{\beta\eta}$ is defined as the closure by reflexivity, symmetry, transitivity and congruence of the following clauses:*

$$(\beta)\ \forall t\ u\ x, (\mathsf{App}\ (\mathsf{Lam}\ x\ t)\ u) =_{\beta\eta} t[x, u]$$
$$(\eta)\ \forall t\ x, x \notin (FV\ t) \to t =_{\beta\eta} \mathsf{Lam}\ x\ (\mathsf{App}\ t\ x)$$
$$(\alpha)\ \forall x\ y\ t, y \notin (FV\ t) \to \mathsf{Lam}\ x\ t =_{\beta\eta} \mathsf{Lam}\ y\ t[x, y]$$

The predicates NF *(being normal) and* AT *(being atomic) are mutually inductively defined by the clauses:*

$$(\mathrm{AtV})\qquad \forall x, (\mathrm{AT\ Var}\ x)$$
$$(\mathrm{AtApp})\ \forall t\ u, (\mathrm{AT}\ t) \to (\mathrm{NF}\ u) \to (\mathrm{AT}\ (\mathsf{App}\ t\ u))$$
$$(\mathrm{NFAt})\quad \forall t, (\mathrm{AT}\ t) \to (\mathrm{NF}\ t)$$
$$(\mathrm{NFLam})\ \forall x\ t, (\mathrm{NF}\ t) \to (\mathrm{NF}\ (\mathsf{Lam}\ x\ t))$$

One can then define the sufficient conditions for the decompilation to return a normal (resp. well-typed) term:

Definition 2 (sem_norm, sem_WT). *Given $T : \mathsf{ST}$, we define the predicates* SNF T *(semantic normal form) and* SWT *(semantically well-typed) both ranging over* $\mathrm{tr}(T)$ *by recursion over T:*

$$\mathrm{SNF}\ \iota\ t \equiv \mathrm{NF}\ t$$
$$\mathrm{SNF}\ A \Rightarrow B\ f \equiv \forall g : \mathrm{tr}(A), (\mathrm{NF}\ A\ g) \to (\mathrm{SNF}\ B\ (f\ g))$$

$$\mathrm{SWT}\ \iota\ t \equiv \mathrm{WT}\ t\ T$$
$$\mathrm{SWT}\ A \Rightarrow B\ f \equiv \forall g : \mathrm{tr}(A), (\mathrm{SWT}\ A\ g) \to (\mathrm{SWT}\ B\ (f\ g))$$

Lemma 4 (decomp_norm). *If* SNF T f *(resp.* SWT T f*), then we have also* NF (decomp T f) *(resp.* WT (decomp T f) T*).*

PROOF.   Separately, by induction over T. In each case, one has to prove simultaneously the dual condition:

$$\forall t\ T, \mathrm{AT}\ t \to \mathrm{SNF}\ T\ (\mathsf{long}\ T\ t)$$

$$\forall t\ T, \mathrm{WT}\ t\ T \to \mathrm{SWT}\ T\ (\mathsf{long}\ T\ t).$$

5 Compilation (Semantics)

We now deal with going from an object t such that WT t T holds to the corresponding object of type $\mathsf{tr}(T)$.

An environment $\mathcal{I}$ is a function which to any identifier x^X associates its semantics (an object of type $\mathsf{tr}(X)$); formally the type of $\mathcal{I}$ is:

```
Definition sem_env := forall (x : id) , tr x.(idT).
```

From there, given $\mathcal{I}$ we want to define the semantics of a term t such that WT t T holds as an object of type $\mathsf{tr}(T)$ through the following, quite straightforward equations:

$$[\mathsf{Var}\ x]_{\mathcal{I}} \equiv \mathcal{I}(x)$$
$$[\mathsf{App}\ t\ u]_{\mathcal{I}} \equiv [t]_{\mathcal{I}}([u]_{\mathcal{I}})$$
$$[\mathsf{Lam}\ x^T\ t]_{\mathcal{I}} \equiv \lambda\alpha : \mathsf{tr}(X).[t]_{\mathcal{I};\alpha\leftarrow<x,X>}$$

Formally however, this definition is not as easy to handle as it seems. The typing is delicate in the case of the application node because it requires $(\mathsf{App}\ t\ u)$ to be well-typed. The idea is that if WT $(\mathsf{App}\ t\ u)$ T, we know there exists $U : \mathsf{ST}$ such that WT u U and WT t $(U \Rightarrow T)$. This in turn implies that $[t]_{\mathcal{I}} : \mathsf{tr}(T) \rightarrow \mathsf{tr}(U)$ and $[u]_{\mathcal{I}} : \mathsf{tr}(U)$ which allows the construction $[t]_{\mathcal{I}}([u]_{\mathcal{I}})$.

If we go into detail however, the hypotheses are : there exists T, U and U', such that: $[t]_{\mathcal{I}} : \mathsf{tr}(U) \rightarrow \mathsf{tr}(T), [u]_{\mathcal{I}} : tr(U')$ and we have a proof that $U = U'$. One then has to use this last proof to transform $[u]_{\mathcal{I}}$ into an object of type $\mathsf{tr}(U)$. But programs constructed that way are very difficult to reason about: because the inner types depend upon values (here the values U and U'), equational reasoning about these values can easily make the goal not well-typed anymore. Also, a naive way to define the compilation would be to have it depend upon the typing judgement. At least in the setting of Coq, this is not a good idea, again for the same reason.

Treatment of Type Equality

Georges Gonthier suggested us a convenient way to treat type equality tests. When U and U' turn out to be equal, the result of the equality test will be used to map an object of some type $A(U)$ to $A(U')$. So we can build this coercion into the equality test's result. This is done by defining:

```
Inductive cast_result (a1 a2 : ST) : Type :=
  | Cast (k : forall P, P a1 -> P a2)
  | NoCast.
```

One then defines the function `cast : ST -> ST -> cast_result` which returns `NoCast` if its arguments are different and `Cast` applied to the identity if they are equal:

```
Fixpoint cast (a1 a2 : ST) {struct a2} : cast_result a1 a2 :=
  match a1 as d1, a2 as d2 return cast_result d1 d2 with
  | Iota, Iota => idcast
  | Arr b1 c1, Arr b2 c2 =>
    match cast b1 b2, cast c1 c2 with
    | Cast kb, Cast kc =>
      let ka P :=
        let Pb d := P (d ==> c1) in let Pc d := P (b2 ==> d) in
        fun x => kc Pc (kb Pb x)
      in Cast _ _ ka
    | _, _ => NoCast
    end
  | _, _ => NoCast
  end.
```

On one hand one then shows that **cast** actually implements the equality test. On the other hand however, one does not need to invoke this property in order to define a function like compilation. Indeed, we want to make the compilation function as robust as possible; instead of asking for the argument to verify WT, the function is defined for any **term** but can return a default value when the argument has no semantics. This means the function returns a result of the following type:

```
Inductive comp_res : Type :=
| Comp : forall T:ST, (sem_env -> tr T) -> comp_res
| NoComp.
```

and the **comp** function is then best described by its actual code:

```
Fixpoint comp (t:term): comp_res :=
let F T := sem_env -> tr T in
  match t with
| Var i => Comp i.(idT) (fun I => (I i))

| Lam i t =>
  match comp t with
  | NoComp => NoComp _
  | Comp U f => Comp (Arr i.(idT) U)
                     (fun I x => (f (esc I i x)))
  end

| App u v =>
  match comp u , comp v with
  | Comp (U1 ==> U2) su , Comp V sv =>
    match cast V U1 with
    | Cast f => Comp U2 (fun I => (su I (f tr (sv I))))
    | NoCast => NoComp _
```

```
      end
  | _,_ => NoComp _
  end
end.
```

The two main remarks are:

- One easily proves that comp correctly re-implements type-checking. That is (comp t) is of the form (Cast T v) if and only if (infer t) reduces to (Some T).
- The big advantage of using cast appears, as expected, in the clause for App t u: we use the cast f in order to construct the result, without having to know that cast actually implements equality. This may look like a technical detail but is crucial for keeping the proofs reasonably small and tractable.

One can prove a first result about compilation, namely that its result verifies the SNF property.

Lemma 5 (comp_norm). *Let $\mathcal{I}$ be such that for all x^A, we have SNF A $(\mathcal{I}\ x^A)$. If (comp t) is of the form (Comp T st) (which is always the case if (WT t T) holds), then we have (SNF T $(st\ \mathcal{I})$).*

Definition 3 (id_env). *The standard interpretation $\mathcal{I}_0$ is defined by*

$$\mathcal{I}_0(x^T) \equiv \mathsf{long}\ T\ (\mathsf{Var}\ x^T)$$

for all x^T.

The lemmas 4 and 5 then ensure:

Theorem 1 (norm_norm). *If (comp t) is of the form (Comp T st), then (NF (decomp $(st\ \mathcal{I}_0)$)). This is always the case when WT t T holds.*

6 The Central Logical Relation

It then remains to show that compilation and decompilation preserve conversion. That is if WT t T and if n and $\mathcal{I}$ are well-chosen, then

$$t =_{\beta\eta} \mathsf{decomp}(T, n, [t]_\mathcal{I}).$$

Exactly like in all the related work, one here has to introduce a logical relation between the syntactic and semantic levels. The definition could not be simpler:

Definition 4 (sem_conv). *If t : term, T : ST and f : tr(T) then $t \simeq_T f$ is a proposition defined recursively by:*

$$t \simeq_\iota st \equiv t =_{\beta\eta} st$$
$$t \simeq_{A\Rightarrow B} st \equiv \forall u\ su, u \simeq_A su \rightarrow (\mathsf{App}\ t\ u) \simeq_B (st\ su)$$

The logical relation allows us to define an extentional equality on the semantical level:

Definition 5 (ext_eq). *If* T : ST, *then* $=_T$ *is a binary relation over* $\text{tr}(T)$ *defined by:*

$$t =_\iota u \equiv t =_{\beta\eta} u$$
$$f =_{A\Rightarrow B} g \equiv \forall(t : \text{term})(f'\ g' : \text{tr}(A)), t \simeq_A f' \to f' =_A g' \to (f\ f') =_B (g\ g')$$

Notice, in the second clause, that we require one of the arguments to be related to some term t. This can be understood as a way to prevent considering "pathological" functions, which, for instance, could depend upon the size of terms, the name of bound variables, etc... Although the formulation is not symmetrical, the definition actually is; since one then shows that the logical relation is extentional.

Lemma 6 (sem_comp_ext1, sem_comp_ext2). *Suppose* $t \simeq_T st$. *Then:*

1. *if* $t =_{\beta\eta} t'$, *then* $t' \simeq_T st$,
2. *if* $st' =_T st$, *then* $t \simeq_T st'$.

7   Putting It All Together

We can then finish the normalization proof by proving the main lemma of the development.

Lemma 7 (sem_comp). *Let* t *be such that* (comp t) *is of the form* (Comp T st), *which is always the case when* WT t T *holds. Let* σ *a substitution and* $\mathcal{I}$ *an interpretation be such that for any* x^A *which is free in* t *we have* $\sigma(x) \simeq_A \mathcal{I}(x^A)$. *Then we have:*

$$t[\sigma] \simeq_T [t]_\mathcal{I}.$$

PROOF.   By induction over the structure of t. It is the longest normalization-related proof of the development. It uses some technical results about free variables and α-conversion, that we have not detailed in this account.

The next lemma 8 states that the "well-behaved" functions, which can be decompiled, are exactly the ones related to some term by $\simeq$. Notice that this means that the lemma 7 can be understood as the real completeness result of the development: it states that the co-domain of the semantics are precisely the "well-behaved" functions.

Lemma 8 (sem_decomp). *If* $t \simeq_T st$, *then* $t =_{\beta\eta}$ (decomp T (st $\mathcal{I}_0$)).

PROOF.   The proof of this lemma proceeds over a simple induction on the types, initially conducted simultaneously with the equivalent property on long. It is the only result relying on lemma 1, but presents no other difficulty.

It is then easy to conclude the weak normalization result:

Theorem 2. *If* WT t T, *then* (comp t) *is of the form* (Comp T st) *and:*

1. $t =_{\beta\eta}$ (decomp T (st $\mathcal{I}_0$))
2. NF (decomp T (st $\mathcal{I}_0$)).

PROOF.   It is a corollary of theorem 1, lemma 8 and the fact that well-typed terms are compilable. For lemma 8, one simply uses the fact that $t =_\alpha t[Id]$.

8   Conclusion and Future Work

We have shown that formal treatment of NbE in provers based on type theory is tractable even when using a formalization style which is very different from the one followed by Catarina Coquand. We have also shown that NbE is possible when using the simple types for the compiled terms, even if, in our case, this comes at the expense of efficiency. Whether one can get rid of this overhead without changing the typing seems however doubtful to us.

A first possible direction of work is to apply similar techniques, and possibly reuse part of this development in order to formalize and implement the related versions of NbE of Berger and his collaborators. This seems at the same time feasible and useful, especially in a framework like Coq, which implements "real" compilation and would thus allow really fast normalization.

A second more prospective but, we hope, promising direction of research is using the present development for making reasoning about structures with binders easier. Indeed, a language with binders can be described by a context of simply typed λ-calculus. For instance, untyped λ-terms can be described as simply typed λ-terms whose free variables are either of the atomic type ι, or equal to one of the two variables:

$$\mathrm{APP} : \iota \to \iota \to \iota; \ \mathrm{LAM} : (\iota \to \iota) \to \iota.$$

This is the idea of higher-order abstract syntax (HOAS [15]) whose possible use inside type theory has already been investigated [11,16]. We hope that by allowing to characterize precisely what are the terms of the type theory which belong to the simply typed fragment and accessing their syntax, our work can be a first step for implementing techniques inspired by HOAS inside existing type theories; possibly in a way similar to [7].

Acknowledgments

We thank Thorsten Altenkirch, Thierry Coquand, Olivier Danvy, Hugo Herbelin, Marino Miculan and Helmut Schwichtenberg for helpful discussions on the topic. Anonymous referees made many useful comments. Special thanks go to Ulrich Berger who pointed out a crucial mistake and Georges Gonthier who provided the useful SSR proof tactic package and suggested the definition of typing as an actual function.

References

1. Altenkirch, T., Dybjer, P., Hofmann, M., Scott, P.J.: Normalization by evaluation for typed lambda calculus with coproducts. In: LICS, pp. 303–310 (2001)
2. Berger, U.: Program extraction from normalization proofs. In: Bezem, M., Groote, J.F. (eds.) TLCA 1993. LNCS, vol. 664, pp. 91–106. Springer, Heidelberg (1993)
3. Berger, U., Berghofer, S., Letouzey, P., Schwichtenberg, H.: Program extraction from normalization proofs. Studia Logica 82(1), 25–49 (2006)

4. Berger, U., Eberl, M., Schwichtenberg, H.: Normalisation by evaluation. In: Möller, B., Tucker, J.V. (eds.) Prospects for Hardware Foundations. LNCS, vol. 1546, pp. 117–137. Springer, Heidelberg (1998)

5. Berger, U., Eberl, M., Schwichtenberg, H.: Term rewriting for normalization by evaluation. Inf. Comput. 183(1), 19–42 (2003)

6. Berger, U., Schwichtenberg, H.: An inverse of the evaluation functional for typed lambda-calculus. In: LICS, pp. 203–211. IEEE Computer Society Press, Los Alamitos (1991)

7. Capretta, V., Felty, A.: Combining de bruijn indices and higher-order abstract syntax in coq. In: Altenkirch, T., McBride, C. (eds.) Proceedings of TYPES 2006. LNCS, Springer, Heidelberg (2007)

8. Coquand, C.: From semantics to rules: A machine assisted analysis. In: Meinke, K., Börger, E., Gurevich, Y. (eds.) CSL 1993. LNCS, vol. 832, pp. 91–105. Springer, Heidelberg (1994)

9. Coquand, C.: A formalised proof of the soundness and completeness of a simply typed lambda-calculus with explicit substitutions. Higher-Order and Symbolic Computation 15(1), 57–90 (2002)

10. Danvy, O., Rhiger, M., Rose, K.H.: Normalization by evaluation with typed abstract syntax. J. Funct. Program. 11(6), 673–680 (2001)

11. Despeyroux, J., Pfenning, F., Schürmann, C.: Primitive recursion for higher-order abstract syntax. In: de Groote, P., Hindley, J.R. (eds.) TLCA 1997. LNCS, vol. 1210, pp. 147–163. Springer, Heidelberg (1997)

12. Gonthier, G.: A computer-checked proof of the four colour theorem (2005), available on http://research.microsoft.com/~gonthier/

13. Gonthier, G.: Notations of the four colour theorem proof (2005), available on http://research.microsoft.com/~gonthier/

14. Krivine, J.-L.: Une preuve formelle et intuitionniste du théorème de complétude de la logique classique. Bulletin of Symbolic Logic 2(4), 405–421 (1996)

15. Pfenning, F., Elliott, C.: Higher-order abstract syntax. In: PLDI, pp. 199–208 (1988)

16. Schürmann, C., Despeyroux, J., Pfenning, F.: Primitive recursion for higher-order abstract syntax. Theor. Comput. Sci. 266(1-2), 1–57 (2001)

17. Stoughton, A.: Substitution revisited. Theor. Comput. Sci. 59, 317–325 (1988)

Mizar's Soft Type System

Freek Wiedijk

Institute for Computing and Information Sciences
Radboud University Nijmegen
Toernooiveld 1, 6525 ED Nijmegen, The Netherlands

Abstract. In Mizar, unlike in most other proof assistants, the types are not part of the foundations of the system. Mizar is based on untyped set theory, which means that in Mizar expressions are typed but the values of those expressions are not.

In this paper we present the Mizar type system as a collection of type inference rules. We will interpret Mizar types as *soft types*, by translating Mizar's type judgments into sequents of untyped first order predicate logic. We will then prove that the Mizar type system is *correct* with respect to this translation in the sense that each derivable type judgment translates to a provable sequent.

1 Introduction

1.1 Problem

The activity of checking mathematical proofs for correctness using a computer is called 'formalization of mathematics'. Systems for doing this are called proof assistants [12]. There are three main classes of proof assistants: the ones based on Church's *higher order logic* (e.g., HOL, Isabelle/HOL, ProofPower, and maybe also systems like PVS), the ones based on Martin-Löf's *type theory* (e.g., Coq, NuPRL, Agda, Epigram), and the proof assistants based on Cantor's *set theory* (e.g., Mizar, Metamath, Isabelle/ZF, the B method). These three 'cultures' are quite different, and people from different cultures sometimes find it hard to get a clear view on what people from the other cultures are doing. The primary aim of this paper is to make the set theoretical system Mizar (and in particular its type system) more understandable to people from the type theoretical and higher order logic communities.

The Mizar proof assistant [7] has been in development in Białystok, Poland, from the seventies until today, by a team led by Andrzej Trybulec. The current version of the system is called PC Mizar and is at version 7. It was originally released in 1989, and is still being actively developed. The library of formalized mathematics that accompanies the Mizar system is called MML (for Mizar Mathematical Library). It is the largest library of formalized mathematics that is currently in existence. At the time of writing it consists of 1.9 million lines of Mizar text, and is the collaborative work of almost two hundred people (the so-called 'Mizar authors.') The large size of the MML library is partly a reflection of the fact that Mizar only gives one moderate automation. Also the Mizar

K. Schneider and J. Brandt (Eds.): TPHOLs 2007, LNCS 4732, pp. 383–399, 2007.

library contains quite a bit of rather obscure mathematics. Still the Mizar library is undoubtedly one of the most interesting libraries of formalized mathematics in the world. The MML contains a formalization of a graduate-level textbook on the theory of continuous lattices, which is being translated quite faithfully into the Mizar language. (This project, which is being led by Grzegorz Bancerek, is currently two thirds finished.)

The Mizar system is based on first order predicate logic with on top of that a slight extension of Zermelo-Fraenkel set theory (ZF). To be precise: the *system* only implements first order predicate logic (together with 'schematic' axioms and theorems[1] – to be able to deal with the 'replacement' axiom scheme of ZF – and with a Hilbert choice operator that is hard-wired into the way the system deals with underspecified functions), but the MML *library* is based on set theory (all of the 1.9 million of lines are fully checked for correctness against only a handful of set theoretical axioms.) It is irrelevant for the rest of the paper exactly which set theory the Mizar library is based on, but to be specific: Mizar's set theory is called Tarski-Grothendieck set theory. It is ZF set theory with one extra axiom added (where '$\sim$' means that the two sets have the same cardinality):

$$\forall N \exists M \big(N \in M \,\wedge$$
$$\forall X \forall Y (X \in M \wedge Y \subseteq X \Rightarrow Y \in M) \,\wedge$$
$$\forall X (X \in M \Rightarrow \exists Z (Z \in M \wedge \forall Y (Y \subseteq X \Rightarrow Y \in Z))) \,\wedge$$
$$\forall X (X \subseteq M \Rightarrow X \sim M \vee X \in M) \big)$$

This axiom states that there are arbitrarily large universes, or, in other words, that there are arbitrarily large strongly inaccessible cardinals. From it one can derive the Axiom of Choice (even without that axiom being hard wired into the logic.) I do not know why Mizar has selected exactly *this* set theory for its foundation. Maybe one of the reasons was that the universes are useful when one wants to do category theory.

Set theory in the style of Cantor, like ZF set theory or von Neumann-Bernays-Gödel set theory (NBG), customarily is an *untyped* theory. Most often there is just one 'sort', the sort of sets. At most there will be two sorts, with the second sort being the sort of 'proper classes'. However, the Mizar system is a *typed* system: it implements a type system on top of its first order predicate logic. And not only does it have a type system, its type system is very powerful, and has many interesting features. In particular: it does support *dependent types*, which are *very* useful if one wants to formalize abstract mathematics.

This raises the question of what the type system of Mizar 'means': what the relation is between the typed version of set theory that one gets in Mizar and the untyped set theories like ZF that one finds in logic textbooks. This is the question that this paper will address.

---

[1] Mizar's notation for set comprehension – in the Mizar community called the 'Fraenkel-operator' – is a alternative version of this.

1.2   Approach

There are at least two ways in which to give an interpretation to Mizar's types:

1. Either one interprets the types of Mizar as *classes of sets*. In that case the set theory of Mizar will be taken to be a set theory like NBG set theory, where proper classes are first class objects.

   In this approach the interpretation of the Mizar type 'Ring' will be the class of rings, while the (dependent) type 'LeftMod of' will be interpreted by the 'class function' that maps each element of this class of rings to the class of the left modules over it. This interpretation of 'LeftMod of' therefore maps *each* element of a proper class to a *different* proper class.

2. Alternatively one can interpret the types of Mizar as *predicates*[2] that the system will keep track of automatically. This approach sometimes is called *soft typing*[3], which is the terminology that we will adopt for it in this paper. In this approach each reference to the type 'Ring' will be interpreted as *actually* being about a unary predicate 'is_Ring', while the type 'LeftMod of' will be interpreted as *actually* talking about a binary predicate 'is_LeftMod_of'.

In this paper we will focus on the second approach, and will not pursue the first possibility. This second approach has the attractive property that it does not need set theory. It allows one to give a meaning to the types of typed first order predicate logic (and even with types that are as powerful as the ones that one find in Mizar), even in the case that the theory in that logic is not set theory.

Mizar uses types in various ways. First, they annotate all variables that occur in a Mizar text: both for bound variables in formulas and for variables in a proof[4] there is a type. For instance, one writes

```
for n being Nat holds ...
```

when one universally quantifies over a variable n that has the type Nat (the type of natural numbers), and one might write

```
let n be Nat;
```

if one is reasoning in a proof about a variable of type Nat.

But types also can be used to create a formula, that states that an expression has a certain type. For instance one can write that

```
i is Nat;
```

---

[2] More generally: a dependent type with n parameters will be interpreted as an $n+1$-ary predicate.

[3] This term originates in the programming languages community [2], where it is used with a somewhat different meaning. In that context it means that you statically type as much as possible, and insert run-time checks for what cannot be statically typed.

[4] Although in logic these are considered variables, in the Mizar community they are often looked at as constants that are local to the proof. In the Isabelle community these are called *fixed variables*.

Here the keyword 'is' is put between a term and a type. This specific example means that the value of the expression 'i' (which for instance could be a variable of type 'Integer') satisfies the defining property of the type 'Nat', i.e., this states that i is non-negative.

This second way of using types does not have a direct counterpart in most of the proof assistants from the higher order logic and type theory traditions. There a type judgment is on a different level from the statements that one reasons about: in those systems type judgments are *outside* the logic, while statements are *in* the logic. But 'soft types' cross this boundary.

Apart from using types for reasoning, Mizar also uses types to disambiguate expressions that involve overloaded notation. Although this feature is very useful (for instance in Mizar a notation like $X + Y$ can mean many different things, depending on what the types of X and Y are) we will not go into this use of Mizar types in this paper.

To reiterate: the interpretation that we give to Mizar types will be to associate a 'hidden' predicate which each type, and to consider references to types to really be about these hidden predicates. We will consider the Mizar type system as being an engine that automatically – behind the scenes – generates statements involving those predicates. For instance, if we call the predicate that corresponds to the 'Nat' type 'is_Nat', then the three example lines of Mizar on the previous page will be interpreted as being an abbreviation of:

```
for n being set holds (is_Nat(n) implies ...)

   let n be set; assume is_Nat(n);

          is_Nat(i)
```

Now we have statements in single sorted predicate logic where all variables are in the sort 'set'.

1.3 Related Work

There already is a paper about the Mizar type system by Grzegorz Bancerek [1]. However, the presentation of the type system in that papers is quite different from the one that is used here. Also, the interpretation of the types in an 'algebra of types' is closer to the first approach that we mentioned on page 385 than to the second approach that we are pursuing here. Andrzej Trybulec also has such an approach, using the notion of what he calls *dependent type algebras*.

The the work of Ingo Dahn [3] and the work of Josef Urban [9,8,10] on translating Mizar into a form that is digestible by first order theorem provers, is based on the same interpretation of Mizar types as soft types that we present in Section 5. In the work of Josef Urban [10] also occurs the view of the Mizar type checker in 'logic programming' style, which is how we interpreted our typing rules in Section 4.

There are other theorem provers that use soft types as a way of pushing the type system of first order predicate logic beyond the customary 'many-sorted' variant of first order predicate logic, where one only has a finite number of types without any further structure. For instance it is used in the SPASS first order theorem prover, see [11].

Joe Hurd showed how to have a layer of soft typing on top of a higher order system [5]. PVS also can be considered to be such a system. However, in PVS the soft typing is not actually a separate *layer*.

1.4 Contribution

The contribution of this paper is threefold:

- It gives a *presentation* of the Mizar type system as a collection of type inference rules, which is the style that is standard in the type theoretical research community. This presentation of the Mizar type system is new.
- It gives an *interpretation* of Mizar's types by systematically translating type judgments to sequents of untyped first order predicate logic. This interpretation was already implicitly present in the work of Ingo Dahn and Josef Urban, but the way it is made explicit in this paper, and the focus that we have on interpreting it as the *semantics* of the Mizar type system, is new.
- It shows that this interpretation is *correct*, in the sense that for any type judgment that is generated by the Mizar type system, the corresponding translation is provable.

1.5 Outline

The structure of this paper is as follows. In Section 2 we present the notation that we will use for Mizar's type judgments. In Section 3 we give a non-trivial example of such a judgment, which we both present in our notation and in the usual Mizar syntax. In Section 4 we present the type inference rules of the Mizar type system. In Section 5 we prove that these rules are correct with respect to a translation into untyped logic. Finally in Section 6 we conclude, and mention some questions for further research.

2 Judgments

In Mizar types have various uses. In particular, they also play an important rôle in the logical language of the system, because type judgments are one of the kinds of atomic formula. However, from now on we will focus on the type system on its own, separately from the logic. That is, we will now just focus on the mechanism that ascribes types to terms.[5] In the Mizar system, this is

---

[5] This might seem to be a strong restriction. In particular the reader might wonder how the type system fits in with the underlying set theory. (In fact, the Mizar type system is completely independent of set theory. The Mizar system and its type theory can be used with *any* first order theory.)

If one translates a Mizar formalization into standard 'unsorted' first order predicate logic (as is done in [9]), then basically three kinds of statements are involved. First, there are the statements that actually occur in the Mizar text, which

implemented in the part of the system that is called ANALYZER. (The logic is implemented in the part called CHECKER.[6])

We will now describe the syntax that we will use for Mizar type judgments. The notation that we will use is specific to this paper. It will make the typing rules of Section 4 much more compact than if we had used the Mizar input syntax. For a non-trivial example of a typing sequent, both in our syntax as well as in the Mizar input syntax, see Section 3.

In our judgments we will have four kinds of variables. Actually, three of the four kinds are not considered to be variables in the Mizar system, but because we bind these symbols in the context part of the judgments[7] we will consider them to be variables of the type judgment. These kinds of variables are:

$$x \qquad \text{term variable}$$
$$f \qquad \text{'functor'} = \text{function symbol}$$
$$\alpha \qquad \text{'attributes'} = \text{type modifier}$$
$$M \qquad \text{'mode'} = \text{type symbol}$$

(The words 'functor', 'attributes[8]', 'mode' and (below) 'radix type' are Mizar-specific terminology.[9])

Apart from these variables, we will use one special symbol, the asterisk, for the root type of Mizar, of which all other types are subtypes:

---

are 'translated' by relativizing all quantifiers to the predicates that correspond to the types. Second, there are the statement that give the definition of the various predicates, functors, modes and attributes. In the Mizar file these are implicitly given by the keywords 'means' or equals'. Third, there are the statements that originate in the type system: the statements occurring in the translations of the type judgments as described in Section 5. Apart from the statements of the second kind, *all* these statements have a proof in the Mizar file.

This means that although it might seem in Section 4 that one is allowed to arbitrarily build a Mizar context, if one wants to have that context in an actual Mizar text, then one will need to *prove* the translation in the style of Section 5 of that context.

[6] Note that neither ANALYZER nor CHECKER has a small 'kernel', as is common in LCF-style systems. To trust the Mizar system, one will need to trust the full code base.

[7] Actually, many of these variables will occur multiple times in the context, because of the presence of redefinitions and clusters. The first occurrence of the variable – corresponding to its original introduction in the Mizar text – is the binding one.

[8] Most systems do not have anything like the attributes of Mizar, which are type modifiers that behave a bit like intersection types. See Section 3 below for an example that shows how attributes are used. In that example the type 'int' of the integers has attributes 'pos' and 'neg' that allow one to talk about the positive and the negative integers. For example the type 'pos int' contains the positive integers. The elements of that type are the objects that *both* satisfy the defining statement of the 'int' type and that of the 'pos' attribute.

[9] Words like 'functor' and 'radix' are used with quite different meanings outside of the context of Mizar, so our use of these words might be confusing. Maybe 'function symbol' or 'operator' for 'functor' and 'base type' for 'radix type' would be more appropriate. However, we decided not to depart from standard Mizar terminology.

*   the root type

In Mizar input syntax this type is called 'set' because it is the type of all sets. It also used to be called 'Any'. (In our interpretation of types as unary predicates it corresponds to the predicate that is constantly true.[10])

Mizar also has *predicate symbols*, which are not treated in this paper. The reason for leaving them out is that although the arguments to the predicates are typed, the predicates will not play any part in generating the types.

Next, here is the grammar that gives the various notions that occur in our type judgments:

$$t ::= x \mid f(\vec{t})$$

$$R ::= * \mid M(\vec{t})$$

$$a ::= \alpha \mid \bar{\alpha}$$

$$T ::= \vec{a}\,R$$

$$D ::= x : T$$

$$J ::= \cdot \mid t : T \mid T \leq T \mid \exists T \mid \alpha/T$$

$$\Delta ::= \vec{D}$$

$$\Gamma ::= \overrightarrow{[\Delta](\vec{J})}$$

In this grammar t are the *terms*, R are the *radix types*, a are the *adjectives* (these are either an attribute α or the negation of an attribute $\bar{\alpha}$), T are the *types*, D are the *declarations*, J are the *judgment elements*, and Δ and Γ are the two parts of the context of a type judgment. The full type judgments that we will derive with our typing rules will have the shape:

$$\Gamma; \Delta \vdash J$$

In this judgement Γ corresponds to the type information of a series of Mizar definitions and registrations. The 'local context' Δ corresponds to the types of the variables that have been introduced *inside* a Mizar definition or proof. We call Γ the global context and Δ the local context of the judgment.

In the grammar from this section we use vector notation. For instance, an expression like $[\vec{x} : \vec{T}](f(\vec{x}) : T')$ should be read as $[x_1 : T_1, \ldots, x_n : T_n]$ $(f(x_1, \ldots, x_n) : T')$. Furthermore all expressions should only be considered 'modulo α-equivalence', so $[x : T](f(x) : T')$ and $[y : T](f(y) : T')$ are really considered to be the same. Finally the 'clusters of adjectives' $\vec{a}$ in front of a type are considered only as sets. In other words, the expression $\alpha_1\bar{\alpha}_2$ is considered to be equivalent to $\bar{\alpha}_2\alpha_1$, $\alpha_1\alpha_1\bar{\alpha}_2$, $\alpha_1\bar{\alpha}_2\bar{\alpha}_2$, and so on.

The instances of the notion of judgment elements J have the following interpretations:

---

[10] In the typing rules of Section 4 the root type plays an essential rôle. One can only introduce new radix types to the context if one already *has* a type (which will be its supertype). So without the root type the rules of Section 4 would not work, as there would not be a starting point for introducing types.

$$t : T \qquad t \text{ has type } T$$
$$T_1 \leq T_2 \qquad T_1 \text{ is a subtype of } T_2$$
$$\exists T \qquad T \text{ is a non-empty type}$$
$$\alpha / T \qquad \alpha \text{ is an attribute of the type } T$$

In Mizar input language $t : T$ is written as 't be T' or 't being T', and $T_1 \leq T_2$ is written as 'T_1 -> T_2'.

The centered dot '$\cdot$' is used if one just wants to state that a context is well-formed. (To indicate that a type T is well-formed one either uses $T \leq T$ or $\exists T$, depending on whether one already knows that the type is non-empty or not.)

3   Example

We now present an example that demonstrates the various features of the Mizar type system. The following type judgment[11] is derivable using the rules of Section 4:

$$\text{int} \leq *, \ \exists \, \text{int},$$
$$\text{pos}/\text{int},$$
$$\text{neg}/\text{int},$$
$$\text{pos int} \leq \overline{\text{neg}} \, \text{int},$$
$$\exists \, \text{pos int},$$
$$\exists \, \overline{\text{pos}} \, \overline{\text{neg}} \, \text{int},$$
$$z : \text{int},$$
$$z : \overline{\text{neg}} \, \overline{\text{pos}} \, \text{int},$$
$$[n : \text{int}](S(n) : \text{int}),$$
$$[n : \text{int}](P(n) : \text{int}),$$
$$[n : \overline{\text{neg}} \, \text{int}](S(n) : \text{pos int}),$$
$$[n : \text{pos int}](P(n) : \overline{\text{neg}} \, \text{int}),$$
$$[n : \overline{\text{neg}} \, \text{int}](\text{list}(n) \leq *), \ [n : \overline{\text{neg}} \, \text{int}](\exists \, \text{list}(n)),$$
$$\text{nil} : \text{list}(z),$$
$$[n : \overline{\text{neg}} \, \text{int}, \, x : *, \, l : \text{list}(n)](\text{cons}(n, x, l) : \text{list}(S(n))),$$
$$[n : \text{pos int}, \, l : \text{list}(n)](\text{car}(n, l) : *),$$
$$[n : \text{pos int}, \, l : \text{list}(n)](\text{cdr}(n, l) : \text{list}(P(n)))$$
$$;$$
$$x : *$$
$$\vdash$$
$$\text{cdr}(S(z), \text{cons}(z, x, \text{nil})) : \text{list}(P(S(z)))$$

This example involves types int and list for integers and lists, the latter being a dependent type with the length of the list as the argument. It has attributes pos and neg on the type of integers for positive and negative integers. Furthermore it has functions S and P on the integers for successor and predecessor and functions nil, cons, car and cdr for the lists.[12] The local context of the judgment is just the

---

[11] We put the first two judgment elements 'int $\leq *$' and '$\exists$ int' on a single line, as in the Mizar text it corresponds to a single definition.

[12] These are not the names that are used in the MML for these notions. There int is called **Integer**, list is called **FinSequence** (although the version that depends on the

variable declaration $x : *$, and the statement of the judgment is that the term 'cdr($S(z)$, cons(z, x, nil))' has among its collection of types the type 'list($P(S(z))$)'.

The judgment that we just presented has the shape

$$\Gamma; \Delta \vdash J$$

of which the part Γ corresponds to a series of definitions and registrations. Here is what this Γ looks like in Mizar syntax:

```
definition
 mode int -> set means ...; existence ...
end;

definition let n be int;
 attr n is pos means ...
 attr n is neg means ...
end;

registration
 cluster pos -> non neg int; coherence ...
end;

registration
 cluster pos int; existence ...
 cluster non pos non neg int; existence ...
end;

definition
 func z -> int means ...
end;

registration
 cluster z -> non neg non pos; coherence ...
end;

definition let n be int;
 func S n -> int means ...
 func P n -> int means ...
end;

registration let n be non neg int;
 cluster S n -> pos; coherence ...
end;

definition let n be pos int;
```

---

length of the list like in the example is called **Tuple**, and that type also depends on the set from which the elements are taken). The attributes **pos** and **neg** are called **positive** and **negative**, and nil is called **{}**. The functions S and P do not exist in the MML, $S(n)$ is just written as $n + 1$ and $P(n)$ is just $n - 1$. The list functions do not exist either: cons(x, l) is written $<*x*>^\frown l$, car(l) is written $l.1$, and cdr(l) is written $l/^1$.

The name **neg** in the MML is not an attribute symbol but a functor symbol, for intuitionistic negation.

```
redefine func P n -> non neg int; coherence ...
end;

definition let n be non neg int;
 mode list of n -> set means ...; existence ...
end;

definition
 func nil -> list of z means ...
end;

definition let n be non neg int; let x be set; let l be list of n;
 func cons(x,l) -> list of S n means ...
end;

definition let n be pos int; let l be list of n;
 func car l -> set means ...
end;

definition let n be pos int; let l be list of n;
 func cdr l -> list of P n means ...
end;
```

For a version of these definitions that has been completed with statements and proofs in the place of the dots see http://www.cs.ru.nl/~freek/mizar/example.miz and <http://www.cs.ru.nl/~freek/mizar/example.voc>.[13]

Note that most of the items in this list of definitions and registrations have proof obligations. This means that they do not, like in the judgments that we show in this paper, behave like assumptions, but that they really are statements that are proved from the existing theory. For example, the part of the context

$$[n : \mathsf{pos\ int}](\mathsf{P}(n) : \overline{\mathsf{neg}}\ \mathsf{int}),$$

that is the 'redefinition' of the predecessor function to give its value the more specific type '$\overline{\mathsf{neg}}$ int' when it is known that the argument has the type 'pos int' is in the Mizar formalization written as

```
definition
 let n be pos int;
 redefine func P n -> non neg int;
 coherence
 proof
   ...
   hence P n is non neg int by ...
 end;
end;
```

where the 'P n' in the **hence** line refers to the earlier definition of the P function. This means that the dots will have to be a proof that amounts to showing that

---

[13] Note that from the point of view of the MML, this is a *very* silly example as it just defines a lot of stuff that is present already, only using different names.

from $n > 0$ it follows that $n - 1 \geq 0$. Under the translation from Section 5 this part of the typing context turns into

$$\forall n \big(\mathsf{pos}(n) \wedge \mathsf{int}(n) \Rightarrow \neg\mathsf{neg}(\mathsf{P}(n)) \wedge \mathsf{int}(\mathsf{P}(n)) \big)$$

and in a real Mizar formalization that statement will have to be proved.

Similarly the other definitions and registrations have appropriate proof obligations (the only judgment elements in the context of the example that do not have proof obligations are the attribute definitions.)

4   Rules

We will now present the Mizar type system as a collection of typing rules. These rules present a slightly simplified version of the Mizar type system:

- There are no structure types.
  Structure types are the 'record types' of Mizar. (For an interesting discussion of how structure types can be understood in terms of the underlying set theoretical foundations of the Mizar system, see [6].)
- In the real Mizar system, symbols can be overloaded. Here we suppose that all symbols have been sufficiently disambiguated. That is, the typing rules that we are presenting should only be instantiated according to the Barendregt convention (variables should never be 'hidden' by later variables.)
- In the real Mizar type system, a redefinition takes priority over the definitions that come before it in the context. However, in this version of the type system the order of the definitions is not taken into account when generating type judgments.
- When reasoning, the set of types of a Mizar expression will be closed under available equalities. For instance, if one of the statements that justifies the inference is $n = n'$ and an expression has type $\mathsf{list}(n)$, then it also will be assigned type $\mathsf{list}(n')$. This kind of equality reasoning is not present in our version of the Mizar type system.

Note that a Mizar term generally does not have just one type (for instance, every well typed expression will always *also* have the type $*$), and can even get a quite large collection of types.

One can consider these rules to be something like a 'logic programming' description of the Mizar type checker:

$$\frac{}{;\vdash \cdot}$$

$$\frac{\Gamma; \Delta \vdash \vec{t} : \vec{T}[\vec{x} := \vec{t}]}{\Gamma; \Delta \vdash J[\vec{x} := \vec{t}]} \, [\vec{x} : \vec{T}](J) \in \Gamma; \Delta \qquad \frac{\Gamma; \Delta \vdash \exists T}{\Gamma; \Delta, x : T \vdash \cdot}$$

$$\frac{\Gamma; \Delta \vdash \cdot}{\Gamma; \Delta \vdash * \leq *} \qquad \frac{\Gamma; \Delta \vdash \cdot}{\Gamma; \Delta \vdash \exists *}$$

$$\frac{\Gamma;\Delta\vdash T\leq T'}{\Gamma;\Delta\vdash T\leq T}\qquad\frac{\Gamma;\Delta\vdash T\leq T'\quad\Gamma;\Delta\vdash T'\leq T''}{\Gamma;\Delta\vdash T\leq T''}$$

$$\frac{\Gamma;\Delta\vdash t:T\quad\Gamma;\Delta\vdash T\leq T'}{\Gamma;\Delta\vdash t:T'}\qquad\frac{\Gamma;\Delta\vdash T\leq T'\quad\Gamma;\Delta\vdash\exists T}{\Gamma;\Delta\vdash\exists T'}$$

$$\frac{\Gamma;\Delta\vdash\alpha/T}{\Gamma;\Delta\vdash\alpha T\leq T}\qquad\frac{\Gamma;\Delta\vdash\alpha/T}{\Gamma;\Delta\vdash\bar{\alpha}T\leq T}$$

$$\frac{\Gamma;\Delta\vdash T\leq T'\quad\Gamma;\Delta\vdash aT'\leq T'}{\Gamma;\Delta\vdash aT\leq T}\qquad\frac{\Gamma;\Delta\vdash T\leq T'\quad\Gamma;\Delta\vdash aT'\leq T'}{\Gamma;\Delta\vdash aT\leq aT'}$$

$$\frac{\Gamma;\Delta\vdash T\leq aT'\quad\Gamma;\Delta\vdash T\leq a'T'}{\Gamma;\Delta\vdash T\leq aa'T'}$$

functor definition:
$$\frac{\Gamma;\vec{x}:\vec{T}\vdash\exists T'}{\Gamma,[\vec{x}:\vec{T}](f(\vec{x}):T');\vdash\cdot}\,f\notin\Gamma$$

mode definition:
$$\frac{\Gamma;\vec{x}:\vec{T}\vdash\exists T'}{\Gamma,[\vec{x}:\vec{T}](M(\vec{x})\leq T'),[\vec{x}:\vec{T}](\exists M(\vec{x}));\vdash\cdot}\,M\notin\Gamma$$

attribute definition:
$$\frac{\Gamma;\Delta\vdash\exists T'}{\Gamma,[\Delta](\alpha/T');\vdash\cdot}\,\alpha\notin\Gamma$$

existential cluster:
$$\frac{\Gamma;\Delta\vdash\vec{a}T'\leq T'\quad\Gamma;\Delta\vdash\exists T'}{\Gamma,[\Delta](\exists\vec{a}T');\vdash\cdot}$$

conditional cluster:
$$\frac{\Gamma;\Delta\vdash\vec{a}T'\leq T'\quad\Gamma;\Delta\vdash\vec{a}'T'\leq T'}{\Gamma,[\Delta](\vec{a}T'\leq\vec{a}'T');\vdash\cdot}$$

functorial cluster:
$$\frac{\Gamma;\Delta\vdash t:T'\quad\Gamma;\Delta\vdash\vec{a}T'\leq T'}{\Gamma,[\Delta](t:\vec{a}T');\vdash\cdot}$$

functor redefinition:
$$\frac{\Gamma;\vec{x}:\vec{T}\vdash\exists T''\quad\Gamma;\vec{x}:\vec{T}\vdash T''\leq T'''\quad\Gamma;\vec{x}':\vec{T}',\vec{x}:\vec{T}\vdash f(\vec{x}):T''''}{\Gamma,[\vec{x}':\vec{T}',\vec{x}:\vec{T}](f(\vec{x}):T'');\vdash\cdot}$$

mode redefinition:
$$\frac{\Gamma;\vec{x}:\vec{T}\vdash\exists T''\quad\Gamma;\vec{x}:\vec{T}\vdash T''\leq T'''\quad\Gamma;\vec{x}':\vec{T}',\vec{x}:\vec{T}\vdash M(\vec{x})\leq T''''}{\Gamma,[\vec{x}':\vec{T}',\vec{x}:\vec{T}](M(\vec{x}):T'');\vdash\cdot}$$

The side-conditions '... $\notin \Gamma$' of the three definition rules mean that the symbol does not occur anywhere in the context Γ. The 'extra arguments' $\vec{x}'$ in the redefinition rules and generally are the empty vector.

In Mizar the types of actual terms always have to be non-empty.[14] This explains all the assumptions of the form $\exists T$ that occur in these rules. However, note that clusters sometimes involve types that have not been shown to be non-empty.

5   Correctness

We will now translate the typing judgments of our Mizar type system into sequents of single sorted first order predicate logic.[15] We will do this in two phases:

- First we introduce an *annotated* version of the Mizar type system, in which all the attributes have explicit arguments. This is exactly the same system that we already presented, but each attribute α now gets a list of arguments. These arguments are the arguments that determine the type on which the attribute was defined.

  The grammar of the judgments stays exactly like it was, except that the rule for an adjective becomes:

  $$a ::= \alpha(\vec{t}) \mid \bar{\alpha}(\vec{t})$$

The derivation rules also stay all the same, apart from the rules that explicitly involve an attribute symbol:

$$\frac{\Gamma; \vec{x} : \vec{T} \vdash \exists T'}{\Gamma, [\vec{x} : \vec{T}](\alpha(\vec{x})/T'); \vdash \cdot} \; \alpha \notin \Gamma$$

$$\frac{\Gamma; \Delta \vdash \alpha(\vec{t})/T}{\Gamma; \Delta \vdash \alpha(\vec{t}) \, T \leq T} \qquad \frac{\Gamma; \Delta \vdash \alpha(\vec{t})/T}{\Gamma; \Delta \vdash \bar{\alpha}(\vec{t}) \, T \leq T}$$

We now have the following theorem, that we present here without proof:

Theorem 5.1. *For every derivable type judgment of the non-annotated version of the Mizar type system, there exists a corresponding type judgment of the annotated version of the Mizar type system which only differs in that after the attributes arguments have been added.)*

---

[14] There is no good mathematical reason for this restriction. It *does* lead to higher quality formalizations, as the formalizer will need to think about whether the types are empty or not. Also, it of course simplifies the implementation of the inference checker. On the other hand it sometimes leads to unnatural mode definitions (like the infamous definition of 'Element of').

[15] In fact the Mizar typing rules can be motivated from this translation. The Mizar type system is designed to combine two opposite goals: to have the system automatically infer as many type judgments as possible for which the translation is provable; but on the other hand to have a type system in which all typing judgments can be efficiently inferred.

Note that the annotated version of the judgment is not always unique. This is the reason that the Mizar implementation internally keeps track of these 'hidden arguments' of the attributes. (There has been discussion in the Mizar community about whether these arguments maybe also should be allowed to be explicit.)

– Now that we have annotated versions of the Mizar type judgments, translating them into first order logic is easy. We define a translation $|\cdot|$ that maps our system into first order logic:

$$
\begin{aligned}
|*|(t) &:= \top \\
|M(\vec{t'})|(t) &:= M(t, \vec{t'}) \\
|\alpha(\vec{t'})|(t) &:= \alpha(t, \vec{t'}) \\
|\bar{\alpha}(\vec{t'})|(t) &:= \neg\alpha(t, \vec{t'}) \\
|a_1 \ldots a_n R|(t) &:= |a_1|(t) \wedge \ldots \wedge |a_n|(t) \wedge |R|(t) \\[4pt]
|t : T| &:= |T|(t) \\
|T \leq T'| &:= \forall x\, (|T|(x) \Rightarrow |T'|(x)) \\
|\exists T| &:= \exists x\, (|T|(x)) \\
|\alpha/T| &:= \top
\end{aligned}
$$

$$
\begin{aligned}
|[x_1 : T_1, \ldots, x_n : T_n](J)| &:= \forall x_1 \ldots \forall x_n (|T_1|(x_1) \wedge \ldots \wedge |T_n|(x_n) \Rightarrow |J|) \\
|\overrightarrow{[\Delta](J)}; \vec{J'} \vdash J''| &:= \overrightarrow{|[\Delta](J)|}, \overrightarrow{|J'|} \vdash |J''|
\end{aligned}
$$

In the first order logic, we take the symbols for types and attributes to be predicate symbols, where the arity as a predicate symbol is one more than the original arity. The idea is that if T is a type, then $|T|(t)$ corresponds to the Mizar statement 't is T'. This explains the order that we chose for the arguments of the symbol taken as a predicate.

(The translation of α/T as just 'true' might be unexpected. One might expect the translation to be:

$$
|\alpha/T| := \forall x\, (|\alpha|(x) \Rightarrow |T|(x))
$$

However, we decided not to do this, as it would be strange to require $|\alpha|(t)$ to imply $|T|(t)$, but not to require the same property for $|\bar{\alpha}|(t)$ ($\bar{\alpha}$ also being an adjective of T). Our translation is interpreting adjectives in the spirit of intersection types.[16])

---

[16] It might be surprising that an attribute can be given whatever radix type one likes. This corresponds to the fact that in Mizar an attribute definition does not need any proof (it does not have a 'correctness condition'): the defining statement of an attribute can be any formula, without any restriction. Note also that there is no such thing as an 'attribute redefinition'.

The following theorem now also is easy:

Theorem 5.2. *If $\Gamma; \Delta \vdash J$ is a judgment of the annotated version of the Mizar type system, then $|\Gamma; \Delta \vdash J|$ is a provable sequent of first order predicate logic.*

Proof. Induction on the derivation of the judgment: each rule of the type system corresponds to a small derivation in first order logic.   □

6   Conclusion

6.1   Discussion

One of the nicest things about interpreting the Mizar type system as a system of *soft* types, is that it shows that the Mizar type system, with all its power, can easily be added 'on top' of any existing proof assistant.[17] It is mainly a matter of defining selected predicates to take the rôle of the types and then to:

- Implement automatic inference of statements about these predicates along the lines of the rules in Section 4.
- Add a layer of parsing and pretty-printing to the system to have syntax for the predicates as types. In this layer the *implicit arguments* that are common in dependently typed systems can be implemented.

This way even the systems from the HOL family of proof assistants [4] can have dependent types!

In fact, even in systems like Coq that have a rather powerful type system already, one often sees the tendency to use 'soft' types on top of the 'hard' types that are already in the system. For instance, in the C-CoRN library from Nijmegen, there is a formalization of integration theory, where instead of using a type for continuous partial functions, there are lines in the development that look like:

```
Variables a b : IR.
Hypothesis Hab : a [<=] b.
Variable F : PartIR.
Hypothesis contF : Continuous_I Hab F.
```

and then the operation called 'Integral' takes the predicate 'contF' as one of its arguments. Clearly this is a rough version of soft typing.

Similarly, a development of Galois theory by Georges Gonthier and Sean McLaughlin (developed in the Microsoft/INRIA institute in Paris) is using a style of having 'soft types on top of Coq'.

---

[17] The work of Joe Hurd [5] already is a version of this (although it of course does not implement the full Mizar type system.)

6.2   Future Work

There are various interesting questions that might be pursued as a continuation of the research presented in this paper:

— A type system really should be *decidable*, but we have not established this property for the type system that we presented here. The implementation of the type system in the Mizar type checker clearly seems to have this property, but then the rules that we presented in this paper do not *exactly* match the type system as it is implemented in the actual system.

It is clear that a naive implementation of our version of the Mizar type system will not work. The redefinition:

```
redefine mode Element of n -> Element of n + 1;
```

(which is allowed in the actual Mizar system!) will with our version of the typing rules give rise to infinite collections of types.[18] This example also shows that a direct Prolog-style implementation of the rules from Section 4 will not always terminate. However, it is might be the case that a less naive algorithm than just generating all possible types for an expression still can implement a type checker for the typing rules from Section 4.

— We have proved that the type system that we present in this paper is *correct*, but one also could consider the question of whether it is *complete*. The theorem to be proved for this would be that if a sequent is a translation of a typing judgment in our system of which the context is already a correct context, and if that sequent is provable in first order predicate logic, that then in fact the typing judgment is derivable in the type system.

We have not yet tried to prove this property, but thus far we do not know of a counter-example either.

— It might be interesting to make the rules that we presented here more realistic, by for example adding structure types or equalities between terms. Maybe even more interesting would be to precisely analyze the differences between our version of the type system, and the corresponding fragment of the type system the way it is implemented in the actual Mizar system. The interesting question would be whether the differences might easily be removed (either by adapting the typing rules, or by changing the implementation), or whether the differences are essential for giving the implementation of the type checker a reasonable performance.

Acknowledgments. It will be clear that this paper was inspired by the papers of Fairouz Kamareddine. When I wrote this paper I had Herman Geuvers in mind as my target audience: I hope that this paper managed to communicate the Mizar type system to him. Furthermore many thanks to Josef Urban, Makarius and the anonymous referees of the TPHOLs conference for their helpful comments on a draft version of this paper.

---

[18] We got this example from Josef Urban.

References

1. Bancerek, G.: On the structure of Mizar types. Electronic Notes in Theoretical Computer Science, 85 (2003)
2. Cartwright, R., Fagan, M.: Soft typing. In: Proceedings of the SIGPLAN '91 Conference on Programming Language Design and Implementation, pp. 278–292 (1991)
3. Dahn, I.: Interpretation of a Mizar-Like Logic in First-Order Logic. In: Caferra, R., Salzer, G. (eds.) Automated Deduction in Classical and Non-Classical Logics. LNCS (LNAI), vol. 1761, pp. 137–151. Springer, Heidelberg (2000)
4. Gordon, M.J.C., Melham, T.F. (eds.): Introduction to HOL. Cambridge University Press, Cambridge (1993)
5. Hurd, J.: Predicate subtyping with predicate sets. In: Boulton, R.J., Jackson, P.B. (eds.) TPHOLs 2001. LNCS, vol. 2152, pp. 265–280. Springer, Heidelberg (2001)
6. Lee, G., Rudnicki, P.: Alternative Aggregates in Mizar (to be published in Mathematical Knowledge Management, 2007)
7. Muzalewski, M.: An Outline of PC Mizar. Fondation Philippe le Hodey, Brussels (1993), http://www.cs.ru.nl/~freek/mizar/mizarmanual.ps.gz
8. Urban, J.: MPTP 0.1: System Description. ENTCS 86(1) (2003)
9. Urban, J.: Translating Mizar for First Order Theorem Provers. In: Asperti, A., Buchberger, B., Davenport, J.H. (eds.) MKM 2003. LNCS, vol. 2594, pp. 203–215. Springer, Heidelberg (2003)
10. Urban, J.: MoMM – Fast Interreduction and Retrieval in Large Libraries of Formalized Mathematics. International Journal on Artificial Intelligence Tools 15(1), 109–130 (2006)
11. Weidenbach, C.: SPASS: Combining superposition, sorts and splitting (1999)
12. Wiedijk, F. (ed.): The Seventeen Provers of the World. LNCS (LNAI), vol. 3600. Springer, Heidelberg (2006)

Author Index

Lecture Notes in Computer Science

Sublibrary 1: Theoretical Computer Science and General Issues

For information about Vols. 1– 4421
please contact your bookseller or Springer

Vol. 4595: D. Bošnački, S. Edelkamp (Eds.), Model Checking Software. X, 285 pages. 2007.

Vol. 4590: W. Damm, H. Hermanns (Eds.), Computer Aided Verification. XV, 562 pages. 2007.

Vol. 4588: T. Harju, J. Karhumäki, A. Lepistö (Eds.), Developments in Language Theory. XI, 423 pages. 2007.

Vol. 4583: S.R. Della Rocca (Ed.), Typed Lambda Calculi and Applications. X, 397 pages. 2007.

Vol. 4580: B. Ma, K. Zhang (Eds.), Combinatorial Pattern Matching. XII, 366 pages. 2007.

Vol. 4576: D. Leivant, R. de Queiroz (Eds.), Logic, Language, Information and Computation. X, 363 pages. 2007.

Vol. 4547: C. Carlet, B. Sunar (Eds.), Arithmetic of Finite Fields. XI, 355 pages. 2007.

Vol. 4546: J. Kleijn, A. Yakovlev (Eds.), Petri Nets and Other Models of Concurrency – ICATPN 2007. XI, 515 pages. 2007.

Vol. 4545: H. Anai, K. Horimoto, T. Kutsia (Eds.), Algebraic Biology. XIII, 379 pages. 2007.

Vol. 4533: F. Baader (Ed.), Term Rewriting and Applications. XII, 419 pages. 2007.

Vol. 4528: J. Mira, J.R. Álvarez (Eds.), Nature Inspired Problem-Solving Methods in Knowledge Engineering, Part II. XXII, 650 pages. 2007.

Vol. 4527: J. Mira, J.R. Álvarez (Eds.), Bio-inspired Modeling of Cognitive Tasks, Part I. XXII, 630 pages. 2007.

Vol. 4525: C. Demetrescu (Ed.), Experimental Algorithms. XIII, 448 pages. 2007.

Vol. 4514: S.N. Artemov, A. Nerode (Eds.), Logical Foundations of Computer Science. XI, 513 pages. 2007.

Vol. 4513: M. Fischetti, D.P. Williamson (Eds.), Integer Programming and Combinatorial Optimization. IX, 500 pages. 2007.

Vol. 4510: P. Van Hentenryck, L.A. Wolsey (Eds.), Integration of AI and OR Techniques in Constraint Programming for Combinatorial Optimization Problems. X, 391 pages. 2007.

Vol. 4507: F. Sandoval, A. Prieto, J. Cabestany, M. Graña (Eds.), Computational and Ambient Intelligence. XXVI, 1167 pages. 2007.

Vol. 4501: J. Marques-Silva, K.A. Sakallah (Eds.), Theory and Applications of Satisfiability Testing – SAT 2007. XI, 384 pages. 2007.

Vol. 4497: S.B. Cooper, B. Löwe, A. Sorbi (Eds.), Computation and Logic in the Real World. XVIII, 826 pages. 2007.

Vol. 4494: H. Jin, O.F. Rana, Y. Pan, V.K. Prasanna (Eds.), Algorithms and Architectures for Parallel Processing. XIV, 508 pages. 2007.

Vol. 4493: D. Liu, S. Fei, Z. Hou, H. Zhang, C. Sun (Eds.), Advances in Neural Networks – ISNN 2007, Part III. XXVI, 1215 pages. 2007.

Vol. 4492: D. Liu, S. Fei, Z. Hou, H. Zhang, C. Sun (Eds.), Advances in Neural Networks – ISNN 2007, Part II. XXVII, 1321 pages. 2007.

Vol. 4491: D. Liu, S. Fei, Z.-G. Hou, H. Zhang, C. Sun (Eds.), Advances in Neural Networks – ISNN 2007, Part I. LIV, 1365 pages. 2007.

Vol. 4490: Y. Shi, G.D. van Albada, J. Dongarra, P.M.A. Sloot (Eds.), Computational Science – ICCS 2007, Part IV. XXXVII, 1211 pages. 2007.

Vol. 4489: Y. Shi, G.D. van Albada, J. Dongarra, P.M.A. Sloot (Eds.), Computational Science – ICCS 2007, Part III. XXXVII, 1257 pages. 2007.

Vol. 4488: Y. Shi, G.D. van Albada, J. Dongarra, P.M.A. Sloot (Eds.), Computational Science – ICCS 2007, Part II. XXXV, 1251 pages. 2007.

Vol. 4487: Y. Shi, G.D. van Albada, J. Dongarra, P.M.A. Sloot (Eds.), Computational Science – ICCS 2007, Part I. LXXXI, 1275 pages. 2007.

Vol. 4484: J.-Y. Cai, S.B. Cooper, H. Zhu (Eds.), Theory and Applications of Models of Computation. XIII, 772 pages. 2007.

Vol. 4475: P. Crescenzi, G. Prencipe, G. Pucci (Eds.), Fun with Algorithms. X, 273 pages. 2007.

Vol. 4474: G. Prencipe, S. Zaks (Eds.), Structural Information and Communication Complexity. XI, 342 pages. 2007.

Vol. 4459: C. Cérin, K.-C. Li (Eds.), Advances in Grid and Pervasive Computing. XVI, 759 pages. 2007.

Vol. 4449: Z. Horváth, V. Zsók, A. Butterfield (Eds.), Implementation and Application of Functional Languages. X, 271 pages. 2007.

Vol. 4448: M. Giacobini (Ed.), Applications of Evolutionary Computing. XXIII, 755 pages. 2007.

Vol. 4447: E. Marchiori, J.H. Moore, J.C. Rajapakse (Eds.), Evolutionary Computation, Machine Learning and Data Mining in Bioinformatics. XI, 302 pages. 2007.

Vol. 4446: C. Cotta, J. van Hemert (Eds.), Evolutionary Computation in Combinatorial Optimization. XII, 241 pages. 2007.

Vol. 4445: M. Ebner, M. O'Neill, A. Ekárt, L. Vanneschi, A.I. Esparcia-Alcázar (Eds.), Genetic Programming. XI, 382 pages. 2007.

Vol. 4436: C.R. Stephens, M. Toussaint, D. Whitley, P.F. Stadler (Eds.), Foundations of Genetic Algorithms. IX, 213 pages. 2007.

Vol. 4433: E. Şahin, W.M. Spears, A.F.T. Winfield (Eds.), Swarm Robotics. XII, 221 pages. 2007.

Vol. 4432: B. Beliczynski, A. Dzielinski, M. Iwanowski, B. Ribeiro (Eds.), Adaptive and Natural Computing Algorithms, Part II. XXVI, 761 pages. 2007.

Vol. 4431: B. Beliczynski, A. Dzielinski, M. Iwanowski, B. Ribeiro (Eds.), Adaptive and Natural Computing Algorithms, Part I. XXV, 851 pages. 2007.

Vol. 4424: O. Grumberg, M. Huth (Eds.), Tools and Algorithms for the Construction and Analysis of Systems. XX, 738 pages. 2007.

Vol. 4423: H. Seidl (Ed.), Foundations of Software Science and Computational Structures. XVI, 379 pages. 2007.

Vol. 4422: M.B. Dwyer, A. Lopes (Eds.), Fundamental Approaches to Software Engineering. XV, 440 pages. 2007.